INDUSTRIAL RELATIONS LAW

Second Edition

Charles Barrow, BSc Econ, LLM, Barrister

Senior Lecturer in Law, University of North London

Cavendish
Publishing
Limited

London • Sydney

Second edition first published in Great Britain 2002 by Cavendish Publishing Limited,
The Glass House, Wharton Street, London WC1X 9PX, United Kingdom

Telephone:	+44 (0)20 7278 8000	Facsimile:	+44 (0)20 7278 8080
Email:	info@cavendishpublishing.com		
Website:	www.cavendishpublishing.com		

© Barrow, C   2002

First edition   1997

Second edition   2002

British Library Cataloguing in Publication Data

Barrow, Charles

Industrial Relations Law – 2nd ed

1 Labour laws and legislation – England 2 Labour laws and legislation – Wales
3 Industrial relations – England 4 Industrial Relations – Wales

I Title

344.4'201

ISBN 1 85941 563 6

Printed and bound in Great Britain

PREFACE

Since the last edition of this book there have been several major developments in industrial relations law – the most significant of which is the passage of the Employment Relations Act 1999. This statute, enacted by the Labour Government elected in May 1997, does not dismantle the 'restrictive' framework of law established by consecutive Conservative administrations from 1979–97. Instead, it makes limited amendments to existing law (for example, on industrial action ballots and discrimination against union members at the workplace), and accords certain additional rights to trade unions and their members (such as the right to recognition and individual representation at work). The rationale for these changes is contained in the White Paper, *Fairness at Work* (Cm 3968), developed after extensive discussion with trade unions and the business community and published in May 1998. The White Paper emphasises that Labour's industrial and economic policy is centred on the development of competitive businesses and the enhancement of wealth creation through the encouragement of the enterprise economy. This, it states, can be more efficiently accomplished where a 'partnership' model of industrial relations operates, underpinned by legal changes at the individual and collective level, that guarantees 'fairness' at the workplace and, thus, more effective and fruitful working relationships. Although it has to be doubted how far the provisions of the Act will achieve this specific outcome, the Act does represent a major departure from previous government policy and should enhance trade union influence at the workplace.

In addition to this initiative, there have been other case law and statutory changes; for example, the introduction of the European Works Council Directive, reform of the Collective Redundancies and Transfer of Undertakings consultation provisions and the implementation from October 2000 of the Human Rights Act 1998, which integrates the European Convention on Human Rights into UK law. The Human Rights Act 1998 will certainly have a considerable impact on the legal interests protected by the Convention. Instead of a situation where civil liberties are safeguarded by negative freedoms (where actions are controlled and limited by statute and the common law), the acts of individuals and associations will now be protected by a framework of positive rights contained in the Articles of the Convention, elaborated by the Strasbourg case law and interpreted and enforced by the UK judiciary.

The Convention, however, is predominantly concerned with the protection of civil and political rights. Apart from Art 11 (which protects the rights of individuals to form and join a trade union for the protection of their interests), there are no other specific Articles promoting trade union or workers' interests and, as international law (largely ignored by the domestic judiciary), it has had little influence, hitherto, on legislative and judicial decision making in the employment field. Nonetheless, on a close reading of the jurisprudence emanating from Strasbourg on Art 11 and other relevant Articles (such as Art 8 on privacy, Art 10 on freedom of speech and Art 14 on discrimination), the incorporation of these Convention rights into UK law could have a marked impact on the employment relationship. In particular, an issue of relevance to this text is how far the elements of industrial relations law that have been left unchanged by the Employment Relations Act 1999 will be in violation of the 1998 Act.

In general terms, the overall objective of this new edition, in a similar vein to the first edition, is to provide a clear, comprehensive and critical account of the law that governs the relationship between workers, trade unions and employers. Consequently, reference to historical developments in the law and industrial relations issues are retained from the first edition – as they aid an understanding of the contemporary framework and functioning of industrial relations law. This edition also preserves the previous structure of three self-contained areas dealing with the regulation of the internal affairs of trade unions, the degree of legal support for free association in trade unions and for collective bargaining, and the extent of legal intervention where industrial conflict arises between union and employer.

I would like to thank Cara Annett, Ruth Massey and all the team at Cavendish for their work in preparing this edition. The law is stated as at 31 January 2002.

Charles Barrow
31 January 2002

CONTENTS

PART 2
FREEDOM OF ASSOCIATION AND COLLECTIVE BARGAINING

PART 3
INDUSTRIAL CONFLICT

TABLE OF CASES

TABLE OF STATUTES

TABLE OF STATUTORY INSTRUMENTS

TABLE OF EUROPEAN LEGISLATION

TABLE OF CAC DECISIONS

TABLE OF ABBREVIATIONS

ACAS.. Advisory, Conciliation and Arbitration Service
APEX.................. Association of Professional Executive Clerical and Computer Staff
ASLEF .... Associated Society of Locomotive Engineers and Firemen
ASRS... Amalgamated Society of Railway Servants
ASTMS .... Association of Technical and Managerial Staff
ATW... Amalgamated Textile Workers Union
AUEW...................................... Amalgamated Union of Engineering Workers

BRB.. British Railways Board

CAC.. Central Arbitration Committee
CCSU .... Council for the Civil Service Unions
CROTUM......................... Commissioner for the Rights of Trade Union Members

EAT .... Employment Appeal Tribunal
ECHR....................................... European Convention on Human Rights
ECJ.. European Court of Justice
EETPU .... Electrical, Electronic, Telecommunications and Plumbing Union

GCHQ .... Government Communications Headquarters
GMBATU .... General, Municipal, Boilermakers and Allied Trades Union
GPMU... Graphical Paper and Media Union

ITWF .... International Transport Workers Federation

JNB.. Joint Negotiating Body
JP .... Justice of the Peace

NALGO .... National Association of National and Local Government Officers
NATSOPA.......... National Society of Operative Printers, Graphical and Media Personnel
NCB .... National Coal Board
NEC .... National Executive Committee
NGA .... National Graphical Association
NUGSAT .... National Union of Gold, Silver and Allied Trades
NUJ... National Union of Journalists
NUM.. National Union of Mineworkers
NUPE .... National Union of Public Employees
NUR .... National Union of Railwaymen
NUS... National Union of Seamen

NUT . . . . National Union of Teachers
NUTGW . . . . National Union of Tailors and Garment Workers

OTWU . . . . Oil Workers Trade Union

POEU . . . . Post Office Engineering Union

QIP . . . . qualified independent person

RMT . . . . National Union of Rail, Maritime and Transport Workers

SOGAT . . . . Society of Graphical and Allied Trades

TGWU . . . . Transport and General Workers Union
TUC . . . . Trades Union Congress
TULR(C)A 1992 . . . . Trade Union and Labour Relations (Consolidation) Act 1992

UCW . . . . Union of Communication Workers
UKAPE . . . . United Kingdom Association of Professional Engineers
USDAW . . . . Union of Shop, Distributive and Allied Trades

CHAPTER 1

TRADE UNIONS – THE HISTORICAL CONTEXT[1]

Trade union attitudes to legal intervention and the relevance of the economic and political framework in which the law operates are more readily explicable if there is some knowledge and understanding of labour history. As a general historical introduction to trade union law, I shall concentrate here on the founding and growth of trade unions and on the criminal and civil liabilities they laboured under during their formative period prior to the First World War. A short historical overview of the development of collective bargaining and of the system of immunities to tortious liabilities is provided at the start of Part 2 and Part 3, respectively.

THE ORIGINS OF EARLY TRADE UNIONS

The Middle Ages to the Industrial Revolution

Wage regulation and the gilds

Prior to the enormous changes to the economy that occurred with the onset of the Industrial Revolution in the late 18th and early 19th centuries, the British economy was predominantly agrarian, serviced by a vast pool of unskilled labour. The few skilled workers were known as journeymen, who traditionally plied their trades travelling around the local district. They were members of a craft association or gild and were employed by a master craftsman after serving a lengthy apprenticeship.[2]

A gild was not exclusively an association of workers but rather a combination of masters and skilled workers with some, albeit limited, identity of interests between them. A gild would have had its own governing body, rules, customs and traditions which controlled all facets of the trade. It would also regulate standards of workmanship, fixed rates of pay, the pricing of the product produced and entry into the craft through the apprenticeship system. No craftsman could work at his craft without being a member, whilst no master could employ any person who was not a member of the gild.

---

1   General reading: Webb, S and Webb, B, *The History of Trade Unionism*, 2nd edn, 1920; Pelling, H, *A History of British Trade Unionism*, 5th edn, 1993; Cole, GDH, *A Short History of the British Working Class Movement 1789–1947*, 2nd edn, 1948; Clegg, H, Fox, A and Thompson, AF, *A History of British Trade Unions Since 1889*, 1964; Hunt, EH, *British Labour History 1815–1914*, 1981; Orth, J, *Combination and Conspiracy: A Legal History of Trade Unionism 1721–1906*, 1991; Hamish Fraser, W, *A History of British Trade Unionism 1700-1998*, 1999; Lewis, R, 'The historical development of labour law' (1976) 14 BJIR 1; Hodge, A, 'The curious history of trade union law' [1989] Denning LJ 92.

2   The gild system of production was based on the supremacy of the master who owned the premises, tools, raw materials and who employed journeymen and apprentices to produce the finished article which he then sold in the locality.

The advent of the Black Death (bubonic plague) in the 14th century decimated the working population by up to a third. The resulting shortage of labour triggered demands for higher wages from both the skilled and unskilled. The response of the State to this unwanted development was the passage of legislation that regulated wages. Under the Statute of Labourers, of 1349 and 1351, wages were fixed by Parliament, based on the customary wages prevailing in the district. Those workers who agitated for higher pay or left their work before the agreed time risked criminal prosecution and imprisonment.

From 1389, under the authority of the third Statute of Labourers, the responsibility for fixing wages passed to Justices of the Peace (JPs), who were empowered to take into account the fluctuation of food prices in the locality before determining wages. Spasmodic labour scarcity caused by the residue of the plague was still a feature of economic life in the 15th century. Consequently, in order to stop labourers from moving from one employer to another in times of labour shortages, legislation in 1423 and 1427 reinforced wage fixing by providing JPs with powers to impose greater penalties on workers who accepted wages above the fixed rate or who took action to improve their conditions of work or wages.[3]

The Tudor and Stuart eras were marked by ever increasing State regulation of the economy. The prevailing doctrine of mercantilism or protectionism preached prosperity through national and individual economic self-sufficiency. Individual self-sufficiency was to be achieved by the tight regulation of the labour market to attain full employment and a minimum standard of living. To achieve these goals, the State imposed further wage and price controls through the Statute of Artificers 1563. This Act repealed all earlier statutes regulating employment and gave JPs greater power to fix the wages of both skilled and unskilled labour. Unlike the previous system, this was done under the supervision of central government. The wages were recorded in the Court of Chancery, proclaimed in public and fixed in a convenient position for the public to view.[4]

Wage fixing for the skilled worker became a form of minimum wage, which was exceeded where masters could be persuaded, through the power of the gild system or by labour scarcity, to improve the established wage. Wage fixing reinforced their status over the unskilled and provided official recognition of their worth. For the agricultural labourer, however, wage fixing underlined their subservient status as, with no skill to sell, there was usually little need for employers to enhance the pay above the very low subsistence rates set by JPs.

Where properly applied, the Act had a beneficial influence on the living standards of many skilled workers, since it was based on the notion that they should be paid a reasonable wage for their labour. However, as the century progressed, the ideals underpinning the Act were subverted by the wayward and erratic application of wage fixing. In some localities, where the supply of skilled labour was plentiful, a low wage was fixed by JPs influenced by employers and so unsympathetic to the notion of a 'reasonable wage'. Others failed to utilise their discretion to fix a new wage every year, so that in some districts it would be many years before a new wage was settled to reflect any

---

3   Although in theory the practice of wage regulation applied equally to the skilled trades, this statutory regulation clashed with the monopoly position of the gilds. Journeymen were able to influence the level of wages for their craft through the gilds and so maintain their privileged position.

4   Like previous regulatory statutes, it was an offence to break an agreement with the master by leaving work earlier than agreed.

increase in prices. Even where a reasonable wage was determined, there was no guarantee in times of economic hardship that all employers would abide by that rate of pay nor that the JPs would enforce that wage against them.

The power of the gilds to fix wages and other conditions of work and to protect the customs of the trade had been seriously weakened by this degree of State regulation of the economy. The gild system of production was now in terminal decline, further loosening the ties between the gilds, masters and journeymen.[5] It was because of the failure of the gilds to adjust to the new conditions of production and to protect the interests of journeymen against the iniquities of wage fixing that groups of journeymen initiated self-help groups that eventually evolved into the first forms of trade unions.

Locally based associations of journeymen had previously existed for recreational and social purposes. The failure of wage fixing to secure acceptable living standards transformed these associations, in the late 17th and early 18th centuries, into societies and clubs for the provision of mutual insurance benefits against sickness, unemployment, old age and death. These self-help groups were the forerunners of what later became known as 'friendly societies' and spread widely across the country throughout the 18th and 19th centuries.

The more permanent social clubs or friendly societies were transformed into pressure groups to petition JPs to act on their powers of wage fixing. For some of these groups, their main concerns were not necessarily over pay, but over the recognition of their status and the erosion of their traditional rights and privileges, formerly guaranteed through the gilds. Thus, it was not unusual for such associations to petition Parliament to secure legislation protecting their restrictive customs and practices on apprenticeships and on the use of substitute unskilled labour. In this way, entry into the trade could be controlled and the supply of labour limited, so ensuring wages would be kept high. Where petitions to JPs or Parliament failed, there is evidence that on occasion some trade associations attempted to negotiate directly with employers, even countenancing strike action against employers who refused to pay the fixed wage.[6]

The response of the State to these new combinations agitating for improved pay and conditions was to legislate against them in specific trades. Legislation was passed, for example, in 1720 making the journeymen tailors association illegal. Legislation in 1725 and in 1749 proscribed the associations of weavers and dyers, respectively. In addition, it was held, in *R v Journeymen Taylors of Cambridge*,[7] that although it was lawful for a combination to seek to enforce the statutory provisions on wage fixing by petition, where persons combined for other, unlawful purposes, such as to raise wages or change conditions of work by negotiation with employers, the common law crime of conspiracy was committed.[8]

---

5   The gild system was replaced by the domestic system whereby masters would be supplied with the raw materials and paid by small time entrepreneurs to produce the finished article which would then be sold by the entrepreneur in the market place.

6   One of the earlier documented cases of strike action concerned the Journeymen Feltmakers in London in 1696. See *op cit*, Webb and Webb, fn 1, pp 28–29.

7   (1721) 8 Mod Rep 10.

8   This was one of the first cases on restraint of trade. The combination restrained the freedom of masters and individual workers to agree their own terms and so was a combination in pursuit of an illegal purpose.

TRADE UNIONS AND THE INDUSTRIAL REVOLUTION

Despite this apparent illegality, many trade associations continued to thrive; operating within the confines of the law by stressing their friendly society rather than their industrial purposes.[9] An important factor in their development during the latter part of the 18th century was the response by skilled workers to the changing economic conditions. As the control economy of the 17th and early 18th centuries, based on the strict regulation of the economy and on the domestic system of production, was discredited by the new ideas of economic laissez-faire,[10] wage fixing declined and lapsed into disuse, eventually being formally discontinued in 1813.[11] This breakdown of wage fixing, combined with the disintegration of the gild system, meant that skilled workers, when they were dissatisfied with their wages, increasingly directed their demands for redress to employers rather than relying on the system of petitioning Parliament or JPs.

As the pace of industrial change quickened in the late 18th century, with increased specialisation and new methods of machine based work, the traditional journeyman was no longer able to aspire to become a master himself, but became a mere permanent wage earner. The skilled worker, in adjusting to the new economic realities created by the system of industrial production, soon recognised that bargaining strength was heightened when workers acted in consort. Consequently, despite residual illegality and hostile employers, by the beginning of the 19th century a form of organised craft unionism[12] had grown out of the original journeymen trade associations and societies.

Trade union illegalities

A feature of the early years of the Industrial Revolution was the rise in the demand for both unskilled and skilled labour as the economy grew. The demand for unskilled labour was satisfied by the movement of agrarian labourers to the industrial centres, creating an urban working class. The demand for skilled labour encouraged local autonomous trade associations to take advantage of the new economic conditions to flex their newly acquired, albeit limited, power. Yet, as the embryonic craft unions grew in confidence, their very existence was threatened by both the new economic and old political interests.

To the owners of capital, combinations of workers were a threat to the profitability of the factories and trade: to the property owning classes, they were agents of revolution and a threat to political stability. The suspicions of the State towards trade unions were generated by political developments at home and abroad. By the late 18th century, public unrest in Europe was widespread. Following the French Revolution of 1789, where the 'workers' had taken control, trade unions in England were regarded as a vehicle for the spreading of revolutionary ideas. At home, unrest in the armed services, with mutinies by sailors at Spithead and the Nore in 1796, food riots in London in the 1780s and the

---

9   See *op cit*, Webb and Webb, fn 1, pp 28–45.

10 Proponents of the ideology of *laissez-faire* believed that, rather than State intervention to determine a 'fair wage', the sole determinant of pay should be the market forces of supply and demand for labour.

11 One of the last attempts to enforce wage fixing, by an association of millers, was made in *R v Justices of Kent* (1811) 14 East 395. The Lord Chief Justice was unwilling, in the new economic climate, to force JPs to act on their discretion.

12 Note, however, the term 'trade union' was not coined until the middle period of the 19th century.

rebellion in Ireland in 1798 contributed to the sense of paranoia prevalent at that time amongst the ruling classes.[13]

It was in this atmosphere of revolution abroad and unrest at home that Parliament reacted to the continuing spread of trade unionism by passing the Unlawful Oaths Act 1797 and the Combination Acts of 1799 and 1800. As we have seen, combinations of workers in particular trades were already illegal as criminal conspiracies under the common law and by specific legislation dating from 1720. The Combination Acts of 1799 and 1800 went further by criminalising workers' organisations in all trades or occupations. A penalty of three months' imprisonment was specified for those who formed an association of workers that had the purpose of raising pay, reducing hours or interfering in any other way with an employer's business or the employment of workers.[14]

The Combination Acts gave employers the right to prosecute for a breach of the statute. The evidence of prosecutions from the surviving records[15] suggests the criminal controls were used selectively by employers. Those employers who needed to keep the goodwill of their skilled artisans to function profitably did not target the established craft associations. However, the law was ruthlessly deployed by employers to destroy any combination of unskilled factory workers and to suppress any organisation of skilled workers in the recently developed textile industries.[16] As direct union activities were proscribed, the only alternative for the new workers in the mills and factories was to follow the path beaten by the older craft associations, by either banding together lawfully for the purposes of mutual welfare through friendly societies or by organising unlawfully in secret.

The banning of trade unions by the Combination Acts did not eradicate organising activity in other sectors of the economy, nor stamp out social dissension. Social and economic factors, such as poor working and living conditions,[17] unemployment, high food prices and low wages, spawned unrest amongst the general population. Workers, unable to combine openly and peacefully, directed their frustration and anger against the new machinery with the 'Luddite' riots taking place from 1811–13. Violence broke out at a demonstration in 1819 in Manchester, resulting in the 'Massacre of Peterloo'.[18] There was also rural unrest and a growth of unionism in agriculture.

To many influential thinkers, the solution to labour unrest was to put into practice the economic doctrines of the time. They argued that the State, by prohibiting unions, was interfering in the free play of market forces in determining the price of labour. Employers should be free to use their capital, and workers to sell their labour, as they see fit. To these

---

13 Deference, obedience and respect was expected of the urban worker. So the rise of the combination was a shock to the ruling establishment and was seen as striking at the foundations of social order.

14 It also criminalised a combination of employers, but the penalties were much lighter and there is no record of prosecutions.

15 See *op cit*, Webb and Webb, fn 1, pp 74–78.

16 Eg, the Philanthropic Society, with members in the cotton and wool industries, was successfully prosecuted in 1818 resulting in its collapse.

17 For an excellent analysis of the brutality and dehumanising nature of the factory system and of the poverty of the new urban working class see Inglis, B, *Poverty and the Industrial Revolution*, 1972.

18 Eleven people were killed and 400 injured when the army broke up a protest meeting. Subsequently, the 'Six Acts' were passed in 1819 restricting the holding of public meetings and controlling the publication of seditious newspapers.

thinkers, such as Francis Place and Joseph Hume, unions were superficially attractive to workers because of their illegality. Once unions were legalised and free to negotiate wages with employers they would soon wither away, as the laws of supply and demand would ensure that unions only secured the market or 'natural' rate for their members. Once this rate was fixed through the free market, there would be no further role for unions.

The view of these radicals influenced a House of Commons Inquiry into the operation of the Combination Acts. As a result of its recommendations, the Combination Act 1824 was enacted which repealed all anti-union legislation and provided, for the first time, some limited protection for unions against the common law offence of conspiracy. However, contrary to the theories of Francis Place and his colleagues, trade union membership did not decline: by contrast, trade union activity flourished in the new climate of legality. Hence, controls on unions were reimposed in 1825. The Combination Act of 1825 permitted workers to meet to discuss wages and conditions. However, this protection was almost worthless. If a union attempted to use this freedom of association to pursue a wage claim, then not only would the common law crime of conspiracy be infringed, but also the union would fall foul of provisions in the Act that criminalised most forms of trade union agitation or industrial action.[19]

Employers and opponents of trade unions also had other weapons to fight the burgeoning union movement. A statute of 1823, the Masters and Servants Act, provided that it was unlawful for an employee to break their contract of employment with the intention of pressurising an employer to improve wages and conditions. Henceforth, each individual worker who followed a strike call was personally open to prosecution.

Criminal liability had also been indirectly imposed on trade unions by the Unlawful Oaths Act of 1797. This Act made it an offence to swear unlawful oaths for seditious purposes. The Act had primarily been intended to deter the secret organisation of mutinies in the armed services and to attack political radicals. The Act's applicability to unions derived from the practice of some unions in the early part of the 19th century to operate 'underground' in order to avoid suppression from the authorities and victimisation from employers. Thus, it was not unusual for new members to swear an oath of secrecy and loyalty to the union.

It was for this offence that five agricultural labourers in Dorset, known as the Tolpuddle Martyrs,[20] were prosecuted and sentenced in 1834 to seven years transportation to Australia. There had been many incidents of rural disaffection throughout England prior to their arrest, which the Home Secretary, Lord Melbourne attributed to the rise of local agricultural unions. As an example to others, he encouraged the Magistrates of Dorchester to deal harshly with the Tolpuddle labourers. Popular protest against their sentences, vigorously pursued by other trade unionists and assorted radicals, was eventually successful in securing their release and repatriation. The strength of this campaign across England attested to the degree of support that now existed for working class organisations.

---

19 These offences: of violence to person or property; of threats or intimidation, molestation or obstruction, 'in order to coerce the will of another' were all subsequently widely interpreted by the judiciary.

20 *R v Loveless and Others* (1834) 6 C & P 596.

The prosecution of the Tolpuddle workers was the culmination of a concerted effort by the State and employers to snuff out the flurry of union activity that had developed during the brief period of legality since 1824. Union growth had been encouraged by the improvement in communications, with transport links improving sufficiently for an attempt to be made at establishing regional or national unions. Workers, who previously only organised locally, were now able to make contact with colleagues within a region and form specific trade federations. For example, in 1827, local building craft trade clubs organised into the General Union of Carpenters and Joiners. This was followed in 1832 with the formation of the Operative Builders Union. There were also attempts at creating general unions that recruited across the trades. In 1830, a 'union of all trades', the National Association for the Protection of Labour was set up in the North of England, chiefly amongst skilled textile workers. In 1834, the social reformer Robert Owen launched the 'Grand National Consolidated Trades Union' which recruited across many industries.[21]

These initiatives were short lived. They disintegrated when faced with hostile employers and the trade depression of 1837–42 which caused large scale unemployment, a severe loss of union membership and an inevitable weakening of union organisation. Despite the collapse of the more experimental forms of unionism, many small localised craft unions continued to exist, sometimes amalgamating within a region to enhance their influence. Other skilled workers fell back on the support of trade associations that existed purely for friendly society purposes.

As workers organisations declined, radical political struggles came to the fore, represented by movements such as the Chartists who campaigned for wider political reform and the extension of the franchise. It was not until the end of the trade depression, with the Victorian economy reaching its peak in the 1850s, that skilled artisans vital to the industrial economy revived trade unionism and spawned the birth of a new generation of strong but cautious unions described by the Webbs as the 'new model unions'.[22]

The foundation in 1851 of the Amalgamated Society of Engineers, formed from a disparate group of smaller unions, has been regarded as a landmark in trade union history as it was the forerunner of other 'new model unions' such as the Amalgamated Society of Cotton Spinners in the textile industry and the Amalgamated Society of Carpenters and Joiners in the building industry. These unions replicated the engineers by recruiting substantial membership, establishing a national headquarters and a sound financial base and quickly winning recognition by employers.

These new unions, based on the old and new skills essential to the economy, were a rather elitist grouping, noted for their 'moderation' in negotiations with employers and belief in the provision of friendly benefits.[23] Where possible, they avoided conflict with employers and courted contact with government to win legal reforms on industrial safety and other matters relevant to their membership.[24]

---

21 The Tolpuddle martyrs had themselves been attempting to set up a local agricultural section of the 'Grand National'.

22 See *op cit*, Webb and Webb, fn 1, p 216.

23 The Webbs styled the five main leaders of the 'new model unions' as 'the Junta'. These five convened the 'Conference of Amalgamated Trades' which met weekly in London to co-ordinate trade union activities.

24 In contrast to other unions of this period, the National Miners Association, founded in 1858, did not fall within this model and challenged employers robustly over safety conditions and pay.

The fight for legality

Although 'new unionism' spread widely in the skilled trades, many employers remained hostile to broader trade unionism. Ample opportunity to eliminate organised labour at the workplace was provided by the criminal restrictions which were still applicable to trade unions. The Combination Act 1825 had given unions a bare legality but, as we saw earlier, when unions attempted to pursue their objects of improving pay and conditions they offended against the penal provisions of the Act. To threaten or to take strike action, to boycott non-union labour or picket peacefully were all illegal.[25]

Some of the harshness of the Combination Act was mitigated by the Molestation of Workmen Act 1859. It was lawful under this Act to attempt to secure changes in wages or hours, '... peaceably and in a reasonable manner and, without threats or intimidation to persuade others to cease or abstain from work'. Yet the courts initially responded to this limited protection by interpreting 'threats or intimidation' quite widely. In R v Druitt,[26] 'black looks' from a picket was sufficiently serious to be classified as 'intimidatory' conduct actionable under the Combination Act;[27] to call someone a 'scab' was an unlawful threat which also attracted criminal liability.[28]

As the economy expanded throughout the 1860s, employers struggled to control the growth of unionism. In 1859, there was a major strike of London building workers supported by other unions. As a direct consequence of this cross-union support, a London Trades Council was established in 1860 to co-ordinate union campaigns. This model was soon followed with the setting up of trades councils in other major cities. The first meeting of the Trades Union Congress (TUC) was in 1868 in Manchester.

The growth of trade unions did nothing to alleviate the residual distrust of unions that existed amongst employers and the State. In 1867, despite opposition from unions, a new Master and Servant Act was passed, replacing the 1823 Act, which criminalised certain misconduct at the workplace such as 'neglecting work' in breach of contract. Prosecutions of individual workers for breach of contract of service was frequently used by employers as a response to strike action and as a way of disciplining their employees.[29]

A further serious setback to trade unions was the decision in Hornby v Close[30] that unions were unlawful associations at civil law.[31] As unions bargained on their members behalf with employers and so interfered with an individual worker's freedom to sell his

---

25   See R v Rowland (1851) 5 Cox CC 437 and R v Duffield (1851) 5 Cox CC 404 – to persuade others to join a strike by peaceful picketing was molestation that coerced the will of the other workers. R v Hewitt (1851) 5 Cox CC 162 – to threaten a strike was molestation of an employer.

26   (1867) 10 Cox CC 592.

27   Later, in R v Shepherd (1869) 11 Cox CC 325, it was clarified that where pickets engage in mere persuasion without abuse, threats or 'black looks', the Act protected pickets from criminal charges under the Combination Act 1825.

28   R v Perham (1867) 5 H & N 30.

29   The Webbs noted that as late as the mid-1870s convictions for breach of this Act were running as high as 10,000 every year. Many of the convictions were of miners who refused on safety grounds to descend unsafe pits.

30   (1867) LR 2 B 153.

31   This applied to trade unions the decision in Hilton v Eckersley (1855) 6 E & B 47, that an agreement between employers on pay was an actionable conspiracy in restraint of trade.

or her labour, unions were organisations in restraint of trade and unlawful at common law. Consequently union rules could not be enforced. This was seen as an attack on a union's internal organisation and on the integrity of trade unions.[32]

In the same year as *Hornby v Close*, 1867, a Royal Commission was established to examine allegations of violence between union members and non-unionists that had occurred in the Sheffield area. As a reaction to the outcry over *Hornby v Close* and the operation of the Combination Act 1825, the Commission was also invited to investigate the relationship of the law to trade unions. The leaders of the unions lobbied the members of the Commission tirelessly and succeeded in persuading a minority of union sympathisers of the merits of a minimum of State regulation and legal intervention in trade union affairs. Despite this, the Commission's majority report was barely favourable to trade unions. Yet it was the minority report, a far more sympathetic document than the majority report, which was accepted by the Government as the basis for legislation.

This was because the new Liberal Government under Gladstone was partly beholden to the support of the trade unions during the 1871 election. However, the passage of two Acts in 1871; the Trade Union Act and the Criminal Law Amendment Act, failed to satisfy fully union reformers. The Trade Union Act 1871 provided unions with an immunity from the civil and criminal consequences of the doctrine of restraint of trade. It also attempted to keep the courts out of union internal affairs by establishing that certain terms of the union membership contract could not be legally enforced. At the same time, it provided unions with a degree of legal status necessary to enable them to protect their property interests and to enforce their agreements with third parties.

The Criminal Law Amendment Act 1871, however, was less favourable to trade unions. Some of the original favourable provisions had been amended by Conservative peers as the Act passed through its stages in the House of Lords. Although the Act repealed the Unlawful Oaths Act 1797 and parts of the Combination Act 1825, it retained some of the penal sections of the 1825 Act, further imposed other criminal liabilities and failed to deal with the problem of common law criminal conspiracy. The importance of this omission became clear when the courts continued to indicate their distaste for trade unions by reviving the offence of conspiracy, which we first saw used in the *Journeymen Tailors* case in 1721.

In *R v Bunn*,[33] gas company employees were prosecuted for common law conspiracy for threatening to go on strike in support of a dismissed colleague. Brett J held that, although a combination of workers in a trade union itself was not a criminal conspiracy, in these circumstances an actionable criminal conspiracy 'to molest' the employer had taken place. What the combination had done was an 'unjustifiable annoyance and interference with the masters in the conduct of their business' which amounted to 'improper molestation'.[34]

---

32 The Webbs report (*op cit*, fn 1, p 262) that Frederic Harrison, a lawyer close to the Junta, was outraged, as the decision had equated unions as '... something like betting and gambling, public nuisances and immoral considerations – things condemned and suppressed by the law'.

33 (1872) 12 Cox CC 316.

34 See also *R v Hibbert* (1875) 13 Cox CC 82. Convictions were secured on conspiracy charges against workers on strike who peacefully picketed their factory.

The response of the trade union movement to the inadequacies of the Criminal Law Amendment Act 1871 and the judiciary's revival of common law conspiracy was to engage in ferocious political lobbying. As a consequence of the 1867 Reform Act, which extended the franchise to many urban skilled workers, trade unionists could no longer be ignored as they now wielded some influence through their voting allegiances. This influence was in its infancy when the Master and Servants Act 1867 and the Criminal Law Amendment Act 1871 were passed. However, with the 1874 election, trade unionist voting intentions became a matter of some importance. With the newly established Parliamentary Committee of the TUC in the forefront, trade unions fought a vigorous campaign for the repeal of the Criminal Law Amendment Act, urging workers to vote for the candidate who pledged their support for this aim.

The result of the 1874 election was the defeat of the Liberals and the formation of a Conservative administration under Disraeli. Many Conservatives had pledged themselves to the reform of the law that criminalised industrial action.[35] A Bill to this effect was brought forward in 1875 which became the Conspiracy and Protection of Property Act. The Criminal Law Amendment Act, the Master and Servants Act[36] and the remainder of the provisions of the Combination Acts were all repealed. Most importantly, the new Act provided an immunity from criminal liability for common law conspiracy where a union was acting in furtherance of a trade dispute. The Act also legalised peaceful picketing by providing that mere attendance at a place for the purpose of peacefully communicating information was lawful. The criminal offences that were introduced were, in comparison to previous criminal liabilities, narrowly defined offences that related solely to picketing that went beyond peaceful persuasion.[37]

This 1875 Act was a milestone in the treatment of trade unions by the State.[38] Previously, criminal controls had been slowly and haphazardly repealed and then reintroduced as policy towards unions wavered. Now, when trade unions represented their members and used their strength in bargaining with employers, the criminal law ceased to play any major part in the process. Employers could no longer rely on the criminal law to rid them of troublesome unions.

Despite union success in achieving legal recognition at both civil and criminal law, the growth of unions amongst the unskilled in the factories of Victorian Britain was limited. Growth was stunted by unhelpful economic conditions that weakened organising activity.[39] It was only after the end of the economic depression in 1882 that the union movement entered the crucial phase of its history with the organisation of the unskilled.

---

35 A Royal Commission on Labour Laws had been set up by the new Government which reported favourably in 1875.

36 This was replaced by the Employers and Workmen Act 1875 which provided that disputes on the contract of employment were now a matter for the civil law only.

37 These provisions, contained in s 7 of the Act, were resurrected during the miners' strike of 1984–85 and are now found in the Trade Union and Labour Relations (Consolidation) Act 1992. They are considered in some detail in Chapter 17.

38 See the rather optimistic conclusions of the Webbs on this legislation, *op cit*, fn 1, p 291.

39 At this time, the skilled craft unions consolidated their power by amalgamation or through the formation of federations.

The rise of general unionism

With much of the criminal law neutralised, and with trade unions gaining an element of legality by the passage of the Trade Union Act 1871, unskilled workers were free to initiate organising activity unfettered by the law. As a response to this new legal climate and to the conditions of a vibrant economy, unions for gas workers, dockers, railway workers and agricultural labourers all emerged in the latter part of the 19th century. These organisations also benefited from changing public attitudes to trade unions, as a consequence of a greater understanding of the often appalling conditions the unskilled workers were expected to tolerate, publicised by the work of numerous social reformers.

One of the earliest celebrated cases of the organisation of the unskilled concerned the 'matchgirls' employed by Bryant and May in London in 1888. These women had gone on strike after the victimisation of one of their colleagues who had complained about the poor conditions and pay. Through their own efforts and those of Mrs Annie Beasant, the editor of a small weekly paper, they campaigned tirelessly for their reinstatement and recognition of their newly formed Matchmakers Union. The campaign galvanised public opinion and focused on pressurising Parliament and Government for support.[40] With substantial financial aid forthcoming from the general public to sustain the strike, the employers, under pressure from all sides, agreed to arbitration conducted by the London Trades Council and a satisfactory settlement was reached.

Other unskilled workers took heart from the triumph of the matchgirls. In 1889, the Gasworkers and General Labourers' Union was formed,[41] which had some immediate success negotiating a reduction in hours worked by gasworks stokers. This success encouraged the leaders of the dockworkers who, as casual labour, had been notoriously difficult to organise in the past, to press for an increase in pay. When this was refused a strike in London quickly spread with, at its height, over 100,000 men on strike all over the country. In a similar vein to the matchgirls' campaign, the dockworkers received the support of other unions and of much of the public. Under the pressure of the strike, the employers granted the strikers' demands and recognised the new dockworkers union, the Dock, Wharf, Riverside and General Workers Union.[42]

The success of the dockworkers' strike paved the way for the formation of many new unions catering for the unskilled labouring class. In the 1890s, new unions were established, for example, in the shipyards, in the building industry and in the chemical industry. These 'industrial' unions, recruiting within a single industry were joined by the emergence of 'general' unions which recruited the unskilled across industries. Such unions expanded rapidly, tapping into the vast pool of non-unionised labour in a multitude of industries ripe for recruitment.[43] The new found freedoms from the law, combined with the proliferation of the new industrial and general unions, gave the union movement strength, confidence and influence. The repercussions of this new found confidence were further demands for recognition and bargaining rights.

---

40 The success of the campaign is described fully by the Webbs, *op cit*, fn 1, pp 402–04.
41 Eventually amalgamating with other smaller unions and becoming the General, Municipal and Boilermakers' Union in 1924.
42 This was the forerunner of the Transport and General Workers Union formed in 1920.
43 Union membership rose rapidly, with 1.5 m members in 1892, rising to 2 m in 1900 and 4m on the outbreak of war in 1914.

These unskilled unions not only differed from the elitist craft unions in their recruitment policies, but also differed in their policy towards employers. They were far more confrontational than the conservative and cautious 'new model unions', who were administratively bureaucratic, often paying more attention to the provision of provident benefits to their members than engaging in 'robust' negotiations with employers and in applying the strike weapon. To the more militant general and industrial unions, inspiration came from the struggles of the dockworkers and the gasworkers.

This growth of unionism was not without its problems. High profile disputes over recognition and attacks on employers who used non-union labour turned public opinion against the unions. Judicial hostility also resurfaced – despite the apparent neutralisation of the criminal law, the courts re-emerged as the bulwark against trade unionism and fought a rearguard action to stem the influence of the unions. Until the case of *Curran v Trevelan*,[44] the courts had consistently decided that a boycott of employers who used non-union labour amounted to intimidation for the purposes of liability under the 1875 Act.[45] In *Lyons v Wilkins*,[46] it was held that peaceful picketing with the object of persuasion was capable of coming within the ambit of the offence of 'watching and besetting' under the 1875 Act, as the Act only rendered it lawful to attend in order to inform, rather than actively persuade. However, these isolated uses of the criminal law were not sufficiently serious to slow down union expansion. Rather, the principal mechanism of judicial control over union activity now passed to the civil law.

The emergence of civil liabilities

As we have noted above, in the last two decades of the 19th century the growth of the unskilled unions coincided with much industrial unrest. With criminal controls on union activity eliminated by statutory intervention, employers increasingly turned to the civil law to provide a remedy against damaging strikes. The courts willingly responded to these concerns by developing a series of civil liabilities enforceable by employers by way of injunctions and damages claims.

The judges developed and refined trade union liability in tort. For example, in *Temperton v Russell*,[47] the tort of inducing breach of contract was applied to the circumstances of an industrial dispute. The House of Lords held that, when a union calls on its members to take strike action, it is committing the tort by persuading members to unlawfully break their contracts of employment.

In *Quinn v Leathem*,[48] the House of Lords held that, when industrial action was threatened or occurred, unions as a combination of workers act unlawfully as a civil conspiracy. Even though the industrial action may have been taken to further a dispute of interest to the workers, they were conspiring together, without justification, to injure the employer economically.

---

44 [1891] 2 QB 545.
45 See, eg, *R v Bauld* (1876) 13 Cox CC 282.
46 [1896] 1 Ch 811. This view was rejected by the Court of Appeal several years later in *Ward, Lock & Co v Operative Printers' Assistants Society* (1906) 22 TLR 327.
47 [1893] 1 QB 715. This tort derives from the case of *Lumley v Gye* (1853) 2 E & B 216.
48 [1901] AC 495.

In *Temperton v Russell*, the House of Lords had established that individuals who organise strike action could be sued, but that unions as organisations remained immune from legal action for the tortious liabilities. However, in the landmark decision in *Taff Vale Rly Co v ASRS*,[49] the House of Lords declared that trade unions themselves possessed sufficient legal status to be held liable in their own name for inducing breach of contract. This case, if it stood for any appreciable length of time, would have bankrupted unions and impaired union ability to prosecute strikes. The judges had in effect, by this decision, turned the law back to the position prior to the 1875 Act where unions were lawful *per se*, but any attempt by them to take action in support of collective bargaining was unlawful.

These civil liabilities seriously disrupted a union's ability to function and threatened all that had been achieved since 1871. The practical outcome of these cases was to give trade unions an impetus to develop their political representation in Parliament in order to reverse these damaging decisions. This tactic had been further encouraged by an extension of the franchise in 1884. Many unions now aligned themselves with the Labour Representation Committee, established in 1900, out of which grew the Labour Party in 1906.

As a result of union disquiet over *Taff Vale*, a Royal Commission on Trade Disputes was set up in 1903 to examine the legal position of trade unions during industrial conflict. The TUC in its evidence to the Commission stated that the civil law had developed in such a way that organised labour was unable to function effectively. It was argued that the civil law had to be reformed to recognise the legitimacy of trade union activity. This was best achieved by the creation of a form of trade union immunity from certain torts so as to protect them from the full rigour of the common law.

The recommendations of the Royal Commission were not overtly sympathetic to the trade union position. However, the reforming 1906 Liberal Government, influenced by their supporters in the union movement, were forced to withdraw a Bill based on the majority report and, instead, took account of many of the proposals from the TUC, which were enacted in the Trade Disputes Act 1906. This Act formed the basis of the present structure, providing the unions with a liberty to strike by granting trade unions an immunity from certain actions in tort, providing the action is taken 'in contemplation or furtherance of a trade dispute'.[50]

This pattern of protection has remained until today, although as will be seen in Chapters 14 and 15, these immunities have often been under judicial attack. The courts have attempted to circumvent the protection provided by the Trade Disputes Act and later consolidating Acts, through their interpretation of the statutory provisions or by outflanking the immunities by creating new civil liabilities unprotected by statute.[51]

As the Trade Disputes Act 1906 had blunted the judicial attack on the unions industrial activities, the courts now turned their attention to union political activities. In *ASRS v Osborne*,[52] the House of Lords concluded that it was unlawful for unions to collect

---

49 [1901] AC 426.

50 Immunity was granted for inducing breach of contract (s 3(1)), unjustified interference in business (s 3(2)) and for conspiracy (s 1).

51 Until 1979 the response of Parliament had been to legislate to re-assert the status quo. Now, legislative changes have made these judicial developments unnecessary.

52 [1910] AC 87.

and apply funds for political, as opposed to industrial, purposes. This was contrary to the objects of a trade union derived from the definition of a trade union in the Trade Union Act 1871. This decision had serious consequences for the fledgling Labour Party as it was cut off from its major source of funding: it also threatened further legislative advances obtained by political lobbying.[53] The legality of these political payments was restored by the Trade Union Act 1913 which permitted such payments after a majority vote in a ballot.

It was during this period, from the late 19th century to 1914, that the system of industrial relations that lasted for much of the 20th century was developed. By the time of the First World War, the State, through the enactment of the Trade Union Act 1871, the Trade Disputes Act 1906 and the Trade Union Act 1913, had removed criminal liabilities, mitigated the worst effects of the civil liabilities and thereby had temporarily halted statutory and judicial interference in union industrial, political and internal affairs. The legitimacy of union action in the pursuit of recognition and collective bargaining was recognised, if not by all employers, then at least by the State. The system of 'voluntarism' or 'collective *laissez-faire*' had now emerged, based on the non-intervention of the law in industrial disputes and on free collective bargaining unhindered by legal constraints. This structure was now entrenched as the basis of British industrial relations for the rest of the century.[54]

---

53 Despite the problems of the *Osborne* decision, union influence played a part in the passage of many social and industrial reforms during this period – the Workers Compensation Act 1906, Old Age Pensions Act 1908, Coal Mines (Eight Hours) Act 1908 and National Insurance Act 1911.

54 The period immediately after the General Strike 1926 and the period between 1971–74 were aberrations, as legislation was passed to regulate formally the system of industrial relations, so creating a high degree of State intervention in industrial matters.

PART 1

THE REGULATION OF TRADE UNION INTERNAL AFFAIRS

PART 1

INTRODUCTION

Trade union freedom from State interference in internal affairs has been a long standing principle of industrial relations since the late 19th century. This principle has increasingly been under attack by statutory initiatives introduced by successive Conservative Governments in power from 1979–97 and so far left in place by the present Labour administration. Legislation now intervenes in trade union affairs by enforcing compulsory union elections, by regulating union financial matters and political activities and by providing the dissident individual member with a comprehensive package of rights to enforce against his or her union. This extensive scheme of statutory regulation exists side by side with judicial control of trade union internal government through the interpretation and enforcement of the union rule book.

The following chapters assesses the extent of this statutory and common law control. Chapter 2 examines the structure and internal government of trade unions, their legal character and the system of financial regulation applicable to trade unions. Chapter 3 considers the role that the rule book plays in the governance of trade unions and what legal action members may take should these rules be broken. Chapters 4 and 5 contain a detailed analysis of common law and statutory protection for those individuals who are denied admission to, disciplined or expelled by their union. Chapter 6 appraises the degree of legal intervention in the area of union elections and Chapter 7 explores the issue of trade union political activities.

First, we examine the role of the Certification Officer – an independent official appointed by government, who plays an important role in the area of internal trade union law.

THE CERTIFICATION OFFICER

The office of Certification Officer has a lengthy historical pedigree. The original forerunner to the Certification Officer was the Registrar of Friendly Societies who administered the registration of unions under the Trade Union Act 1871. Registration under this Act was a voluntary matter with little detriment to a union that declined to register. This was abolished by the Industrial Relations Act 1971 and replaced by a system of registration administered by a Registrar of Trade Unions. Unlike the previous arrangement, registration was necessary to gain the benefits of trade union status and without it unions were subject to substantial liabilities.

After the repeal of the Industrial Relations Act, the Registrar of Trade Unions was replaced by the office of the Certification Officer created by the Employment Protection Act 1975. The Certification Officer is appointed by the Secretary of State for Trade and Industry and is financed and staffed by the Advisory, Conciliation and Arbitration Service (ACAS), although formally independent of both ACAS and government.

Under the Employment Protection Act 1975, the duties of the Certification Officer were limited to supervising trade union compliance with the statutory requirements outlined in the Trade Union and Labour Relations Act 1974 and with administering the list of trade unions and certifying their independence. As the statutory regulation of trade unions has increased during the 1980s and early 1990s, the Certification Officer's administrative role has been supplemented by an expansion in his supervisory and judicial functions.[1]

The main responsibilities of the Certification Officer are contained in the Trade Union and Labour Relations (Consolidation) Act (TULR(C)A) 1992 and include:

(a) maintaining a list of trade unions and employers' associations and certifying the independence of trade unions who are on this list and who apply for a certificate of independence;

(b) seeing that unions keep appropriate accounts and comply with the statutory provisions governing union accounting and superannuation matters;

(c) ensuring compliance with statutory procedures relating to the setting up and operation of union political funds and approving political fund ballot rules;

(d) ensuring the observance of the statutory rules concerning union mergers and transfer of engagements;

(e) hearing complaints over the handling of secret ballots for union elections, over the conduct of merger ballots and for breaches of the political fund rules;

(f) hearing complaints over the failure of a union to compile and maintain a register of members' names and addresses;

(g) hearing and investigating complaints about alleged financial malpractice.

With the abolition of the office of the Commissioner for the Rights of Trade Union Members (CROTUM), the Certification Officer has now, under the Employment Relations Act 1999, been given additional powers to investigate and adjudicate on nearly all alleged trade union breaches of the rule book and statute where previously the CROTUM was empowered to give advice and assistance. The CROTUM was created by the Conservative Government in 1988 in order to provide assistance (by paying legal costs or by obtaining legal advice) to trade union members who wished to take legal action in the courts against their own union for union breaches of certain statutory rights (relating to a failure of administration and governance). The remit of the office was extended by the Employment Act 1990 to include assistance to pursue legal action for alleged breaches of union rules – including rules relating to the appointment and election to union office, balloting of members, disciplinary proceedings and the application of union funds or property.

The CROTUM was established on account of the Conservative Government's concern that there was no guarantee that the new statutory obligations developed in the 1980s to control trade union internal affairs would be enforced unless an agency was founded to help individuals pursue their remedies under the relevant legislation.[2] The creation of the CROTUM was heavily criticised at the time as an unwarranted interference in the private

---

1   For example, the Trade Union Reform and Employment Rights Act 1993 provided the Certification Officer with additional power to act on complaints by individual union members and investigate union financial malpractice.

2   See the arguments contained in the Green Paper, *Trade Unions and Their Members*, Cm 95, 1987, para 6.

affairs of trade unions. There was a fear that dissident union members would take advantage of this legal assistance to cause severe inconvenience to unions and hinder their legitimate activities. However, the worst fears of the trade unions were unfounded. The statistics derived from the Commissioner's annual reports show that the office has had very little formal impact, with the number of applicants given material assistance in single figures year on year.[3] The low figures of assistance suggest that trade unions have been generally complying with rule book requirements and the imposed statutory conditions.

In the Employment White Paper, *Fairness at Work*,[4] issued by the Labour Government in May 1998, it was recognised that the CROTUM had had very limited impact and thus was 'inefficient and unnecessary'. Section 28 of the 1999 Act repealed ss 109–14 of the TULR(C)A 1992 which established the Commissioner's powers and outlined his functions and procedure. As a consequence of this abolition, the Certification Officer's competencies are now extended and redefined. Schedule 6 to the 1999 Act (amending the TULR(C)A 1992) provides for an extension of the Certification Officer's jurisdiction relating to breaches of statutory rights and rule book infractions, and introduces a new enforcement procedure for the Certification Officer's existing jurisdiction. The rationale for this (set out in *Fairness at Work*) was that by giving this responsibility to the Certification Officer trade union members would be able to secure their rights more easily and effectively without the cost and delay associated with court proceedings.

New jurisdiction for breach of statutory rights

Where a union member's right to access to inspect union accounts (s 30 of the TULR(C)A 1992) is violated, Sched 6, para 6 of the 1999 Act amends s 31 of the TULR(C)A 1992 by providing that the Certification Officer now has jurisdiction (in conjunction with the court) to adjudicate on breaches of this right.[5] The Certification Officer should determine the application within six months, is entitled to make 'enquiries as he thinks fit' and give both parties the opportunity to be heard.[6] Where the Certification Officer finds the claim well founded, an order may be made (enforceable in the same way as a court order) to ensure enforcement of the right – to inspect the accounts, to be accompanied by an accountant and to be supplied with extracts or copies of the accounts.[7]

Schedule 6, para 13 inserts a new s 72A into the TULR(C)A 1992 giving the Certification Officer jurisdiction (as an alternative, not as an addition to court proceedings) over complaints of a breach of the statutory rules on the use of general funds for political objects.[8] Similar procedural requirements as outlined above apply –

---

3   For example, in 1993–94, out of 47 formal applications for financial aid only five were granted. In 1994–95 only seven applications were successful. During the passage of the 1999 Act through Parliament it was reported that, in total, only 12 applications had been received throughout 1998 (Standing Committee E, 4 March 1999, col 273). For comment on the earlier CROTUM Annual Reports see Morris, D (1993) 22 ILJ 307.

4   Cm 3968, 1998.

5   However, an applicant cannot apply to both the court and the Certification Officer – s 31(6)(7).

6   Section 31(2A)(C).

7   Section 31(2)(B).

8   Section 71.

although here the application is for a declaration and reasons for the decision must be given.[9] Where the union intends to remedy the breach, the declaration must specify the steps the union needs to take to do so.[10] The Certification Officer also has the authority to issue any necessary order[11] and both declarations and orders are enforceable as if made by the court.[12]

Additional jurisdiction over breaches of union rules

Schedule 6, para 19 of the 1999 Act (creating ss 108A–108C of the TULR(C)A 1992) introduces new powers for the Certification Officer to investigate certain breaches of union rules: previously, the only remedy was a common law action in the civil courts. Now, a member of a trade union has the right to apply to the Certification Officer if there has been a breach or threatened breach of a trade union's rules (including the rules of any branch or section) relating to any of the matters set out in s 108A(2) of the TULR(C)A 1992. The matters are:

(a) the appointment or election of a person to, or the removal of a person from, any office;
(b) disciplinary proceedings by the union (including expulsion);
(c) the balloting of members on any issue other than industrial action;
(d) the constitution or proceedings of any executive committee or of any decision making meeting:
(e) such other matters as may be specified in an order made by the Secretary of State.

The applicant must be a member of the union, or have been a member at the time of the alleged or threatened breach and the application must be made within a six month time limit from the date of the breach, or the conclusion of the internal complaint procedure, or one year from the invoking if that procedure.[13] Once an application has been made to the Certification Officer, the applicant may not complain to the court on the same matter nor may the Certification Officer entertain an application if, alternatively, an application has been made to the court.[14]

The Certification Officer may refuse to accept an application unless satisfied that the applicant has taken all reasonable steps to resolve the claim by the use of any existing union internal complaints procedure.[15] Where the application has been accepted by the Certification Officer, it must be determined within six months of it being made. He has powers to initiate enquiries regarding the claim, must provide the applicant and the trade union with an opportunity to be heard and must give reasons for his decision to make or refuse the declaration asked for.[16]

---

9   Section 72A(2).
10 Section 72A(4).
11 Section 72A(5).
12 Section 72A(7)(9).
13 Section 108A(3)(6)(7).
14 Section 108A(14)(15).
15 Section 108B(1).
16 Section 108B(2).

Where a declaration is made, the Certification Officer may also make an enforcement order unless 'to do so would be inappropriate'. This order imposes on the union one or more of the following requirements:

(a) to take such steps to remedy the breach, or withdraw the threat of a breach, as may be specified in the order;
(b) to abstain from such acts as may be so specified with a view to securing that a breach or threat of the same or a similar kind does not occur in the future.[17]

Where an order imposes a requirement on the union, as in (a) above, the order must specify the period within which the union must comply with the requirement of the order.[18] A declaration or an enforcement order made by the Certification Officer is to be treated as if made by the court.[19] Any union member is entitled to enforce an enforcement order, not just the original applicant.[20]

The commencement date for these provisions was 25 October 1999 and the Certification Officer's power to consider such applications is restricted to alleged breaches occurring on or after 27 July 1999. The Certification Officer's Annual Report for 1999–2000 reported that no decisions have been issued in the period 25 October 1999–31 March 2000, although 10 applications are outstanding.

Enforcement procedure

The 1999 Act provides for a new enforcement mechanism in areas where previously the Certification Officer only had the power to issue decisions and declarations. Binding orders (enforceable as an order of the court) may be granted where:

(a) a union has failed to maintain the register of members;
(b) a union permits an officer (having offended against certain provisions of the TULR(C)A 1992) to hold union office contrary to the statute;
(c) a union has failed to comply with the statutory requirements to hold a balloted election for union office;
(d) a union has failed to comply with the statutory requirements to hold ballots on political resolutions or failed to comply with ballot rules.

Where there is an application to the Certification Officer for an order to force the union to comply with the relevant provision, that individual cannot then apply to the court (and vice versa should the application be first made to the court). However, a different person is not barred from applying to the Certification Officer or court on the same issue; although when considering the new application the Certification Officer or court should have regard to any previous decisions or deliberations on the matter.

The procedure to obtain and enforce an order under this jurisdiction is complex and detailed. In brief, on an application, the Certification Officer should make such enquiries as he thinks are necessary and must give the applicant and trade union the opportunity to

---

17 Section 108B(3).
18 Section 108B(4).
19 Section 108B(6) and (8).
20 Section 108(7).

be heard. A declaration may then be made, specifying the trade union's failure, giving reasons for the decision. Unless the Certification Officer deems it inappropriate, an enforcement order (enforceable by any member of the union) may now be made – ordering the union to remedy the failure (such as to hold a ballot in accordance with political ballot rules or an election ballot in accordance with the statutory requirements) or to abstain from future acts so the failure is not repeated. A declaration or enforcement order is to be treated as if granted by a court.

In addition, the powers of the Certification Officer to investigate trade union affairs are strengthened where complaints are made relating to breach of political fund rules (and where there is a failure to comply with the statutory rules on union amalgamations and transfers).[21] The relevant paragraphs of Sched 6 state that the Certification Officer is entitled to make 'such enquiries as he thinks fit' and that, where information is to be furnished to him in connection with such enquiries, he may still proceed with a determination of the complaint where the requested information has not been provided by a specified due date.

Appeal procedure

The 1999 Act introduces new rights of appeal to the Employment Appeal Tribunal (on points of law) from the Certification Officer's decisions. Paragraph 8, inserting a new s 45D into the TULR(C)A 1992, introduces the right to appeal for an application regarding the duty to maintain a register of members, the request for access to accounts and the duty to ensure that offenders do not hold union office. A new s 56A of the TULR(C)A 1992 (inserted by para 12) provides for an appeal to the Employment Appeal Tribunal for those applications relating to complaints about union balloting arrangements for elections under s 55 of the TULR(C)A 1992. Section 108C provides that an appeal on any question of law arising from a determination by the Certification Officer in rule book proceedings also lies to the Employment Appeal Tribunal.

---

21 Schedule 6, paras 17 and 18.

CHAPTER 2

TRADE UNION GOVERNMENT AND ADMINISTRATION

THE STRUCTURE OF TRADE UNIONS

The internal structure of a trade union, the way it is governed and the distribution of power within it is determined by the provisions of the union rule book which acts as the union's constitution. The rule book defines the place of the branches, districts, regions or councils, conferences and various *ad hoc* union committees in the management of the union. Subject to statutory provisions to the contrary, the rule book also defines the composition of each governing body, its powers, eligibility for membership, and the method of election or appointment to it.

Of course, not all union rule books contain exactly the same provisions. A rule book is written on a union's foundation and amended as circumstances require. Therefore, the peculiar constitutional arrangements of any one union is influenced by matters such as the union's recruitment patterns, its democratic objectives and the changing needs and requirements of its membership. Even though, traditionally, craft, industrial and general unions have had their own distinctive form of organisational structure, within these classifications there has always been a diversity of internal administrative arrangements. This diversity has been amplified over the past 20 years as a result of increasing union rationalisation through amalgamation and the transfer of membership from one union to another and by the broadening of recruitment within and across the traditional categories; both trends precipitated by economic conditions hostile to trade unionism.[1]

While the complexity of organisational structure is a characteristic feature of the British trade union scene, it is possible to identify some broad principles applicable to most unions. Many unions have a unitary structure with a geographical regional division of their administration. In other unions, where there is a more diverse membership, administrative arrangements may be sectionally based, reflecting the many trades or occupations of the membership.[2] Where the structure is federal, with areas or sections separate to the national union, different organisational arrangements will be in place. Members of a federal union usually belong to both the regional union and the national union. Each regional or local organisation is a separate trade union discrete from the national union, and the national body itself is a federation of the local unions and a union in its own right. This form of administrative organisation can have its advantages where a trade union wishes to avoid or limit responsibility for illegalities (see later, pp 29–30).

Most unions also have some common features of internal government. All have the local branch, which is the focus of union activity for the ordinary member.[3] Branches

---

1   In 1979 there were 433 listed trade unions with the number declining to 256 by 1995. The most recent figures show a further fall to 221 (Annual Reports of the Certification Officer for 1979, 1995 and 1999–2000).

2   The Transport and General Workers Union is an example of a union that utilises the trade group structure with separate sections for road haulage, agriculture, dockworkers, etc.

3   It is unusual for a single branch to have more than 300 or 400 members. The majority tend to have less than 100 members. See Millward, N *et al*, *Workplace Industrial Relations in Transition*, 1992, pp 139–43 and Cully, M *et al*, *Britain at Work*, 1999, p 193.

have their own, usually unpaid, officials, such as a chair, secretary and treasurer, who are elected by the local branch membership. How much autonomy a branch has is dependent on the rule book. In some unions, the rule book provides for a substantial degree of autonomy sufficient for the branch to operate independently of the national union.

Within the branch, there will usually be other appointed or elected officials, known as shop stewards, who act as spokespersons and representatives for a defined group at the workplace. In the vast majority of unions, the position of the local shop steward is incorporated into the formal constitution of the union with the rule book providing for a system of election or appointment of shop stewards and incorporating shop steward committees into the branch structure.[4] As most union activity is based at the local level, the shop stewards of an enterprise are of great importance. They deal with shop floor issues on a day to day basis, acting as a channel of communication between members and management and are often involved with colleagues in other unions in negotiating local collective agreements through a joint shop stewards committee.[5]

The next tier of authority within a geographically organised union is usually the district council. All branches from within the district will usually elect or appoint a representative to serve on the district council. Like the branch, the district council will have a chair, secretary and treasurer. At this level, there is also often an employed full time officer, known as the district secretary, who is responsible for the day to day administration of union affairs in that district. Other full time union organisers may be employed to assist the district secretary and to support and advise branches in that district.

Members of the district council are then appointed or elected by their colleagues to serve on a regional council. Members of the regional council are likewise delegated to the final and supreme decision making body of the union, the national council. If a union structure does not include such a body, then supreme authority is exercised by branch and district members nominated or elected to a national delegate conference, convened annually or biennially. Often, such members are mandated by their local branches or districts to support or oppose a particular issue and to vote accordingly. In some unions, the rule book may provide for both bodies, with the annual conference having the ultimate authority for determining union policy.

The implementation of national union policy and authority for the day to day running of the national union is vested in the national executive committee. This committee will usually have specific authority to act in the name of the national council or delegate conference unless overruled by that body. The composition of the national executive differs widely between unions. It may consist of only full time paid officers or a mixture of paid officers and representatives from the districts or branches. The major officers of the union are described in the rule book, which will define the powers and authority of the incumbents. Most unions will have a president who is ordinarily a

---

4   See Clegg, H, *The Changing System of Industrial Relations in Great Britain,* 1979, Chapters 2 and 5 and *op cit,* Cully, fn 3, 1999, Chapter 9.

5   Despite media criticism in the 1960s portraying shop stewards as militants fomenting industrial unrest, the Donovan Commission (Cmnd 3623, 1968, para 110) concurred with the view that shop stewards were a 'reasonable and even moderating influence, more of a lubricant than an irritant'.

nominal figurehead, with little real power, and a general secretary whose role has been compared to a chief executive. Since 1984, all members of the national executive committee, whether full time or lay, paid or unpaid, must be elected by the union membership.[6]

The degree of democratic accountability entrenched in a constitution varies between unions. The aim, not always attained, is to establish a system which reconciles effective leadership with rank and file control. Most unions have a system that delivers a high degree of democratic participation by the membership at all levels of the union organisation, ensuring that the union hierarchy is responsive to the wishes of the membership. At each stage of decision making or policy formulation, there is an exhaustive process of consultation and debate with the membership or their nominated or elected delegates. This arrangement ensures that, ultimately, power is exercised by the membership as a whole.[7]

This degree of internal democratic control over each level of the union structure has been often overlooked by legislators and the judiciary when legal constraints over internal trade union matters are developed. Decisions which have been taken under the authority of the rule book may offend the individualist sensitivities of the judiciary or clash with the ideological convictions of the government; yet such decisions represent the will of the membership. The reality is that legal interference, whether common law or statutory, ignores rule book democracy and takes control of the union out of the hands of the membership as a whole. This is a theme that will be returned to later in this chapter and in subsequent chapters. First, however, the legal status and definition of trade unions is examined.

TRADE UNION LEGAL STATUS

The legal status of a trade union is of some importance, since it is this status that determines the legal capacity of the organisation. For example, whether legal action can be taken by and against a trade union in its own name, the way property is held, the liability of officers of the union, are all matters determined by the particular legal status imputed to a union. The question that arises is whether a union has the legal status of an individual, of a partnership between individuals, of a statutory or private corporation, or has an exclusive category of status reserved to itself.

Although trade unions had become lawful organisations with the passage of the Trade Union Act 1871, this statute did not deal directly with the issue of trade union legal status. Those unions that had registered under the Trade Union Acts of 1871 and 1876 had had conferred on them by the courts a degree of legal personality equivalent to quasi-corporate status.

---

6   See Chapter 6 for further details.

7   An example of the power of the membership is the response of the union hierarchy in the large industrial unions to the growth of the shop stewards movement early in the 20th century. Democratic accountability of these unions was enhanced by the incorporation of workplace representatives into their formal constitutions.

The leading case of this era was *Taff Vale Rly Co v ASRS*.[8] Farwell J in the High Court noted that the Trade Union Acts rendered the purposes of trade unions legal and enabled these purposes to be carried out by virtue of the specific powers provided in the Acts. Furthermore, the Acts, *inter alia*, established a system of union registration, legalised trade union contracts, authorised the ownership of property through trustees and imposed duties of account on officers. Consequently, he concluded that the existence of these specific provisions meant that Parliament must have intended to treat a registered trade union as if it was a legal entity subject to nearly all the same duties and liabilities as an individual or corporation.

Although the Court of Appeal reversed Farwell J's judgment, the majority of the House of Lords[9] strongly approved his opinion that registered unions possessed similar powers and liabilities to a corporate body.[10] This majority decision was subsequently unanimously re-affirmed by the House of Lords in *ASRS v Osborne*[11] with the Earl of Harlsbury asserting that, as a trade union was a statutory body, the Trade Union Acts represented a trade union's charter of incorporation.[12]

This analysis of trade union status was followed in subsequent cases. In *Gillian v National Union of General and Municipal Workers*,[13] the Court of Appeal, relying heavily on *Taff Vale*, propounded the view that as a registered trade union was a distinct legal person separate from the individuals comprising it, a trade union possessed sufficient characteristics of a company so as to have an independent legal personality capable of being defamed. A majority of the Court of Appeal (Uthwatt J and Scott LJ) went close to suggesting that the union should be treated as if it possessed all the attributes of an incorporated body.

In *Bonsor v Musicians' Union*,[14] the issue of legal status was discussed in the context of whether a union member could sue the union for wrongful expulsion in breach of the rule book and whether damages could be awarded against the union itself. Although both Lord Morton and Lord Porter recognised that a union may not possess the full powers of an incorporated body, they concurred with the notion, stemming from *Taff Vale*, that a union possessed most of the attributes of a corporation. Thus, to their Lordships, there was no doubt that the union, as a hybrid, quasi-corporate body, had the capacity to make contracts and therefore to be sued under them.

While these cases show that unions were treated by the courts for many purposes as invested with the characteristics of corporate bodies, it remained unclear what the true extent of trade union quasi-legal status was. Doubts persisted as to whether it was technically correct to treat unions as separate legal entities possessing nearly all, if not all,

---

8   [1901] AC 426.
9   [1901] AC 434.
10 Eg, Lord Brampton said (p 442): '... a legal entity was created under the 1871 Act by registration ... the legal entity ... though not perhaps in a strict sense a corporation, is nevertheless a newly created corporate body created by statute distinct from the unincorporated trade union consisting of many thousands of separate individuals ...'
11 [1910] AC 87.
12 See also *Yorkshire Miners' Association v Howden* [1905] AC 256 (HL).
13 [1946] KB 81.
14 [1956] AC 110. For comment, see Wedderburn, KW (now Lord), 'The *Bonsor* affair: a postscript' (1957) 20 MLR 105.

the attributes of a corporation. In 1968 the Donovan Commission reported that any uncertainty should be ended by statute formally providing for the incorporation of trade unions.[15] This recommendation was resisted by many unions who did not want formal legal recognition as a corporation, perceiving that form of organisation as being based on a hierarchical centralised structure with power residing in a controlling Board of Directors, which was inappropriate to their needs and contrary to their democratic history.

The Industrial Relations Act 1971, however, did provide for the formal incorporation of trade unions, although this full incorporated status was only available to those unions that registered under the Act. Few unions did so for reasons related to the rejection of many of the other provisions of the Act. The Labour Government elected in 1974 repealed the majority of the provisions of the Industrial Relations Act 1971 and replaced it with the Trade Union and Labour Relations Act 1974. The aim of s 2(1) of the 1974 Act was to put on a statutory footing the anomalous status of a trade union as an unincorporated association of workers with specific features usually associated with corporations.

This section first asserted that a 'trade union shall not be, or treated as if it were, a body corporate' and specified that any attempted incorporation under the Companies Acts would be void. It continued by providing specific authority for unions to enter into contracts, for property to be held in trust for the benefit of the trade union as an entity, for unions to be subject to the criminal law, for unions to sue and be sued in their own name and for civil judgments to be enforced as if the union was a company.[16]

The question arose in *EETPU v Times Newspapers Ltd*[17] as to whether the provisions of this section furnished unions with the same level of status as had been bestowed by the courts from 1901–71. An article in *The Times* had alleged that vote rigging had taken place in union elections. The union wished to initiate an action in libel, believing that as an organisation its character had been defamed. Individuals as natural legal persons can, of course, be libelled, as can corporations who, since they possess full artificial legal personality, can sue to protect their trading reputation. For the EETPU to sustain the action, it was necessary that sufficient legal personality be attributed to the union in the same way that it is attributed to companies.

Prior to s 2(1), the Court of Appeal in *Gillian*[18] had, as we saw earlier, established that unions registered under the 1871 Act possessed this degree of separate personality and consequently had a reputation to protect. O'Connor J in *EETPU* held that this was not now the position. Despite the fact that s 2(1) conferred on unions most of the elements of corporate status, the words of the section – 'shall not be treated as a corporate body' – limited union legal status to something less than had previously been the case. As a union specifically did not have corporate powers, it clearly did not possess the reputation of a corporate body. For the union to take action for defamation depended on whether the list of rights and liabilities contained in s 2(1) conferred such a power on a union. As the list did not do so, the EETPU could not maintain an action in their own name in relation to their reputation.

---

15 Cmnd 3623, para 782.
16 Now, see TULR(C)A 1992, ss 10(1) and 12(1)(2) which substantially repeat this formulation.
17 [1980] QB 585.
18 [1946] KB 81.

O'Connor J's decision – that a trade union is not a corporation or quasi-corporation but merely an association of individuals with exhaustively defined collective powers – was affirmed by the Court of Appeal in *Times Newspapers Ltd v Derbyshire CC*.[19] The case concerned the liability for libel of a local authority. In the course of the judgment on the substance of the action, the court made *obiter* comments on the *Gillian* and *EETPU* cases. Two out of the three Court of Appeal judges (Balcombe and Butler-Sloss LJJ) assumed that the right to sue in defamation had been removed by the 1974 Act and that the decision in *EETPU* had been correct.

However, some confusion concerning the issue of whether a union has the capacity to sue for defamation has arisen as a consequence of the judgment by Lord Keith in the appeal to the House of Lords.[20] Lord Keith, who gave the leading speech which was unanimously followed by his colleagues, commented favourably on the decision of the Court of Appeal in *Gillian*, noted the sound reasons for it and discussed *Gillian*'s relevance to other cases concerning non-trading associations. Keith, however, failed to comment on the *EETPU* case or the assumption of the Court of Appeal that *Gillian* no longer represented the correct legal position.

What is clear is that Lord Keith's remarks have not altered the general position on trade union legal status which remains governed by ss 10(1) and 12(1)(2) of the Trade Union and Labour Relations (Consolidation) Act (TULR(C)A) 1992. Rather, the only issue that has been somewhat clouded is the specific issue of whether a trade union may sue in its own name for defamation. As mentioned, Lord Keith failed to consider the judgment by O'Connor in *EETPU*. Until the *EETPU* case is directly reconsidered by a higher court and overruled, it must still be regarded as authority for the principle that a trade union cannot protect its reputation by an action in defamation.

THE DEFINITION OF A TRADE UNION

The statutory definition of what constitutes a trade union is applied by the Certification Officer in determining whether the organisation can be entered on the list of trade unions. Listing is voluntary, but it does have some advantages as entry on the list is the gateway to tax advantages for the union such as tax relief on provident or friendly funds.[21] More importantly, without listing, the union would be unable to apply for a certificate of independence which is a prerequisite for the union to be eligible for certain additional benefits (see p 31).

Section 1(a) of the TULR(C)A 1992 defines a Trade Union as:

... an organisation of ... workers of one or more descriptions and whose principal purposes include the regulation of relations between workers of that description or those descriptions and employers or employers associations.

---

19 [1992] 3 All ER 65.
20 [1993] 1 All ER 1011.
21 Income and Corporation Taxes Act 1988, s 467.

This definition was considered by the Court of Appeal in *British Association of Advisers and Lecturers in Physical Education* (BAALPE) *v NUT*.[22] In 1982, BAALPE terminated an affiliation agreement with the NUT. As a consequence, the NUT in conjunction with other unions, moved to exclude BAALPE from the Soulsbury panel, which was the negotiating body for certain employees in the education field. On the issuing of a writ against the NUT alleging breach of contract, the preliminary issue to be decided was whether BAALPE was a competent body to initiate proceedings. The NUT argued that, as a small and ineffective organisation, BAALPE did not satisfy the definition of a trade union and so was incapable of suing in its own name. The Court of Appeal explained that, so long as BAALPE's principal purpose was to regulate relations between its members and the employer, how effective it was at doing so was not a relevant consideration. By participating in the Soulsbury committee, BAALPE had satisfied this principal purpose test and so qualified as a trade union.

Professional bodies that have the function of administering the profession, rather than representing members in negotiations with employers, are not trade unions. In *Carter v Law Society*,[23] Carter was a director of an organisation that provided cheap conveyancing for its members, undercutting established fees usually charged by solicitors. The Law Society responded by advising all members to refuse to co-operate with the organisation in conveyancing transactions. Carter then took action against the Law Society alleging that the Law Society as a trade union had committed an 'unfair industrial practice' under the legislation then in force, the Industrial Relations Act 1971.

The High Court held there were two grounds why the Law Society did not fall within the definition of a trade union. First, it was not an 'organisation of workers' as it did not wholly or mainly consist of persons who are employed by the Law Society. Second, the Law Society had a variety of functions, of which the 'regulation of relations between workers and employers' was a minor rather than a principal function or purpose of the Law Society.

A year after this case, to avoid any doubt, s 30(1) of the Trade Union and Labour Relations Act 1974, expressly excluded in the definition of 'worker' those persons that provide professional services. This is now found in s 296 of the TULR(C)A 1992 which states:

... worker means an individual who works ... or seeks to work

(a) under a contract of employment, or

(b) under any other contract whereby he undertakes to do or perform personally any work or services for another party to the contract who is not a professional client of his ...

Can a branch be a trade union in its own right?

One consequence of the *BAALPE* decision is that any organisation, which satisfies the definition in s 1(a) of the TULR(C)A 1992, no matter how small or ineffective, may be regarded as a trade union.[24] It is therefore arguable that, if an individual branch or

---

22   [1986] IRLR 497.

23   [1973] ICR 113.

24   Indeed, in *Midland Cold Storage v Turner* [1972] ICR 230, the court was willing to apply the definition to a temporary joint shop stewards' committee comprising only seven members.

section of a trade union carries out sufficient functions to bring it within the definition in s 1(a) and it is organisationally separate from the national union, then it exists as a trade union in its own right.

Statutory provisions give credence to the view that branches or sections of a trade union may exist as legally separate entities to the parent body. The obligations on trade unions with regard to elections contained in the TULR(C)A 1992 ensures, in s 50(3)(c), that '... section of a union includes a part of the union which is itself a trade union'. There are other references in the Act that support the view that branches or sections may exist as separate trade unions in their own right. For example, s 44(3) (dealing with the accounting duties of trade unions) states, '... references to a branch or section do not include a branch or section which is itself a trade union'.[25]

In *NGN Ltd v SOGAT 82*,[26] Stuart Smith J followed the conclusions of the Court of Appeal in *BAALPE* and re-emphasised that the size or effectiveness of the organisation was an irrelevant factor. What was required was that the branch or section satisfied the definition by existing as an organisation of workers, with the purpose of representing such workers in negotiations with employers over terms and conditions of employment.[27] The fact that members of a branch were also members of the main trade union did not prevent the branch from being a trade union in its own right.[28]

One consequence of this decision was that injunctions were granted against individual branches to restrain picketing organised at the branch level. Yet, there may be occasions when a union would wish to take on the guise of a loose grouping of associated but separate units. For example, in a dispute with an employer where the national union has acted unlawfully and has been fined for contempt for failing to adhere to a court order, should the fine remain unpaid, it may be advantageous to allocate national union funds to these legally separate branches or sections to frustrate any attempts at the sequestration of national union assets. National union funds would be protected from seizure so long as they remained the property of the legally separate branches.

Moreover, if industrial action is organised locally, with local branch members or officials breaking the civil law, then it would be the branch, as a separate trade union rather than the national organisation, which would suffer the financial penalty should an employer take an action in damages for loss. Section 22 of the TULR(C)A 1992 provides that the maximum in damages that can be recovered is dependent on the number of members of the union. For example, if the union has less than 5,000 members, the maximum award in damages is £10,000, continuing on a scale up to £250,000 for the

---

25 See also TULR(C)A 1992, s 119, on the interpretation of expressions used in the Act. The term 'branch or section' in the Act '... includes a branch or section which is itself a trade union'.

26 [1986] IRLR 337.

27 In the earlier case of *Midland Cold Storage v Turner* [1972] ICR 230, employers attempted to sue a temporary joint shop stewards' committee that organised industrial action. The court interpreted the definition of a trade union narrowly and held that the committee was not a separate trade union because it was not formally involved in negotiations on the terms and conditions acceptable for a resumption of work. It was merely a pressure group advising the union on industrial action.

28 See also *Express & Star Ltd v NGA* [1985] IRLR 455. In this case, Skinner J concentrated on the issue of whether the branch had real independence from the national union. Because the rules imposed a 'monolithic' rather than federal organisational structure, he held that the union was not a federation of autonomous separate unions: consequently, the national union was liable for the actions of branch officials.

biggest unions. As branches are ordinarily limited in size to well below 5,000 members, actual damages recoverable by an employer would be likely to be far less than if the employer was able to sue the national union.

EVIDENCE OF STATUS AS A TRADE UNION

Where an organisation wishes to be entered on the list of trade unions, s 3 of the TULR(C)A 1992 outlines the procedure for an application to the Certification Officer. Once the Certification Officer is satisfied that the organisation complies with the definition in s 1(a) and so qualifies as a trade union, the name of the trade union is included on the list. The union's appearance on the list is good evidence of status as a trade union and a certificate is issued to this effect.[29] Should an organisation wish to appeal from the decision of the Certification Officer not to enter its name on the list or to remove their name from the list, then an appeal lies to the Employment Appeal Tribunal (EAT) on fact or law. The appeal is in the form of a re-hearing, so the EAT will come to its own independent decision.[30]

This system of certifying status replaced the previous method under the Industrial Relations Act 1971 of the registration of unions. Registration under the 1971 Act was necessary for unions to enjoy the benefit of certain statutory rights. The disadvantages to a union which refused to register were substantial. Without registering, unions were open to extensive legal action by employers for 'unfair industrial practices' if they took industrial action. However, very few unions registered, as that implied complicity in a system of industrial relations based on legal and State control over the internal affairs and external activities of the union, contrary to the system which operated prior to the 1971 Act. Throughout the short life of the Act, most unions refused to register and campaigned for the repeal of the Act, which duly occurred on the fall of the Conservative Government in 1974.

Only listed unions can apply for a certificate of independence.[31] Once in possession of a certificate of independence, trade unions are the recipients of a degree of State support to enhance the effectiveness of their activities. The most important benefits granted are the right of individual members to be protected against anti-union action, so enabling them to join the union and engage in union activities without fear of victimisation or discrimination,[32] and the right of the union to apply for recognition.[33]

Once an independent union has been recognised, various other rights that facilitate collective bargaining are provided, such as the right to information for collective bargaining purposes,[34] right of consultation on redundancies,[35] right of consultation on a

---

29 Section 2(4).
30 Section 9(1).
31 Section 6.
32 See TULR(C)A 1992, ss 146 and 152.
33 See *ibid*, s 70A and Sched A1.
34 *Ibid*, s 181.
35 *Ibid*, s 188.

proposed transfer of an undertaking[36] and the right to time off for trade union officials and members to engage in trade union activities and duties[37] (see Chapters 9 and 11). The aim of this system of listing and certifying independence is not to enhance employer or State control over union affairs, but rather to identify which organisations are genuine trade unions and, thus, deserving of support for their legitimate trade union activities.[38]

The test for independence

The test for independence is devised to identify unions that are independent of the employer and fully represent the workforce. The question the Certification Officer has to consider is whether the applicant organisation is:

(a) not under the domination or control of an employer or group of employers or of one or more employers' associations; and

(b) is not liable to interference by an employer or any such group or association (arising out of the provision of financial or material support or by any other means whatsoever) tending towards such control ...[39]

Disputes over the use of the Certification Officer's discretion were particularly prevalent in the 1970s as a consequence of the large growth in 'white collar' staff associations in the banking insurance and chemical industries. There were some allegations that many of these organisations were management inspired 'sweetheart' staff associations or 'house unions' easily influenced by employers. The purpose behind the test for independence is to exclude such weak and dependent staff associations from obtaining the statutory benefits available to *bona fide* trade unions.

The EAT, in *Blue Circle Staff Association v CO*,[40] and the Court of Appeal, in *Squibb UK Staff Association v CO*,[41] approved the criteria the Certification Officer was using in his application of this test for independence. In determining whether the applicant union is independent, the Certification Officer will take into account information provided under the following headings.

(a) Finance: who provides the finance for the union? If the employer does so, then that is strong evidence that the union is 'under the domination or control of the employer'. If the financial base of the union is weak and the union receives some limited financial assistance from an employer, this implies the union is 'vulnerable to interference' by the employer.

---

36 TUPE Regulations (SI 1981/1794).
37 TULR(C)A 1992, ss 168 and 170.
38 The system of certifying independence to exclude weak employer orientated unions from obtaining benefits which support collective bargaining was first introduced in the Industrial Relations Act 1971 to counter the perceived anti-union bias of the Act as a whole.
39 Section 5. The burden of proof is on the applicant. See *Association of HSD (Hatfield) Employees v CO* [1978] ICR 21.
40 [1977] ICR 224.
41 [1979] 2 All ER 452.

(b) Other support: does the employer provide any other support such as premises and office facilities? If they are provided for free or at low cost, this is evidence of dependence on the employer.[42]

(c) History: was the union originally created by the employer and controlled by the employer? If so, has it now grown from being a 'creature of management into something more independent'.[43]

(d) Membership base: does the union only recruit from one employer or is it a more broadly based union? If it recruits solely from one employer, then it is more likely to be 'vulnerable to interference' from that employer.

(e) Organisation and structure: are the rules settled by the employer so that the employer can control or interfere with the union? The rules should also allow the members of the union to play a full part in the decision making process and exclude the employer or senior members of the management from any involvement in union affairs.[44]

(f) Negotiating record: what is the unions general attitude to negotiations with the employer, is it 'robust', with a good record of success?

The applicant union does not have to pass a test based on each individual factor. The Certification Officer will consider the full circumstances and nature of the case in deciding whether, overall, the union is under the domination or control of the employer or, if not, whether the union is liable to interference by the employer. In the *Blue Circle* case, the EAT approved the refusal of a certificate as the staff association had been created and then dominated by the employer for some years. During these years of domination by the employer, the staff association had been little more than a form of personnel control. Although there was evidence of some progress towards independence, the staff association had still not satisfied the heavy burden of showing that it had divested itself of this control by the employer, as '... the process of asserting genuine and effective independence after some years of such domination by management as has occurred in this case is likely to be protracted'.[45]

Most unions that fail to obtain the certificate of independence do so on the less stringent second limb of the test. In *Squibb UK Staff Association v CO*,[46] the Court of Appeal held that a union is 'liable to interference' if it is 'vulnerable to interference' or 'exposed to the risk' of control without possessing the means to resist such control. Furthermore, the Court of Appeal held that whether it is actually likely, or not unlikely, that the employers will exploit such vulnerability, is not relevant. Any factors that raise a possibility of interference, even if it was unlikely to happen in practice, should result in a certificate being refused.

---

42 In *Squibb*, finance from the employer and the provision of an office, stationery and equipment was accepted as evidence of the union's vulnerability to interference. Ironically, once a union is certified as independent and recognised by an employer, it is expected that it will be the recipient of such facilities to enable it to function effectively. See ACAS Code of Practice on Time Off for Trade Union Duties and Activities, para 28.

43 The union in the *Blue Circle* case was created by the employer and was not able to show that it had developed a sufficient degree of independence.

44 In *Blue Circle*, the employer nominated members of the union executive and could interfere in the selection of union representatives.

45 Cumming Bruce J, p 234.

46 [1979] 2 All ER 452.

In *Squibb*, the provision of financial support and other assistance from the employer combined with the record of ineffective bargaining and the small membership base meant that this staff association was 'exposed to the risk of' interference which would tend towards control by the employer. Even though there was little likelihood of the employer bringing pressure to bear by withdrawing this material support, if it were to be withdrawn, the association would be sufficiently weakened to be unable to resist employer interference and continue independently.

The *Squibb* interpretation of the test was applied by the Certification Officer in *GCHQ v CO*.[47] After the rights of association in trade unions had been withdrawn by the Conservative administration in 1984 from members of staff at GCHQ, the question arose as to whether the new GCHQ staff federation which replaced representation by national trade unions was entitled to a certificate of independence. The GCHQ Staff Federation's application for a certificate of independence was refused by the Certification Officer and the appeal to the EAT was dismissed. Wood J concluded that the employer's previous actions in dismantling the established unions and the subsequent denial of employment protection rights to workers at GCHQ indicated that the very existence of the staff federation was at the mercy of management, which may independently or by instruction from the Government withdraw approval or recognition. As the staff association's ability to negotiate on behalf of its members, its freedom of action and, indeed, its very existence depended on the approval of the management, the staff association was clearly 'exposed or vulnerable or at the risk of interference' and failed to satisfy s 5(b).

Once granted, a certificate of independence is conclusive evidence of independence.[48] But likewise, a withdrawal or cancellation of the certificate of independence under s 7 is conclusive evidence that the trade union is not independent. An appeal on law or fact against a refusal, withdrawal or cancellation of a certificate proceeds to the EAT.[49]

TRADE UNION FINANCIAL AFFAIRS

Trade union property

As a trade union is not a distinct legal person, it cannot hold property in its own name. As an unincorporated association (albeit with special powers), a trade union must hold property vested in trustees. This principle was put on a statutory footing by s 8 of the Trade Union Act 1871, which stated that the trustees of a registered trade union hold property 'for such a trade union and the members thereof'.

It had been argued in a number of cases in the early 20th century that this provision meant that the assets of a union were held both collectively and individually: consequently, it was only the terms of the contract of association which stopped an

---

47 [1993] IRLR 260.

48 Section 8(1).

49 Section 9(2). A union unhappy at the granting of a certificate of independence to a rival organisation cannot itself appeal against this decision – *General Municipal Workers Union v CO & Imperial Group Staff Association* [1977] ICR 183.

individual from claiming his or her share on dissolution of the union.[50] But, in the majority of cases decided at that time, it was held that the primary beneficiary was 'the union' itself rather than individual members.[51] Accordingly, as the trustees held union property for the membership as a whole, an individual member only possessed an indirect interest in the assets of the union and, as such, could not claim a severable share on dissolution of the union or otherwise.

The Industrial Relations Act 1971, in a departure from the legal position established 100 years before, gave registered unions corporate status. Union property was vested directly as corporate property, thus dispensing with the need for trustees. On repeal of the Industrial Relations Act, the Trade Union and Labour Relations Act 1974 restored the non-corporate status of trade unions and specified that '... all property belonging to the trade union shall be vested in trustees in trust for the union'.[52] The words 'and the members thereof' have been omitted from this new formulation. This resolves any residual uncertainty surrounding the exact legal right of the membership over union property. The individual member does not have any direct beneficial interest in the property as the sole beneficiary under this section is clearly stated as 'the union' only. Trade union property is held on trust for the benefit of the membership of the union as a whole.

It is clear now that, as the assets of the union are not held by the trustees on trust for the members individually but rather for the members collectively, a member cannot claim any severable share of the union's funds. Any right members have over union property under the trust is therefore determined solely by any contractual rights contained in the rule book rather than under the general law of trusts.[53] This was confirmed in *Hughes v TGWU*,[54] where Hughes's request for full access to all branch and national union accounts was refused. Hughes argued that he was entitled to see the accounts as he was simply asking for access to information on property he part owned. Vinelott J disagreed, holding that as trustees hold the property for the union as a whole, the individual member does not have any direct interest in the property of the union. Any entitlement to view the accounts depended on the provisions of the rule book which, in this case, clearly denied him this right. (See, now, the statutory right to examine accounts, p 43.)

Trust formalities

The union rule book is the document that sets out the terms of the trust, the trustees powers and duties and the procedure for the appointment and removal of trustees. It may provide for the holders of certain offices of the union to be trustees or for the trustees to be elected by the annual conference. There is no requirement for trustees to be members of the national executive and, often, they are not. However, typically, it is the executive committee

---

50 Some support for this view had been gleaned from the statement of Lord Lindley in *Yorkshire Miners' Association v Howden* [1905] AC 256, p 280, when he said: '... a trade union holds property by trustees; but not being incorporated, there is no one legal person or entity in whom the beneficial interest in the property of a trade union is vested. The beneficiaries are its members collectively and severally.'

51 See, eg, the judgment of the Court of Appeal in *Cotter v NUS* [1929] 2 Ch 58.

52 Now, TULR(C)A 1992, s 12(1).

53 For the most recent exposition of this view, see the comments of Sir Donald Nicholls VC in *Boddington v Lawton* [1994] ICR 478, p 494.

54 [1985] IRLR 382. For comment, see Rideout, R (1986) 15 ILJ 46.

that has the real power to make financial decisions as the trustees are normally required to act in accordance with the lawful directions of the national executive committee.

The rule book may provide for union property to be split between national and local units of the union, with certain property vesting in branch trustees for the benefit of members of that branch. As we shall see later, this has important legal implications if action is taken to satisfy damages claims made against national union property.

A listed union benefits from specific administrative arrangements on the vesting of property. Ordinarily, under the general law where there is a voluntary change of trustees, either through retirement or removal, the Trustees Act 1925 requires certain property to be transferred by deed to new trustees. Sections 12 and 13 of the TULR(C)A 1992 introduce a special regime for unions by making specific provision for the automatic vesting of property in new trustees on death or removal subject to certain formalities. Section 14 facilitates the transfer of stocks and shares to any new trustees.

Common law control over trustees

The trust should be administered in accordance with the terms of the trust deed, that is, the provisions of the rule book. Any disposition of property outside the terms of the trust in the rule book is unlawful and trustees are then liable to the union for breach of trust. Only the union has the authority to take action under the trust.[55] As we have already seen, members only have an indirect beneficial interest in the union assets and so have no 'rights' under the trust. Yet, as Sir David Nicholls VC said, in *Boddington v Lawton*,[56] the trustees hold the society's property '... upon trust for the members on the terms set out in the rules'. Since the terms of the trust are contractual terms contained in the rule book, an action to enforce the rule book would in theory allow individual members a right to sue the trustees for breach of trust.

In these circumstances, the individual member has to overcome the rule in *Foss v Harbottle*[57] (see Chapter 3). This rule provides that an individual member has no right to complain of a breach of rule book, in circumstances where the wrong has been committed against the union as a whole. Thus, it would seem that where *Foss v Harbottle* applies, the member's only option is to publicise the breach and to request the union to take action. However, the rule in *Foss v Harbottle* does not apply in certain circumstances, such as where the action of the trustees is *ultra vires*. The doctrine of *ultra vires* will apply if funds are used for purposes that are not permitted by the rules.[58] In such a situation, the member does have standing to take an action on the basis of the breach of trust arising from the rule book.

---

55 See *Oddy v TSSA* [1973] ICR 524.

56 [1994] ICR 478, p 494.

57 (1843) 2 Hare 461.

58 In practice, the rule book of a union gives the national executive the power to give directions to trustees regarding the disposition of property. The main role of the trustees is thus to obey the lawful instructions of the executive. If these instructions are themselves unlawful and a trustee follows such an instruction, an actionable breach of trust has been committed. Eg, in *Bennett v National Amalgamated Society of Operative House and Ship Painters and Decorators* (1916) 85 LJ Ch 298, union trustees were instructed to buy shares in a commercial concern where there was no power to do so in the rules. As this was an *ultra vires* payment, the individual member had standing to take an action based on the breach of trust derived from the rule book. See also *Carter v Utd Society of Boilermakers* (1916) 85 LJ Ch 289.

An opportunity for individual union members to enforce this form of common law right was provided during the miners' strike of 1984–85. During the strike, fines were imposed on the NUM for contempt of court for refusing to adhere to a series of court orders. The NUM executive declined to pay and as a precaution ordered the trustees of the union to send union funds abroad out of the jurisdiction of the UK courts. As a consequence of the continuing contempt, a sequestrator was appointed to recover the amount due. The trustees refused to authorise payment of the appropriate sums to the court appointed sequestrator and took action to frustrate the efforts of the sequestrator in tracking down union funds.

An NUM member successfully took action to have the union trustees removed from office for breach of trust derived from the rule book. The official receiver was appointed in their place to administer the union's assets. Although the trustees were complying with their duties as trustees under the rule book by obeying the instructions of the national executive committee, these instructions were not in themselves lawful. By complying with unlawful instructions the trustees were, consequently, in breach of the terms of the trust and acting *ultra vires*. Mervyn Davies J concluded that, as the trustees were aware that their actions would very likely result in further substantial fines against the union and a reduction in the size of the funds available for lawful purposes, they were not 'fit and proper persons' to administer the property of the union.[59]

Additional control of union financial matters can be enforced through the general law of trusts. This enables the union to challenge the way the assets are being used, if there has been a breach of a fiduciary duty by the trustees. Individual union members cannot sue directly for breach of fiduciary duty as the duty is owed to the union. However, where a breach of fiduciary duty is alleged, there will usually also have been a breach of the trust deed derived from the rule book and so, subject to the rule in *Foss v Harbottle*, an action would proceed based on breach of contract.

In *Cowan v Scargill*,[60] NUM representatives on the NCB pension fund management committee refused to agree to an investment plan that invested in overseas companies and in the competing oil and gas industries. This plan was contrary to union policy and, in the opinion of the NUM trustees, not in the best interests of the beneficiaries. On an application by the NCB trustees, the High Court found that the NUM trustees were in conflict with their fiduciary duty to ensure the best return on the funds held. The trustees' personal views or moral reservations on the choice of investments were not relevant nor were the requirements of the coal industry or the union. It was solely the interests of the beneficiaries to the pension fund that were relevant and these were not met by excluding high yielding overseas investments or investments in competition with coal.

Union funds, damages and sequestration

Where calls on trade union funds are made as a consequence of a fine or a damages or costs award and the union refuses to pay, a sequestration order may be taken out against union property. *In extremis*, all union property may be seized, making it impossible for the

---

59   *Clarke v Heathfield (No 2)* [1985] ICR 606. See, also, *Taylor v NUM (Derbyshire Area) (No 3)* [1985] IRLR 99, where trustees following an instruction from the national executive misapplied union funds by providing strike pay to miners engaged in an unlawful strike.

60   [1984] IRLR 260. For comment, see Nobles, R (1984) 13 ILJ 167 and (1985) 14 ILJ 1.

union to function effectively. As we have seen earlier, a branch that satisfies the definition of a trade union is a separate trade union in its own right with branch trustees holding branch funds. These funds should not be liable to sequestration on the wrongdoing of the national union or of another branch.

Union funds can, however, be protected by other methods without it being necessary to allocate funds to branches that are themselves separate in law. Even where branches remain a part of the parent union, funds that are vested in separate branch trustees are arguably protected from sequestration, as branch trustees hold property for the individual branch, not the union as a whole. Such funds are therefore safeguarded should there be an attempt at seizure due to a transgression of the national union.

If the rule book creates separate branch funds, branch property vests in branch trustees. Whether branch funds are separate is dependent on the construction of the national or local rule book. Union rules must not only provide for separate trustees but must also give members the right of sole use of the funds.[61] In *NGN Ltd v SOGAT 82*,[62] both the national and branch rules provided for a considerable degree of independence for the London branch and specifically stated that all branch funds were the property of the branch, vested in the branch trustees for the benefit of the branch alone. The rules, therefore, clearly intended that these funds were to be for the exclusive use of the branch and so, consequently, a writ of sequestration against the property of the union as a whole was not applicable to the property of the London branch.[63]

Sequestration was an issue was of some importance in the printing disputes during the early 1980s as both of the unions involved, the NGA and SOGAT 82, were organised through autonomous branches. In a comment on the NGA dispute in 1983, when all the funds of the union was sequestrated, it was stated that, '... in a union not centrally funded like the NGA, if all branches declared UDI and regained funds, sequestration might have been nullified'.[64] This is perhaps an over-optimistic view, as independence itself is not sufficient: what is required is exclusivity of use of the funds.

An alternative method of protecting funds is to earmark certain funds for particular charitable purposes, such as a fund for the benefit of the families of members in times of hardship. Trustees hold the property on special trusts for the benefit of these designated beneficiaries and not for the union.[65]

Statutory control over trustees

After the litigation during the miners' strike of 1984–85, the Conservative Government believed the common law remedies available to union members were inadequate in controlling the abuse of these funds used to further the dispute. Trustees were always

---

61 See *Cope v Crossingham* [1909] 2 Ch 148.

62 [1986] IRLR 227.

63 Contrast *Burnley v ATW* [1986] IRLR 298, where a local branch was unable to take branch funds on secession from the national union as the rules did not provide for it.

64 See Gennard, J (1984) 15 IRJ 16.

65 See *Sansom v LULVW* (1920) 36 TLR 666; *Thomas v NUM (South Wales Area)* [1985] IRLR 136; and *Hopkins v NUS* [1985] IRLR 157. Statute recognises the existence of these special trusts. TULR(C)A 1992, s 23(2)(a), specifically provides that any damages awarded against the union is not recoverable from property belonging to the trustees in 'some other capacity'.

willing to follow unlawful orders given by the NUM national executive.[66] The Green Paper, *Trade Unions and Their Members*, outlined the need to improve safeguards on the use of union assets in the interests of members who contribute to union funds. The Green Paper noted that the safeguard of union funds by trustees '... comes under strain where the union finds itself in conflict with the law', and that '... persons bearing the title of trustees may properly be required to prevent the unlawful use of the assets they are supposed to be protecting'.[67] The authors of the Green Paper were driven to the conclusion that if trustees do not obey the general law any member should have the right to take action quickly and efficiently to remove the offending trustee.

This right was subsequently provided by the Employment Act 1988 which is now contained in s 16 of the TULR(C)A 1992. This section states that where trustees carry out or propose to carry out their functions unlawfully,[68] such as by breaking the union rules, refusing to carry out a court order or by breaking their general fiduciary duties, any member can take action in the High Court which has the power to make a variety of orders. The court may require the trustees to protect or recover property by, for example, carrying out a particular investment policy or by paying a fine so as to recover property from a receiver.

The court has discretion to remove trustees and can appoint a receiver to administer the remaining union property.[69] Where trustees have not been removed, but a court order has been granted, if the trustees propose to apply or do apply any union funds in contravention of that court order, then the court must remove all the trustees of the union, unless one or more can satisfy the court that there is good cause why they should not be removed.[70]

Importantly, interlocutory relief is available where the court 'considers it appropriate'.[71] This allows the court to remove the trustee on an emergency motion. Removal of trustees at the interlocutory stage would normally take place right at the beginning of an industrial dispute and so would cut-off funding during the crucial early period of the dispute. One side effect of preserving union funds by removing a trustee and appointing a receiver is that the court makes it more likely that the employer who is suing the union can recover damages and costs.

The right to ensure trustee compliance with the law exists side by side with the existing common law right to sue for breach of trust.[72] In the future, it is far more likely

---

66   We saw an example of this earlier, in *Clarke v Heathfield*, where the trustees complied with unlawful directions under the rules given by the national executive committee resulting in their eventual removal and the appointment of a receiver.

67   Cm 95, 1987, Chapter 3, paras 3.1 and 3.14.

68   The section does not define 'unlawful' expansively. Therefore, whether this includes the use of funds in support of industrial action where this action is in breach of an economic tort and not covered by an immunity, is not clear. Note that the right to remove a trustee includes situations where they merely 'propose' to carry out an unlawful act. The right of removal at common law only applies if the breach of trust has already occurred.

69   Section 16(3).

70   Section 16(4). Clearly, any deliberate illegal acts would result in removal. Possibly, the 'good cause' defence is satisfied where the illegality occurred inadvertently and the act contravening the court order was made in good faith for the benefit of the membership as a whole.

71   Section 16(5).

72   Section 16(6).

that a member will initiate statutory action rather than an action under the common law. Although, during the miners' strike, the common law action did eventually result in trustees being removed and union property moved out of the reach of union officials, the new statutory right is a potentially quicker, more effective and flexible remedy, giving clear express rights to union members and particular powers to the court. Moreover, the statutory remedy specifically provides for the appointment of a receiver and so resolves the previous uncertainty that existed about whether the court had power under their inherent jurisdiction to provide such a remedy.[73]

Union finances and the 'check off'

The 'check off' is the system under which the employer deducts trade union subscriptions from members' pay on behalf of the union. This arrangement is by far the most efficient way for trade unions to collect subscriptions and provides unions with a steady and predictable income. Check off arrangements also help in stabilising union membership. Where union subscriptions are collected in person at the workplace by local union officials, there is always a danger that some members will miss payments and gradually 'drift' out of the union.

The Employment Act 1988 required employers to stop deducting union subscriptions from pay where a union member had resigned or intended to resign their union membership and had informed their employer of this. This was enforceable in an industrial tribunal as an unauthorised deduction from wages under the Wages Act 1986 (now ss 13–14 of the Employment Rights Act 1996). In the 1991 Green Paper, *Industrial Relations in the 1990s*,[74] the existence of check off arrangements enforced via provisions in a collective agreement was heavily criticised as interfering with the freedom of individuals to choose the way they wish to pay their subscriptions.

Consequently, in the Trade Union Reform and Employment Rights Act 1993, a new provision was introduced, replacing the protection previously contained in the Employment Act 1988. The deduction of union dues from pay was now only lawful where an employee had given express authorisation in writing. In addition, periodic renewal of this authorisation was required every three years and at all times a union member had the right to withdraw authorisation. Should union subscription charges increase during the three year period, an employer did not have to deduct the new amount until the member has received a month's written notice of the increase from the employer. The notice had to include a reminder that withdrawal of authorisation may be made at any time.

As union subscriptions are the foundation of union finances, this legislative attack on the check off system was viewed with some disquiet by the union movement. One concern was that, as the bureaucratic responsibilities of the new system are on the

---

73   The Trade Union Act 1871, s 4, had prevented a receiver being appointed as the section excluded the courts from interfering in any agreement relating to the application of funds of the union. (See *Sansom v London and Provincial Union of Licensed Vehicle Workers* [1920] 36 TLR 666.) The High Court took advantage of the repeal of the Trade Union Act 1871 by the Industrial Relations Act 1971 and by the absence of such a section in the Trade Union and Labour Relations Act 1974 to appoint receivers in some of the miners' cases. Until the events of the miners' strike, there had been no recorded cases where this had occurred before.

74   Cm 1602.

employer, check off facilities would be slowly abandoned by employers unwilling to administer the system.[75] In practice, however, it seems a greater threat was the abandonment of check off by some employers as a punishment for taking industrial action[76] or as a first step to derecognition.

One of the first acts in the employment field of the Labour Government elected in May 1997 was to introduce an Order in Council (SI 1998/1529), issued under the authority of the Deregulation and Contracting Out Act 1994, reversing the Conservative reforms. The requirement for union members to authorise deductions every three years is repealed, as is the need for unions to notify individuals of any increase in union subscriptions. Now, so long a member authorises the deduction arrangement in writing, then this is authority for an indefinite period,[77] subject to the right to cancel that authorisation at any time.[78] There are also complex transitional arrangements contained in the Order in Council for those individuals who provided a three year consent under the previous regime. Essentially, the authority to deduct sums for the three year period is preserved and on its lapse a new authorisation is required.

Statutory regulation of financial administration

As trade unions are funded directly through members' subscriptions and as they control substantial funds to enable them to provide a variety of services to their membership, it is indisputable that there should be a degree of democratic accountability and fiscal regulation to ensure their financial integrity. Due to the serious consequences of improper financial control, unions have never been left to devise their own financial systems without any interference. Noticeably, however, the degree of regulation has increased dramatically in the years since the miners' strike of 1984–85.

Basic controls over union financial affairs and the disposition of union property were provided by the Trade Union Act 1871, mirroring the type of regulation provided by the Companies Acts of 1844 and 1862. Trade unions were under an obligation to produce properly audited accounts and to deposit an annual financial return with the Chief Registrar. This limited statutory regulation of trade unions was increased dramatically with the passage of the Industrial Relations Act 1971 which introduced a full regulatory framework for all trade union activities including financial administration.

On repeal of the Industrial Relations Act 1971, it was accepted that the financial regulation of trade unions should not revert back to the limited control under the Trade Union Act 1871. The Donovan Commission in 1968[79] had examined the issue of financial administration and had found that the lack of regulation had not resulted in any large scale financial corruption or fraud. However, it also found that inefficiency or waste was not easily identified where inexperienced or untrained staff were involved in preparing

---

75   For a survey of union and employer responses to the changes, see 'Checking up on the check off Campaign' (1994) Labour Research, September, p 11.

76   Eg, British Rail unilaterally cancelled its check off arrangements with the RMT after the union held one day strikes in 1993.

77   Section 68(1).

78   Section 68(2).

79   Royal Commission on Trades Unions and Employers' Associations, Cmnd 3623, 1968.

union accounts and other financial documents. The reasoning behind the regime introduced by the Trade Union and Labour Relations Act 1974 was to cure the problems created by reliance on amateur staff to discharge accounting and other financial tasks.

This was achieved by the introduction of a legally enforceable framework of professional support. The substance of these requirements previously contained in ss 10–12 and Sched 2, Pt 1 of the Trade Union and Labour Relations Act 1974 have been retained and consolidated into ss 28–45 of the TULR(C)A 1992.

The system of financial control

Under s 28 of the TULR(C)A 1992, trade unions must have a proper system of financial control. Appropriate accounting records must be kept, either at branch or national level, so as to satisfactorily provide a '... true and fair view of the state of the affairs of the trade union ... and to explain its transactions'.

Section 32 makes it compulsory for a union to submit an annual financial return to the Certification Officer. The return must include the audited accounts (balance sheet and revenue accounts), a copy of union rules, the auditor's report and a note on any change of union officers.[80] The annual return is available for public inspection and a copy of the annual return must be supplied to members and others on request.[81]

The role of union auditors, their specific duties and the content of their report is guided by ss 33–37. These sections establish the principle that independent professionally qualified auditors must be appointed to report on the accounts that are submitted with the annual return.[82] In particular, the auditors must report on: (i) whether the union has kept proper financial records under s 28; (ii) whether the union has maintained a satisfactory system of checking accounts and finances under s 28; and (iii) whether the accounts in the annual return correspond to the union's accounting records.[83] Under s 37, auditors have extensive rights of access to all financial documents, the right to demand information from union officers and to attend and speak at union general meetings.

Offences

Where the union refuses or wilfully neglects to perform these duties, criminal liability is imposed under s 45(1).[84] Furthermore, under s 45(2), liability also accrues to an officer whose duty it was, unless he or she reasonably believed some other competent person had been authorised to carry out the duty and had done so.[85] It is also an offence for any person in the course of performing the above duties wilfully to alter or cause to be altered any financial document with intent to falsify, so as to enable a trade union to evade any of their financial duties.[86]

---

80 Section 32(3).
81 Section 32(5)(6).
82 Sections 33–35.
83 Section 36.
84 The term 'wilfully neglects' suggests that more than mere negligence is required for the union or official to commit this offence.
85 Section 45(3).
86 Section 45(4).

The annual reports of the Certification Officer have indicated that unions had generally complied with the requirements of the Act and that there was little evidence of any serious financial impropriety. As a consequence, the Conservative Government did not intervene in this area until inspired to do so by the experience of the miners' strike of 1984–85. As the strike was called in contravention of the rule book, litigation was initiated by members to challenge the way union finances were applied to prosecute the strike. Furthermore, as the union refused to obey the orders of the court and found itself in contempt, action was also taken by members to safeguard union assets against sequestration. In the Green Paper, *Trade Unions and Their Members*,[87] it was noted that these actions were hampered by the lack of information available to individual members and by the obstructive attitude of the NUM.

The reforms introduced by the Employment Act 1988 were built on the common law decisions during this period and aimed to make it easier for union members to ascertain wrongdoing by establishing their right to demand access to financial information. The reasoning behind these provisions is that, without an unfettered right to obtain such information, a member would not be able to make an informed decision about whether to initiate an action against the union. These obligations have now been consolidated into TULR(C)A 1992 as ss 29–31.

The right to financial information

Under s 29, unions must have all their accounting records available for possible inspection by any member for a period of six years.[88] Failure to do so may be an offence under s 45(1) if the refusal is deliberate or results from 'wilful neglect'. Section 30 permits a member to inspect the past and current accounts of the national union, or of any branch or section of the union, accompanied, if necessary, by an accountant.[89] The member who wishes to inspect union accounts is entitled to take copies as required, subject to reasonable administrative charges.

The union must comply with this request within 28 days. Should access not be forthcoming or if some or all of the requirements outlined in s 30 are denied, a court order can be obtained under s 31 enforcing the right to inspect. Should the order be ignored, the union or union officials will be held in contempt and heavy fines or possible sequestration of funds may be the consequence. Alternatively, an application can be made to the Certification Officer for an order enforceable in the same way as a court order.

---

87 Cm 95, 1987, para 3.25.

88 Note that this right permits any member to obtain information of all national or branch accounts and so deals with the issue that arose in *Hughes v TGWU* [1985] IRLR 382, where a union member was unable to examine the accounts of branches other than his own as the rules did not permit it.

89 Section 30 provides statutory support to the decision in *Taylor v NUM (Derbyshire Area) (No 2)* [1985] IRLR 65. Vinelott J (following *Norey v Keep* [1909] 1 Ch 561 and *Dodd v AMWU* [1924] 1 Ch 116) had held that, where the rule book gives the member the right to inspect the union accounting records, an implied right exists to have an accountant present for the purposes of interpreting the data.

Financial regulation and the Trade Union Reform and Employment Rights Act 1993

Although the Trade Union and Labour Relations Act 1974 and the Employment Act 1988 imposed a comprehensive regime of financial regulation and a package of rights for members to enforce, further State interference was signalled by the Green Paper, *Industrial Relations in the 1990s*,[90] published in July 1991. The Green Paper noted that '... recent events have indicated that these rights are insufficient' to control financial wrongdoing. This was yet another reference to the effect of the miners' strike. As a consequence of allegations in the press that NUM funds had been misapplied during the strike, the NUM had appointed Gavin Lightman QC to conduct an inquiry.[91] As a consequence of his report, the Certification Officer initiated a prosecution of members of the NUM national executive which failed partly due to the inadmissibility of much of the evidence collected for the report.

The response of the Government to the failure of this prosecution was the conclusion in the Green Paper that the relevant law required strengthening, particularly in the area of the investigation of financial irregularities, the offences that may be committed and the provision of financial information to members. The Green Paper suggested that additional powers should be given to the Certification Officer to find and prosecute irregularities and that those convicted of offences should be barred from holding national office. In addition, it was argued that there should be automatic and extensive disclosure of financial information to enable members to assess whether offences have been committed and to enhance the evidence gathering process for prosecutions. Despite opposition from unions, the substance of the Green Paper was enacted in the Trade Union Reform and Employment Rights Act 1993, amending the TULR(C)A 1992.

The annual return and the financial statement

The Trade Union Reform and Employment Rights Act 1993, amends s 32 of the TULR(C)A 1992, by widening the range of information that has to be disclosed in the union annual return to the Certification Officer. It now provides that details of benefits and salary paid to all members of the executive, president, general secretary and other officials must be disclosed.[92]

A new s 32A of the TULR(C)A 1992 now requires a union that has been in existence for more than 12 months to make an annual financial statement to its members no later than eight weeks after the annual report has been sent to the Certification Officer.[93] Either a copy of the statement can be sent to members or it can published via the union's normal channel of communication, that is, publication in the union newspaper or journal. The

---

90 Cm 1602, 1991.

91 See Lightman, G, *The Lightman Report on the NUM*, 1990.

92 The annual return must also now contain information about the number of names on the register of members and the number without addresses. This is of significance in union elections as the register of members acts as the union's electoral roll.

93 The Certification Officer stated in the Annual Report for 1999–2000 that trade unions have, in the main, readily complied with the requirement to provide members with a statement which contained the required information and met the statutory timescale.

annual statement must also be sent to the Certification Officer as soon as reasonably practicable and a copy provided free to any member who requests it.

The financial statement is, in effect, a summary of the union's annual return. It should include the report of the auditors on the union accounts and additionally specify the general income and expenditure of the union, its income from members' subscriptions, income and expenditure of the political fund and details of salaries and other benefits to designated officials. In addition, a specific statement must be included informing members that, if they are concerned about financial irregularity, their concern may be raised with the officials of the union, trustees of the property, auditors, Certification Officer or the police.

Investigation of union financial affairs

The Certification Officer's functions have been extended by the 1993 Act. The Officer now has additional powers to investigate union financial matters at national or branch level and to prosecute irregularities.

A new s 37A allows the Certification Officer, where there is 'good reason', to direct a trade union to produce 'relevant documents', defined as accounting documents or other documents dealing with financial affairs. Where necessary, the Certification Officer may also direct the union, official or agent[94] to provide an explanation of them.[95]

The Certification Officer also possess the power to appoint inspectors to investigate the financial affairs of a trade union.[96] This power of investigation is only activated if it appears that:

(a) the financial affairs of the union are being conducted fraudulently; or

(b) that the union has failed to comply with any duty relating to its financial affairs imposed by the statute; or

(c) that a rule of the union relating to financial affairs has been broken; or

(d) a person concerned with the management of the union has been convicted of an offence regarding the management of union funds.

If an investigation is undertaken, all relevant financial documents in the possession of officials or agents of the union must be produced. Such persons must co-operate with the investigation by attending any meeting with an inspector and by giving any other assistance they are reasonably able to give as required. The same duties are imposed on any other person who appears to the inspector to be in possession of relevant information. Any persons who are required to explain any documents or to assist an investigation are not entitled to refuse on the grounds that it may incriminate them. However, they will be protected from prosecution, unless their financial explanations given are inconsistent with a statement or explanation made previously.[97]

---

94 Agent is defined in TULR(C)A 1992, s 119, as a banker, solicitor or auditor.

95 By s 37E, the CO should consider using the power to examine documents if: (i) the auditor's report is qualified so that the accounts do not give a true and fair view of union finances or raises an issue of financial irregularity; or (ii) where a member complains to the CO of a financial irregularity.

96 Section 37B.

97 Sections 37A(7) and 37B(7). However, refusal to disclose information on the grounds of legal professional privilege is expressly retained by s 37E(3).

Where an investigation is taking place, the inspector appointed must keep the Certification Officer informed and provide the Certification Officer with any information requested.[98] Additionally, the inspector may make a written interim report as directed by the Certification Officer and, on the conclusion of the investigation, a final report must be made. The final published report is distributed free of charge to the trade union, to any auditor of the trade union or branch or section of the union who requests a copy. In addition, a copy must be given to any member on request who has initiated a complaint under s 37B where the Certification Officer considers the report contains findings relevant to the complaint.[99] Most importantly, in the light of the failure of the Lightman prosecution, a certified copy of the report is admissible in any legal proceedings.

Offences

Offences for breach of the duties or requirements concerning inspection and investigation in ss 37A and 37B of the TULR(C)A 1992 are dealt with by a new s 45(5) of the same Act. It is now an offence for an official or agent of a trade union intentionally to conceal the financial affairs of the union. However, where proceedings are brought for failing to produce documents, it is a defence for the accused to prove that they were not in their possession and it was not reasonably practicable for them to comply with the requirement.[100] Where a person purports to comply with ss 37A or 37B and knowingly or recklessly provides a false explanation or statement, an offence is committed as a breach of s 45(9).

In addition, two other offences are specifically created. It is an offence intentionally to defeat the law by destroying, mutilating or falsifying a financial document or by making a false entry in a financial document[101] and fraudulently to part with, alter or delete anything in a financial document.[102]

Penalties

New penalties for all offences relating to the financial administration of trade unions are contained in s 45A. All of the offences are tried summarily in the magistrates' court and may result, on conviction, in either a fine of up to £5,000 for the offences under s 45(1)–(5) or imprisonment for up to six months and/or a fine of up to £5,000 for those under s 45(4) and (7)–(9).

Section 45B provides for a new penalty of disqualification for persons convicted of any of the offences in s 45. A trade union is under a duty to ensure that any member of the executive, or the president, and/or the general secretary is disqualified from a position in the union for five years if convicted of an offence of maladministration under s 45(1)–(5). Where such a person is convicted of the offences of corruption detailed in s 45(4), (7), (8) or (9), the period of disqualification is 10 years. An exception to disqualification arises

---

98 Section 37C.
99 The expenses of the investigation should firstly be met by the CO. However, there is provision for a person convicted under this section to be ordered to contribute some or all of the costs, s 37D.
100 Section 45(6).
101 Section 45(7).
102 Section 45(8).

where the president or general secretary is not a voting member of the executive or holds the position under the rules for only 12 months and has not held the position before.

A member of a trade union who believes the union has failed to comply with s 45B by not disqualifying offenders may apply to the Certification Officer or the court for a declaration.[103] A declaration by the court or the Certification Officer[104] may be enforced by an order requiring the union to take steps to remedy the failure specified in the declaration. This order, once made, is enforceable by any member of the trade union.

Conclusions

In the same way that companies are regulated for the protection of their shareholders, statutory intervention in union financial affairs has been defended as in the best interests of union members because it ensures a relatively high standard of financial probity. Yet, there is clearly a discrepancy of treatment in the regulation of company and union affairs. The level of penalties imposed on unions or their officers for infringement of the law is substantially higher than that imposed on companies or directors. For example, under the Company Directors Disqualification Act 1986, the court has a discretion to disqualify company directors who break financial regulations. Where union officials are concerned, as we have seen, the disqualification is mandatory. Should a company fail to submit accounts on time to Companies House, fixed civil financial penalties are imposed.[105] Should a union fail to submit their financial statement on time to the Certification Officer, the penalty is a fine of up to £5,000.

This discrepancy of treatment between union and company is also noticeable when individual rights of union members and shareholders are compared. Union members have a package of rights to enforce union financial duties and responsibilities. Shareholders are not provided with the same level of statutory rights to intervene in the internal financial affairs of the company they invest in. Moreover, to encourage union members to exercise these rights, the law provides for any complaint by a union member to be investigated by the Certification Officer and for the Certification Officer to adjudicate on certain applications by members. A shareholder concerned about the administration of their company may inform the Department of Trade and Industry, but is not provided with an alternative to the court system in which to sue directors.

---

103 Section 45C.
104 For details of the enforcement procedure, see p 21.
105 Companies Act 1985, s 242A.

CHAPTER 3

MEMBERS' RIGHTS AND THE RULE BOOK[1]

INTRODUCTION

We saw earlier in Chapter 2 how the union rule book operates as the union's constitution, setting out the procedures of how the union is to be governed and administered. The rule book also acts as a contract of association between the union and each individual member. Therefore, where there is a breach of the provisions of the constitution or of other specific rights and obligations outlined in the rule book, any member is entitled to take legal action against their union on the basis that there has been a breach of contract.[2]

Historically, the right of members in principle to sue to enforce the rule book was very limited. Trade unions laboured under a twin handicap. As an unincorporated association of individuals, akin to a social club, a union had no legal existence separate from its membership. An individual member did not contract with 'the union' because such a legal entity did not exist. Rather, the individual was contracting with all the other individual members of the union. Therefore, the rule book, containing the terms of the contract of association, could not be enforced against the union, but only against the membership as a whole.

For an individual to sue an unincorporated body of which he was a member was tantamount to suing himself which legally he could not do.[3] The only device that could be used to commence litigation against an association in these circumstances was the representative action. Here, the complainant would nominate certain named members to represent all the other members of the association. This, however, was fraught with procedural difficulties, and could rarely be utilised.[4]

The second major handicap for trade unions was the decision in *Hornby v Close*,[5] that the rules of a union were unlawful at common law as an unreasonable restraint of trade, as they restrained the right of each member to sell their labour on terms he or she saw fit, and so could not be enforced in any way. Section 3 of the Trade Union Act 1871 exempted unions from this doctrine by providing that trade union agreements and trusts were not void or voidable merely on the grounds of restraint of trade.

Despite this recognition by statute that unions were lawful organisations at civil law, unions agreements could still not be enforced. To limit trade union authority over their membership, s 4 specifically denied unions or members the right legally to enforce most

---

1 See, generally, Elias, P and Ewing, KD, *Trade Union Democracy: Members' Rights and the Law*, 1987, Chapters 2 and 4.

2 This is subject to the rule in *Foss v Harbottle* (1843) 2 Hare 461, discussed on pp 57–66.

3 See eg *Kelly v NATSOPA* (1915) 84 LJ KB 2236.

4 It was necessary for all members of the association to have common personal liability. This meant that any members with individual defences distinct from those of the group as a whole had to be excluded from the action. This also applied to those members who had joined the union after the event which precipitated the litigation. These conditions were particularly difficult to satisfy in large unions with a fluctuating membership.

5 (1867) LR 2 QB 153.

of the rule book. The court was excluded from entertaining any legal proceedings that had the aim of directly enforcing conditions in the rule book relating to terms of employment, payment of penalties or subscriptions and the application of union funds.[6] As the provisions of the rule book were unenforceable in law, neither an individual nor a union could have recourse to the courts to enforce observance of the rule book. Section 4 thus had the important effect of preventing the courts from exercising jurisdiction over the internal management of unions.[7]

By the early 20th century, the non-interventionist stance of the law enshrined in s 4 was challenged by the courts in order to protect the interests of the individual member. To assert control over the rule book the judiciary developed a series of strategies to frustrate the effect of s 4.[8] In *Howden v Yorkshire Miners' Association*,[9] a majority in the House of Lords held that s 4 operated only to limit enforcement of a right under the rule book; it did not have an effect on the courts' ability to restrain a wrong by granting injunctive relief.[10]

The courts were also at times willing to find that union agreements and activities were not in unreasonable restraint of trade. Where the doctrine of restraint of trade was not applicable, trade union agreements were lawful and capable of enforcement.[11] At other times, judges were prepared to sever those rules that were in unreasonable restraint of trade from those that were not. Often, the friendly society rules of a trade union were held to be 'reasonable' and so the membership had a right to enforce observance of these particular clauses in the rule book.

However, the decision of the House of Lords in *Russell v Amalgamated Society of Carpenters and Joiners*,[12] initiated a period where non-intervention again became the norm. The Law Lords declined to intervene in a dispute between a member and the union executive over superannuation benefit due under the rules. A majority of their Lordships refused to treat trade unions as lawful at common law, whatever the purposes outlined in the rule book or the apparent reasonableness of their activities, and refused to sever the friendly society purposes, that is, the rule on the superannuation benefit, from the rules as a whole. Ironically, this decision, which reinforced the position that trade unions were

---

6   This provision had been introduced because of concerns raised in Parliament that if the obligations contained in the rule book were enforceable, unions may use the law to require members to take industrial action contrary to their individual conscience.

7   Where there was intervention to protect members' rights, jurisdiction tended to be based on the wrongful interference with property rights associated with membership. Eg, in *Re Printers' Amalgamation Trades Protection Society* [1899] 2 Ch 184, a member had the right to share in the disposal of the assets of the union only because they were held on a resulting trust for each individual member.

8   For a full and wide ranging analysis of these methods, see Kahn-Freund, O, 'The illegality of a trade union' (1944) 7 MLR 192.

9   [1905] AC 256.

10   The Law Lords approved the decision, in *Wolfe v Matthews* [1882] 21 Ch 194, that an injunction granted to restrain union funds being spent on a proposed amalgamation was merely an indirect enforcement of the rule book and so did not infringe s 4.

11   For example, in *Gozney v Bristol T & P Society* [1909] 1 KB 901, the court held that where the purpose of the union was to use conciliation to settle disputes or even engage in preparatory negotiation with employers on terms and conditions of employment, the union was not acting 'unreasonably' in restraint of trade and so the rule book could be enforced.

12   [1912] AC 421.

unlawful organisations at civil law, was welcomed by trade unions because it resurrected the protection provided by s 4.[13]

A significant shift in judicial attitudes to s 4 was signalled by the House of Lords in *Amalgamated Society of Carpenters and Joiners v Braithwaite*.[14] Here, the plaintiff had been expelled in breach of the rule book. The court held that it was not contrary to s 4 for a declaration on the construction of the rule to be made, as that was not enforcing the rule book.[15] In addition, granting a subsequent injunction based on that declaration was also permissible. An injunction, restraining the union from expelling the member in breach of the rule book, does not directly enforce the contract, it simply preserves the status quo by leaving the relationship between the parties untouched.[16]

It was also during this period, in the early 20th century, that the courts started to develop the concept of the registered union under the 1871 Act as a legal entity, with the attributes of a corporate body – one of which was the power to make contracts in the union name and be bound by them. In the leading case of *Taff Vale Rly Co v ASRS*,[17] the House of Lords had held that a union that registered under the Trade Union Act could be sued in its own name for the purposes of the law of tort. Although the view that a union could be sued under its registered name in contract was not universally held, recourse to the representative action as an alternative way of suing the union became increasingly common with trade union officials selected to represent the rest of the membership.

Both of these issues – the effect of s 4 of the Trade Union Act 1871 and the contractual capacity of trade unions as an entity – were reconsidered by the House of Lords in *Bonsor v Musicians' Union*.[18] The House of Lords summarily dismissed the relevance of s 4 to the proceedings and stated that the full array of civil remedies, including damages, were available to union members to protect their contractual rights. Moreover, the House of Lords held that members could sue to enforce the contract without having to resort to the procedural device of the representative action. As a union registered under the Trade Union Act 1871 had the capacity to make contracts as a quasi-corporation distinct from the membership, either a member could sue the union as a legal entity in its own right or the union could be sued in its own name as the embodiment of all the membership.

When the 1871 Act was repealed by the Industrial Relations Act in 1971, any residual effect that s 4 might have had was eliminated. The Industrial Relations Act 1971 gave unions who registered full corporate status, so that unions had the right to make contracts and to sue and be sued under them. When the Industrial Relations Act was repealed in 1974, s 4 was not revived by the Trade Union and Labour Relations Act 1974. As we saw in Chapter 2, this Act gave trade unions many of the attributes of incorporation, including being able to make contracts and to be sued in their own name, now repeated in s 10(1) of the Trade Union and Labour Relations (Consolidation) Act (TULR(C)A) 1992.

---

13 To ensure the continual benefits of s 4, and the exclusion of the courts from their internal affairs, some unions even went so far as to include clauses in their rule books that made it clear that one of their purposes was to act in unreasonable restraint of trade. See *Miller v Amalgamated Engineering Union* [1938] Ch 669.

14 [1922] 2 AC 440.

15 Following the earlier House of Lords decision in *Howden v Yorkshire Miners' Association* [1905] AC 256.

16 It was conceded that damages was not a possible remedy as that would be enforcing a direct personal benefit of membership which was specifically excluded by s 4.

17 [1901] AC 426.

18 [1956] AC 110.

CONTENT OF THE RULES

We saw earlier, in Chapter 2, that a rule book will have many provisions dealing with the government and financial administration of the union. There will also be a variety of other rules. For example, rules on membership will specify who is eligible to join, outline the categories or classes of membership, subscription rates and any other conditions of membership. Rules on the discipline and expulsion of members will establish the system of fines or other sanctions and outline the procedure to be followed for the imposition of these penalties.

A union objects rule will usually restate the statutory objects, that the principal purposes of the union is the regulation of relations between workers and employers. It may then continue by providing the union with an extensive list of powers to engage in political activities, supply legal services, publish journals, bestow educational grants, etc. As we shall see later in this chapter, the objects rule is of some importance as it fixes the legal capacity of trade unions which is considered by the courts when the *ultra vires* doctrine is applied.[19] Another essential rule is one which describes the procedure for the alteration of the rules, which is usually by a special delegate conference or on a ballot of the members. Otherwise, without such a rule, the union would need the unanimous consent of all its members, which would be well nigh impossible to achieve.

An important element of trade union autonomy from the law has been the freedom of unions to form their own rules without undue State interference. For most of the 20th century, the subject matter and content of the rules was primarily a matter for the union itself. While there has been some statutory interference with the contents of the rule book since 1871, the extent of interference has developed substantially since 1979.

The Trade Union Act 1871 contained a short list of subjects on which the union should have rules. The list was limited to matters such as objects, trustees and arrangements for financial scrutiny of the union books. The Industrial Relations Act 1971 controlled the content of union rules by requiring all rules to conform to 'guiding principles' set out in the statute and required unions to have rules on a series of specified matters. On the repeal of this Act, unions were required by the Trade Union and Labour Relations Act 1974 to have rules on only two particular subjects: to allow a member to terminate his or her membership on reasonable notice and on the appointment and removal of auditors. Both these provisions have been retained in the TULR(C)A 1992 as ss 69 and 33–35, respectively. All rules, of course, must not offend against any general provisions of common law or statute. In particular, rules on admission to membership and the benefits of membership must not be contrary to the prohibitions against race or sex discrimination, or discrimination on grounds of disability.[20]

Few areas of the union rule book have been left untouched by the passage of legislation since 1979. Sections 46–61 of the TULR(C)A 1992 completely replace any

---

19 Where a union does not have an objects clause or the clause is very limited, the court will discern the objects of the union by an examination of the rules as a whole.

20 Race Relations Act 1976, ss 6 and 11; Sex Discrimination Act 1975, ss 12 and 49; Sex Discrimination Act 1986, s 6; and Disability Discrimination Act 1995, ss 13–15. For examples of case law, see *Fire Brigades Union v Fraser* [1998] IRLR 697 and *Diakov v Islington Union 'A' Branch* [1997] ICR 121. Also, note that discrimination between nationals of an EU State is proscribed by EC Regs 1612/68 and 312/76.

existing provisions contained in a union's rules on elections to its executive committee. Where rights on admission are concerned, ss 174–77 of the TULR(C)A 1992 provide all individuals with a right to join a union of their choice. Discipline and expulsion is another area now heavily regulated by statute. Sections 64–67 of the TULR(C)A 1992 give every member the right not to be disciplined unjustifiably. In all these examples, the provisions of the rule book, democratically determined by the representatives of the membership as a whole, are overriden, with statute either nullifying the rules or displacing them.[21]

Judicial control over union rules

Union rules and illegality

Union rules must not be illegal at common law. In *Drake v Morgan*,[22] the National Executive Committee (NEC) of the union resolved, under the appropriate rule, to indemnify members who had been fined for offences committed on picket lines during a trade dispute. The NEC subsequently authorised payment of the fines from union funds. The question that arose was whether such a payment was contrary to public policy and so unlawful on the basis that it incited or aided and abetted the commission of a criminal offence. In refusing the application for an injunction to restrain the payments, Forbes J ruled that since the resolution was made after the offences had been committed and related only to those particular offences, such a payment was not unlawful. However, Forbes J then distinguished this position from the situation where a resolution provided a financial indemnity for future criminal activity. This would be unlawful as contrary to public policy, as it would be tantamount to encouraging a breach of the law.[23]

This common law position has now been altered by s 15 of the TULR(C)A 1992, formerly s 8 of the Employment Act 1988. This section prohibits the use of union funds or other property to pay a financial penalty imposed upon an individual or to indemnify their unlawful conduct in any way.[24] Should the union do so, then the payment or value of the property is recoverable from the recipient by the union.[25] If the union fails to recover funds applied in this manner, any member may apply for a court order to initiate or continue proceedings against the recipients.[26] The section specifically states that this does not affect the availability of appropriate common law remedies.[27] Thus, this statutory provision acts as an alternative or additional remedy for the protesting member.

---

21 The ILO Convention No 87 (1948), Arts 2, 3 and 8, specify that unions have a right to draw up their own constitutions without interference from the State. On a number of occasions, the ILO Committee of Experts has found the UK Government in breach of this Convention. For analysis of the ILO's decisions and the British Government's response, see Ewing, KD, *Britain and the ILO* (1994, Institute of Employment Rights). See also Mills, S (1997) EHRLR 35 and Novitz, T (1998) 27 ILJ 169.

22 [1978] ICR 56.

23 This issue was further considered in *Thomas v NUM (South Wales Area)* [1985] 2 WLR 1081 by Scott J. He agreed with Forbes J in *Drake* that an indemnity for future offences would offend against public policy as such an indemnity encourages others to commit criminal or civil wrongs.

24 Section 15(1).

25 Section 15(2).

26 Section 15(3).

27 Section 15(6).

Interpretation of the rules

Where a member and the union are in dispute over union action which is allegedly contrary to provisions in the rule book, the court can intervene to interpret the relevant provision of the rules to establish whether a breach of contract has occurred and to provide an appropriate remedy. In addition, the courts will examine rule books to ascertain the objects or powers of a trade union. Where a union has acted in breach of the objects of the union derived from the rule book, the courts will declare such action as *ultra vires*, that is, beyond the powers of the union.

This intervention in the administration of union affairs by enforcement of the contract of association or the declaration of *ultra vires* has had profound implications in a variety of areas, such as over the discipline and expulsion of members and over the operation of union elections. Though, as we see later, these are now areas heavily controlled by statute, common law intervention continues to have some relevance as an effective residual power over allegedly wrongful union activity. Many cases heard throughout the duration of the miners' strike, 1984–85, exemplify the application of judicial control both via the interpretation of the rule book and the use of the *ultra vires* doctrine.

The miners' strike and the rule book[28]

In *Taylor v NUM (Derbyshire Area) (No 1),*[29] working miners were suspended by the area union for failing to abide by strike instructions issued by the area and national union. As miners are members of both the national and area union of the NUM, the fundamental issue was whether the strike was a national or area strike and whether it had been called in breach of the national or area rule book. Nicholls J held that the strike was a national one and had been called in breach of national rule 43, which required a national ballot before the calling of the strike. Nicholls J further decided that, even if it was a local area strike, Derbyshire Area rule 68, which required a 55% majority on an area ballot, had not been followed. The area ballot that had been held only resulted in a 49% vote for the strike.

A declaration was thus issued that the strike call was in contravention of the rules and so unlawful. As the action was 'unofficial', the plaintiffs were not breaking union rules in refusing to go on strike and could lawfully disregard union instructions. Furthermore, as the power to suspend contained in the rules only applied to a lawful strike, an injunction would be granted to prohibit any further disciplinary action.

This view, that the strike had been called in breach of union rules, had further serious ramifications for the conduct of the strike. In *Taylor v NUM (Derbyshire Area) (No3),*[30] payments had been made to pickets and to strikers to relieve the hardship of strike action. The High Court held that, as the strike was not authorised under the rules, these payments were *ultra vires* (beyond the powers of the union), since the rule that allowed expenditure for strike purposes must be interpreted to refer to lawful strikes only.

---

28 See, generally, here, Ewing, KD, 'The strike, the courts and the rule books' (1985) 14 ILJ 160 and Lord Wedderburn, *The Worker and the Law*, 3rd edn,1986, pp 730–59.

29 [1984] IRLR 440.

30 [1985] IRLR 99.

Further disputes between dissident members of the NUM and the officers of the union occurred over attempts to discipline these recalcitrant union members. An extraordinary delegate conference of the NUM was called in July 1984 to add a new r 51, allowing for the disqualification of members, branches and areas and the removal of officers who had ignored the strike instructions.

The plaintiffs, who were members of the NUM Nottinghamshire Area, applied to the court for a declaration that the resolutions of the conference which altered the rules were void and for an injunction restraining the NUM President from enforcing the void rule changes. Megarry VC granted both of the applications on the basis that the way the changes had been conducted were themselves in breach of the rules. There had been no meeting of the Nottinghamshire Area and no consultation on the rule changes as is necessary under the rules. As Megarry VC said, '... as long as [the NUM] its own rules and the democratic process for which the rules provide, it must not be surprised if it finds that any changes of the rules made by these means are struck with invalidity'.[31]

In *Taylor and Foulstone v NUM (Yorkshire Area)*,[32] members of the NUM (Yorkshire Area), sought, *inter alia*, an injunction restraining the operation of the disciplinary rule 51 which had been carried by a newly convened NUM conference in August 1984 a month after the the original rule 51 had been struck down, in *Clarke v Chadburn* above. In a similar vein to the situation in the Nottinghamshire Area, by dint of the lack of notice and proper consultation with area representatives, the rule change was declared invalid and an interlocutory injunction was granted to halt disciplinary action.

Litigation during the miners' strike was not solely the province of discontented NUM members. During the Annual General Meeting of the National Union of Seamen (NUS) in 1984, support was expressed for the NUM in their dispute with the National Coal Board (NCB). In response, the NEC of the NUS approved payments to the NUM of £5,000 and £10,000 from the union's general fund. In addition, the NEC resolved to introduce a rule so as to impose a levy on members of 0.25% of salary to provide additional funds for the NUM. The plaintiff, a member of the NUS who believed the NUS rule book was not being followed, sought a declaration that the donation from the general fund was unlawful and an injunction to prohibit the levy.

The High Court considered that the rules did not give the NEC authority to impose the levy as this was the exclusive right of a special general meeting. Neither could the NEC lawfully make substantive alterations to the rules to give itself this power, as the right to alter the rules was also given exclusively to a special general meeting. Therefore, the NEC's actions were *ultra vires* and void and an appropriate declaration and injunction were granted.

However, the court held that the one-off donation could be justified under the provision in the objects clause of the NUS which allowed the use of funds to 'promote and provide for the extension of trade union principles'. Such a payment could promote the trade union principle of solidarity. In practice, however, these general trade union principles would not be promoted by funding the NUM as such payments were likely to be sequestrated, as the NUM was in contempt of court for refusing to adhere to previous

---

31   *Clarke v Chadburn* [1984] IRLR 350, p 352.

32   [1984] IRLR 445.

court rulings. Therefore, as the objects of the NUS could not in practice be furthered, this payment was also unlawful.[33]

Some of these decisions stemming from the miners' strike have been criticised for the way the courts restrictively construed and applied the relevant rules. For example, in the *Taylor and Foulstone* case, the legality of the industrial action arguably depended upon whether the strike was local or national. It would have been feasible for the court to have decided that, on the facts, the action was an area action, governed by the area, rather than the national rules. This was because the Yorkshire Area had initiated action at the Cortonwood colliery on 8 March. It was only on 19 April that a special delegate conference of the NUM was convened which called for national strike action and only after that date was there full co-ordination of the strike by the national union. In the Scottish decision in *Fettes v NUM (Scotland Area)*,[34] Lord Jauncey had observed that an area action could start earlier and run in parallel with a national action and, in the circumstances, the 19 April resolution did not have the effect of turning the already existing Scottish strike into a national strike.[35]

If this interpretation had been applied in the Yorkshire Area, rule 53 of the Yorkshire Area Rules would have had to have been satisfied. This stated that a 55% vote in favour of action would need to be obtained before a strike could be called. Arguably, this rule had been fulfilled as area ballots were taken in 1981 and 1982. The first resulted in an 85% vote in favour of action on the pit closures issue, the second a 56% vote for industrial action on a mixed issue of pit closures and a wage claim. However, Nicholls J decided on the evidence that this was a national strike, which was not sanctioned by a ballot as required in the rule book of the national union. He further stated that, even if he had regarded it as an area action, the ballots taken in 1981 and 1982 were too remote in time to be effective.[36]

The miners' cases also demonstrated the readiness of the High Court to use their powers to issue injunctions and declarations at the interlocutory stage of litigation, before a full trial. Some disquiet was caused when unusually, in *Taylor and Foulstone*, a mandatory injunction on an interlocutory application was granted to enforce the holding of postponed branch elections and branch committee meetings. Nicholls J noted Lord Justice Lane's comment, in *Stephen (Harold) Ltd v Post Office*,[37] that '... it is only in extreme circumstances that this court will intervene by way of a mandatory injunction in the delicate mechanism of industrial disputes ...', but felt that this was a sufficiently exceptional case to justify this form of intervention. In *Clarke v Chadburn*,[38] Megarry VC was willing to take the rare step of issuing a final declaration on the law, on an interlocutory application, without hearing legal argument from the defendants.

---

33   *Hopkins v NUS* [1985] IRLR 157.

34   *The Scotsman*, 25 September 1984.

35   See also the judgment of Scott J supporting this view in *Thomas v NUM (South Wales Area)* [1985] 2 WLR 1081, p 1120.

36   If the court had upheld the lawfulness of the strike, instructions from the NEC in support of the strike would have been lawful, so avoiding contempt proceedings and the sequestration of assets. This arguably would have had a major impact on the success of the industrial action.

37   [1977] 1 WLR 1172, p 1180.

38   [1984] IRLR 350.

During the miners' strike, the use of the law in this manner by discontented members was particularly effective as the court orders were ignored by the NUM, resulting in the union being found in contempt of court. On refusing to pay the fines imposed for contempt, the fine was enforced by a dissident member obtaining a writ of sequestration against the property of the union, weakening the union's financial position. On the continuance of the contempt, receivers were appointed to administer the affairs of the union. Although sequestration of assets to pay the fines for contempt was inevitable once the union had refused to settle the fines voluntarily, receivership was a more serious step. Receivership is the process where all the property of an organisation is in the control of the receiver who manages all its financial affairs.[39]

Starved of funds to distribute to striking members and their families, the union had great difficulty in prosecuting the strike. Furthermore, the weight of litigation and the legal consequences of the finding of illegality and the contempt, sequestration and receivership, created the perception that the union was engaged in serious illegalities which damaged public support for the strike. Yet, these remedies available under the inherent jurisdiction of the court were granted at an interlocutory stage of proceedings, sometimes without representation by the defendant union, and so were all granted on the basis of an 'arguable case', that there had been an alleged breach of the rule book, and on the 'balance of convenience' between the parties.[40]

As Lord Wedderburn has written, these serious consequences flowed merely from '... a breach of an interim order to remedy a possible breach of contract'.[41]

Limitations on the enforcement of contractual rights

The rule in Foss v Harbottle[42]

One argument, that was not fully considered in many of the cases during the miners' strike, was that individual members who took action against the NUM for a breach of the rules did not have legal standing to do so. This point derives from the rule in *Foss v Harbottle*.[43] This is a company law rule partially derived from partnership law which has been extended to apply to all associations able to sue in their own name. There are two limbs to the doctrine, although they are closely interwoven: one is referred to as the proper plaintiff principle, the other is known as the internal management principle.

---

39 The power to appoint a receiver was itself a contentious decision as there was no specific authority for the court to do so in trade union cases. The Trade Union Act 1871, s 4, precluded the courts from doing so until the repeal of the Act in 1971. The decision to appoint a receiver on an *ex parte* application was appealed by the NUM in *Clarke v Heathfield* [1984] ICR 203. Although the Court of Appeal recognised that this use of the court's discretion was 'most unusual', the court felt that it was justified in the circumstances as the union had failed to purge their contempt. For comment on these developments see Kidner, R (1985) 14 ILJ 124.

40 For a further discussion of the use of interlocutory injunctions in industrial disputes, see Chapter 16.

41 *Op cit*, Wedderburn, fn 28, p 737.

42 See, generally, on this rule, Wedderburn KW (now Lord), 'Shareholders' rights and the rule in *Foss v Harbottle*' [1957] CLJ 194 and [1958] CLJ 93.

43 (1843) 2 Hare 461.

The proper plaintiff principle bars an individual of an association from initiating an action where the alleged wrong is a breach of duty by an officer of the association, or a wrong committed by an outsider. The proper plaintiff for such an action is the association itself. For example, a minority of shareholders may wish to take action on behalf of the company against an individual director for a breach of his or her duty to the company. In this type of situation, the proper plaintiff is the company itself which has suffered the wrong and which is capable of suing for these wrongs in its own name, rather than the individual shareholder. Similarly, the proper plaintiff in an action against an officer of the union is the union itself, as represented by the majority of the membership who may initiate action through the usual decision making process. This aspect of the principle, which is primarily concerned with the fiduciary duties of officers of the association, has not often been applied in the union context, as the union will normally not require any prompting to pursue its legal rights against fraudulent officers or outside bodies.

The second principle applies where there is an internal irregularity in the way the association is governed. If this internal irregularity can be condoned by a simple majority of the members of the association, the court will not intervene on an application by an individual member or minority group. In the context of the corporate body, the internal irregularity may involve a breach of the articles of the company, which could be ratified by a majority of the shareholders in a general meeting. For the union, the irregularity is the breach of the rule book, which likewise can be regularised by a resolution of the majority of the members. Thus, on a matter of irregular internal management, the dissenting minority is not entitled to bring an action which could be 'cured' by the majority.

The effect of the rule is to deny to minority members of the association the opportunity to litigate on matters that are of concern only to the association itself and from usurping the rights of the majority to control the organisation. The purpose of the rule is to avoid a multiplicity of actions, some of which may be vexatious.[44] If each member was entitled to sue on an allegation that a wrong had been committed by, for example, an officer of the association, the association may be subjected to numerous lawsuits by fractious and obstreperous members which would result in unwarranted interference in its day to day administration. The rule also avoids wasteful and meaningless litigation. If the wrong is an irregularity which could be ratified in a general meeting by the majority, it would be futile to allow a disgruntled minority member to initiate an action without the consent of the majority, as the majority could ultimately regularise the irregularity, thereby negating any court decision.

---

44 Mellish LJ in *MacDougall v Gardiner* (1875) 1 Ch D 13 justified the rule on the basis that it restrained 'cantankerous litigation'.

The application of Foss v Harbottle to trade unions

For the rule to apply, the central condition which must be satisfied is that the association is a legal entity capable of instituting proceedings in its own name.[45] As a consequence of the powers provided by the Trade Union Act 1871, the courts had on many occasions decided that a trade union has similar attributes to a corporate body, one of which is the ability to initiate action in its own name. Any doubt as to the applicability of the doctrine, due to any residual uncertainty surrounding the exact legal status of a trade union, has been resolved, as statute now clearly establishes that unions have a right to sue in their own name.[46]

There have been a number of cases concerning trade unions where the *Foss v Harbottle* rule has been applied, culminating in the failure of the legal action challenging the union decision. In *Cotter v NUS*,[47] the Court of Appeal refused to grant a declaration and injunctions to the individual member of the union who purported to sue on behalf of the membership. Although a special general meeting was invalidly called, subsequent resolutions providing for a £10,000 loan were not void as the irregularity could be condoned by the majority calling a properly constituted meeting which would pass fresh and effective resolutions on this matter. Lawrence LJ indicated his strong support of the rule with the comment: 'I think that it would be lamentable if a technical breach of the rules were held to entitle a dissentient member or minority to obtain an injunction to restrain the carrying out of a resolution of the union.'[48]

In the earlier case of *Steele v South Wales Miners' Federation*,[49] a levy was imposed on members without the existence of a formal procedure providing for it. The court, applying *Foss v Harbottle*, declared that they would not interfere with the internal administration of the union where the majority of the membership approved of the action, so long as it is within the scope of the purposes authorised by the rules. Another successful application of the rule occurred in *Goodfellow v London and Provincial Union of Licensed Vehicle Workers*,[50] where it was alleged that the rules of the union had not been followed in convening delegates to a union conference. The action was struck out by Peterson J on the grounds that this was '... a question of internal management that could be ratified by a subsequent resolution'.

More recently, Goff J refused an injunction to disgruntled union members in *McNamee v Cooper*,[51] where the union had cast its votes at the Trades Union Congress (TUC) conference, contrary to the decision of the union delegate conference. Although, under the rules, the union was bound by a decision of the delegate conference, Goff J held that, as the executive council's breach of the rules was a matter of internal administration, he was unable to intervene.

---

45 Romer J, in *Cotter v NUS* [1929] 2 Ch 58, summarised this point when he said (p 71): 'The principle, as I understand it, does not depend upon the existence of a corporation. The reasoning of it [*Foss v Harbottle*] applies to any legal entity which is capable of suing in its own name and which is composed of individuals bound together by rules which give the majority of them the power to bind the minority.'

46 For a full examination of trade union legal status, see Chapter 2.

47 [1929] 2 Ch 58.

48 At p 107.

49 [1907] 1 KB 361.

50 (1919) *The Times*, 5 June.

51 (1966) *The Times*, 8 September.

MEMBERS' RIGHTS – THE PERSONAL OR DERIVATIVE ACTION

Exceptions to the rule do exist. These open the door for union members to take either a personal action against the union to protect his or her individual rights or a derivative action to enforce the union's rights.

The personal action

If personal rights of a member are infringed as opposed to the right of the association, then an individual may bring an action, representing themselves and any other member alleging breach of that personal right. Clearly, in this context, in the interests of justice, the majority cannot be allowed to ratify wrongs which directly affect an individual's personal right.

The question which then arises is: what constitutes a personal right of a member and when is it infringed? The cases indicate that interference with a proprietary right is a sufficiently personal infringement for the purposes of the rule. Thus, where qualifications for office or membership benefits are altered contrary to the rule book to the disadvantage of that individual member, then the *Foss v Harbottle* rule is waived and the wronged individual is able to enforce his or her contractual rights.

In *Edwards v Halliwell*,[52] the failure to obtain the required two-thirds majority for an increase in subscriptions was a wrong done to each individual member on a matter of substance as it resulted in an increase in financial commitments for each member and so was an invasion of a personal right. In *Radford v NATSOPA*,[53] Plowman J took an expansive view of a personal right. He said that where a plaintiff's job was in jeopardy because of an unlawful loss of union membership this was capable of amounting to a personal right such that the plaintiff could sue for wrongful expulsion in breach of the rules.

More recently, in *Wise v USDAW*,[54] two members of the union sought to challenge decisions of the executive council on election procedure which they alleged was contrary to the rule book. Chadwick J, after quoting extensively from the judgment in *Edwards v Halliwell*, held that the defendant's reliance on the rule in *Foss v Harbottle* was 'misconceived' as it was an individual right '... not to have the constitution of the union, and in particular the composition of a new executive council, the president and the general secretary, imposed upon them save in accordance with the rules of the union ...'.[55]

---

52   [1950] 2 All ER 1064.

53   [1972] ICR 484.

54   [1996] IRLR 609.

55   At p 614. He was also critical of the rule in general terms, arguing that if a breach or threatened breach of the rules was not actionable by an individual member then the statutory power granted by Parliament to the Commissioner for the Rights of Trade Union Members (now abolished by the Employment Relations Act 1999) to assist actions on the rule book would be nullified.

The derivative action

The derivative action is a procedural device utilised by the membership when the court relaxes the *Foss v Harbottle* rule because the association is controlled by miscreant personnel. The individual minority member 'derives' the right to sue from the union's right to take action, as technically the wrong has been committed against the union itself. The right being enforced is that of the association but, because the wrongdoers have control, the association is prevented from taking action in its name and so, in the interests of justice, the rule in *Foss v Harbottle* is waived. The circumstances when a derivative action can be taken are summarised as follows:

(a) If the act is a fraud on the minority, perpetrated by the majority in control of the association, then the rule is relaxed to allow the minority to recover compensation. Fraud in the authorities in company law has been defined broadly, including circumstances where there has been an abuse of power which results in a tangible benefit to the majority that is denied to the minority. There have been few trade union cases on this exception.

(b) If the matter which is the subject of the action requires a special majority before it can be confirmed in a meeting of the membership then, as a mere majority would not be sufficient to implement it lawfully, the rule does not apply. Essentially, the controlling majority is not entitled to disregard the requirement for a special majority contained in the constitution of the association. This exception was discussed in some detail by the Court of Appeal in *Edwards v Halliwell*.[56] The union rules specified that an increase in subscriptions could only be imposed where, in a ballot of members, there was a two-thirds majority for the increase. The union, instead, purported to raise subscriptions by a decision of the delegate conference. The Court of Appeal held that, as this failure to follow the rules could not be confirmed by a simple majority, it was open for members to take legal action to overturn this decision.

(c) If, in practice, it is not possible to call a meeting to have the wrongful act ratified by the majority, then the *Foss v Harbottle* rule will not be applicable. The authority for this proposition is contained in the judgment of Goulding J in *Hodgson v NALGO*.[57] The NEC of the union instructed NALGO delegates to the TUC conference to vote on an issue at the TUC conference contrary to a resolution of the annual conference of the union. Under the union constitution, as set out in the rule book, the NEC did not have this power. As the TUC Conference was imminent, it would have been impossible to summon the required special conference for the membership to ratify the decision. With no real opportunity for the majority to ratify this decision, the rule barring individual actions did not apply.

Hodgson illustrates the difficulties that unions may have with the requirement that there must be more than a mere theoretical possibility that an irregular decision can be ratified. The majority do not actually have to call a meeting and vote to ratify, but must be capable of doing so. In corporations, extraordinary meetings of shareholders can be called relatively quickly. Under many union constitutions, a special delegate

---

56 [1950] 2 All ER 1064.
57 [1972] 1 WLR 130. For comment, see Prentice, DD (1972) 35 MLR 318.

conference may only be summoned after a lengthy procedure has been followed. If there is no power to summon a special delegate conference then it may be many months before the issue could in practice be considered in an annual conference. Consequently, in the union context this exception is particularly relevant.

(d) Where the wrongful transaction is *ultra vires* the association, the rule does not apply as the majority cannot validly confirm such an act. The *Foss v Harbottle* rule can only protect a union or individual officers who act *intra vires* (within the power), as these are matters capable of being ratified by a majority vote.

So when is a union acting *ultra vires*? *Ultra vires* as a concept in company law was developed to protect the interests of potential investors and shareholders. A company provides in its memorandum of association an objects clause by which the company outlines its purposes. In theory, the outsider is entitled to rely on this exposition of the company's objects in deciding whether to invest and the shareholder can take action to protect his or her investment if the company engages in transactions outside the powers formally provided by the objects clause of the company.

As a trade union does not formally possess a memorandum of association, the court has to determine the 'objects' of a trade union by other means. As union rules act as the constitution of the union, the courts derive the objects or purposes of a union from an examination of the rule book. However, an act that may itself be a breach of the rules because it is an irregular way of doing something provided for in the rules is not *ultra vires*. An *ultra vires* act is not such a procedural irregularity, but a wrong of a more fundamental nature. It is where the union has acted without the capacity to do so – an act that is beyond the scope of a union's rules.[58]

In determining whether a union acts outside its powers, the court has to decide which rules are 'objects' rules. Matters related to the union's classic function of representing workers in collective bargaining and at the workplace would ordinarily be formally outlined in the rule book of most unions as their objects. But individual trade unions may well expand on this with subsidiary objects laid out elsewhere in the rule book. We saw earlier, in *Hopkins v NUS*,[59] how payments to the NUM were not *prima facie ultra vires* as, on examination of the rule book, the objects of the union included a provision whereby funds could be used to 'promote ... trade union principles'. We also saw a similar view being taken many years earlier, in *Steele*, where an object under the rules of the union was to provide funds for political purposes. Although, in allocating funds, the internal procedure in the rule book was not followed, this irregular political payment was still within the scope of the purposes of the union.

A similar view on *ultra vires* was put forward by Lord Denning, in *Sherrard v AUEW*.[60] Denning examined the rules of the union and noted the objects included the furtherance of political aims of any kind. Thus, a one day 'political' strike against government policy was lawful as it was not taken outside the power of the union as it had authority under the rules to call such a strike.

---

58 For example, in *Martin v Scottish TGWU* [1952] 1 All ER 691, a temporary member was admitted. The union had no rules permitting that category of member. As the union had no capacity to act in this way, the decision to admit was null and void.

59 [1985] IRLR 157.

60 [1973] IRLR 188.

The Court of Appeal in *Sherrard* did not pronounce on whether a rule that provided authority for strike action which then attracted liability in tort or that was in breach of contract would remain *intra vires* the rule book. Roskill LJ briefly mused on the importance of this issue but came to no clear conclusions. However, in *Thomas v NUM (South Wales Area)*,[61] it was submitted that unlawful strike action was *ultra vires* as union rules authorising industrial action must be construed to restrict the power of a union to call for a lawful strike only. Scott J differentiated between tortious and criminal acts committed during industrial action. He would have applied the *ultra vires* doctrine if a crime had been committed intentionally during the industrial action, although he was unsure whether a tort committed deliberately would also be *ultra vires*.[62]

This is the use of the doctrine of *ultra vires* on the basis that the act is contrary to the general law as opposed to *ultra vires* the rule book.[63] Importantly, for the purposes of the exception to the rule in *Foss v Harbottle*, both types of *ultra vires* entitle a member to maintain an action to have the strike declared illegal which then nullifies all subsequent union instructions taken under the authority of the rule book.

Ultra vires and the miners' strike

The rule in *Foss v Harbottle* was of some significance in litigation during the miners' strike. Although the union did not defend every action, where they did do so, particular attention was focused on the validity of the *ultra vires* exception to the rule.

The rule in *Foss v Harbottle* was fully considered by Vinelott J in *Taylor v NUM (Derbyshire Area) (No 3)*,[64] one of the few miners' cases fully defended by the union. Here, what was at issue was the legality of providing £1.4 m of strike pay to miners engaged in a strike which was contrary to the rule book. Vinelott J first outlined his understanding that, as an exception to the rule in *Foss v Harbottle*, any member is entitled to insist that the union does not act to apply any of its funds which is not in furtherance of the objects inferred from an examination of the constitution contained in the rule book. Vinelott J noted that there was an object in the NUM rule book permitting the union to provide an allowance to support strikers and their families during industrial action: this, however, did not provide the union with the appropriate capacity to act. These payments were *ultra vires*, as the union objects derived from the rule book only provided financial support for striking miners and their families if the strike was lawful, that is, within the rules.[65]

Therefore, as the *ultra vires* exception to the rule in *Foss v Harbottle* applied, an individual member had standing to apply for the sums to be repaid by the officers who committed the wrong. However, Vinelott declined to make an order for repayment

---

61 [1985] 2 WLR 1081.

62 Scott J also held that it would not necessarily be *ultra vires* for a union to engage in action that carried the mere risk of a crime or a tort being committed.

63 The flexible use of *ultra vires* by the courts is not a new phenomenon. See the House of Lords' judgment in *ASRS v Osborne* [1910] AC 78, where political payments were unlawful as they were 'ultra vires the statute' (the Trade Union Act 1871).

64 [1985] IRLR 99.

65 He cited in support of this contention *Bennett v NASOHSP* (1915) 113 LT 808, *Carter v USB* (1916) LJ Ch 289 and the Court of Appeal decision in *Howden v Yorkshire Miners' Association*, all cases where an injunction was granted on an application by a union member to restrain a misapplication of funds for purposes outside the powers of the union.

because of the circumstances of the case.[66] He suggested that it was open for the union, as represented by a simple majority of the membership, properly to decide that it was not in the best interests of the union to press for restitution. Vinelott noted that, as over 85% of the membership were obeying the strike call, arguably the majority of members approved of this expenditure. There was thus evidence that the majority would take the view that it was not in the best interests of the union to make the defendants personally liable by ordering repayment.

Vinelott was partially influenced in this view by the spectacle of the trustees – all members of the NUM executive – becoming martyrs to their cause. As the trustees would be personally liable to repay the sums expended unlawfully it would only have been a matter of time before the applicants enforced the order with bailiffs seizing the homes and property of the defendants. Yet, in principle, Vinelott's decision that the majority may resolve in good faith to take no action subverts the basis of the *ultra vires* rule. It creates the strange situation where the majority cannot rely on *Foss v Harbottle* to defend the action, but could do so to stop enforcement of any remedy.

This softening of the consequences of the finding of *ultra vires* is one response to the practical difficulties the court found itself in. Yet, an altogether different line of reasoning to Vinelott J's would have been possible in the *Taylor* case. Arguably, the failure to ballot in breach of the rules was a mere procedural irregularity rather than something that the union had no power to do. The union clearly had the power to call a strike under the rules. By not complying with the requirements for a ballot in the rules they simply did not go about calling it in the correct manner. If this was the case, the doctrine of *ultra vires* would not apply and the irregularity could be condoned by a subsequent decision by the majority of union members as provided for under the constitution, such as by a special delegate conference. As we saw earlier, a special delegate conference did take place supporting the NEC resolution on 19 April 1984.

Ultra vires and the Trade Union and Labour Relations Act 1974

A more fundamental objection to the use of the *ultra vires* doctrine in trade union cases has been put forward by Lord Wedderburn.[67] He argues that the doctrine of *ultra vires*, as applied in the past, is now redundant as a consequence of recent legislative changes. Wedderburn notes that the reason why the doctrine has been previously applied was because the Trade Union Act 1871 was interpreted in such a way as to give unions many of the attributes of incorporation, such as the capacity of registered unions under the 1871 Act to be sued in their own name in tort, to make contracts and to sue to protect their reputations. This treatment of unions as analogous to corporations reached its high point in 1971 when full incorporation was provided by the Industrial Relations Act 1971.

However, Wedderburn contends that the regime introduced by the Trade Union and Labour Relations Act 1974, repeated in the TULR(C)A 1992, flags up a change from this. Although s 2 of the Trade Union and Labour Relations Act 1974 lists a series of quasi-corporate characteristics that allows a union to be treated, in many circumstances, as if it

---

66 Note that today he would not be able to exercise his discretion in this manner. TULR(C)A 1992, s 16, states that where there is a breach of duty by trustees, an order for repayment is mandatory.

67 See Lord Wedderburn (1985) 14 ILJ 127; contrast Clayton, R and Tomlinson, H (1985) 135 NLJ 361.

were a company, the section starts with the form of words: 'A trade union ... shall not be, or treated as if it were, a body corporate.' Where the courts have been required to interpret this provision, they have clearly done so in such a way that effectuates Parliament's intention to break from the historical analysis of trade unions as quasi-corporations.[68] The character of a trade union is thus of a voluntary association of individuals with some strictly limited additional powers provided by statute. The consequence is that the corporate doctrine of *ultra vires* should not now be applicable to trade unions.[69]

If Wedderburn's analysis is correct, then although the member can sue for breach of contract to protect an individual right such as an irregular levy, there is no *ultra vires* rule to prohibit ratification of most other breaches of the rules. As these other irregular actions can be validated by the majority, they will be treated as just another ordinary breach of contract and, therefore, subject to the *Foss v Harbottle* rule. Legal action by the disgruntled minority member who wishes to sue their own union will thus be more likely to fail.

Judicial restraint and the rule in Foss v Harbottle

Whatever the uncertainty surrounding the applicability of *Foss v Harbottle* and the proper scope of the exceptions to the rule, the rule has not fettered the courts' discretion to hear cases and to use the common law to control union activity. Where the court wishes to refrain from intervention in the domestic affairs of a union, *Foss v Harbottle* is a useful tool to justify restraint. Likewise where intervention is thought necessary the exceptions are wide enough to permit examination of the rule book. We have seen that, in the union sphere, there have been few cases where the rule has been actively considered by the courts. This suggests that either the rule is ignored by the courts or the rule actively discourages members from initiating action in circumstances where it would have disposed of the case.

The rule in *Foss v Harbottle* is one way the courts articulate a decision not to intervene in the internal administration of a trade union. There is evidence of another approach: of a wider principle of association law which justifies a decision to decline to intervene in certain internal matters of a trade union. This was most recently exemplified by the decision in *Hamlet v GMBATU*,[70] a case about a complaint of breach of the rule book which had been rejected by the union after an internal investigation. In deciding that there was no case to answer, Harman J declared: 'The only duty of courts in considering questions of appeals and internal machinery for resolving disputes in unions is to see that the internal machinery has been properly followed through. The decision is not one which the court has any business to go into.'[71] In explaining this decision Harman J did not refer to *Foss v Harbottle*, but rather cited the *dicta* of James LJ in the administrative law case of *Dawkins v Antrobus*[72] that '... courts have no right to sit as a Court of Appeal upon the decision of members of a club duly assembled'. If this principle was taken to its logical conclusion,

---

68 See *EETPU v Times Newspapers* [1980] QB 585.

69 Note Denning's view on *ultra vires* and unincorporated associations in *Institute of Mechanical Engineers v Cane* [1961] AC 696, p 724.

70 [1986] IRLR 293.

71 At p 195.

72 (1881) 17 Ch D.

internal decision making in areas such as the disciplining of union members by branch committees would be safe from review by the courts so long as correct procedure was followed.

This non-interventionist stance was taken up by the Court of Appeal in *Longley v National Union of Journalists*,[73] a case on whether the union construction of the rules justified disciplinary action. Sir Ralph Gibson commented that trade union standards of behaviour should be taken into account when determining whether the actions of the plaintiff broke union rules and that the courts should proceed with caution when using their power to grant injunctions against a trade union. Concern with precipitous judicial intervention was also raised in *Burnley v ATW*[74] by Skinner J when he said that the courts should be wary of intervening in internal disputes over the interpretation of the union rules. In *Iwanuszezak v GMBATU*,[75] Lord Justice Lloyd went so far as to say that: '... the primary function of a union is to look after the collective interests of its members. When the collective interests of the union conflict with the interests of an individual member, it only makes sense that the collective interests of the members as a whole should prevail.'[76]

This flowering of judicial restraint in the later period of the 1980s may have been as a response to the furore over the courts' decisions during the miners' strike, or may have developed from judicial acceptance that, as common law control over union affairs was in decline (as a consequence of statutory remedies becoming available), there was no need to use an overly restrictive approach to the interpretation of the rule book.[77]

Whatever the judicial motivation for these decisions, these cases of judicial abstentionism[78] are not really characteristic of the usual practice of the courts. In certain areas, particularly in admission, discipline and expulsion from a union, which we turn to in the next chapter, the courts have had particular difficulty in restraining themselves from intervention.

---

73   [1987] IRLR 109.

74   [1986] IRLR 298, p 300.

75   [1988] IRLR 219.

76   At p 223. This conflict between the individual and the collective interest is of great importance in union and judicial decision making and is referred to throughout other chapters of this book. For further analysis of this issue, see Kidner, R, 'The individual and collective interest in trade union law' (1976) 5 ILJ 90.

77   It is difficult to substantiate whether we have entered a period of judicial abstentionism, where the interpretation of the rule book is concerned, as actions on the rule book have drastically declined in response to the new statutory rights now available to malcontent members.

78   See also *Brown v AUEW* [1976] ICR 147 and *Douglas v GPMU* [1995] IRLR 426, discussed in Chapter 6.

CHAPTER 4

ADMISSION, DISCIPLINE
AND EXPULSION I

COMMON LAW CONTROL[1]

Until 1980, control of union decision making in the area of admission, discipline and expulsion was solely based on common law; either through the enforcement of the terms of the contract of association or by reliance on judicially developed common law principles founded on public policy. The common law has now been supplemented by an extensive statutory regime to control internal union decisions in this area. This will be fully considered in Chapter 5. Although recourse to the enforcement of common law rights is likely to be less frequent, the common law still retains an important residual supervisory role, exemplified by the litigation during the miners' strike, considered earlier in Chapter 3.

Common law and public policy

The enforcement of contractual rights has not always been a wholly effective way of regulating union decisions to expel or refuse admission. For example, where contractual requirements are fully observed – such as where a rule clearly allows for the expulsion of the member and full consideration is given to the application of correct procedure – the courts' capacity to intervene on the basis of a breach of contract is severely restricted. Alternatively, where a decision is made to refuse an application for membership, common law control based on a wrongful application of the rule book would be clearly inadequate as there is no contractual relationship between the applicant and the union.

The solution for the courts was to broaden their jurisdiction, supplementing control via the rule book by the generation of additional common law doctrines justified on grounds of public policy. Many of these legal principles were developed to restrain the operation of the closed shop, either where a member was expelled, resulting in a loss of their job, or where an application for membership was refused, denying the applicant the opportunity of working in that trade or occupation.

Now that the closed shop is unenforceable by statutory changes introduced since 1980, the courts have less need to utilise such principles. However, an examination of the way the courts have attempted to develop them is illuminating as it illustrates the interventionist approach of the judiciary to challenge perceived injustices emanating from the closed shop and demonstrates the inherent flexibility of the common law where it is grounded on notions of public policy. Moreover, even if many of these doctrines are now of little practical use, they are not necessarily obsolete. Should the legislative framework alter in the future, resulting in a revival of closed shop arrangements, they may well re-emerge as a tool of regulation.

---

1   See, generally, Elias, P and Ewing, KD, *Trade Union Democracy: Members' Rights and the Law*, 1987, Chapters 3, 6 and 7.

In the forefront of these developments – in moulding the common law by way of public policy, to fit the requirements of 'justice' – was Lord Denning. He eloquently justified this use of public policy in *Enderby Town Football Club v Football Association Ltd*,[2] where, after describing cases of judicial intervention in contractual disputes between members and their associations, he said:

> All these are cases where the judges have decided, avowedly or not, according to what is best for the public good. I know that over 300 years ago Hobart CJ said, 'Public policy is an unruly horse'. It has often been repeated since. So unruly is the horse, it is said that no judge should ever try to mount it, lest it run away with him. I disagree. With a good man in the saddle, the unruly horse can be kept in control. It can jump over obstacles. It can leap the fences put up by fictions and come down on the side of justice.[3]

Common law doctrines and control over admission and expulsion

The 'right to work'

The 'right to work' was developed in a series of cases in the 1960s and 1970s.[4] In *Nagle v Fielden*,[5] the plaintiff claimed she had been unreasonably refused a licence as a horse trainer by the Jockey Club which had a monopoly of control over flat horse racing. Rule 17 of the Jockey Club permitted the club full discretion to grant or withdraw licences to officials, trainers and jockeys. The consequences of denying the plaintiff a licence was that she was unable to practise her chosen profession as a trainer. It was acknowledged by the court that she was being denied a licence merely on the grounds of her sex.

Lord Denning distinguished the legal position of the ordinary social club that had a right to deny membership to any applicant, with that of powerful associations that do not have this unfettered right. The social club has unrestricted power to admit or refuse to admit any person because the applicant who is denied entry does not lose anything as a consequence. By contrast, the applicant who is denied entry to a powerful association such as the Jockey Club which has control over the entitlement to work by the refusal or withdrawal of a licence has lost the right to earn his or her livelihood.

After an examination of earlier 17th and 18th century cases,[6] Denning concluded that the court was entitled to intervene in the exercise of the Jockey Club's discretion, as the common law:

> ... has for centuries recognised that a man has a right to work at his trade or profession without being unjustly excluded from it. He is not to be shut out from it at the whim of those having the governance of it. If they make a rule which enables them to reject his application arbitrarily or capriciously, not reasonably, that rule is bad. It is against public policy.[7]

---

2   [1971] 1 All ER 215.
3   At p 219.
4   For a review of the early cases see Rideout, R, 'Upon training an unruly horse' (1966) 29 MLR 424; Rideout, R, 'Admission to non-statutory associations controlling employment' (1967) 30 MLR 389; and Weir, T, 'Discrimination in private law' [1966] CLJ 165.
5   [1966] 2 QB 633.
6   Such as the case of the *Ipswich Tailors* (1614) 11 Co Rep 53a.
7   At p 644.

Denning continued by examining the position of the union closed shop. By analogy, he explained, the same principles must apply. A union like the Jockey Club is a great power as, through the operation of the closed shop, it can deprive a persons livelihood by refusing or withdrawing union membership. So for a rejected applicant to a union or for a member ousted from membership, the court can grant a remedy based on the 'right to work' without regard to whether or not there was a contractual relationship between the parties.

Unusually, Denning's colleagues in the Court of Appeal agreed with his analysis. Danckwerts LJ stressed that as the case involved important matters of public policy this justified judicial action on the basis that '... the courts have the right to protect the right of a person to work when it is being prevented by the dictatorial exercise of powers by a body which holds a monopoly'.[8] Salmon LJ agreed that the courts are entitled to intervene, on the basis that a man is '... not to be capriciously and unreasonably prevented from earning his living as he wills'.[9]

All three judges were in effect 'riding the unruly horse of public policy' to sustain the argument that where there is a failure by the governing body of the trade or profession properly to consider the merits of the case, such a decision is void on the basis that it conflicts with the 'right to work'.

Lord Denning was given further opportunity to develop this principle in the subsequent trade union case of *Edwards v SOGAT*.[10] The plaintiff was employed in the printing industry where a closed shop was in operation. By an oversight, the plaintiff, who was a temporary member, had failed to pay his union fees for six weeks and was excluded from membership under the rules of the union. His applications for readmission were rejected and he was subsequently dismissed by his employer.

Building on the principles derived from *Nagle*, Denning argued that such an unfettered and uncontrolled right to withdraw membership, which is a prerequisite for employment, is an interference with a person's implied right to work. Sachs LJ agreed that an arbitrary refusal to re-admit was invalid '... as being contrary to public policy for the reasons discussed in *Nagle v Fielden*'.[11] Similarly, rules that provide for expulsion must not be exercised capriciously or arbitrarily, such as where the exclusion from the union is on personal or political grounds.

In *McInnes v Onslow Fane*,[12] Megarry VC discussed the notion of the 'liberty to work'. Megarry preferred the use of this form of terminology because he regarded the 'right to work' as more of a social or political catchphrase than as a justiciable principle.[13] Megarry emphasised that there cannot be an automatic right to admission to membership of a club or society or an automatic right to the grant of a licence to work in a trade or profession,

---

8   At p 650.

9   At p 655.

10   [1971] Ch 354. For comment, see Elias, P [1971] CLJ 15.

11   At p 383.

12   [1978] 1 WLR 1520. Discussed by Elias, P, 'Admission to trade unions' (1979) 8 ILJ 111.

13   Megarry rejected the phrase 'right to work' because he noted that if one party has a right, there must be another party who owes a duty. He saw insurmountable problems in determining which party owed such a duty, as it may naturally be thought that the leading candidate would be the employer.

unless the denial is of major importance to the applicant's livelihood. Therefore, the 'liberty to work' may be exercised when an application is made for union membership where this is a requirement for employment. There will then be some justification on grounds of public policy for the court to intervene to strike the rule down as unreasonable where the evidence is that the body that grants such applications has not acted fairly, honestly and without bias.

This concern with 'powerful associations' that inhibit the 'right to work' or 'liberty to work' was further expressed by Slade J in *Grieg v Insole*.[14] The case dealt with the attempt by the domestic and international cricketing authorities to change their qualification rules so as to ban professional cricketers from county and test matches if they participated in a new 'World Series Cricket' tournament. The plaintiffs, *inter alia*, contended that the changes in the rules were void as they denied them the 'right to work', that is, the freedom to practise their profession as they wished. Slade J in disposing of the case did not apply this principle, but approved the view that rules emanating from a body which has a monopoly over professional activity could be controlled by the courts where it was necessary to protect the right to work on the 'broader grounds that they were contrary to public policy'.[15]

In one of his last cases before retirement, in *Cheall v APEX*,[16] Denning continued to advocate the view that it was a fundamental principle that a man has the right not to be expelled capriciously or arbitrarily without reasonable cause and only where the requirements of natural justice have been followed. Otherwise, the rule itself or the way such a rule was applied was invalid as contrary to public policy. This last attempt by Denning to persuade his judicial colleagues of the existence of such a principle was unsuccessful. In the House of Lords,[17] Lord Diplock, who gave the leading speech, rejected this broad formulation of the right, although he did suggest it may have some merit where the expulsion from the union had the effect of the member losing his job because of a closed shop agreement.

It is extremely doubtful whether the 'right to work' as a substantive principle of law derived from case law of the 1960s and 1970s and the particular industrial circumstances pertaining to that era, is still applicable in the 21st century. First, all the Denning cases were decided in the context of the closed shop. Arguably, the doctrine has no application where a failure to admit or an expulsion from a union takes place in other circumstances. In the vast majority of work situations today, union membership is not a requirement for employment. Thus, this principle would seem to be particularly inappropriate for current use.

Should the closed shop be revived, question marks still remain over the contemporary relevance of the 'right to work' concept. In *Goring v British Actors' Equity Association*,[18] Browne-Wilkinson VC held that a union rule banning members from working in South Africa did not interfere with the plaintiff's 'right to work'. After first commenting that

14   [1978] 1 WLR 302.
15   At p 362.
16   [1982] ICR 543 (CA).
17   [1983] IRLR 215. See the general note on the House of Lords' judgment in 99 LQR 337.
18   [1987] IRLR 122.

'... the exact jurisprudential nature of the "right to work" is obscure ...',[19] he then proceeded to outline the essential features of such a right; the most important of which was that there must be no contractual relations between the parties. Where a membership contract exists, the contents of which are contained in the rule book, a union member cannot complain of disciplinary action or expulsion under the rules, since by joining the union the member has agreed to submit to the authority of the union. Consequently, the right to work could only apply in the limited circumstances where there has been a refusal to admit.

The 'right to work' principle has also been compared to the old doctrine of restraint of trade.[20] A union rule book ensures a union member is bound by terms collectively negotiated by the union. This agreement is in unreasonable restraint of trade since workers are unable to engage in work on terms they please and, as a matter of public policy, the courts refuse to give effect to such agreements.

The 'right to work' principle arguably applies in a similar manner. Where an individual is denied entry to a union or expelled from a union where a closed shop operates, this restrains the right of the worker to earn a living: it restrains the right of the worker freely to enter into his or her trade or occupation on terms he or she wishes to be employed. This hindrance on a worker to pursue a trade or occupation is, therefore, an unreasonable restraint on this right.[21]

If the 'right to work' principle is merely an extension of the old doctrine of restraint of trade, then the immunity to restraint of trade originally contained in s 3 of the Trade Union Act 1871 should have been applied in the same way and the immunity to restraint of trade contained in the Trade Union and Labour Relations (Consolidation) Act (TULR(C)A) 1992 would deny its application today. Some support for this is provided by the comments of Bingham J in the *Cheall* case heard in the High Court. After noting that the expulsion rule was not an unreasonable restraint of trade as it was legitimised by s 2(5) of the Trade Union and Labour Relations Act 1974, he then went on to say: '[Counsel] did rely, as a separate head of public policy invalidity, on the infringement of the right to work, but I cannot see that in this context that concept raises any different issue.'[22]

In conclusion, it is extremely unlikely that the robust version of the 'right to work' as propagated by Lord Denning survives. Rules on expulsion or admission cannot be declared unlawful and struck down as contrary to the 'right to work'. Perhaps, where the union acts arbitrarily, with bias or dishonesty when deliberating on an admission case where a closed shop is functioning at the place of work, the doctrine may have some validity.

---

19 At p 127.

20 See Hepple, B, 'A right to work?' (1981) 10 ILJ 65, pp 78–81.

21 Salmon LJ in *Nagle v Feilden* [1966] 2 QB 633, p 654 said: 'The principle that courts will protect a man's right to work is well recognised in the stream of authorities relating to contracts in restraint of trade.' The judgment of Wilberforce J in *Eastham v Newcastle Utd* [1964] Ch 430, p 432, also implies that the right to work operates in a similar manner to restraint of trade. The system of Football League clubs retaining players' contracts was an interference with the rights of the players to earn a living and to 'seek other employment'. See, also, Slade J in *Grieg v Insole* [1978] 1 WLR 302, p 362.

22 *Cheall v APEX* [1982] IRLR 91, p 100.

This interpretation of the boundaries of the doctrine was most recently put forward by Stuart Smith LJ in the Divisional Court in *R v Jockey Club ex p RAM Racecourses Ltd*.[23] Stuart Smith considered that:

> Where a body enjoys a monopoly position such that it can prevent a person from earning his living by not admitting him ... it will be amenable to a declaratory judgment in an action begun by writ, if it has acted in an arbitrary and capricious way in refusing to permit the applicant's activities.[24]

This may, however, be overstating the effect of the doctrine. Rather than highlighting the right to work as a substantive principle of law, the better approach is to examine the procedural implications of Megarry's 'liberty to work'. Misconduct can, therefore, be challenged more on the basis that it conflicts with the 'duty to act fairly' as set out by Megarry in *McInnes* (examined in more detail later in the chapter), than by reference to the much criticised and imprecise 'right to work'.

The rule book and the bylaw theory

In a series of judgments in trade union cases spanning a period of 30 years until his retirement in 1983, Lord Denning often referred to the contract of association between union and member as a 'legal fiction'.[25] The essence of Denning's view was that union rules were not mutually agreed contractual obligations, but were imposed on a new member who had no choice but to accept the rule book unaltered. Therefore, as union rules were more in the nature of a legislative code or set of regulations laid down by a governing body they could be treated as analogous to statutory bylaws.

By suggesting that union rules could be compared to bylaws, Denning attempted to open the way for the legal regulation of union rules in the same way that statutory bylaws are controlled. Denning, in *Bonsor v Musicians' Union*,[26] adopted the views of Russell LCJ in *Kruse v Johnson*,[27] who said that bylaws created by statutory authorities under powers delegated from Parliament must not be 'unreasonable'.[28]

Denning applied this theory in his powerful dissenting judgment in *Faramus v Film Artistes Association*.[29] The relevant union had a rule which stated that no person who had committed a criminal offence was eligible for, or should retain membership of, the union. *Faramus* was admitted without disclosing convictions from some years previously. He was treated by the union as being wrongly admitted, as if he had never been a member of

---

23   [1993] 2 All ER 225.

24   At p 243.

25   Eg, see *Abbot v Sullivan* [1952] 1 All ER 226; *Bonsor v Musicians' Union* [1956] 3 All ER 518; *Lee v Showmen's Guild of Great Britain* [1952] 1 All ER 1175; and *Boulting v ACTAT* [1963] 1 All ER 716.

26   [1956] AC 110.

27   [1898] 2 QB 91.

28   Russell LCJ said that bylaws must be struck down if they: '... were partial and unequal in their operation between different classes; if they were manifestly unjust; if they disclosed bad faith; if they involved such oppressive or gratuitous interference with the rights of those subject to them as could find no justification in the minds of reasonable men, the court might say, "Parliament never intended to give authority to make such rules; they are unreasonable and *ultra vires*".'

29   [1963] 1 All ER 636. For a discussion of the implications of the case, see Rideout, R (1963) 26 MLR 436.

the union and was, therefore, excluded from the union. He then lost the opportunity to work as a film extra as the union operated a closed shop.

On the basis of the bylaw theory, Denning propounded the view that the union had applied an unreasonable interpretation of the rule and consequently their reliance on it was invalid. The rule did not provide for the automatic disqualification of the plaintiff from membership, but rather, properly interpreted, the rule had given the union a discretion to admit the plaintiff. By automatically disqualifying the plaintiff, without considering the option of admitting him, the union had failed properly to apply their existing discretion.

Both Upjohn LJ and Diplock LJ rejected the argument that the rules must be reasonable in the same way that bylaws of statutory authorities have to be. The doctrine of 'unreasonableness' in the context of a statutory bylaw was limited to where the organisation that created the bylaw was acting *'ultra vires'* in doing so.[30] Such a test could not be applied to the rules on eligibility for joining a trade union which was based on contract not statute. Therefore, Upjohn and Diplock, although critical of the rule, felt unable to intervene.

On appeal to the House of Lords,[31] their Lordships confirmed the view of Upjohn and Diplock that the bylaw theory could not be sustained as it was not possible to compare a bylaw made by a local or public authority with a provision in the union rule book which derived its authority from a contract. The proper interpretation of the rule was that it directed the union to exclude Faramus from the union.

Denning returned to this and his other arguments in *Edwards v SOGAT*[32] and in *Cheall v APEX*.[33] In *Edwards*, he said that a rule which destroys or gratuitously interferes with the right to earn a living is unreasonable and invalid. In *Cheall*, he updated his argument by referring to recent statutory provision (the Unfair Contract Terms Act 1977) which invalidated certain terms in a consumer contract. He strongly argued that as the union contract was a 'legal fiction', as consumer contracts were, union rules on expulsion and discipline should be treated in a similar vein to exemption clauses in consumer contracts, only being valid if they are 'reasonable'.

The House of Lords, some 20 years after first rejecting Denning's analysis in *Faramus*, did so again in *Cheall*.[34] Lord Diplock said that it was untenable for union rules to be invalidated in this manner without specific statutory authority. Diplock further rejected the whole notion of the bylaw thesis by saying that remedies designed for use in administrative law could not be invoked to control union decisions where the relationship between the union and their membership was clearly based on contract.[35]

---

30   For example, the statutory authority did not have the power from Parliament to do so.

31   [1964] AC 925.

32   [1971] Ch 354.

33   [1982] ICR 543 .

34   [1983] IRLR 215. For comment on the House of Lords' decision in *Cheall*, see Ewing, KD [1983] CLJ 207.

35   More recent cases have reaffirmed this view that the internal affairs of private associations cannot be the subject of public law remedies. For further discussion of this, see p 76.

The rule book and restraint of trade

Unions are combinations of workers with the aim of improving wages and gaining other benefits for their members. To achieve this aim, unions engage in collective bargaining with employers. This restrains the right of their members to work on any terms they may wish to. Those members of a union who have agreed in the contract of association to have their terms and conditions collectively negotiated are limiting their individual right to pursue their trade or occupation without interference.

Until 1871, union rules providing for the collective bargaining function were unenforceable and struck down as contrary to public policy on the grounds that they were in restraint of trade. However, s 3 of the Trade Union Act 1871 had reformed this position. Section 3 provided that the objects of a trade union, which are derived from the rule book, were not to be unenforceable merely because they were in restraint of trade.

For Lord Denning, an alternative interpretation of s 3 of the Trade Union Act 1871 was possible. Dissenting from the majority decision in *Faramus*, Denning concluded that s 3 had no application to any rules that are not specifically concerned with the purposes or objects of the union. Rules that deal with the internal management or organisation of the union, such as a rule dealing with entitlement to membership, are not part of the purposes or objects of the union. Therefore, it was open to the court to find that a rule concerned with admission to a union was in unreasonable restraint of trade as it denied the applicant the right to work in a profession of their choice and so was void as contrary to public policy.

On appeal, the House of Lords was unconvinced by Denning's attempt to distinguish between rules establishing the objects of the union and other rules. Their Lordships agreed with the majority decision in the Court of Appeal that, although arguably the rule on admission was *prima facie* in restraint of trade, s 3 of the Trade Union Act 1871 validated not only the purposes or objects of the union but also anything contained in the contract between a union member and a union.[36]

Denning's approach did, however, gain some support in the judgment of Sachs LJ in *Edwards v SOGAT*.[37] Sachs LJ explained that, where trade union membership is a prerequisite for employment, any rule on expulsion that gives a union an absolute right to withdraw membership interferes with the right to work and so is clearly an unlawful restraint of trade. Sachs LJ then went on to say that s 3 of the Trade Union Act 1871 could not possibly protect '... such despotic and capricious action ...'.[38]

Although the House of Lords in *Faramus* had rejected Denning's proposition, to ensure that it would not be resurrected in any subsequent case, Parliament enacted s 2(5) of the Trade Union and Labour Relations Act 1974 expanding the immunity for restraint of trade specifically to cover all the rules of a trade union.[39] Surprisingly, even this enactment, passed to establish beyond doubt that the doctrine of restraint of trade is inapplicable to trade unions, failed fully to eradicate judicial pronouncements on the

---

36 Lord Pearce stated that, even if Lord Denning's view had any validity, the decision of the union to establish a closed shop and to enforce it in this manner was a purpose or object of the union.

37 [1971] Ch 354.

38 At p 382.

39 This is now repeated in TULR(C)A 1992, s 11.

issue. Slade J in *Grieg v Insole* commented that s 2(5) may provide no defence where it is claimed that the rules on admission or exclusion were void on the far broader notion of general public policy. However, he failed to come to any clear conclusion on this point. If, as Slade implies, a wider ground of public policy could be used as an alternative to restraint of trade to strike down union rules, then this certainly would be a serious development for the principle of trade union self-government. However, as yet, this view has not been amplified or applied in any subsequent cases.

More recently, in *Goring v British Actors' Equity Association*,[40] it was asserted that instructions from the NEC which derive their authority from the rules are capable of falling foul of restraint of trade as such instructions are not legitimised by s 2(5). Browne-Wilkinson VC reiterated the conventional opinion that all the rules and purposes of a trade union were lawful by virtue of this provision and that, consequently, instructions given under the authority of the rules should be treated no differently.

An interesting postscript to the issue of restraint of trade was played out in the High Court in 1994. In *Boddington v Lawton*,[41] Nicholls VC mused on the possibility that the issue of restraint of trade *per se* should no longer be applicable to the rules of a trade union. He regarded it arguable that the rules of a trade union are not in unreasonable restraint of trade as union objectives are not now contrary to the public interest due to the well recognised and important role unions play in contemporary industrial relations.

The common law concepts – an evaluation

The significance of these common law developments is not in their effectiveness in controlling union internal decisions – in the majority of cases where the doctrines were propounded they did not settle the case – but rather lies in the willingness of certain members of the judiciary to engage in a 'subversion of the democratic process of trade unions'.[42] The provisions of the rule book are developed and agreed by the membership of the union through their representatives or delegates at union annual or special conferences. Should it be necessary to change or amend a rule because of unfairness in its application, then unions have exhaustive procedures for this purpose. These doctrines, arguably, have the effect of overturning these democratically agreed rules.

What underpinned these doctrines was a barely disguised hostility to the closed shop. The collectivist view of the closed shop, that the restriction of employment to union members helps to ensure job security and protects terms and conditions of employment, does not attract much sympathy from the courts, which are more concerned with the 'rights' of the individual. Interference in this way may be justified if it was clear that injustice was a regular consequence of the closed shop, but, as the Donovan Commission reported, this was not the case.[43] Real injustice to an individual occurred very rarely. The union movement itself, aware of the controversy engendered by a closed shop policy, formed, through the auspices of the Trades Union Congress, an Independent Review

---

40   [1987] IRLR 122.

41   [1994] ICR 478.

42   Wedderburn, KW (now Lord), *The Worker and the Law*, 2nd edn, 1971, p 432.

43   Cmnd 3623, 1968, para 610: 'There is little evidence that applications for membership are dealt with unfairly, or that membership is capriciously refused.'

Committee with a brief to consider complaints of injustice. For the duration of its existence, over a period of 10 years, only 51 complaints were heard and less than 10 formally upheld.[44]

The danger where broad principles such as these are articulated is that they may have an application which goes beyond the original intention behind their creation. For example, a doctrine such as the bylaw theory, which treats all union rules as part of an imposed legislative code, has a potential to be misused to strike out rules other than those on expulsion in a closed shop. Donaldson LJ in the Court of Appeal recognised the significance of this when he said, in *Cheall*, that principles based on public policy provided opportunities for judicial interference in matters best left to the trade unions themselves to resolve. Cheall had been recruited contrary to the TUC Bridlington principles on the poaching of members between unions and had been expelled as required under the principles. Donaldson LJ obliquely criticised his colleagues in the Court of Appeal for determining their positions, partly because of their distaste for the Bridlington principles, even though many on both sides of industry saw them as a factor in reducing inter-union strife and in contributing to securing peaceful industrial relations.[45]

Public law remedies

Given the history of judicial creativity in the realm of trade union law, it may be asked whether in the future the courts will discover new ways of controlling union decision making. One possibility, given the increase in the importance of judicial review in the 1990s, is via the re-affirmation of public law concepts.

As we know, Lord Denning had almost single handedly argued for this form of judicial intervention in many cases from the 1950s until his retirement in 1982. Denning considered that trade unions were not truly private organisations to be treated in a similar manner to unincorporated social clubs, but were rather 'powerful associations' and 'monopolies exercising important functions in society', which justified the application of principles more commonly associated with administrative law to trade union practices.[46]

This view resurfaced in *R v Jockey Club ex p RAM Racecourses*,[47] where Simon Brown J said:

> Cases like [*Nagle v Feilden, Breen v AEU* and *McInnes v Onslow Fane*] had they arisen today and not some years ago, would have found a natural home in judicial review proceedings. As it was, considerations of public policy forced the courts to devise a new private law creature ... But clear recognition of the true, essentially public law, nature of these cases is to be found in the judgment of Lord Denning MR in *Breen v AEU* and I for my part would

---

44   For further analysis of the work of this committee, see Chapter 5, p 96.

45   Donaldson went on to make a plea to his colleagues to control their enthusiasm for making such decisions based on public policy with the comment: '... judges must beware of confusing political policy with public policy ... Whether judges are better or less able than others to assess the merits or demerits of political policies is beside the point, because that is not their function.' *Cheall v APEX* [1982] ICR 543, p 565.

46   See, eg, Denning in *Breen v AEU* [1971] 2 QB 175, p 190. Further explanation may be gleaned from Lord Denning's commentary on these cases in *The Discipline of Law*, 1979, p 147 and from Jowell, JL and McAuslan, JP (eds), *Lord Denning, the Judge and the Law*, 1984, pp 368–77.

47   [1993] 2 All ER 225.

judge it preferable to develop these principles in future in a public law context than by further distorting private law principles. *Nagle v Fielden* was never in my judgment a restraint of trade case properly so called; rather it brought into play clear considerations of public law.[48]

To what extent is Simon Brown's bold statement supported by the authorities? The House of Lords, in *O'Reilly v Mackman*,[49] held that for the courts to have jurisdiction to enforce public law remedies it is necessary for the body in question to exercise some public duty or public function. It may well be arguable that, on occasion, trade unions do exercise some public functions in the realm of industrial relations that affect a wider group of persons other than the membership of a union. This is particularly the case where a closed shop operates in regulating the supply of labour in an industry. However, even if it is accepted that occasionally trade unions play some wider public role, more recent decisions suggest that 'public interest' in a decision is not enough to move an ostensibly private body into the sphere of public law.

In *R v Panel on Takeovers and Mergers ex p Datafin*,[50] the Court of Appeal declared that, in determining whether public law remedies were applicable, the source of power is more relevant than the degree of public function a body exercises. Where the sole source of authority for the decision is contractual and so derived from private law, the action of the body is not subject to public law controls. This conclusion was followed by Rose J in *R v Football Association ex p Football League*,[51] where he held that the Football Association, as a domestic body whose powers arose from private law, was not a body that was ordinarily susceptible to judicial review proceedings.[52] It would therefore seem that authority points towards the proposition that union decisions to discipline or expel cannot be controlled by public remedies as the power to do so is based on contract, which is solely a matter for private law.

This, however, still leaves open the question whether decisions of private bodies to refuse to admit a candidate for membership is also outside the jurisdiction of the courts. It is possibly in this context that Simon Brown's comments in *ex p RAM Racecourses* should be understood. Some support for Simon Brown's opinion that *Nagle v Fielden*, if it arose today, should be dealt with as a public law case was contained in the judgments of Bingham MR and Farquharson LJ, in *R v Disciplinary Committee of the Jockey Club ex p Aga Khan*.[53] Both judges were of the opinion that if a remedy in private law was clearly inadequate because of the absence of a contractual relationship between the parties, then the grant of a public law remedy, such as judicial review of a decision to deny entry, was justified.[54]

In conclusion, it may well be that in the future, if there is no appropriate statutory remedy, applicants to trade unions who are denied admission may find that the courts will entertain an application for judicial review. This does not necessarily impose on trade

---

48 At p 247.
49 [1983] 2 AC 237.
50 [1987] QB 815.
51 [1993] 2 All ER 833.
52 See also the judgments of Neil LJ and Roch J in *R v Jockey Club ex p Massingberd-Mundy* [1993] 2 All ER 207.
53 [1993] 2 All ER 853.
54 At pp 859 and 873, respectively.

unions a great burden. The purpose behind judicial review here is to control any abuses of discretionary power. So long as applications are considered fairly and the discretion to refuse membership is exercised properly, the courts will not strike down such a decision taken reasonably as contrary to the principles of administrative law.

Enforcement of the rule book

The law of contract, through a member's individual contract of association, regulates the relationship between the member and the union. As the rule book outlines the terms of the contract between the member and the union, a member alleging wrongful discipline or expulsion due to a failure of the union to abide by the rules may bring an action to enforce the rules.

Nearly all unions have rules that allow them to discipline their members and to impose sanctions such as the suspension of membership, the imposition of a fine or expulsion. In a survey of union rule books in 1980,[55] Gennard noted that, out of the 79 union rule books considered, 69 had a broad general expulsion or discipline rule permitting punishment for 'action contrary to the interests of the union' or for 'bringing the union into disrepute'. In addition, rule books will usually contain specific disciplinary offences such as 'disobeying an instruction of the union' or 'misappropriating property'.

The rules will also usually outline the disciplinary procedure to be followed including, *inter alia*, the composition of the disciplinary body, the conduct of hearings, the appeal process and often matters such as whether legal representation is permitted. Frequently, the original disciplinary charge will be heard by a branch committee with appeals to a special tribunal appointed for this purpose by the annual conference or national executive of the union.

Compliance with the rules

As judicial control is exercised through the application of the contract of association between member and union, it follows that any failure to comply strictly with the requirements of the rules will render the decision to discipline or to expel unlawful. Consequently, courts will scrutinise the operation of disciplinary rules very carefully to ensure that the rule which is applied by the union clearly does provide the union with the power to act to impose the particular sanction and that all procedural requirements outlined in the rules have been followed.

Moreover, if the power to expel or discipline a member or the power to impose a particular sanction is not explicit but is vague or unclear, then, as it fails to provide the authority for the action taken by the union, the court will declare it unenforceable. Where the power to act does not arise at all under the contract, then the courts will not usually imply a power to discipline or expel a member.[56] However, in 'exceptional and unusual

---

55 Gennard, J, 'Throwing the book: trade union rules on admission, discipline and expulsion' (1980) *Employment Gazette* 591. See also Rideout, R, 'The content of trade union disciplinary rules' (1965) 3 BJIR 153 and the survey of union practice in disciplinary matters in *Industrial Relations Review and Reports* (1982) May, pp 2–7.

56 Eg, in *Spring v National Amalgamated Stevedores' and Dockers' Society* [1956] 2 All ER 221, the union purported to expel the plaintiff to comply with an award of the Trades Union Congress Disputes Committee. As there was no express provision in the union rules permitting it to do so for this reason, the union was restrained from expelling the plaintiff.

circumstances', arising from a matter of principle, a court will permit a union to discipline a member even though there is no express power in the rules.[57]

Substantive compliance

Any divergence from the powers outlined in the rules will be unlawful. In *Blackall v National Union of Foundary Workers*,[58] Blackall was expelled for being 19 weeks in arrears with his subscriptions. The relevant rule allowed for an expulsion where a member was 20 weeks in arrears. As there had not been strict adherence to the rule, the expulsion was unlawful. A similar situation arose in *Bonsor v Musicians' Union*.[59] The relevant rule specified that, if a member was more than six weeks in arrears, then the branch could resolve to expel the member. Bonsor had failed to pay his subscriptions for a year. The branch secretary decided personally to inform the plaintiff he was expelled. As the power of expelling a member was vested in the branch committee and could not be delegated, the expulsion was contrary to the rules and therefore void.

Burns v National Amalgamated Labourers' Union[60] is an example of how the power of the union to impose a particular sanction is strictly limited by what is permitted under the rules. Here, Burns, a local officer of the union, had been barred from holding office for five years. Under the rules, the executive committee had a discretion to suspend or expel members for the offence that Burns had committed. Lawrence J stated that the rules did not give the executive committee power to punish or penalise the plaintiff in this particular way. The penalty, even though less severe than the one provided for in the rules, was unenforceable.

Procedural compliance

In addition to complying with the substantive rules on discipline or expulsion, the union must comply with any additional procedural requirements stipulated in the rules. Thus, the domestic tribunal must be properly constituted and duly convened as required under the rules.[61] Any rules providing for a specific period of notice to be given before the convening of the disciplinary tribunal, or for a right to attend the hearing, must be adhered to[62] and the procedures for investigating a charge outlined in the rules must be followed.[63]

---

57 In *McVitae v Unison* [1996] IRLR 33, the plaintiff had been a member of NALGO before it amalgamated with other unions to form Unison. After the amalgamation had taken place, a Unison disciplinary committee was convened to hear charges relating to the period when the plaintiff was a member of NALGO. The plaintiff argued that Unison had no power to discipline its members in relation to events which occurred prior to its creation. Although there was no express power in the Unison rule book to discipline members for conduct that occurred before its inception, Harrison J was willing to imply a power to discipline in these 'compelling circumstances' where the plaintiff's conduct was contrary to the rules of NALGO and the rules of Unison.

58 (1923) 39 TLR 431.

59 [1956] AC 110.

60 [1920] 2 Ch 364.

61 *Leary v National Union of Vehicle Builders* [1971] Ch 34.

62 *Lawlor v Union of Post Office Workers* [1965] Ch 712.

63 *Santer v National Graphical Association* [1973] ICR 60.

If there is a failure to comply with the appeal procedures enshrined in the rules, the original decision of the tribunal is of course void. That failure may also, in appropriate circumstances, invalidate any subsequent charges. In *Silvester v National Union of Printing, Bookbinding and Paper Workers*,[64] the plaintiff was charged with acting to the detriment of the union for refusing to obey an instruction of the union. The plaintiff continued to defy the union and so further charges were brought against him. His right to appeal under the rules for the first charge was refused as an investigation of the other charges had not yet been completed. The court held that the wrongful denial of the appeal on the first charge invalidated the proceedings and vitiated the decision on all the charges.[65]

Construction of the rules

The domestic disciplinary tribunal is ordinarily regarded as having exclusive jurisdiction over any findings of fact. Yet, where questions of law arise, the findings of a domestic tribunal can be disturbed by the courts as, in matters of law, the courts claim ultimate jurisdiction. It is a question of law whether there is sufficient evidence reasonably capable of supporting the findings of fact by the domestic tribunal. In effect, the court is entitled to take it upon itself to assess the weight of evidence presented to the tribunal.[66]

Even where the facts are clearly supported by the evidence, the decision is reviewable by the courts where the tribunal has incorrectly interpreted the offence cited in the rules. Where the rules have been misapplied in this manner, the courts will find that the conduct of the member is not capable in law of constituting the offence. The right of the courts to intervene in this way was strongly defended by the Court of Appeal in *Lee v Showmen's Guild*.[67] Both Romer LJ and Denning LJ stressed that, where the domestic tribunal has construed the rules wrongly, the right to review the tribunal's decision is reserved exclusively to the courts which are the sole arbiters of the true meaning of the rules.

In *Radford v NATSOPA*,[68] the plaintiff was charged with taking 'wilful action against the union' for consulting a solicitor during a previous dispute with the union. Plowman J justified intervention on the grounds that the courts are 'peculiarly appropriate' bodies to consider the true construction of the rules and to examine the sufficiency of evidence to support findings of fact. On these facts, he unsurprisingly held that consulting a solicitor could not be reasonably construed as satisfying the test of 'wilful action against the union'.

In an attempt to preserve the jurisdiction of the domestic tribunal and to avoid judicial intervention, many unions frame their disciplinary rules in very subjective terms.

---

64 (1966) 1 KIR 679.

65 See also *Braithwaite v EETU* [1969] 2 All ER 859.

66 For example, Denning, in *Breen v AEU* [1971] 2 QB 175, emphasised that where a tribunal has taken into account irrelevant evidence, the court is wholly justified in declaring the decision of the tribunal null and void. See also, here, *Kelly v NATSOPA* (1915) 84 LJ KB 2236. Disciplinary action had been taken against Kelly as it was believed that his daytime employment constituted a safety hazard to his fellow workers on the night shift. The court held that this in itself was not sufficient evidence that Kelly posed a safety hazard to his fellow workers and so disciplinary action for 'conduct detrimental' to the interests of members of the union could not be sustained.

67 [1952] 2 QB 329.

68 [1972] ICR 484.

A rule of this nature will require the domestic tribunal to assess whether, in the tribunal's 'opinion', the offence, such as 'acting to the detriment of the union' has been committed. This phraseology in principle ostensibly operates to exclude the court, since it is for the domestic tribunal to decide what is detrimental to the union, based on its own standards of behaviour. What is required of such a disciplinary tribunal is simply that it acts honestly and in good faith.

Despite *dicta* by Romer LJ in *Lee v Showmen's Guild* that the courts should beware of intervention where such a subjective formulation is used in the rules, and a general acceptance of the use of subjective phraseology in social club cases,[69] the courts have not been inhibited in interceding where trade unions use such a device. Consequently, it is immaterial whether the offence is phrased objectively or subjectively: the courts will still declare a decision of a union domestic tribunal as perverse in law if there is insufficient evidence to support the facts, or to justify the opinion, or if there is an erroneous interpretation of the offence.

The 'reasonable tribunal' test

In theory, the court should not intervene unless satisfied that no reasonable tribunal acting in good faith could have come to the conclusion that was reached on the submitted facts and evidence presented. This approach, if strictly followed by the courts, gives the domestic tribunal some scope in its interpretation of the rule and on the relative weight of evidence. At times, however, the courts have been less than willing to allow unions even this limited degree of autonomy and have substituted their own view of whether the actions of the applicant are capable of satisfying the rule. *Esterman v NALGO*[70] is a somewhat notorious example of this.

During a dispute between NALGO and certain local authorities (and after a ballot which showed 49% of the membership in favour of industrial action), the union, under the rules, instructed members not to co-operate with the holding of local government elections. Esterman defied the instruction and was invited to attend a disciplinary branch meeting which was to consider whether her conduct merited expulsion from the union. Rule 13 stated that members could be expelled for actions 'that render him [*sic*] unfit for membership in the opinion of the executive committee'.

Templeman J held that the failure of the NALGO executive to obtain a majority vote for industrial action entitled the applicant to doubt whether the union had the power under the rules to instruct members to take action. The consequence of this misuse of union power to call industrial action was that the applicant's actions in defying the unlawful instructions could not be interpreted as conduct that 'renders him unfit for membership' in the eyes of any reasonable tribunal.

Templeman J purported to apply the 'reasonable tribunal' test – that the court only interfered because it was satisfied that no reasonable tribunal acting in good faith could have concluded that the member had offended against the rule – yet the reality was that the court was deciding for itself what was reasonable based on a test of what the

---

69 See, eg, *Dawkins v Antrobus* [1879] 17 Ch 615; *Rigby v Connol* [1880] 14 Ch 482; *MacLean v Workers Union* [1929] 1 Ch 602.
70 [1974] ICR 625. Noted by Davies, P (1975) 4 ILJ 112.

'reasonable union member' believes is an appropriate exercise of union power. Such a test merely disguises the fact that the court is substituting the tribunal's view with its own opinion of whether the facts fall within the terms of the disciplinary rule.

Ambiguity

A further safeguard for the disciplined member is that the courts insist that the rule book is construed in such a way so that any ambiguity in the rules is resolved in favour of the individual. This is achieved by the courts interpreting the rules '... so as to give a reasonable interpretation which accords with what in our opinion must have been intended'.[71] This allows the courts some discretion over how the rule book should be construed. The court adopts, what is to the court, the most reasonable interpretation in the circumstances. In *Goring* itself, the rules on internal democracy were contradictory. The House of Lords resolved the ambiguity in favour of the rights of members to express their view through a ballot by all the membership rather than through a general meeting that could not be attended by all the membership.[72]

MacLelland v NUJ[73] is a good example of this method of construction of the rules in the area of discipline. Under r 15 of the union, a chapel (branch) had the power to discipline a member of the chapel where he or she failed to attend a compulsory union meeting. At a monthly meeting of MacLelland's chapel, the committee members designated the meeting as compulsory and instructed the membership to attend. MacLelland only attended one part of the meeting. The court construed the rules in such a way that, even if the meeting had been properly called, there had been compliance with the rule on attendance as the obligation to attend the mandatory meeting did not impose on MacLelland a duty to remain for the full duration.

Ousting the jurisdiction of the court

Denning LJ, in *Lee v Showmen's Guild*,[74] underlined the exclusivity of the court's jurisdiction when he said that: '... the true construction of the contract is to be decided by the courts and by no one else.'[75] This is clear authority that an internal tribunal cannot ordinarily usurp the authority of the court in matters of law. Indeed, any formal attempt to oust the jurisdiction of the court by the provision of a clause in the rule book purporting to exclude the power of the court to intervene will be struck down as void and unenforceable.[76]

---

71 Viscount Dilhorne in *Goring v British Actors' Equity* [1978] ICR 791, p 795.

72 That the courts prefer an interpretation that results in the most 'democratic' outcome is also illustrated by the cases of *Porter v NUJ* [1979] IRLR 404 and *Taylor v NUM (Derbyshire Area)* [1984] IRLR 440; in both cases the rules were interpreted in such a way that industrial action could only be lawfully taken after a full ballot of the membership rather than by a decision of a special delegate conference or the national executive. On this, see also *Gormley v NUM* (1977) *The Times*, 21 October.

73 [1975] ICR 116

74 [1952] 2 QB 329.

75 At p 344.

76 *Scott v Avery* (1856) 5 HL Cas 811 as applied in *Lee v Showmen's Guild*. Note, also, that the mere fact that an applicant assents to the jurisdiction of the internal domestic tribunal by instigating the internal appeal process does not impliedly constitute an exclusion of the court's jurisdiction to inquire into the circumstances of the domestic tribunal's decision – *Annamunthodo v OWTU* [1961] 3 All ER 621.

Partial ouster

The courts have an inherent discretion to stay proceedings until domestic procedures have been exhausted.[77] This discretion, however, cannot be enforced by a formal mandatory provision in the rule book delaying access to the courts, until there has been recourse to domestic proceedings. Such a rule would act to fetter the courts' lawful discretion and is *prima facie* contrary to public policy: yet, it may be valid in appropriate circumstances. Goff J dealt with this issue in *Leigh v NUR*[78] when he said: '... where there is an express provision in the rules that the plaintiff must first exhaust his domestic remedies, the court is not absolutely bound by that because its jurisdiction cannot be ousted, but the plaintiff will have to show just cause why it should interfere with the contractual position.'[79]

What circumstances justify the court's disregarding the contractual position and therefore allowing immediate access were not fully enumerated by the judge. From the authorities it seems that 'just cause' may be satisfied where there is clear evidence of bias in the domestic tribunal, capricious or arbitrary behaviour by the union, excessive delay[80] or, possibly, where the factual issues are not in dispute and so only an issue of law is to be considered.[81] In these limited circumstances, the courts, at common law, may well be willing to recognise and give effect to a partial ouster of their jurisdiction and so use their discretion to stay legal proceedings pending the outcome of the domestic tribunal.[82]

The common law position on the legality of delaying access to the courts has now been supplemented by a statutory provision, s 63 of the TULR(C)A 1992, which provides a right for members to have access to the courts to pursue a grievance against their union, notwithstanding any contrary rule in the rule book. This right, not to be denied access to the courts, is limited to the situation where the member has already made an application under the rules of the union and six months have elapsed from the date of the application without a determination by the union, unless the reason for the delay was because of the unreasonable conduct of the member. If the member enforces their statutory right, the court is bound to adjudicate without regard to any rule limiting its jurisdiction, even if the matter would have been more quickly, efficiently and conveniently disposed of under domestic procedures.

Section 63(6) states that this right is provided without prejudice to any principle of common law. Thus, it is still possible that if 'just cause' is demonstrated, the member may still ignore any rule requiring the exhaustion of domestic remedies, before the six month period has elapsed.

---

77 *Lawlor v UPW* [1965] Ch 712 and *White v Kuzych* [1965] 1 All ER 353.

78 [1970] Ch 326.

79 At p 334.

80 *Leigh v NUR* [1970] Ch 326.

81 *Radford v NATSOPA* [1972] ICR 484.

82 This is, of course, on the assumption that the domestic procedures are effective and will preserve the status quo pending the decision of the tribunal. *Hiles v Amalgamated Society of Woodworkers* [1968] Ch 440.

The pre-emptive injunction

A particularly worrying development for unions is where the court grants an interlocutory injunction prior to the disciplinary hearing. This precludes the domestic tribunal from considering the substance of the charge and so fails to allow the parties to settle their disputes internally. Although intervention in advance was contrary to the previous practice of the court, the provision of such an injunction was another feature of the *Esterman* case.[83] The plaintiff was granted an injunction restraining the disciplinary action prior to the hearing on the basis that no reasonable tribunal acting *bona fides* could uphold the complaint against the applicant.

The House of Lords in *Porter v NUJ*[84] gave further credence to this doctrine by granting an interlocutory application for an injunction to quash the disciplinary decision before the completion of the internal appeal process.[85] Similarly, an injunction was granted prior to the completion of disciplinary proceedings in *Partington v NALGO*.[86] Partington had been expelled from his union for returning to work during industrial action. He did so at the request of his employer to provide emergency cover under the terms of a collective agreement. He was charged with the disciplinary offence of 'conduct unbefitting a member'. The court held that as he was obliged to attend work to provide emergency cover, no reasonable tribunal would expel him in those circumstances and so any branch committee that attempted to do so would be acting unlawfully.

The Court of Appeal, in *Longley v NUJ*,[87] has attempted to limit the application of such injunctions in disciplinary matters. Here, a shop steward defied the National Executive Committee of the NUJ in working at the Wapping headquarters of News International. He was expelled for 'conduct detrimental to the interests of the union' which was defined in the rules as *inter alia*, 'failure without reasonable cause, to comply with an instruction of the NEC ...'. Before the complaint was heard, Longley applied for an interlocutory injunction against the union to stop the disciplinary action. Longley argued that he had reasonable cause to defy a call for industrial action as it was unsupported by a valid ballot required under the Trade Union Act 1984 (now, see s 226 of the TULR(C)A 1992).

The Court of Appeal initially accepted the *Esterman* test that intervention in advance could be countenanced – if it is clear that these were such exceptional circumstances that no reasonable tribunal acting *bona fides* could possibly find against the plaintiff. The court, however, then made it clear that 'exceptional circumstances' should be given a narrow interpretation. What was required was clear evidence of bias or that the issues would be prejudged or that prescribed procedures were being ignored so that it would be totally unreasonable of the domestic tribunal to find against the plaintiff. In the Court of Appeal's judgment the sole evidence of the failure to ballot was not on its own necessarily

---

83 See also *Losinka v CPSA* [1976] ICR 473, where an interlocutory injunction was granted to restrain officers of the union from criticising the plaintiff's conduct.

84 [1980] IRLR 404.

85 For further explanation of the House of Lords' judgment, see Newell, D, 'Trade unions and non-striking members' (1981) 97 LQR 214.

86 [1981] IRLR 537.

87 [1987] IRLR 109.

sufficient to satisfy this test. The Court of Appeal also attempted to introduce a degree of industrial realism into the test by stating that a court should take into account that a disciplinary tribunal's deliberations will be properly influenced by the practices and traditions of the union, which inevitably puts a premium on collective solidarity at the workplace.[88]

In *Ali v Southwark LBC*,[89] a case concerning an internal disciplinary hearing conducted by an employer, the plaintiff applied for a pre-emptive injunction on the grounds that the employer had no evidence to support the charge. Millett J could not find on the facts any 'exceptional circumstances' to justify intervention prior to the hearing and cited approvingly the formula put forward by Knox J in the High Court in *Longley*, that a domestic tribunal which has not completed a hearing '... should not be restrained unless it has acted improperly or it is inevitable that it will do so'.

Conclusions

Judicial decisions in this area can be criticised for failing to respect union freedom to discipline their membership under the rules. The relationship between union and member is based on the contractual model. In theory, this should preserve the authority of the union to take appropriate disciplinary action under the contract of association. On joining the union, a member contracts to observe the rules and on failing to do so to submit to established disciplinary procedures and sanctions. By interfering too readily, the courts are disregarding union contractual rights to deal internally with domestic affairs and challenging their legitimate authority to enforce disciplinary rules that were democratically formulated to protect the interests of the membership as a whole.

Many decisions also betray the judiciary's lack of understanding of the nature and importance of the interests of the collective membership in the decision to take disciplinary action. A union's main purpose is to win enhanced terms and conditions for all its membership through collective bargaining and to protect the job security of its membership. To be effective in this role, it needs to be a disciplined and cohesive organisation. Therefore, where, for example, a member betrays trade union principles by opting out of industrial action undertaken to attain these goals, to the collective membership as a whole this disloyalty should be dealt with by internal disciplinary action.

If we examine cases where members have been disciplined for failing to support industrial action, the courts have consistently attacked these decisions by declaring the industrial action itself to be unlawful in some way. For example, the *Esterman* decision suggested that, where an individual member regards the strike action as illegitimate on grounds of conscience, then disciplinary proceedings are inappropriate. We saw earlier, in *Partington*, that the disciplinary action was ill-founded where the industrial action was in

---

88 Ralph Gibson LJ in the Court of Appeal went further than his colleagues by stating that, even in the circumstances where a tribunal has acted improperly, it may not always be in the interests of justice to grant an interlocutory injunction to prevent members from facing disciplinary hearings.

89 [1988] IRLR 100.

breach of a collective agreement.[90] Denning, in *Sherrard v AUEW*,[91] went so far as to say that it was unlawful internally to discipline a member for refusing to participate if the industrial action did not attract the protection of the statutory immunities in tort. We have already seen in the miners' cases in Chapter 3 how, where strike action was taken without a ballot, all disciplinary proceedings were quashed.

By interfering in this manner, the courts are undermining union collective strength at a crucial time. Solidarity in an industrial dispute is imperative, otherwise the union cannot function effectively in its bargaining role as a counterweight to the economic power of an employer. The cases above demonstrate that, to the courts, the 'rights' of the individual to opt out of industrial action are of paramount importance – more so than the needs of the trade union to secure full, active support for the benefit of the membership as a whole.[92]

More recently, there has been some limited evidence of judicial appreciation that there is a need to strike a sensible balance between the needs of the membership of a union collectively and the interests of the individual. *Longley* is an example of this, particularly the judgment of Ralph Gibson LJ. As we saw in Chapter 3, cases such as *Hamlet v GMBATU*[93] suggest that the courts, in the late 1980s, may have adopted a more non-interventionist approach towards internal trade union matters.[94] This is difficult to assess because the mass of statutory regulation in this area has rendered the common law action almost extinct, as the interests of the individual member are now more effectively protected through statutory regulation.

However, the future may see a revival of common law actions as Sched 6, para 19 of the Employment Relations Act 1999 introduced new powers for the Certification Officer to investigate and adjudicate on certain breaches of union rules – including disciplinary matters (for further details see pp 20–22).

The rules of natural justice

We saw above that, if disciplinary procedures are incorporated into the rule book, the courts will act to enforce this procedure and declare any disciplinary action contrary to the procedure unlawful. Where the procedural safeguards in the rule book are inadequate or incomplete, the courts will still insist that certain minimum requirements are met. These are broadly known as the rules of natural justice.

---

90   The principle that may be extrapolated from this decision is that where there is a failure to participate in industrial action which is in breach of contract, unions do not have the authority to discipline any members that have ignored the call for action. As industrial action is nearly always in breach of an employment contract, this would have serious implications for a union's right to discipline their membership under the rules. However, the Court of Appeal, in *Porter v NUJ* [1979] IRLR 404, rejected such an argument. Shaw LJ stated at 407 that: '... a power to order a member to go on strike ... extends to requiring the member to strike although in doing so he may be in breach of contract with his employer.'

91   [1973] ICR 421. See also the judgment of Astbury J in *National Sailor's & Firemen's Union v Reed* [1926] Ch 536.

92   It is clear that the courts are essentially ill equipped to balance such contrary interests because the English common law is instinctively hostile to collective rights. For further elaboration of this theme see Kidner, R, 'The individual and the collective interest in trade union law' (1975) 5 ILJ 90.

93   [1986] IRLR 293.

94   See the case note to *Hamlet* by S Lee (1987) 103 LQR 330.

The legal authority for the imposition of these principles has been a matter of debate. In the era of intervention in union internal affairs during the period of the closed shop, the general grounds for intervention in union affairs shifted perceptively from a contractual basis towards the application of public law remedies and public law concepts. Thus, there was a general acceptance that administrative law principles of natural justice applied to trade unions. More recent criticisms of unions functioning as public bodies[95] suggest that natural justice is not now founded on public law. Rather, the better view is that there is a need for union tribunals to observe the principles of natural justice owing to the existence of implied obligations of law to that effect in the contract of association. As implied terms of law they cannot be excluded by any contrary provision in the rule book, since such an agreement would be void as contrary to public policy.[96]

The components of natural justice[97]

There are broadly two constituents of natural justice:

(a) the disciplinary decision must have been reached without bias on the part of the panel hearing the charges;

(b) there must be a fair hearing. This means the accused is entitled to appropriate notice of the charges, the right to be heard in answer to these charges, the right to attend and to put his or her case to the tribunal.

Rule against bias

In the vast majority of cases, initial disciplinary hearings are convened at the branch level with the disciplinary panel comprising of local branch officers. Hence, few members of a union disciplinary tribunal can be totally free from any interest or involvement in the issues. To apply the rule against bias stringently – expecting members of a disciplinary panel to be strictly impartial – would impose a great burden on trade unions and emasculate their legitimate powers to control the behaviour of their membership. Rather than expecting all members to be free from any bias or prejudice, the courts accept that it is perhaps inevitable that within a domestic tribunal there may be members of the tribunal who have certain pre-conceived opinions on the issues to be considered.

Consequently, the courts attempt to apply the rule against bias realistically by examining the composition of the disciplinary tribunal with reference to the nature of the complaint. If it is clear that there are members who have strong adverse views about the plaintiff's conduct or who have a personal grudge against the plaintiff, then this may well constitute real bias as there is a danger that they have made their decision in advance before hearing the evidence.

This tolerant approach of the courts was illustrated in *White v Kuzych*,[98] where there was strong and widespread resentment against the applicant by the membership as a

---

95 See pp 76–77.

96 See *Lee v Showmen's Guild* [1952] 2 QB 329; *Radford v NATSOPA* [1972] ICR 484; *Breen v AEU* [1971] 2 QB 175; cf *Lawlor v UPW* [1965] Ch 712.

97 See the classic statement by Lord Hodson on the essential requirements of natural justice in *Ridge v Baldwin* [1964] AC 40, p 132.

98 [1951] AC 585.

whole because of his opposition to union policy on the closed shop. When disciplined for his opposition to union policy, he objected to the presence of one member of the disciplinary panel who was known to be particularly hostile to his point of view. Viscount Simon disagreed with the proposition that this hostility automatically vitiated the decision of the tribunal. Where questions of bias were raised, what was required of the members of a tribunal '... was a will to reach a honest conclusion ... and a resolve not to make up their minds up beforehand on his personal guilt, however firmly held their conviction as to union policy and however strongly they had joined in previous adverse criticism of the respondent's conduct'.[99]

Yet, if there is evidence of a real failure to 'reach an honest conclusion' then the court will intervene. In *Taylor v National Union of Seamen*,[100] the union general secretary had dismissed an official for insubordination and had presided over his appeal to the executive committee of the union. During the deliberations of the committee, the general secretary made prejudicial comments and allegations irrelevant to the charge. The Court of Appeal stated that the executive committee was required to consider in a judicial fashion whether the decision to dismiss was well founded. The presence and behaviour of the general secretary was clear evidence of bias which may well have had a material effect on these judicial deliberations.

In *Roebuck v NUM (Yorkshire Area) (No 2)*,[101] Roebuck had been disciplined because of his support of a newspaper, the *Sheffield Star*, which was being sued for libel by Arthur Scargill, the Yorkshire President at the time. Scargill initiated the disciplinary action, alleging that Roebuck's actions had been 'detrimental to the interests of the union' under rule 42. He sat as chair of the area executive committee which charged the plaintiff and as chair of the disciplinary committee which heard the charge.

Templeman J maintained that the test of bias which should be applied to determine whether a decision of a disciplinary tribunal should be quashed, was not just whether the tribunal was actually biased against the plaintiff but whether '... there is a likelihood of bias in the eyes of the reasonable person who knew nothing of the actual deliberations of the tribunal'. As Scargill acted as the prosecutor and as a judge in his own cause, the '... appearance of bias was inevitable; the exercise of bias conscious or unconscious was probable'.[102]

Fair hearing

Notice of charges

Natural justice requires that the complainant has notice of the charge so as to enable a defence to be prepared. Notice of the charge should ordinarily be put to the member in

---

99 At p 596. This formula espoused by Viscount Simon was followed by Harman J in *Hamlet v GMBATU* [1986] IRLR 293. An appeal was heard by the general council which included four members of the original disciplinary committee. Harman J reiterated that there was no blanket rule that said it was automatically contrary to natural justice for such a committee to include members who had an interest or connection with the case. There was no reason to believe they were not ready to reach an 'honest conclusion'.

100 [1967] 1 All ER 767.

101 [1978] ICR 678. Noted by Newell, D (1979) 8 ILJ 44.

102 At p 682.

writing,[103] although formal notice is arguably not necessary where the case is straightforward and the individual is well aware of the issues to be considered.[104] In addition, information on the potential penalty should be provided, especially where the sanction is of some significance.[105]

If one charge is put to the applicant, then the tribunal cannot move to convict on another which the accused has not received notice of. In *Annamunthodo v OWTU*,[106] the appellant had alleged that the general secretary of the union had defrauded funds from the union. Originally, the union formulated a specific charge against the appellant which had a fine as the penalty, but it was altered without notice to enable the expulsion of the appellant. By failing to give proper notice of the fresh charge, the requirements of natural justice had not been observed.

In *Radford v NATSOPA*,[107] the branch committee had decided to take disciplinary action under the rules against Radford due to his refusal to adhere to an agreement made between the union and his employers dealing with redundancy matters. Before the hearing, the branch committee became aware that Radford had instructed solicitors to act on his behalf. When Radford refused to disclose the nature of his discussions with his solicitor and to hand over certain documents, the committee concluded without hearing from Radford that he had 'taken action ... wilfully against the union' as defined under the rules and so expelled him forthwith. Plowman J had no hesitation in declaring the decision void as no charge had been put to the member and no hearing had taken place: both serious lapses in procedure.[108]

Serious irregularities also occurred in *Ecclestone v NUJ*,[109] where the applicant (the deputy general secretary of the union) was charged with 'serious misconduct' that under the union rules could result in a written warning. Incriminating material relevant to the charges was not made available to the applicant until his appearance at the internal disciplinary hearing. When the applicant's request for an adjournment to study the material at length was denied, the applicant refused to participate in the proceedings. Subsequently, the tribunal proceeded in his absence, passing a motion of no confidence in him and resolving to dismiss him summarily. The High Court held that the tribunal had reached its decisions at a meeting that was conducted in the 'clearest breach of natural justice', as the applicant was denied the opportunity to defend himself against a motion of no confidence that was not originally on the agenda.

---

103 *Santer v NGA* [1973] ICR 60.

104 *Abbot v Sullivan* [1952] 1 KB 189, pp 199 and 211. The same principles of natural justice apply where an official is dismissed, so the notice provided must be specific unless the case is known to all and straightforward. See *Stevenson v Utd Road Transport Union* [1971] ICR 893 and, generally, on officers rights, Kidner, R, 'The right to be a candidate for union office' (1973) 2 ILJ 65.

105 *Payne v Electrical Trade Union* (1960) *The Times*, 14 April.

106 [1961] AC 945. Noted by Wedderburn, KW [1962] CLJ 28 and by Rideout, R (1962) 25 MLR 86.

107 [1972] ICR 484.

108 See also, here, *Lawlor v Union of Postal Workers* [1965] Ch 712.

109 [1999] IRLR 166.

The hearing

A hearing must be held so that the member is given an opportunity to be heard in their own defence. This is an essential requirement no matter how clear the plaintiff's guilt may seem.[110] Ordinarily, a member is entitled to an oral hearing unless the issues are simple and the penalty relatively light, when a paper hearing may be appropriate.[111] The hearing should be at a reasonably convenient time so that the member has the opportunity to be heard and to reply to the allegations. However, if the member fails to take the opportunity to attend to put their case, then the tribunal may still proceed unless the plaintiff had good cause for the failure to attend.[112]

For the disciplinary tribunal properly to be convened, the notice must be sent and received by all those entitled to attend. Once convened properly, it must proceed fairly, with every member of the body given the opportunity to participate.[113] A domestic tribunal does not necessarily have to follow the rules of evidence, so the tribunal may not necessarily allow cross-examination of witnesses. However, as proceedings must be conducted fairly, the individual must be allowed to respond to the evidence and it is arguable that, in the most serious of cases, the right to cross-examine is implied.[114] No prejudicial evidence that is irrelevant to the charge should be admitted.[115]

Legal representation

There is no absolute right to legal representation. If there is a union rule denying the member legal representation, this is not necessarily contrary to natural justice.[116] Where the disciplinary matter is relatively minor and the penalty is light, the substantial delay in the proceedings and the expense of legal representation is not justified. However, a rule banning legal representation will not always necessarily be upheld, as every tribunal has a discretion as a matter of law to permit legal representation.[117] This discretion should be exercised in favour of an accused in the exceptional cases where the issues are complex, or where the matter is serious, such as in the case of an expulsion where the accused may lose their livelihood or where the disciplinary action will have a serious effect on the reputation of the accused.[118]

---

110 Note the comments of Megarry VC justifying this principle in *John v Rees* [1970] Ch 345, p 402.

111 See *Burn v NALUGB* [1920] 2 Ch 364 and *Pett v Greyhound Racing Association* [1969] 1 QB 125.

112 In *Annamunthodo v OWTU* [1961] 3 All ER 621, the plaintiff failed to attend a disciplinary hearing because he was judging a student moot. This was not a suitable excuse.

113 *Leary v National Union of Vehicle Builders* [1971] Ch 34.

114 It appears it is not contrary to natural justice for a union to abandon a hearing and to later re-open or re-hear the disciplinary charge; see *McKenzie v NUPE* [1991] ICR 155.

115 See, earlier, *Taylor v National Union of Seamen* [1967] 1 All ER 767.

116 As Lord Denning said in *Enderby Town Football Club v Football Association* [1971] Ch 591, 'justice can often be done better by a good layman than a bad lawyer'.

117 Therefore, a clause in the rule book that purports to exclude this discretion in these type of cases is void as it is contrary to public policy to fetter judicial discretion on a matter of natural justice; *per* Lord Denning in *Enderby Town Football Club v Football Association* [1971] Ch 591.

118 Denning in *Pett v Greyhound Association (No 1)* [1969] 1 QB 125, p 132, and in *Meynard v Osmond* [1977] QB 240, p 244. Also, see *Walker v AUEFW* 1969 SLT 150; but cf Maugham J in *MacLean v Workers Union* [1929] 1 Ch 602, p 621 and Lyell J in *Pett v Greyhound Association (No 2)* [1970] 1 QB 46.

Appeals

Where an appeal takes place the tribunal should adhere to the same standards of fairness that the original tribunal is subject to. If this is not the case, an unfair hearing on appeal may well render void the decision of an original fair hearing.[119]

The question then arises as to whether a fair and unbiased appeal can remedy bias or unfair procedure at the first instance tribunal, so that the decision taken by the appeal tribunal to confirm the decision by the first instance tribunal is valid. Arguably, in such a case, the member has been deprived of a right of appeal as the appeal is in reality merely the original fair hearing. As Megarry VC said in *Leary v National Union of Vehicle Builders*:[120] 'If the rules and the law combine to give the member the right to a fair trial and the right of appeal, why should he be told that he ought to be satisfied with an unjust trial and a fair appeal?'[121]

In the later non-union case of *Calvin v Carr*,[122] the Privy Council first stressed that there was no absolute rule that an ostensibly fair appeal cures an earlier defective hearing, as it may be that, in the circumstances, a complete rehearing of the case is required. The court then continued by saying that, in the trade union context, the circumstances are such that it is less likely that an appeal will remedy the wrongful verdict of the original tribunal because of the real danger of bias. The appeal tribunal will nearly always be aware of the decision of the original tribunal and the principles of trade union solidarity are such that the appeal committee will inevitably be influenced by the unfair conclusions of the disciplinary tribunal.

Giving reasons

There is no general rule that requires a disciplinary tribunal to provide reasons for its decisions.[123] Lord Denning, however, in *Breen v AEU*,[124] argued that where an individual's livelihood is concerned, or a legitimate expectation is dashed by a domestic tribunal's decision, then reasons should be provided.[125]

Natural justice and admission to a trade union

We have seen how the principles of natural justice are well developed in the context of discipline or expulsion of union members where there is a contractual relationship between the parties. Arguably, an individual who applies for membership also has an, albeit limited, degree of protection in the way their application is considered. Earlier we

---

119 *Hiles v Amalgamated Society of Woodworkers* [1968] Ch 440.

120 [1971] Ch 34.

121 At p 49.

122 [1979] 2 All ER 440. Noted by Elliot, M (1980) 43 MLR 66.

123 See *Weinberger v Inglis* [1919] AC 606.

124 [1971] 2 QB 175.

125 Megarry VC in *McInnes* was less certain that such a right existed. More recent administrative law cases regarding the actions of public bodies suggest that in exceptional circumstances, reasons for decisions should be provided. See *Doody v Secretary of State for the Home Department* [1994] AC 531, *R v HEFC ex p Institute of Dental Surgery* [1994] 1 All ER 651 and *R v Secretary of State for the Home Dept ex p Fayed* [1997] 1 All ER 228.

examined the 'right to work' as a duty to achieve a result that was fair in substance which permits the courts to strike down rules contrary to this right. However, we concluded that the better view of this right was that it created possible procedural rather than substantive rights. Essentially, an applicant to a trade union may expect that certain principles of natural justice, broadly categorised as the 'duty to act fairly', will apply when the union is exercising its discretion in determining eligibility for membership.

Originally, in *Faramus v Film Artistes Association*,[126] the majority of the Court of Appeal and the House of Lords rejected the notion that a provision prescribing a qualification for membership or, indeed, any procedure for membership, is subject to the rules of natural justice and so unenforceable on grounds of public policy. Their Lordships saw a distinction where the procedure for expulsion was concerned, as admission was 'in no sense analogous' to the cases where an employee's contract is terminated due to expulsion. Thus, the 'courts will require that natural justice is observed for an expulsion from a social club but not on an application to it'.

Denning LJ in *Breen v AEU* took the opportunity to develop his dissenting judgment in *Faramus*, that the principles of natural justice apply to trade union internal decision making. Breen had been elected shop steward for his branch and under union rules his election required the confirmation of the district committee, which had unfettered discretion to reject a successful candidate. This committee, in its deliberations, considered certain allegations of dishonesty without informing him of this or providing him with the opportunity to respond. Although these allegations had been investigated some time before and had been found to be groundless, the committee subsequently refused to confirm his election.

Denning argued that this was a case of the plaintiff having a legitimate expectation that he would be confirmed by the district committee. In these circumstances, the discretion of the committee must be exercised carefully and fairly with appropriate regard to the principles of natural justice. Denning then made it clear that the same principles can be applied in the context of a trade union committee performing an administrative function in determining an application to membership of a union where the 'right to work' applies.

Denning's judgment in *Breen* was carefully considered by Megarry VC in *McInnes v Onslow-Fane*.[127] Megarry contended that different categories of cases attracted different levels of procedural safeguards. In so called forfeiture cases, where an existing right was taken away, such as the right to work in an expulsion case, the full panoply of natural justice was appropriate to protect the applicant. At the other end of the scale, for mere application cases, where the only concern of the adjudicating committee is the general suitability of the applicant and where no special rights were infringed, the only obligation imposed would be to act honestly and without bias.

Megarry then outlined a third intermediate category, which he termed the 'legitimate expectation' cases. Where a plaintiff had a legitimate expectation of a successful application to join a society, such as where he was asking for a renewal of a licence that had always been granted in the past or where a person recently elected seeks a formal

---

126 [1963] 1 All ER 636.
127 [1978] 1 WLR 1520.

confirmation, then additional safeguards approaching the full requirements of natural justice were required. The 'legitimate expectation' cases can be extended to situations where an individual is applying for union membership which is necessary for work in the individual's trade, or where in the past membership has been a formality. Therefore, in the majority of cases, whether one of 'pure' admission or 'legitimate expectation', it is arguable, based on the Megarry formula, that an applicant to a trade union can expect to be provided with some degree of protection based on the principles of natural justice. The 'duty to act fairly' therefore arguably imports into the decision making process of unions a sliding scale of protection for a potential member: the exact extent of the protection being dependent on how important the decision is to the individual.

In practical terms, the exercise of such a right will not require the union to admit a plaintiff into membership. Rather, should the union not 'act fairly' in deliberating on the application, the most the court can do is to nullify the decision and order the union to consider the application properly. That still allows for the possibility that the application will be rejected after full and fair consideration.

CHAPTER 5

ADMISSION, DISCIPLINE
AND EXPULSION II

STATUTORY CONTROL

Introduction

Until the passage of the Industrial Relations Act 1971, there was little statutory regulation limiting a union's power to admit, discipline or expel a member. The Trade Union Act 1913 enforced a requirement that a union could not refuse to admit or discipline an individual solely on the grounds that they refused to contribute to the political fund. Other than this very limited provision, control was based solely on judicial construction of the rule book and on doctrines of public policy considered in Chapter 4.

In 1968, the Donovan Commission[1] reported that there was little evidence of abuse of power by unions in unreasonably refusing admission or unreasonably expelling a member. Yet, the Commission did recommend the establishment of an independent committee to investigate and provide redress for the limited number of cases where unreasonable exclusion was alleged.[2] The new Conservative Government responded to this recommendation by including in the Industrial Relations Act 1971 a provision providing for full statutory control over disciplinary matters. Section 65 prohibited arbitrary exclusions or expulsions from a union and unfair or unreasonable disciplinary action with enforcement by way of an application to an industrial tribunal.[3] This section was broader than had been strictly thought necessary by the Donovan Commission as it was not exclusively concerned with admissions or expulsions where a closed shop operated but provided members with a general right of complaint against disciplinary action.

Although the Industrial Relations Act 1971 was repealed by the Trade Union and Labour Relations Act 1974, this particular section was preserved as s 5 of the 1974 Act. The retention of this protection was as a result of a campaign by Conservative peers in the House of Lords. Rather than delay passage of the Act as a whole, the minority Labour Government acceded to the campaign. However, once the Labour Government gained a clear majority, s 5 was repealed.[4] As a consequence of the furore created by this abolition, the Trades Union Congress (TUC) acted upon the recommendations of the Donovan Commission and set up an Independent Review Committee to investigate and deliberate on admission and expulsion cases where a closed shop existed.[5]

---

1   Cmnd 3623, para 610.
2   Paragraphs 612 and 658–69.
3   For example, all unions had to adhere to disciplinary procedure specified in the Act and it was automatically unfair for a union to discipline a member who refused to take unlawful industrial action.
4   Trade Union and Labour Relations (Amendment) Act 1976, s 1(a).
5   The TUC Independent Review Committee differed in certain respects from the body recommended by the Donovan Commission. For details of the distinctions, contrast the terms of reference and procedure of the Independent Review Committee contained in the TUC Annual Report 1976, p 94 with paras 658–69 of the Donovan Report.

Where an allegation of unreasonable exclusion from the union was made, the Committee was charged to investigate the circumstances and attempt to achieve a conciliated settlement. If this was not possible, as a last resort, a formal hearing would be held. Even at this stage the Committee would engage in post-hearing conciliation to attempt to resolve the dispute.[6] If the complaint was upheld, the experience was that all unions complied with any recommendation of the Committee; although there were in fact no legal sanctions had a union refused to implement the award.[7]

The Committee played an important role in controlling overzealous disciplinary action by trade unions. However, after 1980 the role of the Independent Review Committee diminished. The Employment Act 1980 created a new statutory right to complain to an industrial tribunal of unreasonable exclusion from a trade union. Other legislative interventions made it more difficult for trade unions to establish new closed shops and to enforce existing ones. The Independent Review Committee, now effectively redundant, was formally disbanded in 1989.

The Employment Act 1980

A feature of the new Conservative administration elected in May 1979 was the priority attached to the attack on the union closed shop. The first plank of the strategy to undermine the closed shop was the right, introduced in s 4 of the Employment Act 1980, for an individual not to be unreasonably excluded from membership or refused membership or expelled from a trade union where a closed shop operated.[8]

The crucial component of this right was the 'reasonableness' of the exclusion or expulsion. In determining reasonableness, tribunals were to examine each case 'in accordance with equity and the substantial merits of the case'. This was nominally the same type of test that applied where tribunals deliberated on issues of unfair dismissal. In unfair dismissal cases, the reasonableness test is interpreted in the context of whether the employer's response to dismiss fell within the range of responses of a reasonable employer. The tribunals were not, however, directed to interpret unreasonable exclusion in such a manner, that is, by reference to the 'range of responses of the reasonable union'.

First, it was specifically provided by the statute that it was not necessarily reasonable for a refusal to be in accordance with the rules of the union.[9] The rules on admission or expulsion were to be considered purely on their merits. Second, the application of the test was tightly circumscribed by a Code of Practice on Closed Shop Agreements and Arrangements published by the Department of Employment in 1980 and revised in 1983. The contents of the Code were admissible in evidence and both tribunals and courts were directed to take notice of the Code 'where it appears relevant'.[10]

---

6   For an example of this process, see the case of *Mayhew Smith and ACTT* described by Ewing, KD (1979) 8 ILJ 184.

7   For a full account of the first six years of the Committee, see Ewing, KD and Rees, W, 'The TUC Independent Review Committee and the closed shop' (1981) 10 ILJ 84. The TUC Annual Reports 1977–89 are also a source of information on the work of the Committee.

8   For a more detailed explanation of the background to this statutory development, see Elias, P, 'Closing in on the closed shop' (1980) 9 ILJ 201, especially pp 207–14.

9   Section 4(5).

10   Section 3(8).

As any breach of the Code was evidence of 'unreasonableness', the tribunals were in effect expected to take into account the Department of Employment's view of the reasonable union.[11] In practice, whether the union had complied with the Code became the litmus test for determining whether the union had acted reasonably. The Code contained both substantive and procedural elements. Procedurally, the Code stated that rules on exclusion must be clear and well known, with sufficient appeal procedures, and that the principles of natural justice should be observed when taking the decision to exclude the applicant. By far the most controversial element of the Code was the recommendation that no member should be excluded or other disciplinary action taken if a member refused to take industrial action[12] or crossed a picket line.[13]

The Code was also explicit in outlining the specific occasions when the union may exclude an individual. A union could restrict entry by requiring relevant occupational qualifications for membership or where it was necessary to regulate membership to protect existing terms and conditions of employment (due to the oversupply of applicants in the trade or occupation).[14]

Where there was a breach of this provision, the plaintiff was not given the right to compel the union to admit or re-admit them as members. Rather, the aim was to encourage the union voluntarily to admit or readmit: only if this was refused was compensation payable for any loss suffered. There was no need for the applicant, when initiating a claim for compensation, to identify a specific job they had lost as a result of their exclusion.[15]

A complaint of a breach of this right proceeded to an industrial tribunal. Where the tribunal was satisfied that the complaint was proven, a declaration to this effect was awarded. The union then had four weeks to consider its position and act on the declaration. The level of compensation was dependent on whether the applicant had then been admitted or readmitted to the union within that four week period. If the applicant was admitted or readmitted, then the claim for compensation remained in the industrial tribunal which could make a basic and compensatory award, assessed in the same way as the compensation for unfair dismissal.

Should the union refuse to react positively to the declaration, then the applicant could apply to the Employment Appeal Tribunal (EAT) for an enhanced award. This was assessed in the same way as an award for a failure of an employer to re-engage or reinstate after an unfair dismissal. In *Howard v NGA (No 5)*,[16] a global assessment of loss was made so that compensation for loss of future earnings and for opportunity to progress in the trade was combined with a figure for non-pecuniary loss such as injury to feelings and distress suffered as a consequence of exclusion from membership. The EAT

---

11 See the comments of Browne-Wilkinson in *NGA v Howard (No 3)* [1983] IRLR 445, pp 447–48 on the application of the reasonableness test. See also the valuable discussion on reasonableness by Miller, K, 'Reasonableness and section 4 of the Employment Act' (1990) 28 BJIR 69.

12 Paragraph 61.

13 Paragraph 62.

14 Paragraph 49. See the interpretation of this paragraph in *Howard v NGA (No 3)* [1983] IRLR 445 – where the state of unemployment amongst the membership was a relevant and crucial factor in the determination that the exclusion was reasonable.

15 *Clark v NATSOPA* [1985] IRLR 494 (noted by Kidner, R (1986) 14 ILJ 129).

16 [1984] IRLR 489.

was criticised for making such a broad assessment of loss rather than itemising the loss under separate headings in the way unfair dismissal compensation is ordinarily assessed. Consequently, in decisions subsequent to *Howard*, the EAT reverted to the tradition in unfair dismissal cases, thereby introducing a degree of certainty to the calculation of compensation.[17]

As with unfair dismissal cases, an applicant was under a duty to mitigate loss and suffered a reduction in compensation if he or she contributed to the expulsion. In *Howard v NGA (No 5)*,[18] the EAT suggested that deliberately allowing membership to lapse by failing to pay subscriptions was sufficient contributory cause to justify a reduction. In *Saunders v Bakers Union*,[19] the applicant's compensation was reduced by 20% for failing to take up the opportunity of a personal hearing on appeal. It was also suggested, in *Saunders*, that a confrontational attitude to the union by an applicant may, in certain circumstances, have justified a reduction.

The relevance of the remedy provided by s 4 declined as the closed shop became less easy to enforce because of economic conditions and legislative initiatives.[20] The very principle of a closed shop was assailed in stages by provisions in the Employment Acts of 1982, 1988 and 1990.[21] Accordingly, the closed shop became impossible to enforce against an employer or against a non-unionist. Moreover, economic conditions prevailing in the 1980s (especially large scale unemployment) seriously weakened union negotiating power, thus limiting union influence over employers.[22]

The introduction in 1988 of the right for union members to complain of 'unjustifiable discipline' further reduced reliance on s 4 of the Employment Act 1980. Although in 1992, s 4 was consolidated into the Trade Union and Labour Relations (Consolidation) Act (TULR(C)A) as s 174, within a year it was repealed by the Trade Union Reform and Employment Rights Act 1993 and replaced by a new s 174. The new s 174 provides union members with a general right to join and remain a member of their chosen trade union. It is to these two more recent statutory developments – the right not to be disciplined unjustifiably and the right of an individual to join a trade union of their choice – that we now turn.

The right not to be 'unjustifiably disciplined'

The 1988 Employment Act expanded the protection for union members from the limited protection in s 4 against exclusion from a union where a closed shop existed, to include situations where disciplinary sanctions were taken against them, short of exclusion.[23] In

---

17   See, eg, *Saunders v Bakers Union* [1986] IRLR 16 and *Day v SOGAT* [1986] ICR 640. Both cases are discussed by Rawlings, HF (1987) 19 ILJ 121.

18   [1984] IRLR 489.

19   [1986] IRLR 16.

20   This was tacitly acknowledged by the Government by the revocation of the DOE Code of Practice on the Closed Shop in 1991 (SI 1991/1264).

21   See TULR(C)A 1992, s 222 – trade dispute immunity is withdrawn if industrial action is taken to enforce a closed shop.

22   For further discussion of judicial and legislative control over the closed shop, see Chapter 12.

23   For an overview of the cases decided in the first three years, refer to Kidner, R, 'Unjustified discipline by a trade union' (1991) 20 ILJ 284.

the Green Paper, *Trade Unions and Their Members*,[24] which presaged the publication of the Employment Bill, the Government particularly focused its criticisms on trade unions that imposed sanctions on members who refused to take industrial action. The Government took the view that the freedom of choice of the individual to work rather than take industrial action must be unaffected by the threat of discipline and that the common law provided inadequate protection for union members who were in conflict with their union over their right to choose to go to work.[25] This, it was suggested, was supported by the evidence of disciplinary action being unjustly taken during several high profile disputes, such as during the rail dispute in 1982, and most importantly the experience of the miners' strike of 1984–85 and the Wapping dispute in 1986.[26]

Consequently, a new statutory right not to be unjustifiably disciplined was introduced by the Employment Act 1988 to supplement protection provided by s 4 of the Employment Act 1980 and common law rights via enforcement of the rule book. The provisions of the Employment Act 1988, which established this right, have now been incorporated into ss 64–68 of the TULR(C)A 1992. Essentially, a union member, under s 64, has the right to complain of 'unjustifiable discipline' where a disciplinary act, as defined in the statute, has been taken against the applicant.

The disciplinary act

An individual is 'disciplined' by a union if action is taken that falls within s 64(2). This includes matters such as expulsion from the union, the imposition of a fine, or enforcing the payment of other monetary sum, such as by confiscating subscriptions.[27] It also embraces more general action such as where the member is deprived of '... access to any benefits, services or facilities ... of the union',[28] or where a member is subjected to 'some other detriment'.

The EAT has taken a broad view of the meaning of the term 'some other detriment'. In *TGWU v Webber*,[29] the EAT held that refusal to allow the applicant to attend a union meeting was capable of amounting to some 'other detriment'. In *NALGO v Killorn*,[30] the EAT defined 'other detriment' as 'some disadvantage of whatever nature'. Therefore, the action of the union in advertising the names of members in a union newsletter who had

---

24 Cm 95, 1987, paras 210–13.

25 The importance the government attributed to this right to work is clear from the introductory statement to para 210: 'The right of the individual to go to work despite a call to take industrial action is an essential freedom.'

26 In para 213, it was stated that 'These and many other examples give rise to serious concern ... that existing remedies are less than comprehensive'.

27 It is also a disciplinary act if an applicant to a union is refused membership where refusal has been encouraged or advised by another union. This clearly has implications for the operation of the Bridlington Principles.

28 As access to benefits, services or facilities derive from the use of membership any suspension of membership, whether temporary or not, is a deprivation under the Act – see *NALGO v Killorn* [1990] IRLR 464.

29 [1990] IRLR 462.

30 [1990] IRLR 464.

not taken strike action, so causing them embarrassment, was 'other detriment' for the purposes of the Act. Clearly, any slight, no matter how minor, is caught by this section.[31]

The determination

A member is disciplined if a 'determination' is made under union rules, or purportedly under the rules, or is made by an official[32] of the union, to impose a penalty on an individual member. The EAT has held in *TGWU v Webber*[33] that 'determination' meant final disposal of the issue. In this case, uncertainty remained, as Webber had been suspended by his branch, pending expulsion, but had not yet been formally expelled by the only body with the authority to do so, the General Executive Council of the union. As the proceedings in the case had not finished, this was not a determination for the purposes of the Act.

The unjustified reason

The disciplining of the member is 'unjustifiable' if it is for one or more of several reasons outlined in s 65. Originally, under the 1988 Act, this included a union disciplining a member for:

(a) failing to take part in or support a strike or other industrial action,[34] or for opposing such action;

(b) failing to contravene a contract of employment, (such as by obeying an instruction by a manager to cover for strikers) or for encouraging others to comply with their contract of employment (such as by urging others not to take strike action);

(c) asserting that there has been a breach of the rule book or of a statutory requirement or for asserting that the union is proposing to act in this manner or for assisting someone who has made such an allegation, unless the assertion was made knowing that it was false or otherwise made in bad faith;

(d) asking the advice or seeking the assistance of the Certification Officer or Commissioner for the Rights of Trade Union Members (now abolished, see pp 18–19) or of any other person, such as a solicitor.

As a result of further reforms contained in the Trade Union Reform and Employment Rights Act 1993, this list has been substantially increased to include conduct such as:

(e) failing to agree or withdrawing agreement for the 'check off' system of deduction of union subscriptions from source;

---

31   This may be contrasted with the earlier decision of the EAT, in *Reeves v TGWU* [1980] IRLR 307, on the interpretation of a similar provision in the Trade Union Act 1913. This stated that a non-contributor to a union political fund must not suffer 'a disadvantage'. The EAT held that a trivial disadvantage was not a breach of this provision.

32   'Official' is defined in s 119.

33   [1990] IRLR 462.

34   The Court of Appeal, in *Fire Brigades Union v Knowles* [1996] IRLR 617, affirmed the decision of the EAT that a union ban on full time fire personnel taking on additional duties was not 'other industrial action' as it was imposed for safety reasons. Thus, where the applicants had been expelled from the union for contravening union policy on hours of work they not been unjustifiably disciplined. For a more detailed consideration of what constitutes industrial action short of a strike, see Chapter 13.

(f) resigning or proposing to resign from the union or becoming or proposing to become a member of another union;

(g) working with or proposing to work with non-union labour or members of another union, working for or proposing to work for an employer who employs non-union labour or a member of another union.

This is clearly an extensive list, but it is also an exhaustive one. Should a member be disciplined for activities not included in this list, then it will not be lawful under this section. In *Medhurst v NALGO*,[35] Medhurst had secretly tape-recorded a branch executive meeting, had refused to deliver up the tape when discovered and was subsequently suspended. On a complaint to an industrial tribunal that he had suffered unjustifiable discipline, the EAT agreed with the tribunal that the reason for the disciplinary action was not 'unjustifiable' as it did not come under any of the heads listed in the Act.

It should be noted that where an applicant is disciplined for committing several offences of which only one is 'unjustifiable', then the union is still entitled to proceed on those other charges not listed in the Act. For example, a member's opposition to industrial action may result in verbal abuse or violence to an officer of the union. This can be separated from the opposition to the industrial action *per se*, so the union may legitimately take action under the rules against the member for this behaviour.[36]

The time limits

Section 66(2) provides that the applicant must apply to an employment tribunal with the complaint within three months of the determination to impose the penalty which infringes the right. This time limit can be extended if '... it was not reasonably practicable for the complaint to be presented before the end of that period', or 'any delay is ... attributable to a reasonable attempt to appeal against the determination or have it reconsidered or reviewed, within such further period as the tribunal considers reasonable'.[37] This allows members to apply for an internal appeal without any prejudice to their right to complain to an employment tribunal of a breach of this statutory right.

In *NALGO v Killorn*,[38] the applicants had been suspended from membership for refusing to cross a picket line during an industrial dispute. Later Killorn wrote to the branch chair requesting answers to a number of questions and making it clear she did not accept her suspension. Before she had received a reply, she made a complaint of unjustifiable discipline to the tribunal which was out of time by one day. The question arose whether the delay in lodging the complaint was attributable to a 'reasonable attempt' to appeal against the determination or have it reconsidered or reviewed. The EAT concluded that this was a reasonable attempt to appeal, even though the word appeal was not used in the applicant's letter. As no specific method for initiating an appeal is laid down, all the tribunal should assess is whether there was an intention to appeal rather than look for the formality expected in civil proceedings.

---

35 [1990] ICR 687.
36 Section 65(5).
37 Section 66(2)(b).
38 [1990] IRLR 464.

Remedies

The procedure and remedies for breach of this provision operate in a similar manner to those originally developed for a breach of s 4 of the Employment Act 1980.

An application must originally be made to an employment tribunal. The tribunal then has the power to grant a declaration that the application is well founded.[39] Once a declaration has been made, further remedies of restitution of any financial penalty or compensation are available under s 67 in a further application to an employment tribunal or the EAT. An application for compensation or for reimbursement of a payment or fine by the member should be made within six months, but not before four weeks from the time of the declaration. This is to allow the union to reflect on the decision of the tribunal and voluntarily to make amends.

Where the union has acted on the declaration, taken steps to revoke the determination infringing the applicant's right not to be unjustifiably disciplined and has restored the *status quo* by securing the reversal of the penalty imposed, then the application for compensation is to the employment tribunal.[40]

Compensation awarded is dependent on what is considered to be 'just and equitable in the circumstances'.[41] However, the section provides for the duty of the applicant to mitigate loss[42] and that contributory fault by the applicant may justify a reduction in compensation.[43] In the employment tribunal, the amount of compensation awarded should not exceed the maximum basic and compensatory award for unfair dismissal.[44]

Where the union has failed appropriately to revoke the determination, the application for compensation is to the EAT. In assessing compensation, the EAT is subject to the same maximum limits as the employment tribunal. However, there is a minimum amount of compensation the EAT must award; currently not less than £5,500.

The operation of these compensatory provisions was considered by the EAT in *Bradley and Others v NALGO*.[45] After a ballot on industrial action had been taken which resulted in a majority in favour of action, NALGO called out members for one day strike action. The nine applicants refused to take action and crossed picket lines to go to work. All were expelled from the union. The tribunal granted a declaration that the members were unjustifiably disciplined. The union refused to revoke the expulsions and the applicants then applied to the EAT for compensation under s 67.

The applicants argued that an award could be made for loss of earnings and for injury to feelings and distress. The EAT disagreed that in these circumstances an award for loss of earnings could be made. The applicants had not been disadvantaged in the labour market as union membership was not a necessity to obtain employment. However, in

---

39 Section 66(3).
40 See on this *NALGO v Courtney-Dunn* [1991] IRLR 784.
41 Section 67(5).
42 Section 67(6).
43 Section 67(7).
44 Section 67(8).
45 [1991] IRLR 159.

principle, compensation for distress or injury to feelings was permissible, although any award should be of a modest nature. The EAT believed an appropriate award was the statutory minimum; at that time £2,520.[46]

Conclusions

Clearly, this is an expansive right. It covers all disciplinary action, not just expulsions or exclusions, and is not solely limited to cases where a closed shop exists. Furthermore, 'unjustifiable' discipline is not synonymous with 'unreasonable' discipline. An employment tribunal is not required to evaluate the union's justification for the action or the proportionality of the response or to examine the reasoning of the union. Thus, even if, on the facts of the case, the action of the union is warranted and the penalty imposed appropriate, if the reason for the disciplinary action offends against the statutory list, no matter how minor the penalty, it is unlawful.

The direct effect of this right of a member not to be disciplined unjustifiably is that it weakens union control over their own membership.[47] It is a direct attack on the autonomy of unions to regulate their own internal affairs and undermines the notion of collective responsibility and union solidarity.[48]

The issue that perhaps created most controversy was the inclusion of the industrial action provisions – the so called 'scabs charter'. It does not matter whether there has been a secret ballot authorising the action, all dissenters who do not wish to take action are protected against disciplinary proceedings for failing to heed a strike call. Allowing individual members actively to ignore decisions made by the majority in a secret ballot clearly undermines democratic decision making and puts into doubt whether the true aim of Conservative policy was really to 'democratise' trade unions or to sabotage effective industrial action.

In any event, it is arguable that trade union democracy is damaged rather than promoted by this provision. On joining a trade union a member has contractually assented to be bound by the rules as a whole and to disciplinary procedures and decisions in particular. This interference disregards union contractual rights to discipline members according to the rules that have been democratically determined by the membership as a whole.

Further criticisms of the right not to be 'unjustifiably disciplined' have emanated from the International Labour Organisation's (ILO) Committee of Experts which has upheld a complaint brought by the TUC that it is incompatible with Art 3 of the ILO Convention No 87 on Freedom of Association and Protection of the Right to Organise (1948).[49]

---

46 £5,500 is now the minimum that may be awarded.

47 Note, however, in other contexts Conservative policy has been to enforce trade union control over its membership by making the union responsible for the actions of its members – see the provisions on union vicarious liability for industrial action in Chapter 16.

48 See further, on this, McKendrick, E, 'The rights of trade union members – Part 1 of the Employment Act 1988' (1988) 17 ILJ 141, pp 147–50.

49 For further details, see Brown, D and McColgan, A, 'UK employment law and the International Labour Organisation; the spirit of co-operation?' (1992) 21 ILJ 265, pp 272–73.

The right to membership

The Trade Union Reform and Employment Rights Act 1993 introduced a new s 174 into the TULR(C)A 1992, so repealing the protection originally contained in ss 4 and 5 of the Employment Act 1980. This new s 174 guarantees the right of every person to join a trade union of their choice and the right not to be expelled from a trade union unless the exclusion[50] or expulsion is expressly permitted by the statute. Section 174(2) outlines the permissible reasons.

(i) If an applicant or member is excluded because they do not satisfy an 'enforceable membership requirement' contained in the rule book then the exclusion is permitted. The statute continues by stating that a membership requirement in the rule book is only 'enforceable' in three circumstances: if it limits membership by virtue of requiring specified qualifications or experience; if membership is limited to members of a specified trade or profession; or to particular grades or categories of jobs.[51]

(ii) Where the union only recruits in a certain geographical area, or from only one employer, then the rejection of an application from outside that area or from someone who works for another employer, is justified.

(iii) The exclusion or expulsion is permitted if it is wholly because of the conduct of the individual. What constitutes sufficient misconduct for the purposes of the section is clearly open to interpretation. However, certain types of conduct can never be a valid reason for exclusion or expulsion. It would be unlawful to exclude or expel a person for having been or presently being a member of another trade union,[52] or for having been or presently being employed by a particular employer or for having been or presently being a member of a political party. Additionally, conduct which would constitute 'unjustifiable discipline' under s 65 is not a sufficient reason for exclusion or expulsion under this section.[53]

Remedies

The procedures for complaining of exclusion or expulsion and for the assessment of compensation closely parallel those that previously existed under the old s 174 – unreasonable exclusion where a closed shop operated. An application for a declaration is first made to an employment tribunal, within six months from the date of exclusion or expulsion. Once obtaining a declaration that he or she was excluded or expelled contrary to the statute, the applicant may claim compensation after a waiting period of four weeks. Where the applicant has been admitted or readmitted consequent to the declaration, the employment tribunal calculates compensation based on what is considered to be 'just and equitable', subject to the maximum of the basic award and compensatory award available for unfair dismissal.

---

50 In *NACODS v Gluchowski* [1996] IRLR 252, the EAT concluded that 'exclusion' for the purposes of liability under s 174 must be construed strictly. A temporary suspension of membership did not amount to exclusion from the union.

51 Section 174(3).

52 Section 174(4). This thus provides that a refusal of an application because it would result in a breach of the Bridlington Principles on inter-union membership disputes would be unlawful.

53 Section 174(4)(b).

Where the union refuses to readmit or admit, then the application for compensation proceeds to the EAT. Similarly, with an award for 'unjustifiable discipline' there is a minimum the EAT must award: the current minimum is £5,500.[54] Whether the action is initiated in the employment tribunal or the EAT the rules of contributory fault apply.[55]

The relationship between ss 64 and 174

Prior to the 1993 Act, where expulsion infringed the right not to be disciplined unjustifiably, a complaint lay only under the old s 174. Now, if there is a disciplinary expulsion, it is possible that a claim for unjustified discipline and a claim for improper expulsion under s 174 may both be made. Although an applicant can start proceedings for both, he or she can succeed only on one. A declaration by an employment tribunal on one claim will block the proceedings on the other. The remedies are essentially the same: the only differences of note is that the time limits for taking action differ, with the s 174 action having a more generous six month limit. Also, under s 174, there is no provision requiring for the applicant to mitigate his or her loss.

Unlike previous reforms, the law contained in ss 64 and 174 does not strike a balance between individual rights and collective needs. The inherent conflict between individualism and collectivism has been decisively decided in favour of the individualist position.[56] What started as a specific campaign against the closed shop, with tribunals directed to balance individual and collective interests as part of the decision making process has now progressed (despite the demise of the closed shop) to a direct attack on union freedom of action to discipline existing members and to implement and administer a chosen recruitment policy.

The erosion of the Bridlington Principles and Procedures has been particularly contentious.[57] The principles were developed to reduce, *inter alia*, the incidence of inter-union disputes over organisational matters at the workplace (such as demarcation disputes) and over the recruitment of members. For example, Principle 4 established that where a union has good reason to object to a transfer of a former member to another union, the new union should not accept that person as a member and Principle 5 stated that, where a union already has members at a workplace, another union must not start recruitment activities without permission of that union.[58] Enforcement is provided by a

---

54 Considering the levels of compensation now available for those victimised (TULR(C)A 1992, s 146), dismissed (s 152) or refused employment on grounds of non-membership of a trade union (s 137), it is unlikely compensation will be higher than the minimum of £5,500. Compensation will be solely for the hurt of losing membership *per se*; not for the practical effects of this.

55 Section 176(5). For an interpretation of how this sub-section may be applied, see the cases on contributory fault decided under the old s 174.

56 For a further discussion of this and related issues, see Simpson, B, 'Individualism versus collectivism: an evaluation of section 14 of the Trade Union Reform and Employment Rights Act 1993' (1993) 22 ILJ 181.

57 They are termed the 'Bridlington' Principles as they were originally agreed at the 1939 TUC Conference at Bridlington, Yorkshire. All TUC affiliated trade unions should adhere to these principles. Failure to do so can result in suspension and expulsion from the TUC. The most recent example of this occurred in 1988 with the suspension of the EETPU.

58 This principle has been of use in stopping the 'poaching' of members by one union against another. It is also ensures a stable bargaining structure by limiting the number of unions that can recruit at any one workplace.

TUC Disputes Committee which may order the aberrant union to expel any member recruited contrary to these principles.[59]

Section 4 of the Employment Act 1980 did not formally ban expulsion or exclusion on these grounds. The Code of Practice, para 56, stated that infringement of the Bridlington Principles was one factor that may be taken into account by a tribunal in determining whether a refusal of admission was reasonable. The Code, however, was silent as to whether a decision to expel a member in furtherance of the principles would amount to a reasonable expulsion.

The Employment Act 1988 undermined the principles by providing that it was 'unjustifiable discipline' for an applicant to be refused entry to a union where refusal has been encouraged or advised by another trade union. Yet, the culmination of the campaign to undermine the Bridlington Principles was signified by the publication of the Green Paper, *Industrial Relations in the 1990s*.[60] The Green Paper attacked the Bridlington Principles as suppressing individual freedom of choice and as contrary to the principle of freedom of association.

In a response to the Green Paper, several organisations[61] (not normally known for their enthusiasm for trade union principles) indicated their concern that the outlawing of the Bridlington recruitment procedures would result in the proliferation of unions and the fragmentation of collective bargaining. In particular, there was disquiet that this reform would damage the negotiation of single union agreements. Despite these objections, which the Government regarded as groundless, the undermining of the inter-union arrangements in Bridlington was achieved by the passage of s 174. As a consequence of this legislative change, the old Bridlington Principles have been rewritten, taking into account the new law.[62]

The statutory rights – compatibility with the Human Rights Act 1998

The Human Rights Act 1998 is intended to give further effect within the UK legal system to the rights and freedoms guaranteed under the European Convention on Human Rights. This Convention, with the limited influence of an international treaty, has, hitherto, had little impact on domestic judicial decision making. The Human Rights Act, though, provides for Convention rights to be addressed throughout the court system, although they are only directly enforceable in proceedings brought against a 'public authority'.[63] However, in all cases (whether the defendants are private persons or public authorities acting in a private or public capacity), the Act will have an important indirect

---

59　As it is not possible to expel a member without direct authority from the rule book. All TUC affiliated unions have a model rule to allow expulsion in furtherance of a decision of the TUC Disputes Committee. On the workings of the Disputes Committee, see Elgar, J and Simpson, B, 'A final appraisal of Bridlington? An evaluation of TUC Disputes Committee decisions 1974–1991' [1994] BJIR 32.

60　Cm 1602, 1991.

61　For example, the Confederation of British Industry.

62　Published in November 1993.

63　Section 6(3). For further analysis of the definition of 'public authority' see Morris, G, 'The Human Rights Act and the public/private divide in employment law' (1998) 27 ILJ 293 and Bamforth, N, 'The application of the Human Rights Act 1998 to public authorities and private bodies' (1999) 58 ILJ 159.

effect as it provides that, where Convention rights are in question, the court must interpret present and future legislation in conformity with the Convention,[64] decide all cases' (brought under statute or common law) compatibly with Convention rights unless barred from doing so by primary legislation[65] and take account of the Strasbourg jurisprudence in all cases where it is relevant.[66]

By maintaining that both past and future primary and secondary legislation must be 'read and given effect' in conformity with the Convention 'so far as it is possible to do so', the Human Rights Act has created a new rule of statutory interpretation. Where legislation is so clearly incompatible with Convention rights that it is impossible to construe the statutory provision in any other way, then a formal declaration to that effect must be issued by the court.[67] A declaration of incompatibility will not have the effect of invalidating the legislation *per se* but will act as a prompt to government and parliament to initiate amending legislation under a new 'fast track' procedure.[68]

The 'fast track' procedure provides for the relevant government minister to amend the legislation by statutory instrument to ensure compatibility (subject to approval by both Houses of Parliament within 60 days).[69] Where change is required urgently, it may take effect without such approval,[70] although the amending item of secondary legislation will lapse if subsequent consent by both Houses of Parliament is not forthcoming within a period of 120 days.[71]

Undoubtedly, this power to declare legislation incompatible with the Convention could have profound consequences across a range of employment areas.[72] In the context of internal trade union law, it is certainly arguable that the legislation permitting the high degree of intervention in trade union internal affairs reflected by ss 64 and 174 of the TULR(C)A 1992 is susceptible to a declaration of incompatibility.

Strasbourg case law holds that the right to form trade unions under Art 11 (on freedom of association) includes a limited right for trade unions to draw up their own internal rules and to administer their own affairs without undue State interference. For example, in *Cheall v UK*,[73] the applicant was expelled by his union pursuant to a TUC

---

64 Section 3(1).

65 Section 6(1)–(3).

66 Section 2(1).

67 Where a declaration is a possible outcome, the Act provides for the Government to be given the opportunity to intervene and make representations by way of being joined as a party to the proceedings.

68 An alternative recourse for a court is to interpret the domestic legislation in such a 'purposive' manner that there is no need for their declaratory power to be invoked. This is best demonstrated by the application of EC legislation where the meaning of domestic legislation is stretched in order to ensure conformity with the European provision; see, eg, *Litster v Forth Dry Dock Ltd* [1989] ICR 341 on the Acquired Rights Directive and the TUPE Regulations.

69 Section 10(2) and Sched 2(a).

70 Schedule 2(b).

71 Schedule 2(4).

72 For a general review of the potential impact of the Act in the employment sphere, see Ewing, KD, 'The Human Rights Act and labour law' (1998) 27 ILJ 275; Lightman, G and Bowers, J, 'Incorporation of the ECHR and its impact on employment law' (1998) EHRLR 560; Palmer, S, 'Human rights: implications for labour law' [2000] CLJ 168; Ewing, KD (ed), *Human Rights at Work* (2000, Institute of Employment Rights).

73 (1986) 8 EHRR 74.

Disputes Committee decision granting another union the rights to recruit at his workplace. Cheall argued he was entitled to protection by the State from the actions of his union that interfered with his Art 11 rights of association (the right to join and remain a member of a trade union). The Commission declared that an individual has no right inherent in Art 11 to be admitted to, or not excluded from, a union of choice as '... in the exercise of their rights under Article 11, unions must be free to decide, in accordance with union rules, questions concerning admission to and expulsion from the union'. The Commission continued by holding that State interference to protect a member against disciplinary measures is only justified where there was an abuse of a dominant position by the trade union (for example, where the disciplinary measure resulted in exclusion which was arbitrary or unreasonable as it was not in accordance with the rules or where the consequences of exclusion resulted in exceptional hardship – such as the loss of a job because of the operation of the closed shop).[74] In *Johansson v Sweden*,[75] the Commission repeated this view that the Art 11 right only obliges the State to protect a trade union member against disciplinary measures that were clearly unreasonable or arbitrary, stemming from a trade union's dominant position in the labour market.

The European human rights institutions have also indicated in a number of cases that Art 11 incorporates the right of individuals to associate with whom they choose and so to refuse to associate with others (the so called negative right to dissociate).[76] On this basis, interference with a decision by the membership of a trade union to assert this right (of non-association), so as to discipline or exclude an existing member under the rules who acts against their interests, would be a breach of Art 11 (subject, as noted above, to the decision not being arbitrary or unreasonable).

On the face of these arguments – that unions are entitled to administer their own affairs, that members of a union collectively have a right under Art 11 to refuse to associate with others and that the State may only intervene with this right in exceptional circumstances – then domestic legislation on the absolute right to be admitted to a trade union (s 174 of the TULR(C)A 1992) and on protection from 'unjustified discipline' (ss 64–65 of the TULR(C)A 1992) may well be incompatible with the Art 11(1) Convention right unless this degree of State intervention is justified by reference to conditions set out in Art 11(2).

The intervention must be 'necessary in a democratic society ...' and fall within one of the objectives outlined – including for the 'protection of the rights and freedoms of others'. According to the Strasbourg jurisprudence, a restriction in Art 11(2) is only 'necessary in a democratic society' if it meets a 'pressing social need' (which often involves a balancing of legitimate competing interests) and if it goes no further than is strictly necessary to meet that need – that is, it is 'a strictly proportionate response to the legitimate objective pursued'. Therefore, when examining this legislation under the Human Rights Act, the UK court must apply these principles to the government's explanation for legislation that grants individuals an absolute right to belong to, and

---

74 For an example, see *Young, James and Webster v UK* [1981] IRLR 408.

75 (1990) 65 DLR 202.

76 See *Young, James and Webster v UK* [1981] IRLR 408; *Sigurjonsson v Iceland* (1993) 16 EHRR 462; *Sibson v UK* (1994) 17 EHRR 193; and *Gustafsson v Sweden* (1996) 22 EHRR 409.

remain a member of, a trade union, and which protects them from nearly all disciplinary action. It is certainly arguable that many of the 'pressing social needs' identified in the parliamentary debates and the Green Papers that preceded the passage of the original legislation are no longer relevant to the legal and industrial circumstances of the 21st century and that the legislation as a whole fails the proportionality test.

For example, the Green Paper, *Trade Unions and Their Members*,[77] justified strict limitations on a union's ability to discipline members who refused to follow a strike call on the basis that it was required to protect individuals from loss of income whilst on strike, from the possibility of dismissal and any subsequent disadvantage in the labour market and from being sued by their employer for breach of contract. It was also suggested that protection was necessary for those who oppose industrial action on ideological grounds.

However, exclusion or discipline by a union now has little material effect on a member's job prospects as more recent legislative initiatives and changing economic circumstances have seen a reduction in union power and a decline in closed shop arrangements – which, in any event, are no longer enforceable. Dismissal for engaging in lawful industrial action is now automatically unfair under the 1999 Employment Relations Act and, in practice, it is almost unheard of for employers to sue employees directly for their loss. Furthermore, in considering the efficacy of a restriction based on the right of a member to refuse to participate in a strike on ideological or philosophical grounds (the freedom of choice issue), the UK courts ought to have regard to the European Court's concern to uphold other relevant fundamental principles – in this case the principle of democracy. The legislation clearly fails to respect a trade union's internal democratic process where the dissident member is being disciplined for refusing to accept the union's mandate (emanating from a secret ballot) to take action for the benefit of the membership collectively. In addition, to permit non-association to this extent weakens the fundamental right of association of the trade union membership and the capacity of the association to protect their interests (as outlined in Art 11(1)). In this context, an appropriate balance between the competing rights of the union membership and the individual dissident has not been achieved by such a total ban on internal disciplinary action. Furthermore, the blanket nature of the restriction – which applies to all disciplinary action taken against dissenters – is a disproportionate response to a perceived need and so offends against the principle of proportionality.

Section 174 is essentially a direct attack on the Bridlington Procedures – devised by the TUC to avoid damaging inter-union recruitment disputes. It makes it unlawful for a union to expel an employee in order to comply with a decision of the TUC Disputes Committee awarding another union sole recruitment rights. These procedures were examined in some detail by the Commission in *Cheall* (see above) and were found to be compatible with Convention principles, that is, that expulsion in pursuance of a TUC Disputes Committee decision was not arbitrary or unreasonable.

The Green Paper, *Industrial Relations in the 1990s*,[78] attacked the Bridlington Procedures as suppressing individual freedom of choice and as contrary to the principle

---

77 Cm 95, 1987.
78 Cm 1602, 1991.

of freedom of association. This absolute and individualistic view of freedom of association is quite distinct from the Commission's understanding of the principle in *Cheall*[79] – that is, that an individual has no automatic entitlement to associate where the group is unwilling to do so – especially where the exclusion has no negative implications for the applicant and is not arbitrary. As the Commission made clear, the application of the Bridlington Procedures, which may compel an individual to join a particular trade union, does not strike at the very substance of the freedom of association guaranteed by Art 11 unless the individual is truly disadvantaged in some way. In any event, it seems clear that the objective and effect of the provision is to disrupt trade union organisation at the workplace and undermine structured collective bargaining – one of the legitimate ways in which trade unions protect the occupational interests of their members[80]. This ill-intentioned motive undermines the legitimacy of the proffered reason for intervention which cannot be justified by reference solely to this ideological argument when balanced against the needs and requirements of the trade union's membership. With this in mind, it is unlikely that a legitimate social need has been established and that, arguably, that this provision is also in breach of Convention guarantees.

79 This view of freedom of choice and association was also contrary to the House of Lords' view of freedom of association in its deliberations in *Cheall v APEX* [1983] IRLR 215. In the course of a judgment that it was not contrary to public policy to expel a union member to comply with a decision of the TUC Disputes Committee, Lord Diplock said (p 218): '... freedom of association can only be mutual; there can be no right of an individual to associate with other individuals who are not willing to associate with him.'

80 See *National Union of Belgian Police v Belgium* (1975) 1 EHRR 578.

CHAPTER 6

UNION ELECTIONS

COMMON LAW CONTROL

Until the advent of extensive statutory intervention (with the passage of legislation from the Employment Act 1980 to the Trade Union Reform and Employment Rights Act 1993), there was no statutory requirement to hold elections for union positions.[1] Yet, as a matter of general law, if specific provisions on elections and election procedure existed in the union rules then a member could force the union to abide by these provisions by the contractual enforcement of the terms of the rule book. Judicial control in this manner was dependent on unions having extensive rules on election matters and on the willingness of the courts to intervene where there were internal disputes on the interpretation and application of the rules.

Union rule books have always contained comprehensive provisions governing the procedure for elections at all levels in the union. Consequently, there are many examples of judicial intervention where procedure outlined in the rules has not been faithfully followed. For example, after extensive malpractice had been exposed during national elections in the Electricians Union in 1961, legal action ensured that the original election was declared void thereby giving the defeated candidate an opportunity to recontest the election.[2] Another example is provided by *Leigh v NUR*,[3] where the rule book of the NUR stipulated that the union general secretary had the authority to vet nominations for election to the post of president of the union. Where approval was improperly denied to a potential candidate the court granted an injunction to restrain the holding of the election.[4] An action on the rule book was also successful in *Wise v USDAW*[5] where the executive council of the union acted outside of the rules when altering nomination procedure.

There are of course limitations to this system of control. As members' rights are based solely on the enforcement of the rule book, members cannot object to the lack of elections or demand adherence to a preferred procedure if such matters are not contained in the rules.[6] Furthermore, existing rules, even by an interventionist court, can only be construed so far. *Hughes v TGWU*[7] illustrates this point. Hughes was unhappy about the operation of the procedure for counting votes during the election of General Secretary of

---

1   The Industrial Relations Act 1971, Sched 4 and s 65, attempted to impose some general standards on election procedure applicable to registered unions. As most unions did not register under the Act nor co-operate with its implementation, this form of limited control failed.

2   *Byrne v Foulkes* (1961) *The Times*, 29 June; cf *Chapple v ETU* (1961) *The Times*, 22 November.

3   [1970] Ch 326.

4   For a fuller examination of actions on the rule book, see Kidner, R, 'The right to be a candidate for union office' (1973) 2 ILJ 65.

5   [1996] IRLR 609.

6   This is despite Denning's attempt to develop a contrary argument, in *Breen v AEU* [1971] 2 QB 175, that an ordinary member has the right to stand for office regardless of the provisions of the rule book as it is his or her 'legitimate expectation' that he or she will be allowed to do so.

7   [1985] IRLR 382 (noted by Rideout, R [1986] ILJ 46).

the union. After an inquiry, the General Executive Council arranged for a new ballot in Hughes' region. For this rerun election, Hughes applied to the High Court for an order requiring the union to release full information about the result of the election in each branch and for the right to full access to union records to ascertain the accuracy of this information. As the rules did not provide for the release of such detailed information, this request was denied by the court.

Even where there has been an irregularity in the conduct of an election and a breach of the rule book there have been occasions where the courts have refused to arbitrate in a dispute between member and union. We saw earlier in Chapter 3 how the *Foss v Harbottle* principle was applied in *Goodfellow v London & Provincial Union of Vehicle Workers*[8] to justify non-intervention in the circumstances of an irregularity in election procedure. We have also seen in the same chapter how Harman J, in *Hamlet v GMBATU*,[9] refused to intercede where the procedure for internal investigation of the complaint of election malpractice had been correctly employed by the union and the complaint had been rejected.[10]

Non-interference in election disputes has also been justified on more pragmatic grounds. Walton J held in *Brown v AUEW*,[11] that so long as an irregularity in election procedure was only of a minor nature causing no substantial injustice an election result was still valid. In the more recent case of *Douglas v GPMU*,[12] the union executive council ordered a fresh election to the post of general president of the union because of allegations that the plaintiff, who had been elected, had acted in breach of the rules by making unauthorised comments to the press prior to the election. Morison J, in reinstating the result of the original election, adopted the reasoning in *Brown v AUEW*. As the alleged minor breach of the rules would not have truly affected the result of the election the executive council's decision to re-run the election was unreasonable and perverse.

STATUTORY INTERVENTION

The Conservative Government elected in 1979 believed that intervention in the internal democratic process of trade unions was justified for several reasons. Most importantly, not all trade unions maintained the system of direct elections to senior trade union positions favoured by the new administration.[13] There was also, at this time, heavy media and Government criticism of the militant leadership of many unions. It was thought that the existing common law was too weak to prevent these unrepresentative 'union barons' from manipulating the rule book to retain power at the highest levels of the union.

---

8   (1919) *The Times*, 8 September.

9   [1986] IRLR 293.

10 The administrative law principle in *Dawkins v Antrobus* [1879] 17 Ch 615 was applied. The duty of the court was merely to ensure that the correct internal procedure had been followed.

11 [1976] ICR 147.

12 [1995] IRLR 426.

13 For criticisms of union arrangements prior to the statutory changes, see the Green Paper, *Democracy in Trade Unions*, Cmnd 8778, 1983, para 39.

Therefore, legislation was necessary in order to give effective control of the union back to its membership and to establish a minimum standard of democracy.

The legislative strategy described in this chapter (the imposition of direct balloted elections and compulsory election procedure) has been criticised for ignoring the existence of an already well developed system of democracy appropriate to the needs of trade unions. Unions have always had rules governing elections and election procedure at all strata of the union; not just for the national executive. Although unions have not always utilised a system of direct elections to senior positions,[14] the various methods employed reflect the historical development and organisational complexity of trade unions.[15]

If democracy is about ensuring the accountability (and responsiveness) of union officers, from the shop steward to the general secretary, then arguably union arrangements are, as a general rule, sufficiently democratic. This is because the diversity of democratic methods utilised within the decentralised structure of a trade union enables the views of the membership to be communicated to the union hierarchy at a number of levels.[16] Furthermore, the system of democracy that unions typically emphasise is 'democracy in action' or participatory democracy. All members have a right to influence union decision making by actively participating in union affairs at the workplace: such as by attending, speaking and voting at union branch meetings and by involving themselves in policy determination as elected delegates to district or regional councils.

The alternative conception of democracy is quite different. The only legitimate democratic model is a system of representative democracy where candidates for election are selected by a ballot of the whole national membership. This interventionist legislation, enforcing uniformity, undermines the autonomy of trade unions to choose their own models of democratic control and has the (perhaps favoured) outcome of sidelining the union activist. But there are other more fundamental objections to the imposition of this form of democracy. Representative democracy, designed for a system of 'government' and 'opposition' is unsuited to trade unions as it encourages the existence of oppositionist factions or groupings.[17] This potentially damages the necessary cohesion which a trade union requires effectively to represent the interests of its membership in negotiation with employers. If representative democracy disrupts, rather than strengthens collective action, then union ability to exercise this essential function is weakened.[18]

---

14   Undy and Martin (in *Ballots and Trade Union Democracy*, 1984, p 59) noted that 61% of TUC affiliated unions had secret direct elections to the national executive.

15   Methods used differed between unions. Where amalgamations have occurred at different phases of a union's history, special arrangements for election to the national executive may have been in place to meet the needs of special occupational groups or sections. Alternatively, in some unions, indirect elections (such as appointment via a special delegate conference) may have been used to determine membership of all or part of a union's national executive.

16   For a brief outline of the variety of governmental structures trade unions employ, refer to Chapter 2.

17   The danger of hostile groupings in what is essentially a 'fighting organisation' is cogently examined by Kahn-Freund in 'Trade unions, law and society' (1970) 33 MLR 241, p 266. Arguably, groups who object to the actions of the majority in a trade union can secede from the union and form their own organisations.

18   These and other points are discussed in more detail by Davies, P and Freedland, M, *Labour Law Text and Materials*, 1984, pp 670–85, and by Kahn-Freund, O, *Labour and the Law*, 1983, pp 270–90. See also Fredman, S, 'The new rights: labour law and ideology in the Thatcher years' (1992) 12 OJLS 24.

The preoccupation with direct elections is yet another example of the individualisation of British industrial relations. As Wedderburn has commented:

> [A vote] ... may be expressed at home and by post without the inconvenience of collective trade union experience or discussion of policy or candidates at the branch meeting ... the insistence upon the individualised ballot is part of an attempt to prove that 'democracy' consists only in the individual franchise rather than in a wider and collective participation in union affairs.[19]

The first stage of reform

The first stage of the 'democratising' of trade unions in order to enhance membership control was based on a strategy of encouraging rather than compelling trade unions to hold balloted internal elections. Section 1 of the Employment Act 1980 made State funds available for those unions willing to hold secret ballots on a number of matters including national and certain local internal elections.[20] The scheme was administered by the Certification Officer and funds were provided to defray the costs of the printing of the ballot paper, other stationery and postal costs.

To further support union ballots, ss 2 and 3 of the Employment Act 1980 obliged employers to make their premises available for recognised trade unions to conduct workplace secret ballots on matters that fell within the scheme in s 1. When the Employment Act 1988 enforced compulsory postal ballots for election to a union national executive, this right declined in importance and was formally repealed by the Trade Union Reform and Employment Rights Act 1993.[21]

These sections were enacted on the belief that this would be sufficient to ensure that 'responsible' and 'moderate' trade union leaders would be elected.[22] In practice, the operation of the provisions were a disappointment to the Government. Initially, out of all the TUC affiliated unions only the electricians' and the engineers' unions took advantage of the finance available.[23] When it became clear that this approach was not effective in

---

19 Wedderburn, KW, *The Worker and the Law*, 3rd edn, 1986, p 785.

20 Finance was also provided to hold ballots on other matters such as to amend union rules, on amalgamations and on industrial action. Thus, funds for union elections were part of a wider strategy to encourage member participation in union decision-making.

21 Although the statutory right was repealed in 1993, employers may still voluntarily provide such facilities enabling unions to hold local elections at the workplace. Indeed, the Code of Practice on Time Off for Trade Union Activities and Duties, para 21, recommends that employees are allowed reasonable time off during working hours so as to vote in a workplace ballot.

22 Academic research at the time, rebutted this rather simplistic view. See *op cit*, Undy and Martin, fn 14, p 110.

23 For a full list of those unions that applied for recoupment of balloting expenditure during this period, see the Certification Officer reports from 1980–84. In 1984, the funding regulations were altered by the Trade Union Balloting Regulations (SI 1984/1654) to reflect the changes introduced by the Trade Union Act 1984. A consequence of the imposition of compulsory ballots was that TUC objections to this form of State support weakened. So, eg, in 1990, 77 unions (including three of the four largest unions, TGWU, GMB and AEU) took advantage of financial support for balloting. As a consequence of the Trade Union Reform and Employment Rights Act 1993 and the Funds for Trade Union Ballots (Revocation) Regulations (SI 1993/1233), this financial subsidy has now been withdrawn.

changing union methods of democracy, the next stage of reform was to introduce more directive legislation enforcing union elections under a specified procedure.

The second stage of reform

Since the unions themselves could not be sufficiently encouraged by this initial legislation to alter their arrangements, the Government responded by enforcing mandatory elections by secret ballot.[24] The Green Paper, *Democracy in Trade Unions*,[25] put forward the Government's case for the introduction of a prescriptive regime. It alleged that there was evidence that the national executives of certain unions were not properly representative and accountable to the membership as a whole;[26] that union rules were too easily manipulated by the leadership of unions[27] and that allegations of corruption of the election process were too numerous to ignore.[28]

As a consequence of these criticisms, fundamental reforms on compulsory elections and election procedure were introduced by Pt 1 of the Trade Union Act 1984.[29] Important amendments extending statutory control have since been made by the Employment Act 1988 and the Trade Union Reform and Employment Rights Act 1993. All these provisions have now been consolidated into Chapter IV, ss 46–56 of the Trade Union and Labour Relations (Consolidation) Act (TULR(C)A) 1992. This extensive regime for elections, where necessary, displaces any relevant rules of the union.[30]

Duty to hold elections

The original provision in the Trade Union Act 1984 only required voting members of a union's executive committee to be directly elected. The Employment Act 1988 extended this to all members of the executive committee who are entitled to attend and speak or hold national office, whether they have a vote or not,[31] and enforced a requirement that elections to the national executive must be fully postal.[32] Section 46 of the TULR(C)A 1992

---

24 Government disappointment with the failure of s 1 was made clear in the Green Paper, para 13 – despite the availability of funding for balloting since 1980, 'trade unions have made few or painfully slow attempts to reform their internal affairs and electoral practices'.

25 Cmnd 8778, 1984.

26 Paragraphs 1 and 7. It was also stated that not only are members entitled to expect their unions to be democratic institutions but, because of the trade union role in industrial relations, there is a 'wider public interest in seeking to ensure that unions are truly representative'.

27 Paragraph 10.

28 Paragraph 12.

29 The background to the passage of the 1984 Act and the perceived justifications are fully examined by Martin, R, in Fosh and Littler (eds), *Industrial Relations and the Law in the 1980s*, 1985, Chapter 5.

30 If, however, the rules of the particular union are more stringent, eg by requiring direct elections every three years rather than the statutory five years, then it is the rules that must be followed.

31 This became known as the 'Scargill clause' as the NUM president had previously given up his vote on the executive committee to avoid adherence to the 1984 Act.

32 The 1984 Act had originally provided that secret postal ballots were the preferred method of election, but that workplace secret ballots were acceptable in certain circumstances. Even though there were criticisms in the Green Paper (para 5.8) of the organisation of workplace ballots for elections in the TGWU and the CPSA, it was surprising that they were forbidden by the 1988 Act as workplace ballots guarantee a far higher level of turnout and, thus, are inherently more 'democratic'.

now provides for mandatory direct elections by secret postal ballot every five years of any member of the union principal executive committee and those who hold the offices of president and general secretary or their nearest equivalents.

Members of the executive who act as mere advisers are not required to be elected;[33] nor is a non-voting general secretary or president of the union who holds a purely ceremonial position.[34] Special dispensation is also given to those members of the executive committee who have been employees for at least 10 years and are within five years of retirement. Subject to the provisions of the rule book, there is no need for these members to stand for re-election.[35] The rationale for this provision is to protect those loyal employed senior members of the union who would lose their jobs if they were voted out of the executive.

The executive committee is defined as the principal committee of the union exercising executive functions;[36] in other words the union governing body. Should there be a dispute on identifying the relevant union body which acts as the executive committee, then the question to consider is: which body transacts the day to day business of the union and has the authority to make daily administrative decisions?[37]

Exclusion of a candidate for election

It is a basic right that each individual union member is entitled not to be excluded unreasonably from standing as a candidate, nor may a candidate be required to be a member of a political party.[38] Many unions have special eligibility rules (such as a bar on candidates with criminal convictions or a minimum age requirement). Arguably, these would not automatically be a breach of this provision so long as they applied to all candidates. Some guidance as to the interpretation of 'unreasonable exclusion' has been provided by the decisions of the Certification Officer who has held that a policy of requiring particular qualifications or a number of nominations by other members or branches before a member could stand as a candidate is not unlawful so long as the nomination process is well advertised by the union.[39]

However, the exclusion from candidature must be objectively justified. In *Paul v NALGO*,[40] the rules of the union stated that candidates for vice president had to be nominated by the executive or by district councils of the union. Paul argued this was contrary to s 47(1) as an ordinary member would need personally to persuade members of the executive or district council to nominate him or her. Refusal would mean an ordinary member was excluded from standing as a candidate. The Certification Officer upheld this complaint as this was an unreasonably exclusive nomination system that

---

33 Section 46(3).

34 Section 46(4).

35 Section 58.

36 Section 119.

37 See *Re NUM (Yorks Area)* D/4/94 14 April 1994 (CO), *Stone v NATFHE* D/5/87 30 June 1987 (CO) and *Re British Actors' Equity Association* D/1/-2/99 8 April 1999 (CO).

38 Section 47(1) and (2). Prior to s 47(2), discrimination on political grounds had been lawful – *Leigh v NUR* [1970] Ch 326.

39 See *Re NATFHE* D/6/94 20 May 1994 (CO).

40 [1987] IRLR 43.

could not be objectively justified. Although the procedure did not actually preclude members from standing, in practical terms it made it very difficult for them to exercise their right.

The right not to be excluded unreasonably from standing as a candidate is qualified by s 47(3) which permits the rules of a union to exclude a whole class of members. In order to disqualify a class, it must be possible to establish in advance who is within that class.[41] In the *NATFHE* case,[42] the Certification Officer said that a 'class of members' can be defined as a number of individuals possessing some common attribute identifiable by description, such as all new members or retired members, but not, as in this case, those persons 'who are not approved by the NEC'.

In *Ecclestone v NUJ*,[43] the national executive of the NUJ dismissed the deputy general secretary of the union who subsequently sought re-election for the vacant post. The executive attempted to exclude his candidature on the basis that the rules gave them the power to draw up a shortlist of candidates who possessed the 'required qualifications' – namely, that each candidate had to have the full confidence of the executive. Ecclestone's exclusion was held to be in breach of s 47 as the 'class' to be excluded was determined by reference to a subjective test applied by the executive in a prejudiced and unfair manner.

The election address

If a candidate chooses to write an election address, they are not required to bear the expense of producing copies for distribution. The election address, as far as reasonably practicable, must be included unedited with the ballot paper sent to the electorate.[44] The reasoning behind this provision is to secure free speech for all candidates, so that the opinions of candidates critical of the union are still given an airing to the membership as a whole. Quite importantly, s 48(8) ensures that only the candidate who produced the address is liable for any civil or criminal liability consequent upon publication of the address.

The scrutineer and independent counting officer

The office of scrutineer, established by the Employment Act 1988, was introduced to ensure that trade unions administered and conducted their elections fairly. Despite the lack of evidence of widespread malpractice,[45] concern over possible abuse of electoral procedure was cited in the Green Paper, *Trade Unions and Their Members*,[46] as the reason for the creation of the post of scrutineer.

---

41 See *Flavin v UCATT* D/2/87 17 February 1987 (CO) where exclusion of all regional officers (as a 'class of members') under union rules was not in breach of s 47(3).

42 *Re NATFHE* D/6/94 20 May 1994 (CO).

43 [1999] IRLR 166.

44 Section 48. The imposition of certain limitations (such as a maximum word limit) on the election address is permissible so long as they apply to all candidates.

45 See para 5.20.

46 Cm 95, 1987.

The scrutineer's role is to oversee the election and ensure that it is run fairly.[47] The scrutineer is charged with a duty to supervise the production and distribution of ballot papers and, on request from a union member or a candidate, or where it is appropriate to do so, to check the union register of members[48] (which acts as the electoral roll) for accuracy.[49]

All ballot papers must be returned directly to the scrutineer who retains custody of them for at least a year to assist any member who wishes to complain of irregularities in the election. Even where there is an uncontested election and therefore no need for a ballot, the Certification Officer has held that there is still a duty on the union to appoint a scrutineer, despite the fact that he has virtually nothing to supervise or report on.[50]

The name of the scrutineer has to be notified to members individually or through the union journal before he or she commences duties, so that any member has the opportunity to challenge the appointment.[51] The scrutineer is under a duty to make a report on the election detailing the results of the election and commenting on its fairness and whether there has been full union compliance with the statute.[52] A copy of the report must be sent to all members or alternatively the report may be published in the union journal. This report must contain certain specific information, such as the number of ballot papers distributed, number returned, number of valid votes for each candidate, a record of whether the register of members was inspected and the performance of any independent counting officers, if appointed.[53]

The scrutineer is supposed to be competent, impartial and independent of the union. The union is under a duty not to interfere in the scrutineer's work and to co-operate at all times.[54] The Scrutineer Regulations (SI 1993/1909) details who is qualified to act as a scrutineer. A union may appoint a firm of solicitors or accountants that satisfy certain additional conditions or appoint one of three specialist named organisations: Electoral Reform Ballot Services Ltd, the Industrial Society or Unity Balloting Services Ltd.

The Trade Union Reform and Employment Rights Act 1993 amendments to election procedure created the office of the 'independent counting officer'. A union must appoint a counting officer to store, distribute and count the voting papers once they are returned. The section provides that the scrutineer may take on these functions. In practice, this has often been the case. Otherwise the criteria for appointment is similar to that for the scrutineer. Of paramount importance is the independence and impartiality of the appointee.

---

47 Comment was made by Morison J, in *Douglas v GPMU* [1995] IRLR 426, that as the balloting process is under the control of the scrutineer it is doubtful whether a union has any power, even if provided under the rules, to cancel and re-run an election where the scrutineer has expressed satisfaction with the arrangements.

48 A union is required under s 24 to maintain this register.

49 Section 49(3). See *Re Public and Commercial Services Union* D/8-12/98 6 November 1998 (CO).

50 *Re Offshore Industry Liaison Committee* D/7/94 25 November 1994 (CO).

51 Section 49(5).

52 Section 52. The result of the election should not be published by the union until the scrutineer's report has been received – *Re Civil and Public Services Association* D/8/94 30 December 1994 (CO).

53 Sections 52(1), (2A), (2B) and s 52(2B). The scrutineer's report is important evidence when complaints by members or candidates are received and investigated by the Certification Officer.

54 Section 49(6), (7).

The electorate

The union is under a duty, as far as reasonably practicable, to compile and maintain a register of names and addresses of their members which acts as the union's electoral roll. A failure to maintain this register's accuracy is a breach of the statute.[55] A member has the right to inspect this register and the scrutineer has a duty to inspect where he or she is requested to do so by a member.

To ensure that no members are unreasonably excluded from voting, the electorate who are entitled to vote are clearly defined by the legislation. All members are so entitled unless they belong to a specified class excluded by the rules. The classes that may be lawfully excluded are those members who are unemployed, in arrears with their subscriptions, apprentices, trainees, students, new members or those on holiday.[56] Additionally, where a member of the executive represents a particular union constituency, based on a trade group, a geographical area or a section of the union, then it is permissible for the union to limit participation in the election of that representative to the appropriate group of members.[57]

The method of voting

Section 51 permits a union to choose the method of direct election:[58] this may be the 'first past the post' method or the single transferable vote system. Whatever system is chosen, the election must be a fully postal ballot with each vote given equal weighting.[59] The section further requires that votes given are fairly and accurately counted, although an inaccuracy that occurs accidentally which does not affect the result of the election can be disregarded.

The principle of non-interference

All members must be allowed to vote without interference or any constraint imposed by the union, its officials or employees or other members.[60] The purpose of this provision is to ensure that members are free to vote without any undue pressure.[61] But not all conduct that has the aim of influencing the way a member votes will fall foul of the provision. The cases show that it is intimidatory conduct which is caught by this provision. This has been defined as conduct that puts members in fear of voting freely, so preventing them

---

55 Section 24(1). Clearly, the register will not be absolutely up to date as changes in membership are inevitable in those unions with a rapid turnover of membership. Thus, where minor errors arise this will not be a breach of the section, see *Paul v NALGO* [1987] IRLR 43.

56 Section 50(2).

57 Section 50(3).

58 Any form of indirect election (such as elections to an electoral college which appoints or votes for members of the executive) is unlawful – see *Paul v NALGO* [1987] IRLR 43 and *Whiteman v AUEW* D/1/87 3 February 1987 (CO).

59 However, a system weighted to prevent the over-representation of the membership in any one geographical area is permissible – *R v CO ex p EPEA* [1990] IRLR 398.

60 Section 51(3).

61 Yet, the section does not outlaw interference by other parties in the election process (such as the employer or the media).

from exercising their right to vote for a candidate of their choice. The mere direct endorsement by the union of one candidate over another is not an interference or constraint prohibited under the Act.[62]

Remedies and procedure

Should a candidate be elected improperly, that does not invalidate his or her actions as a member of the executive, or as general secretary or president.[63] Rather, where there has been a failure to comply with these detailed requirements, any 'person having sufficient interest' has the option of making a complaint within a year of the default to the Certification Officer or the court for a declaration.[64]

The 'person having sufficient interest' to take an action is defined in s 54(2) as any candidate and any person who was a member of the union at the time of the election. It seems that it is only those 'full' members (that is, those who are entitled in the rules to stand as candidates or vote) who may make a complaint under the statute. This is the logic of the EAT's decision in NUM (Yorkshire Area) v Millward.[65]

A complaint about the conduct of the ballot itself must be made to the Certification Officer[66] or to the High Court[67] within one year of the announcement of the result. Unless the complaint to the Certification Officer is frivolous or vexatious, the Certification Officer will investigate the circumstances and must give the trade union and the applicant the opportunity to present their case before making or refusing the declaration requested. If the Certification Officer believes there is a *prima facie* case to answer, a declaration will specify the provisions the union has broken and what steps the union has to take to remedy the failure to comply with the Act. Whether the Certification Officer makes or refuses the declaration, reasons must be given for the decision.[68]

The application to the court is also for a declaration. If a declaration has already been made by the Certification Officer, then the court is required to have due regard to this and may well restate, in its declaration, the Certification Officer's findings. The Certification Officer and the court also have the discretionary power to make enforcement orders and the court has the authority to grant interlocutory relief.[69] An enforcement order may

---

62 See *Paul v NALGO* [1987] IRLR 43 and *Re USDAW* D/1/94 13 January 1994 (CO). Note that the Certification Officer in *Re NUM (Yorkshire Area)* CO/1994/13 19 May 1994 suggested that comments short of intimidation may be actionable if they are untrue or seriously misleading.

63 Section 61(2).

64 Note, previously, the union could not appeal against a declaration granted by the Certification Officer. The only remedy for the union was to apply for a judicial review of the decision. This lacuna in the law was criticised by Kidner in 'Trade union democracy: election of trade union officers' (1984) 13 ILJ 193, p 209. Now, the Employment Relations Act 1999, Sched 6, para 12, introduces a right of appeal to the EAT from the Certification Officer's decisions (a new s 56A inserted into the TULR(C)A 1992).

65 [1995] IRLR 412.

66 Section 55.

67 Section 56.

68 An odd addition to this section is sub-s (5) which states that reasons 'may be accompanied by written observations on any matter arising from; or connected with, the proceedings'. This seems to encourage the Certification Officer to go beyond the judicial function and to comment on internal matters unrelated to the dispute in question.

69 Sections 55(5A) and 56(4), (7).

require the union to hold the election again in accordance with the provisions of the Act, or to take other steps to remedy the failure specified in the declaration or to abstain from such acts in the future. Once an enforcement order has been made, any member or candidate, not just the original applicant, can act upon the order to enforce it. A failure to adhere to an enforcement order is a contempt of court by the trade union; the ultimate sanction is a fine and sequestration of assets.

It is clear that an application to the Certification Officer by one individual does not automatically preclude an application to the court by another. A complainant has a choice whether to make a single application or consecutive applications to both the Certification Officer and the court, but not concurrent applications.[70]

The relationship between the rules and the statutory framework

Because of the existence of this statutory framework, actions based on the rule book have declined.[71] Where union omissions would result in a *prima facie* breach of a union rule and a statutory requirement, the decision in *Venness and Chalkey v NUPE*[72] suggests that the member is better advised to rely on the statutory right. Here, the challenge to the NUPE executive council election was brought solely on the basis of an alleged breach of the union rules. As required under the rules and by statute, the union had appointed an independent 'scrutineer', the Electoral Reform Society, to oversee the election process. The scrutineer had full control over the administration of the ballot, including distribution of the ballot papers and the declaration of the result. In one branch, due to an oversight by the scrutineer, only a minority of members received voting papers.

The High Court held that the plaintiff had no cause of action as there had been no discernible breach of the rule book. The union had adhered strictly to the requirements in the rule book by properly delegating the conduct of the election to the independent scrutineer. Consequently, the better course of action would have been to claim a remedy under statute in an application to the court or the Certification Officer.

Successful challenges to the union organisation of elections under this legislation have not been numerous. This is because breach of many of the electoral standards are dependent on a degree of union culpability. For example, the duty to ensure every member has the opportunity to vote is not actionable if the breach was accidental.[73] Where irregularities have been documented, they have been mainly caused inadvertently

---

70 For the position prior to the reforms introduced by the Employment Relations Act 1999, see *Lenahan v UCATT* [1991] IRLR 78.

71 Although, note that the Employment Relations Act 1999, Sched 6, para 19, has introduced new powers for the Certification Officer to investigate certain breaches of union rules – including any alleged violation of election rules. For further details, see p 20.

72 [1991] IRLR 76.

73 The duty is to see that 'as far as reasonably practicable' every member has the opportunity to vote. So, where there is an administrative error, there is no breach of this requirement. However, if the failure is deliberate or not in good faith, then no matter how small or insignificant the breach a declaration and enforcement order will be granted.

or accidentally and so have not been the cause of litigation.[74] Furthermore, it seems the imposed legislative regime has failed to have the sort of impact on the political complexion of the union leadership and on union policy making that had been presumed at the time of the introduction of the reforms.[75]

---

74 The evidence is that complaints are running at a very low level. Eg, in 1990, there were seven complaints to the Certification Officer, of which two were upheld. In 1995, two complaints were made, one was upheld. In 2000, the Certification Officer issued the first enforcement order ordering the Musicians' Union to hold fresh elections to the post of general secretary.
75 See Smith, P et al, 'Ballots and union government in the 1980s' (1993) 31 BJIR 365, and Undy, R et al, Managing the Unions: The Impact of Legislation on Trade Union Behaviour, 1996.

CHAPTER 7

TRADE UNIONS AND POLITICAL ACTIVITIES[1]

Trade unions were formed in the late 18th and early 19th centuries to represent and protect their members' interests at the workplace. In this early period, trade union demands of employers were only occasionally successful. However, as the trade union movement developed, negotiation with employers became more widespread and a system of collective bargaining was gradually established with tangible benefits for many trade union members. Yet, collective bargaining could only deliver a partial and uneven level of protection as it depended on the willingness of employers to engage in bargaining in good faith or on the power of the union to draw the employer to the negotiating table.

Towards the end of the 19th century, trade unions increasingly turned to the political system as an alternative means of improving the welfare of their members by securing benefits such as, minimum standards in conditions of employment, greater protection of health and safety, compensation for industrial injuries at work and so forth. Unions at this time were also labouring under the remnants of the anti-trade union legislation from the early period of the 19th century and judge made civil liabilities in tort: both of which inhibited their development and ability to represent their membership. Consequently, in the late 19th and early 20th centuries, the union movement sought political influence to win industrial, social and economic advantages for its mass membership and to secure the repeal of anti-union legislation and the reversal of hostile judicial decisions.[2]

Early union strategy had entailed working within the existing political framework as a pressure group to achieve limited objectives.[3] When the mainstream parties failed to respond to union concerns, the union movement turned to fostering direct Parliamentary representation as the means to win benefits for its mass membership and working class constituency. Trade union influence was predominant in the formation of the Labour Representation Committee in 1900 which, in 1906, changed its name to the Labour Party.[4]

---

1   For general background, see Ewing, KD, *Trade Unions, The Labour Party and the Law*, 1982.

2   For a more detailed analysis of union campaigns in this period see Webb, S and Webb, B, *The History of Trade Unionism*, 2nd edn, 1920, pp 284–90; and Pelling, H, *A History of British Trade Unionism*, 5th edn, 1993, Chapter 4.

3   Although a few individual unions directly funded candidates for election to Parliament, most unions and the TUC, were somewhat more reticent in supporting direct political representation of the working classes. The TUC Parliamentary Committee did engage in the lobbying of Parliament for an extension of the franchise and for changes in the law that penalised trade union activity. However, active participation in the political process itself to achieve these goals was not looked on favourably by the ruling majority in the TUC. A number of unions did, however, form the Labour Representation League in 1870. This organisation sought to persuade the Liberal Party to adopt working class candidates for election to Parliament. Without backing from the major unions and the TUC, it collapsed in 1881.

4   Keir Hardie, who along with other socialists had long campaigned within the union movement for a party to represent workers' interests, formed the Independent Labour Party (ILP) in 1893. Internal disagreements in the TUC prevented the ILP from receiving any substantial support from trade unions. It was only in 1899 that the Parliamentary Committee of the TUC agreed to co-operate with the ILP and other socialist groups to launch a new organisation; the Labour Representation Committee (LRC). In the 1906 election, 29 LRC candidates were elected; by 1910, 42 Labour Party members were in Parliament. For a full account of the role of the trade unions in the establishment of the Labour Party see *op cit*, Webb and Webb, fn 2, pp 677–89, and Pelling, Chapters 6 and 7.

The Labour Party was the vehicle for the representation of union interests and many unions provided funds to support its activities. Of particular importance was the financial sponsorship of Labour MPs as, in that period, they received no salary. The use of funds to support Labour MPs had been challenged in *Steele v South Wales Miners' Federation*,[5] on the basis that unions did not have the legal power to distribute their funds in this way. This argument had been rejected by Darling J who concluded that, so long as the rules provided the authority for this activity, such payments were not *ultra vires* and unlawful.

ASRS v OSBORNE

Union support for the Labour Party was temporarily halted by the House of Lords judgment in *ASRS v Osborne*.[6] Osborne challenged the rule which provided for a compulsory levy for the payment of funds to the Labour Party to support its candidates for election. A majority in the House of Lords (Lords Halsbury, Macnaghten, Atkinson) applied the *ultra vires* doctrine in a hitherto novel manner. They did not follow the reasoning of Darling J in *Steele v South Wales Miners' Federation*, or their colleagues in the earlier case of *Howden v Yorkshire Miners' Association*,[7] that the rule book determined the objects or powers of the union. Rather, in construing the objects of the union, the rule book was ignored.

Instead, the House of Lords examined the definition of a trade union contained in the Trade Union Acts of 1871 and 1876 and concluded that the powers of a trade union were limited to matters that fell within this definition. As Lord Halsbury said, '... what is not within the ambit of that statute, is I think, prohibited to a ... combination; it only exists as a legalised combination having power to act as a person and to enforce its rules within the limits of the statute, whatever those limits are'.[8] As there was nothing in the statutory provisions that indicated that parliamentary representation was a permissible object of a trade union, the funding of political activities was *ultra vires*, that is, outside the powers of the trade union.

This decision, if it had stood for any appreciable length of time, would have dealt a severe blow to the fortunes of the newly emerging Labour Party. Yet, the implications of the case went further than this. Not just was political expenditure illegal (serious as that was), but the use of funds for any purposes, such as for educational or insurance purposes, whether allowed under the rule book or not, was illegal if these purposes did not fall within the statutory definition. The decision was thus viewed with some concern by trade unions, who had for many years engaged in a variety of activities that were authorised under their constitutions, but were now illegal as '*ultra vires* the statute'.

5   [1907] 1 KB 361.
6   [1910] AC 87.
7   [1905] AC 256.
8   At p 93.

THE TRADE UNION ACT 1913

The *Osborne* decision was partially mitigated when Parliament, in 1911, granted MPs a salary. However, this did not deal with the principle that it was still illegitimate for a trade union to attempt to influence legislators for the common good of its membership and to engage in many other ancillary union activities. After the election of 1912, the Liberal Government, under pressure from the Labour Party and wishing to retain some influence with the union movement, piloted through a Bill to reverse the *Osborne* judgment; this became the Trade Union Act 1913. The Act essentially restored the *ultra vires* doctrine to the form which had applied prior to the *Osborne* case. It provided that a union could apply its funds for any object or purpose so long as they were authorised by the rules of the union.

However, in the specific area of political expenditure, the trade unions had to accept some limitations on their freedom to spend their funds. Expenditure for political purposes had to be from a specific 'political fund' administered separately from the union general fund, established by a ballot of the membership and financed by a 'political levy' on individual members. The Act also defined and limited the political activities that could be supported by expenditure from the political fund. Furthermore, as a consequence of Conservative pressure in both Houses, provisions were incorporated into the Act to ensure that no union member would be forced to contribute to the political fund if it was anathema to their personal convictions or conscience and to safeguard them from discrimination within the union.

It is this framework, reformed in crucial respects during the 1980s, that still regulates trade union political expenditure today. The regulations concerning the procedure for establishing a political fund and the uses and limitations of such a fund, altered by the Trade Union Act 1984, the Employment Act 1988 and the Trade Union Reform and Employment Rights Act 1993 have now been incorporated into Chapter VI, ss 71–96 of the Trade Union and Labour Relations (Consolidation) Act (TULR(C)A) 1992.

ADOPTING POLITICAL FUND RULES

A specified procedure for the adoption of political objects was imposed on trade unions by the Trade Union Act 1913. The lawful application of funds 'in the furtherance of political objects' was dependent on the union adopting special rules in compliance with the provisions of the Act and approved by the Chief Registrar.[9] Adoption was only effective if a resolution, incorporating these rules into the rule book, was passed in a once and for all ballot of members. The resolution established the special political fund from which all the political expenditure must come; ensured that any payments to further political objects were made out of the political fund; listed the political objects as contained in the Act; contained provisions permitting any member to contract out of contributing to the political fund; and proscribed discrimination against such a non-contributor.

---

9   The modern day equivalent of the Chief Registrar is the Certification Officer.

In the Green Paper, *Democracy in Trade Unions*,[10] the Government expressed the view that there was a need for this procedure to be tightened up. In particular, the requirement that unions only needed to ballot once was criticised as anachronistic. A ballot held up to 70 years ago could not legitimately represent the wishes of the contemporary membership of a trade union.[11] A regular ballot, every 10 years, was recommended to take into account the wishes of new members and those members whose views had changed. Consequently, the previous 'once and for all' ballot that authorised expenditure on the political objects has now been superseded by the requirement (originally contained in the Trade Union Act 1984) that a postal ballot is necessary every 10 years to affirm this authorisation.[12] As most unions had set up their political fund more than 10 years earlier, a number of fresh 'review ballots' on a new political fund resolution took place in 1985 and 1986.[13]

The statutory procedure for adopting political fund rules, although in many areas similar to the original provisions contained in the Trade Union Act 1913, differ in some crucial respects. The arrangements for the ballot (or reballot) are overseen by the Certification Officer who has a general duty of supervision of the procedure. The Certification Officer has to approve the organisation of the ballot[14] and the political fund rules that are to be incorporated into the rule book as a consequence of the ballot.[15] Although these rules need to be submitted to the Certification Officer for approval, 'model' political fund rules can be provided by the Certification Officer if required. The model rules follow the detailed statutory requirements outlined in s 82(1) regarding the conduct of the ballot, the political objects and the government of the political fund. The model rules on the government of the political fund provide for the separation of the fund from other union funds, allow for the contracting out from the fund and proscribe discrimination for non-contributors, although permitting the exclusion of non-contributors from the control and management of the fund.

The statutory requirements on ballot supervision are very similar to those in force for leadership elections, discussed earlier in Chapter 6.[16] The difference being that these obligations are enshrined in the union rules, so technically any complaint relates to a breach of the rule book rather than to the statute. The rules must provide for the appointment of an independent scrutineer to oversee the ballot and submit a report on the operation of the ballot.[17] On publication, all members are entitled to a copy of the report. An independent counting officer must also be appointed who may be the

---

10   Cmnd 8778, 1983.

11   Paragraphs 84–86.

12   Section 73(3). A simple majority is required to adopt or readopt the political objects resolution.

13   The Certification Officer's Annual Reports of 1985 and 1986 show that all the unions which previously had political funds reballoted successfully. The success of union campaigning to retain political funds is analysed in Steele, M, Miller, K and Gennard, J, 'The Trade Union Act 1984: political fund ballots' (1986) 24 BJIR 443.

14   Section 74(1).

15   Section 74(3).

16   In a similar vein to leadership elections, the supervisory procedure is now quite complex due to the changes introduced by the Employment Act 1988 and the Trade Union Reform and Employment Rights Act 1993.

17   Sections 75 and 78.

scrutineer.[18] The rules will also establish the right of all members to an entitlement to vote and to be given a reasonable opportunity to vote without interference.[19]

THE POLITICAL OBJECTS

The original provisions contained in the Trade Union Act 1913 limited the political activities that could be financially supported by the political fund to clearly defined 'political objects'. Lawful expenditure was limited to:

(a) the payment of any expenses incurred either directly or indirectly by a candidate or prospective candidate for election to Parliament or to any public office, before, during or after the election in connection with his candidature or election; or

(b) the holding of any meeting or the distribution of any literature or documents in support of any such candidate or prospective candidate; or

(c) the maintenance of any person who is a Member of Parliament or who holds a public office; or

(d) (payment) in connection with the registration of electors or the selection of a candidate for Parliament or any public office; or

(e) the holding of political meetings of any kind, or on the distribution of political literature or political documents of any kind, unless the main purpose of the meetings or of the distribution of the literature or documents is the furtherance of statutory objects within the meaning of this Act.

Several cases have provided guidance on a number of issues concerning the interpretation of these political objects rules.

Whether loans to political parties can be regarded as political expenditure for the purposes of the Act was considered in *Richards v NUM*.[20] Funds were loaned to help develop the national headquarters of the Labour Party. Richards alleged that using money from the union general fund in this way was a breach of rules on political expenditure. The Certification Officer regarded the contribution to the development of the building, whether a straightforward commercial investment or not, as 'expenditure' within the meaning of the rule. Therefore, since the principal function of the building was to hold gatherings of a political nature, this was expenditure '... on the holding of political meetings' and so infringed the political fund rules.[21]

A further matter raised in *Richards* concerned payments by the NUM for a lobby of Parliament by union members. The Certification Officer held that a lobby of Parliament to further industrial matters that implicitly supported the Labour Party's political position was improperly funded from the general fund as it was also expenditure on a 'political meeting'.

---

18   Section 77A.
19   Sections 76 and 77.
20   [1981] IRLR 247.
21   See also *ASTMS v Parkin* [1983] IRLR 448.

An issue of some concern to trade unions is whether contributions to campaigns or causes that are not 'party political', although of an ideological nature, ought to be funded solely from the political fund. The Chief Registrar, supported by the High Court in *Forster v National Union of Shop Assistants and Clerks*,[22] thought not.

The Certification Officer followed this view in *Coleman v POEU*.[23] Coleman's union branch contributed an affiliation fee of £8 from its general fund to the local Trade Councils 'Campaign against the Cuts' which had as its object a campaign against Government public spending cuts and economic policies. The fee contributed to the financing of public meetings and the publication of campaign literature. The Certification Officer rejected the argument that this fee should have been paid out of the political fund. 'Political' for the purposes of the Act, meant 'party political'. This literature was merely expressing a general point of view and since it was not expressly in support of a particular political party, the contributions were not infringing the rules.[24]

Government concern over some of these decisions was demonstrated by critical comment on trade union political activity in the Green Paper, *Democracy in Trade Unions*.[25] As a consequence, the Trade Union Act 1984 substantially amended the definition of political objects and broadened the scope of 'political' activities that may only be funded by the political fund.[26] In addition to the activities, noted above, originally contained in the Trade Union Act 1913, the 1984 Trade Union Act included as political objects:

(a) the provision of any service or property for use by or on behalf of a political party;[27]

(b) the production, publication or distribution of any literature, document, film, sound recording or advertisement the main purpose of which is to persuade people to vote for a political party or candidate or to persuade them not to vote for a political party or candidate.[28]

In addition to these changes other elements of the original political objects have been amended. The definition of 'political office' has been expanded to include Members of the European Parliament and any position within a political party.[29] Expenditure on holding conferences or meetings, the main purpose of which includes the transaction of business connected with a political party, is also now explicitly subject to the rules on the political fund.[30]

---

22 [1927] 1 Ch 539.

23 [1981] IRLR 427.

24 Clearly, expenditure to produce documents supporting the election of named candidates and a named political party is 'political' expenditure – *McCarthy v APEX* [1980] IRLR 335.

25 Cmnd 8778, 1983, paras 103–04.

26 See, generally, on the 1984 changes Ewing, KD, 'Trade union political funds: the 1913 Act revised' (1984) 13 ILJ 227.

27 This gives statutory support to the Certification Officer's decision in *Richards v NUM* [1981] IRLR 247 and *Parkin v ASTMS* [1983] IRLR 448.

28 This alteration has the effect of overturning the Certification Officer's decision in *Coleman v POEU* [1981] IRLR 427. It has also brought up to date the means by which political information is disseminated.

29 Thus, union expenditure on internal Labour Party elections (local or national) is now regulated.

30 This includes expenditure incurred by delegates or participants in connection with their attendance.

The High Court was called upon to interpret the scope of the reforms in *Paul v NALGO*.[31] The union did not have a political fund but had initiated a publicity campaign at election time entitled 'Make People Matter' using the general fund. The campaign was aimed at publicising criticisms of public expenditure cuts in the public services. Paul argued this was a political campaign contrary to the new definition as it intended to persuade the electorate not to vote Conservative at the General Election.

Browne-Wilkinson VC thought the crucial issue was determining the purpose of the union in disseminating the information. The main purpose could be surmised by an examination of the content of the literature in the light of all the surrounding circumstances. An important circumstance was the impending election. According to Browne-Wilkinson, the high level of criticism of the Conservative Government and the request to readers to consider their voting intentions with the material in mind was evidence that this was a political campaign to persuade people to vote against the Conservative Party.[32]

THE POLITICAL FUND LEVY AND THE NON-CONTRIBUTOR

The 1913 Act established the principle that a member cannot be compelled to contribute to the political fund. This has been retained under the present system. So long as the member gives notice of his or her objections, then the political fund rules in the rule book must provide for exemption from the obligation to contribute.

The procedure for opting out of the political levy[33] is detailed in s 84 of the TULR(C)A 1992. Once political objects are adopted, the union must issue an 'exemption notice' notifying its members in writing of their right to opt out of the obligation to contribute.[34] The notice must make it clear that paying the political fund is not a condition of membership and indicate how subscription relief will be provided for those who contract out.[35]

It has not always been the case that union members needed to 'opt out' of the political levy. The right to contract out of the fund was substituted in 1927 by the principle that members must themselves make a positive decision to contract into the political fund. This provision contained in the Trade Disputes and Trade Unions Act 1927 was passed subsequent to the General Strike, thereby weakening the union movement's political base and the financial base of the Labour Party. Contracting out of the political fund was reinstated in 1946 when the Labour Party attained office in the 1945 General Election.[36]

---

31 [1987] IRLR 413.

32 Arguably, a campaign funded by the general fund to express disapproval of government policy at any other time would be lawful.

33 The 'political levy' is the only way unions may lawfully finance the political fund (s 83(1)).

34 Section 84(2).

35 Section 85.

36 Trade Union and Trade Disputes Act 1946. The financing of the political fund was considered by the Donovan Commission (1968). The Commission did not recommend any changes to the status quo (paras 912–27 and Appendix 7).

Contracting out was challenged again in the Green Paper, *Democracy in Trade Unions*.[37] The Green Paper noted the high level of trade union members who pay the political contribution and expressed doubt that the vast majority had positively taken a decision not to exercise their right to opt out.[38] It was suggested that inertia and the lack of awareness of this right was the more likely explanation for this failure to contract out.[39] The Trades Union Congress (TUC) successfully forestalled legislative intervention[40] by consulting with Government representatives and agreeing to issue a 'Statement of Guidelines' to affiliated unions to encourage greater openness on financial matters in general and on the political fund in particular.[41]

The statement recommends that unions pay more attention to advertising to members the right to be exempt from the political levy and that they publicise payments from the fund so members are more aware how the political fund operates. This should be done by each union drawing up an information sheet to be given to all new members and any existing member on request. The statement also provides guidelines to unions on how to operate the political fund openly without interfering with any members' rights.

DISCRIMINATION AND THE NON-CONTRIBUTOR

The political fund rules must contain provisions ensuring that a member who is exempt from the obligation to contribute is not excluded from any benefits of the union or is placed indirectly or directly at any disadvantage compared with other members of the union.[42] However, there is a statutory exception; discrimination is permissible in relation to the control or management of the political fund. The right to discriminate is, however, not automatic. It is necessary to have a rule allowing for the exclusion of non-contributors.[43] Within the ambit of the expression 'control and management' are included matters of policy on how to distribute the political fund.[44] Therefore, an exempt member can be excluded from voting on a motion dealing with the reselection of a union sponsored MP.[45]

In *Birch v NUR*,[46] the plaintiff, a non-contributor, was an elected chair of his union branch. As chair, Birch had a multiplicity of union functions to perform, one of which was

---

37 Cmnd 8778, 1983.

38 Paragraph 89.

39 Paragraphs 92–94. For an alternative interpretation, see Ewing, KD and Rees, W, 'Democracy in trade unions: the political levy' (1983) 133 NLJ 100.

40 It is also thought that legislation to enforce 'contracting in' was not brought forward due to a belief that the new procedural changes would see a reduction in political funds.

41 For comment on the TUC Statement of Guidance, see Ewing, KD (1984) 13 ILJ 125.

42 See the interpretation of this in *Richards v NUM* [1981] IRLR 247 – a non-contributor who was excluded from inspecting the political fund accounting records had not been discriminated against as he could not possibly have any interest in such records. Now, cf TULR(C)A 1992, s 30, on the statutory right of access to union accounts.

43 *Hobbs v Clerical and Administrative Workers' Union* (Registrar's Annual Report 1956).

44 See *Double v EETPU* (CO Annual Report 1982).

45 *Parkin v ASTMS* (CO Annual Report 1979).

46 [1950] Ch 602.

the management of the political fund. He was subsequently declared ineligible to hold this position and removed from office.

Birch applied to the High Court for a declaration on the grounds that he was put at a disadvantage by his exclusion from holding union office. Danckwerts J decided that, even though the Registrar had approved the union rules, they still offended against the condition of non-discrimination in the Act. Birch was not just denied the opportunity to manage the political fund, but also excluded from involvement in union affairs as a whole.

The thrust of the decision was that a union cannot bar an individual *per se* from a union office, but only from the duties relating to the political fund. In practice, this would suggest that the constitution of the union should ensure that the control and management of the political fund is separated from other managerial and administrative functions of the union. However, to separate political functions from other administrative matters would be very difficult to achieve at national level without increasing union bureaucracy and diminishing efficiency. For this reason, it has been argued that the decision in *Birch* does not apply to arrangements made at the national level.[47]

Other commentators have argued that this view is difficult to sustain on a reading of the statute and the case.[48] The solution perhaps is not to separate these functions at all, but rather to dispense with any rule that excluded non-contributors from control and management of the fund at the national level. Non-contributors to the political fund are highly unlikely to be elected onto the executive and so be in a position to control such funds.

THE NON-CONTRIBUTOR AND THE 'CHECK OFF'

The positive results of the political fund ballots undertaken since 1984 had undermined Conservative optimism that the political fund would wither away. Consequently, the target for reform shifted away from a direct attack on the political fund to an examination of the 'check off' arrangements for the political levy.

The 'check off' is the deduction of union subscriptions direct from salary by an employer who forwards it on to the union. Often, it is administratively convenient for an employer to deduct the total contribution from each member without adjusting the amount to reflect the reduced subscription rate paid by those who are exempt from contributing to the political fund. Where this is the procedure, the union reimburses a lump sum to the non-contributors.

This procedure was successfully challenged in *McCarthy v APEX*[49] as a form of discrimination contrary to s 82(c). Yet, in *Reeves v TGWU*,[50] the Employment Appeal Tribunal stated that, although it was preferable that the refund should be in advance, it

---

47 Grunfeld, C (1963) 1 BJIR 23 and Grunfeld, C, *Modern Trade Union Law*, 1966, pp 302–03.
48 See Ewing, KD, 'Trade union political fund rules: a note on adjudication' (1980) 9 ILJ 137, pp 143–46.
49 [1979] IRLR 255.
50 [1980] IRLR 307 (noted (1981) 41 MLR 219).

was not unlawful to provide refunds in arrears so long as the refund is provided automatically without the member having to request or apply for it.

The Green Paper[51] criticised the reimbursement of a lump sum as as an affront to individual rights. Consequently, now, s 86 of the TULR(C)A 1992 provides that once an employee certifies in writing to their employer or their union that they are a non-contributor to the political fund, the employer is under a duty to ensure that the check off of union dues reflects this.[52] A potential problem for trade unions is that, where it is administratively awkward to apply a system accurately, employers may be tempted to suspend check off arrangements altogether or simply check off the lower rate for every union member, leaving the union to collect the political levy separately. It has been argued that this reform was motivated more to limit the political funds available to trade unions rather than because of a concern for the individual rights of non-contributors.

REMEDIES

Where the complaint is of a breach of the political fund rules, the Certification Officer and High Court have jurisdiction. In a hearing before the Certification Officer, the trade union will be notified of the complaint and both parties are given the opportunity to make representations. The Certification Officer has a discretion to issue a declaration and make an enforcement order requiring the union to remedy the breach. This is enforceable in the county court.[53]

Where the complaint is that the rules for holding the ballot have been infringed, the High Court also has concurrent jurisdiction with the Certification Officer to grant a declaration and an enforcement order.[54] Where there has been a breach of the statute (such as where the trade union has no political fund rules and yet has made a political donation), the High Court had sole authority to hear the complaint. The Certification Officer, however, now also has jurisdiction (introduced by the Employment Relations Act 1999).[55]

---

51   *Democracy in Trade Unions*, Cmnd 8778, 1983.

52   This right is enforceable in the employment tribunal via a declaration (s 87(4)(a)) and an enforcement order (s 87(4)(b)).

53   There is a right of appeal to the EAT from the Certification Officer's decision (ss 95 and 108(c)). The Certification Officer's Reports show a very low level of complaint. In 1985, there were seven complaints. All were resolved to the satisfaction of the complainants without the need for any formal hearings. In 1995, only two complaints were received; both resolved amicably. Between January 1999 and 31 March 2000, two complaints were received, no declarations were made.

54   The application must be lodged one year from the announcement of the ballot result (s 79(3)).

55   The reforms to the Certification Officer's jurisdiction and procedure are described in detail at pp 17–22.

THE EFFECTS OF THE CONSERVATIVE REFORMS

The changes, introduced in the 1980s to further regulate and limit political expenditure by trade unions, have clearly been counter-productive.[56] The assumption that many of the votes would go against the retention of a political fund has been proved to be woefully inaccurate. At the end of 1982, only 60 out of 462 unions had political funds.[57] By 1987, not only had all the unions that were required to reballot done so successfully, but 20 more unions had balloted to create new political funds.[58]

This can be explained by union reaction to the legal changes. The reforms actually encouraged rather than discouraged unions to adopt political funds. Unions that already possessed political funds were galvanised into organising highly effective campaigns to retain their political funds with the result that the average percentage vote for retention was over 80%. Other unions that did not have political funds were concerned that the minor political activity they had previously engaged in, funded by the general fund, was now potentially unlawful.[59] Although initiated as a precautionary measure, the side effect of the creation of new political funds is that in global terms an even larger amount of funds have now become available for political campaigning.[60]

Ten years on from the introduction of the Trade Union Act 1984, all unions with political funds had reballoted to satisfy the provision requiring express approval every 10 years. Trade unions affiliated to the TUC under the auspices of the Trade Union Co-ordinating Committee have campaigned vigorously to retain the funds. In 1994, it was reported that all 20 review ballots resulted in substantial majorities to retain the fund (indeed, 12 of the unions increased their majorities from 1984–86). In 1995, 12 review ballots were held. All were passed by substantial majorities. The results of these ballots clearly show that there is a broad measure of support for political funds by the majority of membership across the union spectrum.[61]

The success of union campaigns to retain the political fund should not obscure other important issues. For example, the detailed regulation of trade union political activity has been unfavourably compared to the less intrusive legal control imposed on other associations who contribute to political campaigns or political parties. Private companies are entitled to use their funds for whatever purpose without any special legal control, apart from limited control by shareholders. Although companies have to disclose their political donations in excess of £200,[62] ordinary shareholders are not consulted, nor may

---

56   See Steele, M et al, 'The Trade Union Act 1984: political fund ballots' (1986) 24 BJIR 443, pp 463–64.

57   CO Annual Report 1983.

58   CO Annual Report 1988.

59   Of particular concern to public sector unions was the redefinition of political objects. This threatens the legality of expenditure on campaigns critical of government policy.

60   Total funds available for political expenditure soared from £8.5 m in 1984 to £18.1 m by the end of 1994 (CO Annual Reports 1984 and 1995.) More recent figures show a slight fall – with total political funds standing at £15.8 m at the end of 1998 (CO Annual Report 1999–2000).

61   For further details of the balloting process during this period, see Leopold, J, 'Trade unions, political fund ballots and the Labour Party' (1997) 35 BJIR 23.

62   Companies Act 1985, Sched 7, s 235.

shareholders 'opt out' of contributing to these donations by, for example, requesting a higher dividend as compensation.

At a more general level, it could also be maintained that if it is the democratic will of the membership (as expressed by ballot or through other democratic channels), a trade union, in common with any other democratic association, should command the right to engage in any lawful political activity or at least have the discretion within its rules structure to take part in such activity.

PART 2

FREEDOM OF ASSOCIATION
AND COLLECTIVE BARGAINING

INTRODUCTION

The right of workers to join and participate in trade union affairs and a union's freedom to engage in collective bargaining are the cornerstones of the British industrial relations system. These bedrock principles are inextricably linked as, manifestly, without unhindered free association of workers in trade unions, collective bargaining, by its very nature, cannot function. Even with free association, collective bargaining is undermined where unions are unable to organise effectively – such as where trade union members and officials are discouraged or formally penalised for participating in trade union affairs. Furthermore, a prerequisite for collective negotiation is formal recognition of a trade union, for this purpose, by an employer. The overall aim of Part 2 of this book is to examine the response of the law to these interlinked issues: to analyse and assess the role the law plays in underpinning or undermining the freedom to organise and to participate in collective bargaining.

In this introductory section, we examine the growth of the system of free collective bargaining. We enquire how far government policies through the use of the law, supported, encouraged, regulated or inhibited this process. After this historical outline, we examine the contemporary framework of collective bargaining with particular reference to the changes in practice that have occurred since 1979. In the context of these developments, Chapter 8 analyses the legal effects of collective agreements on the employment relationship. Chapters 9, 10 and 11 investigate the extent of legal assistance to enhance organisational strength of trade unions and bolster collective bargaining by the creation of individual rights for union members and officials and collective rights for the union itself. In Chapter 12, we consider how far freedom of association *per se* in trade unions is legally guaranteed.

THE DEVELOPMENT OF
FREE COLLECTIVE BARGAINING

The tacit recognition by the State of the legitimacy of trade unions by the removal of criminal sanctions in 1875[1] from strike action was the precursor of the recognition struggles of the late 19th century which spawned the development of the modern system of collective bargaining. Although the first unions to win some degree of recognition from employers were the 'new model' craft unions in the middle 1800s, these small occupational unions engaged predominately in regional bargaining for their exclusively skilled membership. It was not until the development of 'general unionism' in the 1890s

---

1   The Conspiracy and Protection of Property Act 1875 provided an immunity from criminal liability for the common law offence of conspiracy. For further details on this, see p 10.

(with the recruitment of unskilled workers in a multiple of industries) that a more sophisticated decentralised bargaining structure across and within industries emerged.[2]

Recognition of the more robust general trade unions by employers for the purposes of collective bargaining was not achieved painlessly. Strikes, lock outs and picket line violence between hired strikebreakers and unionists were a feature of the industrial scene in the late 19th century. As a consequence of this industrial strife, a Royal Commission on Labour was set up in 1891 to examine the causes of this conflict and to recommend solutions. The Royal Commission reported in 1894 and identified collective bargaining as an effective system of regulation of economic relations between workers and employers and urged on the Government an industrial policy that took account of the realities of the union-employer relationship. The Commission recommended that the State use its powers to support voluntary agreements between union and employer and provide conciliation mechanisms to help resolve disputes and secure industrial peace.

The response of the State to the burgeoning union movement and the recommendations of the Royal Commission was reluctantly to recognise the inevitability of the expansion of collective bargaining. Within a few years of the Royal Commission's report, the first legislation was enacted to encourage the voluntary resolution of disputes between employer and union and to support, albeit hesitantly, a system of collective bargaining. In 1896, the Conciliation Act was passed which provided for the appointment of a Commission of Inquiry by the Board of Trade into industrial conflicts and for the voluntary arbitration or conciliation of disputes.

Furthermore, the impact of collective bargaining was recognised by the House of Commons Fair Wages Resolutions of 1891 and 1909 which introduced the notion of the State as a 'model' employer. These resolutions required employers who contracted with government departments to observe minimum standards of pay for their employees equivalent to that 'commonly' recognised in the relevant industry. In those industries where workers were denied union representation and so were without proper bargaining structures, the Trade Boards Act 1909 set up machinery to determine guaranteed minimum wages.

These statutes – cautiously promoting rather than controlling collective bargaining – were the foundations of what later became known as the 'voluntarist' or 'abstentionist' approach to labour relations.[3] The overriding guiding principle was that the law did not impinge on the private relationship between union and employer. The bargain struck between employer and union for the price of labour was a matter for the parties

---

2   For a detailed examination of the growth of trade unions and collective bargaining in this period see Webb, S and Webb, B, *The History of Trade Unionism*, 2nd edn, 1922, Chapter 9 and *Industrial Democracy*, 1920, Part 2, Chapter 2; Pelling, H, *A History of British Trade Unionism*, 5th edn, 1992, Chapter 6; and Wrigley, C (ed), *A History of British Industrial Relations 1875–1914*, 1982.

3   See Flanders, A, 'The tradition of voluntarism' (1974) 7 BJIR 352 and Davies, P and Freedland, M, *Labour Legislation and Public Policy*, 1993, Chapter 1. The celebrated labour lawyer, Otto Kahn-Freund, coined the phrase 'collective *laissez-faire*' to describe the relationship of the law to industrial relations from the early 20th century. See 'The legal framework' in Clegg, H and Flanders, A (eds), *The System of Industrial Relations in Great Britain*, 1954; 'Labour law' in Ginsberg, M (ed), *Law and Opinion in England in the 20th Century*, 1959. See also an appreciation of the writings of Kahn-Freund in Lewis, R, 'Kahn-Freund and labour law: an outline critique' (1979) 8 ILJ 202.

themselves. Where disputes arose, the State provided the mechanisms for dispute resolution, but did not formally involve itself in determining the outcome of the dispute. An additional aspect of abstentionism was the acceptance by the State that the common law should not intrude in union-employer disputes arising from a breakdown in collective bargaining. Hence, the Trade Disputes Act 1906 was a crucial component of abstentionism as it provided trade unions with immunities from the civil liabilities committed during strike action and so ensured the neutrality of the law.[4]

This fledgling 'voluntarist' or 'non-interventionist' policy was put under pressure by the inexorable rise of union influence in the early years of the 20th century. As trade unions grew in strength, successful recognition disputes resulted in the growth of collective bargaining across industries with national and regional bargaining superseded in many industries by local bargaining. The consequences of this was the development of a militant unofficial shop stewards' movement which culminated in an expansion of uncontrolled bargaining and further industrial strife in many important industries in the period immediately prior to and during the First World War.

The response of the Government to these developments was to establish the Whitley Committee in 1917 with the remit to advise on securing improvements in industrial relations.[5] The main thrust of the Committee's recommendations confirmed the view that collective bargaining was an effective and efficient system of industrial regulation. Whitley strongly endorsed the 'voluntarist' position that the role of government was not to dictate what should be agreed or interfere in the process through legal means, but to support ordered collective bargaining by creating the means for union and employer to meet and negotiate.

Whitley identified the problem with existing arrangements as being located in the disparate and fragmented framework of unco-ordinated bargaining. Whitley thus recommended that collective bargaining procedures needed to be formalised by the provision of approved fora to facilitate collective bargaining at all levels within industries. In the private sector, the Government encouraged the formation of National and District Joint Industrial Councils and Works Committees as the venue for negotiations between union representatives and employers. Legal regulation was avoided since participation in the councils was voluntary. However, these initiatives were only partially successful. It was in the public sector that the recommendations had the greatest success with the setting up of an integrated system of local and national collective bargaining in all government departments and agencies.

A major concern of the Whitley Committee was how best to avoid the problem of economically debilitating industrial disputes. Compulsory arbitration was rejected as an option as this was contrary to the voluntarist philosophy. It was therefore recommended

---

4   This disengagement of the law from industrial disputes was the major objective of the union movement. Unions lobbied for a non-interventionist and neutral role for the law as a consequence of their experiences of anti-union judicial decisions at the turn of the century in cases such as *Taff Vale v ASRS* [1901] AC 426 and *Quinn v Leathem* [1901] AC 485.

5   Labour shortages at this time had enhanced union bargaining strength further exacerbating industrial conflict. Consequently, the Government was particularly worried that this conflict would sabotage co-operation between union and employers which was necessary for full industrial mobilisation to aid the war effort.

that machinery to facilitate settlement of industrial disputes arising out of the collective bargaining process should be expanded. Accordingly, the Industrial Courts Act 1919 granted the Ministry of Labour authority to assist in the settlement of disputes by conciliation, voluntary arbitration or special inquiry.[6] The Act also set up the Industrial Court – a permanent court of arbitration. This tribunal sat with representatives of both sides of industry to arbitrate on a dispute where both sides had consented to its jurisdiction.[7] The Act also provided the authority for the setting up of occasional 'courts of inquiry'. This body would examine the underlying causes of the dispute, make recommendations for settlement and proposals to avoid similar disputes in the future.[8]

Also stemming from the Whitley Committee proposals was a new Trade Boards Act which was passed in 1918. This Act permitted the Minister of Labour to make an Order establishing a Trade Board in any industry where there was no determination of wages by collective bargaining. Trade Boards were served by representatives of both unions and employers and had the authority to set minimum wages in the relevant trade.[9]

The consequences of the Whitley Council recommendations was an increase in national level bargaining and a marginalisation of the shop steward movement. However, the onset of a serious economic slump in the early 1920s heralded an era of union and social unrest culminating in the general strike of 1926. After the strike had collapsed the Trade Disputes and Trade Union Act 1927 imposed new restrictions on union political activity and on the conduct of industrial disputes. However, voluntary structures for the settlement of disputes remained in place and the promotion of national bargaining remained a focus of industrial policy throughout the 1930s.

The Second World War years were characterised by the imposition of legal regulation justified on the grounds of wartime necessity. The Conditions of Employment and National Arbitration Order (SI 1940/1305) gave legal force to collective agreements enforceable via an award of the National Arbitration Tribunal.[10] Where employers refused to negotiate or renegotiate a new collective agreement, the Order enforced the 'recognised terms and conditions of employment' pertaining in the industry. Where disputes arose, due to

---

6   The Ministry thus took on the role of advising and assisting in a settlement of a dispute similar to the role performed today by ACAS.

7   In the inter-war years from 1920 until 1939, the Ministry of Labour brokered 1,200 conciliation settlements. There were also over 2,000 arbitration awards made by the industrial court or by other *ad hoc* arbitrators under the auspices of the Ministry.

8   Due to a number of serious disputes in the economic depression after the First World War, 20 courts of inquiry were convened in the years immediately after the war. For a detailed examination of their operation from 1919, see McCarthy, W and Clifford, B, 'The work of industrial courts of inquiry' (1966) 4 BJIR 1. The most recent court of inquiry was the Report into the Grunwick recognition dispute by Lord Justice Scarman in 1977 (Cmnd 6922). Although TULR(C)A 1992, s 215, preserves the power of the Secretary of State to refer any trade dispute to a court of inquiry, ACAS (by TULR(C)A 1992, s 214) has less formal powers to investigate trade dispute issues. Consequently, the court of inquiry as an investigative device has fallen into disuse.

9   The trade union response to the Trade Boards was initially hostile as it was believed statutory regulation of wages, creating legally enforceable minimum rates, would tend to weaken trade union efforts to obtain effective collective agreements in the industries covered by the Trade Boards. Yet, the aim of this legislation was to encourage voluntary agreement within the Trade Boards rather than the dictation of wage rates through direct interference. As the Trade Boards were a forum for negotiation between union and employer, there was also an expectation that this would encourage collective bargaining on a number of other issues.

10   For an analysis of the application of this aspect of the order see Kahn-Freund, O, 'Collective agreements under war legislation' (1943) 6 MLR 112.

infringements of a collective agreement or over the 'recognised terms and conditions', the Ministry of Labour would attempt to secure a settlement by encouraging voluntary conciliation under the industry's joint machinery. Only if that failed would reference be made by the ministry to the National Arbitration Tribunal for compulsory binding arbitration. This was the only way unions could enforce a collective agreement as industrial action was specifically prohibited by this Order.[11]

The end of the Second World War did not see the immediate dismantling of the regulatory structures due to the serious economic difficulties experienced in the post-war period. Not all unions called for the unilateral dismantling of this structure as the wartime experience of compulsory arbitration had been advantageous for unions in poorly organised industries. For these weak unions, this was their first opportunity to enforce negotiated agreements and ensure there was a minimum parity of terms and conditions of employment across the industry. It was not until the regulation of all facets of national life, imposed in this period of austerity, was discredited in the early 1950s that the Conditions of Employment Order was repealed in conjunction with the restrictions on the right to strike.[12]

Existing provisions that supplemented and supported collective bargaining were enhanced in this post-war period. The Wages Council Act 1945[13] renamed the Trade Boards and expanded their authority to determine additional terms and conditions of service apart from pay and to examine other industrial matters such as training issues. In effect, Wages Councils operating in poorly unionised workplaces assumed similar functions to the Joint Industrial Councils in other industries. The Fair Wages Resolution was revised in 1946,[14] extending its application to sub-contractors and incorporating collectively negotiated industry-wide standards into government contracts.[15] Furthermore, rather than leaving enforcement to government departments, the new

---

11 The legal sanctions on strike action were only partially successful. Many small localised strikes did take place during the War and during the period of austerity immediately after. In most cases, there was no attempt to enforce the law as it was thought this would inflame the dispute. Indeed, exactly this happened in the infamous prosecution of coal miners at the Betteshanger colliery in Kent in 1941. The strike was not settled until the leaders of the strike were released from jail and the Government gave an undertaking not to enforce the fines meted out to over 1,000 striking miners.

12 A major reason for the repeal of Order 1305 was due to the controversy surrounding enforcement. In 1950, there was a well publicised prosecution of London Gasworkers. The prosecution was the last straw for the TUC which demanded its repeal. The trade unions, however, lobbied to retain the aspects of the Order relating to arbitration awards. Consequently, the Industrial Disputes Order (SI 1951/1376) retained limited provisions for recourse to compulsory arbitration. The Minister of Labour could refer disputes to a new Industrial Disputes Tribunal which had the authority to make awards on terms and conditions of employment. This strengthened the authority of agreements emanating from the existing voluntary system of negotiation and encouraged the upholding of collective agreements. The Order was revoked in 1958, although replaced by a similar provision in 1959 (Terms and Conditions of Employment Act, s 8).

13 Wages Councils were unpopular with the Conservative regimes in the 1980s. The Wages Councils Act 1986 (noted by McMullen, J (1986) 15 ILJ 266) curtailed their powers by removing protection for those over 21 and, in 1988, a consultation paper recommended their abolition, finally achieved in 1993 by the Trade Union Reform and Employment Rights Act. An analysis of Conservative thinking on wage regulation is provided by Keevash, S, 'Wage Councils: an examination of trade union and Conservative misconceptions about the effect of statutory wage fixing' (1985) 14 ILJ 217.

14 For a full description of the history and application of the Resolution see Bercusson, B, *Fair Wages Resolutions*, 1978.

15 The previous Fair Wages Resolution had incorporated the 'prevailing rates in the industry'. This was often less than the officially negotiated rate. The new resolution thus gave priority to the collective bargain. See Kahn-Freund, O, 'The legal aspects of fair wages clauses' (1948) 11 MLR 269.

resolution provided for complaints of a breach of the resolution to proceed to an independent tribunal for arbitration.[16]

For almost a decade from the early 1950s, a degree of consensus existed between the political parties on industrial policy.[17] There was broad acceptance of the role of trade unions within a system of collective bargaining unhampered by State intervention.[18] This era was characterised by relative full employment and an expansion of collective bargaining arrangements at the national level supplemented by plant level agreements. Initially, as this was also a period of economic growth, increased bargaining strength did not lead to inflationary pressures. However, as the economic position in the late 1950s changed, shop steward bargaining at the local level became more tenacious. This plant bargaining resulted in wages being pushed upwards over the formally nationally bargained rates of pay.

This became a matter of grave concern to successive governments in the 1960s, both Labour and Conservative, who believed that trade union bargaining was responsible for initiating inflationary wage-price spirals.[19] The formulation of anti-inflation strategies became a major domestic concern. In the late 1950s, the Government attempted to secure voluntary pay restraint. A Council on Prices, Productivity and Incomes was established in 1958 to encourage employers and unions to take account of the national economic interest in determining wage increases.

On the failure of this voluntary strategy, a non-statutory pay policy was imposed in the public sector in 1961, with employers in the private sector encouraged to follow suit. In 1962, the first Incomes Policy was formally put into place to control collective bargaining between employer and union by imposing pay norms in certain industries. In conjunction with this pay policy, a National Incomes Commission was created to provide advice to employers and unions on the settlement of wages. Both voluntary and imposed pay restraint failed in response to a hostile and unco-operative union movement and selective industrial action.

The new Labour Government's solution to poor economic performance was greater management of, and control over, the economy. Prices and incomes were suppressed whilst higher productivity and greater efficiency in industry were encouraged to negate inflationary pressures. A National Board for Prices and Incomes was created with powers to recommend pay freezes in a particular industry unless they were linked to increases in productivity. As the economic position worsened, an even more comprehensive regulation of prices and incomes was put into place by the Prices and Incomes Act 1966, setting specific upper limits to wage increases. Conflict soon arose between these economic

---

16 The Fair Wages Resolution was rescinded by the House of Commons in 1983. For the background to this decision, see Bercusson, B (1982) 11 ILJ 271.

17 For a detailed account of government policy towards trade unions and collective bargaining in the post-war period, see op cit, Davies and Freedland, fn 3, and Wrigley, C, British Trade Unions and Industrial Politics, 1999.

18 This period, before the onset of wage regulation in the 1960s is regarded as the highpoint of the voluntarist approach to industrial relations (described earlier on p 138). It was at this time that Kahn-Freund produced his influential articles, describing and analysing the system of 'collective laissez-faire'.

19 It was argued that, with full employment, trade union bargaining power is greatly enhanced. Employers therefore pass on increased wage costs through higher prices to the consumer. As prices rise, this triggers off further wage claims.

policies, based on counter-inflationary incomes policies to limit pay increases, and the free operation of the collective bargaining process.[20] A corollary of this was increased industrial action, particularly unofficial action, at the local level.[21]

The response of the Labour Government to the deteriorating industrial situation was to set up a Royal Commission to examine the industrial relations framework.[22] The Commission (known as the Donovan Commission after Lord Donovan, the Commission's chairman) emphasised that industrial conflict was merely a symptom of the underlying problems of ineffective collective bargaining procedures in industry. Consequently, the Commission's predominant concern was how to improve the workings of collective bargaining. The Commission identified the fragmentation of bargaining between the formal industry-wide system and the informal plant approach. This resulted in 'wage drift' where the local agreement, which provided for higher pay, was followed in preference to a national agreement. This local bargaining at shop floor level co-existing with industry-wide bargaining was a recipe for localised conflict and inflationary pressures.[23]

The Donovan Commission believed that a strengthening of central bargaining through comprehensive factory-wide agreements and more effective disputes procedures was required.[24] Yet, the Commission did not support the introduction of formal legal regulation to enforce such bargains. In this, the prevailing status quo was accepted. Instead, the Commission urged that the law should be used to foster and encourage this model of collective bargaining. To help develop a national standardised system of collective bargaining, the Donovan Commission recommended the establishment of an Industrial Relations Commission with a brief to assist voluntary reform by acting as a forum for union/employer negotiations on reducing bargaining levels.

Additionally, legal support for collective bargaining such as a union right to recognition and consultation and to information was proposed. In particular, recognition was identified by the Donovan Commission as a fundamental requirement. Historically, recognition was widespread in the public sector and, as a consequence, industry-wide bargaining in that sector was far more advanced and industrial relations more harmonious than in the private sector. It was felt that a managed expansion of factory and industry-wide bargaining in the private sector would enhance productivity and limit industrial conflict.

---

20 For an analysis of the relationship between labour law and anti-wage inflation policies in this period, see Lord Wedderburn, 'Labour law now: a hold and a nudge' (1984) 13 ILJ 73. See, also, Deakin, S, *Inflation, Employment, Wage Bargaining and the Law* (1992, Institute of Employment Rights).

21 It was during this decade that the phrase 'the British disease' was coined to describe the mushrooming of official and unofficial 'wildcat' strikes. The perception of some commentators at the time that shop steward power had grown uncontrollably, culminating in industrial anarchy was arguably somewhat overstated. See the contemporary analysis by Turner, H, *Is Britain Really Strike Prone?*, 1969.

22 Royal Commission on Trade Unions and Employers' Associations, Cmnd 3623, 1968.

23 Donovan noted that in many industries bargaining operated in conflict rather than in co-operation. With the shift of power from the centre to the periphery there was a 'tendency of extreme decentralisation and self-government to degenerate into indecision and anarchy'.

24 See para 182.

Before any recommendations of the Donovan Commission could be fully implemented,[25] the Labour Government was defeated at the 1970 general election. The new Conservative Government introduced a radical new approach to the organisation of industrial relations, building on ideas imported from the United States. This approach was based on the legal regulation of industrial relations by the provision of legally enforceable rights and obligations for employers and unions. These ideas were embodied into the Industrial Relations Act 1971. The union movement concentrated on the imposed legal obligations[26] and restrictions on union activity and reacted with hostility to what was perceived as overbearing State intervention in the bargaining process and the end of the voluntarist system.

The Act introduced the notion of legally binding collective agreements fixed for a set period. Renegotiation before the end of the period was heavily discouraged as industrial action to force the reopening of negotiation was specifically unlawful. Additionally, *prima facie* lawful industrial action was regulated by specific rules and procedures. Ballots before industrial action were introduced. In certain circumstances, a compulsory 'cooling off' period of 28 days had to be observed before the action could continue. To trade unions this was a restriction on their hard won autonomy from legal intervention. The experiment collapsed amongst industrial chaos far worse than the strife it was designed to cure.[27]

The Labour administration elected in 1974 repealed the Industrial Relations Act and set about introducing a comprehensive package of legal measures (through the Trade Union and Labour Relations Act and the Employment Protection Act)[28] to encourage and underpin collective bargaining. The Advisory, Conciliation and Arbitration Service (ACAS) was created with a brief to promote the improvement of industrial relations by encouraging the extension of collective bargaining and to advise on the improvement and reform of bargaining procedures within industries.[29] The Central Arbitration Committee (CAC) replaced the National Arbitration Board set up in 1971, itself the replacement for the Industrial Court established in 1919.

---

25 The recommendations of the Commission were only accepted after substantial debate and disagreement within the Labour cabinet. Initially, a White Paper, *In Place of Strife*, proposed an Industrial Relations Bill that incorporated legal constraints on the freedom of trade unions to take industrial action. The proposals were finally dropped after the TUC gave a 'solemn binding undertaking' to urge all unions to follow an agreed programme to limit industrial action. A new Bill representing many of the Commission's findings was lost on the fall of the Government.

26 The legal benefits for trade unions (eg, the imposition of collective bargaining procedures on employers, the obligation on employers to disclose information) were only available to those trade unions that registered under the Act. Very few unions did so as a protest against the obligations contained in the rest of the Act.

27 For a comprehensive review of the 1971 Act, an analysis of its provisions and the opposition to it, see Weekes, B, Mellish, M, Dickens, L and Lloyd, J, *Industrial Relations and the Limits of the Law*, 1975. Also, see *op cit*, Davies and Freedland, fn 3, Chapter 7. For a review of the case law decided under the Act see Kahn-Freund, O, 'The Industrial Relations Act 1971 – some retrospective reflections' (1974) 3 ILJ 186.

28 For commentary on these Acts, see Lord Wedderburn (1974) 37 MLR 525 and (1976) 39 MLR 169.

29 ACAS took over the duties of the Commission on Industrial Relations created as a consequence of the Donovan recommendations.

There was enhanced legal support for collective bargaining by strengthening trade union organisation through rights for members and officials to engage in trade union activities.[30] Collective 'props' to bargaining were introduced which provided unions with rights to recognition and consultation and information for bargaining purposes. Furthermore, a 'floor of (individual) rights' (such as maternity pay, guaranteed pay on lay-off) was provided via the incorporation of statutory implied terms into the individual employment contract. The Terms and Conditions of Employment Act 1959 was replaced by Sched 11 to the Employment Protection Act 1975 which introduced procedures for imposing collectively agreed minimum terms on employers within a particular industry.[31] The intention was that the provision of these collective and individual rights would act as a catalyst for further bargaining on these and related matters.

The *quid pro quo* for the provision of these benefits was union co-operation in the drive to conquer inflation by the moderation of their wage demands – this became known as the Social Contract. Initially, this policy was relatively successful in encouraging a move towards more formalised bargaining. In this early period, there was a growth of self-financing productivity bargaining, with better terms and conditions of employment being agreed, in return for changes in working practices and worker performance to improve industrial efficiency.[32]

However, by the late 1970s the Social Contract had broken down, particularly in the public sector which did not benefit from the productivity deals. The Labour pay policy was this time challenged, not by the unofficial wildcat strikes of the 1960s, but by co-ordinated national action. Industrial action in the winter of 1978–79, the so-called 'winter of discontent', ushered in the General Election of 1979 and the Thatcher-led Conservative Government. In the 1980s, management of the economy and the control of prices and incomes was achieved by the application of monetarist economic policies based on the control of the money supply. This, combined with other free market policies, resulted in profound changes in the collective bargaining framework in many industries. It is thus to an examination of the contemporary structure of collective bargaining that we now turn.

---

30 The right of union members not to be dismissed or to have action short of dismissal taken against them for participation in trade union activities; the right for trade union officials to take time off to engage in industrial relations duties.

31 See Wood, P, 'The CAC's approach to Schedule 11' (1978) 9 ILJ 65 and Jones, M, 'Two years of CAC and Schedule 11' (1980) 11 ILJ 28. The repeal of Sched 11 in 1980 struck the first blow against the 'fair wages' policy in poorly unionised industries.

32 Unlike the previous regime introduced under the Industrial Relations Act, there was no formal direct regulation of the union-employer relationship. There was merely support for trade union organisation and for the collective bargaining process with no legal sanction or interference should collective bargaining break down. However, it has been argued that voluntarism was not resurrected by the reforms of 1974–79. There was a shift from the 'organic' approach of the State encouraging union growth and collective bargaining on a purely voluntary basis towards imposing it by indirect legal means via the rights provided to unions and union members and officials. For elaboration of this argument, see Clark, J, 'The juridification of industrial relations' (1985) 14 ILJ 69.

THE ROLE, SCOPE AND STRUCTURE OF COLLECTIVE BARGAINING[33]

Collective bargaining is a central and fundamental institution in British industrial relations. Collective bargaining provides workers, through their trade unions, with greater leverage and equality of negotiating power in the bargaining process with employers. Union representatives, acting on behalf of workers, are able to secure better terms and conditions of employment than could be achieved by individuals negotiating on their own behalf. Collective bargaining deals with all aspects of the employment relationship, not just with the content of the employment contract. The process frequently includes negotiation on matters such as on the content of day to day works rules and on procedural issues important to the worker and the functioning of the union in its relationship with an employer.

It is through this system of collective representation that workers can obtain influence over their employers and become involved in decisions that have a bearing on their experience of work. As the Donovan Commission stated:

> Properly conducted, collective bargaining is the most effective means of giving workers the right to representation in decisions affecting their working lives, a right which is or should be the prerogative of every worker in a democratic society.[34]

Collective bargaining in the United Kingdom is characterised by the multiplicity of bargaining levels and the diversity of bargaining within and between industries. The Donovan Commission,[35] set up in 1965 to report on improving industrial relations, broadly identified two forms of collective bargaining.[36] Agreements made at a national level throughout a particular industry, supplemented by regional or district agreements, were characterised as the product of 'formal' collective bargaining. Formal collective bargaining takes place within a well established negotiating framework. Employers in the relevant industry are represented through an employers' association and a confederation of unions by a joint negotiating panel.

Pressures imposed by unions for further bargaining at a lower level, such as at the individual employer or factory level, may result in the improvement on the terms and conditions agreed at the formal institutional level. This lower level of bargaining often conducted between shop stewards and local managers was classified as 'informal' bargaining by the Donovan Commission. Thus, the term collective bargaining covers an

---

33 For further description and analysis of the changing structure of collective bargaining and industrial relations see Clegg, H, *The Changing System of Industrial Relations in Great Britain*, 1979; Daniel, W and Millward, N, *Workplace Industrial Relations in Britain*, 1983; Millward, N and Stevens, M, *British Workplace Industrial Relations*, 1986; Batstone, E, *The Reform of Workplace Industrial Relations*, 1988; Millward, N *et al*, *Workplace Industrial Relations in Transition*, 1992; Jackson, M, *Decentralisation of Collective Bargaining*, 1993; Millward, N, *The New Industrial Relations?*, 1994; Edwards, P (ed), *Industrial Relations: Theory and Practice in Britain*, 1995; Beardwell, I (ed), *Contemporary Industrial Relations*, 1996; Cully, M *et al*, *Britain at Work*, 1999; Millward, N *et al*, *All Change at Work?*, 2000.

34 Paragraph 212.

35 Royal Commission on Trade Unions and Employers' Associations, Cmnd 3623, 1968.

36 See paras 143–54.

enormous range of bargaining experiences: from national officials negotiating with an employers' association representing multi-national organisations, down to the junior manager dealing with the concerns of the shop steward representing a section of the workforce in a factory.

Across industries there may well be a combination of formal and informal structures in place. Which system predominates in a given industry depends on the history of the industry,[37] the way the industry is organised and evolved custom and practice at the workplace.[38] Government also influences the method of bargaining prevalent across and within industries through industrial and economic policy.[39] One consequence of this vigorous and fluctuating bargaining process is that agreements relating to the same group of workers may operate at different levels. Thus, at times, the content of national, district, company or plant agreements may overlap. Where this occurs, legal solutions may be required to establish primacy.[40]

Once negotiations are completed, the agreements that emerge at whatever level of bargaining can be classified as procedural or substantive. Substantive agreements or substantive clauses establish the terms and conditions of employment for the relevant workers. Procedural agreements or procedural clauses regulate how substantive matters are to be determined, interpreted and applied and how conflicts stemming from the agreement are to be resolved. For example, a recognition agreement is a procedural agreement since it regulates when the parties shall meet, the subject matter or substance to be negotiated, what facilities will be provided to union officials to discharge their bargaining duties, etc.[41] A disputes agreement is procedural in that it provides a mechanism for both parties to bring up their concerns deriving from a substantive agreement or from other sources. These disputes agreements are wide-ranging and may also deal with issues that are particularly relevant to the individual worker, for example relating to procedure to be followed before dismissals and discipline. Accordingly, disputes procedure provides a method of dealing with conflict of whatever nature at the workplace.

Essentially, the British system is flexible and all-embracing. The lack of control by centralised union and employer organisations over the development of autonomous localised bargaining structures has resulted in a fluid and dynamic system of

---

37 The form of collective bargaining that evolved in any one industry was influenced by the type of trade union that predominated. As trade unions across industries developed in a piecemeal and *ad hoc* manner, so collective bargaining structures followed in a similar fashion.

38 For example, in industries dominated by a few large powerful unions, national bargaining has usually been predominant with less scope for local supplementary agreements.

39 The changes in bargaining methods achieved after 1974 were partly due to government initiatives to encourage more formalised company wide bargaining to replace informal plant and work group bargaining. There was also a growth in productivity bargaining-where improvement in terms and conditions is linked to changes in work practices and increases in production. During the time of the Conservative administrations from 1979–97, trends showed an increase in decentralised bargaining induced by explicit government policies which had focused on discouraging national collective bargaining.

40 See Chapter 8.

41 Negotiations dealing with procedural matters are often conducted at the national level and then applied at the local level.

bargaining.[42] Agreements are not normally legally binding between employer and union, nor are they fixed for a specific period. Although both parties to the bargain will regulate observance and agreements are regarded as socially binding or binding in honour, the lack of legal interference and the open-ended nature of agreements ensures that renegotiation and alteration can take place as circumstances dictate.

The system as described above has been traditionally defended as providing benefits to all parties. For the employer, industrial peace is maintained through the involvement of the union in the determination of the terms and conditions of employment of the workforce. Industrial action, if it is threatened, can be dealt with coherently within procedures established in the agreement. The employee will have gained a higher standard of reward than would probably be available by individual negotiation and will generally have some influence over developments at work through their union.

Thus, it is not surprising that since collective bargaining contributes to orderly industrial relations and improvements in the economic performance of industry, governments have nearly always encouraged this process by legal means. However, this broad consensus, both as to the positive advantages of voluntary collective bargaining and as to the appropriate role of the law, was eroded in the 1980s by the vigorous pursuit of an alternative political and industrial agenda.

The election of a Conservative Government in May 1979 heralded a departure in attitudes towards trade unions. Unions lost much of their influence over industrial and economic policy. Unions were no longer regarded as a partner, with industry and government, in the determination of policies to secure economic growth and prosperity. Indeed, the core role of unions in engaging in collective bargaining, was looked upon with some antipathy by the new administration. Collective bargaining merely drove up labour costs and distorted the efficient operation of the market. The argument that collective bargaining was worthy of support as an instrument of conflict regulation at the workplace was not acknowledged. Rather, to the new Government, conflict at work was a symptom of union power.

Policies to counter union influence at the workplace were developed, taking into account the lessons learnt from the debacle of the Industrial Relations Act 1971. All-embracing legal regulation of union activities was not imposed. Rather, change was gradual and came about through a combination of the effects of unfettered market forces and piecemeal restrictive legislation over 16 years. These economic and legislative changes had a dual effect. They resulted in a change in the scope and structure of bargaining and in a reduction in the numbers of workers covered by collective bargaining.

Economic policies encouraging free enterprise, open competition and efficiency produced rationalisation and business reorganisation in the private sector. The result of these economic policies in the public sector has been expenditure cuts, privatisation of nationalised industries and the enforced deregulation of public services. In combination with the severe recession in the early 1980s, which abetted the decline of traditional

---

42   Kahn-Freund contrasted this with the more formal system of collective bargaining applicable in the USA. There 'static' bargaining takes place with agreements of a fixed duration which are rarely altered during the currency of the agreement. See Kahn-Freund, O, *Labour Relations: Heritage and Adjustment*, 1979, Chapter 2 and Davies, P and Freedland, M (eds), *Labour and the Law*, 3rd edn, 1983, p 70.

manufacturing industries, these factors were the cause of unemployment and subsequent loss of union membership.[43]

The shift in the industrial structure of the economy has had a profound effect on the framework of collective bargaining. There has been a decline in the older heavily unionised manufacturing industries and a growth in employment in the poorly unionised service sector and new technology industries. This fragmentation of the labour market and change in the style of employment has altered working arrangements and bargaining patterns. In the newer industries, without previous experience of union representation, often recognition has been achieved only by competing unions agreeing to a single union deal – where one union is given sole representational rights.

In many traditional industries, where working methods have been revolutionised by new technology, national collective bargaining arrangements have been under attack. In some, albeit limited cases, the consequences of a review of bargaining arrangements has been the full de-recognition of previously established trade unions. In other instances, there has been a movement towards simplifying bargaining procedures – such as 'single table bargaining' where one union takes on the representative function for others in the plant or all unions take part together in a single bargaining forum.

Economic change has also had effects on bargaining in other sectors of the economy. Both in the public sector and parts of the private sector, employers have re-examined their relationship with unions as a consequence of organisational change. Increasingly, there has been a movement to devolved management structures within organisations and a reconfiguration of public and private concerns into autonomous self-governing units.[44] Many employers have also moved towards 'flexible working arrangements'[45] and 'performance related' and 'merit' pay where pay and conditions are related to organisational and personal targets. Consequently, there has been a steady shift away from often long standing national or industry-wide pay negotiations towards local devolved bargaining to tie rewards more closely to local labour and product market conditions. Where national negotiations survive, frequently these national agreements merely set a basic minimum, with wide variations between and within localities dependent on plant or workplace agreements tailored to local business needs.

The Conservative Government welcomed the development of these new bargaining relationships. In the publication *People, Jobs and Opportunity,*[46] the Government's view was that national collective bargaining '... runs counter to the objectives of rewarding

---

43   Clearly, one reason for the reduction in the numbers of those covered by collective bargaining is this loss of union membership. In 1980, union membership stood at over 13m. By 1990 it had declined to 9.8 m and by 1995 it had been reduced to 8.23 m (CO Annual Reports 1980, 1990 and 1995). This serious loss of membership caused unions to devise a variety of strategies to attempt to stem the loss. Some unions responded by emphasising the individual benefits of union membership often in conjunction with a high profile marketing campaign. Another union strategy has been to negotiate mergers as a way of securing sufficient economic power to deliver more effective bargaining and better individual services to their membership. For further analysis see Machin, S, 'Union decline in Britain' (2000) 38 BJIR 631.

44   A good example in the public sector is the establishment of NHS trusts and the consequent movement to decentralised bargaining within trusts.

45   Especially in areas where new technology had taken hold, employers were increasingly insisting on 'multi-skilling' productivity agreements to address the issue of union demarcation practices.

46   Cm 1810, 1992.

individual effort and performance and increasing job opportunities and choice through the operation of a more efficient labour market ...'.[47] In conclusion it was stated that '... the government will ... continue to encourage employers to move away from traditional, centralised collective bargaining to systems which reward individual skills and performance; respond to the wish of individual employees to negotiate their own terms and conditions of employment; and take full account of business circumstances'.[48]

Hence, legislation passed throughout the 1980s and early 1990s has expressly or impliedly facilitated these changes in bargaining. For example, statutory reforms[49] damaged the organisational base of trade unions, further exacerbating their loss of membership and weakening union internal structures. The derecognition of unions for bargaining purposes was implicitly supported by initiatives such as the repeal of the provisions on recognition procedure, the Fair Wages Resolution and other previously well established 'props' to bargaining. Even the role of ACAS to promote bargaining was curtailed. Legislation also made it more difficult for unions to utilise their major bargaining weapon of strike action. New restrictions on the right of employees to strike and on the procedural requirements a union has to comply with prior to calling a strike arguably reduced their power and effectiveness in negotiations.

Surveys conducted during this period show that there had been a decline in the number of workers covered by collective agreements,[50] although it was still the case that a majority (54%) of the workforce in 1990 had their terms and conditions of employment determined by collective bargaining.[51] However, by the end of the Conservative period of office, collective agreements applied to only 41% of workers[52] (due to, *inter alia*, the loss of union membership throughout the 1990s, derecognition, the demise of the traditional unionised industries and the rise of new working patterns based on part time, flexible, non-unionised labour). Further decline in the incidence of collective bargaining seems to have been arrested by the election of a Labour Government in 1997.[53] Changes in the law (such as the passage of supportive legislation granting trade unions the legal right to recognition and certain bargaining rights) have stimulated an increase in involuntary and voluntary recognition deals, thereby contributing to a resurgence of workplace bargaining. Whether these initiatives merely stall the decline in traditional forms of collective representation or herald a new era for British employment relations remains to be seen. However, what is certainly the case is that many employers continue to recognise the advantages of conducting workplace relationships with the formality and convenience that collective bargaining can bring and that collective bargaining, local or national, continues to play an established and central role in industrial relations.

---

47 Paragraph 4.3.
48 Paragraph 4.7.
49 Such as the limitations on the operation of closed shop arrangements.
50 See Brown, W, 'The contraction of collective bargaining in Britain' (1993) 31 BJIR 189.
51 *Op cit*, Millward *et al*, fn 33, p 92. This is a greater number than the total of union membership as many non-union personnel also have their terms and conditions determined by collective agreements. This is due to the contractual effect of collective agreements. An agreement negotiated by a recognised union is nearly always incorporated into the individual contract of employment of all employees at that workplace whether or not they are union members.
52 *Op cit*, Cully *et al*, fn 33, p 242.
53 See the Labour Force Survey 2000–01.

CHAPTER 8

LEGAL EFFECT OF COLLECTIVE AGREEMENTS

ENFORCEABILITY BETWEEN UNION AND EMPLOYER

A distinguishing feature of industrial relations in Britain is that collective agreements between trade unions and employers are not legally binding.[1] The Donovan Commission in 1968 noted that this was the case even though there was little legal authority to support such an assumption. The Commission put forward the view that collective bargains between a union and an employer were not legally binding because both parties did not intend the agreement to be enforceable.[2]

The issue was considered a year later in the High Court in 1969, when the Ford Motor Company, attempting to dispute the perceived wisdom of the time, brought an action alleging that the unions who were parties to the collective agreement had broken agreed procedures relating to industrial action.[3] Geoffrey Lane J, in a wide ranging analysis that took into account the academic consensus of the time[4] and the conclusions of the Donovan Commission, declared that the agreement was binding in honour only, since the essential element of an intention between the parties to create legal relations was absent. Although the case was not taken to appeal, Lane J's judgment was authority for the presumption that collective agreements were not legally binding. The presumption, of course, could be rebutted by contrary evidence, such as where an intention to be bound was explicitly stated within the agreement.[5]

In an attempt to control industrial action that arose from a breakdown in collective bargaining, the Industrial Relations Act 1971 created a statutory presumption that collective agreements were legally binding unless the parties declared otherwise. This attempt at imposing legal enforceability on agreements failed since neither employers nor unions wished to be answerable to the courts for their failures to honour procedural agreements. In practice, the vast majority of agreements during this period negated the statutory presumption by including the clause 'This is not a legally enforceable document' (the so called TINALEA clause). When the Industrial Relations Act was repealed and replaced by the Trade Union and Labour Relations Act 1974 the

---

1   For foreign comparisons, see Lord Wedderburn, 'Inderogability, collective agreements and community law' (1992) 21 ILJ 245.

2   Paragraphs 470–74.

3   *Ford Motor Co Ltd v AUEW* [1969] 2 QB 303. Noted by Selwyn, N in 'Collective agreements and the law' (1969) 32 MLR 377. See also the critical article by Hepple, B, 'Intention to create legal relations' [1970] CLJ 122. The *Ford* decision was followed in *Stuart v Ministry of Defence* [1973] IRLR 143.

4   The writings of Kahn-Freund, arguing that collective agreements were not enforceable at the collective level, were particularly influential. See 'Legal framework' in Flanders, A and Clegg, H (eds), *The System of Industrial Relations in Great Britain*, 1959; Davies, P and Freedland, M, *Labour Legislation and Public Policy*, 1993, pp 158–66. For an excellent review of Kahn-Freund's analysis see Lewis, R, 'Collective agreements, the Kahn-Freund legacy' (1979) 42 MLR 613.

5   For a full review of the legal and industrial issues relating to the non-binding nature of collective agreements, see Lewis, R, 'The legal enforceability of collective agreements' (1970) 8 BJIR 313. See also a later analysis by Wilson, A, 'Contract and prerogative: a reconsideration of the legal enforcement of collective agreements' (1984) 13 ILJ 1.

presumption of non-enforceability at common law was put on a statutory footing.[6] In its present form, it is contained in s 179(1) of the Trade Union and Labour Relations (Consolidation) Act (TULR(C)A) 1992. This states that it is presumed that a collective agreement is not legally enforceable unless the agreement is in writing and specifies that it is intended to be legally enforceable.

There are very few examples of unions and employers entering into such formal arrangements. In the early 1990s, the Conservative Government's Green Paper, *Industrial Relations in the 1990s*,[7] outlined the advantages of legally binding collective agreements.[8] Primarily, it was suggested that these arrangements would bring the UK into line with the position in North America and Europe and so would be a way of encouraging foreign companies to invest in the UK. It was also stated that, by legally formalising arrangements, the intermittent revision of agreements by trade unions would be discouraged and industrial relations would become more certain and secure. The Green Paper also noted the increasing acceptance of legal intervention in industrial relations and the movement towards more localised bargaining based on smaller units. It thus surmised that these factors would make enforcement easier than had been the case in the past. As a consequence of these arguments, the Green Paper formally recommended that the statutory presumption should be reversed.[9]

Although there has been no legislation implementing the recommendation of the Green Paper, and unlikely to be in the near future, the proliferation of single union deals in the 1980s, incorporating binding 'industrial peace' obligations, demonstrate that, in certain limited circumstances, employers may insist on partially binding legal agreements.

Single union deals and 'no-strike' clauses

During the 1980s, it became common for foreign companies (intending to set up new factories, and so not in established bargaining units) to attempt to streamline the number of unions they bargain with. Exclusive negotiating rights are offered to just one union which represents all workers – skilled, unskilled and managerial staff. For many foreign organisations, used to these single union deals and binding collective agreements, the trade off for exclusive bargaining rights is usually job flexibility, legally binding dispute

---

6   On the application of the statutory presumption, see *NCB v NUM* [1986] ICR 736 and *Monterosso Shipping Co Ltd v ITF* [1982] IRLR 468.

7   Cm 1602, 1991, Chapter 8.

8   The Donovan Commission (paras 469, 473–82) rejected enforceable collective bargains as unworkable in the industrial circumstances prevailing at that time. In 1981, the Conservative Government's Green Paper, *Trade Union Immunities*, Cmnd 8128, paras 215–44, considered whether a change in the contractual status of collective agreements was appropriate. After a review of the arguments no clear recommendation was made.

9   The object behind making collective agreements contractually binding is to give employers legal sanctions (in the form of damages or injunctions) against unions in breach of disputes procedures. Yet, as we shall see in Chapter 15, industrial action is only lawful in limited circumstances and where the union has adhered to a complex procedure. Thus, employers usually have ample opportunity to take action to stop a strike. Enforceable collective agreements would, arguably, generate additional and unnecessary legal control over trade unions.

arbitration[10] and no strike deals.[11] As we saw above, these exclusive recognition agreements are not legally binding, unless employer and union comply with s 179 of the TULR(C)A 1992. Consequently, many single union deals have included such a provision.

This is a controversial development since single union deals may conflict with the TUC's Bridlington Agreement.[12] This attempts to defuse membership recruitment rivalry between unions at the same workplace. Under Bridlington, the TUC will inquire into the circumstances of the dispute and, if necessary, allocate sole rights of organisation and recruitment to a specified union. Single union arrangements clearly interfere with this internal disputes procedure.[13] In 1985, the TUC resolved that no union should enter into single union arrangements which would have the effect of depriving another union of existing rights of recognition. In 1988, the TUC adopted a Code of Practice to help resolve escalating disputes between unions competing for representation rights. A notification procedure was put in place. Any union intending to agree a single union deal should first inform the TUC. Where other unions have representation in the industry, a conciliation process will be activated before any formal reference to the TUC Disputes Committee.[14]

Any no-strike clause within a single union agreement is still opposed in principle by the TUC. Principle 3 of the Bridlington Procedures states that unions must not make agreements that remove the basic democratic and lawful rights of trade union members to take industrial action. Any TUC affiliated union that accepts such a provision in a collective agreement is in danger of being expelled, as the EEPTU was in 1988 for single-mindedly pursuing single union and strike-free deals. Even if a no-strike (mandatory arbitration) clause is contained in a collective agreement, there is doubt as to its practical legal significance. Whether such a clause is considered legally binding on an individual employee or on a union is considered later.

ENFORCEABILITY BETWEEN EMPLOYEE AND EMPLOYER[15]

Although collective agreements are not ordinarily of any legal significance between employer and union, if they are translated into a contractual relationship between employer and employee, then they do have legal force. To assume contractual validity,

---

10 Often, so called 'pendulum arbitration' arrangements are enshrined in the agreement. Here, the arbitrator does not broker a compromise agreement between the parties but has to choose between the employer's offer and the union's response. See, generally, Wood, J (Sir), 'Last offer arbitration' (1985) 23 BJIR 415 and Lewis, R, 'Strike-free deals and pendulum arbitration' (1990) 28 BJIR 32.

11 It is not always foreign companies that demand these arrangements. Domestic companies that start up new plant or relocate to 'greenfield sites' may also alter their bargaining arrangements. The best known example is where News International relocated to Wapping in 1986 and only recognised the EEPTU for the purposes of collective bargaining.

12 For background to this agreement, see Chapter 6.

13 Single union arrangements are also viewed with suspicion since they are inevitably employer-led initiatives. It is argued that these 'union beauty contests' result in the employer choosing the most compliant union in the weakest bargaining position.

14 For an analysis of how effective the TUC disputes machinery is in resolving disputes over single union agreements, see Elgar, J and Simpson, R, 'A final appraisal of Bridlington: an evaluation of TUC Disputes Committee decisions 1974–91' (1994) 32 BJIR 47, pp 57–62. Refer also to Simpson, R, 'Bridlington 2' (1994) 23 ILJ 170.

15 See generally, on this, Kahn-Freund, O in *op cit*, Davies and Freedland, fn 4, pp 166–84.

the agreement must be incorporated into the contract of employment expressly or impliedly and the relevant clauses of the collective agreement must be capable of being legally binding between the employer and the employee.[16]

Express incorporation

The most effective way for the collective agreement to be incorporated is for the employment contract to refer expressly to the relevant agreement. The reference should be clear and unambiguous. For example, in *Robertson and Jackson v British Gas Co Ltd*[17] the appropriate contract read: 'The provision of the agreement of the National Joint Council ... relating to remuneration and increments will apply to you ...' This was sufficient to incorporate the terms of an incentive bonus scheme negotiated between union and employer into the contract of employment.

The form of incorporation may give advance authority to the union to negotiate subsequent agreements. So, in *NCB v Galley*,[18] miners' written contracts specified that wages were regulated by the 'national agreements for the time being in force'. The particular agreement in force at the time required Galley to work overtime. Galley argued that, since there was nothing specific in his contract referring to the need to work overtime, he had not agreed to it and so it was not a valid term of his contract. The court held on the interpretation of the phrase '... for the time being in force' that Galley had expressly agreed in advance to his wages being determined in this manner. The provision in the renegotiated collective agreement on compulsory overtime had become a valid term of Galley's employment contract without it having to be specifically written into his contract.[19]

The most useful mechanism for express incorporation is often the written particulars of employment or statutory statement that every employer is bound to supply to any new employee. To help identify the most important express terms ss 1–7 of the Employment Rights Act 1996 (previously ss 1–6 of the the Employment Protection (Consolidation) Act 1978 as amended by the Trade Union Reform and Employment Rights Act 1993)[20] establish that within two months of acceptance of employment, an employee must be issued with a statement of his or her particulars of employment. The particulars should include information such as the names of the parties, hours of work, rate of pay, holiday entitlement, etc. This statutory statement or written particulars of employment is good evidence of what has been agreed between the parties and so will often be a binding

---

16 Note that whether a valid collective agreement exists is dependent solely upon whether an agreement between the parties has been reached. This could be through an informal process (such as an exchange of letters), so long as there is a mutual intention on the part of both parties to enter into a bargain – see *Burke v Royal Liverpool University Hospital NHS Trust* [1997] ICR 730 and *Edinburgh Council v Brown* [1999] IRLR 208.

17 [1983] ICR 351. For comment, see Leighton, P (1983) 12 ILJ 115.

18 [1958] 1 WLR 16.

19 See also *Keir and Williams v Hereford and Worcester CC* [1985] IRLR 505.

20 Amendments were made as a consequence of the European Community Directive (91/533/EEC). For the changes introduced by the Directive see Clark, J and Hall, M (1992) 21 ILJ 106.

contractual document, unless there is rebutting evidence of an alternative agreement on different terms.[21]

Prior to the changes introduced by the 1993 Act, it was permissible for details on most of these matters to be notified to an employee by reference to another document, that is, a collective agreement. An express clause of this nature in a statutory statement would ordinarily incorporate the terms of the relevant collective agreement into an individual's contract (subject to rebutting evidence noted above). Now the majority of particulars[22] and any subsequent alterations must be explicitly provided in a full written statement. Additionally, a new provision,[23] introduced in 1993, provides that the statement must contain details of 'any collective agreements which directly affect the terms and conditions of the employment'.

Where the provisions of a collective agreement are fully reproduced in the written particulars of employment, there should be little doubt of their incorporation as part of the individual contract. If, in practice, some employers fail to adhere to the new statutory requirements and refer (as previously permitted) to the collective agreement in name only, that does not necessarily mean that the collective agreement has no effect at the individual level. As the content of the contract is a matter of common law, the express reference[24] will probably still have contractual effect.[25]

Implied incorporation

If the collective agreement is not expressly incorporated through the statutory statement or through any specific written contract, it is still possible for the agreement to have legal effect if the agreement is impliedly incorporated into the contract of employment. In strict legal terms, the courts look for some form of implied agreement that the collective bargain is binding. They consider whether the facts indicate that the employer and employee intended that the relevant part of the collective agreement should be part of the employment contract. Intention can be derived from knowledge of the provisions of the agreement and subsequent conduct. However, problems have arisen over the level of knowledge of the collective agreement and the appropriate conduct necessary to establish intention.

Many industrial relations commentators support the notion that industrial common sense demands that, since a national level collective agreement provides a well accepted standard throughout a particular industry, this is automatically part of a contract of employment on the basis of industrial custom and practice. Kahn-Freund, in his seminal

---

21 See *Gascol Conversions Ltd v Mercer* [1974] ICR 420; *Systems Floors Ltd v Daniel* [1982] ICR 54; *Robertson and Jackson v British Gas Co Ltd* [1983] ICR 351; *Trusthouse Forte Ltd v Adonis* [1984] IRLR 382; *Eagland v British Telecommunications plc* [1992] IRLR 323.

22 Section 2 permits referral to 'some other document' for provisions on sickness and pensions.

23 Section 1(4)(j).

24 As we saw earlier in *Robertson and Jackson v British Gas Ltd* [1983] ICR 351.

25 Note that where the collective agreement provides that the agreement is 'binding in honour only' this does not affect the express incorporation of terms into an individual contract. Such a clause is merely repeating the presumption of non-enforceability at the collective level – *Marley v Forward Trust Group Ltd* [1986] IRLR 369. For comment, see MacLean, H (1987) 16 ILJ 59.

work, *Labour and the Law*,[26] building on earlier writings, characterised this process as 'crystallised custom'. The provisions of the collective agreement are tacitly embodied into the contract of employment by the unexpressed assumptions of the parties; an unchallenged consensus between them. There is no requirement for any particular level of knowledge or positive affirmative response as both parties passively expect that the terms of the employment contract are governed by the existing collective agreement. There is, however, precious little legal authority for this view.

When deciding whether to incorporate a collective agreement on the basis of custom and practice the courts have preferred to apply explicit legal criteria. The custom has to be a well known and accepted practice of a particular industry or trade.[27] In *Duke v Reliance Systems Ltd*,[28] the Court of Appeal restated the test that a collective agreement would need to be 'clear, certain and notorious' before it could be incorporated on the basis of custom. Clarity and certainty may be present but the concept of notoriety requires both a level of knowledge of the agreement and adherence to it for a substantial period of time.[29] Collective agreements that follow the criteria will be incorporated. For example, in *McLea v Essex Lines*[30] the terms of a well established, and therefore well known, collective agreement were incorporated into the contracts of merchant seamen, since evidence was available that it had been followed in the past for a number of years.

Even though 'crystallised custom' as a basis for automatic incorporation has had little legal support, it still has some residual legal importance. This was illustrated by the decision in *Howman and Son v Blyth*.[31] A national agreement on sick pay was not formally incorporated, expressly or impliedly, but since there was a gap in the contract it was necessary to imply a term on sick pay. The clauses in a non-incorporated collective agreement were, therefore, used as a guide in determining on what terms sick pay should be implied.

It is clear that the mere existence of a collective agreement does not mean that it is incorporated through industrial relations practice. However, the fact that both parties have universally observed the agreement at the workplace is evidence of implied agreement: for example, incorporation is readily implied where wage rates have always been fixed by reference to a collective agreement without protest. This presumption of incorporation can be countered where a new collective agreement has been negotiated and the individual worker objects to the new provisions. This is clearly illustrated by *Singh v British Steel Corp*.[32] Singh had previously been a union member and had adhered to all previous collective agreements. After a disagreement, he left the union before a new shift system had been negotiated introducing new hours of work. Singh refused to work the new shift, arguing that his terms of employment were unaffected by the newly

---

26 *Op cit*, Davies and Freedland, fn 4.

27 See *Meek v Port of London Authority* [1918] 1 Ch 415 and *Sagar v Ridehalgh* [1931] 1 Ch 310.

28 [1982] IRLR 347.

29 For a further example of this strict approach to incorporation, see *Hamilton v Futura Floors Ltd* [1990] IRLR 478. However, by contrast, see the EAT's analysis of custom and practice in *Henry v London General Transport Services Ltd* [2001] IRLR 132.

30 (1933) 45 LLR 254.

31 [1983] ICR 416. For comment, see (1983) 99 LQR 494.

32 [1974] IRLR 131.

negotiated collective agreement since it was not expressly incorporated into his contract. The court accepted the argument that, as he had formally rejected the new agreement, any change was a unilateral variation which he was not bound to accept. Although Singh had knowledge of the new agreement there was no evidence that he agreed to it. Any previous implied acceptance through acquiescence was no longer relevant since he had expressly renounced the agreement.[33]

Evidence of acceptance of the new or changed collective agreement does, of course, serve as a basis for implying incorporation of the new agreement. In *Joel v Cammell Laird Shiprepairers Ltd*,[34] the collective agreement introduced job flexibility with a consequent increase in pay. Joel refused to change his work practices, yet did accept the related pay rise. His conduct clearly was good evidence to the court that he had in reality accepted the contents of the collective agreement.

On the basis of an analysis of these cases, it can be said that the extent of the worker's knowledge of the collective agreement and conduct in response to it play a major part in determining whether a collective agreement is impliedly incorporated. The greater the knowledge and subsequent conduct the more likely the agreement is impliedly incorporated.[35]

Incorporation by way of agency

In *Heatons Transport Ltd v TGWU*,[36] the House of Lords cautiously seemed to have approved the principle that trade union members automatically authorise the results of negotiations by union officials on the basis that the union acts as the members' agent. This has not been regarded as an attractive solution to the problem of the incorporation of collective agreements due to the anomalies it would create. As only union members would be bound, non-union employees could opt out of collective agreements. Thus, some workers would be able to enforce and have enforced against them, terms and conditions of employment that did not apply to others. In *Burton Group Ltd v Smith*,[37] the Employment Appeals Tribunal (EAT) dismissed the notion of an agency relationship arising solely by virtue of union membership. Any agency relationship must derive from the particular facts of the case and does not arise automatically from the relationship of union and member.[38]

However, union membership may well be relevant when determining whether a collective agreement has been impliedly incorporated on the basis of the principles discussed above. It may be assumed by the court, as a matter of evidence that, if the employee is a union member, then he or she has greater knowledge of union negotiations than non-members and so mere acquiescence is sufficient to establish incorporation. In

---

33   See also the EAT decision in *Land v West Yorkshire Metropolitan CC* [1979] ICR 452.

34   [1969] ITR 206.

35   Note that, in *Bond v CAV Ltd* [1983] IRLR 360, an alternative device was used to give the collective agreement contractual force. Pain J ruled that the collective agreement was binding on the individual as a supplemental agreement to the contract of employment.

36   [1973] AC 15.

37   [1977] IRLR 351.

38   See also Denning's comments on the agency issue and *Heatons Transport* decision, in *Chappell v Times Newspapers* [1975] ICR 145, pp 172 and 173.

Nelson v The Post Office,[39] the employee was bound by the collective agreement despite his objections to a particular clause after the agreement had been finalised. The fact that he was a member of the relevant union indicated to the court that he had intended to be bound by the agreement. Union membership was also specifically referred to in *Gray Dunn v Edwards*,[40] as a pertinent and major factor in determining intention. Edwards had been disciplined under an agreed disciplinary code. On the question whether this code had been incorporated into his employment contract, Lord McDonald stated: 'Where employers negotiate a detailed agreement with a recognised union, they are entitled to assume all employees who are members of the union know of and are bound by its provisions.'[41]

In conclusion, if the agreement has been expressly incorporated, then it is of direct legal effect. The employee may later attempt to refute the incorporation clause but this would not be of any consequence.[42] Union membership or non-membership is also of no relevance here. The employee has formally pledged acceptance of incorporation. If express incorporation is missing, then the courts look for some deemed acceptance. The degree of evidence required for these purposes is variable, but actual or assumed knowledge of the agreement and subsequent behaviour would be sufficient. There seems to be little clear and unequivocal support for the notion of automatic incorporation *via* 'crystallised custom'.

Incorporation of individual, not collective, clauses [43]

Not all provisions of a collective agreement are suitable for incorporation into an individual's contract of employment. For a clause to be capable of incorporation, it must specifically relate to a substantive issue, that is, an individual's terms and conditions of employment.[44] Matters of industrial policy or procedural matters that are essentially collective in nature, that is, of more relevance to the union than the individual worker, are not capable of incorporation. This is clearly demonstrated in the cases dealing with the withdrawal of recognition from unions. In *Gallagher v The Post Office*,[45] the plaintiff argued that the relevant clause in the collective agreement guaranteeing recognition for the plaintiff's union was incorporated into his contract of employment. Thus, the employer's breach of this clause by withdrawing recognition from the union was a breach of the plaintiff's employment contract. Brightman J held that the content of this clause was a matter of concern only between the union and the employer. It was not a substantive term suitable for incorporation into the employment contract and for enforcement by the plaintiff against the employer.

---

39   [1978] IRLR 548.
40   [1980] IRLR 23.
41   At p 24.
42   See *Tocher v General Motors Scotland Ltd* [1981] IRLR 55.
43   See, generally, *op cit*, Davies and Freedland, fn 4, pp 289–97.
44   It also must be clear and certain, rather than vague and imprecise. See *Lee v GEC Telecommunications* [1993] IRLR 383.
45   [1970] 3 All ER 712.

A similar decision was made by the High Court in *NCB v NUM*.[46] The NUM had been given exclusive recognition for collective bargaining purposes by virtue of s 46 of the Coal Nationalisation Act 1945. The Coal Board unilaterally terminated the provision so as to include the new Union of Democratic Mineworkers (UDM) as a negotiating partner. The question as to whether this exclusive recognition deal had been incorporated into members' contracts was dealt with swiftly. Scott J followed the argument in *Gallagher* that recognition rights contained in a collective agreement are a procedural collective matter and so are not appropriate for incorporation. This is not to say, however, that trade union support agreements are always deemed to be procedural matters. The Court of Appeal has accepted that it was arguable that a sufficiently clear and specific collective agreement which provided workplace facilities for trade union officials is capable of incorporation into the individual contract of a particular shop steward.[47]

The distinction between individual matters that are appropriate for incorporation and procedural matters that are not can at times be a relatively fine one.[48] This can be illustrated by contrasting the decisions in *British Leyland v McQuilken*[49] and *Marley v Forward Trust Group*.[50] In *McQuilken*, a collective agreement was negotiated on redundancy issues. This was not capable of incorporation since it was interpreted by the court as a long term policy statement about how redundancies should be handled should they occur. Thus, as a procedural matter of concern only to the union and employer, this was not suitable for incorporation into individual contracts. By contrast, in *Marley v Forward Trust Group*, the agreement between union and employer contained a detailed plan of action following redundancy. Clauses outlined that employees should be given the opportunity to take on new posts for a six month trial period and that their redundancy rights were not affected if, after the six month period, they did not wish to continue in the trial post. Unlike the case in *McQuilken*, the agreement was specific enough and would sufficiently affect the individual to make it appropriate for incorporation into an employment contract.[51]

Whether a particular clause is suited for incorporation also depends on whether the parties intend it to be incorporated and binding on themselves. In *Marley v Forward Trust Group*, evidence was put forward and accepted that this was the intention of the parties. In *Alexander v Standard Telephones (No 2)*,[52] Hobhouse J regarded the inference of contractual intent as central to the decision on whether a clause is apt for incorporation. Here, the collective agreement was a long and discursive document which included clauses on redundancy procedure. These clauses outlined a selection procedure that included calling for volunteers first, followed, if necessary, by selection based on the 'last

---

46 [1986] IRLR 439. For comment, see Rees, W, 'A minefield for industrial relations' (1987) 50 MLR 100.

47 *NUPE v City and Hackney AHA* [1985] IRLR 252.

48 Note the problems the courts have in deciding whether the provisions of natural justice are appropriate for incorporation – *Lee v Jones* [1980] ICR 310.

49 [1978] IRLR 245.

50 [1986] IRLR 369.

51 For another example of incorporated redundancy procedure, see *Anderson v Pringle of Scotland Ltd* [1998] IRLR 64.

52 [1991] IRLR 286.

in, first out' criteria. When redundancies were required, the employer refuted the agreement. Hobhouse J came to the conclusion that the agreement as a whole was predominantly on industrial issues and so of collective interest only. Although the redundancy clauses were more specific, there was nothing to suggest that these clauses should be treated any differently from the rest of the agreement, essentially because there was no evidence to suggest the parties intended them to be binding.[53]

Incorporation of 'no-strike' clauses[54]

If effectively incorporated into an individual contract of employment, a specific no-strike clause that prohibits or restricts industrial action is a limitation on union activity and on an individual worker's freedom to withdraw their labour. Normally, no-strike clauses do not specifically ban a resort to industrial action, but rather attempt to enforce the exhaustion of agreed procedures before industrial action takes place. Ordinarily, this agreed dispute procedure clause, contained in a collective agreement, is regarded as not being apt for incorporation into an individual contract.[55]

However, as a consequence of legislative developments, a mandatory 'industrial peace' clause is capable of incorporation in certain circumstances. Section 180 of the TULR(C)A 1992 (originally introduced by the Trade Union and Labour Relations Act 1974)[56] provides that such a clause in a collective agreement can be lawfully incorporated into an individual contract of employment where the collective agreement is made by an independent trade union, is readily accessible for workers to consult, is in writing and expressly states that the term is incorporated.

Since industrial action is usually a breach of an employment contract anyway, irrespective of an enforceable clause in a collective agreement, the legal implications of strike action for the individual are the same irrespective of whether such a clause in a collective agreement is violated. A 'no-strike' clause merely serves as a warning to the union of the consequences of industrial action and has a deterrent effect at the individual level.

Conflicting collective agreements

Where there are different levels of bargaining, there is always the possibility of a clash between local and national agreements. Where this occurs, the issue arises of which agreement has legal primacy. The few cases directly on this point have tended to suggest that national agreements have primacy. In *Loman v Merseyside Transport*,[57] Lord Parker CJ

---

53   See also *Young v Canadian Northern Rly Co* [1931] AC 83.
54   See, on this issue, Anderman, S, 'The status quo issue and industrial disputes: some implications for labour law' (1975) 4 ILJ 131, pp 139–46 and *op cit*, Lewis, fn 10, pp 37–43.
55   See *Tadd v Eastwood and Daily Telegraph Ltd* [1983] IRLR 320.
56   Despite a general belief that these clauses were purely of a collective interest and so not enforceable, the Court of Appeal, in *Camden Exhibition v Lynott* [1966] 1 QB 55, inferred that such a clause may well be capable of incorporation into a contract of employment. The Labour Government in 1974 legislated to resolve the uncertainty. The original purpose behind the legislative intervention was to provide safeguards against the incorporation of such clauses. Yet, the provision arguably has the opposite effect.
57   (1968) 3 ITR 108. Noted by Wedderburn, KW (now Lord) (1969) 32 MLR 99.

in the Divisional Court said both 'in law and common sense', where conflict arises between local and national provisions and there is no evidence which has priority, the national agreement should be followed in preference to a local agreement. The Master of the Rolls, Lord Denning, essentially concurred in that view in *Gascol Conversions Ltd v Mercer*[58] – unless there is evidence to the contrary a national agreement should take precedence.[59]

In *Barnett v NCB*,[60] the EAT felt that this was too simplistic an approach to the problem. The crucial issue to consider is the intention of the parties. If the local agreement was made after the national agreement (as a supplement or addition to it), then the parties might reasonably expect that matters in the local agreement, which depart from the nationally agreed terms, would have priority over the national agreement.[61] Alternatively, it could be argued that since the local agreement is usually more immediate there is a presumption that this has priority, whether negotiated before or after a national agreement, unless there is a clear inference from the evidence that the intention of the parties was for the national agreement to take precedence.[62]

Variation and change of a collective agreement

Since relevant clauses of a collective agreement, once incorporated, form part of an individual's employment contract change is governed by the traditional common law rules which emphasise the need for mutual consent. Thus, it is not possible for an employer lawfully to vary or revoke the collective agreement without consent of the employee, nor for the employee to refute a new collective agreement negotiated between union and employer.

The consent of the employee is automatic if there is a valid variation clause contained in a binding statutory statement or other written document.[63] In that situation, the employee is, in advance, expressly agreeing to be bound by the changes to the collective agreement. Such clauses usually presuppose that any variation has been agreed between employer and union, although it is possible for an express clause to be agreed which permits a unilateral change by an employer.[64]

Where there has not been express incorporation of the collective agreement, but implied incorporation, any new collective agreement negotiated with the relevant union, will normally be binding on the employee in the same way as the previous agreement was. Although, as we saw earlier in *Singh v British Steel Corp*,[65] where an agreement is

---

58 [1974] IRLR 155. For commentary and criticisms of this decision, see Hepple, B (1974) 3 ILJ 164.

59 See also *Clift v West Riding CC* (1964) *The Times*, 10 April.

60 [1978] ICR 1102.

61 Also, see *Donelan v Kerby Construction Ltd* [1983] IRLR 191, noted by Freedland, M (1983) 12 ILJ 256.

62 See *dicta* by Lawton LJ to this effect in *Gascol Conversions Ltd v Mercer* [1974] IRLR 155.

63 Such as in *NCB v Galley* [1958] 1 WLR 16, considered earlier.

64 Note that in *Airlie v Edinburgh DC* [1996] IRLR 516, the EAT held that in certain circumstances an employer could have an implied right to vary a collective agreement. Here, the EAT construed the employer's right unilaterally to vary a collectively agreed incentive bonus scheme, from the termination provisions of the collective agreement, and from clauses in the bonus scheme permitting management control over its operation.

65 [1974] IRLR 131.

only impliedly incorporated there is greater scope for an employee to reject the new collective agreement.

Where the employer attempts unilaterally to withdraw from the collective agreement, without the consent of the union or employee, such abrogation has no affect on the individual contract of employment.[66] Termination of the collective agreement does not alter the terms of the individual contract which are already incorporated from the collective agreement. In *Miller v Hamworthy Engineering*,[67] the collective agreement providing for a guaranteed weekly wage was ignored by the employer who instituted a three day week due to a loss of orders. As there was no evidence that the employee or union had consented to the change, the employer was in breach of the employment contract and employees were able to recover loss of wages.

A similar situation arose in *Burroughs Machines Ltd v Timmoney*.[68] The employers' federation negotiated a collective agreement establishing a level of work and guaranteed pay within the industry. Contained in the collective agreement was a provision that guaranteed pay could be suspended during any industrial action. Two years after having resigned from the federation the employer, relying on the collective agreement, refused to provide guaranteed pay during a period of industrial action. It was held that the fact of resignation from the employers' federation had no effect on the contractual position between employer and employees. The agreement had been incorporated at the time of membership: the employer leaving the negotiating forum did not affect this incorporation.[69]

In *Lee v GEC Telecommunications Ltd*,[70] the employer argued that by issuing a new statutory statement of employment particulars, which did not refer to the previously incorporated collective agreement, any employee who did not formally object to the changes in the statement had consented to the variation. The EAT regarded a failure of the relevant employees to respond as insufficient evidence of consent to the change in terms of employment. As the imposed change was a unilateral variation, it was not legally effective at the individual level and the employer remained bound by the incorporated terms of the collective agreement.[71]

However, in the course of the judgment, the EAT indicated that, in the absence of agreement with the appropriate trade union or of a clause in the collective agreement permitting unilateral variation, express (rather than implied) consent of an individual employee to a variation of terms of employment derived from a collective agreement would be valid.

The EAT's comments suggest that consent for change does not have to be directed towards trade unions but may be obtained from individual employees. So, where a trade union refuses to renegotiate a collective agreement, the trade union can be outflanked by

---

66 This principle, thus, applies where unions are derecognised. Any collective agreement at the individual level remains contractually valid.

67 [1986] IRLR 461.

68 [1977] IRLR 404. For comment, see Freedland, M (1976) 5 ILJ 254 and Upex, R (1978) 7 ILJ 133.

69 See also *Gibbons v Associated British Ports* [1985] IRLR 376 and commentary by Napier, B (1986) 15 ILJ 52 on *Cadoux v Central Regional Council* [1986] IRLR 132.

70 [1993] IRLR 383.

71 See also *Davies v Hotpoint Ltd* [1994] IRLR 538.

the employer directly obtaining the consent of the workforce. In circumstances where unilateral change is sweetened by pay rises, individual employees will react differently; some may accept, others reject. The upshot of this is that employees, of the same union and in the same job, may work under different terms and conditions. In these circumstances, the role of a trade union as a channel of communication is undermined as is the notion of collective bargaining itself. Although in practice this rarely occurs, the legality of such a process demonstrates how the framework of the common law, with its emphasis on individual consent, is unable to adapt to take account of the 'collective' nature of collective bargains.[72]

---

72 On whether such a scenario would be contrary to legislation protecting the benefits of union membership, see Chapter 9, pp 184–92.

CHAPTER 9

INDIVIDUAL RIGHTS FOR UNION MEMBERS AND OFFICIALS

The right to associate in trade unions *per se*, without hindrance from the State, was secured by the repeal of the criminal conspiracy laws in the 19th century. This right, however, is of little value where an employer's hostility to trade unions is manifested by discrimination against trade union members at the workplace. Consequently, an important facet of freedom of association in trade unions is the liberty to join trade unions and participate in union activities without retribution from employers.

One strategy for securing effective freedom of association is to rely solely on trade union strength.[1] An alternative approach is to develop a system of legal rights to augment trade union efforts. The Conservative Government, through the Industrial Relations Act 1971, attempted to provide some legal support for freedom of association. As this was dependent upon trade unions agreeing to limit their rights in other areas, it was not a conspicuous success. The Labour Government from 1974, following the recommendations of the Donovan Commission,[2] legislated extensively in this area. According to Wedderburn: 'British law [was] building a collective "right to associate" out of the bricks of certain individual employment rights.'[3]

These individual rights (to paid and unpaid time off, protection against dismissal or victimisation for trade union membership or activities, protection against anti-union hiring policies) clearly have an additional collective dimension. Assertive and strong trade unions are essential for genuine collective bargaining. The provision of rights to individual union members and officials builds union strength by reinforcing the internal organisation of trade unions. It is in this way that the protection of individual rights assists unions in their collective bargaining function.

The original provisions were, of course, created in an era of strong support for collective bargaining and freedom of association. Government policy from 1979–97 was opposed to this way of conducting industrial relations. Hence, legal and economic developments in this era weakened their effectiveness. The Labour administration has made an attempt to reverse aspects of these legislative restrictions and has created a new right for all individual employees to be accompanied (by a union official or other person of the employee's choice) at grievance or disciplinary proceedings (see pp 194–98).

---

1   The Donovan Commission noted in para 243 that the TUC did not press for legislation as it was believed that industrial pressure was the most effective and reliable way of securing freedom of association and collective bargaining.

2   The Donovan Commission (paras 244–46 and 545) supported the legal protection of the positive right to associate as the Commission believed that this would encourage the reform and extension of collective bargaining.

3   Wedderburn, KW (now Lord), 'The Employment Protection Act: collective aspects' (1976) 39 MLR 169.

PAID AND UNPAID TIME OFF

These rights were originally contained in the Employment Protection Act 1975 as part of the Social Contract agreement between the Labour Government and the Trades Union Congress (TUC). They were consolidated into ss 27 and 28 of the Employment Protection (Consolidation) Act 1978, amended by the Employment Act 1989 and then reconsolidated as ss 168–73 of the Trade Union and Labour Relations (Consolidation) Act (TULR(C)A) 1992.

Arguably, trade union officials are more likely to carry out their duties effectively if they possess skills and knowledge relevant to their duties. Therefore, the rationale behind the original provision of these rights was that collective bargaining would be more effectively discharged if workplace representatives had the opportunity to acquire the skills of negotiation and the time to perform their negotiating functions. The efficient performance of collective bargaining is logically in the interests of employers, as well as trade unions. This is the justification for these rights put forward by the Advisory, Conciliation and Arbitration Service (ACAS) in the Code of Practice on Time Off (see below). The Code states that the provisions work to the mutual advantage of both parties in aiding and improving '... the effectiveness of relationships between employers and trade unions'.[4]

It was perhaps not surprising that the operation of these rights caused concern to the Conservative Government, particularly the right to paid time off for trade union duties. This unease was voiced in the White Paper, *Building Businesses – Not Barriers*.[5] Disquiet was expressed at the wide ranging nature of the industrial relations duties for which trade union officials have a statutory right to paid time off and the financial implications for employers.

The consequence of these and other criticisms were amendments to the time off provisions contained in the Employment Act 1989 which narrowly circumscribed the application of the rights. The reforms, however, did not totally dismantle this form of assistance for collective bargaining. They have ensured that, where an employer has voluntarily recognised a union, time off for the purposes of negotiation and training is provided so long as it is restricted solely to those collective bargaining matters the union is specifically recognised for.

ACAS is under a duty[6] to provide practical guidance on the application of these rights. Consequently, the rights outlined in the sections of the statute are developed by reference to the ACAS Code of Practice (No 3) on Time Off For Trade Union Duties and Activities (1997)[7] which sets out advice on the application of the law.[8]

---

4   The Code also notes that, 'to operate effectively and democratically, trade unions need the active participation of members. It can also be very much in the employers' interests that such participation is assured'.

5   Cmnd 9794, 1986, Chapter 7. For further comment, see McMullen, J (1986) 7 *Company Lawyer* 254.

6   TULR(C)A 1992, s 199.

7   This replaced the previous Codes published in 1977 and 1991. For a review of the 1991 Code, see McColgan, A (1991) 20 ILJ 281.

8   For example, TULR(C)A 1992, ss 168(3) and 170(3), state that how much time off should be granted, on what occasions and whether conditions should be attached to the permission are to be determined by reference to what is reasonable in the circumstances having regard to the Code of Practice. The Code is admissible in evidence and may be taken into account by a tribunal or court in determining any question that arises in proceedings.

Paid time off[9]

Section 168(1) provides that an employee who is an official,[10] of an independent trade union recognised by the employer is permitted to take time off during working hours:

for the purpose of carrying out any duties of his, as such an official, concerned with –

(a) negotiations with the employer related to or connected with matters falling within s 178(2) (collective bargaining) for which the trade union is recognised by the employer, or

(b) the performance on behalf of employees of the employer of functions related to or connected within that provision which the employer has agreed may be so performed by the trade union.[11]

The matters of collective bargaining referred to above are further defined by reference to s 178(2) and listed as: terms and conditions of employment, health and safety, recruitment dismissal and redundancy, job allocation and demarcation disputes, discipline, membership or non-membership of a union, facilities for officials of trade unions, recognition procedures and other machinery for negotiation or consultation on the above matters.[12]

Previously, the statutory provision had been more generous by stipulating that paid time off was available to officials for 'duties concerned with industrial relations'. There was no specific statutory limitation that these duties had also to be the subject of a separate recognition deal. Consequently, where time off was requested to engage in collective bargaining, any recognition agreement that limited the topics that were the subject matter of negotiation or limited the bodies of the union that were recognised for negotiating purposes, did not in itself limit the 'industrial relations duties' for which time off could be claimed. Slynn J made this clear in *Sood v GEC Elliot Process Automation Ltd*[13] when he said:

We do not accept ... the argument that the test of an official's duties (concerned with industrial relations) is to be limited by the recognition (agreement). It seems to us that recognition identifies the trade union whose officers are entitled to claim time under this section. It does not limit those duties to collective bargaining or to the precise terms of the recognition.[14]

Amendments introduced by the 1989 Act, however, reverse this case. Even if the matter is an issue of collective bargaining as defined in the Act by s 178(2) and by the Code of

---

9 The right to time off with pay is also provided for union safety representatives to fulfil their functions under the Health and Safety at Work Act 1974 (see the Safety Representatives and Safety Committee Regulations (SI 1977/500) amended by the Management of Health and Safety at Work Regulations (SI 1992/2051)). Additional unpaid leave is available under the Employment Rights Act 1996, s 50, for union members to discharge certain public duties (such as service as lay magistrates).

10 An official is defined in s 119. The definition includes elected or appointed union officers and workplace representatives.

11 Eg, to represent union members in disciplinary or grievance proceedings.

12 This list is developed further by the Code of Practice, para 12.

13 [1980] ICR 1.

14 At p 9. The Court of Appeal specifically approved this interpretation of the section in *Beal v Beecham Ltd* [1982] ICR 460.

Practice, it will not be the subject of paid leave if the employer does not recognise the union for bargaining purposes on that specific subject matter.

The duties undertaken by the official must be 'concerned with negotiations ... related to ... collective bargaining'. Clearly, time off to engage in the actual process of negotiation is covered by this phrase. The question, however, arises whether it is limited to the mere conduct of negotiations or whether a far broader interpretation may be applied which includes planning and preparatory work prior to the negotiations. The older cases interpreting the phrase duties 'concerned with industrial relations' have held that a preparatory meeting prior to negotiations may be the subject of a time off application. All that was required was for the meeting to be directly relevant to the issue of industrial relations that was to be discussed with the employer.[15]

However, this generous interpretation of the phrase concerned with (industrial relations) was restricted by the decision of the Court of Appeal in Adlington v British Bakeries (Northern) Ltd,[16] that attendance at a meeting to discuss strategy for future negotiation must be 'sufficiently proximate' to the actual negotiations. If attendance at a preparatory meeting was too remote in time to actual negotiations or too remote in its purposes from those negotiations, then in practical terms, the attendance will not be concerned with the industrial relations issue.[17]

More recent cases, decided after the 1989 amendments, have continued to interpret the phrase concerned with (negotiations) in a similar vein. In London Ambulance Service v Charlton[18] (decided after the statutory changes had taken effect but before the new Code of Practice was in force), the Employment Appeals Tribunal (EAT) specifically followed the Adlington 'proximity' formulation. The EAT explained that there is no need for actual negotiations to take place between the two sides: a union official is carrying out a duty which 'concerns' these negotiations so long as the genuine purpose of attendance at the meeting was to enable the official to actively prepare for the forthcoming negotiations.

Paragraph 13 of the Code of Practice provides some guidance on the required degree of proximity. It states that the trade union duties '... must be connected with or related to the negotiations or the performance of functions both in time and subject matter'. The Code of Practice thus suggests that the preparatory meeting must be close in time to the actual negotiations and that the preparations must specifically relate to the subject matter of the negotiations that are to take place. Wood J, commenting on para 13 of the Code in Charlton, said: '... it is ... interesting to note that the approach in the guidance given by ACAS under the new code of practice falls into line with our understanding of the wording of the new section ...'[19]

---

15 See *Beal v Beecham* [1982] ICR 460; *Thomas Scott (Bakers) Ltd v Allen* [1983] IRLR 329; *Young v Carr Fasteners* [1979] ICR 844.

16 [1989] IRLR 218.

17 The decision in *Adlington* endorsed the judgment of the EAT in *Ashley v Ministry of Defence* [1984] IRLR 57. Here, it was held that attendance at a union advisory committee which did not decide policy or negotiation strategy was 'too remote' to actual negotiations to satisfy the test of being 'concerned with' industrial relations.

18 [1992] IRLR 510.

19 At p 514.

Reasonableness

Even though the applicant trade union official may have established that the purposes for which time off is required falls within the section, it does not mean the official is now necessarily entitled to the time off. Section 168(3) makes clear the amount of time off to be taken, the purposes for which it is taken, the occasions on which it is taken and the conditions to which it is subject depend on a test of reasonableness. It may not be reasonable in the circumstances to grant the request at all. Alternatively, it may be reasonable for an employer to allow only a limited amount of time off. Guidelines on the circumstances an employer should appraise in determining what is 'reasonable' are found in the Code of Practice.

Paragraph 25 outlines some general considerations to be taken into account – applicable to both paid and unpaid time off. The paragraph notes that '... trade unions should be aware of the wide variety of difficulties and operational requirements to be taken into account by employers when seeking or agreeing arrangements for time off'. These 'difficulties and operational requirements' include the size of the enterprise and of the workforce, the inconvenience to the employer because of the effect on the production process of the absent employee, the need to secure safety and security at the workplace and 'the need to maintain a service to the public'. In *Thomas Scott (Bakers) Ltd v Allen*,[20] the Court of Appeal refused to interfere with the tribunal's view that the request by 11 shop stewards for all to take paid time off to attend a negotiation strategy meeting was properly denied as it would have disrupted the employer's business to an unacceptable level.

Paragraph 32 recognises that each application should be considered on its own merits, but that past time off may be a factor in determining the reasonableness of a present request.[21] This paragraph in the Code of Practice was included in response to comments in *Thomas Scott (Bakers) Ltd v Allen* by May LJ, that the past record of leave is not necessarily relevant when determining the reasonableness of the present request.[22]

Where a dispute arises between an employer and a union as to the issue of reasonableness, arguably the tribunal should take an objective view, independently examining the issue on its merits and then appraising all the evidence before deciding whether time off was unreasonably denied.[23] However, in *Ministry of Defence v Crook*,[24] the EAT asserted that the industrial tribunal should examine the issue from the employer's perspective, asking the question whether the decision to deny time off was within the band of reasonable responses by an employer.[25] It has been argued that this is

---

20 [1983] IRLR 329.

21 Applied in *Borders Regional Council v Maule* [1993] IRLR 199.

22 Arguably, the inclusion of para 32 was not necessary as the EAT had held in *Wignall v British Gas* [1984] ICR 716, contrary to May LJ's *obiter*, that the amount of time off already taken *was* a relevant consideration in determining the reasonableness of the employer's decision.

23 For an example of this approach, see the decision of the EAT in *Wignall v British Gas* [1984] ICR 716.

24 [1982] IRLR 488.

25 In *Thomas Scott (Bakers) Ltd v Allen* [1983] IRLR 329, the Court of Appeal was content to leave the issue of reasonableness to the industrial tribunal 'sitting as an industrial jury'. Consequently, a decision of an industrial tribunal on reasonableness cannot be easily disturbed on appeal; only if the decision was perverse or if there was an error of law.

an incorrect approach, as it imports notions derived from unfair dismissal law which cannot be justified on a reading of the statutory provisions.[26]

Paid time off for industrial relations training[27]

Section 168(2) of the TULR(C)A 1992 provides that an employer:

... shall also permit such an employee to take time off during his working hours for the purpose of undergoing training in aspects of industrial relations –

(a) relevant to the carrying out of such duties as are mentioned in sub-s (1); and

(b) approved by the Trades Union Congress or by the independent trade union of which he is an official.

It is a question of fact and degree whether there is a sufficient link between the training and the specific duties to be discharged for it to be 'relevant' for the purposes of this section. The Code of Practice (Pt 2) provides some guidance on this issue. Paragraph 16 suggests that training is relevant if it is appropriate to the actual role and duties of the union official. This is dependent upon the structure of the union, the level of bargaining arrangements and the scope of the recognition agreement. The Code advises that time off should be considered where the official has special responsibilities or where the official has only recently been elected and has little experience. Another area where training may be required is if existing collective agreements have to be reconsidered because of legislative changes or because of structural changes in the forum for negotiations.[28]

Clearly, training that is very generalist, unconnected to that particular official's duties would not be considered relevant.[29] However, a fairly generous construction of the term was applied in *Young v Carr Fasteners*.[30] Relevance (to the carrying out of an official's duties) was extended to attendance on a course on pension rights where pensions were not as yet, but were in the future, to become an issue for negotiation.[31]

Payment

Once the relevant employee has the required permission from the employer for time off, s 169 details the requirements on payment.[32] Where the employee's pay is calculated by reference to a fixed salary, he or she is entitled to pay 'for the work he would ordinarily

---

26 See Fitzpatrick, B, 'Recent developments in the Court of Appeal' (1983) 12 ILJ 258, p 261.

27 Since 1976 a State subsidy has been provided for the training of trade union representatives. It was announced in 1992 that this funding would cease from 1996.

28 At para 18.

29 For examples, see *Menzies v McLaurin Ltd* [1980] IRLR 180 and *Ministry of Defence v Crook* [1982] IRLR 488.

30 [1979] ICR 844.

31 Also, see *STC Submarines Systems v Piper* [1994] OPLR 13.

32 The EAT, in *Beal v Beecham Ltd (No 2)* [1983] IRLR 317, held that once an employer has decided that time off is reasonable, the official is entitled to be paid. Note the contrary view of May LJ in *Thomas Scott (Bakers) Ltd v Allen* [1983] IRLR 329 criticised by Fitzpatrick, *op cit*, fn 26, p 260.

have been doing ...' during the time of absence.[33] Where pay varies with the amount of work done (such as piecework), pay is calculated by reference to the average hourly earnings of the employee concerned.

Where the union has negotiated a separate agreement on time off, this may be incorporated into their member's employment contract. This contractual provision exists as a supplement to the statutory right, which is a minimum entitlement, a so called floor that the contractual arrangements can improve on, but cannot reduce or exclude.[34] Any payment under the contract will partially or fully discharge an employer's liability under this section and likewise any payment designated as being under this section will discharge an employer's liability under the employment contract.[35]

Both para 14 of the Code on payment for time off for trade union duties and para 19 on payment for time off for training, state that there is '... no statutory requirement to pay for time off where the duty is carried out at a time when the official would not otherwise be at work'. In *Hairsine v Hull CC*,[36] an employee who was an evening shift worker attended with his employer's permission, an industrial relations training course during normal daytime business hours on one day a week for 12 weeks. He requested payment as if he had worked normally. It was submitted on his behalf that if he had been a regular shift worker he would have received time off with pay to attend the course. Consequently, it was argued that the hours he attended on the course should be counted as substitute hours for the work he would normally do for the employer on that day.

Section 168 states that paid time off is only available during an employee's 'working hours' which is defined in s 173(1) as '... any time when in accordance with his contract of employment the [employee] is required to be at work'. The EAT held that, on construction of the sections and with guidance from the Code of Practice, the employer's refusal to pay was justified. Payment only needed to be made where, if he had not been on the course, he would have normally been at work.[37]

Where an official requests paid time off to attend a meeting or a training course where only a proportion of the business transacted is covered by the statutory definition, then the official is still entitled to time off but may find that the assessment of pay is reduced. In *RHP Bearings v Brookes*,[38] the EAT concluded that, where an official was requesting time off for mixed purposes, on the failure of the employer and union to agree to share the reimbursement costs, the tribunal should assess how much of the meeting was devoted to a statutory purpose and award an appropriate level of pay.[39]

---

33 See *McCormack v Shell Chemicals UK Ltd* [1979] IRLR 40 – night shift worker entitled to be paid at the evening shift rate when taking permitted time off during the day. Note that the ECJ in *Arbeiterwohl-fahrt der Stadt Berlin v Botel* [1992] IRLR 423 has ruled that it is a breach of Art 119 and the Equal Pay Directive (75/117/EC) for a part timer (who works a limited number of hours) to be paid less than a full timer for attending the same course where the course extends beyond the normal contractual hours of that part timer. This was followed by the EAT in *Davies v Neath County BC* [1999] IRLR 769.

34 TULR(C)A 1992, s 288, states that 'any provision in an agreement which attempts to exclude or limit the operation of any provision of the Act ... is void'.

35 Section 169(4).

36 [1992] IRLR 211.

37 See also *Davies v Head Wright* [1979] IRLR 170.

38 [1979] IRLR 452. Noted by Bowers, J and Clarke, A (1980) 9 ILJ 56.

39 Although approved by the Court of Appeal in *Beal v Beecham Ltd* [1983] IRLR 192, in the later case of *Beal v Beecham (No 2)* [1982] IRLR 317, the EAT expressed doubts as to whether this was the correct approach.

Unpaid time off for trade union activities

Under s 170(1), an ordinary member of a recognised independent trade union is entitled to take time off work to engage in 'any activities of the union'.[40] The substance of this section was not changed by the 1989 amendments. In contrast to the position in relation to paid time off for trade union duties, this right is not limited within the statute by the need for the activities to be directly connected to matters of collective bargaining or any recognition agreement. However, although 'activities of the union' could thus have a very broad application,[41] the EAT in *Luce v London Borough of Bexley*,[42] has substantially narrowed the application of the phrase.

A number of members of the NUT were refused unpaid leave to attend a lobby of Parliament against the Education Reform Bill. Although the proposed legislation was of vital concern to the members of the union, the industrial tribunal had held on the evidence that this lobby of Parliament was intended to convey a political or ideological message and so was not a appropriate trade union activity for the purposes of the statute.

In the EAT, Wood J held that Parliament could not have intended that all ventures, of whatever nature, were automatically protected trade union activities. The context of the phrasing required that '... in a broad sense the activity should be one which is in some way linked to [the] employment relationship, that is, between that employer, that employee and that trade union'.[43] On this construction of the section, a lobby of Parliament was not sufficiently related to the employment relationship to justify time off.

Wood J is in effect proposing that time off is only available for objectively reasonable trade union activities. Arguably, such a view cannot be justified on a reading of the statute which clearly provides for time off for 'any activities of a trade union' without the need for there to be any link to an individual's employment relationship with their employer. Consequently, the better interpretation is that it is for the trade union subjectively to determine trade union 'activities', not for the tribunal to determine what trade union activities are objectively legitimate and what are not. Of course, where reasonableness is relevant, is in determining the extent of time off for the particular trade union activity.

The Code of Practice does not provide a full explanation of what constitutes 'activities of the trade union'. It merely gives examples of trade union activities in para 21 and does not link the trade union activity with any requirement that it has to be related to the employment relationship.

Section 170(3) repeats the test of reasonableness contained in s 168(3) on paid time off. As is the case with paid time off, once it is has been determined that the activity qualifies under the section the amount of time off has to be reasonable in all the circumstances. General considerations are contained in para 25 of the Code of Practice, dealt with earlier.

---

40 The activities must be union activities not individual activities of a trade unionist. For the distinction, see *Dixon v West Ella Developments* [1978] IRLR 151 and *Chant v Aqua Boats* [1978] ICR 643.

41 Paragraph 21 gives examples of union activities, such as attendance at union meetings to discuss and vote on negotiations with an employer or attendance at meetings with union officials to discuss workplace issues. The Code of Practice, s 170(2) and para 23, makes it clear that industrial action is not an appropriate trade union activity for the purposes of time off.

42 [1990] IRLR 422.

43 At p 425.

Section 170(1)(b) also provides members who are representatives of the union the right to unpaid time off to take part in union activities relevant to their position. Thus, unpaid shop stewards who act as a channel of communication between the membership and the employer are entitled to time off for workplace negotiations with employers. Paragraph 22 of the Code of Practice also expands the statutory provision by recommending that a member who is also a workplace representative of the union should be provided with unpaid time off to discuss union business at branch, area or regional meetings or to attend the union annual conference or national executive committee.[44]

Procedure and remedies

The Code of Practice notes that there are positive advantages in employers and unions coming to formal agreements on the issue of paid and unpaid time off. A formal agreement, which may have to be relatively flexible in smaller organisations, should provide clear guidelines on when time off should be granted, for how long, and whether it should be paid. An individual application can be judged against this agreement thereby ensuring fair and equal treatment and avoiding any misunderstandings that may otherwise arise from an application of the statutory right.[45] The Code stresses that should an agreement be made, this does not of itself supersede the statutory entitlement. The implication is that any agreement cannot provide a worse entitlement than the statutory minimum.[46]

There is no specific procedure outlined in the Act for requesting paid or unpaid time off. The Code of Practice does, however, state in para 29 that where paid time off is requested, as much notice as possible of the application should be provided with full details of the purpose of the time off, the proposed duration and timing and location where it will be used. Similar requirements for paid time off to attend a training course are outlined in para 30.

Where the employer fails to permit time off, the Code of Practice suggests disputes should be resolved internally within the organisation and that any formal agreement on the rights to time off should incorporate procedures to resolve such grievances. This may involve the use of the expertise of ACAS as a conciliator.

Should informal or formal negotiation at the workplace be unsuccessful, then the Code reiterates the right of an official or union member to complain under ss 168(4) or 170(4) to an employment tribunal that their rights to time off have been infringed as the '... employer has failed to permit him to take time off as required by this section'.[47] The

---

44 Arrangements for work place representatives to have time off are inextricably linked to the provision of facilities for union officials. The Code, para 28, recommends that employers may consider making available facilities (such as accommodation, the use of office equipment) 'necessary for them to perform their duties efficiently and to communicate effectively with their members, fellow lay officials and full-time officers'.

45 The Code, para 31, suggests that the agreement on time off should ensure that time off is taken at a time that will minimise disruption to production.

46 See TULR(C)A 1992, s 288, referred to above. Contrast the decision in *Ashley v Ministry of Defence* [1984] IRLR 57, where the EAT gave priority to the agreed procedure which was less generous than the statutory framework.

47 The EAT, in *Ryford Ltd v Drinkwater* [1996] IRLR 16, has held that on a complaint that an employer has 'failed to permit' time off, an applicant has to demonstrate on the balance of probabilities that the request came to the notice of the employer, and having that notice, the employer refused it, ignored it or failed to respond to it.

time limit for lodging a complaint to an employment tribunal is three months from the date of refusal.[48] Where it is not reasonably practicable for the complaint to be presented within that period, then the tribunal has a discretion to extend this time limit.[49]

Should the complaint be successful, the tribunal will issue a declaration that it is well founded. Compensation payable will be what the tribunal considers to be 'just and equitable' in the circumstances which may include compensation for injury to feelings and other non-pecuniary loss.[50] Where a complaint is made that the employee has received time off but the employer has failed to pay the established amount, the tribunal has authority to order payment of what is due.

Protection against dismissal for bringing proceedings to enforce the statutory right to time off or for alleging the employer has infringed this right[51] is provided by s 104(4)(c) of the Employment Rights Act 1996.

PROTECTION AGAINST DISMISSAL[52]

Unlike rights to time off, protection against dismissal on grounds of union membership or union activities were originally found in the Industrial Relations Act 1971. Amended by the Employment Protection Act 1975, these provisions were later incorporated into s 58(1)(a), (b) of the Employment Protection (Consolidation) Act 1978, now contained in s 152(1)(a), (b) of the TULR(C)A 1992.

A dismissal on the grounds of union membership or activity is automatically unfair without the need for any qualifying term of one year's employment or for the employee to show that the dismissal was unreasonable in any way. There is no upper age limit as the usual disqualification based on retiring age does not apply.[53]

General procedure

At the hearing it is for the applicant employee to show the fact of dismissal, that is, a termination at common law or by statute initiated by the employer. Ordinarily, it is then for the employer to establish on the balance of probabilities that the reason for the dismissal was not based on 'union grounds'.[54] If the employer fails to show that there was another reason for the dismissal, then the dismissal is automatically unfair. If the employer does adduce such evidence, the burden of proof in establishing the inadmissible reason then reverts to the applicant. In order to establish that dismissal was

---

48 Section 171.

49 This discretion is not exercised liberally. See the cases on unfair dismissal.

50 Sections 172(1) and 172(2). Compensation is usually nominal as often there is no direct quantifiable loss – see *Corner v Buckinghamshire CC* [1978] IRLR 320 and *Young v Carr Fasteners (No 2)* COIT 820/154 (unreported).

51 So long as the allegations were made in 'good faith'.

52 Protection against selection for redundancy on union grounds is provided by TULR(C)A 1992, s 153. See, as examples, *Driver v Cleveland Structural Engineering Co Ltd* [1994] ICR 372; *West Kent College v Richardson* [1999] ICR 511.

53 Section 154.

54 *Maund v Penwith DC* [1984] IRLR 24.

on trade union grounds, the applicant does not have to show that the employer acted out of malice or was motivated by a deliberate desire to be rid of a trade union activist.[55]

If the employee has less than the appropriate level of continuous employment, a majority of the Court of Appeal in *Smith v Hayle Town Council*[56] held that the applicant bears the onus of proof that he was dismissed on grounds of union membership or activities. Where there is little direct evidence, this can be a difficult burden to discharge.

Where there are two or more reasons for the dismissal, of which union grounds is one, whether the employee attracts the protection of the section depends on what was the principal reason for dismissal. If the principal reason was, for example, misconduct, even if there exists a subsidiary reason based on union grounds the automatic protection of s 152 does not apply.[57]

DISMISSAL FOR UNION MEMBERSHIP

Section 152(1)(a) of the TULR(C)A 1992 states that:

... the dismissal of an employee shall be regarded as unfair if the reason for it ... was that that the employee –

(a) was, or proposed to become, a member of an independent trade union.

This sub-section protects those individuals who are dismissed solely because they possess membership of, or wish to join, a trade union. It thus deals with the more extreme anti-union prejudices of employers. It may be thought that where an employee is actively enjoying the benefits of membership, this is more logically protected by sub-s (1)(b) which protects a union member against dismissal for union activities. However, in *Discount Tobacco v Armitage*,[58] where the employee was dismissed for taking advantage of their union membership, the claim was framed solely by reference to s 152(1)(a).

The plaintiff had asked for a written statement of terms and conditions of employment. When it was not forthcoming, she asked a union official to write to her employer on her behalf. She subsequently received the statement of terms, but also received her dismissal notice. The EAT concluded that making use of union membership in this way was a necessarily incidental act to union membership. Knox J noted that to construe the section in a narrow way would emasculate the protection as '... the scope [of the provision] would be reduced almost to vanishing point, since it would only be just the fact that a person was a member of a union, without regard to the consequences of that membership, that would be the subject matter of that statutory provision ...'.[59]

The construction Knox J put on s 152(1)(a) was explicitly endorsed in the Court of Appeal by Dillon LJ in *Wilson v Associated Newspapers* and *Palmer v Associated British*

---

55 *Dundon v GPT Ltd* [1995] IRLR 403.
56 [1978] IRLR 413.
57 *CGB Publishing v Killey* [1993] IRLR 520.
58 [1990] IRLR 15.
59 At p 16.

Ports.[60] a case on the parallel provision in s 146(1)(a). Dillon LJ approved the view that the concept of membership also includes some use of membership.

> I regard that decision [*Discount v Armitage*] as unquestionably correct ... it is open to an Industrial Tribunal to hold that an employee has been dismissed or penalised for being a member of a union if he has been dismissed or penalised for invoking the assistance of the union in relation to his employment.[61]

However, this expansive view of the protection afforded by s 152(1)(a) was doubted in the House of Lords on appeal.[62] Lord Bridge, who gave the leading judgment, did not directly question the correctness of the decision in *Armitage* but said that the decision did not establish that membership of a union was to be equated with using the essential services of that union, as '... at best it put an unnecessary and imprecise gloss on the statutory language and at worst it was liable to distort the meaning of those provisions that protected union membership as such'.[63]

The EAT, in *Speciality Care v Pachela*,[64] has attempted to resurrect the decision in *Armitage* by distinguishing the *Wilson* and *Palmer* cases on the facts. The EAT held that, where union assistance is enlisted by an individual in a dispute with an employer, it is still open for a tribunal to find that the individual has been dismissed on grounds of union membership.

If the misgivings expressed by the House of Lords are followed in subsequent decisions, then s 152(1)(a) would only be of value where an employer makes a positive decision to dismiss for membership *per se*. Yet, anti-union employers rarely act against the passive union member, they are predominantly concerned with what an individual does with his or her union membership. Thus, unless this area of law is developed by reference to the reasoning in *Armitage*, where union members are dismissed for using the services of the union, the applicants will only be protected if they can show they satisfy the requirements of s 152(1)(b).

DISMISSAL FOR PARTICIPATION IN TRADE UNION ACTIVITIES

Section 152(1)(b) protects individual union members where they have been dismissed for having '... taken part, or proposed to take part, in the activities of an independent trade union at an appropriate time ...'.[65]

There has been far more litigation over the application of this sub-section; predominantly over the interpretation of what constitutes 'activities of an independent trade union' and when is it an 'appropriate time' to engage in these activities.

---

60   [1993] IRLR 336.
61   At p 339.
62   [1995] IRLR 258.
63   At p 264.
64   [1996] IRLR 248.
65   Sections 152 (protection against dismissal) and 146 (protection against action short of dismissal) are complementary rights. Both rights use the common terminology of 'activities of an independent trade union' at an 'appropriate time'. Thus, cases on ss 152 and 146 dealing with these phrases may be taken as authorities for both sections.

At an appropriate time

The statute provides guidance as to when it is an appropriate time to engage in trade union activities. Section 152(2) states that 'appropriate time' means:

(a) a time outside the employee's working hours, or

(b) a time within his working hours at which, in accordance with arrangements agreed with or consent given by his employer, it is permissible for him to take part in the activities of a trade union.

'Working hours' is further defined as '... any time when, in accordance with his contract of employment, he is required to be at work'.

Only at the times above does a worker have the protection of an automatic unfair dismissal claim should he or she be dismissed for trade union activities. This is because an unfettered right to engage in trade union activities at other times could, arguably, interfere with the smooth running of an employer's business.

In *Zucker v Astrid Jewels Ltd*,[66] two specific issues fell for adjudication: the interpretation of the term 'working hours' and the nature of implied consent. The applicant was a vigorous proponent of trade union membership and discussed trade union matters with her colleagues during her tea and lunch breaks and whilst engaging in her duties at work as a machinist. The EAT held that the discussion of union affairs on her employer's premises at a designated break time was not during 'working hours' and so was undertaken at a protected time.[67] Secondly, although conversation at the machines was during the course of work, the employer had always permitted general conversation and had not attempted to control their content. Consequently, the applicant's union recruitment conversations whilst at work was 'in accordance with arrangements (impliedly) agreed with or consented to by the employer'.

However, the Court of Appeal, in *Marley Tile Co v Shaw*,[68] responded with caution to the possibility of inferring consent by silence. The applicant was an employee who had been appointed as shop steward to represent a section of workers at the employer's factory. The employers declined to recognise his status as a shop steward and refused to meet him for the purpose of negotiating on wage rates. The applicant responded by informing the employers that he would call a meeting of the members he represented for consultation. As a consequence of this meeting there was a one hour stoppage. The employers then dismissed the applicant.

The Court of Appeal found that in calling a meeting about the failure of the management to recognise his status as a shop steward he was engaged in trade union activities. However, the employer's failure to ban the meeting or to comment at all to the employee on his course of action could not be regarded as tantamount to implied consent or permission for the employee's action.

---

66 [1978] IRLR 385.

67 On this matter, the EAT followed the House of Lords' decision in *The Post Office v Union of Post Office Workers and Crouch* [1974] IRLR 22. When employees are on recognised breaks they are 'not required to be at work' and so any union activities at this time has the protection of the statute. See also *Carter v Wiltshire CC* [1979] IRLR 331.

68 [1980] ICR 72.

In *Robb v Leon Motor Services Ltd*,[69] the applicant was a coach driver who had been appointed shop steward. During working hours, the applicant had pursued his union activities by attempting to recruit members informally. In response, he was transferred to other duties that restricted his opportunities to make contact with fellow employees. The EAT accepted that he had been transferred because of his union activities. However, the activities had not been pursued at the correct time. There was no specific agreement or implied or express consent to engage in trade union activities during working hours.

Marley and *Robb* do not, however, imply that silence from an employer can never constitute consent. Arguably, if an employee is an accredited shop steward and had called meetings before without dissent from an employer, the employer's previous behaviour is evidence of an established customary arrangement amounting to permission for meetings of that type to be held at that time.[70]

Past union activities

An issue of some importance is whether the section provides protection where the applicant is dismissed due to trade union activities undertaken before he or she joined the present employer. In *Birmingham DC v Beyer*,[71] the plaintiff gave a false name and bogus reference to obscure his past record as a previously active trade unionist which he knew would count against him in obtaining employment. When this became known to the employer, he was dismissed. The industrial tribunal held that Beyer's deceit was a trade union activity as he had had to resort to these tactics because, otherwise, his past record would bar him from obtaining employment.

Kilner Brown J in the EAT strongly disapproved of this reasoning and unequivocally declared that engaging in deceit cannot be a trade union activity, whatever the circumstances. He further went on to say that the section '... could not conceivably refer to activities outside and before employment began'[72] because the statute is limited to protecting trade union activity at an 'appropriate time'.[73]

The same issue was considered by the Court of Appeal some years later in *Fitzpatrick v BRB*.[74] The Court of Appeal first confirmed the decision in *Beyer* that where a dismissal was genuinely for the deceit in failing to inform the employer about past trade union activities, then an applicant would lose the protection of this provision as this would not be a dismissal for 'trade union activities'.

However, the Court of Appeal then went on to note that the section makes it unlawful to dismiss an employee not just for taking part in union activities, but also for 'proposing

---

69   [1978] IRLR 26.

70   The Code of Practice itself suggests that consent may be implied by silence where there is a need for an urgent meeting to discuss an issue such as industrial action and where a union meeting has no detrimental impact on the employer's business.

71   [1977] IRLR 211. Noted by Lewis, R (1977) 6 ILJ 246.

72   At p 212.

73   See also the EAT in *Torr v British Rlys Board* [1977] IRLR 184.

74   [1991] IRLR 376.

to take part' in union activities. To gain the protection of the section, it is not necessary for the activities that the union member 'proposes to take part in' to be precisely identified. If the reason for the employer's decision to dismiss the employee is manifestly because of a fear that such conduct will be repeated in the future, then this is a dismissal for 'proposing to take part' in union activities. The dismissal is clearly initiated by a belief that the employee is proposing to repeat such activities in his or her current employment.[75]

The implications of the case are of some significance. Patently, a union activist has a predisposition to take part in trade union activities. Therefore, subject to evidence of the employer's reason, the dismissal of activists on an employment 'black list' is unlawful.[76]

Appropriate activities

Although there is no statutory definition of 'activities of an independent trade union', the matters listed in the ACAS Code on Time Off for Trade Union Duties and Activities have been construed, for the purposes of this section, as relevant 'activities'. These comprise; attendance at branch meetings, voting in elections and attendance at emergency meetings on industrial action. So long as they are activities undertaken with permission or outside work times, such as at lunchtime, then participation is protected. Local officials (such as shop stewards) will also be protected where they engage in union activities commensurate to their post, such as taking up individual grievances with management or calling a meeting with members.[77]

These examples are not exhaustive and certainly other matters can fall within the scope of appropriate activities. In *Dixon v West Ella Developments Ltd*,[78] employees had complained directly to a union regional organiser about the lack of safety equipment. The union responded by calling in a safety official from the Factories Inspectorate. The employer then victimised the employees who claimed they had been constructively dismissed for reason of their trade union activities.

According to the industrial tribunal, this was not a protected activity. Although ordinary union members are entitled to voice their grievances on health and safety, they would normally proceed with a complaint to a shop steward rather than directly contact a senior official. This approach to the construction of the phrase was rejected by Phillips J in the EAT. To complain to a senior union official about unsafe working conditions was engaging in appropriate trade union activities as the law was '... intended ... to discourage employers from penalising participation in activities of a fairly varied kind and [the section] should be reasonably, and not too restrictively, interpreted'.[79]

---

75 For commentary on these arguments, see Wynn Evans, C, 'Blacklisting unionists revisited' (1992) 21 ILJ 67. See also *Port of London Authority v Payne* [1992] IRLR 447 (EAT).

76 See also the protection originally provided by the Employment Act 1990 (now TULR(C)A 1992, ss 137–43) on anti-union hiring policies discussed at p 192 and the new 'blacklisting' provision introduced by the Employment Relations Act 1999, discussed at p 193.

77 See *British Airways Ltd v Francis* [1981] IRLR 1.

78 [1978] ICR 856.

79 At p 860.

However, this decision by Phillips J may be contrasted with the less generous interpretation of the term 'activities of a ... trade union' applied by Kilner Brown J in *Chant v Aqua Boats*.[80] The applicant had made a complaint that certain equipment he was using did not comply with required safety standards. He acted as the spokesperson for a group of concerned employees and organised a petition under the direction of a local official. After handing it in, he was dismissed purportedly for incompetence, although it was found on the facts to be for the organisation of the petition. Kilner Brown J considered that the actions of the employee in organising the petition did not fall within the definition of an activity of the union. By way of explanation he quoted approvingly from the decision of the industrial tribunal: 'The mere fact that one or two of the employees making representations happen to be trade unionists, and the mere fact that the spokesman of the men happens to be a trade unionist does not make such representations a trade union activity.'[81] As this was a communication of a complaint from an individual who happened to be a member of a trade union, Chant was not entitled to the protection of the section.[82]

Although there is a degree of conflict in the decisions in *Dixon* and *Chant*, it is not now of any great importance where union members raise health and safety matters. This is because of the specific right not to be dismissed or victimised for alleging breach of health and safety legislation (introduced by the Trade Union Reform and Employment Rights Act 1993) implementing the European Framework Directive on Health and Safety.[83]

Trade union organising activity

Where a union is not recognised at a workplace, the recruitment of members may conflict with the anti-union policies of the employer. Can this organising process be protected by an application of the individual right not to be dismissed for union membership or activities? In *Carrington v Therm-a-Star Ltd*,[84] the Court of Appeal subscribed to a cautious approach of the construction of the section. After a recruitment drive by the Transport and General Workers Union, over 90% of the workforce of a new factory had joined or had applied to join the union. The union district official then approached the employer for the purposes of obtaining recognition. In a response to this enquiry, the employer immediately made 20 employees redundant, most of whom were union members or those who had proposed to join.

It was found on the facts that reason for the dismissals was not redundancy, but rather a response to the union's attempt to obtain recognition – as a retaliation against the union. Donaldson MR in the Court of Appeal accepted that the union and the employees had a justifiable grievance, and that the section was clearly aimed at a mischief very similar to that which befell the employees. But, on a true construction of the statute, the section operated only to protect individuals where they have been dismissed for their

---

80   [1978] ICR 643.
81   At p 646.
82   See also *Brennan v Ellward* [1976] IRLR 378.
83   See p 183.
84   [1983] ICR 208. Noted by JMT (1983) 99 LQR 338.

personal trade union activity. The employer's reaction was a blanket response to a general trade union activity.[85]

Where a trade union is already recognised, there is no doubt that, subject to consent, recruitment activity *per se* is protected. It seems trade union officers may go about this function in a robust manner. In *Bass Taverns Ltd v Burgess*,[86] the Court of Appeal noted that, in order to sell the services of the union, it may well be that some implicit or explicit criticism of an employer is made. So long as any criticism is not expressed in bad faith, union officers are still engaging in appropriate trade union activities as there is no obligation on them to perform union functions in a manner approved by an employer.

Industrial action and 'activities of ... trade union'

It has not always been clear whether industrial action is an 'appropriate' trade union activity for the purposes of this section. The EAT, in *Drew v St Edmundsbury BC*,[87] applied a line of reasoning that automatically denied protection to trade unionists who engage in industrial action.[88] The applicant had made several complaints about health and safety standards at his place of work. His union advised him and others to respond to the employer's failure to deal with the complaints by engaging in a 'go slow' in protest. The EAT held his dismissal was not for the legitimate trade union activity of communicating concerns over health and safety matters but for taking part in industrial action, as '... it seems to us quite clear that there is intended by Parliament to be a distinction for the purposes of a claim for unfair dismissal between what is an activity of an independent trade union and taking part in industrial action'.[89]

However, even if industrial action is regarded as appropriate union activity, any claim for dismissal under s 152 would be unlikely to succeed. First, industrial action would have to take place at an 'appropriate time', which as we have seen is outside working hours or with the employer's agreement.[90] The very nature of industrial action is that it rarely takes place after work. However, note that s 238A of the TULR(C)A 1992 (introduced by the Employment Relations Act 1999) now provides a new category of automatically unfair dismissal where an employee takes 'protected' industrial action (discussed in detail in Chapter 13).

---

85   Contrast this with the decision of the EAT in *Lyon v St James Press Ltd* [1976] IRLR 215. The dismissal of Lyon for organising a union branch at the workplace was unlawful as he had personally taken part in the organising activity. Note that the statutory recognition procedures introduced by the Employment Relations Act 1999 provide protection against detriment and dismissal for those workers involved in the statutory recognition process. For further details, see Chapter 10, pp 223–24.

86   [1995] IRLR 596.

87   [1980] ICR 513.

88   Yet, also, see *Rasool v Hepworth Pipe Co Ltd (No 2)* [1980] IRLR 137.

89   Slynn J at 517.

90   Eg, the EAT in *Britool v Roberts* [1993] IRLR 481 was willing to accept that participation in industrial action could be trade union activity but that it was unlikely to gain the protection of s 158 as it could rarely be undertaken at a 'relevant time'. The EAT, however, did distinguish this from the situation where union members were dismissed for organising, rather than participating in, industrial action. As a relevant trade union activity, it would be protected if it was organised outside of worktime.

Remedies

Like claims for unfair dismissal on other grounds, an order for reinstatement or re-engagement[91] is possible but unlikely. An employer can resist a re-employment order if it can be shown that it is 'not practicable' to re-employ the dismissed worker. One factor the tribunal should consider is the effect of the re-employment order on the employer's business arrangements. In *Port of London Authority v Payne*,[92] the Court of Appeal held that when considering the practicability of such an order an industrial tribunal should not substitute its own commercial judgment as to whether the re-engagement was financially feasible for that of the employer. This decision effectively downgrades anti-union dismissal rights by making it easier for employers to persuade tribunals not to grant these orders.[93]

Compensation[94]

There are special compensation provisions for an unfair dismissal on union grounds. A basic award is calculated according to the rules pertaining to ordinary unfair dismissal cases. The number of years of continuous employment, up to a maximum of 20, is multiplied by the figure for one and a half weeks' pay for each year in which the employee was 42 or over, reducing to half a week's pay for each year the employee was under 22. The maximum payable under this formula is £7,200. However, where dismissal was for trade union membership or activities, a minimum figure of £3,300 must be awarded.[95]

The compensatory award is also calculated according to ordinary unfair dismissal rules. This will usually include a sum for future loss. Where an individual has been dismissed for union reasons, it may well be that his opportunity to work in that industry is seriously limited. Thus, if he is unlikely to work again, the figure under this head of loss could be substantial, subject to the maximum allowed of £51,700.

Prior to amendments introduced by the Employment Relations Act 1999, an applicant could also have claimed enhanced compensation in the form of a 'special' award with remuneration of up to 156 weeks' pay available where a re-employment order was granted and not obeyed by the employer.[96] Section 33(2) of the Employment Relations Act 1999 amends the relevant compensation provisions in the Employment Rights Act 1996[97] by replacing the 'special' awards with the 'additional' award.[98] An employee is

---

91   See *Artisan v Strawley* [1986] IRLR 126, noted by Lewis, D (1986) 15 ILJ 203.

92   [1994] IRLR 9.

93   See Bennett, M, 'The practicability of reinstatement and re-engagement orders' (1994) 23 ILJ 164.

94   Figures quoted are current at 1 February 2002.

95   Section 156.

96   These compensation provisions were originally introduced in the 1980s at the same time as the right not to be dismissed on grounds of non-membership of a union. Arguably, this level of (almost punitive) compensation was introduced mainly to deter the operation of the closed shop. In order to be even-handed the Conservative administration extended these compensation terms to persons who were dismissed on union grounds.

97   Section 117(3)(b).

98   The additional award already operates in other cases where reinstatement or re-engagement is requested and an employer fails to comply.

thus entitled to up to 52 weeks' pay should a tribunal order re-engagement or reinstatement and the employer fails to comply.

Interim relief

Under s 161, an interim remedy is available for an applicant who alleges dismissal on the grounds of union membership or union activities. This is in the form of an order for reinstatement or re-engagement. Where the employer refuses to re-employ the dismissed employee, an order for the continuation of the contract of employment will be made. Interim relief thus has the effect of ensuring that the applicant is paid until the hearing of the case.[99] An application for interim relief must be lodged within seven days of dismissal[100] and be supported by a certificate[101] from the union stating that the applicant is or had proposed to become a union member and that there appear to be reasonable grounds for the complaint that the dismissal was on union grounds.[102]

Section 163(1) continues by stating that the relief should not be granted unless it appears to the tribunal that 'it is likely that' they will find the complaint justified. The question that arises is what standard of proof will the tribunals apply when determining the phrase 'it is likely'. In *Taplin v Shippam*,[103] the EAT attempted to provide some guidance on this matter. By emphasising the exceptional nature of the remedy, the EAT held that the applicant had to establish a greater likelihood of success than that based on the ordinary civil standard of proof, the balance of probabilities. An employment tribunal considering whether to make an interim award should consider the question, does the applicant have a 'pretty good' chance of success in claiming unfair dismissal? This, it would seem, is not as high a standard of proof as beyond a reasonable doubt, but it is perhaps a somewhat higher standard than the balance of probabilities.

EMPLOYMENT PROTECTION
AND HEALTH AND SAFETY MATTERS

Many of the cases discussed above have dealt with occasions where the employee has been dismissed or victimised for alleging problems with the health and safety regime at the workplace. Employees have often, because of the interpretation of the phrase 'activities of a trade union', been unable to bring an action under ss 158 or 146. Such employees now have added protection as a consequence of the Framework EC Directive on Health and Safety.[104]

---

99 The reasoning behind this emergency relief, granted in a preliminary hearing, is to forestall unrest amongst the workforce so as to limit the possibility of the dismissal escalating into an industrial dispute.
100 Section 161(2).
101 Section 161(3).
102 The certificate must be signed by an authorised official. It is assumed a full time official has authorisation. Otherwise, express authorisation is required. See *Stone v Charrington and Co* [1977] ICR 248.
103 [1978] ICR 1068.
104 Directive 89/391/EC.

The Trade Union Reform and Employment Rights Act 1993 incorporated the Directive into domestic law; now consolidated into s 100 of the Employment Rights Act 1996. This provision amends the law by providing safeguards for employees dismissed in health and safety cases. A dismissal is automatically unfair if the grounds for the dismissal were for:

(a) carrying out the functions of a health and safety representative;

(b) reasonably bringing to the attention of the employer circumstances harmful to health and safety, where there was no health and safety representative or it was not reasonably practicable to raise the issue with that representative;

(c) leaving or proposing to leave or refusing to return to the place of work, because of a reasonable belief of a serious and imminent danger at the workplace, or for taking or proposing to take appropriate steps to protect himself or others from that danger.[105]

As with dismissal on union grounds, there is no length of service qualification period. The compensation procedures, the additional award and interim relief provisions discussed above are applicable.

ACTION SHORT OF DISMISSAL[106]

The right to claim unfair dismissal for trade union membership and for engaging in trade union activities is supplemented by additional protection where an employer disciplines or victimises an employee for these reasons. The provisions formerly contained in the Employment Protection Act 1975 and then s 23(1)(a), (b) of the EP(C)A 1978 were reproduced (prior to minor amendments introduced by the Employment Relations Act 1999) in s 146(1)(a), (b) of the TULR(C)A 1992 as:

(1) An employee has the right not to have action short of dismissal taken against him as an individual by his employer for the purpose of –

(a) preventing or deterring him from being or seeking to become a member of an independent trade union, or penalising him for doing so;

(b) preventing or deterring him from taking part in the activities of an independent trade union at an appropriate time, or penalising him for doing so ...

The terms 'appropriate activities' and 'appropriate time' were considered earlier when examining protection under s 152. Consequently, the cases on the interpretation of these terms previously considered also apply for the purposes of this section. Schedule 2 to the 1999 Act has replaced the phrase 'has the right not to have action short of dismissal taken against him as an individual' with the expression 'has the right not to be subjected to any "detriment" as an individual'. This merely brings this law into line with other provisions that protect union members from victimisation.

---

105 By the Employment Rights Act 1996, s 44, individuals also have the right not to have action short of dismissal taken against them on these grounds.

106 For a critical general overview of the law on dismissal and action short of dismissal see Evans, S and Lewis, R, 'Anti-union discrimination: practice, law and policy' (1987) 16 ILJ 88.

Actions and omissions

Positive acts, such as demoting an employee, cutting his or her wages, transferring or actively harassing an employee, clearly constitutes detrimental action taken by an employer for the purpose of the section. In appropriate circumstances, threatening to take action which would constitute a detriment has also satisfied the statutory requirement.[107]

Guidance as to whether an omission to act, by for example, withholding a benefit, is regarded as detrimental 'action' for the purposes of the section was provided by s 298 of the TULR(C)A 1992 which stated: 'In this Act, unless the context otherwise requires – "act" and "action" ... includes omission, and references to doing an act or taking action shall be construed accordingly.' Consequently, until recently, the courts have consistently interpreted an employer's failure to provide a benefit to an employee as 'taking action' against that employee.[108]

The omission issue was considered in detail in *NCB v Ridgway*,[109] and *Wilson v Associated Newspapers; Palmer v Associated British Ports*.[110] The Court of Appeal in both these cases held that a failure to grant a pay rise was an actionable omission by the employer. However, the House of Lords in *Wilson* and *Palmer*,[111] by a majority, overruled the Court of Appeal decisions. Lord Bridge, who gave the leading judgment, held that the failure of the employers to pay wage increases to those employees who declined to agree to the termination of union representation on wages and conditions was not 'action' within the meaning of s 146.

Bridge came to this conclusion by dismissing the relevance of s 298. He identified this as a case where an omission should not be treated as if it was an act as 'the context otherwise requires'. Bridge justified this by analysing the language of the section. He noted that if the expression 'omission' was substituted for the word 'action' the section was ungrammatical and incomprehensible. This 'real and substantial' difficulty in the interpretation of the Act could only be resolved by an examination of the legislative history of the section. After considering the statutory history,[112] Bridge held that it was not possible to conclude that an omission was capable of amounting to a contravention of the section.[113] The Labour Government elected in 1997 identified this outcome as a 'loophole' in the protection offered to trade unionists and, subsequently, amended s 146(1) by Sched 2 to the 1999 Act, so ensuring that an omission is considered as an act for the purposes of the legislation.

---

107 See *Brassington v Cauldron Wholesalers Ltd* [1978] ICR 405 and *Grogan v British Rlys Board* (1978) (unreported).

108 Eg, see *Carlson v The Post Office* [1981] ICR 343, refusing a union member a car parking permit, *Department of Transport v Gallacher* [1993] ICR 654, failing to promote a union member.

109 [1987] IRLR 80.

110 [1993] IRLR 336.

111 [1995] ICR 406.

112 At pp 412–15. The original right on action short of dismissal derived from the Industrial Relations Act 1971 did expressly provide protection for omissions to act. Bridge thus argued that the legislative draftsman must have been aware of this when excluding omissions from the statute that now forms the basis of the present right.

113 Lord Keith agreed with Bridge and Browne-Wilkinson came 'regretfully' to the same conclusion. However, both Lords Slynn and Lloyd rejected this view and agreed with the analysis of the Court of Appeal.

Against the employee as an individual

The action taken by the employer must be directed against the employee as an individual. Action taken against the union itself, that then has indirectly negative consequences for the employee, was not 'action short of dismissal' for the purposes of the section.[114] This issue arose in *NCB v Ridgway*.[115] After the defeat of the National Union of Mineworkers (NUM) in the miners' strike, the Union of Democratic Mineworkers (UDM) was formed, consisting of many miners who had opposed the strike. The National Coal Board recognised the UDM for bargaining purposes and negotiated a pay rise with this union. At pits where neither the NUM nor the UDM were in a majority, the NCB decided to grant the pay rise to members of the UDM only. Ridgway and other members of the NUM who were denied the pay rise complained that the failure to increase their pay was action taken against them as individuals which penalised them for membership of the NUM.

The EAT[116] interpreted the provision relatively strictly by maintaining that there was a distinction between discriminating against a union and discriminating against its members as individuals. This action was not aimed against the applicants personally as individuals, as required under the section, but was taken as punitive action against the NUM itself. The applicants were thus only damaged indirectly as a consequence of the general decision to punish the union.

However, the majority of the Court of Appeal in *Ridgway*,[117] with May LJ dissenting, held that the action of withholding a pay award was action against an individual. As individuals, they were penalised by the loss of money, which was a direct loss to them as individuals.[118] This was not merely an attack on the union with indirect consequences for their members.[119]

The 'purpose' of the action

The existence of a mere detriment or disadvantage[120] that prevents, deters or penalises an individual is not enough to satisfy the section. It is also necessary to show the employer's purpose in doing this was to stop the employee from joining or staying in a union or from engaging in union activities.

An issue that has become highly significant is whether members of a particular union who are targeted by an employer (as in *Ridgway*) have the protection of the section where the employer is motivated by hostility to that particular union rather than general hostility to all trade unions at the workplace.

---

114 See *Brassington v Cauldron Wholesale Ltd* [1978] ICR 405.

115 [1987] IRLR 80.

116 [1986] IRLR 379.

117 For comment on this and other issues raised in this case, see Fitzpatrick, B and Rees, W (1987) 16 ILJ 201; Simpson, R (1987) 50 MLR 639; and Howarth, D [1987] CLJ 227.

118 As Nicholls LJ said, at p 88: 'I find it difficult to think of an action, short of dismissal, which an employer can take ... which could more obviously qualify as action taken against him as an individual than a reduction in, or a failure to increase pay.'

119 The majority approved the EAT decision in *Carlson v The Post Office* [1981] IRLR 158. Also, on this issue see *FW Farnsworth v McCoid* [1999] IRLR 626.

120 The disadvantage can be of a very trivial nature – see *Carlson v The Post Office* [1981] ICR 343.

The Court of Appeal, in *NCB v Ridgway*[121] (the facts of which we considered earlier), held that, on a true construction of the section, the protection extends not only to an attack on trade unions generally, but also to an attack on a particular trade union. Accordingly, the section does cover the situation where the employer's purpose is to prevent an employee from becoming a member of a particular trade union or where the purpose was to penalise an individual for joining or being a member of a particular trade union.[122]

However, the Court of Appeal, when making this decision, had clearly focused on the manifestly hostile behaviour of the employer towards the NUM. In *obiter* comments, the Court of Appeal suggested that if the purpose of the discrimination was to further a legitimate industrial relations objective, such as to simplify bargaining structures at the place of work, then that may not be action that offends against the section. This is because the action may not have as its purpose an intention to penalise or deter *per se*.

This was the issue that the Court of Appeal in *Associated Newspapers v Wilson; Associated British Ports v Palmer*[123] had to directly decide. In the first case, the employers had derecognised the union, terminated collective bargaining arrangements and awarded pay rises only to those who agreed to new contracts of employment. In the second, the employers offered a pay rise to staff who entered into a 'personal' contract of employment, with the proviso that they gave up their right to union representation for collective bargaining purposes. Those employees who refused the offer still had their terms and conditions agreed through the collective bargaining system, but were denied the pay rise. In both cases, the common issue to determine was the employer's purpose. Was it to penalise the applicants for their union membership, to deter them from continuing as union members, or merely to further a change in the employment relationship between the employer and their individual employees?

The Court of Appeal refused to disturb the industrial tribunal's view in these two cases. By making the alternative contracts so attractive, the purpose in *Palmer* was to penalise the applicants because they would not abandon their union representation. In *Wilson*, the employer's purpose in providing selective pay increases was ultimately to deter individual journalists from remaining as members.[124] The employer's objective may well have been to ensure contractual flexibility, but that was not the same as the employer's purpose. The purpose of the action was to persuade employees to abandon union representation.

This decision was not favourably received by the Conservative Government, as it impinged on the employer's prerogative to alter industrial relations structures and bargaining arrangements and clearly threatened the whole basis of Government policy towards collective bargaining. The Government's spokesperson in the House of Lords remarked: 'It was never the Government's intention, when the law on action short of

---

121 [1987] IRLR 80.

122 The Court of Appeal approved the similar reasoning of the EAT in *Carlson* and overruled the EAT's decision in *Rath v Cruden Construction Ltd* [1982] IRLR 9. See, also, *Adlam v Salisbury Wells College* [1985] ICR 786.

123 [1993] IRLR 336.

124 In the EAT [1993] IRLR 63, it had been held that the employer's purpose in ending collective bargaining was to achieve business efficiency via greater contractual flexibility.

dismissal was introduced, that it should be interpreted in this way or that it should interfere with an employer's freedom to make such a change.'[125] Thus, the response to the Court of Appeal decision was the introduction of an amendment at a late stage of the passage of the Trade Union Reform and Employment Rights Bill through the Lords.

This amendment in the 1993 Act incorporated a new s 148(3)–(5) into the TULR(C)A 1992. Section 148(1) concerns the burden of proof and provides that the onus is on the employer to show the purpose for which he took the action against the employee. The new sub-s (3) continues by stating that:

In determining what was the purpose for which action was taken by the employer against the complainant in a case where –

(a) there is evidence that the employer's purpose was to further a change in his relationship with all or any class[126] of his employees; and

(b) there is also evidence that his purpose was one falling within s 146,

the tribunal shall regard the purpose mentioned in para (a) ... as the the purpose for which the employer took action[127] ... unless it considers that the action was such as no reasonable employer would take having regard to the purpose mentioned in para (a).

The amended section, therefore, covers the situation where there are two purposes in taking the action; one collectively to alter a relationship with a defined group of employees, the other to penalise or deter union membership or activities. Where this is the case, the tribunal is instructed to ignore the second purpose unless it considers that the act taken by the employer to achieve the change in bargaining relationship was one that 'no reasonable employer would take'.[128] Then, and only then, has the tribunal jurisdiction to examine the employer's actions.

After the passage of the Trade Union Reform and Employment Rights Act 1993, the House of Lords heard the appeal in *Wilson* and *Palmer*[129] from the Court of Appeal. The House of Lords in overruling the Court of Appeal did not require the assistance of the new statutory provision. The House of Lords believed the Court of Appeal had misunderstood the 'ultimate' purpose of the employer's action. According to Lord Bridge, there was insufficient evidence that the ultimate purpose had been to deter the applicants from being members of the trade union or to penalise them for their membership. Rather, the evidence from the hearing at the industrial tribunal indicated

---

125 Viscount Ullswater (Hansard, HL, col 860, 6 May 1993).

126 Class is defined in s 148(5) as 'those employed at a particular place of work, those employees of a particular grade, category or description or those of a particular grade, category or description employed at a particular place of work'.

127 The legitimacy of the employer's purpose is unaffected by how successful the employer has been in changing the relationship with a class of employees (ie where few employees have given up their right to collective bargaining). It is enough that the employer was intending to further that purpose – s 148(4).

128 Presumably, the greater the incentive offered to employees to relinquish union membership the more likely doubts could be raised as to the 'reasonableness' of the employer's actions.

129 [1995] ICR 406.

that the real intention behind the employer's action was to enhance business efficiency by reforming the system of contractual negotiations with employees.[130]

The conclusions of the House of Lords, in *Wilson* and *Palmer*, and the previous statutory changes initiated as a consequence of the Court of Appeal decision have serious implications for the future structure of collective bargaining.[131] First, it is clear that it is not action short of dismissal for an employer to offer differential payments to employees if the object is to encourage them to relinquish their union membership and their right to trade union representation and collective bargaining.

Furthermore, where the employer wishes to streamline bargaining structures by limiting the number of unions representing employees, it would be lawful to offer an inducement to members of one union over another, thereby causing one or more of the other unions to 'wither on the vine'. An employer may also, in pursuance, or as a consequence of a single union deal, derecognise existing unions and entice members by a one off payment to join a sole (new or existing) recognised union. Employers may also lawfully interfere in union recruitment disputes by making payments to encourage employees to remain with one union over another or to join one union rather than another; thereby in certain circumstances subverting decisions of the TUC Disputes Committee. Employers can justify these changes on the grounds that, in all of the above circumstances, the purpose (or one of the purposes) of the employer was to further a change in the relationship with a class of employees.

Action short of dismissal and the Employment Relations Act 1999

The decisions in *Wilson* and *Palmer* and the statutory amendment to the law on action short of dismissal were heavily criticised by trade unionists at the time as they provided employers with the opportunity lawfully to discriminate against union members as individuals and so further limit trade union influence at the workplace. Subsequently, the Labour Government's White Paper, *Fairness at Work*,[132] identified this form of discrimination as '... contrary to its commitment to ensuring individuals are free to choose whether or not to join a trade union'.[133] The White Paper, however, only specifically proposed to change the law in order to ensure that it would be unlawful to discriminate by omission (the first limb of the House of Lords' decision in *Wilson* and

---

130 See also the earlier Court of Appeal decision in *Gallacher v Department of Transport* [1994] IRLR 231. Here, the employer's decision not to promote the applicant employee (as he had little management experience because of his involvement in union affairs), arguably, penalised him for his trade union activities. The Court of Appeal distinguished between the purpose or 'object which the employer desired' or 'sought to achieve' and the effect of the employer's actions. In this case, it was not the employer's intention to penalise the employee for trade union reasons, even though this was the effect of the employer's decision.

131 For a cogent analysis and criticism of the House of Lords' decision in *Wilson and Palmer* and the statutory amendment, see Simpson, R, 'Freedom of association and the right to organise: the failure of an individual rights strategy' (1995) 24 ILJ 235, pp 237–49. See also Auerbach, S, *Derecognition and Personal Contracts: Fighting Tactics and the Law* (1993, Institute of Employment Rights), Chapter 4.

132 Cm 3968, 1998.

133 Paragraph 4.25.

Palmer) and did not explicitly propose to repeal the Conservative amendment or deal with the second limb of the *Wilson* and *Palmer* judgment.

During the consultation period (before the publication of the Employment Relations Bill) and during the passage of the Act through Parliament, trade unions lobbied for explicit changes to the law on all of these issues. However, the Government failed to act decisively. Rather than introducing substantive amendments, the Government instead reserved the right to deal with these issues in the future by the passage of secondary legislation (which, at the time of writing, have yet to be published). Section 17 of the 1999 Act provides the Secretary of State with the power to make regulations:

... about cases where a worker:

(a) is subject to a detriment by his employer, or

(b) is dismissed,

on the grounds that he refuses to enter into a contract which includes terms which differ from the terms of a collective agreement which applies to him.

To complicate matters still further, the Government accepted (during the passage of the legislation in the House of Lords) a Conservative amendment to s 17 that reads:

(4) The payment of higher wages or higher rates of pay or overtime or the payment of any signing on or other bonuses or the provision of other benefits having a monetary value to other workers employed by the same employer shall not constitute a detriment to any worker not receiving the same or similar payments or benefits ... so long as –

(a) there is no inhibition in the contract of employment of the worker receiving the same from being the member of any trade union, and

(b) the said payments of higher wages or rates of pay or overtime or bonuses or the provision of other benefits are in accordance with the terms of a contract of employment and reasonably relate to services provided by the worker under that contract.

This provision reinforces the principle that discrimination by an employer between employees whose terms and conditions are determined collectively and those who accept the determination of terms and conditions individually is permissible and legitimises a rather false distinction between discrimination on grounds of union membership (unlawful) and discrimination against collective bargaining (lawful). It provides that an employee must not be formally victimised for being a union member *per se*, but that it is legitimate to offer individualised contracts that undermine collective bargaining – one of the essential benefits of union membership.

The question that arises for the future is what the relationship will be between s 17(4) of the 1999 Act, existing case law as represented by the House of Lords judgment in *Wilson* and *Palmer*, s 148(3)–(5) of TULR(C)A 1992 and any future regulations issued under the authority of s 17(1) of the 1999 Act. What is certain is that, until regulations or substantive amendments are introduced, an employer may lawfully offer personal contracts and a financial incentive to employees to reject collectively agreed terms – which may have the practical effect of inducing them to leave their union.

The law as it now stands remains in breach of Art 1 of the International Labour Organisation (ILO) Convention No 98 on the Right to Organise and to Collective Bargaining. This Article specifically states that all workers are entitled to 'adequate protection against acts of anti-union discrimination' and acts 'that prejudice a worker by reason of union membership'. The ILO Freedom of Association Committee has, on several occasions, found UK law permitting differential treatment as described above as anti union discrimination for the purposes of Art 1.[134] Of greater legal significance (with the passage of the Human Rights Act 1998) is the likelihood that the present law is contrary to the standards established by Art 11 of the European Convention on Human Rights. Article 11 specifically provides that: 'Everyone has the right to join trade unions ... for the protection of his interests.' European case law, such as *National Union of Belgian Police v Belgium*[135] and *Swedish Engine Drivers Union v Sweden*,[136] has established that a union member is entitled to some form of representation by their trade union on workplace issues. Thus, UK case law and legislation that permits victimisation or discrimination against an individual who wishes their union to represent their interests through the collective bargaining process is potentially in violation of Art 11. In addition, discrimination between different unions at the workplace and between non-members and union members could also amount to a breach of Art 14 (which states that all rights provided by the Convention must be provided without discrimination, unless the discrimination can be objectively justified).[137] The unions in the *Wilson* and *Palmer* cases have lodged a claim with the Strasbourg institutions on this basis that has been declared 'admissible'. Judgment by the European Court of Human Rights is expected later in 2002.

Remedies

The procedure for determining a complaint is contained in s 147. The complaint must be made to an employment tribunal within three months of the action occurring, unless it was not reasonably practicable for the complaint to be presented within the three month period.[138] Should the tribunal find the complaint justified, a declaration must be made to that effect. A compensation order may then be made. Compensation is assessed according to what the tribunal thinks is '... just and equitable in all the circumstances having regard to the infringement of the complainant's rights ... by the employer's act complained of and to any loss sustained by the complainant which is attributable to that action'.[139]

The EAT, in *Brassington v Cauldon Wholesalers Ltd*,[140] rejected the notion that a punitive element of compensation could be awarded under this section. The basis of the discretionary monetary award is purely one of compensation for the employee. Any

---

134 294th Report of the Freedom of Association Committee, paras 192–203; 304th Report of the Freedom of Association Committee, para 498; 309th Report of the Freedom of Association Committee, para 342. Most recently, the Committee of Experts on the Application of Conventions and Recommendations has concurred with the Freedom of Association Committee's conclusions (Report III, Pt 1A, 2000). See, generally, Novitz, T (2000) 63 MLR 379 and Ewing, KD, 'Dancing with daffodils' (2000) 50 *Federation News* 1.

135 (1975) 1 EHRR 578.

136 (1976) 1 EHRR 617.

137 See *Schmidt & Dahlstrom v Sweden* (1976) 1 EHRR 632.

138 See *British Airways Board v Clark* [1982] IRLR 238.

139 Section 149(2).

140 [1978] ICR 405.

actual financial loss is clearly recoverable, such as loss of pay through attendance at the tribunal. However, in addition, the EAT felt that compensation for non-pecuniary loss would be appropriate in certain circumstances, such as where the application has caused stress and anxiety or where the employee has been deprived of union benefits. This was confirmed by the Court of Appeal in *NCB v Ridgway*[141] (with May LJ dissenting). The applicants were entitled to assert a claim for compensation for the frustration and stress caused by having to work alongside other employees who were paid the wage rise for doing the same work.[142]

THE RIGHT NOT TO BE DISCRIMINATED AGAINST IN RECRUITMENT[143]

This right was introduced by the Employment Act 1990, now enacted in ss 137–43 of the TULR(C)A 1992. These provisions provide some protection against anti-union hiring policies and should be considered in conjunction with both the Court of Appeal's judgment in *Fitzpatrick v BRB*[144] which, in some circumstances, protects those who are dismissed for union activities prior to their employment and with the new 'blacklisting' provisions considered below.

Essentially, any individual 'seeking employment' has the right not to be refused employment because he or she is a member of a trade union or specified trade union.[145] Refusal in s 137(5) is defined in some detail, beyond merely refusing an application or enquiry. It also includes causing the withdrawal of an application, refusing to make an offer after an interview or making an offer, but on unreasonable terms or conditions or withdrawing an offer after it has been made. Under s 138, it is unlawful for an employment agency to refuse its services to any person on grounds of union membership.

Complaints of discrimination in recruitment are heard by an employment tribunal.[146] One problem for the those denied employment in these circumstances is that the burden of proof is on the applicant. Where it is impossible to obtain direct evidence of the unlawful reason, the tribunal may accept inferences of anti-union bias from all the surrounding circumstances.[147] If a complaint is upheld, a declaration to that effect will be made. The tribunal also has the authority to make a declaration that the employer takes

---

141 [1987] IRLR 80.

142 See also *Cleveland Ambulance NHS Trust v Blane* [1997] IRLR 332 where £1,000 was awarded as damages 'for injury to feelings' where the complainant had not been shortlisted for promotion as he was an active trade unionist.

143 See, generally, Townshend-Smith, R, 'Refusal of employment on grounds of trade union membership or non-membership' (1991) 20 ILJ 102, and Simpson, R, 'The Employment Act in context' (1991) 54 MLR 418.

144 [1991] IRLR 376.

145 This right also applies to those individuals denied access to employment on non-union grounds. Arguably, the main intention of the provision is to restrict the operation of the pre-entry closed shop. See Government Green Paper, *Removing Barriers to Employment*, Cmnd 655, 1989, Chapter 2.

146 Section 141.

147 Such as leading questions in an interview about union status.

action to eliminate or reduce the effects of the unlawful conduct on the individual. A compensation order may be made which can include an award for injury to feelings.[148]

A question of some importance is whether the union member who is denied access to employment because of his or her known reputation as a union activist will be able to rely on this right. Technically, as the provision only applies to discrimination on grounds of union membership, the answer may well be no. If *Discount Tobacco v Armitage*[149] is still good law, the activist would have a greater chance of protection. This case was authority for the view that making use of membership is merely incidental to, or a manifestation of, union membership *per se*.[150] The House of Lords' decision in *Wilson* and *Palmer* has arguably limited the scope of those activities that can be regarded as 'incidental' to membership.[151] Consequently, protection may be dependent on the way union membership is used: with a distinction being made between the ordinary member who has made a 'legitimate' use of membership, and the activist 'troublemaker' who has not.

In 1991 the TUC complained to the ILO that the Employment Act 1990 did not go far enough in protecting trade unionists at the stage of recruitment. The Committee of Experts, in observing that there had been a breach of Art 1 of ILO Convention No 98, focused on the lack of protection for those trade unionists refused employment on grounds of their past union activities and criticised the problems applicants have in 'proving the real nature of their ... denial of employment'. Additionally, the Freedom of Association Committee of the ILO in 1992 reported that the 'blacklisting' activities of organisations like The Economic League (where lists of active trade unionists are provided to employers for them to cross check against job applicants) was a serious violation of ILO standards.[152]

Partly in response to the ILO judgment, the Government, in *Fairness at Work*,[153] gave a commitment to prohibit the formation and use of such lists.[154] The provisions, however, contained in s 3 of the 1999 Act, do not actually proscribe blacklisting. They provide that the Secretary of State may introduce regulations to prohibit the use, sale or supply of such lists. The regulations will provide a general right for individuals (and/or their trade unions) to complain to an employment tribunal against both the users and compilers of blacklists if they are the subject of discrimination. The new regulations are also likely to introduce criminal sanctions against those compiling blacklists and against those who supply them. The Government is presently consulting all sides of industry on the text of the draft regulations. At the time of writing they have yet to be published.

---

148 Financial compensation is assessed in the same way as the compensatory award for unfair dismissal.

149 [1990] IRLR 15.

150 The Court of Appeal in *Wilson* and *Palmer* had agreed with the EAT in *Armitage* that participation in certain union activity was an extension of union membership.

151 In *Harrison v Kent CC* [1995] ICR 434, the EAT held that a refusal to employ a person because of their union record was a breach of this section. However, this decision relied heavily on the *Discount Tobacco v Armitage* case before it had been criticised by the House of Lords.

152 For further details, see Ewing, KD, *Britain and the ILO* (1994, Institute of Employment Rights).

153 Cm 3968, 1998.

154 The Data Protection Act 1998 (which implements the EC Data Protection Directive (95/46/EC)) will require organisations holding information on individuals to disclose such personal data. However, it is not fully operational until 2007.

THE INDIVIDUAL RIGHT TO BE ACCOMPANIED IN GRIEVANCE OR DISCIPLINARY HEARINGS[155]

The Employment Relations Act 1999, ss 10–15, has created a new right for workers[156] to be accompanied in disciplinary or grievance hearings by a trade union official or a fellow worker. These provisions will allow a trade union official to enter an employer's premises to represent a union member, if the member so requests, even where a trade union (or that particular union) is not recognised. Trade unions will now be able to market their representational services in order to recruit new members at non-unionised workplaces. This right may thus be of particular value to trade unions keen to attract members in order to apply for recognition under the new statutory recognition laws contained in Sched 1A of the 1999 Act (see Chapter 10).

Definition of disciplinary and grievance proceedings

Section 13(4) of the 1999 Act defines a disciplinary hearing as any hearing that could result in:

(a) the administration of a formal warning to a worker by his employer;

(b) the taking of some other action in respect of a worker by his employer (such as demotion, suspension, dismissal);

(c) the confirmation of a warning issued or some other action taken (as in an appeal by the worker concerned).

It seems that the right to be accompanied only applies to hearings that may result in formal disciplinary action taken against the worker or where a worker is challenging disciplinary action at an appeal. Thus, informal interviews or 'chats' with a worker without any record of action noted on a file would be excluded. This view of the scope of disciplinary hearings is confirmed by the new ACAS Code of Practice on Disciplinary and Grievance Procedures (2000)[157] which contains detailed guidance on the operation of the law and is taken into account by tribunals when deliberating on a violation of the right. Paragraph 53 states that:

> Employers often choose to deal with disciplinary problems in the first instance by means of an informal interview or counselling session. So long as the informal interview or counselling session does not result in a formal warning or some other action it would not generally be good practice for the worker to be accompanied as matters at this informal stage are best resolved directly by the worker and manager concerned.

---

155 See also Clancy, M and Seifert, R, *Fairness at Work? The Disciplinary and Grievance Provisions of the 1999 Employment Relations Act* (2000, Institute of Employment Rights).

156 1999 Act, ss 13(1) and 230(3), define a 'worker' as an individual who works under a contract of employment or any other contract where services are personally performed or those persons who are agency workers, home workers, a person in Crown employment or a person employed by Parliament. This definition of 'worker' is wider in scope than the definition of 'employee'. However, individuals who are genuinely self-employed do not qualify as 'workers' as they do not enjoy a *personal* relationship with the hirer of their services. On the test for employment status see, *inter alia*, *Express & Echo Publications Ltd v Tanton* [1999] IRLR 367; *MacFarlane v Glasgow CC* [2000] IRLR 7; *Carmichael v National Power* [2000] IRLR 43; and *Montgomery v Johnson Underwood Ltd* [2001] IRLR 269.

157 This revises and replaces the ACAS Guide on Disciplinary Practice and Procedures previously applied in unfair dismissal proceedings.

The right to be accompanied at a grievance hearing applies only where the grievance issue 'concerns the performance of a duty by an employer in relation to a worker'.[158] This has been further defined in the Code of Practice to mean a legal duty arising from statute (such as an allegation concerning equal pay or health and safety) or common law (such as an allegation that the employer has broken a term of the employment contract). The intention is to ensure that the right is not available where an employee has a grievance on a trivial or irrelevant (to the employment relationship) issue. The Code of Practice also specifically notes that a grievance regarding the future improvement of pay or other terms of the contract of employment is excluded, as it is not a complaint about existing terms.[159] Hence, it is not possible for individuals to declare a grievance on issues that are properly a matter for collective trade union representation.[160]

The scope of the right

The statutory right applies where a worker:

(a) is required or invited by his employer to attend a disciplinary or grievance hearing; and

(b) reasonably requests to be accompanied at the hearing.[161]

The section makes clear that the worker must ask to be accompanied. The employer need not inform the worker of the right and if the worker wants a trade union representative to attend, his or her trade union membership will become known to the employer (with all the dangers that that might entail). Additionally, the right only applies where the worker 'reasonably requests' to be accompanied. This raises the prospect of an employer challenging the worker's request for accompaniment because the subject to which it relates is insufficiently serious. The Code of Practice fails to elaborate on this point apart from unhelpfully stating that it would be up to the courts to ascertain when a request is reasonable in all the circumstances.

Once the worker makes the request, s 10(2) states that the employer must allow the worker to be accompanied at the subsequent hearing by a single companion chosen by the worker, who is either another of the employer's workers or a designated trade union official.[162] The companion is to be permitted to address the hearing (but not to answer questions on behalf of the worker) and to confer with the applicant during the hearing. It is clear that the worker is free to choose the identity of the companion, even to the extent of choosing someone who is an official of another union rather than the one that is recognised. The Code of Practice recommends, however, that where a particular trade union is recognised in a workplace it is appropriate for an official from that union to be

---

158 Section 13(5).

159 See para 55.

160 Thus, the right cannot be used in order to obtain *de facto* recognition.

161 Section 10(1).

162 Section 10(3) states that the union representative may be an employed official as defined in TULR(C)A 1992, s 119, or a local lay official (also defined under s 119, such as a branch secretary) who is 'reasonably certified' by the union as having the necessary experience and training to act as a companion.

selected to accompany the worker at the hearing.[163] The right to accompaniment does not place a statutory duty on the union automatically to provide a companion,[164] although union members may have a contractual right to representation derived from their union rule book.[165]

The companion who accompanies the worker is entitled to reasonable time off with full pay during working hours to prepare for, and attend, the grievance or disciplinary hearing,[166] enforceable by a complaint to an employment tribunal. The Act also states that the accompaniment task is to be treated as a trade union duty or activity for the purposes of the protection contained in ss 168–69 and ss 171–73 of the TULR(C)A 1992.[167]

Section 10(4) of the Act allows for the hearing to be postponed should the worker's chosen companion not be available at the time proposed for the hearing by the employer. In such a case, the employer must postpone the hearing if an alternative time proposed by the worker is 'reasonable' and is within a period of five working days from the day after the date proposed by the employer. If the employer does not postpone, and proceeds without the worker being allowed their chosen companion, it will be treated as a refusal possibly leading to a tribunal claim for compensation.

An important issue that goes to the scope of the right is where the employer does not have a formal disciplinary or grievance procedure. The 1999 Act does not compel employers to introduce formal procedures. The only statutory guidance is contained in s 3 of the Employment Rights Act 1996 which obliges employers with 20 or more employees to inform them of any disciplinary or grievance procedures that are applicable to them. However, case law indicates that all employees (not 'workers') enjoy an implied term in their contracts that the employer must deal reasonably with grievances raised by the employee.[168] If, in order to comply with this contractual obligation, the employer holds a meeting to deal with a grievance, the employee will enjoy the right to be accompanied provided the grievance concerns the performance of a duty by the employer. Also note that the Employment Bill 2002 provides for a statutory grievance, disciplinary and dismissal procedure to be incorporated into every employee's contract of employment.

Remedies

Section 11 of the Act provides a remedy against an employer who has 'failed or threatened to fail' to allow the right of accompaniment under s 10(2) or who has postponed proceedings under s 10(4). A tribunal claim could thus be taken where the employer has threatened to deny a worker the right and the disciplinary matter or grievance is later withdrawn without a hearing. A complaint must be made to an

---

163 Paragraph 58.

164 Paragraph 59.

165 See *English v Unison* (2001) (unreported) where in the county court it was held that a union member does not have an unqualified and absolute contractual right to representation as the relevant rule book provision must be construed subject to a reasonableness test. Thus, where there was little or no merit in the individual's case the union was justified in refusing representational services.

166 Section 10(6) and para 61.

167 Section 10(7).

168 *WA Goold (Pearmark) Ltd v McConnell* [1995] IRLR 516.

employment tribunal before the end of a period of three months, beginning with the date of the failure or threatened failure. This can be extended, at the discretion of the tribunal, if it was not 'reasonably practicable' for the application to be presented in time.

If an employment tribunal finds a complaint well founded, it can make an award of compensation to the worker not exceeding two weeks' pay.[169] This will be subject to the maximum week's pay limits within s 227(1) of Employment Rights Act 1996, which is currently £240 (from 1 February 2001).

Section 12 of the Act also provides protection where a worker has suffered a detriment for exercising the right to be accompanied or to postpone the hearing or where the worker is the chosen companion and has been victimised for seeking to accompany the individual exercising the right.[170] A worker who has been subjected to a detriment, up to and including dismissal, must apply to an employment tribunal within three months of the alleged act by the employer. This period can be extended at the discretion of the tribunal. Dismissal for exercising the rights is automatically unfair and there are no qualifying period or upper age limit restrictions.[171] Note that the unfair dismissal protection ordinarily available only to employees is also made available by s 12(6) to those falling within the wider definition of 'worker'.

Workers who have been subject to dismissal may also claim interim relief. If interim relief is granted, employment is continued (on full pay and benefits) pending the outcome of the full tribunal hearing. This will only be granted where the tribunal is convinced that the substantive claim is likely to succeed at a subsequent full hearing. An application for interim relief has to be submitted before the dismissal or within seven days after the effective date of termination of the employment contract.

Additionally, a failure to initiate a formal disciplinary process before dismissal (in order to avoid the requirements of the provisions) or a refusal to permit accompaniment in a disciplinary hearing that results in dismissal, may support a finding that the employee was unfairly dismissed under s 98 of the Employment Rights Act 1996. Whether an employer has acted unfairly depends on whether the employer acted reasonably in all the circumstances in deciding to dismiss the employee. A failure to comply with procedural safeguards (such as the disciplinary procedure outlined in the ACAS Code) has always been an important element tribunals consider when assessing whether an employer's response to dismiss was unreasonable and therefore unfair. A failure to permit representation as required by s 10 of the 1999 Act may also be a factor which tribunals will consider when deliberating on an employee's claim of unfair dismissal. [172]

---

169 Section 11(3).

170 Section 12(1)(b) establishes that this protection is also available where the worker is accompanying or intends to accompany an individual who is a worker of another employer.

171 Section 12(4).

172 Note that the right not to be unfairly dismissed applies only to 'employees' and not 'workers'. The Government has the power under the 1999 Act, s 23, to extend this protection to other forms of employment relationship but has not, as yet, introduced the necessary regulations.

CHAPTER 10

COLLECTIVE RIGHTS FOR TRADE UNIONS – RECOGNITION

In the previous chapter, the degree to which freedom of association and the process of collective bargaining have been enhanced by individual rights for union members and officials was considered. The next two chapters focus on the development of collective rights for trade unions. Most of these institutional rights (like individual rights) derive from the Labour Government's Social Contract legislation in the 1970s and European Community initiatives.

The only collective right that directly supports trade union bargaining is the right to the disclosure of information from an undertaking prior to negotiation on matters of collective bargaining.[1] The other institutional rights – such as the right to information and consultation on redundancy, on the transfer of an undertaking, health and safety and pensions – indirectly reinforce freedom of association and collective bargaining by promoting trade union influence at the workplace. A major drawback for trade unions is that most of these rights are dependent upon the trade union being recognised by an employer. Furthermore, there is little incentive for workers to join a union which is unable to negotiate on behalf of its members for enhanced terms and conditions of employment. Thus, without recognition, a union is marginalised at the workplace and cannot function in any meaningful or effective way. For the past 20 years, the decision whether or not to recognise a trade union has been solely a matter for the employer. Now, as a consequence of reforms established by the Employment Relations Act 1999, a right to recognition for limited bargaining purposes has been introduced.

This chapter considers the historical background to the issue of State support for recognition, examines the degree to which recognition has been controlled by the law and addresses the question as to how effective the imposition of the new legal duty on employers to recognise and bargain with unions is likely to be.

STATE SUPPORT FOR UNION RECOGNITION

Historically, trade unions have often been ambivalent towards the concept of direct State support for recognition. This has been partly due to a concern that legal interference in voluntary arrangements between employer and union would damage the tradition of 'legal abstentionism' in industrial relations and partly because of a genuine belief held by many trade unionists that there was no need for legal measures to enforce recognition.

For much of the 20th century, recognition was assured in the public sector for both manual and white collar unions as the State, since the Whitley Reports of 1917, had pursued a positive policy of recognition and co-operation with public sector unions.[2] To

---

1   Defined in TULR(C)A 1992, s 178(2).

2   In the State-run industries, provisions for union recognition were included in the nationalisation statutes. Eg, Coal Industry Nationalisation Act 1946, s 46(1); Iron and Steel Act 1949, s 39; Electricity Act 1947, s 53; Gas Act, 1948, s 57.

an extent, recognition and bargaining rights were guaranteed in much of the private sector by trade union strength. This was particularly true in the traditional heavy industries which had a record of very high union membership and a history and culture of solidarity and collective action. Certainly, in evidence to the Donovan Commission, the TUC thought there was no need for legal support as '... trade unions in Britain have succeeded through their own efforts in strengthening their organisation and in obtaining recognition without relying on the assistance of government through legislation'.[3]

The Donovan Commission regarded this as a somewhat complacent view. In the less unionised industries, recognition issues were still a major source of conflict between employers and unions. The Commission also identified a weakness in the developing white collar unions in the private sector. Without a history of solidarity and collective action, few white collar unions were able to achieve recognition in the face of employer opposition.

As the Donovan Commission proceeded on the basis that the pursuit of orderly industrial relations was best served by an extension of collective bargaining, this inconsistency of recognition across and between industries was unsatisfactory. To secure collective bargaining in all sectors of the economy an effective means of dealing with the problems of recognition was required. The Commission recommended the establishment of an independent tribunal to which recognition disputes could be referred. This tribunal would investigate all the circumstances of the dispute and would have the power to make recognition recommendations.[4]

In response to these proposals, the Labour Government in 1968 set up by Royal Warrant the Commission on Industrial Relations. One of the roles of this Commission was to facilitate recognition by providing conciliation services where there was a recognition dispute. It could also inquire into the circumstances of a dispute and make recognition recommendations. A serious weakness, however, was the Commission's lack of enforcement powers.

Before the success of this tribunal could be evaluated the Labour Government lost the 1970 election. The Conservatives, in the Industrial Relations Act 1971, put the Commission on Industrial Relations onto a statutory footing and provided registered trade unions with full rights of recognition. However, union hostility to the Act meant that these provisions never operated effectively. For the returning Labour Government in 1974, the broadening of collective bargaining throughout industry was a central theme of its industrial and economic policy. An essential element of this policy was the extension of recognition. For the first time, this was to be achieved through an enforcement procedure contained in ss 11–16 of the Employment Protection Act 1975.

---

3   Royal Commission on Trade Unions and Employers' Associations, Cmnd 3623, 1968, Appendix 2.
4   Paragraphs 253–56.

The statutory recognition experiment 1976–80

The s 11 procedure[5]

The statutory recognition procedure relied heavily on persuading employers to recognise trade unions by conciliation and mediation. It was only after an exhaustive process intended to encourage employers voluntarily to recognise and negotiate with unions that enforcement procedures were applied. Where an employer refused voluntarily to recognise a union for collective bargaining purposes, the union had the option of referring this refusal to the Advisory, Conciliation and Arbitration Service (ACAS) under s 11 of the Act. If initial conciliation between the parties was unsuccessful, ACAS was then required to comply with a protracted procedure outlined in the statute before a recommendation of recognition could be made. This procedure provided for a process of consultation and inquiry with the employer, the union and all relevant employees. Where the employer refused to comply with a recommendation of recognition, ACAS was empowered to make a second attempt to settle the matter by conciliation.

If this was unsuccessful, the statute then provided for the union to apply to the Central Arbitration Committee (CAC) for an arbitration award. The practice of the CAC was to make an award which enhanced terms and conditions of employment, equivalent to the bargain, which recognition, had it been granted, would have provided. The CAC did not regard it as within its role to penalise reluctant employers by imposing punitive awards.[6]

ACAS and judicial review

The only remedy for employers dissatisfied by an ACAS decision was to seek a judicial review of that decision by way of a declaration that ACAS was in breach of its statutory duty. This depended upon ACAS wrongly exercising its power to recommend recognition by failing to comply with the procedure outlined in ss 11–16. Although the scope for judicial intervention was relatively narrow, this did not stop the courts from vigorously examining the basis of ACAS decision making.

Much of the litigation surrounded the interpretation of s 14(1) of the Employment Protection Act 1975. This provided that during the course of its inquiries and before making a recommendation of recognition, ACAS '... shall ascertain the opinion of the workers to whom the issue relates by any means it thinks fit ...'. This section arguably gave ACAS discretion as to how it should ascertain the workers opinion. This discretion, however, was seriously limited by judicial understanding of the ACAS role.

In *Powley v ACAS*,[7] both the ASTMS union and a staff association had substantial membership amongst employees at the employer's workplace. On being refused recognition by the employer, ASTMS referred the question of its recognition under s 11 to ACAS. ACAS, as part of the investigation and inquiry stage under s 14, issued a

---

5   For a full description of the procedure, see Dickens, L, 'ACAS and the union recognition procedure' (1978) 7 ILJ 160.
6   See Doyle, B, 'A substitute for collective bargaining? The CAC's approach to s 16 of the Employment Protection Act 1975' (1980) 9 ILJ 154.
7   [1978] ICR 123.

questionnaire to all the employees to establish the support for ASTMS amongst the workforce. The employer alleged that this was a procedural irregularity as the questionnaire had failed to address the issue of the support for the staff association.

Browne-Wilkinson J in the High Court emphasised the rights of individual workers to join a union of their choice and to decide their own form of representation. He thus argued that the section had to be construed as far as possible in favour of the individual and in a way that did not deprive workers of this right. Consequently, as s 14(1) required ACAS to find out the employees' true wishes on the issue of representation, ACAS had misdirected itself and exercised its discretion unlawfully by using a questionnaire that was biased against the staff association.[8]

A narrow construction of this section was also favoured by the Court of Appeal and House of Lords in *Grunwick Ltd v ACAS*.[9] Here, the majority of the workforce took strike action over the employer's failure to recognise the union and to negotiate on terms and conditions of employment. In conjunction with strike action, the union put into motion the compulsory recognition procedure under s 11. ACAS, applying its discretion under s 14(1), sent confidential questionnaires to union members and the dismissed workers. However, ACAS was unable to send the questionnaire to the remaining employees still at work as the employer refused to release their names and addresses.

The employer contended that the subsequent recommendation for recognition was void since not all the affected workers were asked their views on the issue. Denning MR in the Court of Appeal argued from the premise that the statute provided unions with a 'great power' to enforce recognition on unwilling employers and unenthusiastic workers. To control this power it was necessary to construe the protection provided by s 14(1) in a way that safeguarded the liberty of individual workers to be free to choose their union representation. Therefore, by not consulting with all the Grunwick workforce, as was required, ACAS had failed to fulfil its duty under s 14(1).

Browne LJ preferred to examine the words of s 14(1) without referring to the effects of the section. The duty, he felt, was to construe the Act as it stands whatever the practical consequences. ACAS had failed satisfactorily to perform its duties as consultation with all workers was a mandatory requirement of the section. On appeal to the House of Lords, Lord Diplock (who gave the leading judgment) followed this reasoning. On the true construction of s 14(1) – on the need to consult the workforce – he held that the statutory intention was that ACAS must take account of all the views of all the workers. The employer was under no legal obligation to co-operate with ACAS during its consultations or inquiries. So long as ACAS was in ignorance of the opinions of a substantial portion of the workforce, ACAS had failed to follow the duty imposed on it by statute.[10]

---

8   Browne-Wilkinson's interpretation required ACAS to act fairly between competing organisations at the place of work. Yet, the competing organisation in this case was the staff association which was not applying for recognition and, not being an 'independent union', was not entitled to make an application.

9   [1978] ICR 231 (CA); [1978] IRLR 38 (HL). For comment, see Napier, B, 'Grunwick and after' [1978] CLJ 32, and James B, and Simpson, R, 'Grunwick v ACAS' (1978) 41 MLR 573.

10 Lord Salmon expressly agreed with Denning's remarks in the Court of Appeal that ACAS recommendations and CAC awards were infringements of individual liberty and that safeguards for workers needed to be construed liberally. Lord Keith concurred and Lords Edmund-Davies and Fraser agreed with the reasoning of Lord Diplock.

The high watermark of the judicial attack on ACAS decision making came in the Court of Appeal decision in *UKAPE v ACAS*.[11] Unlike the other cases discussed so far, this case concerned an inter-union conflict over recognition. UKAPE was a small unrecognised union that had formally referred the issue of recognition to ACAS. ACAS carried out its function of inquiry and consultation with the employer, other trade unions and the workforce. There was evidence from the ballot organised by ACAS that the workforce was strongly in favour of recognition and representation by UKAPE. However, all other parties were opposed to this, arguing that representation by UKAPE was unnecessary and would lead to an inter-union dispute and industrial strife.

In the light of this opposition, the ACAS report did not recommend recognition, reasoning that it would be disruptive to the existing collective bargaining arrangements and lead to the fragmentation of bargaining and possible industrial action. The plaintiff union argued that ACAS had unduly stressed its duty to promote the improvement of industrial relations at the expense of the equally important duty of encouraging the extension of collective bargaining. The High Court and Court of Appeal agreed. ACAS had misdirected itself by believing that its statutory powers required that any recommendation for recognition had to be consistent with existing collective bargaining arrangements. The particular duty of ACAS to encourage the extension of collective bargaining had priority over the general duty to promote the improvement of industrial relations and collective bargaining stability.[12] The courts refused to accept the argument that the resolution of the conflict between these separate duties was a matter best left to ACAS itself.

In general terms, what is striking about judicial control over these ACAS decisions is the transparency of judicial attitudes to this form of legislation and to the role of ACAS.[13] Judges such as Denning in the Court of Appeal and Salmon in the House of Lords examined the legislation on the basis that it deprived workers of control over their right to be free to choose their own form of representation. Where there was any conflict between the collective needs of workers (to enhance their bargaining power through union recognition) and individual choice, the conflict was resolved in favour of individual rights rather than collective needs.[14]

Other judges in the Court of Appeal (Browne and Brandon LJJ) and House of Lords (Lords Diplock and Keith) preferred to take a strict literal view of the statutory provision. This still frustrated the general intention behind the Act of securing union recognition at the workplace where a majority of workers consented. Both approaches illustrated a lack

---

11   [1979] ICR 303.

12   Lord Denning in the Court of Appeal went so far as to advocate that the wishes of the 'big battalions' of the employer and union should be ignored where they were in conflict with the rights of individual trade unionists to be represented by the trade union of their choice, following the principle of freedom of association under the European Convention on Human Rights, Art 11.

13   Other State agencies regulating the employment relationship (ie the EOC and the CRE) have suffered a similar fate at the hands of the judiciary. See eg *Science Research Council v Nasse* [1979] QB 144; *R v CRE ex p Hillingdon BC* [1982] AC 779; and *CRE v Prestige Group plc* [1984] ICR 473.

14   For a fuller discussion of these cases and criticisms of judicial decision making see Simpson, R, 'Judicial control of ACAS' (1979) 8 ILJ 69, and Elliot, M, 'ACAS and judicial review' (1980) 43 MLR 580.

of sympathy with the aims of the legislation and, at times, a lack of understanding of the process of collective bargaining and the practical operation of industrial relations.[15]

The decision of the Court of Appeal in *UKAPE* precipitated the ACAS Board to write to the Secretary of State of Employment outlining its concerns over the judicial interpretation of the legislation. This led ACAS to conclude that '... in the light of the increasing difficulties which we are encountering we cannot satisfactorily operate the statutory recognition procedures as they stand'.[16]

At the same time that ACAS was making clear its dissatisfaction at judicial interference, the House of Lords heard the ACAS appeal in *UKAPE*[17]and provided welcome guidance on the proper role of judicial review. Lord Scarman (giving the leading judgment) stressed that for the provisions to operate effectively the independent discretion of ACAS needed to be preserved. Where ACAS has exclusive discretion, the courts should not interfere by substituting an ACAS decision with their own view of the facts. Consequently, it was solely for ACAS to decide whether the extension of collective bargaining took precedence over the improvement of industrial relations.

This advice on the proper operation of the recognition procedure was, however, too late to have a positive effect on judicial decision making. The new Conservative Government had already decided to repeal these provisions in the 1980 Employment Act.

From all sides of industry, the demise of the recognition procedures went unlamented. There was, from the beginning of the experiment, strong evidence of employer opposition. Over the period of the compulsory recognition experiment, ACAS made 158 recommendations for recognition. One hundred employers failed to comply. Only approximately 16,000 workers obtained rights of recognition through formal recommendations.[18] As Wedderburn has commented, 'so much for the rule of (this) law'.[19]

Unions were dissatisfied with the lack of any effective enforcement procedure to deal with recalcitrant employers who were determined to resist recognition claims and with the extensive delays whilst ACAS went through the exhaustive procedure outlined in the statute. ACAS was unhappy with the legal restrictions imposed by the courts which obstructed its inquiries and undermined its decisions. In the ACAS Annual Report for 1978, ACAS reported an additional unease with the procedures. To undertake effectively its other conciliation and arbitration duties the service needed to be seen to be independent and impartial. The report noted a growing perception by employers that it

---

15   Eg, Salmon in *Grunwick* [1978] IRLR 38, p 44, and Browne-Wilkinson in *Powley* [1978] ICR 123, p 128, believed that one reason why recognition procedures need to be strictly controlled was because recognition of a trade union diminishes the right of each individual to regulate his or her working life by determining their own terms and conditions of employment. This view not only assumes that individuals wish to negotiate their own terms, but also that the outcome of individual contractual negotiations results in mutually satisfactory agreed terms. The reality of the employment relationship for the vast majority of employees is that when they act as individuals, terms are imposed, not negotiated. The only real power individuals have in the negotiation of terms and conditions of employment is when they join together in a trade union and utilise the collective power that brings.

16   ACAS Council letter, 29 June 1979.

17   [1980] IRLR 124. See also the House of Lords judgment in *EMA v ACAS* [1980] IRLR 164. Both cases are noted by Simpson, R (1980) 9 ILJ 125.

18   ACAS Annual Report 1980.

19   Lord Wedderburn, *The Worker and the Law*, 3rd edn, 1986, p 284.

operated the procedures in a biased manner (partly as a consequence of the high profile judicial review cases), thereby compromising its impartiality in employers' eyes.[20]

In conclusion, the statutory recognition procedure was not an unqualified success.[21] Arguably, the sanction of an award of improved terms and conditions of employment was not a suitable disincentive to the employer who wished to retain a workplace free of union influence. Judicial interference sapped the power of ACAS to pursue energetically its duties under the Act. Once it became clear that ACAS could be obstructed and that the sanctions imposed by the CAC were limited, employer non-co-operation increased accordingly.[22]

Tighter procedure and stronger enforcement powers might have improved the rates of forced recognition. Yet, the principle of voluntary collective bargaining which had informed labour relations for many years militated against the introduction of such a coercive system.[23] This experience of legislative intervention in recognition disputes has implications for the application of the recognition law introduced by the 1999 Act (considered below).

RECOGNITION POLICY 1979–97

Repeal of the statutory recognition procedure was the first stage in a Conservative legal strategy (allied with industrial and economic policy) to undermine existing recognition agreements, limit the incidence of new agreements and to forestall the expansion of collective bargaining. As already noted, it was standard practice in those industries nationalised in the late 1940s for the recognition of unions to be guaranteed by placing management under a duty to consult and recognise relevant unions.[24] In other parts of the public sector, there existed similar provisions; such as s 1 of the Remuneration of Teachers Act 1965, which set up collective bargaining machinery (the Burnham Committee) to determine teachers' pay and conditions.

With most of the nationalised industries and public utilities now in the private sector, the obligation to consult and negotiate with appropriate trade unions no longer applies.[25] Recognition agreements in local and central government have been undermined by the

---

20 See the ACAS Annual Report for 1978, p 30.

21 There were some positive aspects. Especially in the first few years, many claims were settled by conciliation without the need for a formal recommendation for recognition by ACAS or a referral to the CAC.

22 For further evaluation of the recognition procedure, see Davies, P, 'Failure to comply with recognition recommendations' (1979) 8 ILJ 55 and Townshend-Smith, R, 'Trade union recognition legislation – Britain and America compared' (1981) 1 *Legal Studies* 190.

23 Wedderburn, KW (now Lord) in 'The Employment Protection Act 1975: collective dimensions' (1976) 39 MLR 169, p 183, commented that the lack of effective enforcement procedure was 'not too high a price to be paid for the maintenance of what will still be fundamentally a voluntary system of collective labour relations'.

24 See fn 2.

25 There are few examples left of this form of statutory recognition. Where there is a duty to recognise, the courts have consistently held that it cannot be enforced at the collective or individual level. See *Gallagher v The Post Office* [1970] 3 All ER 712, *ASTMS v The Post Office* [1980] IRLR 475 and *NCB v NUM and Others* [1986] IRLR 439; all considered in Chapter 8. However, note that in *R v British Coal Corp ex p UDM* [1988] ICR 36, the High Court granted a judicial review of British Coal's decision, under the Coal Industry Nationalisation Act 1946, s 46(1), not to consult with the UDM clerical section.

compulsory competitive tendering process, market testing and subsequent contracting out of public services.[26] In other areas of the public sector, the right to recognition was attacked directly through legislation. The Burnham Committee, as a forum for negotiation with teachers' unions, was abolished in 1987 by the Teachers' Pay and Conditions Act. It was replaced by a committee with advisory powers only. The Secretary of State could ignore the views of the committee when determining national terms and conditions of employment. This development resulted in the International Labour Organisation twice condemning the UK for a breach of Art 4 of Convention No 98 on the Right to Organise and to Collective Bargaining (1949)[27] which establishes that national governments have the responsibility for ensuring that measures are taken to support and promote the voluntary negotiation of collective agreements.[28]

The extent and nature of recognition during the 1980s and 1990s was also shaped and directed by economic forces. Some employers, in response to the new economic conditions created by free market and monetarist policies, reassessed their relationship with trade unions and embarked on policies of derecognition and non-recognition (especially in the new high-tech and white collar industries).[29] Where unions are faced with a reluctant employer who refuses recognition, or who withdraws recognition, the traditional response is to challenge such developments by resorting to collective action to force concessions from the employer.[30] The capacity of trade unions to rely on such a strategy has been seriously handicapped by legislative changes. New limits originally introduced by the Employment Act 1982 do not make recognition disputes themselves unlawful but do weaken union ability to put pressure on employers to expand union recognition requirements across industries.[31]

---

26 A limited legal remedy may be open to some employees in the public sector where they have a 'legitimate expectation' that there would be a form of consultation prior to derecognition. See *R v Secretary of State for Foreign Affairs ex p CCSU* [1985] IRLR 28; *Re NUPE and COHSE* [1989] IRLR 202 and *R v Bradford City Metropolitan Council* (1988), unreported, cited in Fredman, S and Morris, G, *The State as Employer: Labour Law in the Public Services*, 1989, p 163.

27 See the 256th Report of the Freedom of Association Committee (Case No 1391) and the 275th Report of the Freedom of Association Committee (Case No 1518).

28 Bargaining in the schools sector is now covered by the School Teachers' Pay and Conditions Act 1991. The limited powers of the new statutory review body (with employer and union representation) were criticised by Fredman, S and Morris, G (1992) 21 ILJ 44. However, in 1994, the ILO Committee of Experts reporting on UK compliance with the Convention failed to condemn these arrangements.

29 There is some evidence that the incidence of derecognition is declining, although a refusal to bargain with unions or for recognition deals to be conditional on trade union co-operation in areas such as multi-skilling and 'flexible work practices' has been particularly prevalent at new 'greenfield' sites. For a full analysis of the trends, see Claydon, T, 'Union derecognition in Britain in the 1980s' (1989) 27 BJIR 214; Millward, N *et al*, *Workplace Industrial Relations in Transition*, 1992, pp 70–76; Smith, P and Morton, G, 'Union exclusion and the decollectivization of Industrial Relations in Contemporary Britain' (1993) 31 BJIR 97; Purcell, J, 'The end of institutional industrial relations' (1993) 64 Pol Q 6; Gal, G and McKay, S, 'Trade union derecognition in Britain' (1994) 32 BJIR 433; Gall, G and McKay, S, 'Developments in union recognition and derecognition in Britain 1994-1998' (1999) 37 BJIR 601; Millward, N *et al*, *All Change at Work?*, 2000, Chapters 4–5.

30 Derecognition is often the precursor of bitter industrial conflict. Ewing, KD and Napier, B, in 'The Wapping dispute and labour law' [1986] CLJ 285 highlight the practical industrial consequences of derecognition and the defects in UK law for trade unions battling against an employer who refuses to recognise and bargain.

31 For an analysis of the original provisions, see Lewis, R and Simpson, R, 'Disorganising industrial relations' (1982) 11 ILJ 227, pp 227–33. See, also, Short M, 'A practitioner's response' (1983) 12 ILJ 99–101 for comment on arguments deployed by Lewis and Simpson.

Section 225 of the Trade Union and Labour Relations (Consolidation) Act (TULR(C)A) 1992 provides that the immunity for industrial action is withdrawn where action is taken or threatened against an employer to induce the incorporation into a commercial contract of a term or condition which requires that services are only performed, or goods only supplied, by a contractor that recognises trade unions or a particular trade union. The immunity is also withdrawn where action is taken to disrupt the supply of goods and services from a supplier who does not recognise trade unions.[32] This exposes trade unions to actions in tort for the losses caused by the industrial action or for an injunction to stop the action, enforceable via contempt of court proceedings. It is also now unlawful for organisations – such as local or public authorities sympathetic to trade unions – to attempt to enforce recognition via their contractual arrangements with suppliers.[33] Section 186 of the TULR(C)A 1992 states that a term or condition of a contract for the supply of goods or services is void where it purports to require the party to the contract to recognise, consult or negotiate with one or more trade unions.[34] This is strengthened by s 187 of the TULR(C)A 1992 which provides that '... a person shall not refuse to deal with a supplier or prospective supplier', on the grounds that the supplier or prospective supplier does not, or is not likely to recognise, negotiate or consult with one or more trade unions.[35]

Since 1979, the role of law has been reversed. Instead of broadly promoting recognition and collective bargaining, legislation explicitly shackles the efforts of unions themselves to advance recognition. Conservative policies encouraging derecognition and the dismantling of collective bargaining have forced the union movement to reassess strategies to acquire recognition and rekindled interest in legal solutions to the recognition problem. Against this background of the decline in union recognition, broad support for some form of legal machinery to secure, protect and maintain recognition has been growing in the union movement, and in the Labour Party, since the end of the 1980s.[36]

---

32   For further explanation of industrial action and the statutory immunities see Part 3.

33   Sections 144 and 145 applies the same approach to arrangements attempting to secure the recognition of a single union by the use of closed shop arrangements.

34   Section 17 of the Local Government Act 1988 has also forbidden local authorities to insert any non-commercial clauses (such as 'fair wages' clauses) into contracts with suppliers. The Local Government Act 1999, s 19, does, however, provide the Secretary of State with the power to remove this restriction.

35   A 'refusal to deal' with another is defined in s 187(2) as excluding another person from tendering for a contract or by excluding them from a list of approved suppliers of goods or services or otherwise refusing to enter into a contract with them. The imposition of a recognition term in a contract or a refusal to deal is also a tortious breach of statutory duty. It is actionable by the contracting party against whom it is aimed or 'any other person who may be adversely affected' by it.

36   During this period the debate was informed by a burgeoning academic literature on the issue. For example, see Chapter 4 of McCarthy, W, 'Freedom at work: towards the reform of Tory employment laws' (1985) *Fabian Tract* No 508; Townley, B, 'Union recognition: a comparative analysis of the pros and cons of a legal procedure' (1987) 25 BJIR 177; Ewing, KD, 'Trade union recognition – a framework for discussion' (1990) 19 ILJ 209; Simpson, R, *Trade Union Recognition and the Law* (1991, Institute of Employment Rights); Ewing, KD, 'Democratic socialism and labour law' (1995) 24 ILJ 103, pp 122–27. The TUC also published consultative documents on the recognition issue: see 'Trade union recognition' (1991), 'The future of trade unions' (1993), 'Representation at work' (1994) and 'Your voice at work' (1995).

RECOGNITION AND THE EMPLOYMENT RELATIONS ACT 1999

The Labour Party elected in May 1997 was committed to a legal right to recognition for the purposes of collective bargaining.[37] The new administration outlined the substance of the right in the Employment White Paper, *Fairness at Work*,[38] published in May 1998. After extensive consultation with both sides of industry and some amendment to the original proposals, the Employment Relations Bill containing the recognition provisions was introduced in January 1999 and received the royal assent in July of that year. The provisions of the Act on recognition in Sched 1 (inserted into TULR(C)A 1992 as Sched A1 and enforceable since 6 June 2000) amount to over 40 pages and 172 paragraphs. The Schedule was drafted in such great detail and length precisely in order to avoid the pitfalls of the previous experiment on compulsory recognition contained in the 1975 Employment Protection Act. The Government's view was that the major shortcoming of the 1975 Act was its lack of detailed criteria and procedures for making decisions and its failure to provide ACAS with appropriate guidance as to how it should exercise its discretion.[39] Consequently, the 1999 version of a statutory right to recognition is far more comprehensive in its application. A description and commentary on the complex procedure is provided below.[40]

The application to the Central Arbitration Committee[41]

The process of applying for recognition under the statutory scheme is initiated by the union writing formally to the employer requesting recognition. The union must ensure the letter identifies the union and the proposed bargaining unit (defined as the 'group of workers' in respect of whom the union seeks to conduct collective bargaining) and states that it is made under Sched A1 of the 1992 Act.[42] The request will automatically fail if the employer to whom it is made is below the small employer threshold or because the union making the request does not hold a certificate of independence.[43] Small employers are

---

37 See the Labour Party documents 'Looking to the future' (1990), 'Building prosperity – flexibility, efficiency and fairness at work' (1995), 'New Labour, New Life for Britain' (1996), 'Equipping Britain for the future' (1997).

38 Cm 3968.

39 See the statement by Michael Wills, Minister for Small Firms, Trade and Industry, elaborating on this theme (Hansard HC Standing Committee E, col 345, 16 March 1999).

40 For further critical appraisal, see Simpson, R, 'Trade union recognition and the law, a new approach – Parts I and II of Schedule A1 of the Trade Union and Labour Relations (Consolidation) Act 1992' (2000) 29 ILJ 193; Lord Wedderburn, 'Collective bargaining or legal enactment: the 1999 Act and Union recognition' (2000) 29 ILJ 1; Ewing, KD (ed), *Employment Rights at Work: Reviewing the Employment Relations Act 1999* (2001, Institute of Employment Rights), Chapters 1 and 2; and Novitz, T and Skidmore, P, *Fairness at Work: A Critical Analysis of the Employment Relations Act 1999*, 2001, Chapter 4.

41 The CAC is the body with the primary responsibility to administer the new procedures. In exercising its functions under Sched A1 it must 'have regard to the object of encouraging and promoting fair and efficient practices and arrangements in the workplace'. Unlike ACAS, under the 1975 Act, there is no duty on the CAC to promote or encourage collective bargaining, and thus the CAC is expected to remain strictly neutral as regards the merits or otherwise of collective bargaining. For further explanation of the role of the CAC, see Rideout, R, 'Trade union recognition and the CAC' (2000) 50 *Federation News* 77.

42 Paragraph 8.

43 Paragraph 6. See Chapter 2, pp 32–34.

defined as those having fewer than 21 workers either on the date the employer received the request for recognition, or, if the employer had more than 21 workers on that date, the average workforce over the 13 weeks preceding that date was fewer than 21 people. The workforce of the employer must include any workers employed by an associated employer or employers.[44] The small employer threshold may be revised by the Secretary of State if its operation proves to be unsatisfactory.[45]

If the request satisfies these basic requirements, then the parties then have an initial 'first period' of 10 working days in which to conduct negotiations and possibly agree a bargaining unit and recognition.[46] If the employer recognises the union and the bargaining unit is agreed then no further steps can be taken under the statutory procedure. If the employer does not accept the request for recognition but informs the union that it is willing to enter into negotiations, then the parties then have a 'second period' of 20 working days, or an agreed longer period,[47] in which to agree the bargaining unit and the question of recognition. During this period, ACAS may be asked by either party to help in conducting the negotiations.[48] Once the parties reach agreement on both issues, then the union claim under the statutory procedure is terminated.[49] If no agreement has been reached during either the first or the second period, or the employer has rejected the request or failed to respond to it before the end of the first period,[50] the union may apply to the CAC for a declaration of recognition.[51] The role of the CAC is then to decide whether the bargaining unit proposed by the union is appropriate and, if not, whether some other unit is appropriate, and whether the union has the support of a majority of workers within the bargaining unit for the purposes of automatic recognition.[52]

Determination of the bargaining unit

Once the CAC has accepted an application, it must then, within a period of 20 working days or such longer period as it may notify, try to assist the parties to agree on the appropriate bargaining unit.[53] If the parties have not agreed an appropriate unit within the 20 working day period, the CAC must then decide what is the appropriate bargaining unit within 10 working days or such longer period as it may decide.[54]

In order to ensure that pre-existing bargaining arrangements are not disrupted, a recognition application will also not be admissible if the CAC is satisfied that any workers within the relevant bargaining unit (as proposed by the union or agreed with the employer) are already covered by a collective agreement between the employer and

---

44   Paragraph 7(1). For the definition of 'associated employer' see TULR(C)A 1992, s 297.
45   Paragraph 7(6)(a)(b).
46   Paragraph 10(1)(6).
47   Paragraph 10(7).
48   Paragraph 10(5). If the union rejects ACAS assistance then the claim fails (para 10(4)).
49   Paragraph 10(4).
50   Paragraph 10(1)–(3).
51   Paragraphs 11(1)(a)(b) and 12(1)(a)(b).
52   Paragraphs 11(2) and 12(2).
53   Paragraph 18.
54   Paragraph 19(2).

any other recognised union.[55] The exceptions are where an existing union with a limited collective agreement makes an application to obtain negotiating rights (that it previously did not have) on pay, holidays and hours or if the pre-existing agreement was made by the employer with a non-independent union in order to forestall a statutory application by another independent union.[56]

In deciding the appropriate unit, a number of matters may be taken into account by the CAC, including: the views of the employer and of the union or unions; existing national and local bargaining arrangements; the desirability of avoiding small fragmented bargaining units; the characteristics of the workers falling within the proposed unit; and the location of the workers.[57] However, the overriding criterion which the CAC must consider is the need for the unit 'to be compatible with effective management'.[58] This suggests that the employer's view of the composition of the appropriate bargaining unit will be the CAC's paramount concern. This is a very important issue as the determination of the bargaining unit will often be decisive to the outcome of the application for recognition – especially where a union is well organised amongst a particular group of workers or at a particular site, but is much weaker across the whole organisation. If the appropriate bargaining unit is widened to the workforce as a whole, then this clearly has implications for the outcome of the ballot.

The practice of the CAC is, however, to take a balanced view – assessing all the evidence submitted by both parties when deciding whether the bargaining unit is 'compatible with effective management' and thus appropriate. For example, in *Benteler Automotive UK and ISTC*,[59] the ISTC had proposed that the bargaining unit should consist only of shop floor weekly paid production operatives and material handlers and not include monthly paid technical, supervisory or administrative staff who, it alleged, had no common interest with shop floor production staff and who were, in practice, treated differently by management in a number of ways. Management contended that the union had formulated its proposal without understanding the management desire to project a 'whole company' philosophy and that a split of this nature would damage the culture of partnership and team working and undermine 'effective management'. The CAC rejected the employer's submissions, holding that '... the current position at the company does not yet accord with the whole-company, one team culture and approach to which Benteler aspires ...' and thus, as the bargaining unit actually reflected existing management organisation and practice, it was clearly compatible with effective management. In *GPMU and Red Letter Bradford Ltd*,[60] the dispute arose over the union proposal to include shop floor workers in Despatch, Production and IT (who made up the vast majority of employees) in the bargaining unit and exclude management staff who enjoyed significantly different terms and conditions of employment. The employer argued that the exclusion of management was divisive and damaged team spirit – given the company ethos of partnership between all grades. In

---

55   Paragraph 35(1).
56   Paragraph 35 (2)(4).
57   Paragraph 19(4).
58   Paragraph 19(3).
59   (2000) TUR1/4/00.
60   (2000) TUR1/15/00.

rejecting this argument, the CAC found that, as there were patently significant distinctions between these two different types of employee, the union's proposed bargaining unit was 'compatible with effective management'.[61]

Once the bargaining unit has been agreed by the parties, or the unit is determined by the CAC, then the next issue for the CAC is to adjudicate on whether the union has sufficient support within the bargaining unit in order to initiate the balloting process or to justify an automatic recognition declaration.

Automatic recognition

If agreement has been reached on the question of the bargaining unit, but not on the question of recognition itself, then the CAC has the task of determining whether the majority of workers within the bargaining unit support the union before ordering recognition.[62] Unless the union has a majority of members at the bargaining unit (see below), the CAC must decide whether the union has *reasonable support* within the unit. Paragraph 36 defines this as meaning that at least 10% of the proposed unit must be members of the relevant union, and also that a majority of the workers in the unit 'would be likely to favour recognition of the union'.[63]

The 10% threshold test is satisfied by the union providing recent membership records (which may be challenged by the employer). The legislation does not make it explicit how the CAC should arrive at its decision as to whether a majority of workers 'would be likely to favour recognition'. However, the White Paper, *Fairness at Work*, expected that survey or other evidence such as a 'petition signed by a sufficient number of employees' would be sufficient and, in practice, the CAC has followed the suggestions of the White Paper. For example, in *New Millenium Experience Co Ltd and British Actors' Equity*,[64] a 'straw poll' conducted by the union was regarded as sufficient evidence of support for recognition, whilst, in *TGWU and Stadium Electrical Components Ltd*,[65] a petition of the requisite number of employees satisfied the CAC on this point.[66] Once it is established that this level of support exists, the next stage is for the CAC to organise a ballot of all workers at the bargaining unit (see below).

If there is already 50% or the membership in the bargaining unit, the automatic recognition provisions apply and the CAC will normally make a declaration (without the need for a ballot) that the union is to be recognised as entitled to conduct collective bargaining on behalf of the relevant workers.[67] However, the CAC must arrange for a

---

61 See, also, *AEEU and Via Systems Ltd* (2000) TUR1/18/00; *Utd Road Transport Union and Winerite Ltd* (2001) TUR1/26/00; *GPMU and Eastern Counties Newspapers* (2001) TUR1/51/01; and *ISTC and Hygena Ltd* (2001) TUR1/33/00; *MSFU and Uniport DCM* (2001) TUR1/94/01.

62 Paragraph 12(3)(4).

63 Where there is a joint application, the 10% membership threshold refers to an aggregation of all the members of all the unions involved.

64 (2000) TUR1/6/00.

65 (2000) TUR1/10/00.

66 A potential problem for the applicant union is access to the workplace in order to organise a petition or poll. The duty imposed on employers to grant the relevant union reasonable access to their employees for the purposes of the ballot does not apply at this stage. For the CAC's commentary on this issue see *BECTU and MTU Europe* (2001) TUR1/128/01.

67 Paragraph 22(1)(2).

ballot to be held if one of three qualifying conditions are found to exist, namely: the CAC is satisfied that a ballot should be held in the interests of good industrial relations; a significant number of the union members within the unit inform the CAC that they do not want the union to conduct collective bargaining on their behalf; or evidence of membership is produced which leads the CAC to conclude that there are doubts as to whether a significant number of the union members within the unit want the union to conduct collective bargaining.[68]

The parties involved in a recognition dispute are likely to have different ideas as to how 'good industrial relations' is defined and whether a ballot is necessary to preserve or foster those relations. A declaration of recognition and the process of collective bargaining (where it has not existed before) will obviously involve substantial changes to the way that an employer deals with and communicates with its staff, but of itself this should not be regarded as a threat to 'good industrial relations'. The CAC may be faced with difficulties if confronted by an employer who declares that unless a ballot is held it would not regard any declaration of recognition as legitimate and would refuse to bargain in good faith with the union.[69]

The second condition is where a significant number of the union members inform the CAC that they do not want the union to conduct collective bargaining on their behalf. The question arises as to what would be a 'significant number of union members'. The answer will depend on the size of the bargaining unit, and 'significant' is likely to mean a number that is large enough to affect the outcome of the ballot. Having regard to the 40% threshold that the union must win to obtain a declaration of recognition, 'significant' could be a relatively small number. This will potentially give employers the opportunity to offer small groups of union members incentives or inducements to inform the CAC that they do not want the union recognised and there is nothing specifically in the legislation that prohibits the offering of such inducements.

The third condition is where membership evidence is produced which suggests that there are doubts as to whether a significant number of the union members within the bargaining unit want the union to conduct collective bargaining on their behalf. Membership evidence can either relate to the circumstances in which members joined[70] or to the length of their membership. This may include evidence that members did not join voluntarily and felt pressured into doing so by more militant colleagues. It has been suggested that if the employer can show that a significant number of union members have recently cancelled their check off authorisations and appear to be leaving the union, that might prompt the CAC to hold a ballot.[71] Although evidence of

---

68 Paragraph 22(4)(a)–(c).

69 Note that in *ISTC and Fullarton Industries Ltd* (2001) TUR1/29/00 the union had 51% membership in the bargaining unit. Evidence of poor industrial relations persuaded the CAC to reject the employer's submissions and refuse to order a ballot as it would 'exacerbate an already difficult situation'. See also *TGWU and Daryl Industries Ltd* (2001) TUR1/45/01 and *GPMU and Statex Press (Northern) Ltd* (2000) TUR1/21/00.

70 See *AEEU and Huntleigh Healthcare Ltd* (2000) TUR1/19/00 where 90% of the relevant workforce had taken up free membership which had been provided expressly for the purposes of the recognition claim. The CAC believed that this did raise doubts as to whether significant numbers wanted the union to conduct collective bargaining on their behalf.

71 See the statement by Michael Wills, Minister for Small Firms, Trade and Industry in Standing Committee E, 16 March 1999, col 388.

mass cancellation of check off arrangements by a 'significant' number of members might indeed suggest that a ballot is necessary, this may itself be evidence of employer interference.[72]

The balloting process[73]

The ballot must be conducted by a qualified independent person (QIP), appointed by the CAC, and must take place within a period of 20 working days (or such longer period as the CAC may specify) starting with the day after the QIP was appointed.[74] Once the CAC has decided to arrange the ballot, it must 'as soon as reasonably practicable' inform the employer and the union of that decision, the name of the QIP, the period within which the ballot must be conducted, whether the ballot is postal, and – if the ballot is not postal – details of the workplace or places where the ballot is to be conducted.[75]

In deciding whether to choose workplace or postal ballots, the CAC must have regard to the likelihood of the ballot being affected by: unfairness or malpractice if it were conducted at a workplace; costs and practicality; and any other matters it considers appropriate.[76] Unions would generally prefer secret ballots to be conducted in the workplace where possible, as this would tend to maximise voter turnout, although postal ballots are ingrained into the culture of union regulation and employers may argue that they remove the possibility of disputes about fairness or corruption. In *Red Letter Bradford Ltd and GPMU*,[77] however, the CAC did not accept the argument that a postal ballot is necessarily fairer or more confidential than a workplace ballot, because it regarded the presence of the QIP as a safeguard against unfairness or malpractice.

The employer's duties in the balloting process

The legislation states that the employer has three main duties in relation to the conduct of the ballot. First, the employer must co-operate generally in connection with the ballot, with the union and the QIP.[78] Secondly, the employer must give the union '... such access to the workers constituting the bargaining unit as is reasonable to enable the union to inform the workers of the object of the ballot and to seek their support and their opinions on the issues involved'.[79] The final duty concerns the provision of information to the CAC. Within 10 working days, starting with the day the employer was informed about

---

72 Note that para 166 gives the Secretary of State the power to amend the provisions concerning automatic recognition 'in any way he thinks fit', if the CAC expresses the view that the provisions are having 'an unsatisfactory effect'. This may become necessary if the provisions prove susceptible to union or employer manipulation.

73 Provision is made for ballots at various stages throughout the statutory recognition procedure. Ballots are to be held to determine whether the union should be recognised, to secure changes to the bargaining unit where a new unit has been determined by the CAC, and in derecognition applications. In all cases, the process for the conduct of ballots is virtually identical and the gross costs of the ballot are divided equally between the employer and relevant union/s.

74 Paragraph 25(3).

75 Paragraph 25(9).

76 Paragraph 25(5).

77 (2000) TUR1/12/00. See also *BALPA and EasyJet* (2001) TUR1/12/01.

78 Paragraph 26(2).

79 Paragraph 26(3).

the ballot, the employer must give the CAC the names and home addresses of the relevant workers and, 'as soon as reasonably practicable', the employer must inform the CAC of the name of any worker who subsequently joins or leaves the bargaining unit.[80]

If the employer fails to comply with any of the above statutory duties, the CAC may order the employer to remedy the failure. If the employer then fails to comply with that order, the CAC may make a declaration of recognition and dispense with the need to conduct a ballot. However, this is not mandatory, so even if the employer completely denies access to the union for the purposes of the ballot, the CAC is not bound to take any steps against the employer and, if it does not do so, then the ballot will have to be held regardless.

Additionally, employers must comply with the Department of Trade and Industry Code of Practice (Access to Workers During Recognition and Derecognition Ballots), published in May 2000 and laid before Parliament under s 204(2) of the TULR(C)A 1992. The intention behind the Code is to ensure that, during the 'access period' (the period from when the CAC informs the parties of the name of the QIP to the actual date of the ballot), unions have a reasonable opportunity to canvass support for recognition in the relevant bargaining unit. The introduction to the Code on Access states that its purpose is '... to encourage reasoned and responsible behaviour ... and to ensure that acrimony is avoided'. In order to encourage responsible behaviour and co-operation, the Code provides that parties should avoid the use of defamatory material, provocative propaganda, personal attacks and personalised negative campaigning.

The Code suggests that the parties should begin preparations as soon as the CAC notifies its intention to conduct a ballot and, in particular, encourages parties to establish an access agreement covering the union's programme for where and when it will contact the workers, and a mechanism for resolving any disputes that may arise during the operation of the agreement. Subject to any agreement, the Code continues by laying down guidelines on matters such as: who is to be granted access; where and when access is to take place; the frequency and duration of union activities; written communications; and atypical workers.

The Code states that employers should grant access to full time union officials or such of their employees who are nominated lead union representatives, whether at the particular workplace or (in the case of a multi-site organisation) at another workplace, unless it is not practicable in the circumstances. The method of access will generally be determined according to the employer's usual method of communicating with the workers: if mass meetings are held by the employer in a meeting room then the union should have the same facilities.

The Code declares that, in order to avoid disruption to the employer's business, access should normally be arranged during less busy periods of working time, particularly where a large meeting is to be held (for example, a lunch hour or at the end of a shift). In terms of frequency and duration, the Code recommends one mass meeting of 30 minutes' duration for every 10 days of the access period, unless the employer holds similar meetings more often, in which case equality of access should be conferred on the union. In addition, it is suggested that the union should have at least one day in the

---

80   Paragraph 26(4).

access period for union 'surgeries' whereby a union representative or official would be able to see individual workers (or small groups of two or three workers) for short periods of time (15 minutes) in order to discuss the issues. The employer should allow workers time off with pay[81] for this purpose, unless the surgery takes place outside normal working hours. Access to atypical workers should take account of the particular working arrangements and patterns of these workers.

As regards distribution of written material, the Code states that the employer should put a prominent noticeboard at the union's disposal and should not interfere with any material so displayed. The union should also be allowed to place additional material, such as leaflets, near the noticeboard. Electronic forms of communication, such as internal email, intranets, and access to the union website, should be permitted within the parameters expressly or impliedly allowed by the employer in other contexts.

Breach of the Code will not result in any legal sanction as such but, by virtue of s 207 of the TULR(C)A 1992, its provisions are admissible in evidence and may be taken into account in any proceedings before any tribunal, court or the CAC. In considering whether to make orders and/or award of recognition, the CAC will therefore have regard to the compliance by employers and unions with the provisions of the Code. The CAC has the power to order the employer to make good any failure to comply with its duties to allow reasonable access[82] and, in the event of further failure (after the issuing of an order by the CAC), to grant a declaration of recognition. The Code recommends that in the event of minor disputes the parties should attempt to resolve the differences themselves – utilising the conciliation facilities of ACAS if necessary or the good offices of the QIP, before referring the issue to the CAC.

The general duty of co-operation contained in the Code does not inhibit the employer from campaigning vigorously itself against recognition. Thus, it is not necessarily the case that an employer would be in breach of its duty of co-operation by, *inter alia*, distributing what might be regarded as anti-union propaganda, such as warnings that jobs would be lost in the event of recognition. The Code's exhortation to avoid 'provocative propaganda', 'personalised negative campaigning' and 'behaviour likely to cause unnecessary offence' ought to restrict the scope for hard-hitting negative campaigns that some employers may have had in mind. However, the Code is limited in that it only applies during the period of access, and since recognition campaigns will, in reality, begin several weeks or even months before that, employers will still have scope for negative campaigns.

The consequences of a declaration of recognition

As soon as 'reasonably practicable' after the result of the ballot is determined by the QIP, the CAC must inform the union and the employer of the result.[83] If a majority of those

---

81 This is subject to the employer's ability to arrange adequate cover for any particular worker or workers.

82 An order enforcing access arrangements was made in *GPMU and Red Letter Bradford Ltd* (2000) TUR1/12/00.

83 Paragraph 29(1).

voting, and at least 40% of the workers constituting the bargaining unit vote in favour of recognition, a declaration of recognition will be made.[84] However, gaining recognition is the first hurdle for the union. The next is actually to establish a viable procedure for conducting collective bargaining. The parties must agree (with or without the help of ACAS) a method by which they will conduct collective bargaining or the CAC will specify one. The parties will be expected to conduct negotiations – within what is known as the 'negotiation period' – with a view to agreeing an appropriate method. They are given 30 workings days in which to do this, which can be extended by agreement.[85]

If no agreement on the method to conduct collective bargaining is made during the negotiation period, either party may apply to the CAC for assistance. If at the end of a 20 day period the parties have still not agreed the method by which they will conduct collective bargaining, the CAC then has the authority to impose a model method.[86] The specified procedure is deemed to have effect as though it were contained in a legally enforceable contract made by the parties.[87] The parties may agree that either the whole or parts of the method specified by the CAC should not have legally binding effect – or they may vary or replace the method specified by the CAC.[88]

The model method for collective bargaining

The Trade Union Recognition (Method of Collective Bargaining) Order[89] was laid before Parliament on 12 May 2000 and came into force on 6 June 2000. This model makes provision for the establishment of a Joint Negotiating Body (JNB), whose members are to comprise equal numbers of union and employer representatives (with at least three on each side). The employer's representatives must have authority to take final decisions, or make recommendations on final decisions, about pay, hours and holidays. A six stage bargaining process is set out, starting with the submission by the union side of its claim, followed by a meeting of the JNB to consider the claim, submission of a response by the employer, a further meeting of the JNB to consider the employer's response, another meeting in the event of a failure to agree and, finally, the involvement of ACAS. Strict time frames are set for each stage.

Agreements on pay, hours and holidays are to be set in writing as a legally enforceable collective agreement (by way of an order for specific performance). Information must be disclosed by the employer in accordance with the ACAS Code of Practice on disclosure of information for collective bargaining purposes. Union representatives who are employees of the employer are to be given paid time off to prepare the claim and attend meetings, and to hold meetings with workers within the bargaining unit to discuss the claim. The employer must also make certain facilities available to the union side of the JNB.

---

84 Paragraph 29(2).
85 Paragraph 30(4).
86 Paragraph 31(3).
87 Paragraph 31(4).
88 Paragraph 31(5).
89 SI 2000/1300.

Enforcement of recognition

The notion of collective agreements being legally enforceable is a new departure for British law, which has always traditionally regarded such agreements as being binding in honour only between the parties (see Chapter 8). The reason why the Government felt it necessary to give agreements stemming from the statutory recognition procedure contractually binding status was in order to create an enforcement framework in the event that one of the parties failed to observe the method stipulated.[90] The enforcement mechanism specified for a failure to observe the terms of a method imposed by the CAC is an application to the court for an order for specific performance.[91] Failure to comply with an order for specific performance will be a contempt of court punishable by a fine and, in rare cases, imprisonment. This procedural remedy is not accompanied by a substantive sanction, such as in the form of a claim for improved terms and conditions, as was the case under the Employment Protection Act 1975. It has been argued that this reliance on a procedural model for enforcement may well allow a recalcitrant employer to delay and prevaricate – accepting the form of recognition but denying the substance.

In addition, the remedy of specific performance may well prove to be inadequate as specific performance is an equitable remedy and the courts retain discretion over whether to make such an order in any particular case. Matters to be taken into account in making an order for specific performance include whether the party seeking the order has 'clean hands'. This may mean that unions that have resorted to industrial action, prior to issuing court proceedings, may be unable to obtain appropriate orders. Courts have also generally been reluctant to grant specific performance to force parties to maintain and observe private contractual relationships. For example, it has been held that the courts are particularly reluctant to make an order for specific performance where the nature of the contract was such that it required close court supervision.[92] Thus, if the courts maintain their traditional caution regarding orders for specific performance there is a danger that the recognition provisions will be largely emasculated. In addition, doubts have also been raised as to whether, should an order be flouted by an employer, the judiciary will in practice always be willing to countenance union actions for contempt of court against employers with, for example, pressing 'business reasons' for non-compliance.

Changes to the bargaining unit after a declaration of recognition has been issued

Where either party believes that there have been material changes to the bargaining unit after the CAC has declared recognition, they may apply to the CAC for a determination as to whether the original unit is still viable and/or for a declaration of a new bargaining unit.[93] The CAC will only accept such an application where it is satisfied that there is

---

90   It should be noted that any agreement reached by the parties during the negotiation periods (not the CAC imposed method) will not be legally binding unless it states clearly that it is intended to have legal effect.

91   Paragraph 31(6).

92   See *CH Giles & Co Ltd v Morris* [1972] 1 WLR 307.

93   There is also a specific procedure that employers can activate where the bargaining unit has 'ceased to exist'. The relevant union can challenge the application by applying to the CAC for a determination as to whether this is the case.

prima facie evidence that the original unit is no longer appropriate because: there is a change in the organisation or structure of the business carried on by the employer; a change in the business activities pursued by the employer; or a substantial change in the number of workers employed in the original unit.[94]

It has been argued that this approach grants too much discretion to employers to object to a previously agreed or determined bargaining unit. For example, on a strict reading of the expression, 'a change in the organisation or structure of the employer's business', a change in ownership or management, or the introduction of a performance-related pay scheme may all fall within this phrase. A 'substantial change in the numbers of workers in the bargaining unit' is likely to mean a number large enough to affect the outcome of a recognition ballot. Depending on the size of the bargaining unit in question, this may be a relatively small number.

The CAC must decide whether or not to accept an application for decision within 10 working days after the date it was received, or such longer period as it considers appropriate. If the CAC does accept the application for decision, the parties then have an initial 10 working day period – or such longer period as they might agree – in which to agree a new bargaining unit or units that differs from the original bargaining unit.[95]

If the parties manage to agree a new unit or units, the CAC must then issue a new declaration of recognition that replaces the original declaration, with modifications as to the method of collective bargaining if required.[96]

If the parties cannot agree on a new unit or units the CAC must then decide whether the original unit continues to be appropriate; if not, whether another unit is (or units are) appropriate. In deciding this issue, the CAC must follow the same process as it carried out when determining the appropriateness of the original bargaining unit.[97] If the CAC decides that the original unit is no longer appropriate, and that another unit is (or units are) appropriate and there is no overlap with other units, then, depending on the level of support within the new unit, a new declaration of recognition will be made. If the CAC decides that the level of support does need to be assessed, then the inquiry process concerning the level of support for recognition that was carried out in relation to the original unit must be repeated again, up to and including a new ballot if necessary. Where there is any overlap (that is, one or more workers) between the new unit or units and any statutory or voluntary outside bargaining unit, the CAC must declare that the bargaining arrangements for the workers in the new unit or units, and for each overlapping outside unit to the extent of the overlap, shall cease to have effect.[98]

An important point to note is that there is no limitation on either party's ability to challenge the appropriateness of the existing bargaining unit, in the sense that such an application could be made within weeks of the original declaration of recognition. Similarly, there does not appear to be any limitation on the number of times such applications could be made, unlike the applications for recognition and derecognition, which can only be made once every three years.

---

94   Paragraph 67(2).
95   Paragraph 69(1)(4).
96   Paragraph 69(1)(3).
97   Paragraph 70(4)(5).
98   Paragraph 83.

Joint and competing applications

One of the difficulties with the 1975 Act concerned demarcation disputes and competing claims by different unions over the same groups of workers. The provisions on joint applications attempt to remove any likelihood of a repetition of these problems by effectively stating that, if more than one union wishes to make an application for recognition over the same group of workers, they must do so together and co-operatively.

Thus, where a number of unions make a joint application, that application will not be admissible unless the unions show that they will co-operate with each other in a manner likely to secure and maintain stable and effective collective bargaining arrangements; and if the employer wishes, they will enter into single-table bargaining arrangements.[99] The question arises as to the meaning of 'stable and effective collective bargaining arrangements', and concerns have been raised as to the evidence unions must provide to the CAC to demonstrate their ability to deliver this. A union may have to show a history of successfully operating single-table bargaining arrangements at other workplaces in conjunction with other unions.

Where the CAC has accepted an application from a union in relation to a bargaining unit, an application by another union in relation to another bargaining unit would not be admissible if there is any overlap of employees between the two.[100] However, if the competing application has also satisfied the 10% 'reasonable support' test then the original application will be cancelled. If the CAC has received an application but not yet accepted it, and another application is then made, which satisfies the 10% rule, then the CAC must proceed with that application only.[101]

The three year rule and repeat applications

Once the CAC has accepted an application and decides to dismiss the claim, another application must not be made in relation to the same or substantially the same bargaining unit by the same union within a period of three years from the date after the day on which the CAC gave notice of acceptance.[102] However, once an application has been accepted by the CAC, the union can still withdraw it (if new evidence comes to light which suggests, for example, that a ballot would not succeed) without the three year rule coming into effect, so long as it is prior to a declaration of recognition being made or notification being given by the CAC of its intention to hold a secret ballot of the relevant workers.

Semi-voluntary recognition

Part II of Sched A1 makes special provision for 'agreements for recognition'. These are recognition agreements (where the employer has recognised the union as entitled to conduct collective bargaining) reached at any stage after the statutory procedure has been

---

99 Paragraph 37(2).
100 Paragraph 38(1)(2).
101 Different rules apply where there are multiple competing applications – see para 14.
102 Paragraph 39.

commenced, but before the CAC has conducted a ballot or made an award of automatic recognition. The scheme of Pt II is to enable the parties to such an agreement to apply to the CAC with a request to specify a method by which collective bargaining is to be conducted.[103] It also provides that 'agreements for recognition' are to last for a period of three years, after which time they may be terminated by either party. Originally, Pt II was intended to bring purely voluntary recognition agreements within the statutory framework, but it was conceded that this would introduce unnecessary complexity and legalism into areas where voluntary recognition had been operating successfully.

Derecognition[104]

The statutory procedure allows for derecognition applications to be made where the employer contends that the size of its workforce has fallen below 21 workers;[105] where the employer or workers believe that there is less than majority support for the collective bargaining arrangements;[106] where the original declaration of recognition was made automatically on the basis of majority union membership and the employer believes that membership within the bargaining unit is now less than 50%;[107] and where a group of workers want to end voluntary recognition of a non-independent union.[108] The derecognition procedure (for all categories except an application by workers to derecognise non-independent unions) cannot be invoked until three years have passed following the date of the CAC's declaration of recognition.

Where an employer believes that its workforce has fallen to an average of less than 21 workers, the procedure is commenced by the service of a notice by the employer to the union and CAC of an intention to end the bargaining arrangements.[109] Once the CAC decides that the notice is valid,[110] the parties must be notified and the bargaining arrangements will end on the date specified by the employer, unless the union applies to the CAC challenging the accuracy of the employer's assessment of the size of its workforce.[111] A union application to the CAC objecting to the derecognition notice must be made within 10 working days, starting with the day after the date on which the employer's notice was given, and the union must serve a copy of the notice and any supporting documents on the employer. [112]

If the CAC decides that the union's application is 'admissible' (that is, there have been no previous applications within the last three years), it must notify the parties of this within 10 days and consider their views before deciding the issue. If the CAC decides in

---

103 Once the CAC has accepted the application the procedure and enforcement process is the same as applies under Part I above.

104 The derecognition procedure only applies to statutory recognition. Employers who are party to voluntary recognition agreements can still end them by simply giving the appropriate notice specified by the agreement.

105 Paragraphs 96–103.

106 Paragraphs 104–21.

107 Paragraphs 122–33.

108 Paragraphs 134-48.

109 Paragraph 99(2).

110 The notice must comply with certain formalities outlined in para 99(3).

111 Paragraph 103(3)(4).

112 Paragraph 101(1)(3).

favour of the union, the bargaining arrangements continue and the employer's notice fails. Otherwise, the bargaining arrangements shall cease on the date specified by the employer in the notice or the day after the decision, whichever is later.[113]

Where the employer believes that there is no longer majority support for collective bargaining, the process effectively mirrors that which is followed once a recognition request has been served by a union on an employer under Pt I of Sched A1. Once a written request to end the bargaining arrangements is served on the union, the parties then have two periods in which to conduct negotiations with a view to ending the bargaining arrangements. The union can agree in the first period (10 working days following the day on which the union received the request) to end the bargaining arrangements.[114] Alternatively, it can state that it does not accept the request but is willing to negotiate (with the assistance of ACAS if requested), in which case the parties have a period of 20 working days or a longer period as agreed in which to conduct negotiations.[115]

If the union rejects or fails to respond to the employer's request within the first period or no agreement is reached within the second period, the employer can then apply to the CAC for a secret ballot to be held on whether the bargaining arrangements should end.[116]

The CAC must not proceed with the derecognition application unless it is satisfied that at least 10% of the relevant workers want an end to the bargaining arrangements and there is *prima facie* evidence that a majority of those workers would support a derecognition proposal. Just as is the case with unions seeking to gain recognition, employers desiring derecognition will need to canvass the relevant workers in order to satisfy these requirements. If the CAC decides that the formal admissibility requirements are satisfied, it must accept the application, notify the parties of the acceptance and proceed to conduct a secret ballot on the derecognition question.[117]

The balloting process (set out in paras 117–21) is the same as that undertaken when a union makes an application for recognition under Pt I. The employer is under the same three statutory duties and the same 40% threshold applies. If the result of the ballot is that a majority of workers voting and at least 40% of workers in the bargaining unit favour derecognition, then the CAC will declare that the bargaining arrangements are to end on a specified date.[118]

A simplified derecognition procedure will apply in cases where recognition has been automatic (that is, without a ballot) by virtue of the levels of union membership.[119] Where the employer's application alleges that the number of union members has now dropped below 50%, the employer and union have 10 working days or an agreed longer period in which to conduct negotiations with a view to ending the bargaining arrangements.[120] Where there is no agreement, the employer may apply to the CAC for

---

113 Paragraph 103(1)–(3).
114 Paragraph 105(1)(6).
115 Paragraph 105(2)(7).
116 Paragraphs 106, 107.
117 Paragraphs 111(5), 117(1)(3).
118 Paragraph 121(3).
119 Paragraph 122.
120 Paragraph 128(1)(3).

the holding of a secret ballot on the derecognition question. If the CAC is satisfied that less than half of the workers in the bargaining unit are union members, then it will proceed to conduct a secret ballot on derecognition.

A worker or workers disaffected with the recognised union may also seek to press for a derecognition ballot. If the CAC decides that the application is admissible (evidence having been provided as to the decline in union support), it must accept the application and proceed to assist negotiations (within a 20 day time frame) conducted with a view to ending the bargaining arrangements, or the workers withdrawing their application, pending the conduct of a secret ballot should there be no agreement.[121]

The final type of derecognition application enables a union to eliminate employer bargaining arrangements with house staff associations so as to allow the union itself to apply formally for recognition. Thus, where an employer has a voluntary recognition agreement with a non-independent union, a worker or workers within the bargaining unit covered by the agreement may apply to the CAC for a derecognition ballot. The request by the workers to the employer must comply with the usual admissibility requirements,[122] including the requirement that at least 10% of the workers in the bargaining unit desire an end to the bargaining arrangements and a majority of the unit would similarly favour a cessation of the present arrangements.[123]

Once the application is accepted, there then follows a 20 day negotiation period (which may be extended by consent).[124] If there is no agreement on derecognition or withdrawal of the application, then the balloting provisions as discussed above apply. Where the CAC accepts a derecognition application and then it becomes aware that the non-independent union has made an application for a certificate of independence to the Certification Officer, the application will be suspended until the Certification Officer's decision. If the Certification Officer refuses the application, the derecognition procedure continues, even if the union appeals against the Certification Officer's verdict. If a successful appeal is made, the workers' application will lapse at whatever stage it has reached.

Note that if a union that has a statutory declaration of recognition or an agreement for recognition with an employer loses its certificate of independence, then the statutory bargaining arrangements cease to have effect and the parties will be deemed to be in a relationship of voluntary recognition.[125] If the union succeeds in an appeal against the loss of its certificate of independence, then, from the date of reissue of the certificate, the statutory bargaining arrangements will revive.[126]

---

121 Paragraph 115(2)(3)(6).
122 The application would, of course, not be admissible if the union faced with derecognition could demonstrate it possessed a certificate of independence.
123 Paragraphs 137, 139.
124 Paragraph 142.
125 Paragraph 152.
126 Paragraph 153.

Protection against detriment and dismissal

Part VIII of Sched A1 confers special protection against detriment, dismissal and selection for redundancy for workers involved with the statutory recognition and derecognition process.[127] Workers have the right not to be subjected to any detriment by their employer by an act or a deliberate failure to act on any one of eight grounds.[128] The eight grounds are that the worker:

(a) acted with a view to obtaining or preventing recognition of a union by the employer under Sched A1;

(b) indicated that s/he supported or did not support recognition of a union by the employer under Sched A1;

(c) acted with a view to securing or preventing the ending of bargaining arrangements under Sched A1;

(d) indicated that s/he supported or did not support the ending of bargaining arrangements under Sched A1;

(e) influenced or sought to influence the way in which votes were to be cast by other workers in a ballot arranged under Sched A1;

(f) influenced or sought to influence other workers to vote or abstaining from voting in such a ballot;

(g) voted in such a ballot; or

(h) proposed to do, failed to do, or proposed to decline to do, any of the matters referred to above.

A worker will not be protected if the detriment or dismissal occurred because the worker committed an 'unreasonable act or omission'.[129] There is little guidance as to what consists of 'unreasonable' conduct. Thus, this provision is likely to involve tribunals in making fine judgments on the merits of particular cases. For example, if a union meeting during a ballot lasts longer than originally agreed with the employer, and the employer subjects the workers to a detriment, or if two or three workers are disciplined for discussing the recognition issue at work[130] at a time when the employer has expressly forbidden such discussion, the question arises as to whether such conduct would be 'unreasonable' for the purposes of this protection.

A further issue concerns the scope of actions that might be said to be a 'detriment'. This might be important in the context of information being distributed by an employer in the course of a contested recognition ballot. For example, the distribution of letters to employees saying that jobs will be lost if the union is recognised, and other similar

---

127 Employees subjected to a detriment because of their involvement with a purely voluntary recognition process do not have this special protection but may be protected under the existing law preventing victimisation of trade union members on the grounds of trade union membership and activities (see Chapter 9).

128 Paragraph 156(1)(2).

129 Paragraph 156(3).

130 There may be human rights implications here taking into account the requirements of the right to freedom of expression contained in the European Convention, Art 10, and enforceable by the Human Rights Act 1998.

negative campaigning tactics, may arguably be the threat of a 'detriment' rather than merely the provision of information to the workers about the issues involved.

Actions for alleged infringements of the right not to be subjected to a detriment are to be brought to an employment tribunal, within three months of the act (or, if the act is part of a series, the last of the acts) taking place. A deliberate failure to act (which causes the detriment) is to be treated as having happened when it was decided upon. In the absence of any contrary evidence, an employer will be deemed to have decided upon the failure to act when either he does an act inconsistent with doing the failed act, or when the period expires within which the employer may reasonably have been expected to do the failed act.[131] The burden of proof is on the employer to establish the ground on which he acted or failed to act.

Compensation is to be awarded on a just and equitable basis, having regard to the infringement complained of and any loss sustained by the complainant that is attributable to the act complained of. The loss will include any expenses reasonably incurred as a consequence of the act or failure in question, together with the loss of any benefit that the worker might otherwise have expected to receive. Compensation can be reduced on a just and equitable basis where the worker contributed to the loss and workers must take reasonable steps to mitigate their loss.

Where the detriment amounts to a dismissal, employees are protected by specific provisions prohibiting unfair dismissal. The same cap on compensation that applies to employees making claims for ordinary unfair dismissal under the Employment Rights Act 1996 will apply.[132] Employees can also make applications for interim relief provided that any such application is lodged within seven days of the effective date of termination. Selection for redundancy will be automatically unfair if the reason or principal reason for dismissal is that the employee was redundant, but the circumstances constituting the redundancy applied equally to other employees holding similar positions who were not dismissed, and the reason for the employee's selection (or principal reason) was one of the grounds set out in para 156 above.

In the case of the termination of the contract of a worker who is not an employee, the provisions on detriment still apply with compensation levels subject to the maximum for unfair dismissal.

Conclusions

One of the major problems ACAS found when implementing the 1975 version of recognition was the protracted consultation and inquiry procedure that it was obliged to carry out. The procedure took too long – references took a year, on average, to reach the final report stage, and more than a fifth took 18 months. In the 1999 Act, there are prescribed time limits for every stage of the process, with scope for extension where necessary. Even so, the new legislative timetable allows for a period of up to 80 working days – excluding extensions by agreement or as determined by the CAC – from the initial trade union request for recognition to the holding of a ballot on the issue. This could

131 Paragraph 157.
132 Paragraph 160.

cause difficulties for the trade unions involved, not least on a purely practical level of maintaining the employees' interest in the issue. Experience of operating recognition legislation in the United States shows that the longer the delay before a ballot is held, the less likely it is that the union will win.[133]

Secondly, in the 1975 version of compulsory recognition there were problems with inter-union disputes, where more than one union sought recognition over the same group of workers. The TUC was effective in resolving some of these disputes in accordance with the Bridlington Procedures, but serious difficulties still occurred when non-TUC unions or staff associations were competing with TUC affiliates. It remains to be seen how far the 1999 procedure on joint and competing applications deals successfully with this issue taking into account the requirements of co-operation laid down in the procedure.

The question of outright employer opposition to the idea of compulsory trade union recognition also remains one of the most problematic areas for legislation in this field. Many employers will have never had any experience of collective bargaining and others will have become accustomed to excluding unions from the workplace. Coupled with creative legal advice and legislation that is extremely complex, employer opposition to union attempts to secure recognition could well find a fruitful outlet in litigation. Although the procedure was drafted in great detail in order to circumvent court challenges, judicial review applications may well be initiated if the CAC is perceived by determined employers to have failed to exercise its functions or discretion fairly without sufficient reference to the statutory provisions. Employers may also utilise the opportunity provided by the Human Rights Act 1998 to argue that the procedure is in breach of European Convention safeguards. Employers may have concerns that CAC decision making may, in exceptional circumstances, be in breach of their Art 6 right to a fair hearing in civil proceedings – such as where decisions of the CAC (which have an impact on an employer's civil obligation to recognise trade unions) are taken without employer representation. A further issue is that trade union entry onto premises in pursuance of the Access Code may interfere with an employer's right to peaceful enjoyment of private property, contrary to Art 1 of the First Protocol of the European Convention.[134]

The success or failure of such litigation will depend, to a degree, on the attitude of the judges. The operation of the 1975 scheme suffered from a hostile judiciary unsympathetic with the idea of employers being forced to negotiate with trade unions, viewing it as a draconian incursion on the right of an individual to regulate his or her own working life and an attack on employer autonomy. Accordingly, they adopted a deliberate policy of construing the provisions in a narrow, legalistic manner. It remains to be seen how far judicial attitudes towards pro-union legislation have moderated. It may be that this more dynamic process combined with tighter legislative drafting will neutralise the threat of

---

133 The UK method of statutory recognition closely resembles the US model. This has arguably not proved to be a success as the US has one of the lowest rates of unionisation in the industrialised world. For comparison and analysis of the US system, see Ewing, KD (ed), *Recognition Laws – Lessons from Abroad* (1998, Institute of Employment Rights); Wood, S and Goddard, J, 'The statutory recognition procedure in the Employment Relations Bill: a comparative analysis' (1999) 37 BJIR 203; Adams, J, 'Why statutory recognition policy is bad labour policy' (1999) 30 IRJ 96; Brown, W *et al*, 'The limits of statutory trade union recognition' (2001) 32 IRJ 180.

134 For further discussion, see Ewing, KD (ed), *Human Rights at Work* (2000, Institute of Employment Rights), Chapter 8.

judicial review and protect the process from the form of undue judicial interference which had emasculated the operation of the s 11 procedure.[135]

Another criticism of the procedure is the narrow scope of the recognition award. Where the CAC makes an award of recognition to a trade union for the purpose of conducting collective bargaining, this will only apply to negotiations on 'pay, hours and holidays';[136] although the parties may voluntarily broaden the coverage of an agreement for recognition[137] and employers must consult and inform the recognised trade unions on matters to do with training of workers in the relevant bargaining unit.[138] In addition, the CAC imposed model method only enforces (by an order for specific performance) a procedural remedy culminating in the parties meeting for negotiations: it does not enforce actual negotiations on the substantive issues.[139] Disquiet has also been raised over the small employer threshold[140] and the balloting rules that require over 40% of those balloted to vote for recognition, contrary to the ordinarily acceptable democratic principle of the simple majority.[141]

The experience of the CAC indicates that, since the coming into force of the recognition law, unions have been cautious in submitting applications, avoiding bringing cases they were not fully confident of winning, although the CAC has reported increased demand for CAC adjudication as the parties have become more aware of the procedure.[142] There is also evidence of an indirect impact of the recognition law, with unions having had some success in persuading previously reluctant employers to conclude voluntary recognition agreements, particularly where more than 50% of the workforce are union members. At the beginning of 2000, the TUC reported the results of a survey that showed that unions achieved 74 new recognition agreements, covering over 21,000 workers, in the first 10 months of 1999.[143] ACAS has also reported that, in the year to August 2000, it has been asked to assist in 263 voluntary recognition cases – double the number on average during the 1990s.[144]

On their own, the recognition provisions are unlikely to reverse the culture of individualism and anti-trade unionism encountered since 1979. Arguably, to resurrect trade union influence, a legal mechanism for recognition needs to be combined with industrial policies and labour law reforms which encourage organising and recruiting

---

135 The CAC Annual Report 2000–01 states that in the period covered by the report there have been two applications for judicial review of CAC decisions. In the first reported case – *Fullarton Computer Industries Ltd v CAC* [2001] IRLR 752 – the employer unsuccessfully argued that the CAC had acted *ultra vires* by delegating powers of decision to a case manager and that the CAC had taken account of irrelevant matters when deciding against a ballot.

136 Paragraph 3(3).

137 Paragraph 3(4).

138 1999 Act, s 5, inserting ss 70B and 70C into TULR(C)A 1992.

139 It is of course doubtful whether any sanctions could effectively guarantee enforcement of a 'duty to bargain'. As bargaining presupposes a degree of mutual co-operation between the parties, it is questionable whether truly recalcitrant employers can be induced to negotiate in good faith. The experience in the USA is that even compulsory unilateral arbitration and mandatory court injunctions do not deter the determined anti-union employer. See Hart, M, 'Union recognition in America – the legislative snare' (1978) 7 ILJ 201.

140 The TUC has estimated that this has resulted in 5 m employees being excluded.

141 Paragraph 29(5) does give the Secretary of State power to amend the 40% threshold.

142 CAC Annual Report 2000–01.

143 *Financial Times*, 7 January 2000.

144 ACAS Annual Report 2000–01; ACAS Press Release, 11 September 2000.

activity and which assist voluntary action by unions to secure recognition. This, however, would entail a radical departure from policies of the last 20 years which presently have a degree of bipartisan political support. What is more likely is that any future programme of trade union rights will be heavily influenced by the social policy initiatives deriving from Europe, considered in some detail in the following chapter.

VOLUNTARY RECOGNITION

The statutory recognition procedure does not affect the rights and responsibilities of the parties who have negotiated a voluntary recognition agreement. Where the union is not formally recognised, the informal relationship between the employer and the union takes on an added significance. The courts may determine that, at a point in the relationship between union and employer, there exists implied recognition in law due to a course of dealing between the parties. This is of some significance as unions are entitled to certain rights on recognition – such as, *inter alia*, the right to information for collective bargaining purposes and to consultation on collective redundancies and on a transfer of an undertaking. What is required is for the employer, in practice, to negotiate with the union on one or more of the matters contained in s 178(2), that is, terms and conditions of employment, working conditions, discipline, termination and suspension of employment, facilities for trade union officials, membership or non-membership of a trade union and machinery for negotiation and consultation relating to these matters or to trade union recognition.[145] A union thus must have the agreement of the employer to negotiate on issues concerning one or more of these topics to qualify for the collective bargaining rights.[146]

A strict criteria is rigidly employed to determine whether there has been implied recognition. The approach of the courts is epitomised by Lord Denning's comment, in *NUGSAT v Albury Bros Ltd*,[147] that '... a recognition issue is a most important matter for industry; and therefore an employer is not to be held to have recognised a trade union unless the evidence is clear ...'. This evidence may be clear from a previous course of dealing. In *NUTGW v Charles Ingram & Co Ltd*,[148] actual negotiations on a variety of matters took place over an extensive period of time. The bald statement from the employers that the union was not recognised was insufficient as it was contradicted by the practical evidence of co-operation.[149]

In the EAT in *NUGSAT v Albury Bros*,[150] Phillips J suggested that the acts relied on as evidence of implied recognition must be 'clear and unequivocal and will (usually) involve

---

145 In the course of his judgment in *NUGSAT v Albury Bros Ltd* [1979] ICR 84, Eveleigh LJ made it clear that even if an implied agreement can be discerned from the evidence it must be on an issue of collective bargaining specified in s 178(2).

146 Section 178(3). See *USDAW v Sketchley* [1981] ICR 644 where the EAT held that a limited express agreement for union representation of employees grievances did not confer on the union general collective bargaining rights. See also *TGWU v Coutenham Products Ltd* [1977] IRLR 8.

147 [1979] ICR 84, p 89.

148 [1977] IRLR 147.

149 Thus, whether there has been recognition is judged objectively on the facts rather than on the subjective view of either of the parties. See also *J Wilson & Sons Ltd v USDAW* [1978] ICR 614.

150 [1978] ICR 62.

a course of conduct over a period of time'.[151] The Court of Appeal[152] agreed with Phillips J that recognition is not to be presumed lightly. In this case, the mere entering into discussions by the employer over the payment of trade association rates for members was not sufficient evidence of implied recognition. Although a beginning had been made on negotiations, the consultation between the parties was too limited and inconclusive. There was no real evidence of an agreement to bargain; to strike a deal.[153]

A union may be recognised for limited bargaining purposes. What is required is a sustained course of conduct between the parties indicating that there is an agreement to negotiate on at least one of the listed matters of collective bargaining in s 178(2). For example, on the facts in *Sketchley v USDAW*,[154] there existed an implied recognition agreement on redundancy issues. When it had become known to the union that the employer wished to dismiss workers for reason of redundancy, the union threatened strike action. As a consequence, the employer met with the union and it was agreed that certain advance information would be provided should redundancies occur. Although there was not sufficient evidence here for there to be implied recognition of the union for general bargaining purposes, it was arguable that rights of consultation on redundancy had been granted to the union in consideration for their withdrawal of the threat of industrial action.

The union, in *Cleveland CC v Springett*,[155] also argued that the employer had recognised the union for limited purposes. The Association of Polytechnic Teachers was not formally recognised by the employers, but was, in practice, permitted to appoint health and safety representatives to safety committees and to represent members in grievance proceedings. The EAT rejected the submission that the appointment of safety representatives (which was a statutory benefit for recognised unions under the Safety Representatives Regulations) had inferred recognition on matters of health and safety. The statutory provision provided rights to already recognised unions and did not of itself grant rights of recognition *per se*.

More recently, the CAC examined the issue of implied recognition in the context of a claim by the NUM under the statutory recognition procedure.[156] The NUM had submitted an application that it should be recognised for collective bargaining purposes by RJB Mining (UK) Ltd. The CAC refused to proceed with the application as it held that a recognition agreement was already in force. The employer had existing national

---

151 At p 65.

152 [1979] ICR 84.

153 The Court of Appeal in *Albury* also rejected the submission that recognition could come about by an agency relationship. A union is not recognised by a particular employer merely because that employer is a member of an employers' federation which negotiates with the trade union seeking recognition. Whether a particular employer recognises a trade union is dependent on the test of consent between the actual parties. See, also, *Cleveland CC v Springett* [1985] IRLR 131 where the Secretary of State had appointed an unrecognised union to the Burnham negotiating committee which determined national terms and conditions of employment. Recognition was not inferred from this act as 'there is no place in any satisfactory system of employment law for the concept of enforced or automatic recognition thrust upon an employer by a third party' (p 135).

154 [1981] ICR 644.

155 [1985] IRLR 131.

156 *NUM and RJB Mining (UK) Ltd* (2000) TUR1/32/00.

consultation arrangements with the union on Transfer of Undertakings and Working Time issues and negotiated locally on redundancy and pay issues. Although a formal recognition agreement had not been concluded, this was sufficient evidence of implied recognition.

CHAPTER 11

COLLECTIVE RIGHTS FOR TRADE UNIONS – INFORMATION AND CONSULTATION

THE RIGHT TO INFORMATION

The right to information was originally contained in ss 17–21 of the Employment Protection Act 1975,[1] now found in ss 181–85 of the Trade Union and Labour Relations (Consolidation) Act (TULR(C)A) 1992. The object of the legislation at the outset was to encourage the flow of relevant information to trade unions so as to enhance and promote the conduct of ordered collective bargaining. This measure was retained during the Conservative period of office from 1979–97 because it was thought that disclosure served an important economic function in limiting union claims.[2] Where a trade union has knowledge of a business's financial position it would scale down any unrealistic demands and strike realistic bargaining positions.[3]

Recognition and the release of information

Information for collective bargaining purposes is only available to recognised unions. This is a major weakness of the right as employers have the option of lawfully restricting the release of information by refusing to recognise trade unions or by withdrawing recognition.[4] In the vast majority of cases where a trade union is recognised and included in negotiations, an employer will release information as a matter of course. It is precisely those employers who refuse to recognise and negotiate who deny trade unions information.[5]

Recognition for collective bargaining purposes means recognition for the purposes of negotiations on the matters listed in s 178(2).[6] Furthermore, a union is only entitled to

---

1   See Gospel, H, 'Disclosure of information to trade unions' (1976) 5 ILJ 223 for background to the passage of this measure.

2   See Dicken, L, 'What are companies disclosing for the 1980s?' (1980) *Personnel Management* 28.

3   This argument, of course, presupposes poor company performance and greedy 'unrealistic' unions.

4   Note, however, that where a union is recognised at the time the request for information is made, an employer cannot defeat that particular claim by derecognition – *Ackrill Newspapers and NUJ* (CAC Award 92/1) and *HM Prison Service and POA* (CAC Award 95/1).

5   There is an additional legislative requirement encouraging the release of information contained in the Companies Act 1985 (s 234 and Sched 7, para 11) which is not predicated on recognition. In companies employing more than 250 people, a statement must be made in the annual report concerning employee involvement in the affairs of the company. The statement must describe what action has been taken: to '... introduce, maintain or develop ... arrangements' to disseminate relevant information to employees; consult with employees on decision making which is likely to affect their interests; encourage employee share schemes; achieve employee awareness of financial and economic factors affecting company performance. Thus, as a matter of general policy, businesses are encouraged to keep employees informed. Most commentators, however, regard the provision to be of little practical value. See Morris, P (1986) 7 *Company Lawyer* 161.

6   See p 227.

information on a matter for which it is explicitly recognised by an employer.[7] Consequently, the extent of the recognition controls the extent of disclosure. This is demonstrated by the decision in *R v Central Arbitration Committee* (CAC) *ex p Tioxide*.[8] Here, the employer introduced a job evaluation scheme for the reassessment of salary scales. The union was given the opportunity to make representations on behalf of individuals during the process of job evaluation, but not to negotiate on the terms of the scheme.

The union submitted that, as the scheme dealt with an issue of pay, which was a matter related to terms and conditions for which the union was recognised, it should have been provided with relevant information on the application of the scheme. Forbes J held that the employer could lawfully withhold this information. Although salary determination via a job evaluation scheme was a matter related to terms and conditions of employment for which the union was ordinarily recognised, the union was not specifically recognised for negotiating purposes on the application of the scheme.

The type of information to be disclosed

A general duty is imposed on an employer who recognises an independent trade union for collective bargaining negotiations to release information for this purpose. There are, however, checks on the flow of information.[9] Whether the information should be disclosed is dependent on the application of a dual test. It must be information '... without which the trade union representatives would be to a material extent impeded in carrying on collective bargaining ... and which it would be in accordance with good industrial relations practice' to disclose.[10]

For a trade union to be impeded to a 'material extent' in carrying on collective bargaining, the information denied by an employer must be both of a relevant and significant nature; of some importance to the bargaining process.[11] Hence, information which is of no relevance or of little relevance to matters of collective bargaining can be legitimately withheld.[12]

Good industrial relations practice

Section 181(4) of the TULR(C)A 1992 establishes that, in determining what is in accordance with good industrial relations practice, regard should be had to the ACAS

---

7   Forbes J, in *R v CAC ex p Tioxide* [1981] ICR 843, explained the operation of the right to information by reference to a three stage test. An employer is only obliged to disclose information where it is required for the purposes of negotiation; where it is on a matter listed in s 178(2); and where it was a matter for which the union was specifically recognised.

8   [1981] ICR 843.

9   An employer is not required to produce original documents for inspection or for copying; information requested may be conveyed in an edited document. Nor is an employer required to compile or assemble information '... where it would involve work or expenditure out of all reasonable proportion to the value of the information in the conduct of collective bargaining'. See on this *Hoover Ltd and GMWU* (CAC Award 79/507).

10 Section 181(2)(a), (b).

11 *Beecham Group Ltd and ASTMS* (CAC Award 79/337).

12 See *Civil Service Union v CAC* [1980] IRLR 274.

Code of Practice on Disclosure of Information to Trade Unions for Collective Bargaining Purposes (1997). The Code holds that it is good practice for employers to release information which influences the formulation, presentation or pursuance of a trade union claim.[13]

The Code encourages the parties to conclude a voluntary agreement on what items will be disclosed, when and to whom.[14] The CAC in its annual reports has reiterated the usefulness of such an agreement in limiting potential conflict between employer and union over disclosure of information and noted that agreement to disclose and share information was particularly important in an economic climate where rapid change at the workplace destabilises industrial relations.

If no separate agreement is made between employer and union, then, the substantive content of the Code is evidence of 'good industrial relations practice'. The Code makes it clear that the degree and detail of information disclosed will necessarily vary, depending upon the circumstances of the case and that it is not possible to compile an exhaustive list of items that should always be disclosed. The Code does, however, outline in para 11 examples of material that might be the subject of disclosure. This list includes information on such matters as pay and benefits, recruitment policies and redundancy, promotion and other staffing plans, investment and financial information. In adjudicating on whether information should have been released, the CAC does not have to rely exclusively on the Code and may proceed by reflecting on what is common practice amongst good employers in that industry.[15]

Exceptions to the right

Even where this dual test has been exercised, a union is not entitled to demand information where one of five exceptions applies.[16] An employer is not obliged to give the applicant union the information requested if disclosure of the information is: against the interests of national security;[17] would result in the contravention of a statute;[18] is related specifically to an individual and consent has not been obtained for its release;[19] is obtained by the employer for the purpose of legal proceedings; has been communicated in confidence or obtained in confidence or would cause substantial injury to the undertaking.

---

13 Paragraph 9.
14 Paragraph 22.
15 *Standard Telephones & Cables Ltd and ASTMS* (CAC Award 79/484).
16 Section 182(1).
17 Section 183(6) specifies that a certificate signed by or on behalf of a Minister of the Crown to the effect that the disclosure of the information is against the interests of national security is conclusive evidence of that fact.
18 Eg, refusal of disclosure was justified in *Joint Credit Card Co and NUBE* (CAC Award 78/212) because the release of information would otherwise be a breach of copyright.
19 Refusal was justified in *Chloride Legg Ltd and ACTSS* (CAC Award 84/15) because the union had requested personal information on salaries of staff who were not the subject of the pay claim by the union.

Refusal to disclose information on the ground that the information has been obtained or communicated 'in confidence' is only a sound defence where the confidentiality has been imposed by the party who originally supplied the information. The courts will independently assess whether the information, once in the employer's domain, has remained confidential. The more people who have access to the information, the less likely the employer can deny disclosure on grounds of confidentiality.[20] In *Civil Service Union v CAC*,[21] the High Court upheld the CAC's decision that, given the commercial sensitivity surrounding the competitive tendering process, information on cleaning bids by private companies may be withheld on grounds of confidentiality.

In deciding whether information is legitimately withheld as release would otherwise cause 'substantial injury to the undertaking', the CAC is guided by paras 14 and 15 of the Code of Practice. The Code suggests that substantial injury to an undertaking occurs where the release of information would cause the loss of customers to a competitor; or difficulty would be experienced with suppliers of goods or services; or the ability to raise finance would be seriously impaired if the information was released. Illustrations of the type of information that may cause substantial injury are listed in the Code as including detailed analysis of investment, marketing and pricing policy and the make up of tender offers.[22] This is the type of information that would be very useful to a competitor in fixing future competition strategy as it would be to a union in fixing a negotiation strategy.[23]

Procedure for disclosure and remedies for non-disclosure

Section 183(1) of the TULR(C)A 1992 provides that a complaint of failure to disclose information must be presented to the CAC who, initially, will refer the complaint to ACAS to settle the matter by conciliation. If the complaint is not referred because the CAC believes it is not reasonably likely to be settled by conciliation, or it is referred and the conciliation fails, the CAC will hear the complaint from the trade union. The CAC will normally consider representations from the union and the employer[24] and, where the CAC finds the complaint wholly or partly well founded, a declaration is made to this effect. The declaration specifies a timescale by which the employer should comply with the disclosure of the information.[25]

Should the employer fail to comply with the declaration, s 184 provides for a further complaint to the CAC. If the CAC finds the complaint proved, another declaration is issued.[26] The union, on or after presenting the further complaint to the CAC, may apply to the CAC under s 185 for a formal award of enhanced terms and conditions for the

---

20   This was the thrust of the reasoning of the Court of Appeal in *Sun Printers v Westminster Press Ltd* [1982] IRLR 292. Here, a report on changes in working practices was not sufficiently confidential as it had been distributed to 60 junior and middle managers and 28 directors.

21   [1980] IRLR 274.

22   This sensitive information, highly prejudicial to the operation of the organisation, must be information that is not ordinarily in the public domain. Information which is publicly available, eg, under the Companies Acts, is not relevant information for the purposes of this exemption.

23   The burden of proof that disclosure would cause substantial injury lies with the employer.

24   Section 183(3).

25   Section 183(5).

26   Section 184(2).

employees who are the subject of the claim. This award may reflect the terms and conditions specified in the claim or it may reflect what would have been achieved by collective bargaining if the information had been released by the employer.[27]

The new terms and conditions incorporated into the employment contracts of employees cannot be superseded or varied by a later collective agreement or by any subsequent implied or express agreement, unless the agreement is more favourable than the CAC award.[28] This is to prevent employers from pressurising employees to revert back to their previous terms and conditions.

It has been argued that the remedy for a refusal to disclose is inadequate as the union is not entitled to enforce release of the information to which it is entitled.[29] When the provisions were originally adopted the intention was to avoid overt legalism; to produce a system where the law facilitated the release of information rather than enforced disclosure. It was hoped that, in practice, complaints would be resolved through conciliation rather than by formal proceedings.

It seems that to a great extent this has been the experience of the CAC.[30] Very few cases proceed to an enforced award against an employer; disputes are settled by conciliation or information is provided voluntarily once a formal claim is made.[31] For example, during 1994 there were 24 complaints, of which only one resulted in a formal award. Fourteen were settled by conciliation in an informal meeting in the presence of an ACAS officer. The CAC Annual Report for 1999–2000 noted that since the enactment of the provisions, to the end of 1999, 480 complaints had been received with fewer than 15% proceeding to a full hearing.

RIGHTS TO CONSULTATION

Employers are under a statutory obligation to consult with recognised trade unions in the areas of redundancy, on the transfer of an undertaking, on matters relating to health and safety at work and the administration of pension schemes and on issues of training.

---

27 An award can only relate to matters for which the union is recognised by the employer.

28 Section 185(5).

29 See *Holokrome Ltd and ASTMS* (CAC Award 79/451).

30 For a critical evaluation of the disclosure process and a review of CAC awards, see: Mitchel, F *et al*, 'Disclosure of information: some case studies' (1980) 11 IRJ 53; Gospel, H and Willman, F, 'Disclosure of information: the CAC approach' (1981) 10 ILJ 10; Hillman, P and Gospel, H, 'Role of codes – the case of disclosure' (1983) 14 IRJ 76; Gospel, H and Willman, P, 'Trade unions and the legal obligation to bargain' (1983) 21 BJIR 343; and Gospel, H and Lockwood, G, 'Disclosure of information for collective bargaining: the CAC approach revisited' (1999) 28 ILJ 233.

31 One explanation for the low caseload (favoured by the CAC itself in the Annual Report 1993, para 3.4) is that it merely reflects the widespread good practice of company disclosure on a voluntary basis.

REDUNDANCY

The law on consultation in the event of redundancy developed as a response to European Community obligations contained in the European Directive on Approximation of Laws Relating to Redundancies.[32] The provisions of this Directive were enacted into domestic law during the period of the Social Contract as ss 99–107 of the Employment Protection Act 1975;[33] now found in ss 188–92 of the TULR(C)A 1992 as amended by the Trade Union Reform and Employment Rights Act 1993 and by the Collective Redundancies and Transfer of Undertakings (Protection of Employment) (Amendment) Regulations 1995[34] and 1999.[35]

Throughout the 1980s, there was persistent criticism that the UK had not correctly implemented the Directive.[36] As a consequence, the European Commission in 1992 initiated infringement proceedings against the UK on the grounds that the domestic law defined redundancy dismissals too narrowly; failed to ensure that effective sanctions were in place to deter breach of the consultation provisions; did not require employers to consult 'with a view to reaching agreement' and supply the degree of information as prescribed in the Directive; and omitted to lay down appropriate consultation provisions where there was no recognised union at the place of work.

The last complaint was of particular importance.[37] Employers could effectively avoid community obligations by refusing to recognise, or by derecognising trade unions prior to the announcement of dismissals. This was clearly contrary to the Directive which imposed an absolute obligation on employers to consult with 'worker representatives'.

In response to the action by the European Commission and in anticipation of an adverse judgment by the European Court of Justice (ECJ), amendments were made by the Trade Union Reform and Employment Rights Act 1993 on three of the four areas cited by the European Commission.[38] Although the revised legislation on consultation now complied more closely with the requirements of the Directive, there was still one glaring omission – the failure to extend the right of consultation to employee representatives where a trade union was not recognised.

---

32 The Collective Redundancies Directive (75/129/EEC). For an analysis of the Directive, see Hepple, B, 'Community measures for the protection of workers against dismissal' (1977) 14 CMLR 489. See also Bercusson, B, *European Labour Law*, 2nd edn, 2001, Chapters 11 and 17, and Barnard, C, *EC Employment Law*, 2nd edn, 2000, Chapters 7 and 8.

33 The Labour Government's implementation was in certain respects more favourable than the minimum requirements of the Directive (such as the application of the consultation provisions on the redundancy of a single worker). The linking of consultation with union recognition was not, at the time, regarded as a major issue because of the policy initiatives in favour of union recognition and collective bargaining. See further on this Freedland, M, 'Employment protection: redundancy procedures and the EEC' (1976) 5 ILJ 24.

34 SI 1995/2587.

35 SI 1999/1925.

36 See, eg, Hepple, B and Byre, A, 'EEC labour law in the United Kingdom – a new approach' (1989) 18 ILJ 129, pp 138–41.

37 This was also a criticism of the Transfer of Undertakings Regulations implementing the Acquired Rights Directive. This is considered at pp 244–48.

38 See Ewing, KD (1993) 22 ILJ 165, pp 176–78.

In 1994, the ECJ held that, on all of the four grounds above, the UK was in breach of the Directive.[39] The ECJ decision thus confirmed that the UK Government was obliged to ensure that all workers had the opportunity to be consulted on redundancies whether or not their union was recognised. Consequently, in late 1995, the Government introduced, by way of a statutory instrument, additional changes to the consultation provisions and transfer of undertaking regulations to conform with the ECJ decision.

Following the passage of the 1995 Collective Redundancies and Transfer of Undertakings (Protection of Employment) (Amendment) Regulations[40] the duty imposed on an employer was to consult with 'appropriate representatives' of employees who may be dismissed, that is, representatives of a recognised[41] independent trade union or elected representatives of those employees.[42] The employee representatives may be elected specifically for the purpose of redundancy consultation or they may be already elected for a different purpose (such as for health and safety consultation).[43]

The most controversial aspect of the Regulations was that they gave no preference to consultation with recognised trade unions. Under the Regulations, an employer could choose to consult with an *ad hoc* group elected for this purpose rather than with officials of a recognised union – thereby bypassing established employee representatives, sidelining union objections to a particular course of action and effectively frustrating the whole basis of the consultation provisions. The Regulations also allowed the employer to have a free hand in organising the election. The Regulations did not lay down any detailed rules on how the election should be administered nor provide any safeguards to ensure the independence of the elected representative from the employer. More than one commentator noted the disparity between this minimalist approach and the detailed regulations governing internal union elections.

Union critics contended that the amendment Regulations still did not faithfully transpose the Directive. The lack of specific rules on nomination and election procedure allowed the employer to manipulate the election of employee representatives contrary to the intention of the Directive that employers should consult with workers' representatives who are independent of any employer influence. Accordingly, on this basis, a challenge to the Regulations was mounted in the Divisional Court.[44]

The court, however, refused to countenance granting a declaration. Otton LJ held that the lack of detailed safeguards against abuse of the election process did not amount to a defective implementation of the Directive. Yet, Otton LJ further went on to observe that the legal obligation is on the employer to consult 'appropriate' representatives. Although the Regulations did not define this term, the courts had the jurisdiction to assess objectively the fairness of an employer's arrangements to elect these representatives. The

---

39 *Commission of the European Community v UK* [1994] IRLR 392 (Case 383/92). Noted by Davies, P (1994) 23 ILJ 272.

40 For comment, see Barker, J (1995) 24 ILJ 371.

41 On recognition for the purposes of consultation, see *Northern Ireland Hotel and Catering College v NATFHE* [1995] IRLR 83.

42 Regulation 3, which substituted a new TULR(C)A 1992, s 188(1), (2).

43 Section 196(1).

44 *R v Secretary of State for Trade and Industry ex p Unison and Others* [1996] IRLR 438.

subjective determination of employee representatives 'at the whim of an employer' would be manifestly contrary to the Regulations.

The system of collective consultation was most recently the subject of additional amendments introduced in 1999 to counter the criticisms above. New Regulations[45] now provide that, where a trade union is recognised, union representatives of that union must be automatically consulted (even where some of the affected workers are not trade union members)[46]. Where a recognised union is not present at the workplace, explicit detailed regulation of the process of electing employee representatives has been introduced, with the onus on the employer to ensure the election is fair. Employee representatives must be elected in accordance with prescribed procedures in a secret ballot; no affected employee may be unreasonably excluded from voting or for standing as a representative[47] or be unfairly dismissed or suffer a detriment for taking part in an election of employee representatives.[48]

The elected employee representatives have the same rights and protection as trade union representatives to assist them in the performance of their duties. Thus, they should be provided with appropriate facilities, such as accommodation and a notice board, and access to the employees who elected them.[49] They are also entitled to reasonable time off[50] and the right not to be dismissed or suffer other detriment when discharging their duties.[51]

The proposal to dismiss

The duty to consult with appropriate representatives of employees who may be affected by the dismissals, or 'affected by measures taken in connection with the dismissals',[52] arises as soon as the employer is 'proposing to dismiss' 20 or more employees on grounds of redundancy.[53] In *Hough v Leyland Daff Ltd*,[54] Knox J construed the expression

---

45   SI 1999/1925.

46   Section 188(1B)(a).

47   Section 188(1B)(b).

48   Where affected employees fail to elect representatives, having had a genuine opportunity to do so, the employer may discharge the duty under the Act by providing appropriate information to the employees directly.

49   Section 188(5A).

50   Employment Rights Act 1996, s 61.

51   *Ibid*, ss 103 and 47.

52   Section 188(1).

53   Note that the 1993 revision of the legislation (in response to the European Commission's criticisms) widened the definition of redundancy for the purposes of consultation to bring the UK law into line with the Directive. Consultation must take place where dismissals occur 'for a reason not related to the individual worker concerned'. This means that the provisions are applicable wherever there are dismissals resulting from any form of business reorganisation. Eg, in *GMB v Man Truck & Bus UK Ltd* [2000] IRLR 636, this broader definition of redundancy was applied where the employer sent letters to the relevant employees giving them notice of termination of their existing contracts and offering them fresh employment on new terms. According to the EAT, this was a collective redundancy dismissal as the employer was proposing to dismiss on a group basis and not for any reasons related to the particular individuals. Additionally, the EAT held that those employees who had opted for voluntary redundancy were also entitled to the protection of the legislation – the compensation package paid was not evidence of termination by mutual agreement, but compensation for the dismissals.

54   [1991] IRLR 194.

'proposing to dismiss' to mean that consultation only needs to begin when the actual decision has been made to make the employees redundant; when 'matters ... have reached a stage where a specific proposal has been formulated and that is a later stage than the diagnosis of a problem and the appreciation that at least one way of dealing with it would be by declaring redundancies ...'.[55]

The Directive, however, states that consultation should commence once an employer is 'contemplating' redundancies.[56] The view has thus been expressed by Glidewell LJ in *R v British Coal Corp ex p Vardy*[57] that the term 'proposing to dismiss' infringes the Directive as the 'contemplation' of redundancies occurs at an earlier stage, before the employer has formed a definite view on the need for the redundancies.[58] This raises the possibility that the UK courts should interpret the expression 'proposing to dismiss' in a way that complies with the Directive, as evinced by the purposive approach of the House of Lords to domestic legislation in *Litster v Forth Dry Dock Ltd*.[59]

However, the judgment of Blackburne J in *Griffin v South West Water Services Ltd*[60] casts doubt on the need to interpret the domestic law in this manner. Blackburne J argued that the requirement to consult under the Directive arises when an employer is able to identify the workers likely to be affected and can supply the information required. This is a later stage than that envisaged by Glidewell J in *ex p Vardy*.[61] In any event, even if Glidewell's proposition is correct, Blackburne J further went on to state that the Directive could not be directly enforced against the public body as it was insufficiently precise and unconditional to be of direct effect.

More recently, in *Scotch Premier Meat Ltd v Burns*,[62] the Employment Appeals Tribunal (EAT) held that once an employer had decided on a plan of action which had two alternative scenarios, one of which included potential dismissals, then the employer was 'proposing to dismiss' within the meaning of s 188.

---

55 At p 198.
56 Article 2(1).
57 [1993] IRLR 104. Noted by Pitt, G (1993) 22 ILJ 211.
58 See also Lord McDonald's comment in *APAC v Kirvin Ltd* [1978] IRLR 318, p 320, when he said that a proposal to dismiss 'goes beyond the mere contemplation of a possible event ... [as] the employer must have formed some view as to how many [employees] are to be dismissed, when this is to take place and how it is to be arranged'.
59 [1989] IRLR 161. For comment, see Collins, H (1989) 18 ILJ 144.
60 [1995] IRLR 15. See Eady, J, 'Collective dismissals, consultation and remedies' (1994) 23 ILJ 350.
61 Morrit J, in *Re Hartlebury Printers Ltd* [1992] IRLR 516, p 519, construed the expression 'contemplation' of redundancies in a similar vein as Blackburne J. This approach to the construction of the expression seems to go directly against the opinion of the Advocate General, in *Dansk v Nielsen* [1985] ECR 533, that the 'contemplation' of redundancies takes place at the planning stage which is at an earlier point in time to when a 'proposal' to make redundancies is made. This raises the question as to whether individual workers would be able to claim appropriate compensation for losses (under the principle established in *Francovich v Italian Republic* [1992] IRLR 84 and applied in *R v Secretary of State for Transport ex p Factortame Ltd (No 3)* [1996] IRLR 267) caused by the Government's failure properly to implement the Directive. See further on this, Curtin, D, 'State liability under community law' (1992) 21 ILJ 74; Hervey, T, 'After *Francovich*: State liability and British employment law' (1996) 25 ILJ 259; Hervey, T, '*Francovich* liability simplified' (1997) 26 ILJ 74.
62 [2000] IRLR 639.

The nature and degree of consultation

The object of the statutory duty on employers is to give the representatives of the affected employees the opportunity to influence the decision by making constructive proposals to avoid or limit the effects of the redundancies. During the consultation process, the union may suggest alternative methods of achieving the employer's objectives or ways of limiting the number of redundancies.

To facilitate and enhance the consultation process, the appropriate representatives have the right to receive certain information on the employer's proposals for redundancy.[63] The employer must disclose, in writing, the reasons for the redundancies, the number of employees of a particular description to be made redundant, the total numbers of employees of that description, the proposed selection procedure, the proposed method of carrying out the dismissals and how any extra-statutory redundancy payments are to be calculated.[64] Whether the quality of information provided is sufficient to enable meaningful consultation to take place is a matter to be determined on the facts.

An amended s 188(2) of the TULR(C)A 1992 provides guidance on the extent of consultation. The employer is required to engage in discussion '... about ways of (a) avoiding the dismissals, (b) reducing the number of employees to be dismissed, and (c) mitigating the consequences of the dismissals'. The section further states that this consultation must '... be undertaken by the employer with a view to reaching agreement with the appropriate representatives'. The employer who refuses to consider union ideas or who does not make reasonable efforts to reach agreement will clearly fall foul of the law.[65] The provisions will also be broken where the consultation takes place, but it is a sham as the dismissal notices have already been issued,[66] or where little time has been allocated for the consultation exercise.[67]

The consultation must take place 'in good time',[68] but only where at least 20 employees are dismissed.[69] This is subject to a certain statutory minimum period which must elapse before the start of the first of the redundancies. Where 20 or more employees are to be dismissed, consultation must start at least 30 days before the first dismissals take effect. Where 100 or more employees are to be dismissed consultation must take place at least 90 days before the first dismissals.[70]

---

63 Section 188(4) as amended.

64 The statutory consultation period does not run until this information has been provided – *MSF v GEC Ferranti Ltd (No 2)* [1994] IRLR 113.

65 The 1993 Act deleted the previous requirement on employers to outline reasons for rejecting any suggestions put forward during the consultation exercise. For discussion of the requirements of 'fair consultation' (albeit in a different context) see *R v British Coal Corp ex p Price* [1994] IRLR 72, p 75.

66 *NUT v Avon CC* [1978] IRLR 58.

67 *E Green & Son v ASTMS* [1984] IRLR 135.

68 Section 188(1A), replacing the previous requirement that consultation had to be 'at the earliest opportunity'.

69 Previously, before the 1993 amendments, an employer was under an obligation to consult where any number of employees were to be made redundant. On revising the legislation in 1993, the Government took the opportunity to introduce these more restrictive provisions permitted by the Directive.

70 As redundancies create social dislocation and a financial call on State agencies, employers who intend to make at least 20 employees redundant must also notify this to the Department of Trade and Industry. The advance notification period corresponds to the same period for trade union consultation. This obligation is enforced by criminal sanctions.

The defence of special circumstances

If, because of special circumstances, 'it is not reasonably practicable' for the employer to comply with the requirement of consultation within the time frames above or to disclose the necessary information or to engage in the consultation required by s 188(2), then the employer is only under a duty to take 'steps ... as are reasonably practicable in those circumstances'.[71]

The courts have interpreted this provision relatively strictly and have not generally been willing to accept business difficulties as a special circumstance justifying a failure to provide information and to consult. The Court of Appeal in *Clarks of Hove Ltd v Bakers' Union*[72] held that a special circumstance was something 'out of the ordinary, something uncommon'. Here, a decision to cease trading after a period of business difficulty, with the gradual running down of the business to eventual insolvency, was not sufficient to amount to a special circumstance.[73]

However, a sudden financial or physical disaster that results in the immediate closure of the business may well be a special circumstance if it was caused by something out of the control of the employer.[74] In *USDAW v Leancut Bacon Ltd*,[75] there was a failure by the prospective purchaser to carry through the purchase of the business. Almost immediately the bank withdrew credit facilities and a receiver was appointed within days. This sudden development was held to be sufficiently grave to amount to a special circumstance.[76]

There is an additional statutory provision, introduced by the Trade Union Reform and Employment Rights Act 1993, to put into effect the EC amendment Directive on Collective Redundancies.[77] It is not a special circumstance for an employer to argue that the requisite information was not provided because the decision leading to the redundancy was taken by a controlling company that refused to release the information required.

Remedies

Should an employer fail to comply with the duties to inform and consult, s 189 outlines the procedure to be followed on the presentation of a complaint. The first stage is for the union or elected employee representative to make an application to an employment tribunal, either before the dismissals take place or within three months of them taking place.[78]

---

71 Section 188(7). The burden of proof is on the employer to prove special circumstances existed and that all reasonably practicable steps were taken to comply with the duty to consult.

72 [1978] IRLR 366.

73 See also, on insolvency, *AEEU v Clydesdale Group plc* [1995] IRLR 527.

74 See the comments of Merritt J in *Re Hartlebury Printers Ltd* [1992] IRLR 516, p 520. The case is noted by Davies, P (1993) 22 ILJ 55.

75 [1981] IRLR 295.

76 See also *Hamish Armour v ASTMS* [1979] IRLR 24 – a failure of an application for a government loan was a special circumstance; *GMB v Rankin and Harrison* [1992] IRLR 514 – redundancies made to make the business more attractive to purchasers was not a special circumstance.

77 EC Directive (92/56/EC). For an explanation of the minor changes that this Directive introduces, see Dolding, L, 'Collective redundancies and community law' (1992) 21 ILJ 310.

78 Unless it was not reasonably practicable for the complaint to be made within this period.

If the complaint is well founded, then the tribunal will grant a declaration to this effect and may make what is termed a protective award for the benefit of the affected employees. This award is calculated by reference to a 'protected period'. The employer is ordered to pay a sum of money equivalent to a week's pay for every week in the protected period. This period runs from the date the dismissals take effect or the date of the award, whichever is the earlier,[79] and '... is of such length as the tribunal determines to be just and equitable in all the circumstances having regard to the seriousness of the employer's default ...'.[80]

When assessing compensation for breach of these provisions, the tribunals will often consider what is 'just and equitable' by reference to what the employees have lost in wages if the proper period of consultation under the statute had taken place. However, the severity of the employer's default may also be a factor to be taken into account in determining compensation. In circumstances where an employer has not been consulted, but it is clear that everything has been done to avoid the redundancies, then a nominal award may be appropriate. Conversely, where there is a severe and deliberate breach of the statute, a higher award than that based on the statutory period may well be justified.[81]

This approach was supported by the EAT's decision in *Sovereign Distribution Services Ltd v TGWU*,[82] that so long as a tribunal did not intend to penalise the employer for serious breach of the provisions, a consideration of the severity of the default was a legitimate exercise of a tribunal's discretion. Here, the EAT refused to intervene in the tribunal's discretion to make an award close to the upper limit where the employer had failed to provide the relevant information required by s 188(4) and had informed the union of the redundancy dismissals on the same day as the employers were given notice of dismissal, and did not engage in any meaningful consultation before the dismissals took effect.

However, the protected period is subject to a maximum,[83] which previously was dependent on the statutory consultation period that the employer had failed to follow. The maximum period was 30 days' pay if the failure was to consult within the timescale as established by s 188(1A)(b) (that is, the 30 day consultation period where 20–99 employees were involved), which was extended to up to 90 days' pay if the failure was to adhere to s 188(1A)(a) (where 100 or more employees were involved). The 1999 Regulations have increased the maximum amount that a tribunal can award to 90 days' pay in all cases.

Should an employee be fairly dismissed or unreasonably terminate their own contract during the protected period, then s 191 provides that entitlement to payment for the reminder of the protective period lapses. An employee is also not entitled to payment if the employee is made an offer by the employer, before the protected period, to renew the contract on similar terms and conditions of employment and this offer is unreasonably

---

79 See *TGWU v Ledbury Preserves Ltd* [1986] IRLR 492.
80 Section 189(4)(b).
81 See *Spillers-French (Holdings) Ltd v USDAW* [1980] ICR 31.
82 [1989] IRLR 334.
83 Section 189(4) as amended.

refused. If the offer is made during the protective period, then the employee loses entitlement to the protective award from the date it is refused.

Even if the offer of a new contract differs from the provisions of the employee's previous contract, then, so long as it is an offer of 'suitable employment' which is unreasonably refused, then refusal will also result in the termination of the protective award. However, s 191(4) does provide that the employee is entitled to a trial period of four weeks. If the employee terminates the new contract within this period the benefit of the protective award is not lost unless the employee acted unreasonably in doing so.

Prior to amendments contained in the Trade Union Reform and Employment Rights Act 1993, if an employer paid out a sum equivalent to the full protective award then the need to consult with trade unions at the workplace was avoided. Also, there was no requirement on an employer to make extra payments for the breach of contract in giving little or no notice before dismissal. This was because the employer could 'set off' this payment, ostensibly for the breach of contract, against the liability to pay a protective award.[84] An amendment deriving from the 1993 Act now makes the buying out of employee rights in this manner unlawful by providing that employees are entitled to the protective award in addition to any sum for breach of contract.

Conclusions

For any trade union, the fundamental purpose behind consultations with an employer is to limit the loss of jobs. Yet the evidence suggests that trade unions have had limited influence over the determination of policy on workforce reductions.[85] Certainly, in the period of high unemployment in the early 1980s, there were few examples of employers modifying decisions to shed employees after consultation with trade unions.[86] Unions were more likely to be successful in negotiating higher redundancy payments for individuals and in persuading employers to opt for voluntary, rather than compulsory redundancy schemes.[87]

In general terms, the fight against job losses and plant closures has been undermined in the past by employers engaging in 'redundancy management'.[88] By making superficially attractive enhanced redundancy payments[89] and by welcoming consultation at an early stage to neutralise union resistance, redundancies can be effected with the minimum of disruption to business.[90]

---

84 See *Vosper Thornycroft Ltd v TGWU* [1988] IRLR 232.

85 For a more positive analysis of the effect of the provision, see Hall, M and Edwards, P, 'Reforming the statutory redundancy consultation procedure' (1999) 28 ILJ 311.

86 See Cross, M (ed), *Managing Workforce Reduction*, 1985, pp 67–90, and Levie, H *et al*, *Fighting Closures*, 1984.

87 See Millward, N *et al*, *Workplace Industrial Relations in Transition*, 1992, Chapter 9.

88 See White, P, 'The management of redundancy' (1983) 14 IRJ 32.

89 In *R v British Coal Corp ex p Price* [1994] IRLR 72, the High Court held that voluntary severance payments made prior to the completion of consultation do not affect the legitimacy of the consultation process. Employers may, thus, lawfully subvert the purpose behind consultation by offering attractive terms to encourage voluntary redundancies.

90 For a description of the management of workforce change in the 1980s, see Daniel, W, *Workplace Industrial Relations and Technical Change*, 1987, Chapter 9.

The changes to the statutory provisions have not altered the essentially procedural nature of the consultation requirements. Even though consultation is 'with a view to reaching agreement' on specified matters, employers are not obliged to take account of union views and so move towards the union position in order to strike a compromise agreement. Nor is it necessary for employers to justify their rejection of union suggestions.

Moreover, the efficacy of redundancy consultation has been weakened by what was described by the Conservative Government at the time as a 'deregulation measure' to help small businesses. An employer must propose to dismiss at least 20 employees before there is a need to consult with unions or employee representatives. In practical terms, as the bulk of redundancies are small scale, unions have lost the opportunity to influence employers' plans in a large number of cases. It is also arguable that, even after the 1999 amendments, sanctions for breach of the consultation requirements are still not a credible deterrent to the determined employer who can buy out the duty to consult and that the protective award may not satisfy the European Community requirement that sanctions for breach of European law must be 'effective, dissuasive and proportionate'.[91]

ON A TRANSFER OF THE UNDERTAKING[92]

Rights of consultation on the transfer of an undertaking originally derive from the EC Directive on Acquired Rights.[93] The main objective of this Directive is to protect the employment rights of employees where the ownership of an undertaking changes. The Directive was enshrined into domestic law by a reluctant Conservative Government in 1981 by the passage of the Transfer of Undertakings (Protection of Employment) Regulations (TUPE).[94] On a 'relevant transfer', the terms and conditions of affected employees are transferred to the new undertaking, thus protecting their continuity of employment.[95] Also transferred are the contents of any existing collective agreement[96] and any union recognition agreement.[97] A duty is also imposed on both parties to inform and consult with employee representatives on measures to be taken in connection with

---

91 A stronger and possibly more appropriate sanction would be to permit the courts to grant injunctive relief prohibiting the redundancies until proper consultation had taken place. Despite the problem of enforcement, the court in *R v British Coal Corp ex p Vardy* [1993] IRLR 104 granted a declaration that no redundancies should take effect until the statutory review procedure (under the Coal Industry Nationalisation Act 1946) had been followed.

92 See, generally, McMullen, J, 'Takeovers, transfers and business re-organisations' (1992) 21 ILJ 15; Elias, P and Bowers, J, *Transfer of Undertakings: The Legal Pitfalls*, 1994; McMullen, J, *Business Transfers and Employee Rights*, 1998; Bercusson, B, *European Labour Law*, 2nd edn, 2001, Chapters 11 and 18; Barnard, C, *EC Employment Law*, 2nd edn, 2000, Chapter 7.

93 77/187/EEC.

94 SI 1981/1794. See Hepple, B, 'The TUPE Regulations' (1982) 11 ILJ 29 and Davies, P and Freedland, M (1980) 9 ILJ 95, pp 109–13.

95 Regulation 5.

96 Regulation 6.

97 Regulation 9.

the transfer that affect employees.[98] Additionally, subject to an exception, it is automatically unfair to dismiss an employee for a reason connected with the transfer.[99]

A relevant transfer of an undertaking (defined as 'any trade or business') may take place by a 'sale or some other disposition'.[100] A takeover of a business by the purchase of shares is explicitly excluded. Where that occurs, there is no change in the legal identity of the employer so the continuity of employment of an employee is preserved. However, as it is not an operable transfer for the purposes of the Regulations, there are no rights of consultation on any subsequent changes to the structure of the undertaking.

The domestic courts originally construed the expression 'transfer of an undertaking' to mean a transfer of a business as a 'going concern'. It was not a relevant transfer for the purposes of the Regulations if no assets, or only some assets of an undertaking were transferred, or if 'goodwill' was not included in the transfer. Thus, if certain services were contracted out from an existing undertaking to a third party, to be performed on behalf of that undertaking, this was not a 'relevant transfer' as it was not a transfer of a 'going concern'; a viable business in its own right.[101]

This restrictive analysis was doubted on several occasions by the ECJ which initially had taken a much broader approach as to whether there had been a transfer for the purposes of the Directive. A transfer within the meaning of the Directive depended on whether the business 'retains its identity' after the transfer. This was signified by the operation continuing or resuming under the new employer as before. It was not contingent on a transfer of physical assets (stock, plant or premises) or 'goodwill'.[102] The UK courts subsequently followed this line of authority by interpreting the Regulations in the context of the Directive, which meant that the contracting out of services previously carried out 'in house' now attracted the protection of the Regulations.[103] These decisions clearly had important implications for the restructuring of public services by privatisation and the operation of the compulsory competitive tendering and market testing process.[104]

More recent ECJ judgments have, however, resiled from this expansive approach. In *Rygaard v Stro Molle*[105] the ECJ held that where there was a transfer of an activity which was limited to the performance of a one-off contract this was not a 'relevant transfer' for the purposes of the Directive unless a body of assets was also transferred. Although, in

---

98 Regulation 10.

99 Regulation 8.

100 Regulation 3(2).

101 *Curling v Securicor Ltd* [1992] IRLR 549.

102 See *Dr Sophie Redmond Stichting v Bartol* [1992] IRLR 366; *Rask v ISS Kantineservice* [1993] IRLR 133; *Christel Schmidt v Spar* [1994] IRLR 302, discussed by McMullen, J (1994) 23 ILJ 230.

103 See *Perry v Intec Colleges Ltd* [1993] IRLR 56; *Porter v Queens Medical Centre* [1993] IRLR 486; *Wren v Eastbourne BC* [1993] IRLR 425; *Dines v Initial Health Care Services Ltd* [1994] IRLR 336; *Charlton v Charlton Thermo Systems and Ellis* [1995] IRLR 79; *Birch v Nuneaton BC* [1995] IRLR 518.

104 Under the Local Government Act 1988, all local authorities had to engage in compulsory competitive tendering of services to outside contractors. Market testing was a similar exercise, undertaken by central government agencies. See further on this, Napier, B, *CCT, Market Testing and Employment Rights* (1993, Institute of Employment Rights). The policy of contracting out of public services was not abolished by the Labour Government elected in 1997 but has been revised to take account of 'best value' requirements in the bidding process.

105 [1996] IRLR 51.

Merckx v Ford Motors Co Belgium SA,[106] the ECJ returned to the analysis exemplified by the decisions in *Rask* and *Schmidt*,[107] further uncertainty has been caused by the decisions in *Suzen v Zenhnacker Gebaudereinigung GmbH Krankenhausservice*[108] and *Oy Liikeine AB v Liskojarvi*,[109] where the ECJ indicated that the Directive only applied where there had been a transfer of significant tangible or intangible assets or a transfer of the majority of the workforce who provided the service prior to the change of contractor.[110] If the ECJ's view was strictly followed, this would have serious implications for dismissed workers in the more labour intensive and asset-poor sectors of the economy. However, the domestic courts have tended to side-step the negative effects of the ECJ pronouncements by noting the contradictions in the ECJ case law and preferring (with some exceptions) the pre-*Suzen* interpretation of the Directive.[111]

In a similar vein to the criticisms levelled at the collective redundancies legislation, it had been argued by the European Commission that the original 1981 Regulations did not faithfully incorporate the requirements of the Directive as they: had excluded the transfer of non-commercial ventures;[112] had failed to specify that consultation must take place 'with a view to seeking agreement'; did not provide adequate sanctions that conformed to European Community standards; and had failed to identify appropriate employee representatives in the absence of trade union recognition.

In response to infringement proceedings initiated by the Commission, changes were made to the Regulations by the Trade Union Reform and Employment Rights Act 1993.[113] However, as was the case with the Collective Redundancies Directive, the Government failed to ensure that proper consultation provisions were in place where a trade union was not recognised. The infringement proceedings thus culminated in the decision of the ECJ, in *Commission of the European Community v UK*,[114] that the UK remained in breach of the Directive on this ground.[115] As we saw earlier, the UK Government attempted to comply with this judgment by providing for employee representatives to be elected at the workplace for the purposes of consultation prior to the transfer.[116] The 1999 amendment

---

106 [1996] IRLR 467.

107 For an analysis of ECJ decisions during this period, see McMullen, J (1996) 25 ILJ 286.

108 [1997] IRLR 255.

109 [2001] IRLR 171.

110 For comment on the two cases and their implications see, McMullen, J (1999) 28 ILJ 360 and Davies, P (1997) 26 ILJ 193 and (2001) 30 ILJ 231.

111 See, as examples, *ECM (Vehicle Delivery Service) Ltd v Cox* [1999] IRLR 559; *RCO Support Services Ltd v Unison* [2000] IRLR 624; *Argyll Training Ltd v Sinclair* [2000] IRLR 630; *Cheesman v R Brewer Contracts Ltd* [2001] IRLR 144; *ADI (UK) Ltd v Firm Security Group Ltd* [2001] IRLR 542, discussed by McMullen J (2001) 30 ILJ 396.

112 The ECJ had consistently held that the exclusion of non-commercial organisations from the Regulations was contrary to the requirements of the Directive – see *Dr Sophie Redmond Stichting v Bartol* [1992] IRLR 366, applied by the Court of Appeal in *Kenny v South Manchester College* [1993] IRLR 265.

113 See Ewing, KD (1993) 22 ILJ 165, pp 173–76.

114 [1994] IRLR 412 (Case 382/92).

115 Those workers who have been involved in transfers before the ECJ decision and who have been disadvantaged by the defective implementation of the Directive may be able to mount claims on the basis of the principle of State liability elaborated in *Francovich v Italian Republic* [1992] IRLR 84. See, also, fn 61.

116 Collective Redundancies and Transfer of Undertakings (Protection of Employment) (Amendment) Regulations 1995 (SI 1995/2587).

Regulations,[117] specifying the procedure to be followed for the election of representatives and for the primacy of trade union representation, also now apply for the purposes of TUPE consultation.

Additionally, a new amendment Directive on Acquired Rights[118] has been introduced by the European Council, codifying the case law on certain issues, and clarifying the rights of workers on a transfer. The Articles of the Directive provide for new rules on the transfer of pension rights,[119] joint and several liability for both transferor and transferee employer,[120] a requirement on a transferor to notify the transferee of the rights and obligations to be transferred[121] and new rules on insolvent transferors.[122] The Directive is yet to be transposed at the national level in the UK, although the Government was under an obligation to do so by 17 July 2001. In September 2001, the Government announced a consultation process prior to making any substantive changes to the TUPE Regulations. It remains to be seen whether it will take a limited or progressive view of the requirements of the Directive or utilise fully the power provided by s 38 of the Employment Relations Act 1999 to introduce secondary legislation to amend the TUPE Regulations in a way that goes beyond the requirements of the original or amendment Directive.[123]

The consultation and information provisions

Where there is 'a relevant transfer' (as discussed above) and where employees may be affected 'by measures[124] taken in connection with it' (such as redundancy or a change in working conditions), reg 10 provides that both undertakings involved in the transfer must inform the relevant employee representatives of the proposed arrangements in some detail.

The requisite information must cover when the relevant transfer is to take place, the reasons for the transfer, the 'legal, social and economic implications' for the affected employees of the transfer and the measures that each employer envisages will be taken that will affect their employees.[125] The information must be provided '... long enough before a relevant transfer to enable consultations to take place'.[126] The consultation must take place 'with a view to seeking agreement' on the measures put forward.[127] During

---

117 Collective Redundancies and Transfer of Undertakings (Protection of Employment) (Amendment) Regulations 1999 (SI 1999/1925).

118 98/50/EC. For comment see Davies, P (1998) 27 ILJ 365; Hunt, J (1999) 24 ELR 215.

119 Article 3(4).

120 Article 3(1).

121 Article 3(2).

122 Article 4.

123 It appears that these additional powers have been reserved in order to deal with the uncertainties caused by the ECJ decisions in the areas of contracting out of services and the transfer of administrative functions. However, it is uncertain whether the Secretary of State will initiate such measures in order to enhance employment protection on a transfer of an undertaking, although the consultation document does envisage the introduction of amendments to the Regulations to resolve uncertainty in these areas.

124 'Measures' includes 'any action, step or arrangement' – *IPCS v Secretary of State for Defence* [1987] IRLR 373.

125 Regulation 10(2).

126 See *IPCS v Secretary of State for Defence* [1987] IRLR 373.

127 Regulation 10(5) as amended. For a discussion of the meaning of this phrase see p 240.

this process, representations may be made by the appropriate employee representatives. The employer must consider these representations and, if rejected, state the reasons for doing so. There is no minimum period by which time consultation has to commence or last – the more complex the issues that arise on a transfer, the longer the period an employer should allow for consultations.

Similarly to the compulsory consultation provisions on redundancy, a failure to inform and consult on a transfer of undertakings is not actionable where there are special circumstances, making it not reasonably practicable for the employer to perform the duty. An employer is only obligated to take whatever steps of consultation are practicable in the circumstances. It may be assumed that the redundancy case law on this defence will also apply here.

Remedies

On a failure to consult or inform recognised trade unions in advance of the transfer, reg 11 states that a complaint may be presented by the relevant trade union or employee representative to an employment tribunal.[128] If the complaint is well founded, the tribunal will make a declaration to that effect and award compensation to the relevant employees as the tribunal considers '... just and equitable having regard to the seriousness of the employer's default'.

Until amendments contained in the 1993 Act, the maximum award could not exceed two weeks' pay and employers were also able to set off this compensation against a redundancy protective award. As a consequence of criticism by the European Commission that this was not a credible and effective sanction, the compensation levels were increased in 1993 to a sum not exceeding four weeks' pay and the requirement of set off was abolished.[129] Due to criticisms that this was still not an appropriate deterrent, the 1999 Regulations[130] have raised the limit of compensation payable to a maximum of 13 weeks' pay.

HEALTH AND SAFETY AND PENSIONS[131]

By virtue of the powers provided under the Health and Safety at Work Act 1974, the Safety Representatives and Safety Committees Regulations,[132] which came into force in

---

128 The complaint must be made within three months of the date the transfer is completed unless 'not reasonably practicable'. There is no need to wait for the transfer to take place before presenting the complaint – see *South Durham HA v UNISON* [1995] ICR 495. It even appears that the complaint may proceed even if the transfer does not in fact take place – see *BIFU v Barclays Bank plc* [1987] ICR 495.

129 Note the ECJ decision in *Marshall (No 2)* [1993] ICR 893 that compensation limits *per se* undermine the effectiveness of sanctions.

130 SI 1999/1925.

131 A detailed consideration of health and safety and pensions law is beyond the scope of this book. See, generally, Smith, I, Goddard, C and Randall, N, *Health and Safety, the New Legal Framework*, 1993; James, P, *The European Community: A Positive Force for UK Health and Safety Law* (1993, Institute of Employment Rights); Hendy, J and Ford, M, *Redgrave, Fife and Machin: Health and Safety*, 1995; Beck, M and Woolfson, C, 'The regulation of health and safety in Britain: from Old Labour to New Labour' (2000) 31 IRJ 35.

132 SI 1977/500.

1978, introduced the right of recognised trade unions to appoint safety representatives. Section 2(6) of the Health and Safety at Work Act 1974 places a duty on employers:

> ... to consult safety representatives with a view to the making and maintenance of arrangements which will enable (the employer) and his employees to co-operate effectively in promoting and developing measures to ensure the health and safety at work of employees and in checking the effectiveness of such measures.

Where requested by two or more safety representatives in writing, the employer must set up a safety committee within three months of the request. The employer should consult with safety representatives and any relevant union as to how it should function. The powers of the committee and terms of reference are determined by reference to guidance notes provided by a Code of Practice under the Safety Representatives Regulations.

Should an employer refuse to consult with a recognised union about the setting-up of a safety committee after a request by the safety representatives, the union may complain to an inspector from the Health and Safety Commission. An improvement notice may then be issued requiring the committee to be established. It is possible for a recalcitrant employer to be prosecuted under the Act for failing in this duty.

In addition, the Management of Health and Safety at Work Regulations 1992 (amended by the 1999 Regulations),[133] enforcing the European 'Framework Directive' on Health and Safety,[134] contain further requirements on health and safety matters generally and consultation in particular. Regulation 4(a) extends rights of consultation to ensure that every employer will consult 'in good time' on:

(a) the introduction of any measure that may substantially affect health and safety;

(b) arrangements for the appointment of employees to assist with health and safety and with the implementation of procedures where there is serious and imminent risk;

(c) the type of health and safety information provided to employees;

(d) the planning and organisation of health and safety training;

(e) the health and safety implications of the introduction of new technology.

The framework Directive requires (similarly to the Collective Redundancies and Acquired Rights Directives) that consultation must be with 'designated workers' representatives'. Regulations have therefore been introduced to ensure compliance with European law and the ECJ decision in *European Commission v UK*.[135] The Health and Safety (Consultation with Employees) Regulations 1996 have extended rights of consultation to workers in non-unionised workplaces.[136]

Where an employer wishes to opt out of the State pension scheme by operating an occupational company pension for employees, the employer must obtain a contracting out certificate from the Occupational Pensions Board. Before doing so, any relevant trade union must be consulted. Once an occupational pension scheme is in operation, s 113 of the Pensions Schemes Act 1993 and the Occupational Pension Schemes Regulations[137]

---

133 SI 1999/3242.

134 89/391/EC.

135 [1994] IRLR 412.

136 See James, P and Walter, D, 'Non-union rights of involvement: the case of health and safety at work' (1997) 26 ILJ 35.

137 SI 1996/1172.

provide that certain information must be released to members of the scheme and their union representatives recognised for the purposes of collective bargaining.

TRAINING

Where an independent trade union is recognised in accordance with the statutory recognition procedure and a method of collective bargaining has been specified by the CAC, that trade union is entitled to be consulted on training issues within the relevant bargaining unit.[138] The employer is under a duty to call a meeting with trade union representatives within six months to consult on the employer's training policy and on arrangements for training in the following six month period. Follow-up meetings should take place within six months of the previous meeting.[139] Two weeks prior to the meeting, the employer must provide the union with certain relevant information – that without which the union would be impeded to a material extent in participating in the meeting and which it would be in accordance with good industrial relations to disclose.[140] This repeats the formula applied to the right to information for collective bargaining purposes discussed earlier in this chapter, and the same restrictions on disclosure apply. The employer must also 'take account' of written representations from the union stemming from matters raised at a consultative meeting.[141]

Where an employer has failed to comply with this duty to consult on training matters, the union concerned may complain to an employment tribunal for a declaration to this effect and for an award of compensation equivalent to two weeks' pay for each individual member of the relevant bargaining unit; enforceable by the individual, rather than the union complainant.[142]

THE EUROPEAN DIMENSION[143]

The principle of employee information, consultation and participation as an aspect of European social policy has been supported by Community institutions since 1974. The early initiatives in this area were the Acquired Rights Directive and the Collective Redundancies Directive discussed earlier. These two Directives arose out of the 1974–76 Action Programme on Social Policy undertaken by the Commission to harmonise the laws of Member States on employment matters. Although worker participation was a theme of the Action Programme, the Commission failed to develop initiatives on this issue as a consequence of the opposition of a number of Member States to the harmonisation of labour standards in this area.

---

138 TULR(C)A 1992, s 70B(1), (2).
139 Section 70B(3).
140 Section 70B(4).
141 Section 70B(6).
142 Section 70C.
143 See, generally, Nielsen, R and Szyszczak, E, *The Social Dimension of the European Community,* 1993, Chapter 5; Bercusson, B, *European Labour Law,* 2nd edn, 2001, Chapters 19 and 20; Barnard, C, *EC Employment Law,* 2nd edn, 2000, Chapters 1 and 2.

The first attempt by the European Commission to secure a degree of worker information and consultation was the 'Vredling' Draft Directive.[144] This was developed to provide rights of information and consultation to employees of undertakings with complex structures. Where there was a parent undertaking with one or more subsidiaries, the original Directive required the disclosure of wide ranging and explicit financial, economic and strategic information every six months by the dominant undertaking to the representatives of employees of its subsidiaries. Additional financial information concerning the relevant subsidiary had also to be disclosed.

As a consequence of widespread alarm in the European business community, amendments to the original draft Directive were made in 1983. The amended Directive[145] was to apply to both national and multinational corporations with subsidiaries that employ at least 1,000 employees. The same degree of information was to be disclosed to employee representatives, but on an annual, rather than six monthly, basis. Despite these amendments, the draft Directive was still not implemented.[146] It has now been dropped by the Commission. However, many of the Vredling requirements have resurfaced in a different guise via European company law directives and the European Works Council Directive.

In 1986, the Single European Act amended the Treaty of Rome, creating Art 118a which gave the Council powers to legislate by qualified majority voting on health and safety measures. In 1989, the Community Charter of Fundamental Social Rights of Workers (the Social Charter) was adopted by the Council of Ministers in conjunction with an Action Programme to develop new legislative measures.[147] This was the social policy complement to the completion of the single internal market approved by all members of the community except the UK.[148]

The Social Charter Action Programme (1989) spawned the draft Directive on Information and Consultation of Workers Within European Scale Undertakings.[149] As this was a measure harmonising labour standards, the implementation of this draft Directive required a unanimous vote of all States under Art 100. With the UK vetoing this

---

144 OJ C297 1980.

145 OJ C217 1983.

146 For a review of the early history of the Vredling Directive and its contents, see Daubler, W, 'The Employee Participation Directive – a realistic Utopia?' (1977) 14 CMLR 457 and Docksey, C, 'Information and consultation of employees: the UK and the Vredling Directive' (1986) 49 MLR 281.

147 The Community Charter of Social Rights had no specific legal status but was a solemn declaration of agreed principles in the area of social and employment policy. To implement these principles the Council adopted the Action Programme.

148 For an extensive analysis of the Social Charter and background to the Action Programme, see Bercusson, B, 'The European Community's Charter of Fundamental Social Rights of Workers' (1990) 53 MLR 624; Hepple, B, 'The implementation of the Community Charter of Fundamental Social Rights' (1990) 53 MLR 643; Vogel-Polsky, E, 'What future is there for a social Europe following the Strasbourg summit?' (1990) 19 ILJ 65; and Watson, P, 'The Community Social Charter' (1991) 28 CMLR 37. See also Lord Wedderburn, *The Social Charter, European Company and Employment Rights* (1990, Institute of Employment Rights) and 'The Social Charter in Britain – labour law and labour courts' (1991) 54 MLR 1.

149 This was the original draft European Works Council Directive (OJ C39 1991). For discussion of its aims, see Hall, M, 'Behind the European Works Council Directive: the European Community's legislative strategy' (1992) 30 BJIR 547.

Directive,[150] the remaining 11 States turned to implementation procedures under the Maastricht Social Protocol. In 1992, as an addition to the Treaty on European Union (Maastricht Treaty), all members of the EU except the UK reaffirmed their commitment to minimum labour standards and the harmonisation of labour law across the EU. As the UK opposed the extension of community competence in this area, an Intergovernmental Protocol on Social Policy, annexed to the Maastricht Treaty, was agreed by the remaining members to enable implementation of the Social Charter Action Programme.[151]

The European Works Council Directive[152] was finally passed under the Social Policy Protocol procedure and adopted by the Council of Ministers on 22 September 1994, with an implementation deadline of two years from that date.[153] The aim of the Directive is to establish a consistent system of worker participation in all transnational European enterprises so as to ensure that workers are informed and consulted about decisions taken in other Member States. Works councils (committees of workers' representatives), must be set up in all undertakings which have at least 1,000 employees in the EU and have a minimum of 150 employees in at least two other Member States.

Where these conditions are met and where at least 100 employees or their representatives so request,[154] the Directive calls for the 'central management' of the undertaking to organise the setting-up of a 'special negotiating body' between employee representatives and management to negotiate and agree in writing the composition, nature, functions, competences and operating rules of a works council. If negotiations within three years fail to agree to the structure and powers of a works council, the Directive imposes a default model of minimum standards.[155]

The default model lays down that the works council should consist of between three and 30 employees (at least one from each relevant Member State) appointed by all employees or by employee representatives as determined by 'national law or practice'. The works council should meet with management at least once a year to be informed and consulted on the economic and financial situation of the undertaking, on investment proposals and any other company developments of relevance to employees, such as organisational change or the introduction of new working methods. A works council can

---

150 Not surprisingly, at the time, the UK Conservative Government was opposed to the Social Charter and to the Action Programme on the grounds that it was contrary to free market and anti-regulation policies. See the Department of Employment publication, *People, Jobs and Progress: The UK in Europe,* 1991. For an analysis of the economic effects of the Social Charter, see Addison, J and Siebert, S, 'The Social Charter: whatever next?' (1992) 30 BJIR 495; cf Deakin, S and Wilkinson, F, 'Rights v efficiency? The economic case for transnational labour standards' (1994) 23 ILJ 289.

151 This is otherwise known as the Social Policy Agreement. See Fitzpatrick, B, 'Community social law after Maastricht' (1992) 21 ILJ 199; Watson, P, 'Social policy after Maastricht' (1993) 30 CMLR 481. The legal status of the agreement is in some doubt, see Bercusson, B, 'The dynamic of European labour law after Maastricht' (1994) 23 ILJ 1 and Whiteford, E, 'Social policy After Maastricht' (1993) 18 ELR 202, pp 211–18.

152 94/45/EC.

153 See, generally, Gold, M and Hall, M, 'Statutory European works councils: the final countdown?' (1994) 25 IRJ 177.

154 The ECJ has held in the *Bofrost* case [2001] IRLR 403 that employees or their representatives have the right to request information from their employer in order to ascertain whether a European undertaking exists for the purposes of the Directive. In the UK, Regulations enacting the Directive into domestic law already provide for rights to information at this early stage.

155 Many European undertakings have agreed voluntary transnational consultation arrangements (permitted by Art 13 of the Directive) that go beyond the minimum standards required.

insist on additional meetings where business decisions are to be made on matters (for instance, on closures) likely to have a serious effect on the interests of employees.

Despite the UK opt out of the Social Policy Protocol, British employees of large transnational undertakings have benefited from the requirements of this Directive. Although purely domestic companies have been exempt, a UK undertaking which operates in two or more Member States is directly affected. Such companies, although not compelled to introduce works councils in Britain, have needed to do so in their European outlets. Multinationals based in the EU, but with some British operations, have also been required to set up works councils in continental Europe. For both types of undertakings, it has been proved inconvenient and inefficient to structure industrial relations arrangements separately for the UK branch of their operations. Thus, research has suggested that for industrial and personnel reasons over 100 UK based companies and up to 260 companies based within the EU with operations in the UK have voluntarily introduced works council arrangements for their UK employees.[156]

As a consequence of the reversal of the UK opt out of the Social Policy Protocol agreed by the Labour Government at the Amsterdam Conference of June 1997, a new Directive[157] was promulgated to extend the terms of the 1994 Directive to the UK. The Transnational Information and the Consultation of Employees Regulations 1999[158] have now been introduced (under the authority of the European Communities Act 1972) to implement the Directive. The Regulations as a whole reflect the requirements outlined in the Directive with additional detail provided on the issues of enforcement and employee representation.[159] In the absence of a valid voluntary Art 13 or Art 3 agreement,[160] employee representatives who are entitled to trigger the 'special negotiation body' procedure are representatives (who take part in negotiations) of independent trade unions recognised for collective bargaining purposes or any other employee representatives (but excluding specialist representatives such as those elected for the purposes of health and safety or collective redundancy consultation).[161] Members of the 'special negotiation body' are to be elected by supervised ballot of the workforce unless an elected committee already exists – in which case members may be nominated from that group.[162] Members of the works council itself may be elected by employee representatives where they represent all UK employees or by a supervised ballot of all employees. Management will be able to withhold sensitive information to the works council where release might '... seriously harm the functioning of the undertaking concerned or would be prejudicial to it'.[163] The failure to release information on this ground can be challenged by an appeal to the CAC which can

---

156 See ACAS Annual Reports for 1994, p 24 and 1995, p 9; McGlynn, C, 'European works councils: towards industrial democracy' (1995) 24 ILJ 78, p 81; Cully, M *et al, Britain at Work*, 1999, pp 100–01; Carley, M and Hall, M (2000) 29 ILJ 103, pp 106–09.

157 97/74/EC.

158 SI 1999/3323.

159 See Carley, M and Hall, M, 'The implementation of the European Works Council Directive' (2000) 29 ILJ 103.

160 This must provide for meaningful EU wide consultation of the undertakings entire workforce.

161 Regulation 2.

162 Regulations 11–15.

163 Regulations 23–24.

release the information if appropriate. To assuage employers' commercial concerns, the improper disclosure of confidential information has been made a breach of statutory duty enforceable in the courts.

Members of the special negotiating body or the works council have the same rights – to time off with pay to carry out their duties and protection from victimisation and dismissal (unless the action taken against them was due to the improper disclosure of confidential information) – under the Employment Rights Act 1996 that are available to existing employee representatives, enforceable in an employment tribunal.[164]. The CAC has the responsibility to adjudicate on disputes regarding the validity of an Art 13 or Art 3 agreement, compliance with the procedures leading up to the establishment of a special negotiating body or a works council and on whether information is being unreasonably withheld from legitimate employee representatives.[165] Non-compliance with an order of the CAC is enforceable via contempt proceedings. Where a complaint refers to a refusal to co-operate in the setting-up of a special negotiating body or a works council, the EAT has jurisdiction with the power to levy a civil fine on a transgressing employer of up to £75,000.[166]

For those UK companies that are pan-European, this is a major change in the minimum rights employees can expect under domestic law. The requirement on such employers to inform and consult with the workforce is on a far broader range of topics than previously required under British law and is not dependent on union recognition. Moreover, even though under the Directive and the Regulations trade unions do not have the exclusive sole right to representation on a works council, the employee representation structures are based predominantly on the trade union model. The so called 'twin track'[167] pattern of workplace representation that caused some alarm in trade union circles in the 1980s and 1990s (where an employer could opt to inform and consult elected non-union employee representatives rather than elected union representatives) has not been revived by the 1999 Regulations although some disquiet has been caused by the diversity of employee representational structures permitted under the Regulations.

The Works Council Directive is one of the few examples of a recent Commission proposal coming to fruition under the Social Policy Protocol in the labour law area. However, the European Commission has also been successful in promoting a new information and consultation Directive to be applied at the national level. The progress of the Directive was given fresh impetus by the highly public failure of the car manufacturer Renault to inform and consult workers before a decision was taken to shut down a major car plant in Belgium. In the wake of the Renault (and later, in the UK, Rover) closures, concerns were raised concerning the effectiveness of the obligations imposed by the Collective Redundancies and European Works Council Directives.[168] In 1998, the Commission proposed a new framework of minimum standards of information and

---

164 Regulations 25–33.

165 The CAC (to 31 March 2001) has reported that only one reference has been made under this jurisdiction: CAC Annual Report 2000–01.

166 Regulations 20–22.

167 For further details, see Davies, P, 'A challenge to single channel' (1994) 23 ILJ 272; Hall, M, 'Beyond recognition? Employee representation and EU law' (1996) 25 ILJ 15; Hyman, R, 'The future of employee representation' (1997) 35 BJIR 309.

168 For background to the Rover controversy, see Villiers, C (2000) 29 ILJ 386.

consultation at the national level in all undertakings with 50 or more employees on issues concerning contractual and workplace change, threats to employment and the development of employment and economic policy. The UK Government was initially opposed to the Directive but assented in principle after transposition amendments were agreed at the June 2001 EU Council of Ministers conference. The amendments provide for an extended transposition period of seven years; with the qualifying level of employees set at one hundred and fifty after three years, reducing to fifty after seven years. In January 2002, further amendments were made to the draft Directive, with smaller companies employing more than fifty but less than one hundred employees being exempt from the requirements of the Directive for a period of six years.

A further opportunity to promote information and consultation arrangements is provided by the draft EU Charter of Fundamental Rights[169] adopted by the European Council at Nice on 7 December 2000. Article 25 provides for the right of workers or their representatives to information and consultation '... in good time in the cases and under the conditions provided by Community law and national law and practices'. Other provisions include Art 28 on the right to collective bargaining and to take strike action; Arts 21 and 23 on discrimination and equality and Art 30 on the right to protection against unfair dismissal. However, there is some doubt as to its exact legal status.[170] It is arguably a political declaration of existing rights and principles (contained in directives, case law and in the 1989 Community Charter and European Social Charter) and is not directly legally binding. The ECJ may, however, refer to it in its judgements as an aid to interpretation and in that way it may have an indirect influence.

Other proposals, based on developing workers' rights through their participation in company decision making have been attempted through the harmonisation of European company law and are yet to gain full support. Both the proposed European Company Statute Directive and the proposed Fifth Company Directive, derive from initiatives taken in the early 1970s. As part of the new focus on employee representation in the 1989 Action Programme, both Directives were revived in 1991. The intention is that they should complement and supplement the Works Council Directive.[171]

The draft Fifth Company Directive[172] provides for worker participation on the basis of one of three models:

(a) worker representatives having one-third to one-half of the seats on the management board of the company; or

(b) worker representation and consultation facilitated by the formation of a workers' council separate from the management structure, which is kept informed and consulted before important decisions affecting the workforce (such as closures or relocation) are taken; or

---

169 See, Feus, K (ed), *The European Charter of Fundamental Rights*, 2000; Hepple, B, 'The EU Charter of Fundamental Rights' (2001) 30 ILJ 225.

170 Article 51(2) states that the Charter '... does not establish any new power or task for the Community or the Union, or modify powers and tasks defined by the Treaties'.

171 For an analysis of an early draft of the Fifth Directive, see Welch (1983) 4 *Company Lawyer* 78. For this wider view of the role of company law, see Lord Wedderburn, *Social Charter, European Company and Employment Rights* (1990, Institute of Employment Rights) and 'Companies and employees: common law or social dimension?' (1993) 109 LQR 220.

172 OJ C7 1991.

(c) another form of consultation is agreed, providing at least the same level of rights as option (b) (which could be based on a model of collective bargaining).

The draft European Company Statute[173] only applies to European-wide companies as opposed to national companies. It provides for worker representation on the management board of such companies. The models of representation are to be chosen within establishments. As with the draft Fifth Directive, all the models guarantee the right of workers to be consulted before major decisions are made.

The proposed European Company Statute and the Fifth Company Law Directive would promote worker influence within a company by cultivating their participation at board level so that they had an input into strategic investment decisions. The Collective Redundancies and Acquired Rights Directives, the European Works Council Directive and the proposed National Consultation Directive focus on the provision of information and consultation short of decision making. Neither the company law nor the labour law Directives are intended to provide a platform for collective bargaining in the British sense. Rather they support a form of industrial democracy which highlights consultation, dialogue and co-operative decision making.[174] In the UK context, it is questionable whether employee participation strategies (which may not be based solely on a model of trade union representation) are a suitable and effective substitute for the resolution of industrial issues by collective bargaining between employer and trade union and it remains to be seen whether the European approach to workers' representation will act as a catalyst for union recognition or obscure the goal of the promotion of collective bargaining.

The British experience, in the late 1970s, of experimental models of European style industrial democracy in the steel industry and in the Post Office demonstrates the incompatibility of union participation in power sharing with the traditional trade union industrial role.[175] The trade union nominated directors were regarded by their membership as co-responsible with management for taking unpopular decisions and were unduly influenced by managerial presentations. In any event, employee directors had little positive impact upon decision making because the discussions reflected, rather than resolved, the fundamental conflict of interest between labour and capital.[176]

Despite the publicity surrounding the worker participation Directives, there has been little progress in securing their passage. The lack of political consensus across Europe on company law and collective labour standards and the diversity of national industrial relations and employee representation systems have stalled the advance of a number of

---

173 OJ C138 1991.

174 There are various methods of achieving 'industrial democracy', ie, worker influence over company decision making. It could be argued that statutory support for voluntary collective bargaining is a highly effective way of achieving industrial democracy. What is clear is that the individualised labour market, where workers have no collective voice, is the antithesis of industrial democracy.

175 These experiments arose from the recommendations of the *Bullock Report on Industrial Democracy* Cmnd 6706, 1977, noted by Lewis, R and Clark, J (1977) 40 MLR 323. See also Davies, P and Wedderburn, KW (now Lord), 'The land of industrial democracy' (1977) 6 ILJ 197 and Kahn-Freund, O, 'Industrial democracy' (1977) 6 ILJ 65. For an analysis of the debate, see Elliot, J, *Conflict or Co-operation? The Growth of Industrial Democracy*, 1984.

176 See Batstone, E *et al*, *Unions on the Board*, 1983.

harmonisation provisions. Further Community initiatives are unlikely to be developed through EU harmonisation procedures but, instead, are likely to continue to proceed through the Social Policy Protocol mechanism.[177] An alternative vehicle for the enforcement of European labour law was revived by the European Commission in the White Paper on Social Policy (COM (94) 333). This envisages the implementation of community obligations via collective agreements on a European-wide level. There has, however, been little progress towards translating this into a proper framework of bargaining at the European level. [178]

---

177 For specific analysis of the development of the social dialogue model, see Bercusson, B, 'Democratic legitimacy and European labour law' (1999) 28 ILJ 153.
178 See, generally, here, Hepple, B, 'The crisis in EEC labour law' (1987) 16 ILJ 77, pp 85–87; Adinolfi, A, 'The implementation of social policy directives through collective agreements?' (1988) 25 CMLR 291; Bercusson, B, 'The dynamic of European labour law after Maastricht' (1994) 23 ILJ 1, pp 15–26; Hepple, B, European Social Dialogue – Alibi or Opportunity (1993, Institute of Employment Rights); Lord Wedderburn, 'Consultation and collective bargaining in Europe: success or ideology' (1997) 26 ILJ 1.

CHAPTER 12

THE RIGHT TO ASSOCIATE
IN TRADE UNIONS

This chapter is concerned with the extent to which individuals have a bare right, guaranteed by the State, to form or join a trade union and, conversely, whether individuals have a right not to be forced to associate in a trade union. Unlike the position in many other countries in Europe, the lack of a written constitution or Bill of Rights in the UK means that the civil rights of individuals are not protected by a system of positive rights enshrined in a form of 'higher law'. Rather than a right to organise, workers have a liberty to organise, which may be freely exercised subject to restrictions imposed by the civil or criminal law. As we saw in the historical introduction in Chapter 1, freedom to organise has existed since the 19th century, with the Combination Act 1825 permitting a bare association of workers, and with the common law civil restrictions on the formation of trade unions – restraint of trade – repealed in 1871. This was followed in 1875 by the repeal of the remaining criminal provisions on association.[1] Thus, by 1875, both civil and criminal legal obstacles to trade union formation or membership had been removed.

However, a bare liberty to associate in trade unions is of little value unless workers are able to organise effectively and use their collective power when bargaining with employers. This is dependent on a political consensus on both the right of trade unions to exist and on the positive role of trade unions at the workplace. This consensus, which held firm for much of the 20th century, arguably broke down on the election of a radical Conservative Government in 1979. Conservative strategy, however, had not been to broadly restrict the right of trade unions to exist, as this was clearly a recipe for acute political and industrial conflict, but rather to undermine union effectiveness at the workplace by championing the positive right of individuals to dissociate from trade unions, by restricting the liberty to participate in union affairs and by reducing trade union protection from legal action by employers.

Nonetheless, in one carefully selected area, at the Government Communications Headquarters (GCHQ) at Cheltenham, a direct attack was made against the principle of freedom of association in trade unions. The *GCHQ* case demonstrates how the liberty to form or join trade unions can be undermined purely by the application of current provisions of domestic law.

THE GCHQ CASE[2]

The GCHQ is a State intelligence gathering agency administered through the Foreign and Commonwealth Office. In early 1984, the Government withdrew union representation rights for GCHQ workers because of a concern that the work of the facility could be damaged by union inspired industrial action. This was achieved by the Prime Minister (by her authority as Minister for the Civil Service), revising the conditions of service for

---

1   Trade Union Act 1871 and the Conspiracy and Protection of Property Act 1875.
2   See Morris, G and Lee, S, 'The ban on trade unions at Government Communications Headquarters' [1985] PL 177.

certain designated employees at GCHQ so as to exclude the right of membership of a trade union. Rights to complain of unfair dismissal or of unlawful restrictions on trade union membership or activities were also withdrawn on the grounds of national security.[3] Affected staff were offered a gratuity of £1,000 to leave the union and join a staff association or face dismissal. The Government refused to reverse the decision despite an extensive publicity campaign undertaken by the affected unions and an offer by them to follow, on any industrial action, a 'no disruption' code of practice.

Access to an industrial tribunal for those employees who were dismissed for refusing to give up their union rights was blocked by the exemption of GCHQ staff from employment protection legislation. The only legal remedy for the affected workers was by way of a judicial review of the administrative decision taken by the Prime Minister under the authority of the royal prerogative. Thus, the Council for the Civil Service Unions (CCSU), sought a declaration that the instructions varying the conditions of service were invalid, on the grounds that the decision to exclude union rights exceeded the Prime Minister's powers and that by failing to consult with the union before taking the decision the Prime Minister had failed to observe basic rules of natural justice.

Much of the legal argument surrounded the issue of whether in administrative law, a decision taken under the royal prerogative, which did not derive from statute, was technically reviewable by judicial review. Glidewell J in the High Court[4] answered this question in the affirmative and then went on to agree with the submission of the union that the employees had a legitimate expectation that there would be some form of consultation before a decision is made which denies them employment rights and that, consequently, this procedural impropriety rendered the decisions invalid.

However, in the Court of Appeal,[5] a strongly non-interventionist stance was taken. The Court of Appeal held that judicial review proceedings were not an appropriate method to challenge the way the royal prerogative is exercised because it is for the government, not the courts, to judge national security requirements. So long as the decision to ban unions was taken with a *bona fide* belief that national security would be otherwise compromised, it would be constitutionally inappropriate for the court to intervene.

The House of Lords[6] rejected the Court of Appeal's analysis that an executive decision in pursuance of a power derived from the royal prerogative was not susceptible to judicial review. Actions taken under the authority of a prerogative power attract the same duty to act fairly as acts derived from statutory power. However, the substance of their Lordships' judgment was profoundly disappointing for the plaintiff. The House of Lords concluded that the requirements of national security overrode the legitimate expectations of the employees to prior consultation before their employment conditions were altered. Whether prior consultation was or was not in the interests of national security was solely a matter for the executive. All that was required was that the decision not to consult was genuinely motivated by national security considerations.

---

3   At that time, under the Employment Protection (Consolidation) Act 1978, s 138(4) and Sched 9, para 2, and the Employment Protection Act 1975, s 121(4).
4   *R v Secretary of State for Foreign and Commonwealth Affairs ex p CCSU* [1984] IRLR 309.
5   [1984] IRLR 353.
6   [1985] IRLR 28, noted by Fredman, S [1985] 14 ILJ 42.

GCHQ – European and international standards

In the *GCHQ* case, submissions were made to the domestic courts that international treaty obligations on freedom of association had been broken by the Government decision to ban unions at GCHQ. Counsel for the unions paid particular attention to the provisions of the European Convention on Human Rights (ECHR) and Conventions of the International Labour Organisation (ILO) a specialist branch of the United Nations.

Article 11 of the ECHR provides:

(1) Everyone has the right to freedom of peaceful assembly and to freedom of association with others, including the right to form and join trade unions for the protection of his interests.

(2) No restrictions shall be placed on the exercise of these rights other than those prescribed by law and are necessary in a democratic society in the interests of national security or public safety, prevention of disorder or crime, for the protection of the rights and freedoms of others. This Article shall not prevent the imposition of lawful restrictions on the exercise of these rights by members of the armed forces, of the police or of the administration of the state.

As an international treaty that has not been formally enshrined into UK law, this Convention was not legally binding before the domestic court. However, the Convention was cited as persuasive authority in order to clarify the ambiguities of the domestic law on this issue. Although there have been a number of cases where the judiciary have been influenced by the standards of the Convention in their interpretation of the domestic law, in this instance, the courts failed to consider whether UK law was in compliance with the Convention.

The Civil Service Unions now attempted to obtain a remedy by a direct application to the European Court of Human Rights. Although decisions of the Court of Human Rights are not directly binding in UK law, the Government, as a signatory of the Convention, is bound by the Treaty to follow its decisions. Consequently, if the Court found that there had been a breach of the Convention, the Government would be honour bound to rescind its actions.

The application to the European Court of Human Rights was first made to the Commission on Human Rights which acted as a filter, eliminating applications that are incompatible with the Convention. The complaint by the CCSU fell at this hurdle. The Commission found that the complaint was inadmissible.[7] Although there had been an interference with the right of association, the restrictions were lawfully implemented under Art 11(2) as GCHQ workers were 'members ... of the administration of the state'. The Commission accepted the argument that the GCHQ employees were engaged in work of a highly confidential nature which mirrored, to an extent, the role of the security services such as the army and police. The common thread was that they all played a vital role in protecting national security.

The view the Commission took in this case was criticised on a number of grounds.[8] The Commission had failed to follow previous jurisprudence of the Convention, which

---

7   *CCSU v UK* (1988) 10 EHRR 269.

8   See the note on the case by Fredman, S and Morris, G (1988) 17 ILJ 105 and Lord Wedderburn, 'Freedom of association or the right to organise' (1987) 18 IRJ 244.

had interpreted this exception narrowly. Furthermore, the expansive interpretation of who are members of 'the administration of the state' was inconsistent with the far narrower limitations on freedom of association contained in other international instruments, such as in the ILO Conventions, the Universal Declaration of Human Rights and the European Social Charter. It could also be argued that the decision sets a bad precedent. It implicitly provides a justification for governments across Europe to limit union activity, not only in defence departments but also in other areas of 'sensitive' government work.[9]

A complaint was also lodged under the European Social Charter,[10] which augments the Convention in relation to trade union matters. Under Art 5, only the Police and Army are exempted from the basic right to join a union. However, the Committee of Independent Experts, charged under the Charter with the responsibility to adjudicate on complaints, failed to do so in this instance because of jurisdictional problems. Under the Charter, the committee has no power to intervene where worker representation still exists at the complainant's place of work. As, on the demise of union representation, a departmental staff association had been set up at GCHQ, the committee failed to pursue the complaint.

The unions also challenged the Government's decision by referring a complaint to the ILO.[11] As a signatory of the UN Charter, the UK is bound in international law to the provisions of ratified ILO Conventions. ILO Convention No 87 on Freedom of Association and Protection of the Right to Organise establishes in Art 2: 'Workers and employers, without distinction whatsoever, shall have the right to establish and, subject only to the rules of the organisation concerned, to join organisations of their own choosing without previous authorisation.' The only limit on this right is expressed in Art 9(1): 'The extent to which the guarantees provided for in this Convention shall apply to the armed forces and the police shall be determined by national laws or regulations.'

The Court of Appeal had held that the Government's actions were in accordance with the ILO treaties. The court had concluded that ILO Convention 151, which acknowledges that some public servants including those in 'highly confidential' positions can be exempted from protection against anti-union discrimination, took precedence over the more general provision of Convention 87.

However, where the same issue was considered by the ILO Freedom of Association Committee, their interpretation of the relevant Conventions differed appreciably from the Court of Appeal's.[12] The Committee noted that Convention No 87 gives workers an explicit right to join a union of their own choosing without distinction and the only denial of this right is to members of the armed forces and police. As the GCHQ workers were

---

9   The decision of the Commission demonstrates that incorporation of the Convention into UK law will not necessarily result in more effective protection of civil liberties such as freedom of association.

10   See, generally, Shrubshall, V (1989) 18 ILJ 39 and the note by Hepple, B (1988) 17 ILJ 124.

11   An extensive account of the ILO decisions is provided by Ewing, KD, *Britain and the ILO* (1994, Institute of Employment Rights), Chapter 5, and by Creighton, B, 'The ILO and the protection of freedom of association in the UK', in Ewing, KD, Gearty, C and Hepple, B (eds), *Human Rights and Labour Law*, 1994. See also Corby, S, 'Limitations on freedom of association in the civil service and the ILO's response' (1986) 15 ILJ 161; Napier, B, 'The ILO and GCHQ' (1989) 18 ILJ 255; Brown, D and McColgan, A, 'UK employment law and the ILO' (1992) 21 ILJ 265.

12   234th Report of the Freedom of Association Committee (Case No 1261).

not members of the police or armed services and their roles could not be considered analogous to the functions of the police or armed forces, the complaint was accordingly well founded.[13] The ILO Committee of Experts (which has the jurisdiction to make annual reports on compliance by Member States with the Conventions) fully endorsed the Freedom of Association Committee's findings.[14]

The views of both of these ILO agencies were rejected by the British Government which preferred the Court of Appeal's interpretation of the Conventions.[15] As a consequence, the Committee on the Application of Standards, which annually examines the report of the Committee of Experts, has, several times, drawn attention to the seriousness of the breach in their reports to the governing body of the ILO.

On the failure of these legal attempts to reverse Government policy, many affected employees left the union and joined the departmental staff association. This 'house union' was denied a certificate of independence as a trade union in 1993 because of the clear risk of interference by the management at GCHQ.[16] Those union members who remained suffered a degree of discrimination against them in the form of a promotion bar and the withholding of pay awards. The Government continued to refuse to enter into discussions with the union on the possibility of a 'no-strike deal' as a compromise solution. In the autumn of 1988, the threat to dismiss remaining union members was realised with the dismissal of 13 workers. Since the change of government at the May 1997 general election the ban on union membership has been revoked, although a prohibition on industrial action has been agreed with the civil service unions.[17]

THE RIGHT TO DISSOCIATE

Freedom of association and the closed shop[18]

If, in general terms, a worker has the liberty to join a union, the question that also arises is whether a worker has a reciprocal liberty to refuse to do so. Much of the debate has focused on the operation of the 'closed shop' – 'a situation in which employees come to

---

13 The Committee furthermore rejected the House of Lords argument that this key freedom for workers was weakened or tempered by Convention 151.

14 See Report of Committee of Experts (1985) Pt 4 A pp 193–95.

15 The Committee of Experts accepted that the relationship between the Conventions involved a number of complex legal issues. The committee recommended that a reference to the International Court of Justice was made by the UK Government for a definitive interpretation. That option was not pursued by the Conservative administration.

16 *GCHQ v Certification Officer* [1993] IRLR 260.

17 DFEE Press Release, 15 May 1997.

18 See generally, McCarthy, W, *The Closed Shop in Britain*, 1964; Purcell J and Sisson, A, 'Management and closed shops', in Bain, G (ed), *Industrial Relations in Britain*, 1983; Dunn, S and Gennard, J, *The Closed Shop in British Industry*, 1984; Dunn, S, 'The law and the decline of the closed shop in the 1980s', in Fosh, P and Littler, C (eds), *Industrial Relations and the Law in the 1980s*, 1985; Millward, N *et al*, *Industrial Relations in Transition*, 1992, pp 96–101; Dunn, S and Wright, M, 'Managing without the closed shop', in Metcalfe, D and Milner, S (eds), *New Perspectives on Industrial Disputes*, 1993; Millward, N *et al*, *All Change at Work?*, 2000, pp 145–49.

realise that a particular job is only to be obtained and retained if they become and remain members of one of a specified number of trade unions'.[19]

There have been broadly two forms of the closed shop – the pre-entry and post-entry closed shops. The pre-entry closed shop is the more exclusive form of arrangement; to be considered for employment an individual already had to be a member of the relevant union. Where vacancies arose the union would sometimes operate as an unofficial or informal employment bureau, supplying to employers a list of eligible applicants from those on the membership list of the union. The post-entry closed shop operates in a somewhat different manner. Workers are required, if they are not already members, to join the appropriate union once they have been appointed to a position.

Both types of closed shop were either formally organised, with the relevant union negotiating an exclusive agreement with an employer, or alternatively existed informally, sanctioned by the employer for the sake of good industrial relations. The practice of enforcement also varied between and within industries. Some unions tolerated a minority of non-members and did not insist on the dismissal of workers who refused to join the union.

The arguments for and against the closed shop have been well rehearsed over the years. Essentially, the debate has reflected the conflict, on the one hand, between the need for collective solidarity as a counter-weight to management strength and, on the other, the rights of the individual in a liberal democracy to choose freely with whom they wish to associate.[20]

Proponents of the closed shop have argued that the bargaining strength of a union depends on its organisation amongst the workforce. The more members the union has, the more likely an employer will engage in serious negotiations, for the benefit of all employees.[21] In this way, the closed shop helps to counter-balance the inequality of bargaining power between union and employer and is the tangible effect of group solidarity in the face of organised capital.

The closed shop can also be defended as promoting industrial relations stability. If all workers are unionised, a clear single avenue of communication is established between employer and the workforce. The interests of management are served as all grievances and disputes are channelled through the union.[22] Closed shop agreements also encourage formalised plant level collective bargaining and ameliorate the problem of multi-unionism so clearly noted in the Donovan Report as the scourge of British industrial relations. The closed shop (particularly the pre-entry closed shop) also, of course, protects the interests of workers in that industry. It keeps workers' pay and conditions high and creates secure employment by avoiding the over supply of labour.[23]

---

19 McCarthy, W, *The Closed Shop in Britain*, 1964, p 9.

20 Note Kahn-Freund's comment in Davies, P and Freedland, M (eds), *Labour and the Law*, 3rd edn, 1983, p 244: 'The case for the closed shop can only be made in terms of the need for an equilibrium of power (between management and labour) and can be defended ... only in terms of social expediency.'

21 As collective agreements are normally binding on all of the workforce, whether they are union members or not, the closed shop ensures there are no 'free riders' enjoying the benefits of collective negotiation without paying the cost – either in the form of subscriptions to the union or in suffering the hardships of strike action to obtain an enhanced deal from the employer.

22 See Hart, M, 'Why bosses love the closed shop' (1979) *New Society*, 15 February.

23 A negative side effect of this limitation of the supply of labour is the creation of skills shortages in those industries. This has been a particular criticism of the pre-entry closed shop.

To those who champion individual rights, however, there is a basic philosophical objection to the closed shop. It is contrary to the concept of freedom of choice, an individual liberty that underpins the liberal democratic society. If there is a right to join a union, then an individual has an equally fundamental right to refuse to join on grounds of individual choice. This right to choose counter-balances the arguments of 'social expediency'. There are other objections to the closed shop. By its very nature, the closed shop grants substantial power to trade union officials. In a minority of cases, a union may refuse admission or expel a member for an unjust reason that has a serious effect on that individual's capacity to earn their livelihood.[24]

The closed shop and legislative control

Historically, in the post-war period, the post-entry closed shop has been strong in the nationalised industries and in the major private industrial conglomerates, such as the chemical, engineering and car industries. The pre-entry closed shop has been prevalent in the smaller craft industries, such as the printing trade, and in the docks.[25] Until the 1970s, there was little statutory control over the operation of the closed shop.[26] Whether the the closed shop should be restricted was considered in some detail by the Donovan Commission.[27]

The Donovan Commission considered that the liberty or right to join a trade union does not automatically lead to an equal assertion of a right not to join a trade union. A right to join encourages trade union organisation and through that the extension of collective bargaining; a right not to join tends to undermine collective bargaining and to frustrate its development.[28] The Commission, however, did not recommend compulsory membership enforceable by legal means. Individuals should have the right to opt out of union membership in specific circumstances where they show 'reasonable grounds'.[29] Kahn-Freund, a member of the Commission, also supported limited control of the closed shop, not on the basis of reasoning from analogy with the freedom to organise, but because of the economic implications of the closed shop. He argued that the restriction of the supply of labour is an inefficient use of resources and robs people of opportunities to obtain employment.

The recommendations of the Commission were not implemented by the new Conservative regime elected in 1970. As part of the Conservatives' new regulated approach to industrial relations, the right to dissociate was given full legal support and in general terms closed shops were only permitted where unions registered under the Act,

---

24 Examples often quoted include cases such as *Huntley v Thornton* [1957] 1 All ER 234 and *Rookes v Barnard* [1964] 2 AC 1129.

25 In 1964, McCarthy estimated that 3,750,000 members of trade unions worked in a closed shop (around 750,000 in a pre-entry closed shop). By 1978, the height of the closed shop's popularity, Dunn and Gennard found that over 5 m employees were covered by closed shop arrangements. See Dunn, S, 'The growth of the post entry closed shop since the 1960s' (1981) BJIR 275.

26 See Chapter 4 for an analysis of common law control applicable in the absence of legislative restrictions.

27 Royal Commission on Trade Unions and Employers' Associations, Cmnd 3623, 1968, paras 588–602.

28 Paragraph 599.

29 See paras 563–64 and 603–31 for discussion of appropriate statutory and voluntary safeguards.

which few unions did.[30] The returning Labour administration in 1974 replaced the Industrial Relations Act 1971 with the Trade Union and Labour Relations Act 1974. This Act (in conjunction with an amendment Act of 1976) legalised the operation of the closed shop[31] and provided that dismissals for refusal to join a union were fair unless the dismissed employee had refused to join on genuinely held religious grounds.[32]

This limited legislative protection was supplemented by a voluntary system set up by the Trades Union Congress (TUC) to protect those union members unreasonably expelled from their union. In this period, the TUC Independent Review Committee played an important role in resolving membership disputes.[33] There was also a degree of judicial control over the closed shop based on grounds of public policy.[34]

The election of a Conservative Government in 1979 ideologically unsympathetic to the notion of closed shops heralded the demise of this form of employment arrangement. The Employment Act 1980 introduced the statutory remedy of 'unreasonable exclusion' for those members who had been excluded from a union that operated a closed shop.[35] Furthermore, dismissals or other victimisation for failing to join a trade union were only fair if the closed shop arrangement was supported in a ballot by 80% of the relevant workforce. In any event, the Act added to the list of specially protected persons. Even if the closed shop was approved by a ballot, dismissal was unfair if the employee objected to membership of any, or of a particular trade union, on the grounds of 'conscience or other deeply held personal conviction';[36] or was already in employment when the closed shop agreement was made; or had been 'unreasonably excluded or expelled' as defined in the Act or was subject to a written code of professional conduct that banned participation in industrial action.[37]

The decision to legislate to limit and then, later, essentially to eliminate the closed shop was given further impetus and a degree of legal and moral justification by the decision of the European Court of Human Rights in the case of *Young, James and Webster v UK*.[38] Here, three employees of British Rail were lawfully dismissed when they refused to join a trade union on the grounds of political beliefs. At the time of their employment, there had not been a requirement to join any specified union, but when, some years later,

---

30 See Weekes, B *et al*, *Industrial Relations and the Limits of the Law*, 1975, pp 295–304.

31 The closed shop was technically defined in the statute as a Union Membership Agreement, ie, an agreement or informal arrangement concerning employees of an identifiable class.

32 See *Saggers v BRB* [1977] ICR 809. For a review of the closed shop arrangements in this period, see Weekes, B, 'Law and practice of the closed shop' (1976) 5 ILJ 211 and Benedictus, R, 'Closed shop exemptions' (1979) 8 ILJ 160.

33 See Ewing, KD and Rees, W, 'The TUC Independent Review Committee and the closed shop' (1981) 10 ILJ 84.

34 For more on this, see Chapter 4.

35 See Chapter 5.

36 For the interpretation of this expression see *Sakals v Utd Counties Omnibus Co Ltd* [1984] IRLR 474; *Home Delivery Services Ltd v Shackcloth* [1984] IRLR 470; *McGhee v Midland British Road Services* [1985] IRLR 198.

37 The implementation of the statute was supplemented by a Department of Employment Code of Practice on Closed Shop Agreements and Arrangements, revoked in 1991. On the 1980 Act, see Elias, P, 'Closing in on the closed shop' (1980) 9 ILJ 201 and Lewis R and Simpson, R, *Striking a Balance? Employment Law After the 1980 Act*, 1981.

38 [1981] IRLR 408. Noted by Forde, M (1982) 11 ILJ 1; Von Prondzynski, F [1982] CLJ 256.

British Rail concluded a closed shop agreement with three recognised unions, membership of a union became a condition of employment.

The main issue for the court was whether Art 11, which guarantees the positive right to freedom of association in trade unions, could, by implication, guarantee a negative right not to be compelled to join a trade union. The majority of the Court of Human Rights held that although Art 11 does not expressly guarantee a negative right, the concept of a freedom implies some measure of choice in its exercise. The complainants had no real freedom of choice, since if they did not join the union, they would lose their jobs and livelihood.[39]

The court then went on to consider whether this compulsion could be justified by virtue of para 11(2), that is, was it 'necessary in a democratic society' for the closed shop restrictions to apply in order to achieve an objective for the 'protection of the rights and freedoms of others'. The union submitted that the closed shop was 'necessary' in order to achieve the objective of industrial relations stability which was of benefit to the majority of workers and employers. This argument failed to sway the court. The fact that it was 'desirable, useful or advantageous' to organise union/employer relations in this manner could not be equated with the meaning of 'necessary' in the Convention. Moreover, any restriction must be proportionate to the aim pursued. The protection of workers' interests could have been achieved without requiring compulsory union membership.[40]

Wedderburn has remarked that: 'Rarely, ... has such a strange judgment been so misunderstood and misrepresented.'[41] At the time, it was widely reported that the judgment was full square against the principle of the closed shop. The majority decision was, however, exclusively concerned with the particular circumstances of the application. As Wedderburn has pointed out, the majority did not say a negative right to associate was co-terminus with a positive right.[42] Rather, on the facts of the case, compulsory trade unionism was incompatible with the Convention because the complainants were not aware of the obligation to join at the time of their employment, and refusal to join resulted in a loss of livelihood.[43]

---

39 The majority also held that enforcement of the closed shop which compelled someone to join a union contrary to their personal beliefs was a breach of Arts 9 and 10 which guaranteed the right to personal opinion.

40 See also *Reid v UK* (1984) 6 EHRR 387 on levels of compensation for breach of Art 11.

41 *The Worker and the Law*, 3rd edn, 1986, p 377.

42 Although six judges, who concurred with the majority, did go so far as to hold that the negative aspect of freedom of association was inseparable from the positive aspect and so was fully protected by Art 11.

43 In this context now see the judgments of the ECHR, in *Sibson v UK* (1994) 17 EHRR 193 and *Sigurjonsson v Iceland* (1993) 16 EHRR 462. In *Sibson*, the applicant had left his union and had been transferred from one job to another by his employer as a consequence of trade union pressure. The court rejected his contentions that this constituted a violation of Art 11. The Convention did not automatically protect the negative freedom to dissociate. On the facts, there was no breach of Art 11 as Sibson had no objection to union membership *per se* and Sibson had not suffered any serious consequences as a result of leaving the union. In *Sigurjonsson*, on somewhat different facts, there was held to be a violation of the Convention. A requirement in law that a taxi licence holder must be a member of a taxi drivers' association was contrary to Art 11 since the applicant was already a licence holder when the requirement was imposed and because of the serious effect this had on the applicant's livelihood.

In *Webster*, the minority dissenting judgment by three judges failed to receive much publicity. The dissenters argued that it was clear from the *travaux preparatoires*, a record of the negotiations leading up to the drafting of the Convention, that there was no agreement amongst the original signatory States on whether a negative right not to associate should be protected through the Convention. As the framers of the Convention deliberately excluded the negative right, Art 11 could not be interpreted as including it. The dissenters also identified Art 11 as a collective right that could only be exercised by an association of individuals. Article 11 enhanced an individual's right to pursue common interests and to actively participate in activities with others. The negative right weakens the entitlement to associate collectively and goes against the purpose of Art 11.[44]

The Conservative Government responded to this judgment by further constraining the operation of the closed shop through provisions in the Employment Act 1982.[45] The Act altered the balloting requirements to legitimise a closed shop. It had now to be approved by a secret ballot held every five years on a majority of 80% of those entitled to vote or 85% of those voting. If a ballot was not held or the required majority not attained, then any dismissals on grounds of non-union membership were unlawful. Furthermore, an employer or employee could join the union in the unfair dismissal action where the dismissal was induced by union pressure to enforce the closed shop. The industrial tribunal could then apportion damages for the unfair dismissal accordingly between the employer and union. The Act also substantially increased the levels of compensation available for this type of dismissal and provided such employees with the right to apply for 'interim relief' – an order continuing the contract of employment until the complaint has been resolved by the industrial tribunal.[46]

The assault on the closed shop also took on a broader perspective. The Employment Act 1982 outlawed any terms in a contract for the supply of goods or services that purported to enforce 'union only' labour requirements.[47] It was also unlawful to 'refuse to deal' with a supplier of goods or services on union membership grounds, for example, by maintaining a list of approved suppliers and excluding those who did not employ union only labour.[48]

The Conservatives voiced further dissatisfaction with the closed shop in 1987, alleging in the Green Paper, *Trade Unions and Their Members*,[49] that despite statutory control, abuses of closed shop power still continued. Consequently, the aim of further legislative curbs introduced in the Employment Act 1988 was to end all legal protection for the closed shop, so creating an unfettered right for all employees to refuse to join a trade union or any particular union. This was achieved by the repeal of all the closed

---

44 The dissenters noted that the absence of this negative aspect of freedom of association from the European Convention was consistent with the provisions of most other international human rights instruments.

45 See Lewis, R and Simpson, R, 'Disorganising industrial relations' (1982) 11 ILJ 227 and Napier, B, 'The new law of the closed shop' (1983) 46 MLR 453.

46 The 1982 Act also introduced a retrospective compensation scheme for those employees who had been dismissed from their jobs in the period from 1974–80. See Ewing, KD and Rees, W, 'Closed shop dismissals 1974–80' (1983) 12 ILJ 148.

47 Now, s 144 of TULR(C)A 1992.

48 Now, s 145 of TULR(C)A 1992.

49 Cmnd 95.

shop exceptions for dismissals in conjunction with all other provisions on the closed shop. This meant that all dismissals or any action short of dismissal on grounds of non-union membership were automatically unfair.[50] The Act also removed the trade dispute immunity from actions in tort where the reason, or one of the reasons, for taking industrial action is the 'fact or belief' that an employer 'is employing, has employed or might employ ...' non-trade union members or members of a particular union or has failed or might fail to discriminate against them.[51]

In 1989, the Green Paper, *Removing Barriers to Employment*[52] was published, which particularly targeted the pre-entry closed shop; accusing it of being an inefficient restrictive practice that destroyed jobs by raising labour costs and depressing profitably. To end the pre-entry closed shop, the Employment Act 1990 provided a right of complaint to an industrial tribunal for any prospective employee unlawfully refused employment on grounds of non-membership of a trade union.[53]

By 1990, enforcement of both forms of closed shop became, for practical purposes, impossible. Although the closed shop itself as an institution is not formally unlawful, it is now essentially inoperable without infringing the law of unfair dismissal. Not surprisingly, there has been a dramatic decline in the numbers covered by closed shop arrangements caused by the legislative squeeze on the closed shop, unfavourable economic conditions and changing employer attitudes.[54] It has been all but wiped out in the public services and in the newly privatised industries. In manufacturing, where the closed shop was traditionally strong, industrial change has accounted for a dramatic decline in the workforce with closed shop arrangements formally terminated or lapsing into disuse. In the newer, high-tech industries, employers have been unwilling to negotiate this type of employment arrangement, preferring alternatives such as the single union deal. The Labour Government has not repealed any of the restrictive legislation controlling the operation of closed shops and has no intention of doing so. Thus, it is highly unlikely that in the near future there will be any increase in closed shop agreements.[55]

---

50 TULR(C)A 1992, ss152(1)(c) and 146(1)(c).

51 *Ibid*, s 222.

52 Cmnd 655.

53 TULR(C)A 1992, s 137.

54 In 1984 it was reported that 3.5 m workers were still covered by closed shop agreements (Millward, N and Stevens, M, *British Workplace Industrial Relations*, 1986). By 1990 it was estimated that no more than 300,000–500,000 employees were members of a closed shop (Millward, N *et al*, *Workplace Industrial Relations in Transition*, 1992, p 99). For an analysis of the reasons for decline in this period see Wright, M, 'The collapse of compulsory unionism' (1996) 34 BJIR 497.

55 The most recent research shows that 2% of workplaces were still maintaining closed shops in the late 1990s. See Cully, M *et al*, *Britain at Work*, 1999, p 89.

PART 3

INDUSTRIAL CONFLICT

INTRODUCTION

The major purpose of trade unions is to regulate the terms and conditions of employment of their membership by engaging in collective bargaining with employers. Industrial action predominantly takes place where this process has broken down. The 'right to strike' – to take disruptive action – is an essential component of union collective power and goes some way towards balancing the inequality of power between the individual worker and employer. Without the option to engage in strike action as a final resort, unions would be unable to bargain effectively and an employer would be in a position to dictate terms rather than have to engage in negotiation and compromise.

This introduction will consider the peculiarly British approach to 'the right to strike'; focusing on the reasons behind the development of the system of 'immunities' which protects trade unions from legal action and summarising the effects of restrictions on their operation. Following this, the growth in the process of conciliation and arbitration of disputes and the contemporary role of State agencies expressly charged with these duties will be examined. The remainder of Part 3 investigates the extent of legal intervention in industrial disputes. Chapter 13 explores the impact the law has on the individual worker who takes industrial action. Chapter 14 outlines the essential components of the tortious liabilities the organisers of industrial action may commit. Chapter 15 assesses the operation of the statutory immunities and the restrictions on their use. Chapter 16 considers the extent of trade union liability for unlawful industrial action and examines remedies. The final chapter, Chapter 17, analyses the legal implications of action by strikers and others to support or enforce a strike through picketing.

THE 'RIGHT TO STRIKE'

Unlike the position in many European jurisdictions (for example, Germany, France and Italy), British trade unions do not have the 'right' to take strike action guaranteed by any written constitution or Bill of Rights. The extent of the 'right to strike' in the UK is dependent upon the legal sanctions that are imposed by the ordinary common law and statute. Thus, to ascertain how far there is a right, or more accurately, a liberty to organise or participate in industrial action is dependent on an examination of the current law. This, as we shall see in subsequent chapters, requires an analysis of complex common law and statutory rules.[1]

Historically, the common law has always been hostile to trade unions *per se*, not only when they take collective action to secure their objectives. As we saw, in the historical

---

1   Any consideration of the right to strike must also take into account the legal limitations on the individual. The right of an individual to take strike action is restricted by the law on unfair dismissal (see Chapter 13) and by the exclusion of social security benefits for strikers and their families (see Social Security Contributions and Benefits Act 1992, Sched 11 and Jobseeker's Act 1995, s 14). Also note that for certain workers, eg, the police and members of the armed forces, withdrawal of labour is prohibited by the criminal law.

introduction in Chapter 1, the courts in the later 19th century expanded trade union tortious liability on industrial action.[2] On committing one or more of these torts, unions were exposed to substantial damages claims and subjected to injunctions to prohibit further action.

The response of the union movement to these developments was to agitate for legal protection from the judge made common law – not in the form of a positive right to strike – but for a system of immunities to these specific civil liabilities. Unions organised, through the Trades Union Congress (TUC), a campaign to reverse these damaging decisions through Parliament. As a consequence of this campaign, a Royal Commission on Trade Disputes was set up in 1903 to consider reform of the law. Although the final report of the Commission was not overly favourable to the union position, the Liberal Government, elected in 1906, implemented many of the TUC proposals in the Trade Disputes Act. The 1906 Act granted trade unions an immunity against legal action for the torts of inducing breach of contract and conspiracy to injure, so long as the industrial action was in 'contemplation or furtherance of a trade dispute'.[3]

A central question that arises is why the union movement pressed for 'immunities' from the civil law rather than a positive right to take strike action. The answer can be found by reference to the history of the trade union movement.[4] The trade unions which dominated in the late 19th century were the exclusive craft unions and 'new model' unions which were solely concerned with attaining practical benefits for their membership by industrial means.[5] These trade unions did not have any interest in engaging in any wider political debate on the needs of the working class as a whole, nor were they allied to any wider working class movement.[6]

Consequently, during the period in the late 19th century when liabilities were increasingly being imposed, trade unions did not have a political 'positive rights' agenda underpinned by any coherent theoretical class analysis of the struggle between labour and capital. Trade union concerns remained purely pragmatic; to be attained by 'self help' measures. It was not until the early 20th century that trade unions developed a 'political wing' with the formation of the Labour Representation Committee in 1900 and the Labour Party in 1906. By then it was too late for socialist thinkers to alter union priorities.[7]

The upshot of the pragmatic approach and the emphasis on self-help was that the trade union movement did not react to liabilities, unlike its counterparts in continental

---

2 See *Temperton v Russell* [1893] 1 QB 715; *Taff Vale v ASRS* [1901] AC 426; *Quinn v Leathem* [1901] AC 495.

3 This system of protection – dependent upon the act being 'in contemplation or furtherance of a trade dispute' – was originally employed in the Conspiracy and Protection of Property Act 1875 to protect the organisers of industrial action against criminal conspiracy.

4 For a full appraisal of the origins of the immunities, see Lord Wedderburn, 'Industrial relations and the courts' (1980) 9 ILJ 65.

5 In any event, their political influence was limited as their working class constituency at this time did not have voting rights.

6 For example, the Chartists movement, active in the mid-19th century, supported a programme of constitutional change and political rights for the working class, but did not attract enthusiastic union support.

7 By the time revolutionary thought and political activism had permeated through to the union movement, in the period leading up to the First World War, the system of immunities was well established.

Europe, by demanding collective 'rights', but merely wished for the law to 'leave them alone'. In any event, the codified continental system of law, associated with 'rights', was somewhat alien to the experience of trade unions familiar with the British system of an unwritten constitution and the primacy of the common law.[8]

The bedrock of the contemporary right to strike remains these 'immunities', conceived in the early 20th century, to protect unions from the full rigour of the civil law. Indeed, as we shall observe in later chapters, wherever the judiciary attempted to undermine the effect of the immunities,[9] the response of government was to legislate to renew trade union protection. The immunities were protected in this way because they were an essential element of the system of industrial relations known as 'voluntarism' or legal 'abstentionism'.[10] They ensured that the law remained neutral between the parties to the dispute.

However, the election of a radical Conservative Government in 1979 saw a shift in policy towards trade unions and industrial disputes. Reducing trade union propensity to strike was a major aim of the new Conservative administration, having been elected on the back of a high profile and politically damaging (to the Labour Government) strike by public sector workers during the 'winter of discontent' of 1978–79. Strikes were to be restricted by giving employers and others the opportunity to use legal means against 'disruptive' trade unions.[11]

To this end, the system of immunities guaranteeing the liberty to strike has been gradually dismantled by legislation so that the scope for lawful industrial action is now considerably narrower than in 1906. The definition of a trade dispute has been greatly constricted; reducing the number of disputes that will qualify for immunity protection. In addition, where industrial action is taken in furtherance of a trade dispute, the immunities will not apply unless the action has the support of a ballot conducted in accordance with detailed statutory requirements and specified information has been provided to the relevant employer(s). Legislation has also now ensured that the immunities are not operative where the industrial action consists of secondary action or is action taken to enforce union recognition, a closed shop or certain union only practices at work or consists of action taken in support of other workers dismissed for unofficial industrial action.[12]

As industrial action is now far more likely to be tainted with illegality, injunctions to prohibit industrial action are more easily obtained. This, combined with the deterrent

---

8   See Kahn-Freund, O, 'The impact of constitutions on labour law' [1976] CLJ 240.

9   The judiciary were intrinsically hostile to the immunities, perceiving them as 'privileges' for trade unions. Eg, see *Rookes v Barnard* [1964] AC 1129, where the tort of intimidation was expanded to outflank the immunities contained in the 1906 Act. This decision was subsequently reversed by the Trade Disputes Act 1965. See also the comments of Lord Denning in *Express Newspapers v McShane* [1979] ICR 210, p 218, and of Lords Diplock and Keith in *Duport Steel Ltd v Sirs* [1980] 1 All ER 529, pp 541 and 550.

10 The system of 'abstentionism' was briefly overturned between 1971–74 by the experimental and ultimately doomed Industrial Relations Act which imposed an entirely new framework of legal regulation on trade union activity.

11 For the Government's justification of legal restrictions see the Green Paper, *Trade Union Immunities*, 1981, paras 3–6.

12 For further details, see Chapter 15.

effect of the legislation and the greater fear of unemployment amongst workers has effected a steady reduction in the incidence of strike action throughout the 1980s and 1990s.[13] For example, days lost through strike action had declined to 3.5 m in 1987 from the high in 1979 of 29 m.[14] In 1990, the number of days lost through industrial action fell to its lowest level since 1935 with 1.9 m days lost. By 1995, the number of days lost had dramatically declined to 0.41 m.[15] More recent evidence indicates that the decline in trade union recourse to industrial action is continuing.[16]

This legalistic approach to industrial relations – reversing the abstentionist approach of previous administrations and compromising the principle of State neutrality – although ostensibly successful in limiting strike action, requires further assessment. First, the assumption, that Britain since the Second World War was 'strike happy' – gravely in need of a new approach to industrial relations, with a very poor record of industrial relations compared to its industrial competitors – is arguably misleading.[17] It has been pointed out by Wedderburn[18] that, since the Second World War, the number of days lost by strike action has been rarely more than one for each employee. Even in the period of industrial turmoil in the late 1970s, during the winter of discontent, with 29 m days lost through industrial action, the UK was a middle-ranking country in the international league table of industrial action. Countries such as the USA, Italy and Australia had worse records.

Furthermore, there are alternative ways of reducing the number of days lost; such as by promoting policies that engender industrial harmony and, where disputes arise, by focusing on voluntary settlement. For instance, at the start of the Social Contract period between unions and government, where a policy of co-operation, rather than conflict with trade unions was favoured, a comparable number of days were lost through industrial action as were lost in the mid-1980s.

It should also be noted that a statistical decrease in days lost through strike action does not necessarily equate to a reduction in employment disputes. At the same time as days lost through strike action declined, the requests for collective conciliation and arbitration from the Advisory, Conciliation and Arbitration Service (ACAS) reached a record high.[19] This indicates that even though the use of strike action as a negotiating tactic fell, the number of actual disputes did not necessarily decrease. Clearly, greater legal regulation and unfavourable economic conditions do not stop unions from pursuing solutions to genuine grievances.[20]

---

13 Although it should be noted that there were several high profile and large scale disputes in the early 1980s. Eg, in 1984 (the year of the miners' strike) 26.6 m days were lost.

14 *Employment Gazette*, September 1980.

15 The annual average of days lost between 1985–94 was 2.4 m. See *Labour Market Trends*, June 1996.

16 For an analysis of recent trends, see Millward, N *et al*, *All Change at Work?*, 2000, pp 177–79.

17 See Turner, H, *Is Britain Really Strike Prone?*, 1969.

18 *The Worker and the Law*, 3rd edn, 1986, p 573.

19 See the ACAS Annual Report 1999–2000, pp 22 and 26.

20 In any event, the statistics on days lost do not show the true pattern of industrial strife. They exclude disputes which do not result in a stoppage of work: 'go-slows', 'a work to rule' and other manifestations of action short of a strike are not recorded. It may well be that to avoid legal action against them trade unions have turned to these forms of industrial pressure. See Millward, N *et al*, *Industrial Relations in Transition*, 1992, pp 277–309. It is also interesting to note that during the period that collective industrial action has substantially declined, individual conflict between employers and employees has, by contrast, rapidly expanded. See Cully, M *et al*, *Britain at Work*, 1999, p 245.

The right to strike and the Human Rights Act 1998

Article 11 of the European Convention on Human Rights (introduced into English law by the Human Rights Act 1988) provides for the right of individuals to join trade unions for the protection of their interests, but does not explicitly provide for a 'right to strike'.[21] The ability to take strike action is, however, an essential means by which members' interests are protected; such as where a collective agreement needs to be enforced or to deter the victimisation of union members. The European Court of Human Rights acknowledged this view in *Schmidt and Dahlstrom v Sweden*,[22] but went on to specify that the exercise of industrial action could be legitimately limited (although not extinguished) by the requirements of national law. In *Gustafsson v Sweden*,[23] the applicant employer (who refused to join the relevant employers' association and so be bound by a collective agreement) complained of a lack of State protection from consequential industrial action that interfered with his Art 11 right of non-association. The court held that there was no violation of Art 11 as a trade union's right to strike and so impose economic pressure – in order to protect their members' interests by forcing the employer to comply with a collective agreement – takes precedence over the employer's competing right of non-association and subsequent refusal to engage in collective bargaining. This majority decision did not go so far as to explicitly support union use of the strike weapon without restrictions, but is implicit support for the legality of trade union action in pursuant of legitimate aims – such as the enforcement of collective bargaining.

The Strasbourg jurisprudence thus provides that under national law trade unionists should be enabled to strike through the medium of their organisations to protect their occupational interests. There is an obligation on States to facilitate trade union action, although States are permitted a 'free choice of means' by which to comply with this obligation. Where the means applied by the State in order to secure this obligation are so restrictive that, in practice, the 'right' is rendered worthless then, arguably, the State is in violation of the Article. The question that arises from this proposition is whether the extensive regulation of collective action in the UK (both at the individual and collective level by reference to common law and statute) deprives trade unions and their members of the opportunity to take action in order to protect their own interests.

Development of anything resembling an effective 'right to strike' (by a successful application under the Human Rights Act 1998 for elements of the statutory regime controlling industrial action to be declared incompatible with the 1998 Act) is highly dependent on the domestic courts taking into account other international instruments when interpreting Art 11 and the relevant case law. For example, the Committee of Experts of the Council of Europe have condemned the restrictive nature of UK strike law (in general and specific terms)[24] as contrary to Art 6 of the European Social Charter (the

---

21 For further detailed analysis, see Hendy, J, 'The Human Rights Act, Article 11 and the right to strike' [1998] EHRLR 582; Ewing, KD (ed), *Human Rights at Work,* (2000, Institute of Employment Rights), Chapters 5 and 8; Ewing, KD (ed), *Employment Rights at Work* (2001, Institute of Employment Rights), Chapter 4.

22 (1976) 1 EHRR 632.

23 (1996) 22 EHRR 409.

24 Particularly with regard to the impediments to secondary action and the lack of unfair dismissal protection for those dismissed for engaging in industrial action.

European Convention's sister document on social and economic rights) which explicitly guarantees strike action to secure the benefits of collective bargaining.[25] The preamble to the Social Charter makes it clear that it is to be read in conjunction with the Convention and it has been recognised by the Court of Human Rights[26] that appropriate Articles and decisions of the Social Charter supervisory machinery should be taken into account when analysing a relevant right under the Convention. As s 2(1) of the 1998 Act provides that a domestic court must take account of the Strasbourg jurisprudence in all relevant cases, the Social Charter ought to have an indirect, if peripheral, influence on domestic judicial decision making.

It is unlikely that the UK judiciary, taking into account the scope of the discretion accorded by the Strasbourg institutions to the State when legislating in this area, would accept an argument that the freedom to withdraw labour, crucial although it is to the proper balance of power in industrial relations, should be protected as an 'indispensable' trade union right to the extent of dismantling the framework of law that regulates industrial action. It is perhaps more possible that a bold judiciary (applying the positive aspects of the Strasbourg decisions and the exhortations of the Social Charter and other international instruments) could hold that specific targeted provisions are incompatible with Art 11; such as the present ban on certain recognition disputes (taking into account that public policy now promotes collective bargaining through the statutory recognition scheme set up by the 1999 Employment Relations Act).

THE CONCILIATION AND ARBITRATION OF DISPUTES[27]

Support for the voluntary conciliation and arbitration of disputes has always been an essential element of the system of State non-intervention in industrial conflict. This recognises that where industrial disputes arise, the best solution for all parties is the resolution of the dispute without recourse to industrial action. The aim of the law is to aid the parties to reach a solution by bringing the parties together and encouraging dialogue so enhancing the prospect of a settlement. This is consistent with the abstentionist framework as the law does not enforce settlements; it merely encourages them.

The emphasis by the State on the peaceful resolution of disputes through conciliation and arbitration (rather than by a coercive use of the law) has a lengthy history. In 1896, the passage of the Conciliation Act resulted in the setting up of the first conciliation and arbitration service administered through the Board of Trade (responsibility for dispute conciliation was later bequeathed to the Ministry of Labour and the Department of Employment). The Board of Trade's arbitration role was enhanced by the provision of proper machinery for the arbitration of disputes under the Industrial Courts Act 1919.

---

25 For an analysis of the UK's record of compliance with Social Charter obligations, see Ewing, KD, 'Social rights and human rights: Britain and the Social Charter – the Conservative legacy' [2000] EHRLR 91.

26 See, eg, *Swedish Engine Drivers Union v Sweden* (1976) 1 EHRR 617 and *Sigurjonsson v Iceland* (1993) 16 EHRR 462.

27 See, generally, Wedderburn, KW (now Lord) and Davies, P, *Employment Grievances and Disputes Procedures in Britain,* 1969; Wood, J (Sir), 'Dispute resolution – conciliation, mediation and arbitration', in McCarthy, W (ed), *Legal Intervention in Industrial Relations: Gains and Losses,* 1992.

This Act provided for the setting-up of the Industrial Court which, despite its title, was not a court of law, but an arbitrational body, where disputes could be referred for resolution with the agreement of the parties.

Under the scheme introduced by the Industrial Relations Act 1971, the Industrial Arbitration Board replaced the Industrial Court. The Commission on Industrial Relations, set up in 1969 in the wake of the Donovan Report, was put on a statutory footing by the Industrial Relations Act 1971 and given the conciliation duties previously held by the Department of Employment. On repeal of the Industrial Relations Act 1971, the new Labour Government set up ACAS and the Central Arbitration Committee (CAC) as successors to these organisations to facilitate settlements between employer and union.[28]

THE ADVISORY, CONCILIATION AND ARBITRATION SERVICE[29]

ACAS was established by the Employment Protection Act 1975 as a single unifying agency to take over the responsibilities of conciliation and aspects of arbitration previously held by the Department of Employment and the Commission on Industrial Relations. ACAS was also charged under the Employment Protection Act with the broader remit, previously undertaken by the Commission on Industrial Relations, of '... promoting the improvement of industrial relations, and in particular of encouraging the extension of collective bargaining and the development and where necessary, reform of collective bargaining machinery'.

This requirement to promote and encourage the extension of collective bargaining was repealed by the Trade Union Reform and Employment Rights Act 1993 and substituted by a reaffirmation of ACAS's conciliation and arbitration duties in s 209 of the TULR(C)A 1992. This section stated that the duty of ACAS was now '... to promote the improvement of industrial relations, in particular, by exercising its functions in relation to the settlement of trade disputes (by conciliation and arbitration)'.[30]

In the White Paper, *Fairness at Work*,[31] ACAS's advisory mediation and dispute resolution functions (see below) were identified as being of particular relevance to modern day industrial relations. ACAS was seen as a proponent and facilitator of the 'partnership at work' principle that is the main focus of present employment policy. In order to enhance ACAS's role in dispute prevention s 26 of the 1999 Act repeals much of the wording that was introduced in 1993, leaving the statutory terms of reference of ACAS to be solely 'to promote the improvement of industrial relations'.[32]

---

28 This was in response to union criticisms that the Department of Employment conciliation service was not sufficiently independent; being too preoccupied with Government pay policy when brokering settlements.

29 See Weekes, B, 'ACAS – an alternative to law' (1979) 8 ILJ 147.

30 The new priorities of the service were encapsulated in the ACAS 'mission statement' – '... to improve the performance and effectiveness of organisations by providing an independent and impartial service to prevent and resolve disputes and to build harmonious relationships at work'.

31 Cm 3968, 1998.

32 For a ministerial explanation for the amendment, see the statement by Michael Wills (Hansard HC Standing Committee E, col 268, 4 March 1999). On the basis of this affirmation of ACAS's work in this field, ACAS may benefit from 'partnership' funding provided under the Employment Relations Act 1999, s 30.

Conciliation

ACAS engages in both collective and individual conciliation. Individual conciliation takes place where employment tribunal proceedings are initiated as a consequence of disputes between individual workers and their employer. The bulk of these cases concern unfair dismissal claims.

The procedures concerning collective conciliation are contained in ss 210 and 211 of the TULR(C)A 1992. Where one or both parties to a 'trade dispute'[33] request the assistance of the services of ACAS, an officer of ACAS may be appointed to offer assistance to the parties '... with a view to bringing about a settlement'. The parties are encouraged by the ACAS conciliator to settle the dispute using their own agreed procedure. Intervention by a conciliator will not normally happen until these procedures have been exhausted.[34] Often a referral to ACAS is written into collectively agreed dispute procedures as a final stage after the effort to resolve the dispute internally has failed.

The success of the conciliation of collective trade disputes is dependent on the parties' willingness to accept the good offices of ACAS and to submit in good faith to the process. Statistical evidence suggests that both sides of industry frequently have recourse to ACAS[35] and are satisfied with this aspect of ACAS work.[36] Conciliation remains popular as the parties are merely assisted by the ACAS conciliation officer in finding common ground and are not pressurised to alter their own bargaining position.

Arbitration and mediation

Voluntary arbitration is the process where a dispute has been referred to an arbitrator for settlement with the consent of both parties. Usually, the parties accept the binding nature of the arbitrator's award. Dispute mediation occurs where the parties have agreed to refer the issues in dispute to a mediator, but they have not necessarily agreed to accept the mediator's findings, although the mediator's recommendations may form the basis of a settlement. Unlike conciliation, the mediator takes an active role, putting forward possible solutions which are considered by both sides.[37]

ACAS has a brief under s 212 of the TULR(C)A 1992 to administer the arbitration process. ACAS does not provide arbitrators directly from its staff, but, on the request of one of the parties and with the consent of both, will appoint an independent person from a panel it maintains or refer the dispute to the CAC. ACAS should normally recommend arbitration only after internal disputes procedures and conciliation have failed.[38] An arbitrator has sole authority on matters of procedure and will usually take written and oral evidence before making an award. The decision of an arbitrator is not legally

---

33   Defined for these purposes in TULR(C)A 1992, s 218.

34   *Ibid*, s 210(3).

35   During 1999–2000, 1,500 requests for conciliation were made and settlement or progress towards settlement was reported in 92% of cases – ACAS Annual Report 1999–2000.

36   See, eg, ACAS Annual Report 1999–2000, pp 23–25.

37   ACAS has authority by TULR(C)A 1992, s 210, to offer this form of assistance.

38   *Ibid*, s 212(3).

binding[39] although it is unusual for the parties to refuse to accept an award as they have explicitly consented to the process and ACAS policy is to strongly advise the parties, before the arbitration process is initiated, that adherence to an award is expected.

Similarly, with the movement to formal conciliation clauses in collective agreements, there has been a growth in standing arbitration clauses in disputes procedures.[40] Here, the parties, on exhaustion of negotiation, will refer the matter to a nominated arbitrator. This is private arbitration, rather than arbitration under the TULR(C)A 1992, and so the Arbitration Act 1950 is not excluded. This development was particularly marked in the 1980s and early 1990s in the new high technology industries and other industries where single union deals and the no-strike agreement were popular. A feature of this form of arbitration is that the parties do not put a bargaining case to the arbitrator but both make a final submission. The arbitrator then has to choose between the two submissions.[41] This lack of flexibility in the procedure where the arbitrator is given little discretion is discouraged by ACAS.

Despite such developments, in general terms, arbitration has become less popular with both unions and employers. For unions, it compromises the autonomy of the bargaining process. For employers it compromises the right to manage: to impose change on employees. Consequently, requests for ACAS arbitration and dispute mediation have been consistently declining since the 1970s, from an average of 300 in that decade to an average of 200 in the 1980s, falling to 170 in the early 1990s.[42] In 1994, there were 156 requests for arbitration or mediation, which fell to 136 in 1995. Between 1999–2000, ACAS dealt with 66 arbitration cases.[43]

Advisory services

ACAS has the authority to act in a general advisory role on matters of industrial relations and employment policies.[44] Of particular importance over the last decade has been the development of advisory mediation (identified by the Labour Government elected in 1997 as a process of dispute prevention whereby organisations can identify and resolve problems at work so helping to establish a new 'partnership' culture at the workplace). Advisory mediation is a means of 'addressing underlying difficulties affecting the employment relationship'. So, for example, where conciliation has been requested over a particular issue, it may be the case that ACAS identifies a broader problem that requires longer term solutions. ACAS may facilitate the setting-up of a joint working party, with

---

39 The provisions of the Arbitration Act 1950, Pt 1, are specifically excluded by TULR(C)A 1992, s 212(5).

40 See *op cit*, Millward, fn 20, pp 208–11; *op cit*, Millward, fn 16, p 157.

41 See Wood, J (Sir), 'Last offer arbitration' (1985) 23 BJIR 415; Lewis, R, 'Strike free deals and pendulum arbitration' (1990) 28 BJIR 32; and Bassett, P, *Strike Free: New Industrial Relations in Britain*, 1986, pp 86–122.

42 A further explanation for the fall in the use of arbitration is that it reflects the reduction in the number of recorded stoppages.

43 ACAS Annual Report 1999–2000, p 26.

44 TULR(C)A 1992, s 213.

staff from ACAS chairing, to consider these broader issues. In 1999–2000, ACAS engaged in 595 advisory mediation projects.[45]

This role has expanded over the last decade, in part due to economic changes and industrial policies. Industrial reorganisation caused by the privatisation of public sector organisations, mergers and the development of new industries have all contributed to the restructuring of collective bargaining with an emphasis on decentralised bargaining arrangements. This has been a serious cause of conflict between employers and unions. ACAS, through the setting-up of advisory joint councils, has advised and encouraged consultation, both before the changes in collective bargaining are formalised and during the implementation of any changes.

ACAS also disseminates information on industrial relations through the publication of booklets and leaflets and the organisation of conferences and public speakers. This, ACAS sees as a means of promoting good industrial relations practice. Since April 1994, ACAS has been able to charge[46] for its publications and conference service and has reported a significant decline in the orders for its publications. A telephone advisory service is provided for general queries on employment issues. In 1999–2000, a record number of enquiries were received.[47]

Independent inquiry

Section 214 of the TULR(C)A 1992 provides ACAS with the authority to conduct wide-ranging investigations into any question of industrial relations, which may include an inquiry into a particular industrial dispute. The successful conclusion of an inquiry is dependent upon the voluntary co-operation of the parties as ACAS has no powers of compulsion.

The Secretary of State (previously, of Employment, now of the Department of Trade and Industry) has more specific powers under s 215 of the TULR(C)A 1992, originally deriving from the Industrial Courts Act 1919, to order a 'court of inquiry' into a trade dispute. This is a more formal process than an ACAS inquiry. Procedure is regulated by the Secretary of State,[48] with witnesses usually compelled to attend and be examined on oath. The report of the court of inquiry must be laid before Parliament. There are few recent examples of this type of inquiry and it now seems to have lapsed into disuse.[49]

45　ACAS Annual Report 1999–2000, p 27. See, also, ACAS Occasional Paper No 55, 'Joint problem solving: does it work?' and Kessler, I and Purcell, J, 'Joint problem solving and the role of third parties' (1994) *Human Resource Management Journal* (January).

46　ACAS is directed to do so by a new s 251A of TULR(C)A 1992, introduced by the Trade Union Reform and Employment Rights Act 1993.

47　714,921.

48　TULR(C)A 1992, s 216.

49　The most recent example was Lord Justice Scarman's report into the Grunwick dispute (Cmnd 6922, 1977). For an analysis of earlier reports, see McCarthy, W and Clifford, B (1966) 4 BJIR 39.

Codes of Practice

ACAS is required to issue Codes of Practice,[50] after consultation with interested parties, on the statutory provisions regarding the disclosure of information for collective bargaining purposes and time off for trade union members and officials.[51] ACAS also has general authority to issue Codes on other industrial relations matters for the purpose of promoting the improvement of industrial relations. The only other Code issued by ACAS has been on disciplinary matters at work.[52]

These Codes are designed to provide practical guidance on how the detailed legislative provisions should be applied and provide examples of good practice. Once submitted to the Secretary of State and approved, the Code is laid before Parliament and brought into force through a statutory instrument. The Codes do have a significant legal status. They are admissible in evidence in tribunal or arbitrational proceedings and any provision of the Code that is relevant to an issue arising in proceedings must be taken into account in determining that question.[53]

The Secretary of State has also had power to issue Codes of Practice since 1980 'for the purposes of promoting the improvement of industrial relations'.[54] Under this authority two Codes have been issued: on picketing in 1980 (revised in 1992) and on the closed shop in 1983 (revoked in 1991). Further statutory authority to publish Codes of Practice for the purposes of promoting appropriate practices in the conduct of trade union ballots and elections was provided by the Employment Act 1988.[55] There is an exhaustive procedure which has to be complied with before publication. The Secretary of State has to consult with ACAS on the production of the Code,[56] issue a draft and consider representations before submitting the Code to Parliament. Like the ACAS Codes, they are intended to contain practical advice on how to apply the relatively complex and detailed legislation and can be used as evidence of good practice.[57]

Section 207(3) of the TULR(C)A 1992 specifies that these Codes are admissible not only in tribunal or arbitrational proceedings, but also before a court. Similarly to ACAS Codes, where a provision of the Code is relevant to a question arising in the proceedings the Code 'shall be taken into account in determining that question'. These departmental Codes are on relatively contentious issues in industrial relations and, it has been argued, merely support the Government's view of how the legislation should be applied.

---

50 TULR(C)A 1992, s 199.

51 ACAS Codes on Disclosure of Information to Trade Unions for Collective Bargaining Purposes (1977, revised 1997) and Time Off for Trade Union Duties and Activities (1977, revised 1991 and 1997).

52 Disciplinary Practices and Procedures in Employment (1977, revised 1997); now incorporated into a new Code – Disciplinary and Grievance Procedures (2000).

53 TULR(C)A 1992, s 207(2).

54 Authority was provided by the Employment Act 1980. Now see TULR(C)A 1992, s 203.

55 See the Code on Trade Union Ballots on Industrial Action (1991). This was revised in 1995 and 1999 (to take account of changes introduced by the Employment Relations Act 1999) and reissued as the Code on Industrial Action Ballots and Notice to Employers.

56 Due to the controversy surrounding the provisions of the Codes on picketing and the closed shop, ACAS refused to participate in the development of these Codes on the grounds that to do so would damage its reputation for impartiality.

57 The Employment Relations Act 1999 also provides the Secretary of State with the power to publish a Code on union access to workers during a recognition or derecognition ballot.

Consequently, this statutory authority requiring the courts to consider the provisions of the departmental Codes has caused some disquiet. For example, in *Thomas v NUM (South Wales Area)*,[58] the Code on Picketing (para 31), which recommended that no more than six pickets should be present at the entrance to a workplace, was followed by Scott J in the High Court when granting an injunction to restrain picketing by any greater numbers.[59]

THE CENTRAL ARBITRATION COMMITTEE

The Central Arbitration Committee (CAC) was established as a separate body within ACAS by the Employment Protection Act 1975, inheriting many of the duties formerly exercised by the Industrial Arbitration Board. The CAC's original jurisdiction was extensive. The CAC had the responsibility to adjudicate on recognition disputes where the employer had refused to comply with a decision of ACAS to recommend recognition. If the CAC subsequently ordered recognition, and the employer refused to comply, the CAC could award the workers involved in the dispute improved terms and conditions of employment. The recognition provisions of the Employment Protection Act 1975 were repealed by the Employment Act 1980.

Another major function of the CAC was to consider applications by unions under Sched 11 of the Employment Protection Act. Under Sched 11, if, in the absence of agreement, an employer was failing to observe terms and conditions that were generally applicable in the relevant trade or industry, the CAC had the authority to make an award. Schedule 11 operated in a similar manner to the Fair Wages Resolution whereby government contractors had to pay wages of a comparable level to that generally accepted in the relevant industry. The Sched 11 formula was repealed in 1980 and the Fair Wages Resolution was rescinded in 1983.

The focus of the CAC's remaining work has been on voluntary arbitration in collective disputes (although there were no references to the CAC during 2000–01)[60] and on the adjudication of complaints where employers have failed to disclose information to recognised unions as required by ss 181–85 of the TULRCA 1992.[61] The Employment Relations Act 1999 has, however, substantially altered, and expanded the CAC's role. The CAC has the primary responsibility to oversee, administer and determine a recognition application under Sched 1A to the 1999 Act – to decide the appropriate bargaining unit and whether the union enjoys an appropriate level of support, to arrange the secret ballot, through to the award of recognition. In order better to administer the complex recognition procedure, the CAC decision making powers have been streamlined and the appointment system has been restructured.

---

58 [1985] IRLR 136.
59 See, also, *NGN Ltd v SOGAT 82* [1986] IRLR 337. For criticism of this practice of treating the Codes as having the force of law, see Lewis, R, 'Codes of practice on picketing and closed shop agreements and arrangements' (1981) 44 MLR 198 and Baldwin, R and Houghton, J [1986] PL 239, pp 264–67.
60 CAC Annual Report 2000–01.
61 Nine complaints by trade unions were received for the period 2000–01.

Section 25 of the 1999 Act amends s 263 of the TULR(C)A 1992 (which deals with proceedings before the CAC) and inserts a new s 263A. This section states that when discharging its functions under the recognition (and de-recognition) scheme, the CAC shall consist of a panel of three appointed by the chairman of the CAC. This must include the chairman or deputy chairman and one representative of each side of industry.[62] If the panel cannot reach a unanimous decision, but a majority of the panel agree (that is, two out of three), it is their opinion that decides the case. Otherwise, if there is no majority at all (that is, all three have different opinions) then the chairman of the panel has the authority to decide the issue.

The 1999 Act also introduces minor alterations to the appointment process to the CAC. Section 24 amends s 260 of the TULR(C)A 1992 by substituting two new subsections. Previously, ACAS had an input into appointments to the CAC, with members appointed from a list submitted by ACAS. The new provisions leave the choice of appointments (of chairman, deputy chairman and members) solely to the Secretary of State, after consultation with ACAS. The only proviso is that all must be experienced in industrial relations as an employer or employee representative. The reasoning behind this change was to ensure the Secretary of State had a wider group of members to choose from than had previously been the case (as ACAS nominations have tended to be from its own panel of arbitrators).

Another new area of jurisdiction for the CAC is to determine applications under the Transnational Information and Consultation of Employees Regulations 1999 (implementing the European Works Council Directive) regarding disputes over the establishment and constitution of works councils.[63]

---

62 Section 263A(1), (2).
63 One application was received by the CAC for the period 2000–01.

CHAPTER 13

INDUSTRIAL ACTION
AND THE INDIVIDUAL WORKER

INDUSTRIAL ACTION AND THE COMMON LAW

Industrial action has wide-ranging legal implications of both an individual and collective nature. Ordinarily, strike action (which is the total withdrawal of labour) results in a fundamental breach of an employment contract.[1] On this repudiatory breach, the employer may lawfully summarily dismiss the employee at common law without notice, sue for the loss arising from this breach of contract,[2] or refuse to pay any further wages until the employee returns to work.[3] An employer, however, cannot enforce a return to work by way of an order for specific performance of the contract, or injunction to restrain a breach or threatened breach of the employment contract.[4] The breach of the contract of employment is also a component of the tort of inducing breach of contract which union organisers of industrial action may commit resulting in the vicarious liability of the union itself.

There are also a variety of ways of engaging in industrial pressure short of a strike.[5] A common example is the refusal to perform specific duties whilst at work. This will constitute a breach of contract unless such duties are truly voluntary. Other, more imaginative forms of industrial action short of a strike include 'working to rule', 'working without enthusiasm', the 'go-slow' or withdrawing 'goodwill'. Concerted action of this nature is an effective weapon if it has the desired effect of putting pressure on an employer and if it has the advantage of legality. If there is no breach of contract, an employee can still be expected to be paid normally and cannot be dismissed lawfully without the employer complying with the notice provisions in the contract. Furthermore, the organisers will not be subject to an action in tort for inducing breach of an employment or commercial contract. However, judicial decisions suggest that in the vast majority of cases these forms of industrial action will still result in a breach of contract.

INDUSTRIAL ACTION SHORT OF A STRIKE

The 'work to rule'

Employees 'work to rule' when they refuse to do any work that is above and beyond their strict express contractual commitments delineated in their contract of employment. In

---

1   See *Simmons v Hoover* [1977] ICR 61, p 76.
2   For an example of such an action, see *NCB v Galley* [1958] 1 WLR 16 where the calculation of damages for the loss flowing from the breach of the employment contract was based on the cost of hiring a replacement worker.
3   *Wiluszynski v London Borough of Tower Hamlets* [1989] IRLR 259.
4   TULR(C)A 1992, s 236.
5   As Donaldson J commented in *Seaboard World Airlines Inc v TGWU* [1973] ICR 458, p 460 – 'the forms of industrial action are limited only by the ingenuity of mankind'.

Secretary of State for Employment v ASLEF (No 2),[6] the union had instructed their members to 'work to rule' by complying to their contracts and to the provisions of the work's rule book. This meant that employees refused to work on rest days or to volunteer for overtime, causing disruption of railway services.

In a wide-ranging judgment, the Court of Appeal concluded that, although this irregular industrial action short of a strike did not cause a breach of an express term of the employment contract, there had been a breach of an implied term. However, the three Court of Appeal judges explained the content of this implied term in contrasting ways.[7]

Roskill LJ considered that there had been a breach of an implied term of fact – that the instructions in the rule book should be performed in a reasonable and efficient manner – which was automatically incorporated into the employment contract to enable it to function effectively. An express term of this nature had not been necessary at the time of the formation of the contract as the parties had thought such a term self-evident.[8]

Roskill LJ had noted, although not relied on, the alternative ground of breach of the implied obligation of faithful service or fidelity implicit in every employment contract. This was the implied duty that Buckley LJ referred to as 'within the terms of the contract the employee must serve the employer faithfully with a view to promoting those commercial interests for which he is employed'.[9] By 'working to rule', the employees had performed the contract in such a way as to frustrate, rather than promote, the commercial objectives of the employer.

Denning MR identified an implied duty on all employees to perform their tasks in 'good faith'. Wilful obstruction of the employer's business by the unreasonable construction of the works rule book and by the concerted course of non-co-operation amounted to a breach of this implied term. These judgments (especially Denning's and Buckley's) extended the already well established implied duties employees owe to their employer to obey orders and to act with loyalty and fidelity: arguably creating an obligation to co-operate.[10]

The duty to co-operate continues to be of some importance in circumstances of industrial action. In *Cresswell v Board of Inland Revenue*,[11] clerical officers refused to retrain on new technology because of a fear that the introduction of computerisation would bring redundancies. Walton J made it clear that employees were under an obligation to co-operate by accepting a reasonable degree of change in the method of performing their job, as '... an employee is expected to adapt himself to new methods and techniques

---

6   [1972] 2 QB 455.

7   For a full examination of the reasoning in this case, see Napier, B, 'Working to rule – a breach of the contract of employment' (1972) 1 ILJ 125. See also the commentary on the case by Rideout, R (1973) 36 MLR 73, and Kahn-Freund, O (1974) 3 ILJ 186, pp 191–94.

8   This formulation of the implied term of fact was based on an application of the 'officious bystander' test derived from *Shirlaw v Southern Foundaries Ltd* [1939] 2 KB 206.

9   At p 498.

10 This 'duty of co-operation' has been the basis of the development of the mutual duty of trust and confidence implied term which has been of some importance in unfair and wrongful dismissal cases. There have been a number of cases where this implied term has been used to establish constructive dismissal for the purposes of these claims. See *Lewis v Motorworld Garages Ltd* [1985] IRLR 465.

11 [1984] ICR 508.

introduced in the course of his employment'.[12] By failing to do so, the employees were in breach of the implied term to co-operate and the employers were entitled to act upon that failure by withholding pay.

Scott J, in *Sim v Rotherham MBC*,[13] discussed the notion of the duty to co-operate in the context of the professional obligations of school teachers. He held that as professional workers possess a high degree of discretion in the way they work a duty of co-operation with the employer exists in order to ensure the effective discharge of their functions. On this view, the more senior the employee (who usually has wider and more general tasks to perform), the more applicable the implied term is.

The leading case is now *British Telecommunications plc v Ticehurst*.[14] Ticehurst was a manager, who in furtherance of an industrial dispute had withdrawn her co-operation with her employers by working strictly to her hours in the contract. As a consequence of her refusal to desist from this campaign, she was sent home without pay. Ralph Gibson LJ, in allowing the employer's appeal from the decision of the High Court, endorsed the decisions of Buckley LJ and Denning MR in *Secretary of State v ASLEF (No 2)* and had no doubt that an implied term 'to serve the employer faithfully' could be imputed into the contract in these circumstances.[15]

Gibson LJ also endorsed Denning's focus on the motive or intention behind the act which caused the disruption. Intention to obstruct an employer's business can be implied by the employee's decision to engage in a course of action (such as the withdrawal of goodwill) that was inconvenient to the employer. He left open the possibility that, where the intention exists but there has been no actual disruption, there could still be a breach of the implied duty. However, it seems difficult to see how an employee could be liable for a breach of contract where the motive has been to cause disruption but there has been no disruption of any kind.

'Working without enthusiasm' and the 'go-slow'

Working without enthusiasm and the go-slow are both manifestations of employees purposefully working in an inefficient manner. By failing to work to full capacity, the employee is working less than contractually required and so is in breach of contract. This was confirmed by the Privy Council of the House of Lords in *General Engineering Services v Kingston & St Andrew's Corp*.[16] The operation of a 'go-slow' in furtherance of the fire fighters' industrial dispute, which resulted in a fire engine taking 17 minutes to attend a fire when normally it would take three minutes, was a wrongful repudiation of an

---

12   At p 518.
13   [1987] Ch 216.
14   [1992] ICR 383.
15   Note Gibson's LJ statement, p 398, which seems to support the view that the implied term is of particular relevance to those in skilled or managerial positions who have discretion in how they perform their tasks: 'It is, in my judgment, necessary to imply such a term in the case of a manager who is given charge of the work of other employees and who therefore must necessarily be trusted to exercise her judgment and discretion in giving instructions to others and supervising their work. Such a discretion, if the contract is to work properly, must be exercised faithfully in the interests of the employers.'
16   [1989] IRLR 35.

essential obligation of the fire fighters' contract of employment to obey reasonable orders in a reasonable manner.[17]

The manipulation of the implied terms is not the only device courts have at their disposal to locate a breach of employment contract. Another approach, exemplified by the decision in *MBC of Solihull v NUT*,[18] is the identification of an additional contract supplemental to the employment contract, which is broken by the industrial action. Here, the NUT had instructed their members to refuse to cover for absent teachers and not to perform certain functions at lunchtime and outside school hours. The union had contended that withdrawal from these services was not in breach of contract as most of these activities were not formal contractual duties and so had been undertaken voluntarily by teachers. The High Court, however, explained the breach of contract on the basis that teachers had entered into oral contractual obligations. For example, teachers who agreed to supervise pupils at lunchtimes were doing so in return for the consideration of a lunch provided by the school, hence, a failure to engage in lunchtime supervision was a breach of this collateral contract.

Strike action – breach or suspension of contract?

If action short of a strike is a breach of contract, we may well presuppose that a full withdrawal of labour in the form of strike action is also a breach of contract. At common law, an employer is entitled to dismiss an employee for refusing to work (as it is a fundamental obligation that an employee must be willing and able to serve the employer and obey reasonable orders) and it makes no difference that the refusal occurs in the course of a strike.[19] This conventional view was disputed by Lord Denning in *Morgan v Fry*.[20] Where strike notice is given, the 'contract of employment is not terminated, but it is suspended and revives once the strike is over'.[21]

Denning justified this proposition on the basis that it must be implied in a trade dispute that ordinarily both sides do not wish the legal relationship to be terminated. Employees take strike action to gain an alteration, not termination, of the contract. The employer rarely wishes to act on the employees' repudiation, to 'scatter their labour force to the four winds'. As neither side in the strike expects relations to be broken off at the end of the strike, the true intention of the parties is to suspend the contract for the period of the strike. Arguably, Denning's formulation reflects the practice and experience of industrial relations. The vast majority of disputes are settled ending in a negotiated return to work by the striking employees.

Denning's unorthodox opinion was considered by the Donovan Commission which reported that it would not be practicable to introduce such a doctrine into the law as '... considerable technical difficulties would be encountered if the doctrine of unilateral

---

17 Donaldson J, in *Seaboard World Airlines Inc v TGWU* [1973] ICR 458, had earlier identified this form of inaction as in breach of contract when he said, p 460: '... any concerted form of working without enthusiasm, of prolonged tea breaks, or (prolonged) departures for the relief of natural pressures ... constitutes irregular industrial action short of a strike and are prohibited.'

18 [1985] IRLR 211, noted by Hutton, J (1985) ILJ 255.

19 *Laws v London Chronicle Ltd* [1959] 1 WLR 698.

20 [1968] 2 QB 710.

21 At p 728.

suspension of contracts of employment by strike action were to be made part of our law'.[22] This concept was also firmly rejected in subsequent cases. In *Simmons v Hoover Ltd*,[23] Denning's thesis was contradicted by Phillips J in the Employment Appeals Tribunal (EAT) who refused to be bound by *Morgan v Fry* and held that the effect of a strike at common law (preceded by proper notice or not) allows the employer to dismiss the participating employees for their repudiation of their contract of employment.[24] He could find no authority before *Morgan v Fry* for the proposition that strike action suspends a contract of employment and treated this formulation by Denning as a mere device that had been developed solely to avoid a particular result in that case. To find otherwise would 'revolutionise the law' on the subject of the legal relationship between employer and employee, something that, Phillips J believed, Lord Denning could not have intended.[25]

Where there is a specific clause in the contract of employment (usually incorporated by a collective agreement) providing for the suspension of the contract of employment where industrial action is taken, then, where an employer acts upon the clause, the contract will not be at an end. This contractual right of suspension cannot ordinarily be implied by circumstances.[26] However, it has been argued that where a 'no-strike' deal has been negotiated which forbids industrial action until a particular disputes procedure has been exhausted (the terms of which have been incorporated into individual contracts),[27] on full compliance by the union with the terms of the agreement, subsequent industrial action by the relevant employees is permissible under the contract. However, there is no legal authority for the view that the exhaustion of collectively agreed procedures is grounds for 'suspension' of the contract so avoiding breach of contract at the individual level.

Strike notices[28]

We noted earlier that one of the consequences of strike action is that an employer may lawfully dismiss all employees on strike and that the breach of employment contract deriving from the strike call puts the union into the position of being liable for inducing breach of contract, an economic tort.[29]

If the union gives notice of strike action, equivalent in length to the employees' contractual notice period, then it may be argued that, on expiry of the notice and the withdrawal of labour, there is no breach of a contract as the strike notice, given by the union on behalf of the strikers', acts as a collective resignation notice. This was Lord

---

22 Royal Commission on Trades Unions and Employers' Associations, Cmnd 623, 1968, para 943.

23 [1976] IRLR 266.

24 This case is noted by Napier, B, 'Strikes and the contract of employment' [1977] CLJ 34. For a wider discussion of the issues raised, see Napier, B, 'Judicial attitudes towards the employment relationship – some recent developments' (1977) 6 ILJ 1, pp 11–14.

25 See also Kilner Brown J in *Haddow v ILEA* [1979] ICR 202.

26 See *Hanley v Pease & Partners Ltd* [1915] 1 KB 698 and *Puttick v Wright & Sons* [1972] ICR 457.

27 By complying with TULR(C)A 1992, s 180(3).

28 See, generally, on strike notices, Foster, K, 'Strikes and employment contracts' (1971) 34 MLR 275; (1973) 2 ILJ 28 and O'Higgins, P (1973) 2 ILJ 152.

29 Considered in detail in Chapter 14.

Denning's understanding of the effect of a strike notice in *Morgan v Fry*,[30] as otherwise the strike notice must be construed as a threat of breach of contract for the purposes of the tort of intimidation and that '... would do away with the right to strike in this country'.[31]

There has been very limited support for this notion. Saville J in *Boxfoldia Ltd v NGA*[32] held that the effect of a strike notice is dependent upon the meaning of the words used and the context in which it is given. Notice of industrial action will only avert a breach of contract if it is an unambiguous formal notice of termination written and submitted by the strikers personally or if it can be reasonably construed as being written and communicated, on behalf of all the union members concerned, by the union acting as the strikers' agent. However, as Saville J pointed out, an agency relationship between union and the membership is not automatic. Authorisation for the union to act as an agent for its membership cannot be implied by the mere fact of union membership.[33] For a union to act in this way on behalf of the membership requires evidence of express authority.[34]

The more orthodox view is that a strike notice is a threat of a future breach of contract – the withdrawal of labour at a designated date in the future.[35] Such a threat may cause the employer to anticipate a repudiatory breach of contract and so any dismissal in response to this threat would be lawful at common law.[36] Also, note that a strike notice, as a threat to break an employment contract, has additional implications for the purposes of the tort of intimidation (see Chapter 14).

In conclusion, a strike, entailing the full withdrawal of labour, is a failure to discharge all employment duties and so is a repudiatory breach of contract that the employer must accept, rather than waive, to lawfully dismiss at common law. Other forms of industrial action, which put pressure on the employer by a partial withdrawal of labour, also result in a breach of contract. This is the case whether the action is failing to discharge a material part of express contractual duties *per se*, or by discharging express duties in such a way as to be in breach of the implied obligations of the contract of employment.

Industrial action and loss of pay[37]

Where a worker is on strike, he or she is not performing any contractual obligations and the well established common law principle of 'no work, no pay' will apply. Where

---

30 [1968] 3 All ER 452. For comment on the case, see O'Higgins, P, 'The legal effect of a strike notice' [1968] CLJ 223.

31 At p 456. Denning received some limited support from Davies LJ although Russell LJ refused to accept that a strike notice had this effect.

32 [1988] IRLR 383.

33 See *Dixon v Wilson Walton* [1979] ICR 438.

34 This authority is not normally contained as a matter of course in union rules. See on this *Ideal Casements Ltd v Samsi* [1972] ICR 408 and *Heatons Transport (St Helens) Ltd v TGWU* [1972] ICR 308.

35 *Bowes & Partners v Press* [1894] 1 QB 202; *Chappell v Times Newspapers Ltd* [1975] ICR 145.

36 *Rookes v Barnard* [1964] 1 All ER 367, p 396, *per* Lord Devlin.

37 See Napier, B, 'Aspects of the wage-work bargain' [1984] CLJ 337; Morris, G, 'Deductions from pay for industrial action' (1987) 16 ILJ 185; Fredman, S and Morris, G, 'The teachers' lesson: collective bargaining and the courts' (1987) 16 ILJ 215, pp 217–25: McLean, H, 'Contract of employment – negative covenants and no work no pay' [1990] CLJ 28; and Ewing, KD, *The Right to Strike*, 1991, Chapter 3.

employees are engaged in industrial action short of a strike, such as in the form of a 'go-slow' or 'non-co-operation', there is only part performance of express or implied obligations. In this case, not only may a proportionate amount of pay representing the value of the lost services be deducted[38] but also, in appropriate circumstances, an employer may lawfully deny all pay to a worker who is not fully performing their contractual duties.

In *Wiluszynski v London Borough of Tower Hamlets*,[39] employees took limited industrial action by boycotting certain enquiries from council members. They continued to perform the vast majority of their duties but were informed by their employer that they would not be paid unless they worked normally and that any work they did would be treated as being undertaken voluntarily. On an application to recover the salary that had been withheld during the duration of the industrial action, the Court of Appeal held that where an employee is not fully complying with the terms of the contract, and the employer makes it clear in advance that partial performance of the contract is not accepted, then the employer is entitled to refuse to remunerate the employee in any way.[40]

The *Wiluszynski* decision was followed by the Court of Appeal in *British Telecommunications plc v Ticehurst*,[41] the full facts of which were considered earlier. Ticehurst had engaged in a campaign of non-co-operation and refused to sign a pledge that she would work normally. As she was unable to show she was willing and able to discharge her full obligations, once the employers made it clear partial performance was not acceptable, they were entitled to refuse to pay her until after the dispute was settled.

Where an employer has not made it clear that partial performance is unacceptable, the legal position is somewhat more confused. In these circumstances, there are a number of possibilities. Arguably, this could be evidence that the employer has waived the breach of contract. In those circumstances, the employee is entitled to full payment under the contract.[42] Alternatively, the court may come to the conclusion that the employer has accepted incomplete performance of the contract, thereby permitting the employee to make a *quantum meruit* claim for a proportional payment from the employer.[43] In *Sim v Rotherham MBC*,[44] Scott J indicated that where partial performance is accepted the

---

38 In *Miles v Wakefield MDC* [1987] ICR 368 (noted by McMullen, J (1988) 51 MLR 234) the employee, on instructions from his trade union, refused to perform one part of his duties (as a registrar of births, deaths and marriages) on Saturday. The House of Lords held that this was clearly a breach of contract and unless waived by his employers, it justified the deduction of a *pro rata* proportion of salary. This was followed in *Jakeman v South West Regional HA* [1990] IRLR 62, where the High Court refused the employee's claim for interlocutory relief where the employer had deducted a proportion of pay after refusing to accept partial performance.

39 [1989] IRLR 259.

40 The Court of Appeal in coming to this conclusion relied on *dicta* from the House of Lords in *Miles* that where an employer has failed to pay remuneration, and has made it clear that partial rendering of services is unwanted, a court is entitled to refuse an employee's damages claim for wages lost as the employee has not shown willingness to discharge all of his or her contractual obligations. This reasoning – that the party in breach is unable to enforce the contract – was also applied by the Court of Appeal in *Henthorne v CEGB* [1980] IRLR 361 and *McPherson v London Borough of Lambeth* [1988] IRLR 470.

41 [1992] ICR 383.

42 *Royle v Trafford BC* [1984] IRLR 184. Noted by Fentiman, R (1985) 14 ILJ 51.

43 *Miles v Wakefield MDC* [1987] ICR 368, *per* Lords Templeman and Brightman.

44 [1986] IRLR 391.

plaintiff is entitled to be paid in full, subject to an employer's cross-claim for damages deriving from the employee's breach of contract. In such a situation, the equitable doctrine of 'set off' should apply. In practice, this means the employer is entitled to deduct an appropriate amount equivalent to the loss they have suffered. A final possibility, where an employer has accepted imperfect performance, is that the court may find that a contract, supplemental to the main employment contract, has been agreed for the work completed.[45] In all these circumstances, an employee is still only entitled to a proportion of their salary reflecting the actual work undertaken.

These decisions give employers a powerful alternative to dismissal when reacting to industrial action.[46] If employers utilise their legal powers to refuse to pay any salary on making it clear that partial performance is not accepted, then it may be that action short of a strike will lose its popularity amongst workers. The danger for employers, however, is that, in refusing to pay any salary at all, the dispute may be inflamed, so worsening industrial relations.

INDUSTRIAL ACTION AND UNFAIR DISMISSAL

Until the passage of the Employment Relations Act 1999, a dismissal of an employee for participating in industrial action was automatically 'fair' unless the employer had discriminated between the participants by selective re-engagement or selective dismissal. The policy behind restricting the right to claim unfair dismissal purportedly derives from the principle of legal abstentionism; the non-intervention of the law in the area of industrial conflict between employer and employees. Otherwise, it is argued, by examining the circumstances of the dismissal the tribunal would be adjudicating on the merits of the industrial action and would be in danger of compromising its neutrality.[47]

Such a policy fails to distinguish between the different reasons for industrial action. For example, the employee who is dismissed for action taken in support of a pay claim is treated the same as an employee who takes action in response to an employer's provocative action to change unilaterally their terms and conditions of employment. An employer may also attempt to goad employees into taking industrial action so as to dismiss them to avoid redundancy payments or other legal obligations.[48]

In *WJ Thompson v Eaton Ltd*,[49] Phillips J argued that, where a strike had been engineered by an employer's 'gross provocation', it was conceivable that the employer, not the employee, was guilty of conduct that amounts to a repudiation of the

---

45 *Bond v CAV Ltd* [1983] IRLR 360.

46 Deductions made as a consequence of industrial action cannot be challenged under the jurisdiction of the Wages Act 1986 (now incorporated into the Employment Rights Act 1996). See s 14(5) of the 1996 Act and *Sunderland Polytechnic v Evans* [1993] IRLR 196.

47 For further elaboration of this argument, see Phillips J in *Gallagher v Wragg* [1977] ICR 174, p 178, and contrast this with the views of Sir Hugh Griffiths in *Heath v JF Longman (Meat Salesman) Ltd* [1973] IRLR 214, p 215. Note, also, the comments of Lord Scarman on the role of the courts in trade disputes in *NWL v Woods* [1979] IRLR 478, p 486.

48 For an example of this tactic, see Ewing, KD and Napier, B, 'The Wapping dispute and labour law' [1986] CLJ 285, p 291.

49 [1976] IRLR 308, p 311. Noted by McMullen, J [1977] CLJ 32.

employment contract. This may then justify, at common law, an employee's response of accepting breach, treating the contract as at an end and withdrawing labour. Furthermore, in this situation, a purported dismissal was not for the reason of participation in a strike, but to dispense of an employee for economic or other reasons. Although this approach may have had much to commend it, both Kilner Brown J, in *Wilkins v Cantrell & Cochrane Ltd*,[50] and Talbot J, in *Marsden v Fairey Stainless Ltd*,[51] refused to follow this analysis and confirmed that (prior to the Employment Relations Act amendments), so long as no victimisation takes place, industrial tribunals did not have jurisdiction to examine the fairness of such dismissals, whatever the reason for the industrial action.[52]

Industrial action dismissals and the Employment Relations Act 1999

As a consequence of complaints by trade unions of the unfairness of the dismissal provisions (whereby employers could effectively break a lawful strike by simply dismissing all the workforce), and observations by international bodies that the lack of protection for employees on strike was in breach of international law,[53] the Labour Party in opposition committed itself to reviewing and reforming the relevant legislation. In the White Paper, *Fairness at Work*,[54] it was proposed that employees dismissed whilst engaging in lawful industrial action should have the right to complain of unfair dismissal.[55] During the consultation period with employers and unions, the White Paper proposal was substantially amended. The provision that emerged in the 1999 Act provides that where an employee takes 'protected' industrial action, a dismissal is only unlawful where it takes place eight weeks from the start of industrial action – although dismissal could still be unlawful after eight weeks if the employer has not taken reasonable procedural steps to resolve the dispute.

The key legislative change is brought about by Sched 5 to the 1999 Act introducing a new s 238A into the TULR(C)A 1992. Industrial action is 'protected' if the relevant employee is induced to take part in industrial action by an act (or a series of acts) that, by virtue of s 219, is not actionable in tort.[56] The provision therefore requires that the industrial action is both supported by the union, in the sense that is 'official' action (defined below), and also lawful in that the trade union is protected by the immunity in tort law for inducing it.[57] When determining a claim under s 238A, the tribunal will thus

---

50 [1978] IRLR 483.

51 [1979] IRLR 103.

52 For commentary on these decisions see Napier, B [1980] CLJ 52 and Collins, H (1979) ILJ 109. For further analysis of the legal ramifications of a strike in response to a repudiatory breach by an employer, see Elias, P, 'The strike and breach of contract: a reassessment', in Ewing, KD, Gearty, C and Hepple, B (eds), *Human Rights and Labour Law*, 1994.

53 For instance, ILO institutions have consistently criticised this state of affairs as inconsistent with the right to withdraw labour, contrary to collective labour standards enshrined in Convention No 87 (see, as examples, the 277th report of the Freedom of Association Committee, Case No 1540, 1991 and the report of the Committee of Experts, 1995, pp 199–200). For further details, see Novitz, T (1998) 27 ILJ 169, pp 189–90; (2000) 63 MLR 379, p 387.

54 Cm 3968.

55 See paras 4.21–23.

56 Section 218A(1).

57 For criticisms of these preconditions, see Ewing, KD (1999) 28 ILJ 283, p 292.

have to examine the legality of the action by reference to the industrial action provisions contained in the TULR(C)A 1992. This will involve a consideration of a number of factors, ranging from whether the action is in furtherance or pursuance of a trade dispute, whether the union has gone through the appropriate balloting and notification procedures and whether there are factors such as unlawful picketing activities, which take the action outside the bounds of lawfulness (see Chapters 15–17 inclusive). This may have been determined by earlier High Court proceedings, in which case the tribunal will be bound by the previous decisions of the higher court. However, it is not difficult to conceive of circumstances whereby these issues have not been previously litigated and tribunals will have to examine areas of law that were the preserve of the superior courts in injunctive proceedings.

Protection only extends to dismissal that take place within eight weeks from the day on which the employee started to take protected industrial action,[58] or where dismissal has taken place after eight weeks but the employee had already gone back to work before the end of the eight week period.[59] If the dismissal has taken place after eight weeks and the employee is still engaged in industrial action, the employee will lose this protection unless the employer has failed to take 'reasonable' steps in order to resolve the dispute to which the protected industrial action relates.[60] When determining whether or not an employer has acted reasonably, s 238A(6) states that the tribunal should have regard to four specific issues: whether the employer or a union have complied with procedures established by any applicable collective or other agreement; whether the employer or a union offered or agreed to commence or resume negotiations after the start of the protected industrial action; whether the employer or union unreasonably refused, after the start of the protected industrial action, a request for conciliation services to be used: and whether the employer or a union unreasonably refused, after the start of the protected industrial action, a request that mediation services be used in relation to procedures to be adopted for the purposes of resolving the dispute. Clearly, the nature of the steps which the tribunal must consider in determining the fairness of the dismissal are exclusively procedural, with the tribunal explicitly directed by s 238A(7) not to consider the merits of the dispute.

A key distinction that will have to be drawn is between unofficial and official action, with only employees who take official action having the specific protection afforded by s 238A.[61] All action that an employee participates in will be classified as unofficial action unless the employee is a member of a trade union and the action is authorised or endorsed by that union, or he or she is not a member of a trade union but there are members of a trade union taking part in the action that has been authorised or endorsed.[62]

---

58 Section 238A(3).
59 Section 238A(4).
60 Section 238A(5).
61 Note, however, that ss 237(1A) and 238(2A) provide that it is unlawful to dismiss participants in industrial action where the real motivation for their dismissal is for certain reasons related to, *inter alia*, maternity, family or health and safety activities or for acting as an employee representative.
62 Section 237(2).

Whether action is authorised or endorsed is governed by s 20 of the TULR(C)A 1992, which states that a wide category of union officials can endorse the action, including: the principal executive committee, the president, the general secretary, any committee of the union constituted in accordance with the rules, any official, whether employed or not, (which can include a shop steward), and any group of persons of which any official was a member. The union can avoid liability where the executive, president or general secretary repudiates the industrial action induced by other employed or lay officials (for further details see Chapter 16). Section 238A(8) specifically states that if an employee continues to take industrial action the day after the union's repudiation, then the entitlement to claim unfair dismissal under s 238A is lost.[63]

Where a dismissal has been found to be unfair by virtue of s 238A, there are some specific provisions dealing with the powers of the employment tribunal in relation to remedies. A new s 239(4) inserted into the Employment Rights Act 1996 prohibits the issuing of reinstatement or re-engagement orders until after the ending of the relevant industrial dispute. Further, there is a power for the Secretary of State to make regulations to provide that hearings of claims under s 238A may be adjourned or renewed or for the holding of a pre-hearing review. Thus, a tribunal may be given the power to prevent a claim from being heard during the duration of the industrial action, arguably undermining the effectiveness of this new right.[64]

Unfair dismissal and victimisation[65]

Where the provisions of the Employment Relations Act 1999 do not apply, strikers may still be able to claim unfair dismissal under s 238 of the TULR(C)A 1992. This legislative provision is unaffected by reforms introduced by the 1999 Act. The original position as enacted in the 1970s was that employees who were taking strike action would have the right to claim unfair dismissal unless all employees taking that action had been dismissed and none had been selectively re-engaged. The law was amended by the 1982 Employment Act[66] which provided that the employer could selectively re-engage employees after a grace period of three months and still retain an effective immunity from the dismissed employees having a right to claim unfair dismissal. The Employment Act 1990 introduced a new regime, whereby a difference was drawn between official and unofficial industrial action (seen above with regard to the protection offered by s 238A). The same basic scheme – whereby all employees have to be dismissed with no selectivity – was retained in relation to official action, but the ability to dismiss selectively, with no

---

63 Another issue a tribunal may have to consider is whether the employee was actually dismissed by reason of participation in industrial action, discussed on p 300.

64 The Minister of State at the Department of Trade and Industry argued (during the Standing Committee debate, 9 March 1999) that pre-hearing reviews could help stimulate negotiations to settle the dispute. Where an employer had an early indication that the unfair dismissal case was strong, it could encourage a settlement with the union on the underlying trade dispute.

65 See, generally, Ewing, KD, 'The right to strike' (1986) 15 ILJ 143, pp 149–53; Napier, B, 'Strikes and the individual worker – reforming the law' [1987] CLJ 287; Ewing, KD, *The Right to Strike*, 1991, Chapter 4.

66 For an examination and criticism of the amendments, see Wallington, P, 'The Employment Act 1982 s 9 – a recipe for victimisation' (1983) 46 MLR 310 and Ewing, KD, 'Industrial action: another step in the "right" direction' (1982) 11 ILJ 209.

employee having the right to claim unfair dismissal,[67] was introduced in relation to unofficial action.[68]

The amended s 238 now provides that an employment tribunal has no jurisdiction to determine whether a dismissal is fair or unfair (for taking part in a strike or other official industrial action or where the employer was conducting or instituting a 'lock out'),[69] unless, at the date of dismissal: (a) one or more of the relevant employees have not been dismissed, or (b) a relevant employee has been offered re-engagement[70] within three months of the dismissal[71] and the complainant has not.[72]

There is no detailed statutory definition of 'strike', 'other industrial action' or 'lock out' for the purposes of this provision.[73] Where the courts have been called upon to interpret these phrases, they have generally held that whether a strike, other industrial action or lock out has occurred is generally a matter for the industrial tribunal to decide on the facts.[74] However, a tribunal does not have an unfettered discretion to characterise whatever it chooses as a strike or industrial action. Judicial decisions provide some guidance, as a matter of law, as to the meaning of these expressions.

---

67 Note that where none of the participants are union members industrial action is not classified as unofficial and so in this situation the tribunal retains its jurisdiction to examine the fairness of any discriminatory dismissals.

68 The purpose of the legislative change was to reduce the incidence of unofficial action. For further elaboration of the reasons for the reforms, see the Green Paper, *Unofficial Action and the Law*, Cm 821, 1989, Chapter 3. Note, also, that by TULR(C)A 1992, s 223, any industrial action in response to dismissals for unofficial action is unlawful and will result in the trade dispute immunity being lifted.

69 A 'lock out' occurs where an employer reacts to a dispute by closing the workplace or by refusing employees permission to enter the workplace.

70 This refers to an offer of reinstatement into the same job or some other suitable position: s 238(4). See *Williams v National Theatre Board Ltd* [1982] IRLR 377 and *Crosville Wales Ltd v Tracey* [1993] IRLR 60. Even where the re-engagement of a striker takes place as a consequence of a mistake, it is possible for that re-engagement to be effective for the purposes of the section (if the employer has actual or constructive knowledge of the reason for dismissal). This then triggers the tribunal's jurisdiction to examine the fairness of the dismissals of the other strikers – see *Bingham v GKN Kwikform Ltd* [1992] IRLR 4.

71 The three month qualifying period was introduced by the 1982 Act, so weakening the original protection. The employer has now only to wait for the three month period to expire before selectively re-engaging at will.

72 Where the tribunal has jurisdiction, it should proceed by examining the circumstances of the dismissal by reference to the test of reasonableness contained in s 98 of the Employment Rights Act 1996. Eg, see *Edwards v Cardiff CC* [1979] IRLR 303; *Cruickshank v Hobbs* [1977] ICR 725; *Laffin v Fashion Industries (Hartlepool) Ltd* [1978] IRLR 448; *Thompson v Woodland Designs* [1980] IRLR 423.

73 In earlier decisions on the construction of these phrases, tribunals and courts had applied the definitions of 'strike' and 'lock out' contained in the Employment Protection (Consolidation) Act (EP(C)A) 1978, Sched 13, para 24 (now, s 235 of the Employment Rights Act 1996) which were provided for the purposes of calculating continuity of employment for, *inter alia*, redundancy payments. Sole reliance by tribunals on these definitions was disapproved by the Court of Appeal in *Express and Star Ltd v Bundy* [1987] IRLR 422. A definition of 'strike' has existed since 1984 for the purposes of the law on strike ballots and is now repeated in TULR(C)A 1992, s 246. This statutory definition – a 'concerted stoppage of work' – adds very little to the judicial interpretation of the term 'strike' discussed above.

74 For example, the Court of Appeal in *Express and Star Ltd v Bundy* [1987] IRLR 422, p 425, expressed the view that no definition can truly cover all the manifestations of industrial action. Thus, tribunals, experienced in industrial relations matters, are entitled to a high degree of autonomy in deciding whether a lock out or industrial action has taken place. However, of course, the danger of allowing tribunals this level of autonomy is inconsistency between different tribunals as two different tribunals could, without error in law, take opposite views on the same set of facts.

In *Rasool v Hepworth Pipe Co Ltd (No 2)*,[75] Waterhouse J, in the EAT, held that in principle whether certain action constitutes a strike or other industrial action is dependent upon whether the purpose of the action was to apply pressure against an employer so as to secure or obtain an advantage.[76] Thus, attendance at an unauthorised union meeting to discuss future wage negotiation was not industrial action because the purpose of the absence from work was not to put industrial pressure on the employer but to obtain employees' views on this issue.

Whether there has also been a breach of employment contract is not always relevant.[77] This can be criticised on the grounds that an employee is unable to rely on his or her contractual rights. A dismissal for industrial action is automatically fair even though summary termination by the employer at common law would be unlawful. For example, employees locked out by an employer because of their failure to agree to new conditions of employment, and then dismissed, have no protection against unfair dismissal (unless there has been victimisation), even though they are willing and able to work and it is the employer who has engaged in the repudiatory breach of the contract.[78]

Industrial action does not, it seems, depend on concerted pressure being applied by workers acting collectively. The EAT, in *Lewis and Britton v E Mason & Sons*,[79] contrary to *dicta* by Lord Denning in *Tramp Shipping Co v Greenwich Marine Inc*[80] and by Eveleigh LJ in *Coates v Modern Methods & Materials Ltd*[81] reasoned that an industrial tribunal was entitled to conclude that industrial action had taken place even where only one individual had refused to follow orders in a personal dispute over the terms and conditions of his employment.

If tribunals in the future follow this approach, unscrupulous employers will be able to avoid their statutory obligations by dismissing employees purportedly for industrial action rather than misconduct. A strong case can be argued that, where an employee is dismissed for unilaterally refusing an employer's order, in consequence of an individual dispute with that employer, it should be categorised as a misconduct dismissal; thereby

---

75 [1980] IRLR 137.

76 On this test, a tribunal should examine the facts of the case to see if pressure was applied as a bargaining tool. This is a classic, although limited, view of industrial action, as it seems to exclude action taken for political or ideological reasons which is not necessarily aimed at an employer. The Court of Appeal, in *Knowles v Fire Brigades Union* [1996] IRLR 617 (in a different statutory context), preferred a more expansive analysis of the terms based, not only on the object which the union seeks to achieve, but also on the nature and effect of the action.

77 For example, in *Power Packing Casemakers Ltd v Faust* [1983] IRLR 117 (noted by Morris, A (1983) 12 ILJ 251) employees refused to do voluntary overtime and were dismissed as a consequence. Stephenson LJ agreed with the submission of the employer that the tribunal did not have jurisdiction as '... once an industrial tribunal, in the exercise of its good sense decides that an employee was, at the date of dismissal, taking part in industrial action, whether in breach of contract or not, with the object of applying pressure on his employer or of disrupting his business, the tribunal must refuse to entertain the complaint or to go into questions of the employers motive or reasons for dismissal'. However, more recently, Neil LJ, in *Knowles v Fire Brigades Union* [1996] IRLR 617, suggested that whether a breach of contract occurs is one of many factors to consider when determining whether industrial action has taken place.

78 This tactic is described by Miller, K and Woolfson, C, in 'Timex: industrial relations and the use of the law in the 1990s' (1994) 23 ILJ 209.

79 [1994] IRLR 4. Noted by Dolding, L (1994) 23 IRLR 243.

80 [1975] ICR 261, p 266.

81 [1982] IRLR 318, p 323.

giving the employment tribunal jurisdiction to examine all the circumstances behind the dismissal. It may be that the adoption in 1992 of the definition of a strike as a 'concerted stoppage of work' has made this more likely.

Participation in industrial action

Jurisdiction to consider the fairness of a dismissal is removed from an employment tribunal only where all the employees dismissed are 'taking part' in a strike or other industrial action. In *Coates v Modern Methods and Materials Ltd*,[82] the majority of the Court of Appeal (Stephenson and Kerr LJJ) held that the employees' subjective motivation was not a relevant factor in determining whether an employee had been 'taking part' in industrial action.[83] Participation in a strike is to be judged by what that employee does, not the motive behind the action, as in 'the field of industrial action those who are not openly against it are presumably for it'.[84]

The implication of this decision is that the onus is on the employee to show that he or she is not 'taking part' in industrial action. Employees who stay away from work when others are on strike are likely to be deemed to be participants in the strike, unless they make plain their disagreement or objection to the action[85] or have some valid explanation for their absence.[86] It may also be assumed by an employer that an employee's unexplained absence during industrial action is for this purpose, as there is an obligation on employees to dissociate themselves from a dispute.[87] There is, however, a distinction between participating in industrial action and merely supporting it. In *Rogers v Chloride Systems Ltd*,[88] Rogers was legitimately off sick for the duration of the industrial action. When questioned over the phone by her employer, she intimated support for the strike but that did not amount to 'taking part' in the strike. It has also been held, in *Midland Plastics v Till*,[89] that a mere threat to take industrial action cannot be construed as participation in it.

Since the test for determining participation in a strike is an objective test based on the facts known, an employer's subjective belief that employees are participating in industrial action is also irrelevant. In *Manifold Industries v Sims*,[90] a majority of workers voted not to

---

82 [1982] IRLR 318.

83 Eveleigh LJ, in a strong dissenting judgment, relying on Court of Appeal *obiter* in *McCormick v Horsepower Ltd* [1981] IRLR 217, rejected this construction of the expression 'to take part in a strike'. Eveleigh believed that '... the mere fact that an employee is away from work when a strike is on does not lead inevitably to the conclusion that he is taking part in a strike'. A major factor to consider was the employee's motive or intention to withdraw labour in support of fellow employees and their claim.

84 *Per* Stephenson LJ, p 323.

85 *Ibid*.

86 Such as where an employee is certified sick at the commencement of the action – *Hindle Gears Ltd v McGinty* [1984] IRLR 477. Cf *Williams v Western Mail & Echo* [1980] ICR 366. Note, however, that as the test is objective, even where an employee is on sick leave he or she could be 'taking part' if there is clear evidence to this effect – see *Bolton Roadways Ltd v Edwards* [1987] IRLR 392.

87 *McKenzie v Crosville Motors Ltd* [1989] IRLR 516.

88 [1992] ICR 198.

89 [1983] IRLR 9.

90 [1991] IRLR 242.

co-operate with a work study to secure improvements in productivity. Before the work study commenced, the complainants were dismissed for their refusal to co-operate. The EAT held that these workers were not participating in 'other industrial action' at the time of dismissal because they were merely stating in advance their intention not to co-operate and so were not objectively 'taking part' in industrial action.[91] Similarly, in *Naylor v Orton & Smith Ltd*,[92] employees were not participating in industrial action where they attended a meeting, voted for a ban on overtime but did not actually engage in it.[93]

Relevant employees

For an employment tribunal to consider the fairness of any dismissals depends upon whether there has been discrimination in treatment between the complainant and one or more 'relevant employees'. For the purposes of a lock out, a 'relevant employee' is one who is 'directly interested' in the dispute that causes the lock out.[94] Whether employees are 'directly interested' in the dispute is judged at the time of the lock out, not at the time of dismissal. Hence, an employee who was originally locked out, but has returned before the dismissals, remains a relevant employee for the purposes of the unfair dismissal action.[95]

A 'relevant employee', in relation to strike or other industrial action, is defined in s 238(3)(b) as someone who is employed at the same establishment as the complainant[96]and who was taking part in the action at the date[97] of the complainant's dismissal. Prior to the changes introduced by the 1982 Act, a 'relevant employee' included all employees who were on strike at the commencement of the action (rather than the date of the complainant's dismissal). Therefore, if those who returned to work early were not also dismissed, the tribunals retained jurisdiction to consider the fairness of all the dismissals.[98]

The issue of ascertaining whether there has been any discrimination in dismissals is a matter for the tribunal to consider at a preliminary hearing on jurisdiction. If by the end of that hearing discrimination has been shown by the complainant, then the substantive hearing may proceed. However, if an employer dismisses the 'relevant employee' before the end of the preliminary hearing, then tribunal jurisdiction will lapse and the

---

91 See also *Jenkins v P&O European Ferries (Dover) Ltd* [1991] ICR 652.

92 [1983] IRLR 233.

93 Contrast *Winnett v Seamarks Bros Ltd* [1978] IRLR 387, where participation was deemed to be immediate when a collective decision was made to take industrial action, even though some employees were not contractually required to attend work until later in the day. Also, see *dicta* in *Lewis and Britton v E Mason & Sons* [1994] IRLR 9, to the effect that an employee takes part in action from the time he or she evinces an intention to do so.

94 Section 238(3)(a).

95 See *Fisher v York Co Ltd* [1979] IRLR 385 and *H Campey & Sons v Bellwood* [1987] ICR 311 (noted by Napier, B (1988) 17 ILJ 50).

96 Therefore, where there is common industrial action at a multi-plant employer, an employer may dismiss all strikers at one plant whilst retaining strikers at another.

97 By s 238(5), dismissal takes place at the date notice was given or, if no notice was given, at the effective date of termination. In *Heath v JF Longman* [1973] IRLR 214, 'date' was interpreted as the 'time' of dismissal.

98 See *Stock v Frank Jones (Tipton) Ltd* [1978] IRLR 87.

complainant(s) will be unable to proceed.[99] This was the practical outcome of the Court of Appeal's decision in *P&O Ferries v Byrne*.[100]

Industrial action over unilateral changes in terms and conditions of employment had resulted in substantial numbers of union members being dismissed. In order to challenge the employer's actions, a series of unfair dismissal claims were lodged. The applicants had alleged existence of a 'relevant employee' who had also been on strike, but had not been dismissed. In response, the employers sought particulars of the identity of the relevant employee. The Court of Appeal held that the tribunal should grant a disclosure order at the conclusion of the proceedings to determine jurisdiction so the employer knows the case that has to be answered: thereby, in practice, enabling the employer to dismiss the individual, so forestalling employment tribunal jurisdiction for the majority of claims.[101]

Remedies

Where an employee has been successful in their claim, an employment tribunal will first consider whether to make a re-employment order, that is, to re-engage the employee in the job previously held or in a different job which would be 'reasonably suitable in his case'.[102] If the applicant does not wish for such an order to be made or if the tribunal decides against making such an order, the tribunal will proceed to the calculation of compensation. Compensation is assessed according to the general principles of unfair dismissal computation as outlined in ss 118–24 of the Employment Rights Act 1996. This consists, ordinarily, of a basic and compensatory award. A basic award is assessed according to a set criteria based on the employee's age, length of service (up to a maximum of 20 years) and gross weekly pay. The current ceiling (2002) on a week's pay for the purposes of this calculation is £240. The maximum amount that can be awarded is £7,200.

The compensatory award compensates for the loss the employee has actually suffered as a result of dismissal. The factors considered in determining the level of compensation include: actual and future loss of earnings; loss of fringe benefits; loss of pension rights; and loss of statutory employment rights. The award is subject to a current maximum of £51,700. If a re-employment order has been granted and the employer refuses to comply with it, an additional award will be made of up to a further 52 weeks' pay, subject to a maximum of £12,480.[103]

In ordinary cases of unfair dismissal, ss 122(2) and 123(5) of the Employment Rights Act 1996 permit tribunals to reduce both the basic and compensatory award where it is 'just and equitable' to do so because of the conduct of the applicant.[104] One question that

---

99 A claim based a failure to re-engage can also be defeated by the employer offering re-engagement to the complainant before the end of the tribunal hearing – *Highland Fabricators Ltd v McLaughlin* [1984] IRLR 482.

100 [1989] IRLR 254.

101 In deciding this interpretation of the section, the Court of Appeal had ignored contrary *dicta*, in *McCormick v Horsepower Ltd* [1981] IRLR 217, that the cut-off date for determining discrimination between employees was at the start of the hearing, not at the end.

102 Section 238(4).

103 On the additional award, see *Artisan Press v Strawley & Parker* [1986] IRLR 126.

104 See, eg, *Morganite Electrical Carbon Ltd v Donne* [1988] ICR 18.

has arisen is how far a tribunal is precluded from examining the reason for the applicant's decision to take industrial action or their behaviour during industrial action for the purposes of reducing compensation.

The EAT, in *Courtaulds Northern Spinning v Moosa*,[105] concluded that it was not appropriate for an industrial tribunal to consider whether an employee's reasons for taking industrial action justify a reduction in compensation. This was because the purpose of excluding tribunal jurisdiction was to prevent tribunals from examining the merits of industrial disputes. Consequently, if they were permitted to assess whether it was 'just and equitable' to reduce compensation, tribunals would become embroiled in such issues, contrary to the intention of Parliament.

This reasoning was not accepted in the subsequent case of *TNT Express (UK) Ltd v Downes*.[106] A differently constituted EAT held that, once a tribunal has jurisdiction to consider whether the dismissal was fair or unfair, then it was entitled to consider a variety of factors in coming to that conclusion, based on fairness and reasonableness. Thus, when assessing compensation, the tribunal is also entitled to consider whether it would be 'just and equitable' to reduce the level of compensation based on an examination of the circumstances surrounding dismissal (that is, whether the industrial action is 'wholly unmerited') in determining whether the employee contributed to the dismissal.[107]

However, the most recent House of Lords authority has re-affirmed the EAT's decision in *Moosa*. Policy dictates that where an employee is merely taking part in industrial action tribunals must not consider the issue of contributory fault. But it is permissible for a tribunal to consider an applicant's conduct where they have gone beyond participation in the normal way, such as by engaging in violent picketing.[108]

---

105 [1984] IRLR 43.

106 [1993] IRLR 432.

107 For examples of contributory fault in this context, see *Thompson v Woodland Designs* [1980] IRLR 423 and *Gibson v British Transport Docks Board* [1982] IRLR 228.

108 *Crosville Wales Ltd v Tracey (No 2)* [1997] IRLR 691.

CHAPTER 14

CIVIL LIABILITIES

A trade union, in seeking to achieve its objectives, must occasionally force an employer to the bargaining table by the tactical use of industrial action. Employees who respond to the call for industrial action will be in breach of their employment contracts. Strike action will also usually cause breaches of commercial contracts between the employer (against whom the industrial action is directed) and other persons with whom the employer is doing business. Moreover, additional commercial contracts may be broken where employees in other enterprises take supportive secondary action to cut off supplies or the distribution of goods to the employer in the primary dispute.

In the circumstances described above, it is almost inevitable that one or more of the 'economic torts' (that is, inducing breach of contract, interference with trade or business, conspiracy or intimidation) will have been committed. An unfettered application of these torts – with employers, suppliers or other parties taking legal action for damages or for an injunction to stop the action – would seriously hinder trade union industrial activities and render them powerless to protect their members' interests. Consequently, as we saw in the introduction to Part 3, since 1906 unions have been provided with certain 'immunities' to these torts, so long as the action taken is 'in contemplation and furtherance of a trade dispute'. Since 1979, the scope of these immunities have been gradually reduced making it easier for employers and others to challenge industrial action in the courts.

An approach that has much to commend it is to examine trade union liability in three phases. This is the framework employed by Brightman J in *Marina Shipping v Laughton*,[1] subsequently approved by Lord Diplock in *Merkur Island Shipping Co v Laughton*.[2]

(a) Has, *prima facie*, one or more of the economic torts been committed?

(b) If so, do any of the immunities now found in the Trade Union and Labour Relations (Consolidation) Act (TULR(C)A) 1992, s 219 apply?

(c) Has the immunity been withdrawn by the legislation since 1980?

Stage 1 of this framework is considered in this chapter. Stages 2 and 3 are considered in Chapter 15.

---

1   [1982] QB 1127.
2   [1983] IRLR 218.

THE ECONOMIC TORTS[3]

Inducing breach of contract

This tort has its roots in the Statute of Labourers 1381,[4] although the action in its modern form dates from *Lumley v Gye*,[5] a case concerning the inducement of breach of a contract of service. Here, the defendant impresario persuaded an opera singer, who was under a contract to sing at the plaintiff's theatre, to break her contract with the plaintiff so as to perform at the defendant's theatre. The principles contained in *Lumley v Gye* were subsequently applied to trade union strike action; extending the scope of the tort to include the inducement of breach of commercial supply contracts and contracts for the hire of goods and services.[6]

Inducing breach of contract is committed where the instigator of industrial action induces or procures without justification, knowingly and intentionally, directly or indirectly, a breach of an employment or commercial contract.

For example, direct inducement of breach of employment contracts occurs where union official A instructs union members to take strike action against company B. *Prima facie*, company B can sue A, the organiser of the action, in damages or for injunctive relief.

Direct inducement to break a commercial contract arises where union official A persuades company B not to honour a supply contract to company C. Company C is then in a position to sue A.

Where A instructs union members to take strike action against company B, in order to stop the delivery of goods to company C, liability is for directly inducing a breach of employment contract *and* for indirectly inducing breach of a commercial contract of supply.

Components of the tort

In the course of his seminal judgment in *DC Thomson Ltd v Deakin*[7] Jenkins LJ identified the necessary elements that comprise the tort of direct and indirect inducement of a breach of contract. He held that the tort was confined to cases where:

---

3 See, generally, Hughes, A, 'Liability for loss caused by industrial action' (1970) 86 LQR 181; Heydon, J, *The Economic Torts*, 1978; Elias, P and Ewing, KD, 'Economic torts and labour law: old principles and new liabilities' [1982] CLJ 321; Carty, H, 'Intentional violation of economic interests: the limits of common law liability' (1988) 104 LQR 250; Sales, P and Stilitz, D, 'Intentional infliction of harm by unlawful means' (1999) 115 LQR 411; Cane, P, *Tort Law and Economic Interests*, 1996; Weir, T, *Economic Torts*, 1997; *Clerk and Lindsell on Torts*, 18th edn, 2000, Chapter 24.

4 Under this statute (which owed its origins to the system of serfdom), the law recognised the tort of 'enticement' of a servant from a master.

5 (1853) 2 E & B 216.

6 *Bowen v Hall* (1881) 6 QBD 333; *Temperton v Russell* [1893] 1 QB 715; *DC Thomson & Co v Deakin* [1952] Ch 646.

7 [1952] Ch 646.

... first, that the person charged ... knew of the existence of the contract and intended to procure its breach; secondly, that the person so charged did definitely and unequivocally persuade, induce or procure the employees concerned to break their contracts of employment with the intent I have mentioned; thirdly, that the employees so persuaded, induced or procured did in fact break their contracts of employment; and, fourthly, that breach of the (commercial) contract forming the alleged subject of (the indirect) interference ensued as a necessary consequence ...[8]

Jenkins LJ also confirmed that for the purposes of liability for indirect inducement of breach of contract, the additional element of unlawful means was required.

Knowledge of the contract

The central question that arises is what degree of knowledge of the contract is required; is it knowledge of the existence of the contract which is broken or must there be an awareness of the actual terms of the contract? Ordinarily, an instigator of industrial action is fully aware that employees work under a contract of employment and for employees to stop work is a breach of that contract. This is not always the case with complex commercial contracts of supply.

Lord Denning, in *Emerald Construction Co Ltd v Lowthian*,[9] rejected an argument to the effect that liability cannot be imposed where a defendant is unaware that breach of the terms of the contract will result from his or her actions. He held that it was not necessary for the union organisers of industrial action to have knowledge of the precise terms of a contract so long as they had '... the means of knowledge – which they deliberately disregarded ... Like the man who turns a blind eye'.[10] Both the Court of Appeal, in *DC Thomson Ltd v Deakin*,[11] and the House of Lords in *Stratford v Lindley*[12] indicated that it may only be necessary for the defendant to have a cursory knowledge of the existence of the contract broken by the inducement.[13]

Where the contract that has been broken is one regularly employed in the defendant's trade or industry, a form of constructive knowledge of its terms can be ascribed to the defendant. We can see the application of this principle in *Merkur Island Shipping Co v Laughton*,[14] where a union instruction calling for strike action resulted in a breach of a complex 'merchant charter party' contract of hire concerning the sub-leasing of several ships. The House of Lords accepted the contention that even though the union official was not privy to the complex terms of the contract (and so did not know for certain exactly who the other parties were or that the action would cause a breach of the contract of hire), it could be assumed that such an official was well informed about these types of contracts common in the shipping industry.[15] The use of the device of 'deemed

---

8   At p 697.
9   [1966] 1 WLR 691, p 700.
10   See also *Daily Mirror Newspaper Ltd v Gardner* [1968] 2 QB 762, p 780. The case is noted by Wedderburn, KW (now Lord) (1968) 31 MLR 440.
11   [1952] Ch 646.
12   [1965] AC 269. Noted by Wedderburn, KW (now Lord) (1965) 28 MLR 205.
13   See also *Timeplan Education Group Ltd v National Union of Teachers* [1997] IRLR 457, p 461.
14   [1983] IRLR 218.
15   See also Lawton LJ in *Associated News Group v Wade* [1979] ICR 664, p 699.

knowledge' was reaffirmed in *Middlebrook Mushrooms Ltd v TGWU* [16] by the Court of Appeal.

An intention to break the contract

Intention to cause a breach of contract must not be confused with motive. It is not necessary for the plaintiff to show that the defendant acted out of spite or ill will,[17] or that the defendant's aim was to damage the plaintiff *per se*.[18] The authorities link intention with foreseeability – if the defendant can foresee that the consequences of his or her actions will be a breach of contract, the defendant intends its breach. On this test, intention is inextricably linked to the level of knowledge the defendant has of the contract. A defendant intends to cause the breach where he or she takes deliberate steps knowing that breach will be a consequence of his or her actions. In the more straightforward cases of inducing breach of an employment contract, a union defendant is clearly aware that employees who follow a strike call will invariably break their contracts of employment.[19]

As we saw earlier, where commercial contracts are concerned, it is not always the case that the defendant knows that his or her actions will precipitate a breach of contract (due to the defendant's ignorance of the terms of such contracts). Diplock LJ in *Emerald Construction v Lowthian*[20] refused to accept the assertion that, in these circumstances, a defendant does not possess the necessary intent to cause breach.[21] Mere knowledge (actual or constructive) that a contract exists will suffice.

Once the defendant possesses (or is deemed to possess) knowledge of the contract, the defendant has the necessary intention to cause its breach even where he or she does not act deliberately, but is 'recklessly indifferent' to whether a breach occurs or not.[22] This broad test was applied in the county court in *Falconer v ASLEF and NUR*,[23] where a commuter sued the rail unions for inducing a breach of his contract of travel with British Rail. Although the industrial action was aimed at British Rail, rather than the plaintiff, the court held that the breach of the plaintiff's contract was a foreseeable and unavoidable consequence of the action. In such circumstances (where the unions knew of the contract

---

16 [1993] ICR 612, p 621, *per* Neil LJ: '... in many cases a third party (to a contract) may be deemed to know of the almost certain existence of a contract and indeed of some of its likely terms.'

17 Lord MacNaghten in *Quinn v Leathem* [1901] AC 495, p 510; *South Wales Miners' Federation v Glamorgan Coal Co Ltd* [1905] AC 239, p 246; and Slade J in *Grieg v Insole* [1978] 1 WLR 302, pp 336–38.

18 In a departure from previous case law, Henry J in *Barretts & Baird v IPCS* [1987] IRLR 3, p 10, had argued that liability could not be imposed for this tort unless the defendant's predominant purpose was to cause injury to the plaintiff rather than to promote their own self-interest. This view was subsequently rejected by Stuart-Smith LJ in *Edwin Hill & Partners v First National Finance Corp* [1989] 1 WLR 225, p 234, and by Dillon LJ in *Lonhro v Fayed* [1989] 2 All ER 65, p 74.

19 Jenkins LJ in *Cunard Co v Stacey* (1955) 2 LR 247, p 258.

20 [1966] 1 WLR 691.

21 At p 697. See, also, Slade J in *Grieg v Insole* [1978] 1 WLR 302, p 337 and Diplock's further comments on intention in *Merkur Island Shipping Co v Laughton* [1983] IRLR 218, p 222.

22 Denning MR in *Emerald Construction v Lowthian* [1966] 1 WLR 691, p 701 stated: '... if the officers deliberately sought to get this contract terminated, heedless of its terms, regardless whether it was terminated by breach or not, they would do wrong. For it is unlawful for a third party to procure a breach of contract knowingly, or recklessly, indifferent to whether it is a breach or not.' See Dean, M, 'Recklessness and inducing breach of contract' (1967) 30 MLR 208.

23 [1986] IRLR 331. Noted by Rubin, G (1987) JBL 308.

and the risk of breach), the defendant's possessed the requisite intention as they were 'reckless to the consequences' to the plaintiff.[24]

The application of the 'recklessness' test in this way has been strongly criticised as it expands the range of potential plaintiffs from a limited number of employers and suppliers to members of the public who, as part of a determinable class, are caused incidental loss as a by-product of the action. Arguably, the defendant's action must also be directed or targeted against the plaintiff; the fact that the plaintiff is a foreseeable victim of the defendant's conduct is not enough.[25]

Thus, in conclusion, the requirement for intention is satisfied where either the defendant acts with the specific intention to cause a breach of the contract, as in actually foreseeing that a breach would occur and desiring these consequences, or is reckless as to the consequences of their actions to a particular plaintiff.[26]

Inducement to break the contract

The requirement that the defendant should induce the breach of contract provides the link of causation between the intention to commit the unlawful act and the loss suffered by the plaintiff. The clearest example of inducement is where union members are instructed to take industrial action, or threatened or coerced into doing so, resulting in a breach of an employment contract. A threat against a commercial company that strike action will be taken unless they break a commercial contract with a business the union is in dispute with, also constitutes inducement.

However, there are a variety of ways of intervening in contractual relations short of this active inducement of breach. The Donovan Commission[27] identified a clear boundary between the giving of mere advice or information to an individual and actively encouraging, persuading or instructing a person to break a contract:

> a trade union official who advises a customer of an employer in dispute that he should consider his business relations with that employer in the light of the dispute, commits no tort even if in consequence of such advice the customer breaks his contract ... [nor] will it ... constitute an inducement to break a contract even if he calls attention to the possible dangers for the customer of continuing to deal with the employer in dispute.[28]

In *DC Thomson Ltd v Deakin*, Jenkins LJ suggested that general exhortations issued in the course of a trade dispute such as 'Stop supplies to X', 'Refuse to handle X's goods', were not necessarily unlawful inducements as, '... in general, appeals to others to prevent a given

---

24 Members of the public now have an explicit statutory right to take action in circumstances similar to the *Falconer* case. This is examined below, p 323.

25 Jenkins LJ, in DC *Thomson Ltd v Deakin* [1952] Ch 646; Dillon LJ, in *Lonhro plc v Fayed* [1989] 2 All ER 65; Neil LJ, in *Middlebrook Mushrooms Ltd v TGWU* [1993] ICR 612.

26 Note that a defendant may still possess the necessary intent to cause a breach even where there is an honest (but false) belief that the action will not cause a breach of contract – *MBC of Solihull v NUT* [1985] IRLR 211 (belief that withdrawal of 'goodwill' was not a breach of contract), cf *BIP Ltd v Ferguson* [1938] 4 All ER 504.

27 Royal Commission on Trade Unions and Employers' Associations, Cmnd 3623, 1968 .

28 Paragraph 891.

person from obtaining goods or services ... is a purpose capable of being lawfully carried out, and there can, therefore, be nothing unlawful in advocating it ...'.[29]

In other cases, however, inducement has been given a much wider interpretation. Winn LJ in the Court of Appeal, in *Torquay Hotel Co Ltd v Cousins*,[30] was of the opinion that the mere provision of information or advice could amount to inducement in appropriate circumstances as:

> ... it would surely be said that a father who told his daughter that her fiance had been convicted of indecent exposure, had thereby induced her ... to break the engagement. A man who writes to his mother-in-law telling her that the central heating in his house has gone down may thereby induce her to cancel an intended visit.[31]

In *Square Grip Reinforcement Co Ltd v MacDonald*,[32] Lord Milligan also believed that statements or advice had to be construed in the context of the circumstances.[33] Hence, an inducement had occurred where union officials provided workers with certain information concerning a recognition dispute elsewhere, knowing that on hearing this information the workers were highly likely to take industrial action.

Despite the narrower interpretation of 'inducement' applied by Templeman J in *Camellia Tanker Ltd v ITWF*,[34] the Court of Appeal reverted to the much wider construction of the term in *Union Traffic v TGWU*.[35] The court ruled that even where pickets are not actively persuading employees to break their employment contracts their mere presence at the entrance to a workplace may be sufficient to amount to an inducement.

The modern position is therefore to construe the requirement of inducement quite widely. If the gist of the words used or the act committed, in the prevailing circumstances, effects a breach of the contract, then the element of inducement of breach has been satisfied.

Actual breach of the contract[36]

As noted earlier, in Chapter 13, employees who take industrial action commit a fundamental breach of their contract of employment. Whether there is an actual breach of a commercial contract depends on an examination of the terms of that contract. Moreover, Jenkins LJ, in *DC Thomson Ltd v Deakin*, considered that where the plaintiff is alleging indirect inducement of breach of a commercial contract of supply it must be shown that, because of the withdrawal of the services of the employees concerned, the contract breaker was in practice unable to perform the contract.[37] So, for example, where a commercial

---

29   At p 698. See also Evershed MR, p 686.

30   [1969] 2 Ch 106.

31   At p 147.

32   1968 SLT 65. Noted by Wedderburn, KW (now Lord) (1968) 31 MLR 550.

33   See also Lord Pearce in *Stratford v Lindley* [1965] AC 269, p 333.

34   [1976] ICR 274. Noted by Wedderburn, KW (now Lord) (1976) 39 MLR 715.

35   [1989] IRLR 127.

36   Since liability is based on breach of an existing contract there is no liability for persuading a third party to refuse to make a contract (*Middlebrook Mushrooms Ltd v TGWU* [1993] ICR 612, cf *Union Traffic Ltd v TGWU* [1989] IRLR 127) or for persuading a third party to rescind a voidable or illegal contract (*Grieg v Insole* [1978] 1 WLR 302), unless unlawful means are used.

37   Jenkins LJ, in *DC Thomson Ltd v Deakin* [1952] 1 Ch 646, p 696.

contract of supply is broken (due to strike action by lorry driver employees), but the goods or services could be provided by some other alternative means (such as by hiring alternative transport), liability will not ensue as there has not been a breach of the contract of supply as a 'necessary consequence' of the defendant's act.

Although this analysis of loss deriving from the breach of contract is correct *per se*, the requirement for breach is not as important as it once was as a consequence of the judicial development of the tort of interference short of breach, considered later in this chapter. On the basis of 'interference' rather than breach, the Court of Appeal in *Dimbleby & Sons Ltd v NUJ*,[38] were prepared to impose liability and grant an injunction even though there had been no overt disruption of the contract of supply.

The defence of justification[39]

Where all the ingredients of the tort are present it may still be possible for the defendant to escape liability if it can be shown in the particular circumstances of the case that there was 'sufficient justification' in law for the inducement of breach. Although there is no complete and satisfactory definition of the common law defence of justification, the parameters of the defence do not extend to the circumstances of an industrial dispute. Trade union action in inducing breach of contract for the purposes of achieving benefits for their membership is not sufficient justification; even where the defendant trade unionist was acting in good faith and with an absence of malice.

This was the essence of the judgment of Romer LJ in the Court of Appeal in *South Wales Miners' Federation v Glamorgan Coal Co*.[40] Miners were paid on a sliding scale dependent on the selling price of coal. The scarcer coal was, the higher the price of coal and the higher the miners' wages. To increase their members' wages, the trade union persuaded its members to turn up for work intermittently, so as to limit the supply of coal. Although the union had no dispute with the employer and took action genuinely believing that it was in the best interests of their members and of the employer, Romer LJ refused to apply the defence as:

> ... a defendant sued for knowingly procuring such a breach is not justified of necessity merely by showing that he had no personal animus against the employer or that it was to the advantage or interest of both the defendant and the workman that the contract should be broken.[41]

The defence has only been successfully invoked in cases where the defendant has acted in furtherance of a moral duty or in the public interest. For example, in *Brimelow v Casson*,[42] the defendant justifiably induced chorus girls to leave the plaintiff's employment because there was evidence that they were paid such low wages that they resorted to prostitution. Simonds J in *Camden Nominees v Foray*[43] doubted the decision in *Brimelow* and attempted

---

38   [1984] IRLR 67.
39   See, generally, Hansen, B (1975) 38 MLR 217 and O'Dair, R (1991) 11 OJLS 227.
40   [1903] 2 KB 545.
41   At p 574. See, also, Slade J in *Grieg v Insole* [1978] I WLR 302, pp 340–42.
42   [1924] 1 Ch 302.
43   [1940] Ch 352.

to narrow the defence with the argument that the defence should be restricted to cases where persons act in pursuance of a legal, rather than moral duty: for example, a doctor who is in a legal relationship with his patient may instruct an employee to give up work for health reasons without attracting liability for inducing breach of the patient's contract of employment.[44]

Interference with contract or with trade and business

As a consequence of an expansionist and innovative approach to trade union liability, the tort of directly or indirectly inducing breach of contract has been supplemented in recent years by the tort(s) of interference with contract and with trade or business short of breach.

The components of the tort of interference with contract was discussed in some detail by Denning MR in *Torquay Hotel Ltd v Cousins*.[45] The plaintiff hotel owner had criticised the defendant's actions in a dispute the union had with other hotel owners in the region. In response, the union telephoned the oil company Esso, advising them directly that oil supplies to the plaintiff's hotel should cease and that any supplies delivered would be met by a picket line. The contract for the supply of oil between the hotel and Esso included a *force majeure* exemption clause which limited Esso's liability in circumstances where a failure to supply oil was due to an industrial dispute. Arguably, on the construction of the contract there was no breach, a necessary element of the tort of inducing breach of contract.[46]

Denning MR declared that, although there had not been a breach of contract, interference short of breach was in itself actionable, as '... [t]he time has come when the principle (of inducing breach of contract) should be extended to cover deliberate and direct interference with the execution of a contract ...'.[47] Liability for interference with the performance of a contract short of breach would be imposed so long as the interference was deliberate, the defendant had knowledge of the contract or at least turned a blind eye to its contents; and, if the interference was indirect, unlawful means was present.

Lord Diplock in the House of Lords took the opportunity to re-evaluate Denning's judgment in Torquay in *Merkur Island v Laughton*.[48] Here, the International Transport Workers Federation (ITWF), in its campaign against low wages, organised the boycotting of a Liberian registered ship by tugs in the River Mersey resulting in the disruption of a contract of hire between the owners and the hirers of the ship. The contract included a clause which provided that cancellation of the contract was permitted, and payment for hire would cease, if the ship was boycotted due to an industrial dispute.

---

44 See also *Pritchard v Briggs* [1980] 1 All ER 294, pp 327–28; *Edwin Hill & Partners v First National Finance Co* [1988] 3 All ER 801, pp 805–06; and *Timeplan Education Group Ltd v National Union of Teachers* [1997] IRLR 457, p 460.

45 [1969] 2 Ch 106, noted by Grabiner, A (1969) 32 MLR 435.

46 Wynn and Russell LJJ proceeded on the basis that there had in fact been a breach of the commercial contract. The exemption clause merely prevented the hotel from suing under the contract.

47 At p 138.

48 [1983] IRLR 218. Noted by Carty, H (1983) 12 ILJ 166.

Lord Diplock held first that these exclusion clauses did not affect the liability of the defendants for indirectly inducing breach of contract by unlawful means (the unlawful means being the union's inducement of the tugmen to break their contracts of employment). There had been a breach of a primary obligation in the contract, even though the secondary obligation to pay the hire charges or damages for breach had been removed by the exclusion clause.[49] Diplock also concurred with Lord Denning's radical opinion that there existed the tort of interference with the performance of a contract short of breach, arguing that:

> Parliamentary recognition that the tort of actionable interference with contractual rights is as broad as Lord Denning stated in Torquay ... is in my view to be found in s 13(1) of the TULRA 1974 which refers to inducement not only 'to break a contract' but also 'to interfere with its performance' and treats them as being *pari materia*.[50]

Critics of Diplock's judgment have focused on his citation of Denning's very wide formulation of the tort that interference short of breach unaccompanied by any unlawful means is actionable, that is, that direct or 'bare' interference with contract is tortious. It is suggested that this cannot be correct as a tort of this nature is contrary to established precedent stemming from *Allen v Flood* [51] that direct interference requires some form of unlawful means.[52]

In *Torquay v Cousins*, Denning had also endorsed the views of Lord Reid and Viscount Radcliffe in *Stratford v Lindley* [53] that there existed a wider tort; of interference with trade or business intentionally caused by the defendant's use of unlawful means.[54] The existence of this tort of unlawful interference with trade or business was confirmed by the Court of Appeal in *Hadmor Productions Ltd v Hamilton*.[55] The plaintiff was an independent TV production company which was engaged in contractual negotiations with Thames TV concerning the transmission of certain of their programmes. During the dispute, the defendants threatened to instruct their members at Thames TV to refuse to transmit any programmes produced by the plaintiff.

Lord Denning MR in the Court of Appeal held that this was an actionable indirect interference with the plaintiff's trade and business by the unlawful means of threatening to induce breach of employment contracts by strike action. Hadmor had a reasonable commercial expectation that a contract would be finalised and the programmes would be broadcast. This expectation had been shattered and frustrated by the union's boycott.

---

49 Diplock's treatment of this type of clause was applied by the county court, in *Falconer v ASLEF* and *NUR* [1986] IRLR 311, and approved by the Court of Appeal in *Associated British Ports v TGWU* [1989] 1 WLR 939.

50 Parliament had, however, amended the scope of this immunity in 1974 as a cautionary response to the judgment in *Torquay v Cousins*. Patently, the fear that the courts might continue to expand the tort of inducing breach to outflank the immunities in exactly the manner illustrated by the judgment in *Torquay v Cousins* was well founded.

51 [1898] AC 1.

52 See Lord Wedderburn, 'Lawmakers and craftsmen' (1983) 46 MLR 632.

53 [1965] AC 269, pp 324 and 328. See the note by Wedderburn , KW (now Lord) (1965) 28 MLR 205.

54 See further on this tort, Carty, H (1983) 3 *Legal Studies* 193 and Wedderburn, KW (now Lord) (1972) 35 MLR 184.

55 [1981] ICR 690.

Lord Diplock in the House of Lords[56] referred to this tort approvingly although in deciding *prima facie* first stage liability he preferred to found liability in the tort of intimidation.[57]

As we have seen, this tort is primarily the invention of Lord Denning in the Court of Appeal, assisted by Lord Diplock in the House of Lords. Few other senior members of the judiciary have been quite such enthusiastic proponents.[58] More recent judicial statements[59] have recognised the existence of the tort, but as it has rarely been directly at issue, there is still some doubt as to the exact boundaries of liability. The tort thus awaits further clarification by the House of Lords.

Unlawful means

A direct inducement to break (or interfere) with a contract is unlawful in itself, so there is no additional requirement for any form of unlawful means. Where there is an indirect inducement to break or interfere with a contract, such as where a breach of an employment contract prevents the performance of another commercial contract, unlawful means is required.

In this example, unlawful means is straightforward – the tort of direct inducement to break the contract of employment. However, this common form of unlawful means in industrial disputes (as well as the torts of intimidation and conspiracy) is not unlawful means for the purposes of indirect liability where the action taken is 'in contemplation or furtherance of a trade dispute'. This is because the statutory immunities provide that such torts 'are not actionable', which has been interpreted to mean that they are not 'unlawful'.[60] Therefore, the courts have resorted to finding new forms of illegalities, outside the protection of the immunities, to act as unlawful means.[61]

---

56 [1982] IRLR 102. The Court of Appeal and House of Lords judgments are noted by Simpson, B (1982) 45 MLR 447; Newell, D (1982) 11 ILJ 111; and JMT (1982) 98 LQR 342.

57 In *Merkur Island*, Lord Diplock considered that inducing breach of contract and interference with contractual performance were aspects of the wider generalised tort of interference with trade or business by unlawful means. He also introduced a requirement into this tort that the defendant must have 'an intention to injure or harm' the plaintiff. There is some uncertainty as to how far this requirement differs from the degree of intent required for inducing breach of contract; cf the judgment on this issue of Henry J in *Barretts & Baird v IPCS* [1987] IRLR 3 and the Court of Appeal in *Associated British Ports v TGWU* [1989] 1 WLR 939.

58 Although, see the judgment of the Court of Appeal in *Dimbleby & Sons Ltd v NUJ* [1984] IRLR 67.

59 Dillon LJ, in *Lonrho v Fayed* [1989] 3 WLR 631, p 636; Stuart Smith LJ and Neil LJ, in *Associated British Ports v TGWU* [1989] 1 WLR 939; Bingham LJ, in *Union Traffic Ltd v TGWU* [1989] ICR 98, pp 105–06.

60 See the House of Lords' judgment in *Hadmor Productions Ltd v Hamilton* [1982] IRLR 102, p 110.

61 Despite Lord Denning's statement in *Torquay* [1968] 2 Ch 106, p 139, that unlawful means is any act a defendant 'is not at liberty to commit', the modern approach is to look for an act that is actionable in tort (such as nuisance or trespass: *MGN Ltd v NGA* [1984] IRLR 397). With this in mind, some of the older examples of unlawful means must be doubted. See *Daily Mirror Newspaper Ltd v Gardner* [1968] 2 QB 762 (operating an agreement contrary to restrictive practices legislation); *Camellia Tanker v ITWF* [1976] ICR 274 (alleged breach of local bylaws); *Acrow (Automation) Ltd v Rex Chainbelt Inc* [1971] 1 WLR 1676 (contempt of court); *Associated Newspapers v Wade* [1979] IRLR 201 (interference with the freedom of the press contrary to Art 10 of the European Convention on Human Rights).

One question of some significance which arose in *Barretts & Baird Ltd v IPCS*[62] is whether an employee's own breach of employment contract committed during strike action could be unlawful means for the purposes of inducing breach of a commercial contract or interference with business. The House of Lords in *Rookes v Barnard*[63] thought that it was the threat of breach, not the breach itself that was unlawful means.[64] To ensure that no future expansionist court resurrected the issue, the Labour Government piloted through a provision in the Trade Union and Labour Relations Act 1974 which stated that 'for the avoidance of doubt' a bare breach of contract was not unlawful means for the purposes of establishing liability in tort. However, on the repeal of this provision by the Employment Act 1980, the law was returned to a state of some uncertainty.

Consequently, in *Barretts & Baird*, Henry J held that it was arguable that a breach of an employment contract *per se* can be unlawful means for the purposes of an action by a third party for breach of commercial contracts caused by the strike action so long as there was an intent to injure the third party plaintiff.[65] As this case was not appealed to a higher court, it must remain an open question whether the reasoning in the case is correct. Should this be followed in future cases it would have dramatic consequences. It would mean that those on strike would be liable in tort for inducing breach of commercial contracts[66] whilst the organisers of the strike would continue to enjoy the protection of the immunities.

INTIMIDATION

This tort has a direct and indirect form: it is committed where unlawful threats are made directly to the plaintiff or to a third party with the intention of causing the plaintiff loss.

An example of a direct threat is where employer A is compelled to improve pay because of threats of personal violence made against him by B, a union official. The indirect form of the tort occurs where employee A is dismissed by employer B because union official C threatens physical destruction of employer B's business unless A is dismissed, or where union A threatens violence against employee B, to force him or her to strike so as to damage company C.

The tort of intimidation can be traced back to 18th century cases, such as *Tarleton v McGawley*,[67] where the master of a trading ship A, off the coast of Africa, fired a warning shot at a canoe, the third party, which was about to trade with another ship, B, a commercial rival of ship A. As a result, the canoe turned back and the rival trading ship B

---

62   [1987] IRLR 3. For discussion of the wider implications of this case, see Fredman, S (1987) 104 LQR 176; Napier, B [1987] CLJ 221; Simpson, B (1987) 50 MLR 506; Benedictus, R (1987) 16 ILJ 191.

63   [1964] AC 1129.

64   See Weir, T [1964] CLJ 225.

65   We saw earlier that this requirement of 'intent to injure' may be an overstatement of the degree of intention required.

66   Strikers would only be liable in damages as TULR(C)A 1992, s 236, precludes the granting of an injunction or an order of specific performance which has the effect of compelling an employee to perform his or her employment contract.

67   (1793) 1 Peake 270.

lost business and subsequent profits. It was this threat of violence against the third party resulting in loss to ship B which was actionable as tortious intimidation.

In the industrial field, unions can secure their aims by the threat of industrial action and ordinarily do not need to resort to violent tactics.[68] Consequently, until the landmark case of *Rookes v Barnard*,[69] this tort was rarely committed by trade unionists threatening strike action. The House of Lords in *Rookes v Barnard* revolutionised the law on intimidation by holding that a threat to break an employment contract (that is, a threat to go on strike) was an unlawful threat for the purposes of the tort of intimidation.[70]

The Court of Appeal[71] had refused to extend 'this obscure, unfamiliar and peculiar cause of action ...' to cases where '... there is only a threat to break a contract'.[72] The Court of Appeal noted that, if the law was extended, it would undermine the privity rule in contract – as a plaintiff cannot sue for loss which results from actual breach of a contract to which he was not a party – it was surely questionable that he should be entitled to sue for loss which results from a mere threat to break a contract to which he was not a party.

By contrast, Lord Devlin in the House of Lords found such arguments unconvincing and went on to hold that the threat to break or to induce others to break a contract of employment was as much an illegal threat for the purposes of the tort as a threat to commit violence to person or property, as '... all that matters to the plaintiff is that, metaphorically speaking, a club has been used. It does not matter to the plaintiff what the club is made of – whether it is a physical club or an economic club, a tortious club or an otherwise illegal club'.[73]

Lord Devlin was strongly supported by the other members of the House of Lords. Lord Reid believed 'intimidation of any kind was objectionable ...' and found no difference in principle between a threat to break a contract and a threat to commit a tort as 'threatening a breach of contract may be a much more coercive weapon than threatening a tort, particularly when the threat is directed against a company or corporation'.[74]

This decision of the House of Lords caused understandable alarm in the union movement.[75] Kahn-Freund described the decision as a 'frontal attack upon the right to strike'. Wedderburn observed that it was '... one strange result [of] the common law'[76] that a mere threat to strike was unlawful when actual strike action itself was not.

---

68 For examples of actionable intimidation caused by threats of violence, see *NGN Ltd v SOGAT 82* [1986] IRLR 337.

69 [1964] AC 1129.

70 Here, threats were made by a full time union official and two employed branch officers that, unless a non-union employee was removed or transferred, strike action would be taken against the employer. As a consequence of the threats, the plaintiff was subsequently dismissed.

71 [1963] 1 QB 623.

72 *Per* Pearson LJ, p 695. For comment on the High Court and Court of Appeal decisions, see Wedderburn, KW (now Lord) (1961) 24 MLR 572 and (1962) 25 MLR 513.

73 [1964] AC 1129, p 1209.

74 At p 1169. The threat must be of substance; of sufficient seriousness to induce or coerce the third party or plaintiff to submit to the wishes of the defendant and must be capable of being carried out: *Hodges v Webb* [1920] 2 Ch 70, applying *Conway v Wade* [1909] AC 506, p 510.

75 For an analysis of the House of Lords' decision in *Rookes v Barnard* and its implications, see Wedderburn, KW (now Lord), 'Intimidation and the right to strike' (1964) 27 MLR 257; Hoffman, L, '*Rookes v Barnard*' (1965) 81 LQR 116; Hamson, C [1964] CLJ 159

76 *The Worker and the Law*, 3rd edn, 1986, p 42.

In *Morgan v Fry*,[77] Denning MR had suggested that, in some circumstances, justification may be a defence to this tort.[78] For example, threats may be justified where a union official had issued threats against union members working with members of a break away union, if the break away union were 'really trouble makers who fomented discord ... without lawful cause or excuse'.[79]

The development of this new tort was a highly effective method of 'outflanking' the existing immunities, until the Trade Disputes Act 1965, a year later, closed off liability by explicitly bestowing an immunity on strike organisers and union members for threatening to induce a breach of an employment contract or threatening to break an employment contract.

CONSPIRACY

Until 1875, trade unions committed the crime of criminal conspiracy when taking concerted action to raise wages or generally to protect their members' interests. Although s 3 of the Conspiracy and Protection of Property Act 1875 abolished the notion of criminal conspiracy, it left untouched the concept of tortious conspiracy. Two forms of the tort of conspiracy may be distinguished; general conspiracy to injure, often known as simple conspiracy, and the more specific conspiracy to commit an unlawful act.

Conspiracy to injure

This form of conspiracy occurs where two or more persons combine for the intended purpose of injuring another without justification. It may well be that the activity in itself is lawful if undertaken by an individual. However, the law on tortious conspiracy has developed on the basis that acts done in combination may make 'oppressive or dangerous that which if it proceeded only from a single person would be otherwise'.[80]

Thus *prima facie*, economic loss caused to an employer by interference with workers' contracts is actionable as a conspiracy to injure unless it could be said the union's actions were justified in some way.

In the commercial case of *Mogul Steamship Co v McGregor, Gow & Co*,[81] the Court of Appeal had held that an association of shipowners who had driven a rival shipowner out of business by lowering their charges had not committed an actionable conspiracy as they had acted merely to protect their legitimate trade and their profits which was a justifiable aim of their competitive pricing policy. The real purpose of the combination was to advance the commercial interests of the association, not to cause the loss to the plaintiff.

---

77 [1968] 2 QB 710, p 729.

78 See also Denning's comments in *Cory Lighterage Ltd v TGWU* [1973] ICR 339, pp 356–57. The case is noted by Hepple, B (1973) 36 MLR 545.

79 Lord Devlin raised the issue of justification in *Rookes v Barnard* [1964] AC 1129, p 1206, but failed to elaborate fully on its relevance to the tort of intimidation.

80 Bowen LJ in *Mogul* (1889) 23 QBD 598, p 616. Lord Diplock, in *Lonhro v Shell Petroleum Ltd* [1982] AC 173, pp 188–89, doubted the logical basis for this tort but recognised that it was 'too well established to be discarded, however anomalous it may seem today'.

81 (1889) 23 QB 598.

In *Quinn v Leathem*,[82] trade union interests were barely recognised by the House of Lords. The defendants, wishing to enforce a closed shop, prevailed upon an important customer not to trade with the plaintiff after the plaintiff had refused to dismiss non-union staff. The House of Lords justified a finding of actionable conspiracy on the grounds that the combination of workers had intentionally caused loss to the plaintiff and their main purpose in doing so was not to further their own legitimate interests in setting up a closed shop, but to injure the plaintiff for reasons of revenge.

This decision was a serious blow to trade union attempts to obtain benefits for their membership via industrial action and was one of the catalysts for the passage of the Trade Disputes Act 1906 which provided an immunity for this and other torts. However, the immunity for conspiracy is now rarely required as, in a change of judicial attitudes after the First World War, trade union objects were legitimised by a number of judgments.[83] The House of Lords' decision in *Crofter Handwoven Harris Tweed Co v Veitch*[84] confirmed that no liability will attach to a trade union engaged in a genuine trade dispute with a plaintiff; such as on an issue concerning terms and conditions of employment. Once the *bona fide* trade union purpose is established, whether or not the defendants knew damage to the plaintiff was a consequence of their actions is not relevant;[85] nor is the fact that that the conspirators behave in 'a selfish, tyrannous and irresponsible' manner.[86]

Where there are mixed motives for the union's action, such as where the main purpose is to protect or enhance a legitimate interest, but another reason for the action is because of a degree of ill will towards the plaintiff, the legitimate interest must be 'predominant'.[87] For instance, in *Huntley v Thornton*,[88] members of a strike committee pressurised the employer to take action against a non-striking member of the union. This was an actionable conspiracy as the defendants 'were not furthering a trade dispute but a grudge ... or personal matter'.[89]

Conspiracy to commit an unlawful act

This second form of conspiracy occurs where a combination intentionally inflicts damage on another by the use of unlawful means. The conspirators have committed a separate unlawful act and this, committed in combination, is the additional tort of conspiracy. In the industrial context there may be liability for conspiracy to commit the tort of inducing breach of contract, or conspiracy to commit the tort of intimidation. Pickets during a

---

82 [1901] AC 495.
83 See *White v Riley* [1921] 1 Ch 1; *Reynolds v Shipping Federation* [1924] 1 Ch 28; *Sorrell v Smith* [1925] AC 700.
84 [1942] AC 435.
85 Viscount Simon, p 445.
86 *Stratford v Lindley* [1965] AC 269, p 300, *per* Salmon LJ.
87 On the judicially defined legitimate objectives of trade unions and their members, see also *Scala Ballroom (Wolverhampton) Ltd v Ratcliffe* [1958] 1 WLR 1057; *Stratford v Lindley* [1965] AC 269.
88 [1957] 1 WLR 321.
89 Harman J, p 350.

dispute may, by their actions, individually commit the tort of nuisance. They may together be additionally liable for the tort of conspiracy to commit a nuisance.[90]

As these acts above are unlawful in themselves, there may be little need to frame an action in conspiracy because each of the individual conspirators will be liable for the wrong they have committed. Very occasionally, such an action in conspiracy may be used to sue an individual who has not committed any wrong but who was involved in the dispute. This occurred in *Rookes v Barnard*.[91] The full time union official could not have been sued for the tort of intimidation in threatening to break a contract of employment because he was not employed by the third party employer and so did not have a contract to break. But, in organising the threats to break the contracts of employment, he was sued for conspiring to commit the tort of intimidation.

The ambit of the tort was substantially narrowed by the judgment of the House of Lords in *Lonhro Ltd v Shell Petroleum Ltd*.[92] It was held by Lord Diplock that, for liability to arise, the conspirator's predominant purpose must be to injure the plaintiff rather than to further or preserve their own legitimate interests. Otherwise, he said, the tort would be extended beyond its natural parameters.

However, more recent House of Lords authority has cast doubt on Diplock's judgment. In *Lonhro Ltd v Fayed*[93] the House of Lords refused to accept Diplock's reasoning in *Shell* and concluded that, as there must be a distinction between the two forms of conspiracy, an intention to injure the plaintiff was an issue relevant only to simple conspiracy.[94] Consequently, if the conspiracy was unlawful – in that the parties were actively engaged in some illegal activity, such as breach of contract, tort or crime – then the predominant purpose of the combiners was irrelevant, whether or not the purpose was to further or protect a legitimate interest of their own.[95]

OTHER LIABILITIES

In order to outflank the immunities, the courts have not only expanded the basis of unlawful means but have also generated further illegalities which provide employers with new causes of action in civil law unconstrained by the immunities; the most important being inducing breach of a statutory duty, economic duress and breach of an equitable obligation.

---

90 A question that arises is what is unlawful means for the purposes of this tort. In *Lonhro Ltd v Shell Petroleum Ltd*, the House of Lords refused to extend liability in tort for a conspiracy to commit criminal acts where no tortious liability arose *per se*. In *Rookes v Barnard*, Lord Devlin was unsure whether conspiring to break a contract *per se* could be unlawful means for this tort. On whether a breach of statute constitutes unlawful means sufficient to ground an action in conspiracy, see *Michaels v Taylor Woodrow Developments Ltd* [2000] 4 All ER 645.

91 [1964] AC 1129.

92 [1982] AC 173.

93 [1991] 3 All ER 303.

94 *Per* Lord Bridge, p 312: '... I am quite unable to accept that Lord Diplock or other members of the Appellate Committee concurring with him, of whom I was one, intended the decision in *Lonhro v Shell* to effect ... such a significant change in the law as it had been previously understood.'

95 For further discussion on the issue of intention in conspiracy, see Sales, P [1990] CLJ 491.

Inducing breach of a statutory duty

Industrial action may result in the contravention of a statutory duty imposed on employees or on employers. In certain limited circumstances, employers or third party suppliers may have a remedy for this illegality. A clear example is provided in *Cunard Co v Stacey*[96] where the Court of Appeal construed the Merchant Shipping Act 1894 in such a way as to permit the employers to sue the union organisers of industrial action in tort who had induced their members to break provisions of the Act that criminalised strike action.

However, not every breach of a criminal statute is necessarily unlawful at civil law, as not every crime is a tort. In *Gouriet v UPW*,[97] Post Office workers, by delaying mail to South Africa, had *prima facie* committed criminal offences under the Post Office Act 1953. The High Court decision to refuse to permit an action in tort against the defendant on the grounds that there was no power within the statute for the plaintiff to sue for breach of statutory duty was subsequently supported by the House of Lords.[98] This judgment was further endorsed by the House of Lords in *Lonhro Ltd v Shell Petroleum*.[99] Their Lordships made it clear that a breach of statutory duty (which may have criminal or civil ramifications) does not by itself give rise to a civil action by a particular plaintiff unless it can be shown, on the construction of the statute, that a duty is explicitly owed to the plaintiff as a member of an identifiable class.

Lord Denning MR[100] attempted to develop a wider general rule in *Meade v Haringey BC*,[101] which does not depend upon the scope and language of the statute.[102] Here, the parents of children who were unable to go to school because of strike action by ancillary staff issued writs to enforce the local authority to perform their statutory duty to provide full time education under the Education Act 1944. As, according to Denning, '[t]he trade unions were the dominating influence in requiring the schools to be closed ...',[103] this was a call on the local authority to break its statutory duty to provide full time education which was arguably unlawful means for the purposes of an action in tort by those injured by the action.

Likewise, in *Associated Newspapers v Wade*,[104]Denning argued that a refusal by printers across the newspaper industry to handle the advertisements and notices of public bodies interfered with their statutory duty to publish. This constituted unlawful means for the tort of indirectly inducing breach of contract and was actionable in its direct form of hindering performance of statutory duties, as '... trade union leaders have no immunity when a public authority is disabled from performing its statutory duties'.[105]

---

96 [1955] 2 LR 247.
97 [1978] AC 435.
98 See further on this case Simpson, R, 'Gouriet: labour law aspects' (1978) 41 MLR 63.
99 [1982] AC 173.
100 Assisted by Eveleigh LJ.
101 [1979] 2 All ER 1016.
102 See also Lord Wright in *Crofter* [1942] AC 435, p 462, who enunciated a more general approach to determining an actionable breach of statute.
103 At p 1026.
104 [1979] IRLR 201, noted by Simpson, R (1979) 42 MLR 701.
105 At p 206.

Considering the extent of public services regulated by statute, Denning's approach, if correct, would be of some significance, and of some concern, to public sector unions. However, Denning's broad formulation,[106] which gives third parties automatic rights of action on breach of statute, has been disavowed in subsequent cases which have re-emphasised the strict 'construction' test for establishing an actionable breach of statutory duty.[107]

Consequently, inducing breach of statutory duty is only germane to liability where the statutory duty is interpreted appropriately. By way of an example, in *Barretts & Baird v IPCS*,[108] fatstock officers, employed by the Meat and Livestock Commission (which had the statutory function of inspecting and certifying animals for slaughter) took industrial action via a series of one day strikes, causing loss to the plaintiff meat producers. Henry J held that, on the construction of the duty imposed by statute, the plaintiff did have a cause of action which could amount to the tort of inducing breach of statutory duty or constitute unlawful means for the purposes of interference with contract.[109]

In *Associated British Ports v TGWU*,[110] the trade unions objected to proposals to abolish the statutory scheme regulating the supply of dock labour.[111] After negotiations with employers failed, the unions threatened to take strike action. A clause in the scheme established by statute was '... to work for such periods as are reasonable in the circumstances of the case'.

Although the Court of Appeal accepted that, on the construction of the statute, this clause was not actionable at the suit of the plaintiff, there was an arguable case that by calling for industrial action the union was inducing a breach of a (non-actionable) statutory obligation, that is, inducing a breach by the registered dockworkers of an obligation to work – which constituted unlawful means for the purposes of any other subsequent liability to commercial suppliers. The House of Lords believed this clause solely imposed a contractual rather than a statutory requirement to work; therefore, the issue of breach of statutory duty and unlawful means did not arise. Their Lordships, however, failed to reject directly the Court of Appeal's view that a non-actionable breach of statute could be unlawful means for the purposes of the other economic torts.

Economic duress

Economic duress is a contractual doctrine, whereby a contract is declared void if it is entered into on the basis of duress. Usually, the doctrine operates where one party is in such a strong bargaining position that the will of the other party is coerced by the other's

---

106 Also strongly argued by Denning in *ex p Island Records* [1978] Ch 122, p 136.

107 See *Lonhro Ltd v Shell Petroleum Ltd* [1982] AC 173, p187; *RCA v Pollard* [1983] Ch 135, noted by Lord Wedderburn (1983) MLR 224; *CBS Songs Ltd v Amstrad Electronics* [1988] Ch 61; *Lonhro v Fayed* [1990] 2 QB 479, p 489; *X (A Minor) v Bedfordshire CC* [1995] 3 All ER 353; *O'Rourke v Camden London BC* [1998] AC 188; *Michaels v Taylor Woodrow Developments Ltd* [2000] 4 All ER 645.

108 [1987] IRLR 3. Note that the indirect form of the tort of inducing breach of statute would require unlawful means.

109 However, on the facts of the case, Henry J concluded that the one day strikes were not interfering sufficiently with the work of the abbatoirs for there to have been a breach of the statute.

110 [1989] IRLR 305 (CA); IRLR 399 (HL). Noted by Simpson, B (1989) 18 ILJ 234, p 237.

111 For details of the scheme, see Brodie, D (1989) 18 ILJ 230.

actions.[112] In these circumstances, the coerced party may claim restitution of monies paid under the contract.

The use of the doctrine in the context of industrial disputes was first discussed in *Universe Tankships Inc of Monrovia v ITWF*.[113] A ship owned by the plaintiff was boycotted by members of the union on its arrival at the port of Milford Haven. In order to lift the boycott, the plaintiff agreed to pay a sum to the union's welfare fund. The plaintiff made a claim for restitution of this sum on the grounds that consent for entry into this special agreement was vitiated by the industrial pressure imposed by the union on the plaintiff.

Although the majority of the House of Lords agreed that the use of economic duress to induce another person to part with money or property is not a tort *per se*,[114] it was decided that the contractual doctrine was *prima facie* applicable in these circumstances.[115] Lords Diplock and Scarman continued, however, by stating that if the duress was applied 'in contemplation or furtherance of a trade dispute' then for reasons of 'public policy' the action for economic duress must fail.[116] Somewhat surprisingly, on the facts of the case, it was held that this was not a trade dispute and so the plaintiff was entitled to restitution of the funds obtained by the duress.

These issues were partially reconsidered by the House of Lords in *Dimskal Shipping v ITWF*.[117] The facts were very similar, in that a ship owned by the plaintiff was boycotted by the defendant, held in port and not released until the owners complied with the defendant's demands. These demands were, *inter alia*, that all crew received ITF employment contracts, back dated pay and the payment of sums to the ITF welfare fund. Following and affirming the previous House of Lords decision in *Universe Tankships*, it was held that this use of illegitimate economic pressure was a form of actionable duress. Consequently, as the payments were induced by duress the contracts were voidable at the instance of the plaintiff.

Inducing breach of an equitable obligation

In *Prudential Assurance Co v Lorenz*,[118] during an industrial dispute, union officials representing insurance agents working for the plaintiff company induced the agents not to submit their collected premiums to the plaintiff company. Plowman J believed there was sufficient authority for the proposition that the defendants were interfering, not just with a contractual obligation under the agents contract with the plaintiff, but with a general equitable duty 'to account' implied by the general law relating to fiduciary duties.[119]

---

112 See *Barton v Armstrong* [1976] AC 104; *Pao On v Lau Yiu Long* [1980] AC 614; *B & S Contracts Ltd v Victor Green Publications Ltd* [1984] ICR 419; *CTN Cash & Carry v Gallacher* [1994] 4 All ER 714.

113 [1982] IRLR 200. Noted by Lord Wedderburn (1982) 45 MLR 556 and Napier, B [1983] CLJ 43; and discussed by Tipaldy, D (1983) 99 LQR 188 and Sterling, M (1982) 11 ILJ 156.

114 With Lord Scarman dissenting.

115 The majority also noted that the form the duress takes may provide evidence of the tort of intimidation.

116 This must be right as otherwise, if industrial pressure *per se* constituted duress, the whole notion of collective bargaining would be put in doubt.

117 [1992] IRLR 78. The Court of Appeal judgment [1990] IRLR 102 is noted by McKendrick, E (1990) 19 ILJ 195; Phang, A (1990) 53 MLR 107.

118 (1971) 11 KIR 78.

119 For criticism of the decision, see *op cit*, Lord Wedderburn, fn 76, p 649.

As there is no immunity for causes of action based on breach of equitable obligations, if this head of liability was expanded by a creative and innovative judiciary into a general liability for inducing breach of trust, unions would be open to substantial legal action. However, in *Metall und Rohstoff AG v Donaldson Inc*,[120] the Court of Appeal refused to extend liability to other equitable liabilities by specifically stating that there was no such tort of inducing breach of trust, so limiting the common law action to the facts of *Prudential*.[121]

The right to secure the provision of goods or services

In the Green Paper, *Industrial Relations in the 1990s*,[122] it was argued that the '... distinctive feature of strikes and other forms of industrial action in the public services is that they are often targeted on the life of the community'.[123] It was thus proposed that those members of the public who were seriously inconvenienced by unlawful industrial action (such as commuters stranded by a transport strike) should be given the right to enforce the provision of these services by legal action.

In the Green Paper, this right was exclusively linked to the non-performance of public services. In the draft legislation, it was extended to services provided by all sectors of the economy. Despite the combined efforts of the CBI[124] and the TUC all representations for amendments to the draft legislation were rejected and the provisions were enacted in the Trade Union Reform and Employment Rights Act 1993; incorporated as ss 235A–C of the TULR(C)A 1992.[125]

The right operates where a trade union[126] or other person induces another to take part in unlawful industrial action[127] and the effect or likely effect of the industrial action is or will be to '... prevent or delay the supply of goods or services or reduce their quality ...'.[128] In these circumstances, an individual member of the public (whether or not legally entitled to the supply of the goods or services)[129] can apply to the High Court for an

---

120 [1989] 3 All ER 14. Noted by Eekelaar, J [1990] 106 LQR 223.

121 Approved by Hoffman LJ in *Law Debenture Trust Corp v Ural Caspian Oil Corp Ltd* [1993] 1 WLR 138, p 151.

122 Cm 1602, 1991, Chapter 4. The right was first proposed in the *Citizen's Charter*, Cm 1599, 1991.

123 Paragraph 4.5.

124 The CBI was critical of the proposal because an employer may be legitimately hesitant in enforcing the law so as not to disturb the chances of a negotiated settlement. Where members of the public are entitled to do so, the results may be catastrophic for industrial relations.

125 See, generally, Morris, G, 'Public or private? The citizen's right of action in industrial disputes' [1993] PL 595 and Morris, G, ' Industrial action: public and private interests' (1993) 22 ILJ 194.

126 By s 235A(6), an act of inducement by a trade union is assumed if it has authorised or endorsed the act of another.

127 Industrial action is unlawful if it is actionable in tort *per se* by an employer. The Act also provides that it is unlawful if a valid ballot has not been held and the applicant is a union member with the right of complaint under TULR(C)A 1992, s 62. This provides a right of action to the citizen should the industrial action not be in breach of contract (a necessary component of the tort of inducing breach of contract).

128 Section 235A(1) and (2).

129 Section 235A(3).

injunction to prohibit the action.[130] There is no requirement on the individual taking action to show they have been actually inconvenienced or suffered loss.

The provision at the time was criticised for providing third parties who are not involved in the dispute an opportunity to interfere in union-employer relations whatever their individual motivation. It was noted that an employer who is directly involved may have good reasons for not wishing to take action in the courts. The 'concerned citizen' is thus able to override the employer's wishes despite (or because of) the possibility of settlement. Although very few applications under this section have been made, it still remains in force.[131]

---

130 The Commissioner for the Protection Against Unlawful Action was also established by the 1993 Act explicitly to provide financing for these actions. This office has now been abolished by the Employment Relations Act 1999.

131 An example of an unsuccessful attempt to use provision is provided by *P v NAS/UWT* [2001] IRLR 532, discussed on p 329.

CHAPTER 15

TRADE UNION IMMUNITIES

Where, as a consequence of the actions of trade union members or officials, one or more of the common law torts have been committed, the second stage of determining trade union liability is to ascertain whether any of the statutory immunities are applicable to the tortious act at issue.

As we have already observed, amendments to the Trade Disputes Act 1906 were necessary in the 1960s and 1970s as a consequence of judicial decisions which circumvented the immunities by expanding the scope of the established torts and by developing new forms of tort liability. The amended immunities were consolidated into the Trade Union and Labour Relations Act 1974. In contrast to previous legislative policy, statutory (rather then judicial) changes, initiated during the 1980s, have narrowed the circumstances when the immunities apply and enlarged the number of exceptions to them. The core immunities and all relevant amendments are now found by reference to the Trade Union and Labour Relations (Consolidation) Act (TULR(C)A) 1992.[1]

Protection for inducing breach of contract or for interfering with the performance of a contract in the direct or indirect form or for the use of the tort as 'unlawful means' is provided by s 219(1)(a).[2] Immunity for the tort of intimidation (that is, threatening to induce a breach or interference with the performance of a contract) is found in s 219(1)(b) and for the tort of conspiracy to injure in s 219(2).[3]

These immunities only apply where the act that generates common law liability has been committed 'in contemplation or furtherance of a trade dispute'. This has become known as the 'golden formula'.[4] If the industrial action falls outside this formula, then the immunities will be suspended and an interlocutory injunction may be granted to halt the action and damages will be awarded against the organisers and the union. If the industrial action falls within this formula, then the immunities will apply unless they are withdrawn because the industrial action offends against or more of the exceptions examined later in this chapter.

---

1   As amended by the Trade Union Reform and Employment Rights Act 1993 and the Employment Relations Act 1999.

2   The Trade Union and Labour Relations (Amendment) Act 1976 (noted by England, G and Rees, W (1976) 39 MLR 698) extended the immunity for inducing breach of employment contract to include interference with the performance of any contract (employment or commercial) short of breach. The 1976 Act thereby protected breach or interference with contract in the direct or indirect form. Protection for interference with business or trade was originally included in the Trade Union and Labour Relations Act 1974. This was, however, repealed by the Employment Act 1982.

3   This is not extended to conspiracy to commit an unlawful act, eg, conspiracy to commit a trespass or a statutory tort.

4   This expression was first coined by Wedderburn KW (now Lord) in *The Worker and the Law*, 1st edn, 1965, p 222.

THE 'GOLDEN FORMULA'

Contemplation ... (of a trade dispute)

The classic meaning of these words is contained in the speech of Lord Loreburn in *Conway v Wade*.[5] His Lordship said that, for the industrial action to be 'in contemplation ... of a trade dispute', it is necessary for the dispute to be imminent and the act to be done 'in expectation of and with a view to it'.[6] Thus, where a union makes a genuine claim on an employer to improve the conditions or pay of its members and the employers reject the claim, a trade dispute is in contemplation even though no active dispute has yet arisen.

In *Cory Lighterage v TGWU*,[7] the Court of Appeal had held that, where a dispute does not arise because the employer has unexpectedly acceded to union demands, any pre-emptive union action is not 'in contemplation of a dispute'. This interpretation of the formula was reversed by the Trade Union and Labour Relations Act 1974 – now enacted as s 244(4) of the TULR(C)A 1992. This establishes that an act, which if resisted would have led to a trade dispute, is to be treated as being in contemplation of a trade dispute, even though no dispute has in fact arisen because the other party has submitted to the demand.[8]

Furtherance ... (of a trade dispute)

In order to 'further' a dispute, it must already be in existence. Acts taken in the course of the dispute must be discharged so as to support or aid and assist in the dispute.

In a trio of cases – *Express Newspapers Ltd v McShane*,[9] *NWL Ltd v Woods*[10] and *Duport Steel v Sirs*,[11] the Court of Appeal held that whether a particular act was 'furthering' a trade dispute should be interpreted objectively and must not be so remote that it has no real effect on the trade dispute. This meant that purely sympathetic secondary action, which did not in practical terms apply any pressure on the employer in the primary dispute, was unlawful. The reasoning of the Court of Appeal is illustrated by the judgment in *Express Newspapers Ltd v McShane*.[12]

Primary action was taken by the NUJ in Bolton to bring pressure to bear directly on the employers of journalists on local papers in that area. To make the action more effective, the NUJ called on its members in the Press Association to refuse to supply news to these local papers and, additionally, called on all members in national newspapers to

---

5   [1909] AC 506.

6   At p 512.

7   [1973] IRLR 152.

8   However, where the act is done in the belief that no dispute will arise at all, then as it is not 'in expectation of a dispute or with a view to it', it is unprotected.

9   [1979] ICR 210.

10   [1979] IRLR 321.

11   [1980] IRLR 112.

12   [1979] ICR 210. Noted by RWB (1980) 9 ILJ 45.

boycott Press Association copy so as to raise the morale of those journalists who had gone on strike and to persuade other journalists at the Press Association to join them.

The Court of Appeal held that both the primary action and the first secondary action was in furtherance of the trade dispute, as both were bringing pressure to bear on the employer in Bolton. But the second instruction, to boycott all Press Association copy, was not in furtherance of the dispute as it would have no influence on the employer in Bolton.[13]

The House of Lords,[14] with Wilberforce dissenting, disagreed with this analysis. Their Lordships asserted that 'furtherance ... of a trade dispute' should be examined in the context of what the union subjectively believed. Did the defendants honestly and genuinely believe the action they were taking would further union objectives in that dispute? If so, then they were acting in furtherance of the dispute.[15]

The overruling of the Court of Appeal[16] on this issue meant that purely sympathetic secondary action remained lawful. In response, one of the first acts by the new Conservative Government (which had welcomed the Court of Appeal's decisions) was to legislate to withdraw the immunities in these circumstances. However, secondary action which was likely to achieve its objective continued to be protected, that is, action which disrupted a contract to supply goods or services to the primary employer or where secondary action was taken against an associated company because the primary employer had switched production to that associated company.[17] These 'gateways' to legality were removed by the Employment Act 1990. Consequently, all secondary action is now unlawful and will result in a withdrawal of the immunities.

Trade dispute[18]

A dispute has been defined as a 'fairly definite' difference of opinion.[19] Whether a dispute has arisen is not determined by the subjective view of the parties, but is to be reasonably inferred from the facts of the situation. For example, in *Bents Brewery Co Ltd v Hogan*,[20] a trade union official sent out a questionnaire to members of the union, who were employed as managers of public houses, requesting information on takings, wage bills,

---

13   As Lord Denning explained, at p 218, 'an act must give practical support to one side or the other and not merely moral support'.

14   [1980] ICR 42. Noted by Lord Wedderburn (1980) 43 MLR 319.

15   Both Lords Salmon and Diplock considered that whether the organiser of the action is acting with 'genuine and honest belief' is a matter for the evidence. Evidence of a bad motive (such as where an embittered fanatic acts out of spite) casts light on the honesty of the intention. The modern approach to motive is perhaps encapsulated in the comment of Millet J in *Associated British Ports v TGWU* [1989] IRLR 291, p 300, that an improper motive is only relevant if it is 'so overriding that it negatives any genuine intention to promote or advance the dispute'.

16   See the House of Lords judgments in *NWL Ltd v Woods* [1979] IRLR 478 and *Duport Steel Ltd v Sirs* [1980] 116. Also, on this 'objective-subjective' debate, Simpson, R (1980) 43 MLR 327 and Ewing, KD (1979) 8 ILJ 133, pp 138–41.

17   For further explanation of the 'gateways' to legality see Benedictus, R (1980) 9 ILJ 215 and Lord Wedderburn (1981) 10 ILJ 113.

18   For an historical analysis of this term, see Simpson, R, 'Trade dispute and industrial dispute in British labour law' (1977) 40 MLR 16.

19   Lord Loreburn in *Conway v Wade* [1909] AC 506.

20   [1945] 2 All ER 570.

etc, in order to have this data available for a future wage claim. The disclosure of this information was in breach of the managers' contract of employment.

On an action against the union for inducing breach of contract, the court accepted the argument that, as the questionnaire had simply been used to collect information for future collective bargaining purposes, there was no current dispute; no 'difference of opinion' in being or 'imminent'.[21] A dispute would only arise if, after the results of the questionnaire had been considered, a claim was submitted and rejected.[22]

Whether the same objective test can be applied to determining when a dispute ends is open to doubt. In the majority of circumstances, a dispute ends in an agreement between the parties or where one side has abandoned the dispute. In *Stratford & Sons Ltd v Lindley*,[23] the House of Lords took account of objective evidence in deciding that the union had withdrawn from the recognition dispute. Contrary to this authority, the Court of Appeal, in *Newham BC v NALGO*,[24] introduced a subjective element to the test by suggesting that a dispute may continue for so long as one side genuinely believes that it has not been settled.

Once it is established that there is an actual or imminent dispute, the next issue to resolve is whether the dispute is a 'trade' dispute. Arguably the proper role of trade unions is to engage in collective bargaining on behalf of their members for improved terms and conditions of employment and to represent their members on all issues and disputes that arise at the workplace. Accordingly, it is not legitimate for a trade union to go beyond this narrow industrial role by seeking to influence government policy or to restrict an employer's freedom of action on other matters. The concept of the 'trade dispute' in the statute is, for that reason, drafted so as to distinguish genuine industrial disputes (where trade unions can legitimately expect to be protected from legal action) from political or personal grievances.

The definition of a trade dispute is contained in s 244 of the TULR(C)A 1992.

(1) In this Part a 'trade dispute' means a dispute between workers and their employer which relates wholly or mainly to one or more of the following:

    (a) terms and conditions of employment,[25] or the physical conditions in which any workers are required to work;

    (b) engagement or non-engagement, or termination or suspension of employment or the duties of employment, of one or more workers;

    (c) allocation of work or the duties of employment between workers or groups of workers;

    (d) matters of discipline;

    (e) a worker's membership or non-membership of a trade union;

    (f) facilities for officials of trade unions; and

---

21 The mere possibility of a dispute arising at an unknown future date could not satisfy the test of 'imminent'.

22 See also *Health Computing Ltd v Meek* [1980] IRLR 437.

23 [1965] AC 269.

24 [1993] IRLR 83.

25 An expansive interpretation of this phrase is favoured. See Lord Diplock in *Hadmor Productions Ltd v Hamilton* [1982] IRLR 102, p 108.

(g) machinery for negotiation or consultation, and other procedures, relating to any of the above matters, including the recognition by employers or employers' associations of the right of a trade union to represent workers in such negotiations or consultation or in the carrying out of such procedures.

In *BBC v Hearn*,[26] the union attempted to overcome the distinction between industrial and political or ideological disputes by contending that the dispute was about the failure of the employer to agree to the inclusion of a contractual term permitting their members to engage in an activity excluded by s 244. Here, television technicians threatened to prevent transmission of the FA Cup Final to South Africa because of the policy of the union to oppose the apartheid regime in South Africa. Counsel for the union submitted that this was a trade dispute about terms and conditions of employment, as the union wished to vary their members contracts to introduce a term that would allow them to opt out of work that involved broadcasting to South Africa.

The Court of Appeal took the view that this was a straightforward coercive 'political' action unconnected to a trade dispute issue. The contractual device was a mere ruse to give a semblance of legality to the union's actions. However, in the course of the judgment, the Court of Appeal stated *obiter* that if there had been evidence of a previous attempt to renegotiate contracts of employment – to allow employees to opt out of broadcasts they found obnoxious – a trade dispute may well have been in existence on that issue.

This approach to the issue did not find favour with the majority of the House of Lords, in *Universe Tankships Inc of Monrovia v ITWF*.[27] Lord Cross made it clear that a dispute that in reality has no connection with terms and conditions of employment cannot suddenly become such a dispute merely on a demand by a union that a term, permitting the employees' action, is incorporated into a contract of employment. However, Lords Scarman and Brandon dissented on this point and Lord Diplock referred approvingly to the Court of Appeal's judgment in *Hearn*, in *NWL Ltd v Woods*[28] and in *Hadmor Production Ltd v Hamilton*.[29]

In *P v NAS/UWT*,[30] the union successfully balloted its members for industrial action at a school where the staff had been directed by the headteacher to continue to teach a disruptive pupil against their wishes. P sought an injunction to restrain the industrial action arguing, *inter alia*, that the industrial action was exclusively coercive, challenging the headteacher's legitimate powers to issue a lawful order and had not 'matured' into a trade dispute about terms and conditions of employment. The Court of Appeal, however, found that this was a trade dispute. It concerned the entitlement of the headteacher to issue an instruction that impacted on the working conditions of the teaching staff: a matter that clearly did concern terms and conditions of employment.

---

26 [1977] IRLR 275. For comment, see Lord Wedderburn (1978) 41 MLR 80 and Collins, H (1978) 7 ILJ 123.
27 [1982] IRLR 200. Noted by Lord Wedderburn (1982) 45 MLR 556.
28 [1979] IRLR 478.
29 [1982] IRLR 102.
30 [2001] IRLR 532.

Disputes with government

It is often argued that disputes that involve the government of the day tend to be motivated by political considerations and, therefore, cannot be genuine trade disputes. This is the implication of the decision in *National Sailors' and Firemen's Union v Reed*,[31] where a general strike called by the Trades Union Congress (TUC) in support of workers already taking action did not have the protection of the Trades Disputes Act 1906. Astbury J held that the strike was not in furtherance of a trade dispute as 'no trade dispute does or can exist between the Trades Union Congress on the one hand and the government and the nation on the other'.[32]

Where union members are in dispute with a government department that employs them, then clearly a trade dispute will exist so long as it is on an appropriate subject matter, such as terms and conditions of employment. This is the case no matter what the organiser's motive or whether the action has political ramifications or not.[33]

A trade dispute with government can also occur even where it stems from conflict over wider government economic policy. All that matters is that the political and economic decisions of the government have a direct effect on the terms and conditions of employment of the employees in dispute. This was the essence of the decision in *Sherrard v AUEW*,[34] where a one day strike was called at the behest of the TUC, in protest at the Government's counter-inflation policies which froze pay across industries. Denning MR first approved the view of Astbury J that, in general, a dispute between the TUC and the government was not a trade dispute. However, he then stated that those members of unions in government installations who are directly affected by the pay freeze are engaged in a dispute with the Government as an employer, because ministerial authority was required before a pay rise could be authorised.[35]

Conversely, where the industrial action is not aimed at the government as an employer and is not on one or more of the matters listed in s 244 of the TULR(C)A 1992, but is action taken generally to oppose social and economic policy, there is no trade dispute. This is demonstrated by *Express Newspapers Ltd v Keys*,[36] where strikes were held to protest against government economic policies during a collective 'day of action' called by the TUC. This was classified by the High Court as a political protest strike: the outstanding characteristic of which is that the employer is in no position to do anything about the demands of the union.[37]

---

31 [1926] Ch 536.

32 At p 540. See the influential article by Goodhart (1927) 36 Yale LJ 464 attacking Astbury's reasoning.

33 Note the comments of Lord Diplock to this effect in *NWL Ltd v Nelson* [1979] IRLR 478. A bad motive may, however, in exceptional situations cast doubt on the honesty of the intention to 'further' the dispute. See fn 15.

34 [1973] ICR 421.

35 Note that s 244(2) specifically provides that a dispute between government and workers shall be treated as a trade dispute if the dispute has been referred to a joint body for resolution on which there is ministerial representation or if the dispute cannot be settled without the minister's approval (eg, see the provisions of the School Teachers' Pay and Conditions Act 1991 and *Wandsworth BC v NAS/UWT* [1993] IRLR 344).

36 [1980] IRLR 247.

37 See also *Associated Newspapers Ltd v Flynn* [1970] KIR 17.

The dividing line between industrial relations issues, which fall within the scope of the golden formula, and political issues, which do not, was widened by the 1982 Employment Act. Before this Act, a trade dispute had only to be 'connected with' the list of matters outlined in s 244. Now the dispute must relate 'wholly or mainly to' one or more of these items.[38]

Prior to this change, mixed motives for taking action, partly industrial and partly political, satisfied the test. For example, the golden formula still applied in *NWL Ltd v Nelson*,[39] where the dispute was partly a political campaign against 'flags of convenience' ships and partly concerning the poor wages of the crew.

Now that the industrial nature of the dispute must be predominant, there is a greater danger of trade unions losing their immunity where the dispute is in anyway linked to government policies. This is illustrated by *Mercury Communications v Scott-Garner*.[40] The plaintiff company was the beneficiary of the Government's liberalisation of the telecommunications industry. The plaintiff, as a newly licensed operator, planned to establish a digital communications network by using the British Telecom (BT) system. The Post Office Engineering Union supported BT's monopoly and instructed their members employed by BT not to connect Mercury to the system.

The union argued that this campaign of industrial action was necessary to avoid redundancies and protect conditions of employment for their members in the industry. Donaldson MR in the Court of Appeal refused to accept this:

> ... I find it impossible to conclude on the present evidence that the risk to jobs was a major part of what the dispute was about ... on the other hand there is massive evidence that the union was waging a campaign against the political decisions to liberalise the industry and to privatise BT.[41]

The decision in *Scott-Garner* demonstrates that, where political decision making has a direct effect on terms and conditions of employment (or on other matters included in s 244(1)), the resulting dispute will only be a trade dispute if the effect on members' terms and conditions is the union's main concern. Consequently, a union must be careful in the way it expresses its objections to change. For example, in early 1989 the Government announced its intention to abolish the National Dock Labour Scheme which had, since 1947, provided a degree of guaranteed employment to dockworkers at ports covered by the scheme. After negotiations between union and port employers had broken down on the replacement for the scheme, a ballot for strike action was held which produced a large majority in favour.

In the High Court,[42] Millet J rejected the employer's submissions that the dispute over the breakdown of collective bargaining was a mere pretext for a politically inspired dispute with the Government over their abolition of the statutory scheme. There was

---

38 See, generally, on the changes introduced by the 1982 Employment Act, Simpson, B (1983) 46 MLR 463 and Ewing, KD (1982) 11 ILJ 209.

39 [1979] IRLR 478.

40 [1983] IRLR 494. Noted by Ewing, KD and Rees, W (1984) 13 ILJ 60.

41 At p 500. May LJ was even more forthright: he was convinced that 'the present action springs from a political and ideological campaign seeking to maintain the concept of public monopoly against private competition'.

42 *Associated British Ports v TGWU* [1989] IRLR 291.

evidence from the failed negotiations and from the literature that accompanied the ballot paper that the true reason for the dispute was the employer's rejection of the union demand for new national conditions to replace the statutory scheme. In effect, the strike was not directed at the Government *per se*, but concerned the industrial consequences of the political decision to abolish the scheme.

The distinction between an ideological objection to government policy and an objection based on that policy's effect on terms and conditions of employment was also the central question in *Wandsworth BC v NAS/UWT*.[43] The Education Reform Act 1988 established a national curriculum for school pupils and required teachers to stage additional tests and assessments. The defendant unions balloted their members to participate in action short of a strike to boycott the tests required under the national curriculum.

Neil LJ, delivering the unanimous judgment of the Court of Appeal, rejected the council's submissions that this was a dispute about opposition to educational policy *per se* and as such was a dispute with the Government. He concluded that, on the evidence, it was clear that the unions believed the reforms increased teachers' workloads excessively and unreasonably and that that issue was the primary impetus for the dispute.[44]

Issues of public policy also arose in *Westminster CC v Unison*,[45] where the council proposed (as part of its policy of 'externalisation' of services) to transfer housing advice staff to a private sector company that was taking over housing services on behalf of the council. In a ballot of relevant Unison members, the majority opposed this process and voted for industrial action. The question arose whether there existed a genuine trade dispute between the parties or whether the opposition to the council's plans was motivated by an ideological objection against the policy. The Court of Appeal held that, although the union itself was opposed in principle to the policy of privatisation, it was the membership's state of mind that was solely relevant. As the evidence suggested that the membership was predominantly concerned about the likely consequences of the change in employer on their terms and conditions of employment, this was a trade dispute.[46]

Any action taken to pursue a personal grievance that a union has with an employer will clearly fail the definition of a trade dispute: such as where the union was motivated by a desire merely to suppress criticism of the union's existing dispute with other employers in the area.[47]

---

43 [1993] IRLR 344.

44 The evidence of the specific phrasing of the question and of the literature that accompanied the ballot which made it clear that the members were voting on a trade dispute issue was regarded as being of particular importance.

45 [2001] IRLR 524.

46 See also *University College Hospital NHS Trust v Unison* [1999] IRLR 31, where the union organised a strike ballot in response to the trust's refusal to guarantee that staff transferred to a new hospital (built and run by a private company under the Private Finance Initiative scheme) would continue to enjoy equivalent terms and conditions of employment as those who were not transferred. The Court of Appeal believed that this was not a dispute motivated by ideology or policy objections but that rather the union's primary intention was to protect the terms and conditions of employment of their members.

47 *Torquay Hotel v Cousins* [1969] 2 Ch 106. See also *Conway v Wade* [1909] AC 506, p 509; *Huntley v Thornton* [1957] 1 WLR 321, p 349.

It should be noted, however, that mere ill will between the employer and the union does not turn what is *prima facie* a trade dispute into an unprotected personal dispute. The dispute may be carried on zealously due to personal animosity between the parties but, so long it is motivated by an issue deriving from the list in s 244 of the TULR(C)A 1992, it remains a trade dispute.[48]

THE PARTIES TO THE TRADE DISPUTE

The trade dispute must involve the correct parties. The form of words defining a trade dispute in the Trade Union and Labour Relations Act 1974 stated that it was 'a dispute between employers and workers, or between workers and workers'. The amendment introduced by the Employment Act 1982 (incorporated into s 244(1) of the TULR(C)A 1992) provides that the dispute must now be between 'workers[49] and their employer'.

Internal union disputes

Disputes between unions at the workplace over recognition, recruitment or demarcation matters would previously have been classified as between 'workers and workers'. Thus, where a dispute subsequently damaged an employer the unions involved would be safeguarded from any legal action. These purely internal disputes are not now protected. However, employers often intervene in internal disputes so as to eliminate or reduce a particular union's influence. Where this happens, the immunities are applicable as the dispute is not a purely internal dispute but one between an employer and their workers.[50]

Under the formula contained in the Trade Union and Labour Relations Act 1974, unions and employer associations *per se* were legitimate parties to a trade dispute. Thus, a union could initiate a dispute purely on its own behalf. This has always been important for unions who start recognition disputes without having members at the workplace.[51] A union now however, cannot engage in a dispute on its own account to recruit members without running the risk of legal action.

Furthermore, as the dispute must solely be driven by the interests of the membership at the workplace, not by the interests of the union *per se*, a union cannot intervene where there is no ongoing dispute. In the usual course of events, once a dispute arises, the union is called in by the membership and acts on their behalf. Where this does not happen, a union cannot ignore its members' wishes by calling a dispute of its own accord. This change clearly hampers campaigns such as the the ITWF campaign against 'flags of convenience' ships where employers employ foreign crews on poor conditions and low pay. Before the amendment, the union could raise a dispute with the employers even though there was no

---

48   See *Stewart v AUEW* [1973] IRLR 57.

49   By s 244(5), this includes former workers whose employment has been terminated in connection with the dispute.

50   Refer also to Chapter 9. It is not necessarily action short of dismissal to limit pay awards to members of one union so as to encourage membership of another union.

51   See *Torquay Hotel v Cousins* [1969] 2 Ch 106.

evidence that the workers themselves were dissatisfied with their pay[52] and where the employer did not have any union members amongst its staff.[53]

Identity of the employer

It is perhaps self-evident that an employer is the organisation that employs the workers who are taking strike action. However, where employers have complex legal structures strike organisers may have some difficulty in establishing with some certainty exactly who the correct party is to take action against. For example, several interconnecting companies may exist, so that the real controlling party which has the decision making power to resolve the dispute is a legal entity that is not technically an employer of the workers who are taking action. If each company is a separate legal entity, the question arises as to whether the courts will lift the 'veil of incorporation' to permit action against the party with the real influence in the decision making process.

The authorities indicate that, where an employer alters their legal structure with the sole aim of defeating the trade dispute immunities, then the veil of incorporation can be set aside.[54] Where, however, the corporate structure of parent and subsidiary companies has been developed for genuine commercial reasons, the separate legal identities will be honoured by the courts, even though on the face of it the subsidiary companies are controlled by a parent organisation. In these circumstances, a union has to be particularly careful in choosing against which party to take action.[55]

In *University College Hospital NHS Trust v Unison*[56] the hospital trust entered into negotiations with a private consortium under the Private Finance Initiative (PFI) for the consortium to build and run a new hospital. The trust refused the union's request to include a term in the contract to the effect that employees transferred to the new hospital (and any future employees) would receive equivalent terms and conditions to those employees who remained with the trust. The union subsequently balloted for industrial action. The Court of Appeal found that the dispute was about terms and conditions that would apply to workers after their employment with the trust had ceased and about workers not yet identified and not presently employed by the trust. As this was a dispute about the terms and conditions a new or future employer would impose, and so not a dispute between existing employees and their current employer, the requirements of s 244 had not been satisfied.[57] As a consequence of this decision, Unison launched an action in

---

52 The ITWF campaign was based on both challenging the exploitation of foreign workers and on the effect the acceptance of poor pay and conditions had on undermining the terms and conditions of employment of union members in the developed world.

53 See *Camellia Tanker v ITWF* [1976] IRLR 190 (noted by Lord Wedderburn (1976) 39 MLR 715) and *NWL Ltd v Nelson* [1979] IRLR 478.

54 See *Examite Hire Ltd v Whittaker* [1977] IRLR 312, where the employer formed a new company expressly for the purpose of exacerbating union liability; and *The Marubo Porr* [1979] 2 LR 331 where shipowners attempted unsuccessfully to outflank the immunities by arranging for an outside agency to contract with the crew of their ship.

55 See *Dimbleby v NUJ* [1984] IRLR 161.

56 [1999] IRLR 31, noted by Hendy, J (2000) 29 ILJ 53.

57 By contrast, in *Westminster CC v Unison* [2001] IRLR 524, as the identity of the new employer was known, and the transfer of the employment was imminent, the immediate and practical concerns of the employees was the effect of the transfer on their terms and conditions of employment.

the European Court of Human Rights arguing that this analysis of English law denies workers the opportunity to protect their future terms and conditions of employment through strike action and, as such, is in breach of Art 11. At the time of writing, no decision on this application has been made.

THE LOSS OF IMMUNITY

The third and final stage is to consider whether, as a consequence of the legislation since 1979, the actions of the organiser of the industrial action cause the removal of the trade dispute immunity, so restoring the original liability for the common law tort.

The trade dispute immunity is lost in six specific circumstances where:

(a) the industrial action takes place without a valid ballot (ss 226–34) or without giving appropriate notice of action (ss 226A and 234A);

(b) the industrial action consists of prohibited secondary action (s 224);

(c) unlawful picketing takes place during the industrial action (s 219(3));

(d) the industrial action is taken to impose a 'closed shop' (s 222);

(e) the industrial action takes place to enforce recognition of a union or the use of union only labour (s 225);

(f) the industrial action is taken because of the dismissal of unofficial strikers (s 223).

INDUSTRIAL ACTION TAKEN WITHOUT A VALID BALLOT OR WITHOUT PROVIDING THE NECESSARY NOTICE[58]

Prior to the passage of the Trade Union Act 1984, the only procedure a trade union had to follow when contemplating industrial action was found by an examination of the provisions of the rule book. This would determine whether there was any requirement for a ballot, and if so, the type of ballot required (for example, workplace or postal) and other matters such as whether any special majorities were necessary. In 1983, the Conservative Government through the Green Paper, *Democracy in Trade Unions*,[59] expressed concern that industrial action was often initiated without a secret ballot and undertaken reluctantly by the majority of 'moderate' and 'sensible' trade unionists, who were obligated to take action against their wishes by trade union shop stewards and leaders. Statutory intervention to ensure secret ballots before industrial action was thus justified as a method of extending trade union members' democratic rights and as a way of curtailing irresponsible industrial action.

Amendments to the original provisions contained in the Trade Union Act 1984[60] were made in response to issues that arose from the 1984–85 miners' strike. Although strike

---

58 See, generally, Simpson, B, 'Strike ballots, the judiciary, government policy and industrial relations practice' (1993) 22 ILJ 287.

59 Cm 8778, 1983, Chapter 3.

60 For an analysis of the Act, see Hutton, J, 'The Trade Union Act 1984 Part 2' (1984) 13 ILJ 212.

ballots were required under the rule book, the Coal Board was reluctant to initiate legal action when the strike started without a valid ballot. It was left to individual dissident union members to do so. It was argued in the Green Paper, *Trade Unions and Their Members*,[61] that although employers may decline to take action in response to an unlawful strike, unions owed a duty to their members not to initiate action without the legitimacy of a ballot.

As a consequence, the Employment Act 1988 provided a statutory remedy (which supplements the common law remedy of an action under the rule book) for a union member to apply for an order restraining industrial action where a ballot had not been held or a majority for action had not been obtained.[62] The Act also granted the Secretary of State the authority to issue a Code of Practice on balloting for industrial action.[63] The first Code was issued in 1989.[64] It was superseded in 1995 by a new Code on Industrial Action Ballots and Notice to Employer which was criticised for unduly elaborating on the provisions contained in the statute.[65] The latest Code of Practice (taking into account the changes introduced by the Employment Relations Act 1999) was published for consultation purposes in April 2000 with the new revised Code taking effect in September 2000.[66]

Research, based on the requirement for statutory ballots under the Trade Union Act 1984, has shown that these statutory ballots have often been used as bargaining tools in themselves. A majority vote for industrial action, which shows employee support for the union position, is more effective than a vague threat to call a strike. Thus, strike ballots have often been incorporated into a union's bargaining strategy.[67] Partly to temper the use of ballots in this manner, further amendments to the balloting provisions were introduced by the Trade Union Reform and Employment Rights Act 1993. This Act enforced compulsory postal ballots;[68] the independent scrutiny of ballot procedure; a requirement to give at least seven days' notice of the ballot and of the industrial action to relevant employer(s); and the right for individuals to apply for an injunction to stop unballoted action that interferes with the supply of goods or services. Not surprisingly, the tactical use of ballots became less popular.[69]

---

61 Cm 95, 1987.

62 This right can be exercised irrespective of whether the action constitutes breach of contract or whether a tort has been committed.

63 The power of the Secretary of State to issue Codes of Practice is now contained in TULR(C)A 1992, s 203.

64 Noted by Simpson, B (1990) 19 ILJ 29.

65 See Simpson, B (1995) 24 ILJ 337.

66 Discussed by Simpson, B (2001) 30 ILJ 194.

67 See ACAS Annual Report for 1987, p 11 and 1993, p 16; Martin, R *et al*, 'The decollectivisation of trade unions? Ballots and collective bargaining' (1991) 22 IRJ 197; Millward, N *et al*, *Industrial Relations in Transition*, 1992, pp 297–302; Elgar, J and Simpson, B, 'The impact of the law in industrial disputes in the 1980s', in Metcalf, D and Milner, S (eds), *New Perspectives in Industrial Relations*, 1993.

68 Ballots are expensive to hold. Thus, it was a major blow to trade unions when it was announced that the State subsidy for balloting costs, in place since 1980, was to be withdrawn from April 1996 (Funds for Trade Union Ballots (Revocation) Order 1993).

69 For an up to date analysis, see *Labour Research*, September 1995, p 15; Elgar, J and Simpson, B, *Industrial Action Ballots and the Law* (1996, Institute of Employment Rights); Undy, R *et al*, *Managing the Unions: The Impact of Legislation on Trade Union Behaviour*, 1996; Millward, N *et al*, *All Change at Work?*, 2000, p 179.

Further reforms were proposed in the Conservative Green Paper, *Industrial Action and Trade Unions*.[70] In order to give employers even more time to prepare for industrial action it was recommended that unions should provide 14, rather than 7, days' notice of the commencement of industrial action. The Green Paper suggested that the simple majority threshold to legitimise action should be raised to a majority of those *entitled to vote*, thereby, in practice, making it far more difficult for unions to secure an immunity for action. A further reform would have required unions to re-ballot at regular intervals once the action has started, so ensuring that there exists continued support for the action amongst the membership. It was proposed that, where continuous strike action is taken, a fresh ballot should be organised every two or three months. Where the action is discontinuous (for example, one day strikes) the new ballot should take place after a specified number of instances of action. If enacted, these changes would have been a serious organisational hurdle and financial burden on trade unions taking industrial action and would have further undermined the 'right to strike'.

The Labour Government has not abolished these Conservative measures on balloting but has introduced significant amendments *via* Sched 3 to the Employment Relations Act 1999 in order to simplify some of the more complex and controversial provisions.

In the present scheme, there are no circumstances where a trade union can divest itself of responsibility to hold a ballot. In *Shipping Co Uniform v ITWF*,[71] a ballot had not been held because the ITWF was a federation of unions and had no individual members. Staughton J held that this did not mean that there was no requirement of the ITWF to hold a ballot; rather the union rules should have been changed to allow members of the federated unions to vote.

THE CONDUCT AND ORGANISATION OF THE BALLOT

All immunity for industrial action is removed if it is not supported by a ballot that satisfies the detailed and complex provisions of the Act. Unions need to take considerable care in preparing the content of the ballot paper, the literature that accompanies it and in adhering to the procedure once the ballot has been completed.

The content of the ballot paper

The identity of the person authorised to call the industrial action after a successful ballot must be on the ballot paper,[72] with the name of the independent scrutineer[73] appointed

---

70 Cm 3470, 1996.
71 [1985] IRLR 71.
72 Section 229(3).
73 Section 229(1A).

by the union to oversee the conduct of the ballot[74] and the address to where it should be sent and date by which it should be returned.

Before amendments introduced by the Employment Relations Act 1999, all ballot papers had to include a so called 'industrial health warning' – a bare statement which said: 'If you take part in a strike or other industrial action, you may be in breach of your contract of employment.' Although nearly all industrial action is a breach of employment contract (see Chapter 13). some may not be; such as a ban on voluntary overtime. Even if a ban of this nature is all that is called for, the unamended statement still had to appear on the ballot paper.

The 1999 Act does not abolish this provision but, by amending s 229(4) of the TULR(C)A 1992, expands on it, using it as an opportunity to inform employees considering lawful industrial action that a new limited right to protection against dismissal is available. The statement on the ballot paper now reads: 'If you take part in a strike or other industrial action, you may be in breach of your contract of employment. However, if you are dismissed for taking part in strike or other industrial action which is called officially and is otherwise lawful, the dismissal will be unfair if it takes place fewer than eight weeks after you started taking part in the action, and depending on the circumstances may be unfair if it takes place later.'

The question to be answered in the ballot must require a 'yes' or 'no' answer. If the union believes members may be called out to take industrial action short of a strike and actual strike action, then two separate questions are required.[75] This ensures the union has approval for both courses of action.[76] The problem for the union that wishes to implement a strategy of graduated sanctions with action short of a strike – followed, if necessary, by a full scale strike – is that the ballot only has currency for a four week time period. So, if the limited action takes over four weeks, the second question on strike action is out of time, requiring the union to initiate a fresh ballot.

Where a union has expressly limited the wording of the question on the extent of industrial action called for, by, for example, asking for support for a 24 hour strike, then that is the only action authorised by the ballot. Furthermore, literature sent out with the ballot paper may also have the same effect.[77]

Several issues regarding the framing of the question arose in *London Underground v NUR*.[78] Here, there were originally four matters of dispute between the union and the employers. Before the ballot the union had failed to publicise to the membership that

---

74 The scrutineer must report to the union within four weeks after the ballot on specific matters, such as whether reasonable grounds exist for believing a contravention of the statute has occurred and whether the balloting arrangements generally were satisfactory (ss 226B(1), (2) and 231B). Any person entitled to vote and his or her employer is entitled to a copy within six months (s 231B). The union must not interfere in the scrutineer's functions and must comply with all reasonable requests (s 226B(3), (4)).

75 Section 229(2). The union in *The Post Office v UCW* [1990] IRLR 143 fell foul of this provision because a single rolled up question referring to both forms of action was asked.

76 As each question is considered individually, a bare majority only on one question is valid authorisation for the action specified in that question. See *West Midlands Travel Ltd v TGWU* [1994] IRLR 578.

77 *Blue Circle v TGWU* (1989) unreported, 7 July. See Simpson, B (1989) 18 ILJ 234.

78 [1989] IRLR 341.

three of the issues were no longer matters in dispute. Consequently, the employers successfully argued that the resulting ballot was invalid as the members of the union had voted on a single question whether to take strike action, influenced by a belief that all four matters were current.[79]

This can be contrasted with a decision of the High Court in *Associated British Ports v TGWU*,[80] where there were other issues in dispute unidentified by the literature sent with the ballot paper. Millett J declined to declare the ballot invalid, as '... what matters is that a majority supported the strike; it does not matter why they did so'.[81]

Both cases illustrate the importance of the provision of accurate information to the membership, either before the ballot or with the ballot paper, so it is clear to the membership what they are voting on. The Code of Practice recommends that background information on the issues to which the dispute relates should be provided.[82]

A more recent issue that has arisen is how to distinguish between a 'strike' and 'action short of dismissal'. In *Connex South Eastern Ltd v RMT*[83] the union successfully balloted for strike action and instructed members to ban overtime and rest day working. The employer argued that the ballot was flawed, as this form of action, was, in reality, action short of a strike that required a separate question on the ballot paper. The Court of Appeal disagreed, holding that this was 'strike action' as it is defined in s 246 of TULR(C)A 1992 as a 'concerted stoppage of work' – which this was, albeit for a limited period of time. The decision meant that only where a union was balloting for action that does not technically require a stoppage of work – such as a go-slow or work to rule – will a question on the ballot paper on action short of a strike be required. However, a statutory amendment to s 229, introduced by the 1999 Act, has overturned this decision. Section 229(2A) now categorically states that for the purposes of the balloting provisions an overtime ban and call out ban both constitute industrial action short of a strike.

Entitlement to vote

Entitlement to vote must be accorded equally to all members who it is reasonable at the time of the ballot for the union to believe will be induced to take part in the action.[84] It does not matter that some are not called upon to take action, so long as the union reasonably believed at the time of the ballot that they would be. Section 227(2) also stated that where any member who is induced to take part is denied their entitlement to vote, then the ballot is invalid. In the case law, these obligations were read in conjunction with s 230(2), which qualified the above by providing that a trade union is only under an obligation to provide a ballot paper to those entitled to vote, 'as far as reasonably practicable'.

---

79 Simon Brown J did, however, reject the employer's contention that where there are four separate issues in conflict between the parties there should be four separate questions. All the issues can be wrapped up into a single question so long they are current live issues of dispute.
80 [1989] IRLR 291.
81 At p 301.
82 Paragraph 36
83 [1999] IRLR 249.
84 Section 227(1).

In *British Rlys Board v NUR*,[85] the question arose as to the validity of a ballot where approximately 200 out of a membership of 70,000 who were called upon to take industrial action had not received ballot papers because of an inadvertent oversight by the union. The Court of Appeal understood this as not being a case of a wilful denial of an entitlement to vote, but rather as an failure to provide an opportunity to vote. As there is no absolute obligation to provide everyone with a ballot paper, and as only a trifling number of voters were affected, the omission did not nullify the ballot.[86]

Since s 227(1) requires the union to ballot all those employees who are to be called on to strike, the question arises whether the action remains lawful where new employees are called out on strike who have not voted, as they were employed after the ballot had been held and before the action started. The Court of Appeal intimated that so long as the numbers are *de minimis* – small enough to have no effect on the result – the validity of the ballot is unaffected.[87]

Alternatively, it may be the case that during the industrial action there is a change in the composition of the workforce. It may then be argued that, if a substantial minority of workers have not voted, the campaign of industrial action has not been legitimised by the ballot. In *The Post Office v UCW*,[88] Donaldson MR indicated that small changes in the composition of the workforce would not necessarily invalidate industrial action taken over a sustained period of time so long as that action is continuous, rather than a series of self-contained actions. However, as regards large, as opposed to *de minimis*, changes in the workforce, the ballot may well be invalidated as any call for industrial action 'should be limited to those employed by the employer who had the opportunity to vote'. However, another Court of Appeal interpretation of the ballot provisions rejected this analysis and held that what is of concern is whether a majority of those voting at the time the action was called have voted in favour.[89]

This realistic approach by the Court of Appeal to the organisation of the ballot was generally welcomed. It would have been virtually impossible for large unions to comply with provisions that made it an absolute necessity to ballot all members without any wastage whatsoever. There will always be a shortfall between the number of members sent ballot papers and those returned, due to the vagaries of the postal service, just as there will always be individuals who have not voted because they have been employed just before or during industrial action.

In order to clarify the position on ballot failures, Sched 3, para 4 of the 1999 Act repealed s 227(2) replacing it with a similar provision, s 232A. This repeats the formula of s 227(2) stating that, where members who are induced to take part in industrial action are denied their entitlement to vote, then the ballot is invalid. However, it also adds the provision that it must be reasonable for the union to believe at the time of the ballot that

---

85   [1989] IRLR 349.

86   Another feature of the case was that the plaintiff complained that the ballot was invalid because a high number of persons did not actually vote in the ballot. As the court pointed out, there is an inevitable shortfall between those who are entitled to vote and those who actually exercise their right. Those who fail to participate of their own accord are not truly disenfranchised.

87   *British Rlys Board v NUR* [1989] IRLR 349, p 352.

88   [1990] IRLR 143. Noted by Auerbach, S (1990) 19 ILJ 120.

89   *London Underground v RMT* [1995] IRLR 636. See also *RJB Mining (UK) Ltd v NUM* [1997] IRLR 621.

the member would be induced to take part in the action. Thus, this makes it explicit that the immunity is not lost if the union induces some members to participate in the action who were not included in the balloting process because they were new or transferred employees who only joined the balloted workplace after the ballot had closed. Additionally, a new s 232B has been introduced affirming the case law that minor accidental failures to comply fully with the provisions on the entitlement to vote[90] and the supply of a ballot paper,[91] that do not affect the result of the ballot, can be disregarded.[92]

Requirement for balloting separate workplaces

Prior to changes made to these provisions by the 1999 Act, all employees who are likely to be called out on industrial action who had 'different places of work' had to be balloted separately, in respect of each of those places of work. The requirement for a separate ballot at each workplace meant that an immunity would only attach to those workplaces that have obtained a majority 'yes' vote.[93]

The intention behind this requirement was to limit the opportunity for a union to 'gerrymander' the vote by including in the ballot workers at a workplace who have a reputation for militancy to out-vote other more moderate workers at other workplaces. The strictness of this provision outlawing the aggregation of votes was tempered in circumstances of a common claim. Aggregation was permitted where the union reasonably believed members had some factors in common relating either to their terms and conditions of employment or their occupational status and all of those members with common factors were balloted, or where it was reasonable for the union to believe that all balloted members had the same place of work.

This provision took into account the realities of national bargaining. Aggregation is essential where the same union members work in different geographical places for different employers with their terms and conditions of employment negotiated nationally.[94] The operation of these conditions was, however, found to unworkable due to their complexity. In order to clarify and simplify the law, Sched 3, para 5 of the 1999 Act repealed the original sections and substituted new ss 228 and 228A of the TULR(C)A 1992. Section 228 re-iterates the general principle that in any dispute separate workplace ballots are necessary, subject to the exceptions contained in s 228A. Section 228A establishes that a union may hold an aggregated ballot across more than one workplace[95]

---

90 Section 227(1).

91 Section 230(2).

92 For a recent application of this section, see *P v NAS/UWT* [2001] IRLR 532.

93 See McKendrick, E (1988) 17 ILJ 141.

94 See, eg, *University of Central England v NALGO* [1993] IRLR 81.

95 Section 228(4) describes 'workplace' as the premises from which the employee works or with which the employee has the closest connection. In the original definition, place of work was defined as premises occupied by the employer at which the employees worked or premises with which the employees had the closest connection. On the problems associated with this earlier definition, see *Inter City West Coast Ltd v RMT* [1996] IRLR 583.

if each workplace contains at least one member who is 'affected by the dispute',[96] or where the union reasonably believes all the members balloted are of a particular occupational description or descriptions who are employed by an employer or employers with whom the union is in dispute, or where the union ballots all of its members who are employed by the employer or employers with whom the union is in dispute. This now means that unions ought to be free to carry out aggregate ballots in selective workplaces where previously this would not have been permitted. This is particularly the case with regard to the first exception. An aggregate ballot of members across a limited number of workplaces operated by the same employer is now permissible provided that at least one affected member works at each workplace where the balloting is to take place.

Notice requirements

The Trade Union Reform and Employment Rights Act 1993 added a new s 226A to the TULR(C)A 1992 which requires the union to take reasonable steps to ensure all employers whose employees are entitled to vote have seven days' written notice of any ballot. The union should also provide a sample voting paper to the employer(s) at least three days before the ballot commences.[97]

This is an attempt to avoid employers being thrown off-guard by quickly organised industrial action.[98] This change gives an employer time to obtain advice on the general legality of the industrial action, whether there are any grounds to object to the ballot and, if so, to prepare an application for an injunction to restrain the action.[99]

The most controversial aspect of this duty was the requirement that the union had to include in the written notice a description, 'so that he can readily ascertain them', of 'the employees of the employer who it is reasonable for the union to believe ... will be entitled to vote in the ballot'. How controversial it was is illustrated by the practical application of the law in *Blackpool & Fylde College v NATFHE*.[100] The union was engaged in a dispute with the college over the introduction of 'flexible' contracts for newly appointed staff. The union in an attempt to comply with s 226A, sent the employer a notice that they intended to 'hold a ballot of all our members in the college'. After a successful ballot, a similar second notice was sent to comply with the provisions of s 234A (see p 344).

---

96 This is defined as a dispute relating wholly or partly to a decision that the union believes the employer has made or will make concerning an issue connected to a 'trade dispute' (outlined in s 244(1)) that has directly affected the member.

97 A new s 226A(3B) introduced by the 1999 Act specifies that a sample voting paper need only be sent to an employer in respect of that employer's own employees. Previously, where a number of employers were involved, s 226A(3) required the union to send a sample of all the ballot papers to all the affected employers.

98 The experience of quickly organised industrial action in the transport sector in the late 1980s was cited in the Green Paper, *Industrial Relations in the 1990s*, Cm 1602, 1991, as a reason for the inclusion of notice provisions in the 1993 Act.

99 Where there is a failure to comply with this requirement any liability for subsequent industrial action is only actionable by the employer who was entitled to the information or by individual union members utilising their statutory right of action.

100 [1994] IRLR 227.

The Court of Appeal held that the reference to members employed at the college in general terms was not a sufficient description as the employer could not 'readily ascertain them', that is, identify who they are. To comply with these provisions, the union must either specify a readily identifiable category of persons who are union members (so the employer can easily find out who they are) or, where that is not possible, the union must provide a full list of individual names.

The union responded to this decision by complaining to the European Human Rights institutions that this amounted to a breach of Arts 8 and 11 of the European Convention. The claim failed at the initial admissibility stage as the European Commission of Human Rights did not consider that the requirement to inform an employer of union names was an unjustified interference with the union's right to protect its members' interests, nor was it a violation of any individual rights.[101] The Labour Government, in the White Paper, *Fairness at Work*,[102] subsequently pledged to amend the law so that specific names of union members taking industrial action would not have to be disclosed. The Employment Relations Act 1999 has now repealed the offending provision. A new s 226A(2)(c) requires a union to identify its members in a notice to an employer only to the extent that it contains '... information in the union's possession as would help the employer to make plans and bring information to the attention of those of his employees who it is reasonable for the union to believe (at the time when the steps to comply with that paragraph are taken) will be entitled to vote in the ballot'. Additionally, s 226A(3A) specifies that if the union does possess information as to the number, category or workplace of the relevant employees, then the notice must contain that information,[103] but it then goes on to qualify the requirement by stating that the notice does not have to include the names of those employees.[104]

Union participation in the ballot

Section 230(1)(a) makes it clear that the electorate must be permitted to vote without interference from, or have any constraint imposed by, the union, its members or officials.[105] However, the Court of Appeal has held that a union is permitted to be partisan in its views and to campaign for a 'yes' vote in the ballot. What matters is that the union does not induce members to take action before the ballot result is known.[106]

---

101 *NATFHE v UK*, App No 28910/95.

102 Cm 3968, 1998.

103 On the application of the new obligations, see *Westminster CC v Unison* [2001] IRLR 524, where the notice identified those entitled to vote by reference to the occupation of the workers at a specific geographical site and relevant check off arrangements. However, note, in *RMT v London Underground Ltd* [2001] IRLR 228, a general statement that 5,000 members employed in all categories at all workplaces would be balloted was not sufficient detail to satisfy the legislative requirements. The union was required to provide further information related to specific workplaces and grades of workers. For commentary on this case see Lord Wedderburn (2001) 30 ILJ 206.

104 The same amendments are made to the notice requirements imposed on a trade union before calling industrial action (contained in s 234A).

105 Such a restraint is not imposed on employers or any other person unconnected with the dispute. As employers are provided with full details of who is to be induced to take action, employers have an opportunity to contact employees directly to lobby for a 'no' vote.

106 See *Newham LBC v NALGO* [1993] ICR 189.

There is, however, a thin line between the mere provision of information on the issues and persuasion and inducement.[107]

PROCEDURAL REQUIREMENTS AFTER THE BALLOT

By s 234A, unions are required to give seven days' notice to every relevant employer before the start of industrial action. The notice must include (similarly to s 226A(2)) information about the employees whom the union intends to induce to take part in the industrial action. Furthermore, the union should identify: the starting date of the action, whether the action is intended to be continuous or discontinuous (that is, a series of one day strikes) and, if the action is to be discontinuous, the dates on which the action will be held.[108]

Once the ballot has been held, s 231 requires the union, as soon as is reasonably practicable, to provide all those entitled to vote with a breakdown of the result. A new s 231A introduced by the Trade Union Reform and Employment Rights Act 1993 obliges the union to provide the same information to the employers of the employees who were entitled to vote.[109] The scrutineer's report (which deals with the fairness of the ballot) must also be made available to employers and employees for a period of six months after the ballot.[110]

Action within four weeks

The industrial action must take place within four weeks from the date of the ballot.[111] Where, on obtaining the majority for action, the union is restrained by a temporary injunction or an undertaking given by the union, this period can be extended for up to 12 weeks.[112] Guidelines for determining an application for an extension, set out in s 234(4), state that no order should be made if it appears to the court that the result of the ballot 'no longer represents the views of the members concerned', or if it is clear that circumstances have so changed (such as the receipt of a subsequent pay offer) that the membership would vote against industrial action if another ballot were to be held.

If the industrial action does not start within the statutory time limit, the union must either hold a fresh ballot or abandon the planned industrial action. In *Monsanto plc v TGWU,* [113] and *The Post Office v UCW,*[114] the Court of Appeal considered the problem of whether action initiated within this time scale is still lawful where the action is suspended for negotiations and resumes after their breakdown, and where the action is a series of discontinuous intermittent strikes over a substantial period of time.

---

107 See also s 233(3)(a).
108 Section 234A(3)(b).
109 A new s 226(3A) provides that in a multi-employer ballot the protection of the ballot will be lost only in respect of the employer or employers who have not been informed of the result.
110 Section 231B(2).
111 Section 234(1). See *RJB v NUM* [1995] IRLR 556.
112 Section 234(2)–(6).
113 [1986] IRLR 406. Noted by Bradgate, J (1987) 16 ILJ 261.
114 [1990] IRLR 143. Noted by Auerbach, S (1990) 19 ILJ 120.

In *Monsanto v TGWU*, the Court of Appeal rejected the notion that, once industrial action is discontinued for negotiations, then the ballot is invalidated once the strike starts up again. The reason for stopping the action was all important – if it was merely to suspend the action temporarily for the purposes of negotiations, rather than an abandonment of the dispute, then the time limit was suspended.

The Employment Relations Act 1999 has also provided an additional degree of flexibility to the four week rule by introducing a new s 234(1)(b). This specifies that, subject to agreement between the union and each relevant employer, the currency of the ballot can be extended up to a period of eight weeks.[115]

However, note that, where no agreement for suspension exists, then, according to Donaldson MR in *The Post Office v UCW*, where a union has formally discontinued action, a new ballot is required even if the issues remain substantially the same. Donaldson MR explained that this is the case even where there had been numerous but intermittent strikes over a lengthy period of time, as a union's mandate for industrial action is not of an indefinite duration as attitudes in industrial relations change rapidly. Therefore, '... it is implicit that, once [action has] begun, it shall continue without substantial interruption, if reliance is to continue to be placed upon the verdict of the ballot'.

The call for industrial action

Should the ballot approve the industrial action, s 233 holds that the action is only protected if the person specified on the ballot paper calls the action. This specified person provision was enacted so as to avoid the confusion of minor officials initiating action, where the leadership of the union has yet to do so because, for example, they are still engaged in negotiations. It is another provision that puts the responsibility of industrial action on to the leadership of the national union, in an attempt to control the 'hotheads' in local branches.

How far the provision permits the delegation of this task was considered in *Tanks & Drums Ltd v TGWU*.[116] Neil LJ in the Court of Appeal accepted that on the construction of the section a conditional authorisation can be given. However, a blanket authority to local officials to call for industrial action could not be permitted as that would subvert the plain meaning of the statutory provision. A conditional authorisation is only lawful where explicit authority is given to named or defined officials.

SECONDARY ACTION

Secondary industrial action occurs where employees who are not involved in the primary dispute take action against their own employer, to cut supplies to the employer in that dispute. Such action clearly interferes with the business of a 'secondary' employer who is

---

115 Note that a new s 234A(7B) provides that a union and employer may agree for action to be suspended and to be resumed at a future date without the need for a new notice to be issued by the union. Section 234(7A) also states that a new notice need not be provided to an employer on the resumption of industrial action temporarily suspended in order to comply with a court order.

116 [1991] IRLR 372.

not a party to the dispute. This form of secondary action has historically been of some importance to employees on strike, enabling them to put tangible pressure on the employer to settle the dispute.

Sympathetic secondary action (action which symbolically demonstrates support for workers in the primary dispute without necessarily having any effect on the dispute in question) was outlawed by the Employment Act 1980. The legality of other types of more effective secondary action was generally not affected by the reforms in the 1980 Act. Thus, coercive secondary action was lawful so long it was organised to disrupt the immediate or primary supplier of goods or services to the employer in the dispute; or was aimed at an associated employer where work had been transferred to that associated employer from the primary employer.[117]

By the late 1980s, the Government's position on secondary action had changed. It was argued in the Green Paper, *Removing Barriers to Employment*,[118] that the immunities for secondary action were unjustified and required amendment. The view was expressed that there was 'no good reason' why employers who are not party to a dispute should be subject to disruptive industrial action. It was also stated that secondary action had the effect of deterring new, predominately foreign employers, from investing and setting up new businesses in the UK.[119] The third reason put forward in support of reform was that the law was so complicated that those involved in industrial action would not be able easily to determine whether they were engaged in unlawful action.

As a consequence, the Employment Act 1990 repealed the limited protection deriving from the Employment Act 1980 and has replaced it with what is now s 224 of the TULR(C)A 1992. By this section, secondary action takes place where a person induces a breach of a employment contract or interferes with its performance and 'the employer under the contract of employment is not the employer party to the dispute'.

Thus, a union inducing employees' breach of contract at one employer's geographical site, in support of the dispute at another, will be in danger of losing the trade dispute immunity.[120] It also seems that to organise lawful national action against more than one employer is dependent on showing that there exists a dispute with each individual employer.[121]

In addition, the definition of 'contract of employment' has been extended by s 224(6) to include those who work under a contract for services, thereby allowing for the possibility that secondary action which results in a breach of a contract with a independent contractor is also actionable.

Faced with the above provisions, the only alternative for a trade union that wishes to cut off the supply of goods or services to the primary employer would be to engineer a primary dispute at the secondary employer who is providing support to the employer

---

117 See further on this Lord Wedderburn (1981) 10 ILJ 113.

118 Cm 655, 1989.

119 See para 3.10.

120 This is particularly the case where an employer has several subsidiaries. They may seem to be one and the same legal person but, because of the legal structure employed, they are regarded as technically separate employers.

121 Section 224(4) states that, 'where more than one employer is in dispute with his workers, the dispute between each employer and his workers shall be treated as a separate dispute'.

with whom the union is in dispute. However, as we have already seen, the motives and reasons for any dispute will be carefully monitored by the courts to ensure it is a genuine trade dispute.

UNLAWFUL PICKETING

Apart from possible criminal offences that pickets may commit, such as public order charges or obstruction, and certain civil wrongs such as nuisance and trespass, picketing may result in the tort of inducing breach of contract. Pickets by their very nature attempt to persuade workers to break their contract of employment by not entering work. They may also attempt to stop supplies entering the workplace by inducing transport workers to refuse to deliver, thereby directly inducing breach of employment contracts and possibly indirectly inducing breach of a commercial contract.

So long as the picketing adheres to the requirements in s 220 of the TULR(C)A 1992, that is, that it is in contemplation or furtherance of a trade dispute, peaceful, and occurs solely at or near the workers place of work, then pickets are protected from liability.[122] Violent or secondary picketing will result in the immunity being lifted. For further analysis of the operation of this section and picketing generally, see Chapter 17.

ACTION TAKEN TO ENFORCE UNION RECOGNITION OR THE USE OF UNION ONLY LABOUR

The trade dispute immunities are withdrawn where the purpose of the industrial action is to interfere with the supply of goods or services so as to force a supplier to recognise a union or to force the employer to contract only with those who employ union-only labour. Interference with the supply of goods or services can take place in three different ways. First, if the purpose of the industrial action is to encourage or compel an employer or other person to impose a union-only clause[123] or union recognition clause[124] into a contract for the supply of goods or services.[125]

The immunities are also withdrawn where a trade union commits an act which induces or attempts to induce another to 'refuse to deal' with a supplier or prospective supplier on the grounds of union membership[126] or union recognition.[127] Finally, protection is removed under s 225(2) where the union induces employees of an employer to break their employment contracts, resulting in interference with the supply of goods or services to another employer and one of the grounds for this is that the second employer

---

122 Section 219(3).
123 Section 223(3)(a).
124 Section 225(1)(a).
125 These clauses are rendered void by virtue of ss 144 and 186. See Evans, S and Lewis, R, 'Labour clauses: from voluntarism to regulation' (1988) 17 ILJ 209.
126 Section 222(3)(b).
127 Section 255(1)(b).

does not, or might not, recognise or consult or negotiate with a union or a particular union.[128]

As the section makes clear, the union recognition issue does not have to be the sole or major reason for the action against the second employer. Furthermore, the section operates even where there is only a belief that there may be a future recognition dispute with that employer.

ACTION TAKEN TO ENFORCE TRADE UNION MEMBERSHIP OR A CLOSED SHOP

Under s 222(1), the statutory immunity does not apply where the reason or one of the reasons industrial action has been taken is the:

... fact or belief that a particular employer:

(a) is employing, has employed, or might employ a person who is not a member of a trade union; or

(b) is failing, has failed or might fail to discriminate against such a person.

The provision includes situations where the action is aimed against a person who is a member of any union or branch or section of a union.[129] Thus, inter-union disputes over membership recruitment will be unlawful.

Discrimination for the purposes of s 222(1)(a), (b) is defined in the same way as in the Sex Discrimination Act 1975 and Race Relations Act 1976, that is, where a non-union member is treated less favourably than a union member.[130] For example, industrial action organised to force an employer to agree a collective agreement that applies only to union members, or only certain union members, would be unlawful discrimination. This can be contrasted with the provisions permitting an employer to discriminate against union membership in order to encourage union members to leave their trade union to enable a change in bargaining structure.[131]

DISMISSAL OF UNOFFICIAL STRIKERS

This is one of many measures passed since 1990 to discourage unofficial action.[132] The protection of the immunities are removed if 'one of the reasons' for the organisation of industrial action is the 'fact or belief' that an employer has dismissed one or more employees who are engaged in unofficial industrial action.[133]

---

128 Contravention of this section and s 222 is a statutory tort actionable by any person 'adversely affected'.
129 Section 222(5).
130 Section 222(2).
131 See Chapter 9.
132 See, further, Chapter 13.
133 Section 223.

Industrial action is unofficial where the union successfully repudiates the actions of its local officers. In these circumstances, should an employer dismiss workers who are on strike they are not entitled to claim unfair dismissal. Although action on an issue of reinstatement is a trade dispute matter, should the strikers' colleagues organise industrial action on their behalf, as a general protest, or to secure their reinstatement, the immunity they would normally have is withdrawn. It does not matter that this additional industrial action is official, backed by the union leadership and taken in compliance with all other procedures.

CHAPTER 16

UNION LIABILITY FOR INDUSTRIAL ACTION

STATUTORY VICARIOUS LIABILITY

Prior to the landmark decision in *Taff Vale Rly Co v ASRS*,[1] it was not possible to sue trade unions for committing tortious acts because they were unincorporated associations and so did not have the capacity to be sued. Employers who believed they had a cause of action were, instead, able to sue in damages or for an injunction against the individuals who organised the action. This was often a less than satisfactory remedy, as individuals usually did not have the finances to meet a damages claim and an injunction was only of limited value, as it only bound the named defendant.

Following *Taff Vale*, unions were held to be quasi-corporations under the Trade Union Acts of 1871 and 1875, with the capacity in civil law to sue and be sued.[2] Consequently, as a union could be sued in its own name, injunctions could formally bind the union itself. More seriously, *Taff Vale* opened up the possibility of union bankruptcy as their funds were now put at risk by employers pursuing large damages claims for the effects of industrial action. The intervention of the law in the guise of the Trades Disputes Act 1906, which was passed in direct response to *Taff Vale*, gave trade unions total immunity from any action in tort[3] and partial immunity to individuals where the action taken was 'in contemplation or furtherance of a trade dispute'.[4]

The practical consequence of this reversal of *Taff Vale* was that the law reverted back to the previous position. Unions could not be sued for damages or be restrained by an injunction, in their own name or by a representative action. Where unlawful industrial action was organised, employers had to resort to claiming an injunction against a named organiser, usually a senior officer, such as a general secretary. The practice emerged, however, that where an injunction was granted, the union treated it as if it had been awarded against the union itself.

This was the legal position until the Employment Act 1982 abolished trade union immunity from liability for the industrial torts[5] by stipulating that a trade union could be sued in its own name, directly for damages, or for an injunction, should the industrial action fail to be protected by the immunities.[6] Although individuals remain liable, the scheme of the section is such that it is only in rare circumstances that employers would need to revert to suing organisers in person. This is because the section provides for a form of statutory vicarious liability of trade unions for the actions of their members and

---

1   [1901] AC 426.
2   See further on this Chapter 2.
3   Section 4.
4   Section 3.
5   Specified in s 20(1) as inducing breach of contract, interference with contract short of breach, intimidation and conspiracy to injure.
6   See Ewing, KD (1982) 11 ILJ 209, pp 218–25.

officers. A trade union will be held liable for the unlawful industrial action of its membership where such action was '... authorised or endorsed by the trade union ...'.[7]

Section 20(2) further provides that:

An Act shall be taken to have been authorised or endorsed[8] by a trade union if it was done, or was authorised or endorsed –

(a) by a person empowered by the rules to do, authorise or endorse acts of the kind in question; or

(b) by the principal executive committee or the president or general secretary; or

(c) by any other committee[9] of the union or any other official of the union (whether employed by it or not).

This is an amended version of the list of persons who can authorise or endorse industrial action. The original provision in the Employment Act 1982 referred only to persons defined in sub-ss 2(a) and (b) above. When, in 1989, there was a spate of unofficial lightning strikes on the London Underground, the docks and on construction sites, organised by local unpaid branch officials, the Government responded with proposals in the Green Paper, *Unofficial Action and the Law*,[10] to extend trade union responsibility to those lower down in the trade union hierarchy. Hence, the Employment Act 1990, amending the Employment Act 1982, expanded the range of persons who could authorise or endorse industrial action to those individuals defined in s 20(2)(c) of the TULR(C)A 1992 above.

For the purposes of s 20(2)(c), a 'committee of the union' may be temporarily set up for a specific purpose; such as a local *ad hoc* strike committee. Moreover, a union will be held responsible, even if only one member of that committee calls for action. All that is required is that an official was a member of the group at the time the call was made.[11]

Prior to these reforms, whether an action was official or not was determined by a consideration of the rule book to see who had authority to call for, or endorse, action. Now the provisions of the rule book are irrelevant because they are expressly overriden by the statute.[12] In short, nearly all industrial action will be now be deemed official unless repudiated according to complex rules found in s 21 of the TULR(C)A 1992.

Repudiation

Prior to the Employment Act 1990, a union could escape liability where an individual's call was repudiated by senior national union officers (members of the executive, president

7   Section 20(1)(b).
8   Whether a person 'authorises or endorses' action is not further defined in the statute. It will, thus, be a matter for the court to determine on the facts of the case. In *(Richard) Transport Ltd v NUM (South Wales Area)* [1985] IRLR 67, there was evidence from newspaper and other media reports that the union was in support of certain picket line actions. This was sufficient for the court to infer that the union had endorsed or authorised these activities.
9   Defined in s 20(3)(a) as any group of persons 'constituted in accordance with the rules of the union'.
10 Cm 821, 1989, Chapter 2.
11 Section 20(3)(b).
12 Section 20(4).

or general secretary). However, the 1990 Act introduced an important limitation on the right to repudiate. Unlike the previous position under the Employment Act 1982, repudiation is now only valid where it is undertaken to avoid liability for a call for action by persons specified in s 20(2)(c). Moreover, to be effective, a repudiation must comply with the detailed requirements of s 21(1)–(6) of the TULR(C)A 1992.

Where, *prima facie*, the union is responsible for an act undertaken by individuals under s 20(2)(c), a written repudiation by the executive, president or general secretary must be sent, 'as soon as reasonably practicable', to the individual or committee in question, once one of them becomes aware of the act.[13] Additionally, the union 'must do its best' to give all members individual notice of the repudiation, who it believes are taking part or will take part in the action, and notice to all employers involved.[14] A specific statement must be included in the notice to affected members: 'Your union has repudiated the call (or calls) for industrial action to which this notice relates and will give no support to unofficial industrial action taken in response to it (or them). If you are dismissed while taking unofficial industrial action, you will have no right to complain of unfair dismissal.'[15]

The executive, president or general secretary must not act inconsistently with any repudiation,[16] that is, the repudiation must not be a sham.[17] Section 21(6) states that where a party to a commercial contract (the performance of which has been or may be interfered with by the action) requests confirmation of the repudiation within three months of it, then the union must confirm the repudiation in writing 'forthwith'. If no confirmation is forthcoming, any actual repudiation that otherwise would be valid is ineffective.

The introduction of vicarious liability is designed to encourage unions to 'police' their own local officials and members more effectively and to inhibit their proclivity to take industrial action. If the union does not disown its more 'militant' members, the cost is potentially severe. If an injunction is issued against the union, and local officers ignore it, the national union will be held in contempt, possibly fined, and assets sequestrated, if the fines are not paid. In general terms, unions are uncomfortable with the centralisation of control that this statutory intervention enforces as trade unions are not traditionally hierarchical bodies. For the national executive to dictate to the membership is contrary to union democratic principles and, arguably, stimulates schisms within the union. Consequently, in many disputes, the union leadership prefers to condone, rather than condemn, local actions, since otherwise they would be in danger of losing all credibility with their membership.

---

13 Section 21(1).
14 Section 21(2).
15 Section 21(3).
16 Section 21(5).
17 See *Express and Star Ltd v NGA* [1985] IRLR 455: the court found that the union's purported repudiation had been half-hearted and that union officials had encouraged action after the repudiation 'by nods, winks, the turning of blind eyes and similar clandestine methods of approval'.

VICARIOUS LIABILITY FOR OTHER TORTS COMMITTED DURING INDUSTRIAL ACTION

During industrial action, other torts may inevitably be committed, such as nuisance, trespass, defamation, etc. For these torts, the statutory scheme of vicarious liability does not apply. To determine whether the union itself could be liable for these torts committed by officials or members requires an examination of ordinary common law principles.

The leading case on this is *Heatons Transport Ltd v TGWU*.[18] The House of Lords ruled that a union is liable for the actions of its employed officials committed in the course of his or her employment, and is also liable for the actions of its 'agents' committed within the scope of their authority.

The House of Lords regarded ordinary union members and local officials as 'agents' of the union. The scope of their authority could be derived from the rule book, custom and practice, or from agreed union policy derived from delegate conference decisions. Thus, in this case, the House of Lords held that shop stewards, acting in accordance with union policy, had implied authority to organise industrial action.[19]

Scott J, in *Thomas v NUM (South Wales Area)*,[20] relied on *Heatons Transport* as authority for his conclusion that the South Wales Union was responsible 'on ordinary grounds of vicarious liability' for the torts of nuisance and unreasonable interference with the right to use the public highway committed by local union officers in organising picketing on behalf of, and in the name of, the South Wales union.

In some circumstances, unions may be liable directly for the acts of its national officers. In the picketing case of *NGN Ltd v SOGAT 82*,[21] Stuart-Smith J noted that in nuisance a landowner who has control over land can be liable for continuing or adapting a nuisance originally committed by some other person on his or her land.[22] He therefore extended the application of this principle by holding that, as a trade union has control over its membership, a union itself could be liable for 'adopting' or 'authorising' a nuisance committed by its own membership, if it is aware of the nuisance and fails to use its powers to control its members' actions.

REMEDIES

If the industrial action has been authorised or endorsed by a responsible person (defined in s 20(2)), and is not protected by the statutory immunities (either because it is not 'in contemplation or furtherance of a trade dispute' or because it is prohibited action), the employer may initiate legal proceedings against the union for an injunction to stop the action, or for damages representing the loss they have suffered, should the action go ahead.

---

18 [1972] 3 WLR 431. Noted by Hepple, B (1972) 1 ILJ 197 and Kahn-Freund, O [1974] 3 ILJ 186.
19 See also *General Aviation Services Ltd v TGWU* [1976] IRLR 224. Noted by Davies, P (1976) 5 ILJ 251.
20 [1985] IRLR 136.
21 [1986] IRLR 337.
22 See *Sedleigh-Denfield v O'Callaghan* [1940] AC 880.

Damages

It is relatively unusual for trade unions to be sued for damages, as most employers are more concerned to avoid disruption to their business by applying for an interlocutory injunction to bring the action to an end as soon as possible. Where action is taken against unions for damages, s 22 of the TULR(C)A 1992 limits the level of damages that may be recovered by an employer.[23]

This restriction is of some importance as the financial consequences of the loss of production caused by strike action could be substantial. If such an employer could recover all their losses, then unions would be in the same position as they were in immediately post-*Taff Vale*. Employers would, in effect, be able to bankrupt unions if they strayed beyond the tight parameters of lawful industrial action imposed by recent legislation.

The level of damages that can be claimed is dependent on the size of the union, that is, the number of members it has.[24] A sliding scale operates, with the largest unions with over 100,000 members being subject to claims for up to £250,000 damages: for those with more than 25,000 members, but fewer than 100,000, the maximum claim is £125,000; for unions of 5,000 or more members but fewer than 25,000 members, the maximum is £50,000; for the smallest unions with fewer than 5,000 members, the maximum award of damages is £10,000. Section 23(2) establishes that certain funds which are separate to the union general fund, such as the political fund or any benevolent fund, is 'protected' property and may not be used to meet a damages claim (nor an award of costs or expenses).[25]

Despite this provision, damages actions may still be a serious drain on union resources as the limitations on damages apply to each plaintiff. Where there are several plaintiffs, on account of the action causing indirect as well as direct interference with contractual relations, substantial claims may be submitted by each employer. Thus, the union may well be liable for a sum well in excess of the statutory maximum.[26]

Secondly, these limitations on damages have no relevance where a union is arraigned for contempt, as a consequence of refusing to accept an order of the court.[27] Where this happens, a union may be fined an unlimited amount. If this fine is not paid, a sequestrator may be appointed to take control of the union's finances to pay the fine and a receiver appointed to administer generally union financial affairs.[28] Litigation during

---

23 This restriction does not apply to those torts stemming from claims for personal injury, product liability or torts such as nuisance or trespass which are 'in connection with the ownership, occupation, possession, control or use of land'.

24 Section 22(2).

25 It also specifies that the private funds of a union's trustees, officials and members is 'protected'. Note that it is possible that an employer's claim on union funds can be frustrated where a branch or section of a union operates independently of a national union or has its own separate funds. See Chapter 2.

26 There may also be a multiplicity of plaintiffs where regional or national action is taken.

27 See, generally, on enforcement proceedings, Kidner, R, 'Sanctions for contempt by a trade union' (1986) 6 *Legal Studies* 18; Lord Wedderburn, 'Contempt of court: vicarious liability of companies and unions' (1992) 21 ILJ 51. See also *NGN Ltd v SOGAT 82* [1986] IRLR 227 and *Kent Free Press v NGA* [1987] IRLR 267.

28 See further on this Chapter 2.

the *Stockport Messenger* dispute in 1983 demonstrates the serious financial implications of defying a court order. For organising unlawful industrial action, the NGA was ordered to pay damages of £125,000.[29] On refusing to obey an injunction against picketing and to pay damages, the union was fined £650,000 for contempt of court and union finances were sequestrated. The legal and administrative costs of the action and of the sequestration were almost as much as the damages and fine combined.[30]

The interlocutory injunction[31]

The interlocutory injunction is by far the most popular remedy sought by employers. This form of relief is usually requested on an emergency basis, either before the action has started[32] or at the very beginning of the action. The real danger for the union defendant is that an interlocutory injunction, granted to stop strike action until a full trial, is usually fatal to a union's campaign of industrial action.[33] It is in the nature of industrial action that it can be promoted most effectively only so long as it is possible to strike 'while the iron is hot'. Once postponed, it is difficult to revive, as general enthusiasm may have waned and the procedure for a lawful strike, such as the requirement for balloting, would need to be repeated. Thus, the grant or refusal of the injunction usually disposes of the action.

It is for this reason that the principles of procedure that the courts apply in determining an application for an interlocutory injunction is of crucial importance to the success of a union's campaign of industrial action. Prior to the House of Lords' decision in *American Cyanamid Co v Ethicon Ltd*,[34] the courts had proceeded on the basis that the plaintiff applying for an interlocutory injunction had to make out a strong *prima facie* case or had to have a real probability of succeeding at the trial of the action. The House of Lords, in *American Cyanamid*, reconsidered the principles applicable to the granting of an injunction and crucially reduced the obstacles facing the plaintiff.

The court should first consider whether there is a 'serious question to be tried', that is, that on the evidence brought before the court the claim was not frivolous or vexatious. If a serious question arises, the court should then consider the 'balance of convenience'. This means that the court should balance the extent to which the plaintiff would not be compensated by damages if the injunction were not granted and if he won at trial, against the loss the defendant would suffer if the injunction was granted, if he won at trial. Where the inconvenience to the parties is evenly balanced, then an injunction should be granted so as to preserve the status quo.

---

29 This included a sum for 'aggravated' damages and 'exemplary' damages to punish the union for its unlawful conduct.

30 *MGN Ltd v NGA* [1984] IRLR 397.

31 See, generally, Anderman, S and Davies, P, 'Injunction procedure in labour disputes' (1973) 2 ILJ 213 and (1974) 3 ILJ 30; Gray, C, 'Interlocutory injunctions since *Cyanamid*' [1981] CLJ 307; Evans, S, 'The use of injunctions in industrial disputes' (1985) 23 BJIR 23 and (1987) 25 BJIR 419; Auerbach, S, 'Injunction procedure in the seafarers' dispute' (1988) 17 ILJ 227; Lord Wedderburn, 'The injunction and the sovereignty of Parliament' (1989) 23 LT 4 (also, Chapter 7 in *Employment Rights in Britain and Europe*, 1991); Gall, G and McKay, S, 'Injunctions as a legal weapon in industrial disputes' (1996) 34 BJIR 567.

32 For a *quia timet* injunction.

33 See *Dimbleby v NUJ* (1984). Noted by Simpson, B (1984) 47 MLR 577.

34 [1975] AC 396.

The *Ethicon* test, applied in the industrial context, has been criticised for the ease with which employers are able to obtain a 'labour injunction'. The initial allegation of an economic tort having been committed often satisfies the court that there is a 'serious question to be tried', and a demonstration that their business interests would be seriously damaged if an injunction was not granted persuades the court that the 'balance of convenience' is in the employer's favour.[35]

In an effort to limit the grant of the interlocutory injunction, a statutory modification to the test was introduced in the Trade Union and Labour Relations Act 1974 (now s 221(1) of the TULR(C)A 1992). This section stipulates that where a defendant union claims a trade dispute defence, or the court thinks that such a defence is likely, the court must not grant interlocutory relief unless satisfied that all reasonable steps have been taken to ensure the union has been given notice of the application so it has an opportunity to put this defence to the court.[36]

In 1975, a further provision was enacted in the Employment Protection Act (now s 221(2) of the TULR(C)A 1992), specifying that in interlocutory proceedings the court must also 'have regard' to the likelihood of the defendant succeeding at trial with a trade dispute defence, before granting an injunction.[37] The relevance of this statutory reform was discussed in some detail by Lord Diplock in the House of Lords in *NWL Ltd v Woods*.[38] Lord Diplock recognised that 'in this unique and exceptional area' the balance of convenience will ordinarily lie with the employer and the 'practical realities' mean that the granting of an interlocutory injunction will dispose of the case. The section thus reminded judges that the likelihood of the success of a trade dispute is a factor that the courts must consider when assessing the balance of convenience. Lord Diplock concluded that courts should refuse an application for an injunction if it 'was more likely than not' on the balance of probabilities, that the defendant has a relevant trade dispute immunity.[39]

Lord Diplock's affirmation of the value of the trade dispute defence must be considered in conjunction with his further comments that the section could be disregarded where the consequences of industrial action for the employer, public or third party, were particularly serious. Moreover, colleagues (such as Lord Fraser) believed that judicial discretion in assessing the balance of convenience was not fettered by the statutory direction, even where the trade dispute was applicable, if the industrial action caused an 'immediate danger to public safety or health'.

Other members of the senior judiciary have also emphasised the exceptions to the application of the statutory guidelines. The Court of Appeal, in *McShane v Express Newspapers* and *Associated Newspapers v Wade*,[40] asserted that risks to fundamental public

---

35 By contrast, unions can only show that they have been 'damaged' by the loss of a tactical advantage.
36 This provision was introduced because of the growing use of *ex parte* applications where proceedings were held without the presence of the defendant.
37 See Wedderburn, KW (now Lord) (1976) 39 MLR 169.
38 [1979] ICR 867. Noted by Simpson, R (1980) 43 MLR 327.
39 For examples of where this defence has succeeded see *Cayne v Global Natural Resources Ltd* [1984] 1 All ER 225; *Monsanto plc v TGWU* [1986] IRLR 406. The likelihood of a trade union establishing this defence has, of course, been reduced by the changes to the definition of a trade dispute discussed earlier in Chapter 15.
40 [1979] ICR 644. Noted by Doyle, B (1979) 8 ILJ 173.

rights (such as freedom of the press) must be taken into account. In *Duport Steel Ltd v Sirs*,[41] Lord Scarman opined that there exists a residual judicial discretion to grant an injunction where the possible effects of the threatened act would have a devastating and immediate impact on the plaintiff's person or property.[42]

The High Court has also, at times, been culpable of ignoring the statutory provisions or has amplified the 'exceptional circumstances' of the case to justify the grant of an injunction in order to forestall industrial action. For example, Stuart-Smith J merely paid lip-service to the statutory provisions when granting an injunction against picketing in *NGN Ltd v SOGAT 82*.[43] Warner J, in *Metropolitan Borough of Solihull v NUT*,[44] in deciding whether to grant an injunction requiring the union to rescind its advice to members to refuse to perform certain functions out of school hours, ignored the statutory requirement and examined the balance of convenience almost exclusively from the point of view of the plaintiff education authority and of the affected school pupils.

A more recent analysis of the effect of s 221(2), undertaken by the Court of Appeal in *Associated British Ports v TGWU*,[45] has confirmed that the judicial discretion to grant an injunction is still preserved, even where there is a 'real probability' that the defence will succeed, if it can be shown that it would be in the 'public interest' to do so.[46] The Court of Appeal applied this principle in deciding that, in circumstances of a dockers' strike, with substantial financial loss to the employer and damage to the national economy, the High Court exercised its discretion correctly in granting the injunction.[47]

It is not only employers who may apply for this kind of remedy. Litigation during the miners' strike of 1984–85 brought into sharp focus how effective the injunction can be when granted against a union on the application of a single union member.[48] In *Clarke v Chadburn*,[49] Megarry VC held on the 'balance of potential injustice' that, where there is an arguable case that a strike was in breach of union rules, the 'risk of injustice' to the plaintiff union member by not granting the injunction outweighed any risk of inconvenience the union may suffer. This was because: '... the right to work is a very precious right and the loss of union membership is an extremely grave loss; a union member who lives in fear on either score must of necessity suffer a personal injury which could only be quantified with great difficulty ... for the defendants, on the other hand, there might be loss of face and some suspension of activities ... but nothing to prevent a strike after a [proper] ballot.'

---

41 [1980] ICR 161.

42 Also, see *Dimbleby & Sons Ltd v NUJ* [1984] IRLR 67, where the House of Lords noted that the 1982 Act made it possible for unions to be sued in damages. Thus, as interlocutory proceedings would not necessarily now 'dispose of the action', Lord Diplock's warning in *NWL Ltd v Woods* had lost much of its currency.

43 [1986] IRLR 337.

44 [1985] IRLR 211. Noted by Hutton, J (1985) 14 ILJ 255.

45 [1989] IRLR 305.

46 The 'public interest', as construed by the judiciary, is a notoriously elusive and malleable term.

47 See Simpson, B (1989) 18 ILJ 234, pp 239–41.

48 The miners' litigation also demonstrates the dire consequences for a trade union (contempt of court, fines, sequestration of assets and receivership) where a court order is flouted. See Lightman, G, 'A trade union in chains: Scargill unbound – the legal constraints of receivership and sequestration' (1987) 40 CLP 25, and O'Regan, C 'Contempt of court and the enforcement of labour injunctions' (1991) 54 MLR 385.

49 [1984] IRLR 350.

A final point concerns the practicalities of an application for an injunction. As we have already observed, employers are entitled to seven days' notice of industrial action (as well as notice of the strike ballot). On the face of it, this gives an employer ample time to prepare an application for an injunction. Yet paradoxically, this may be to an employer's detriment. An employer who requests an emergency *ex parte* application (application without notice) hours before action starts (normally decided on scant affidavit evidence provided by the employer)[50] may now find the courts are less than willing to oblige where the employer has received the full notice of the action as required under the statute.

---

50 For an example of such an application, see *Barretts & Baird Ltd v IPCS* [1987] IRLR 3 and the comments of Simpson on the case at (1987) 50 MLR 506.

Loan Receipt
Liverpool John Moores University
Library and Student Support

Borrower Name: Whitfield,Ian
Borrower ID: **********2115

Public order :
31111013862279
Due Date: 27/09/2013 23:59

The police, public order, and civil liberties :

31111002256384
Due Date: 25/04/2013 23:59

Total Items: 2
18/04/2013 12:13

Please keep your receipt in case of
dispute.

CHAPTER 17

THE CONDUCT OF INDUSTRIAL DISPUTES

PICKETING[1]

An enduring feature of strike action is that those who are engaged in it will seek to persuade others to support them or join them so as to enhance the effectiveness of the strike. This is known as picketing and, historically, has been an established feature of the conduct of industrial disputes in Britain. Picketing may have several objectives. It may be intended to persuade workers not on strike to join the dispute or to discourage or prevent substitute labour from attending the workplace. Alternatively, the object may be to disrupt the supply of goods and services to the workplace by, for example, asking lorry drivers not to pass the picket line and deliver to the employer. Where secondary picketing takes place, employees involved in the primary dispute picket other places of work; usually to encourage those workers to join them on strike so as to cut off the supply of goods and services to the primary employer.[2] A secondary 'information picket' may merely aim to publicise the dispute rather than actively disrupt economic activity at the workplace.

Clearly, picketing is in the interests of those on strike who wish to prosecute the strike as effectively as possible. However, it inevitably conflicts with the interests of other parties, such as employers and working employees and, where picketing results in disruption to public order, it impinges on the interests of the general public. As a consequence, picketing has always been subject to the vagaries of the criminal and civil law.

Criminal liability[3]

Obstruction of the highway

Any static assembly on the pavement or road is a potential obstruction of the highway contrary to s 137 of the Highways Act 1980: 'If a person, without lawful authority or excuse, in any way wilfully obstructs the free passage along a highway he shall be guilty of an offence ...' Members of the public have 'lawful authority or excuse' to make ordinary and reasonable use of the highway, such as to pass and repass along the highway and to do things incidental to that.

Whether the activity on the highway is a reasonable use of the highway is a question of fact dependent on an examination of all the circumstances of the situation. Factors,

---

1   See, generally, Kahn, P *et al*, *Picketing, Industrial Tactics and the Law*, 1983; Fosh, P and Littler, C (eds), *Industrial Relations and the Law in the 1980s*, 1985, Chapters 5 and 6.

2   Individuals who are not directly involved in the dispute but who join picket lines in support of those who are in dispute are also characterised as 'secondary pickets'.

3   See generally, Kidner, R (1975) Crim LR 256.

such as the duration of the obstruction, the place where it occurs and the position of the obstructor, the purpose for which it is done, and the extent of the obstruction, are all relevant in determining whether the use of the highway is lawful under the section.[4] For instance, an individual who is waiting for a bus or who is window shopping is considered to be engaging in activity which is *prima facie* a reasonable use of the highway.

Case law, however, reveals that picketing with the intention of stopping workers or supplies from entering a workplace is not so regarded.[5] In *Tynan v Balmer*,[6] pickets on duty outside factory gates on the public highway were led by the defendant in a continuous circular movement to avoid arrest for obstruction of the highway. Nevertheless, the court did not regard this as an incident of legitimate passage and re-passage along the highway. The object of the action was to block the highway, to force vehicles approaching the factory to stop; it was therefore an unreasonable use of the highway and a *prima facie* obstruction.[7]

Once unreasonable use has been established, the extent of the obstruction is irrelevant. Obstructing 'free passage' includes a partial obstruction of the highway for a relatively trivial amount of time.[8] Furthermore, the requirement that the obstruction be 'wilful' does not import an intention to obstruct, simply an intention to do the act which causes the obstruction.[9]

There also exist local powers which may prohibit picketing, such as local authority bylaws provided under local government legislation to regulate the uses of the highway. Other Acts of Parliament, such as the Metropolitan Police Act 1839, additionally permit the police in the metropolitan area to make regulations or give directions to prevent an obstruction of the highway.

Obstructing or assaulting a police officer in the execution of his or her duty

The police have a common law duty to keep the peace. Therefore, where they reasonably apprehend a breach is about to take place, they are acting in the execution of their duty should they take action to avoid its commission. For example, where a disturbance is likely to break out or has broken out, orders may be given to disperse the crowd.[10] If individuals refuse, they are liable to arrest under the Police Act 1996 for obstructing or assaulting a police officer in the execution of his or her duty.[11] These preventive powers

---

4   *Nagy v Weston* [1965] 1 All ER 78, p 82, *per* Lord Parker. See also *Hirst v Chief Constable of West Yorkshire* (1986) 85 Cr App R 143.

5   See Wallington, P (1972) 1 ILJ 219, pp 226–28.

6   [1967] 1 QB 91.

7   See also *Broome v DPP* [1974] AC 587; standing in front of a lorry to force it to stop so as to peacefully persuade the driver to turn the lorry round was also an actionable obstruction of the highway.

8   *Arrowsmith v Jenkins* [1963] 2 QB 561. Here, the defendant had attended a meeting on the highway to address a small crowd. Liability was imposed, even though meetings had been held at that location in the past and the obstruction was of a partial and minor nature.

9   'If anybody, by an exercise of free will, does something which causes an obstruction, then an offence is committed.' *Arrowsmith v Jenkins* [1963] 2 QB 561, p 562, *per* Lord Parker.

10 See, generally, *Beatty v Gillbanks* [1882] 9 QB 308; *Wise v Dunning* [1902] 1 KB 167; *Thomas v Sawkins* [1935] 2 KB 249; *Duncan v Jones* [1936] 1 KB 218; *R v Howell* [1982] QB 416.

11 Section 89.

apply as much to rowdy picket lines as large scale unruly demonstrations or any other disturbances[12] and equip the police with a measure of discretion in the way they manage and control picketing.

When using their preventive powers, police officers must have reasonable grounds for anticipating that a breach of the peace will occur. Lord Parker CJ, in *Piddington v Bates*,[13] held that police officers have reasonable grounds where there is 'a real possibility of a breach occurring'. In such a case, a police officer is entitled to 'take such steps as he thinks proper' to deal with the threatened breach. This may entail controlling the number of pickets at the place of work.[14]

It is immaterial who is going to cause the breach of the peace; the pickets, employees who wish to work, or bystanders. So long as the police have reasonable grounds for believing disorder may occur (from whatever source), police officers may act to prevent it happening. This is clear from the decision in *Kavanagh v Hiscock*[15] where a picket was arrested for refusing the orders of a police officer to stop picketing when he was not an aggressor. May J, in refusing his appeal on conviction, held that, if a police officer reasonably anticipates that a breach of the peace may occur, caused by spectators or supporters of the pickets or of the working employees, a police officer is still justified in taking whatever steps are necessary to prevent this anticipated breach of the peace. This may include dispersing the picket or requiring the pickets to refrain from picketing or limiting their number.

For the police lawfully to utilise their powers, they must also reasonably apprehend that a breach of the peace is 'imminent', otherwise, should they arrest a person for refusing a police order, they would not be acting in the execution of their duty. The meaning of this expression was considered in a number of cases that arose from the miners' strike of 1984–85. The police had developed an 'intercept' policy whereby pickets from other collieries travelling by car to the site of the picket were turned back some miles before reaching their destination. In *Moss v McLachlan*,[16] striking miners from Yorkshire who travelled in their cars to Nottinghamshire were instructed to turn back several miles from collieries where there had been previous disorder. On their refusal, the defendants were arrested for obstruction. It was argued before the court that this was an abuse of police preventive powers as no breach of the breach was 'imminent' or proximate in the context of time and distance to the picketing event.

Even though the pickets were not in the immediate vicinity of the target workplace, the Divisional Court held that the police action was justified because, on the evidence of

---

12 A picket may be arrested for the common law offence of breach of the peace itself. See *R v Chief Constable of Devon and Cornwall* [1982] QB 458 (noted by Morris, G (1982) 45 MLR 454). Also, see *Percy v DPP* [1995] 3 All ER 124; *Nicol v DPP* [1996] Crim LR 318.

13 [1960] 1 WLR 162.

14 In *Piddington*, the police refused to allow more than two pickets to be present at the entrance to the workplace because of a belief that unrest would occur otherwise. The defendant insisted on joining the picket line but was prevented from doing so by the police officer and arrested. Lord Parker did 'not see that there was anything wrong with the action of the police inspector ... as a police officer charged with the duty of preserving the Queen's Peace must be left to take such steps as on the evidence before him he thinks are proper'.

15 [1974] QB 600. Discussed by Wallington, P (1974) 3 ILJ 109.

16 [1985] IRLR 76. Noted by Newbold, A [1985] PL 30 and Morris, G (1985) 14 ILJ 109.

previous disorder at the collieries, a serious breach of the peace was 'very likely' if the pickets had attended.

In *Foy v Chief Constable of Kent*,[17] miners on their way to picket the Nottinghamshire pits were turned back at the Dartford tunnel, over 100 miles from the area where any confrontation would occur and several hours before any picketing would have taken place. Those that refused were arrested for obstruction. Similarly, as in *Moss v McLachlan*, the Divisional Court was unwilling to interfere in police discretion where the threat of breach of the peace was real, despite it not being an 'imminent' or immediate threat.

The Public Order Act 1986[18]

The major system of control over the conduct and regulation of public assemblies, meetings, demonstrations and marches is provided by the Public Order Act 1986. The public order offences that may be committed by those involved in picketing range in seriousness from riot[19] to violent disorder,[20] affray,[21] threatening behaviour[22] and disorderly conduct.[23] Although all of these offences could possibly occur where violence or the threat of violence occurs on or near the picket line, ss 4–5 of the Public Order Act 1986 are the most relevant.

Threatening behaviour under s 4 is a repeat of s 5 of the now repealed Public Order Act 1936. The offence is committed where a picket uses threatening, abusive, or insulting words or behaviour towards another person and that person believes unlawful violence will be used against him. The victim's fear of violence is an important component of the offence.[24]

The least serious criminal offence in the Public Order Act 1986 is disorderly conduct. This occurs where the defendant uses threatening, abusive or insulting words or conduct which causes harassment, alarm or distress. This covers behaviour which falls short of violence or the threat of violence. There is no need for the words or behaviour to be aimed at a specific individual.[25] Thus, on the face of it, this type of offence is easily committed by pickets who gesticulate or shout at those who cross the picket line. However, the mere fact that a bystander or some other person suffers harassment, alarm or distress is not sufficient; the defendant must subjectively intend or be aware that the threatening, abusive or insulting words or behaviour will do so.[26] Section 154 of the Criminal Justice and Public Order Act 1994 has now inserted a new s 4A into the Public Order Act 1986,

---

17 (1984) unreported, 20 March.

18 See, generally, Thornton, P, *Public Order Law*, 1987; Card, R, *Public Order: The New Law*, 1987; Smith, AHT, *Public Order Offences*, 1987; Carty, H, 'The Public Order Act 1986' (1987) 16 ILJ 46; Bonner, D and Stone, R, 'The Public Order Act 1986' [1987] PL 202.

19 Section 1.

20 Section 2.

21 Section 3.

22 Section 4.

23 Section 5.

24 During the miners' strike of 1984–85, over 4,000 miners were prosecuted for the 'threatening behaviour' under the Public Order Act 1936, s5.

25 *DPP v Orum* [1988] 3 All ER 449.

26 *DPP v Clarke* (1991) 94 Cr App R 359. See also *Morrow v DPP* [1994] Crim LR 58.

creating the additional offence of intentionally causing harassment, alarm or distress directed at an individual. This is a more serious offence which is reflected in the maximum penalty that may be passed of up to six months' imprisonment or a fine of £5,000. [27]

The Public Order Act 1986 has also codified police controls over public assemblies and demonstrations. Section 14 is primarily directed at picketing.[28] The section empowers the police to impose conditions on public assemblies where there are 20 or more persons involved. Conditions can be imposed if the public assembly may result in '... serious public disorder or serious damage to property or serious disruption to the life of the community ... and the purpose of the organiser is the intimidation of others with a view to compelling them not to do an act they have a right to do, or to do an act they have a right not to do'. The reference to 'the right to do or not to do an act' refers to the right of workers to refuse to take strike action or the 'right to work'.

The Act stipulates that controls may be imposed both before or during a picket.[29] The Chief Constable for the region may give written directions before a static assembly such as a picket takes place. Alternatively, where a senior police officer reasonably believes the test in the section is satisfied, then oral directions may be given as to the place, duration of the assembly and the maximum numbers that may be involved.[30] The police may thus restrict a picket by location, instructing the picket to move away or to stay over the road from the entrance to the workplace, or impose conditions on numbers, reducing even further the effectiveness of the picket. It is a criminal offence to fail to comply with these instructions whether as organiser or participant.[31]

The Trade Union and Labour Relations (Consolidation) Act 1992 (s 241)

The offences contained in s 241 of the Trade Union and Labour Relations (Consolidation) (TULR(C)A) Act 1992 derive originally from s 7 of the Conspiracy and Protection of Property Act 1875.[32] It was rarely applied to the circumstances of industrial disputes, until resurrected by the prosecuting authorities in the early 1980s.[33] The penalty for infringing this section was increased by the Public Order Act 1986 from a maximum of three months' to six months' imprisonment and, on the consolidation of labour relations legislation in 1992, it was incorporated into the TULR(C)A 1992 as s 241.

---

27 Picketing may also offend against the Protection from Harassment Act 1997 which makes it an offence for an individual to engage in a course of conduct which amounts to harassment of another (which includes alarming a person or causing them distress) where he or she knows or ought to know that it constitutes harassment. There is also (in s 4 of the Act) a more serious offence of pursuing a course of conduct which puts a person in fear of violence. For further details, see Barratt, B (1998) 27 ILJ 330.

28 Prior to the passage of the Bill, the Government White Paper, *Review of Public Order Law*, Cmnd 9510, 1985, identified unruly picketing as a major concern and s 14 in the Act was devised with this in mind.

29 Section 14(3).

30 Section 14(2).

31 Section 14(4), (6).

32 See Bennion, F, 'Mass picketing and the 1875 Act' [1985] Crim LR 64.

33 For example, during the miners' strike of 1984–85, there were over 200 arrests for offences under this section.

This section provides that five separate offences can be committed by individuals engaged in industrial action.

These are committed where a person[34] 'wrongfully and without legal authority':

(a) intimidates another by putting them in fear by an exhibition of force or violence or a threat of force or violence;[35] or

(b) persistently follows another from place to place;[36] or

(c) hides any tools or clothes[37] or other property or deprives or hinders him in using them; or

(d) watches or besets[38] the house or any other place the person is in occupation; or

(e) follows a person in a disorderly manner,

with a view to compel another to abstain from doing or to do any act that person has a right to do.[39]

A limitation on what seem to be offences of a very broad nature is provided by the requirement within the section that the actions of the pickets must be wrongful and without legal authority. This means that, before picketing gives rise to liability, the conduct must first constitute some other civil or criminal wrong.[40] Whether this is a major hurdle for a successful prosecution is thus dependent on the extent to which picketing offends against other civil or criminal liabilities.

A second limiting factor is the requirement that the act is done 'with a view to compel'. The necessary degree of coercion for the purposes of the section was examined in *DPP v Fidler*.[41] The Divisional Court held that demonstrators outside an abortion clinic, who were shouting slogans to shame and embarrass the patients were not guilty of the offence of 'watching and besetting' as that did not amount to compulsion for the purposes of the section. The defendants' purpose was to persuade the patients to refuse an abortion not to compel them to do something they did not want to do. This departs from the meaning of 'coercion' ascribed to it by previous authorities. One possible implication, should courts follow this reasoning, is that where pickets use strong words to persuade working employees to desist from work, no crime of 'watching or besetting' will have been committed.

---

34 The Criminal Law Act 1977, s 1(1) (as amended by Criminal Attempts Act 1981) and TULR(C)A 1992, s 242, provide that where an offence has been made out accomplices can be convicted of criminal conspiracy.

35 *R v Jones* [1974] ICR 310.

36 See *Elsey v Smith* [1983] IRLR 292, where the defendants followed non-strikers home in their car in a 'disorderly manner' and in such a way so as to amount to conduct calculated to harass and annoy.

37 *Fowler v Kibble* [1922] 1 Ch 487.

38 *R v Bensall* [1985] Crim LR 150. See, also, *Galt v Philp* [1984] IRLR 156 (noted by Miller, K (1984) 13 ILJ 111), where employees engaged in a 'work in' where liable for 'besetting' the premises. On worker occupations generally, see *Plessey Co Ltd v Wilson* [1982] IRLR 198 (noted by Miller, K (1982) 11 ILJ 115) and the Criminal Justice and Public Order Act 1994 which has created a new offence of remaining in adverse possession of property after being requested to leave.

39 Section 241(3) provides a police constable with the power to arrest without warrant.

40 See the Court of Appeal's judgment in *Galt v Philp* [1984] IRLR 156 and Scott J in *Thomas v NUM (South Wales Area)* [1985] IRLR 136.

41 [1992] 1 WLR 91. Noted by Smith, A [1992] Crim LR 63.

Conclusions

The police clearly possess an overriding right to control picketing. We have seen that any picket on the highway, of whatever size, is a *prima facie* unlawful obstruction of the highway and, should pickets refuse to follow police instructions to 'move along', they run the risk of being arrested for obstruction of a police officer under s 89 of the Police Act 1996. In addition, the police possess substantial powers to control picketing, with the Public Order Act 1986 supplementing common law powers to prevent a breach of the peace. It, therefore, appears that any form of picketing will almost inevitably involve the commission of an offence, 'unless the pickets remain quiet and orderly, do not obstruct the street or the footway, and do as they are told by the police'.[42]

Consequently, the extent to which there exists a liberty to picket is dependent, not on the existing state of the law, but on the way that law is enforced. In practice, the evidence suggests that, in the absence of violence or disorder, picketing is tolerated. Once the police believe violence has or will flare up on the picket line, then picketing is perceived as a public order issue rather than a private industrial matter between employers, workers and strikers. In those circumstances, criminal sanctions will be applied. This point is illustrated by the experience of police action during the miners' strike of 1984–85 where 'mass' picketing resulted in mass prosecutions.[43]

During the miners' strike the defeat of the picketing campaign contributed in a large measure to the failure of the strike to achieve its objectives. At the time, criticism was made of police tactics and the robust use of their powers.[44] Criticism heightened when it became clear that police forces were co-ordinating their strategy on a national basis under central government direction.[45] Police relations with the strikers were further soured by the use of the 'intercept' policy discussed earlier.[46] Another area of concern during the miners' strike was the failure of the courts to review effectively police discretion when they exercised their powers.[47]

Although there may be no evidence that indicates in general terms that the law is applied narrowly or oppressively, the fact that picketing is only legitimised by the exercise of police discretion[48] to refrain from fully enforcing the law has implications for the exercise of freedom of speech, association and peaceful protest. Moreover, there are practical objections to the liberty to picket being dependent on police discretion; arguably, legal constraints should be clear and unambiguous (rather than uncertain and

---

42 Wallington, P (1972) 1 ILJ 219, p 222.

43 See the Appendix to McCabe, S and Wallington, P, *The Police, Public Order and Civil Liberties: Legacies of the Miners' Strike*, 1988. This shows that 9,808 pickets were arrested and 7,917 charged with a variety of public order offences ranging from riot to breach of the peace.

44 For an analysis of the role of the police in the miners' strike, see *ibid*, Chapter 7.

45 See Loveday, B (1986) 57 Pol Q 60.

46 See further on this Coulter, J, Miller, S and Walker, M, *A State of Siege*, 1984; Fine, B and Millar, R (eds), *Policing the Miners' Strike*, 1985; Wallington, P, 'Policing the miners' strike' (1985) 14 ILJ 145.

47 Moreover, during the strike, magistrates' courts were imposing standard bail conditions on pickets arrested during disturbances banning them from rejoining the picket line without regard to the particular circumstances of each individual case. This blanket policy was upheld by the Divisional Court in *R v Mansfield Justices ex p Sharkey* [1985] 1 All ER 193.

48 A discretion that is fully recognised by the Code of Practice on Picketing 1992, paras 45–47.

inconsistent in application) so pickets are aware of what is, and what is not, in breach of the criminal law.[49]

Civil liability [50]

If picketing is in breach of the civil law then the plaintiff, such as the employer who is the target of the picketing or the employer's supplier,[51] may obtain an injunction[52] to stop the picketing or obtain damages against the perpetrators and organisers. The two commonest civil obligations broken are trespass and nuisance.

Trespass

Trespass to land occurs where there is a direct interference with the rights of landowners to exclusive possession of their land. Clearly, any picket that enters an employer's land is committing an actionable trespass. Pickets are also trespassing if picketing takes place outside an employer's premises on a private highway owned by the employer. Where pickets are stationed on a private highway not owned by the employer, it is still possible that trespass to the employer's land has taken place. Even though another person or private authority owns the surface, the sub-soil is presumed to belong to the owner of the land on either side of the highway.[53]

To avoid liability for trespass to the soil of adjoining landowners, the activity on the highway must be a 'reasonable use', incidental to passage and repassage, such as queueing for a theatre ticket or for a bus. Whether peaceful picketing was a reasonable use of the highway was considered in detail in *Hubbard v Pitt*.[54] Forbes J argued that the picketing of premises, even if orderly, was potentially an unreasonable mode of using the highway and so *prima facie* a trespass, subject to proof of ownership of the surface or sub-soil.

In *Tynan v Balmer*,[55] to avoid an action in trespass where the employer owned the adjacent land between the highway, the pickets attempted to pass and repass on the highway by walking slowly around in a circle outside the workplace. The court held they were not truly exercising their public right of way nor were they engaged in activity that could be said to be a 'reasonable use' of the highway.[56]

---

49 Note that there are also civil liberty concerns if exacting civil law constraints are imposed on picketing.
50 See, generally, Carty, H, 'The legality of peaceful picketing on the highway' [1984] PL 600.
51 Or even in exceptional circumstances individuals who are enjoined to take strike action.
52 See on this Evans, S, 'Labour injunctions and picketing' (1983) 12 ILJ 129.
53 Lopes LJ, in *Harrison v Duke of Rutland* [1893] 1 QB 142, p 154, defined the position as follows: '... the easement acquired by the public is a right to pass and repass at their pleasure for the purpose of legitimate travel, and the use of the soil for any other purpose, whether unlawful or lawful, is an infringement of the rights of the owner of the soil.' See also *Hickman v Maisey* [1900] 1 QB 752.
54 [1976] QB 142.
55 [1967] 1 QB 91.
56 For a reaffirmation and explanation of the expression, see *DPP v Jones* [1999] 2 All ER 457.

If the pickets are on the public highway, both the surface and the sub-soil is usually owned by the highway authority, that is, a local or public authority.[57] In that case, a private employer would not have a cause of action.[58]

Private nuisance

Pickets may commit this tort where they unreasonably interfere with the use and enjoyment of the plaintiff's land. This is an indirect interference. Pickets adjacent to the plaintiff's land act in a manner which detracts from the way the plaintiff wishes to use his or her land. This so called 'amenity' nuisance is usually committed where undue noise or other interference, such as an obstruction to the entrance or exit of premises, occurs. In the industrial context, there has been some doubt as to whether peaceful picketing *per se* was an actionable private nuisance.

In *J Lyons & Sons v Wilkins*,[59] the Court of Appeal held that mere attendance at the workplace to persuade others to decline to work was capable of amounting to a nuisance. Lord Lindley, who gave the leading judgment, said that '... such conduct seriously interferes with the ordinary comforts of human existence and ordinary enjoyment of the house beset [by the pickets] and such conduct would support an action ... for a nuisance at common law'.[60]

The Court of Appeal contradicted itself several years later in *Ward, Lock & Co v Operative Printers Assistants Society*.[61] The Court of Appeal concluded that inherently peaceful picketing, without violence, obstruction or molestation of any kind, that is merely providing information with a view to persuading members of the workforce to decline to work, did not interfere with the comfort of the plaintiffs or of the enjoyment of their property and so no common law nuisance had been committed.[62]

The majority of the Court of Appeal in *Hubbard v Pitt*,[63] with Lord Denning dissenting, characterised *Ward Lock* as a decision made on the particular facts of the case and preferred to rely on the earlier authority of *J Lyons & Sons v Wilkins* when holding that picketing a person's premises did amount to the tort of nuisance. This analysis was followed by Fitzhugh J in *Mersey Docks and Harbour Board v Verrinder*,[64] where the pickets had blocked off access to a container depot in a protest against the employer's use of unregulated labour. Although there was no obvious physical molestation or violence, Fitzhugh J held this to be an actionable interference in nuisance with the right of the plaintiff to enjoy his property as he pleases. He emphasised that a factor of some importance here was the intention of the pickets not merely to inform or communicate information but to compel the plaintiff to take action against their customers who employed unregulated lorry drivers.

---

57   Highway Act 1980, s 1.
58   Where relevant, a public authority has a right of action: see *Department of Transport v Williams* (1993) 138 SJ (LB) 5.
59   [1899] 1 Ch 255.
60   At p 267.
61   (1906) 22 TLR 327.
62   Followed in *Fowler v Kibble* [1922] 1 Ch 487.
63   [1976] QB 142: discussed by Bercusson, B (1977) 40 MLR 268.
64   [1982] IRLR 152.

Denning's dissenting judgment in *Hubbard v Pitt* has, however, been vested with some authority. Denning's assertion that '... picketing does not become a nuisance unless it is associated with obstruction, violence, intimidation, molestation or threats ...'[65] was followed by Scott J in *Thomas v NUM (South Wales Area)*[66] and by the Court of Appeal in *Galt v Philp*.[67]

Although the precise relationship of the tort of nuisance to peaceful picketing is somewhat unclear due to conflicting judicial authority, there is no doubt that a private nuisance will be committed where more aggressive forms of picketing are utilised. For example, in *NGN Ltd v SOGAT 82*,[68] large numbers of pickets attended the premises of the plaintiff in connection with the dispute over the printing of News International titles at Wapping. The picketing and associated demonstrations attracted liability in private nuisance due to the weight and numbers of demonstrators interfering with the plaintiff's right of access to their property.[69]

In *Thomas v NUM (South Wales Area)*, Scott J noted that the tort of nuisance is only actionable by employers whose enjoyment of land is interrupted by the picketing. This left a gap in protection for those working employees who were subjected to intimidatory picketing. For these reasons, he created a new form of civil wrong closely associated with nuisance termed 'unreasonable harassment', tortious at the suit of a working employee. Liability was imposed for an unreasonable interference with the right of the plaintiff to use the highway for the purpose of going to work.

However, this proposition was doubted by Stuart-Smith J, in *NGN Ltd v SOGAT 82*,[70] and rejected as a principle of law by Peter Gibson J in *Khoransandijan v Bush*,[71] although revived in *Buris v Azadani*.[72]

Public nuisance

Public nuisance is defined as an unlawful act that materially affects the health and safety or comfort and convenience of a class of Her Majesty's citizens, or obstructs them in the exercise of a right.[73] It occurs where there has been an unreasonable obstruction of the highway or where some physical damage afflicts a community as a whole. Although public nuisance is technically a common law criminal offence, a plaintiff may sue for their loss where it is over and above the loss suffered by the community.

---

65 At p 152.

66 [1985] IRLR 136. Note that Scott J was, however, prepared to hold that in exceptional circumstances, where a residential house, rather than an entrance to an employer's premises, is picketed peacefully, an unreasonable interference sufficient for liability in nuisance has taken place.

67 [1984] IRLR 156.

68 [1986] IRLR 337.

69 See Auerbach, S (1987) 16 ILJ 227. Stuart-Smith J also found the union directly liable (on the basis of the principle in *Sedleigh-Denfield v O'Callaghan* [1940] AC 880) that, having knowingly created the nuisance by the organisation of the picketing, the union had therefore 'adopted' it.

70 [1986] IRLR 337.

71 [1993] QB 727, pp 743–44.

72 [1995] 4 All ER 802.

73 *AG v PYA Quarries* [1957] 2 QB 169, p 184, *per* Romer LJ.

This was an additional head of liability imposed by Stuart-Smith J in *NGN Ltd v SOGAT 82*.[74] The second plaintiff in the action, Times Newspapers (which did not own the land in Wapping that was picketed), successfully argued that the weight of numbers of pickets demonstrating against News International constituted an obstruction of the highway that was itself the crime of public nuisance and that they had suffered special damage, greater than that suffered by the general public, by way of extra security and transport costs.[75]

Picketing and the economic torts

In the vast majority of situations, the object of a picket line is to discourage workers from attending their place of work. Where the arguments or exhortations of pickets have this effect, the tort of inducing breach of employment contract will occur.[76] In addition, pickets may interfere with the performance of commercial contracts where lorry drivers are persuaded not to deliver supplies to the employer. Thus, *prima facie*, pickets by their actions will normally commit one or more of the economic torts.

Protection for those torts specified in s 219(1) and (2) is provided by s 219(3) of the TULR(C)A 1992 where the requirements of s 220 of the Act are satisfied. This section holds that an immunity only applies where a person:

... in contemplation or furtherance of a trade dispute attends –

(a) at or near his own place of work, or

(b) if he is an official[77] of a trade union, at or near the place of work of a member of the union whom he is accompanying and whom he represents, for the purpose only of peacefully obtaining or communicating information, or peacefully persuading any person to work or to abstain from working.

Although nearly all secondary picketing is excluded from the protection of this section,[78] an exception is made for certain officials of the union.[79] The Code of Practice justifies this on the grounds that the official is then in a position to secure order and ensure the picketing adheres to the guidelines within s 220.[80]

For the purposes of the legality of picketing, the definition and construction of the term 'place of work' is of particular import. For workers dismissed by an employer during a trade dispute, the '... former place of work shall be treated ... as being his place of

---

74 [1986] IRLR 337.

75 See also *R v Coventry CC ex p Phoenix Aviation* [1995] 3 All ER 47.

76 It seems there is no need for pickets to actively persuade workers to break their contract of employment. The Court of Appeal in *Union Traffic v TGWU* [1989] ICR 98, p 106, asserted that the mere presence of pickets could be sufficient to constitute inducement if their presence is intended to induce breach of contract and if it has that effect.

77 Defined in ss 220(4) and 119.

78 In one situation, secondary action will be protected. Eg, where a picket induces the breach of a lorry driver's contract of employment that is technically secondary action as the lorry driver is not employed by the employer in the dispute.

79 Section 220(4) reiterates that a local official is regarded for the purposes of the section as representing only members of the group that elected or appointed him or her (see, also, Code of Practice, paras 22–23).

80 See Code of Practice on Picketing 1992, paras 54–57.

work'.[81] For those workers, such as lorry drivers, who may have no one place of work or others for whom it is 'impracticable' to picket their place of work,[82] picketing may take place at or near '... any premises of his employer from which he works or from which his work is administered'.[83]

One limitation of these statutory definitions became clear during the Wapping dispute in 1986. Printworkers at News International – based at Grays Inn Road – were dismissed and their former place of work shut down. All production was transferred to another geographical site at Wapping. These former employees of News International were not able to avail themselves of the protection of the section when they picketed the new site as it was not a former place of work, nor was it a place where they had previously worked.[84]

If the courts had subsequently taken a purposive approach to the construction of the section then this gap in protection for employees could have been closed. However, this has not been the case. The Court of Appeal preferred a very narrow construction of the statutory provision, in *Union Traffic v TGWU*.[85] Here, lorry drivers had been made redundant and their depot closed. It was thus futile for them to picket their former place of work – the closed depot. Instead, they picketed a transport site from which they had very occasionally worked some 13 miles from the main depot. Lloyd LJ, who gave the leading judgment, refused to construe the section in such a way as to permit picketing there. He held that the primary intention of the section was to allow workers to picket their 'principal' workplace only, not a subsidiary place of work.

This very strict approach to the legislation by Lloyd LJ is in stark contrast to the Court of Appeal's decision in *Rayware v TGWU*.[86] The court noted that the intention of the section was to confer on employees a liberty to picket peacefully: thus, a wide construction of the term 'at or near place of work' should be utilised to permit picketing 1,200 metres from the employer's premises where the pickets were unable to get any closer.[87]

Section 220 and other liability

Due to this section's distinctive legislative[88] history, it has often been stated that peaceful picketing within the ambit of s 220 provides an immunity for other torts, or even crimes, that *prima facie* have been committed. It is argued that, if picketing is peaceful and at or near the worker's place of work, it is sanctioned by statute and so should be regarded as a 'reasonable' use of the highway for liability in trespass, nuisance or for any offences committed on the highway.

---

81 Section 220(3).
82 Eg, where it is physically dangerous or impossible to picket (such as where the place of work is a North Sea oil rig).
83 Section 220(2)(b).
84 See *NGN Ltd v SOGAT 82* [1986] IRLR 337.
85 [1989] ICR 98.
86 [1989] IRLR 134.
87 Both cases are noted by Auerbach, S [1989] ILJ 166.
88 See Kidner, R, 'The development of the picketing immunity 1825–1906' (1993) 13 *Legal Studies* 103.

One of the earliest cases on the forerunner to s 220 (s 7 of the Conspiracy and Protection of Property Act 1875)[89] was *J Lyons & Sons v Wilkins* where the immunity proviso was defined narrowly. The Court of Appeal held that, although the communication of information was lawful, notwithstanding the statutory provision, the active persuasion of workers was not.

In the later Court of Appeal decision in *Ward, Lock & Co*, it was held (contrary to *Lyons*) that where pickets were engaged in peaceful persuasion (that is, within the ambit of the immunity), neither the tort of nuisance nor the crime of 'watching and besetting' was committed.[90] In any event, it could be argued that the dichotomy between the two judgments is of little relevance today as, where picketing is peaceful, it is unlikely that all the elements of a tort or crime will be present to establish liability.

This issue was, however, further raised in *Broome v DPP*.[91] The defendant had been arrested for obstruction of the highway (contrary to the Highways Act 1959) where he had stood in the middle of the road with a placard urging the driver of a lorry not to deliver goods to the employer. The House of Lords responded to his contention that he possessed a right to picket peacefully guaranteed by s 134 of the Industrial Relations Act 1971 (a precursor of s 222) by asserting that the lawful attendance of pickets for the purpose of communicating information must be exercised reasonably. There was no implied right stemming from the provision that permitted the defendant to compel the potential recipient of the information to stop and submit to the persuasion.[92]

The decision in *Broome v DPP* was followed in *British Airways Authority v Ashton*[93] where employees were arrested and charged with the contravention of bylaws that banned public demonstrations within the perimeter of the airport and gave a constable the right to require persons to leave the airport. The court dismissed the relevance of the protection of the immunity, holding that it did not confer a right to attend on land contrary to a public authority by law as it did not render lawful that which was palpably unlawful.[94]

In conclusion, s 220 may well protect pickets from actions where a possible technical nuisance or trespass has been committed, but will not operate to legalise manifestly unreasonable use of the highway or the commission of any other common law or statutory criminal acts.[95]

---

89 The statutory immunity found in the 1875 Act deemed attendance for the purpose of obtaining or communicating information would not constitute liability for the offence of 'watching and besetting'.

90 Supported by the judgment of Forbes J in *Hubbard v Pitt* [1976] QB 142.

91 [1974] ICR 84. Noted (1975) 91 LQR 173 and discussed by Wallington, P (1974) 3 ILJ 109 and Kidner, R [1975] Crim LR 256.

92 Lord Reid noted that any picketing activity that goes beyond this limited function outlined in the section would be a *prima facie* obstruction. Lord Salmon was somewhat more willing to import a degree of protection for picketing that stayed within the limits of the immunity.

93 [1983] ICR 696.

94 See also *Tynan v Balmer* [1967] 1 QB 91, actions that amount to obstruction are not legitimised by an immunity provided by statute solely for the economic torts; *Kavanagh v Hiscock* [1974] ICR 282, the immunity does not render picketing a lawful and reasonable user of the highway *per se*; *MGN Ltd v NGA* [1984] IRLR 397.

95 The Code of Practice specifically states in para 41 that s 220 does not grant immunity from criminal liability.

The Code of Practice

The Code of Practice on Picketing was first issued by the Department of Employment in 1980[96] and revised and reissued in 1992. It provides an official view of how picketing should be organised and conducted. A breach does not create any liability itself but, as s 207(3) directs and the cases show, the courts take account of its provisions in their deliberations.

For example, the Code in para 51 discourages 'mass' picketing by suggesting that the maximum number of pickets should not exceed six at any entrance or exit and 'frequently a smaller number will be appropriate'. The courts have, on occasion, taken this as a 'guide to a sensible number for a picket line in order that the weight of numbers should not intimidate those who wish to go to work'.[97] Thus, Scott J in *Thomas v NUM (South Wales Area)* held that where there were more than six pickets on duty the picketing was an actionable nuisance and an unreasonable harassment of the working miners in the exercise of their right to use the highway to travel to work.[98]

Picketing and the Human Rights Act 1998

The imposition of criminal and civil restrictions on picketing have important civil liberties implications in the area of freedom of speech and assembly. The relevance of the European Convention Articles on freedom of speech and assembly in potentially limiting these restrictions have been noted on several occasions by the courts prior to the introduction of the Human Rights Act 1998.[99]

As a consequence of the introduction into domestic law of the European Convention by the Human Rights Act, it may well be the case that picketing limitations, formally examined by reference to the Convention, will be found to be in violation of Convention rights. In particular, the courts may well consider that certain of the restrictions offend against the principle of proportionality and are so broad in their application that their interference with the rights contained in Arts 10 and 11 cannot be justified. Commentators have suggested that the wide discretionary powers of the police to control picketing through their powers to prevent a breach of the peace, the Picketing Code of Practice (which restricts no more than six pickets from gathering at a place of work) and the application of s 241 of the TULR(C)A 1992 (which criminalises the commission of a tort in an industrial dispute) are all matters that may well offend against the Convention.[100]

---

96   See Drake, C (1981) 10 ILJ 46.

97   See Scott J, in *Thomas v NUM (South Wales Area)* [1985] IRLR 136, p 151, and Stuart-Smith J, in *NGN Ltd v SOGAT 82* (1986) IRLR 337. See, also, Lee, S (1986) 102 LQR 35 and Carty, H [1985] PL 542.

98   This advice has also been followed by the police in numerous disputes when using their discretion to limit picketing on the highway.

99   See, eg, Neil LJ in *Middlebrook Ltd v TGWU* [1993] ICR 612, p 620.

100 For a general analysis in this area, see Fenwick, H, 'The right to protest, the Human Rights Act and the margin of appreciation' (1999) 62 MLR 491; Mead, D, 'The Human Rights Act – a panacea for peaceful public protest?' (1998) 3 J Civ Lib 37; Fitzpatrick, B and Taylor, N, 'Trespassers might be prosecuted. The European Convention and restrictions on the right to assemble' [1998] EHRLR 292.

INDEX

375

I